Vernacular Buildings of Shropshire

Vernacular Buildings of Shropshire

by
Madge Moran

Logaston Press

LOGASTON PRESS
Little Logaston, Logaston,
Woonton, Almeley, Herefordshire HR3 6QH

First published by Logaston Press 2003
Reprinted 2004
Copyright © M. Moran 2003

ISBN 1 873827 93 8

Set in Baskerville & Times by Logaston Press
and printed in Great Britain by CPI

Front cover: The hall at Moat House, Longnor, by Noel Shepherdson

This book is dedicated to the memory of Don and Pat

'On clear evenings ... one could see the centuries in the house, like ferns in a fossil ... the place had been patched and enlarged by successive generations ... the result ... a mansion to the majority, a prison to the few'.
The House in Dormer Forest by Mary Webb, a Shropshire writer (1920)

'However, I reflected as I walked away: "Well, I am certainly wiser than this man. It is only too likely that neither of us has any knowledge to boast of; but he thinks that he knows something which he does not know, whereas I am conscious of my ignorance. At any rate it seems that I am wiser than he is to this small extent, that I do not think that I know what I do not know".'
Plato's Apology (Defence) of Socrates (420 - 347 B.C.)

or, more concisely—

'There are more questions than answers,
and the more that I find out the less I know'.
Words and music by Johnny Nash, singer and lyricist, (1972)

Contents

Acknowledgments

I owe a tremendous debt of gratitude to the many householders who have welcomed me into their homes, given me freedom to roam and tolerated disruption by my companions wielding tape measures, measuring sticks, roof ladders and torches. Some I now count as close friends. Another group of friends consists of people who have helped me over the years with discussion, exchange of knowledge and/or practical help with measuring and drawing. Chief among these are Henry Hand and the late Eric Mercer. The latter I thank for his unfailing support and his encyclopaedic knowledge of architecture on which I have freely drawn and the former for his recording skills and keen observation. Many of the drawings in the book are Henry's.

As mentioned in the Preface, Jim Tonkin kindled my interest, and I thank him for that early initiation. I also thank members of my Whitchurch class who have helped me greatly, in particular Jean North and Pat Gates. The late Fred Powell and his wife Irene introduced me to most of the delights of south Shropshire and I owe Fred much gratitude. His death in 1998 was a sad loss. Ian West is a friend who helped me greatly, and David Lloyd is another friend to whom I owe much, and he has kindly read through and corrected the Ludlow chapters. Similarly, another friend, David Pannett, helped me with the geological details.

To Noel Shepherdson I extend grateful thanks for permission to include his remarkable drawings of Ludlow Guildhall and his evocative depiction of the hall at Moat House, Longnor shown on the front cover. In this the architectural details are from measurements, but it amused Noel to include Margaret Richards and myself as standing figures.

I also thank Gerwyn Lewis for the illustrations of 2 Pride Hill, Shrewsbury and the details of Upton Cressett (both on the rear cover); Malcolm Hislop for the drawings of Lane End Cottage, Muckleton; Richard Raven for the Plato reference on p.*vi* and Jean North for the illustration of medieval cruck building (also on the rear cover). Where appropriate other acknowledgments are made in the footnotes.

A bonus of writing a book like this at such a time is having the benefit of dendrochronolgy and it pleases me greatly to record that Dan Miles, the dendrochronologist with whom I work now regards Shropshire as his second home. Latterly Michael Worthington has become his associate and together they run the Oxford Dendrochronology Laboratory. Dendrochronology is expensive, and for financial grants I thank chiefly the Owen Family Trust without whose support the project would be much poorer. Other grants came from the British Academy, The Society of Antiquaries, the Royal Archaeological Institute, the Vernacular Architecture Group, the Marc Fitch Fund, the Shropshire Archaeological and Historical Society, Ludlow Historical Research Group, Ludlow Civic Society, Shrewsbury Civic Society, Shropshire County Council, North Shropshire District Council, other smaller authorities and trusts and many private householders. George Baugh took on the administration of the finances and has helped me in many other ways.

Many fellow-members of the Vernacular Architecture Group have helped me over the years. They are too numerous to mention individually but will recognise themselves, and

I would also like to thank the staff of bodies such as the Shropshire Records and Research Centre, the Victoria County History and the library of the Society of Antiquaries.

The chapter on Decoration owes much to discussion and exchange of information with Kathryn Baird, Conservation Officer for North Shropshire who has a particular interest in the subject.

I thank the Owen Family Trust for financial support towards the publication of this book, and I thank my publisher, Andy Johnson of Logaston Press. Most publishers seem to regard their main duty as putting as many obstacles in a writer's path as possible. Andy and his associate, Ron Shoesmith, are different. Their policy is to work *with* their authors.

Finally I thank my long-suffering family. Sadly Don, my husband and Pat, my daughter did not live to see the years of work come to fruition, but I can thank my son, William for the photography in the book and my elder son, Tom for his support.

Madge Moran
Shrewsbury, 2003

Preface

This book is the result of a hobby that got out of hand and became more of an obsession. I became involved with vernacular architecture many years ago through attending an evening class run by J.W. Tonkin B.A., F.S.A. from Herefordshire under the auspices of Birmingham University Extramural Department, and Jim must take the blame for changing the course of my life. When he wanted to give up his Shropshire class in order to concentrate on Herefordshire the Department offered me the chance to take his place. This gave me access to people and houses in various parts of Shropshire, and my membership of the Vernacular Architecture Group broadened my horizons greatly.

Shropshire is the largest non-coastal county in Britain and I am very much aware that there are parts of it which I know only slightly. It is a long way from Shrewsbury to Neen Sollars or to Bettwys-y-Crwyn and when time is limited through other commitments inevitably such areas cannot receive the same coverage as, say, Much Wenlock. I feel sure that many architectural riches remain untapped, especially in south-east Shropshire. The north-east of the county was fairly well covered by the work of my own extramural class in Whitchurch which resulted in the book *Vernacular Buildings of Whitchurch and Area and their Occupants*, published by Logaston Press in 1999, and therefore only passing mention of houses in that area is made in the present work. Similarly, houses in some of the south-western parishes are described in chapter 14 of *The Gale of Life* which was my contribution to the millennium book of the South-west Shropshire Historical and Archaeological Society, also published by Logaston Press.

Architectural historians in some parts of Britain seem able to group their houses into neat typological formats such as 'Hearth-passage Plans', 'End-stack and Direct-Entry plans', 'Houses with Central Service Rooms' etc. I wish it was as straightforward in Shropshire. Shropshire seems to be a melting-pot of many different trends and influences and I feel it would be a brave person who employed such a method here. Each writer is an individual and the approach I have used in this book, I must admit, seems to have suggested itself. I can only hope that it is acceptable and gives the reader an overview of the vernacular delights which lie hidden in the county. Many of the houses have been fully recorded by measured drawings and written reports, but it was felt that a book of this nature was an inappropriate vehicle for such detailed work. If anyone wishes to consult my archive, then please write to me c/o the publisher, Logaston Press.

I debated whether to include a chapter on the 18th-century vernacular scene, but this would have made the book top-heavy and, I have to admit, my real interest is in earlier building practices, but there are references to late Stuart and Georgian work where appropriate. Brickwork as a subject is another absentee. Again, it is an aspect which should have greater coverage than is possible here.

The chapter which summarises the Shropshire Dendrochronology Project includes some repetition of details discussed in earlier sections. The reasons for this is that it puts the points into a concise context and enables readers to 'fast forward' if they so wish. Also, the project has been part of my life over recent years and I owe such a summary to the many sponsors and helpers who have supported me so loyally.

Location Map for the Parishes of Shropshire

Location Map for the Parishes of Shropshire

208 Onibury
209 Stanton Lacy
210 Bitterley
211 Hopton Wafers
212 Neen Savage
213 Bromfield
214 Stowe
215 Bucknell
216 Bedstone

217 Ludlow
218 East Hamlet
219 Ludford
220 Caynham
221 Coreley
222 Cleobury Mortimer
223 Richard's Castle
    (Salop)
224 Ashford Bowdler

225 Ashford Carbonell
226 Greete
227 Whitton
228 Hope Bagot
229 Nash
230 Boraston
231 Milson
232 Neen Sollars
233 Burford

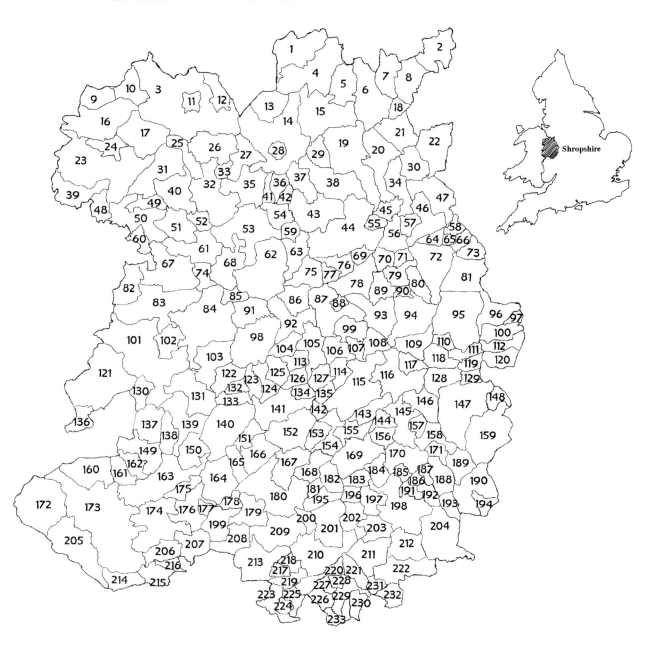

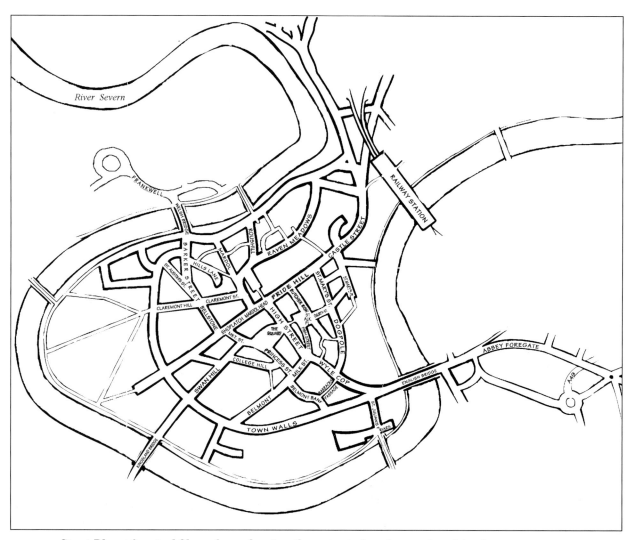

Street Plan of central Shrewsbury showing those streets largely mentioned in the text

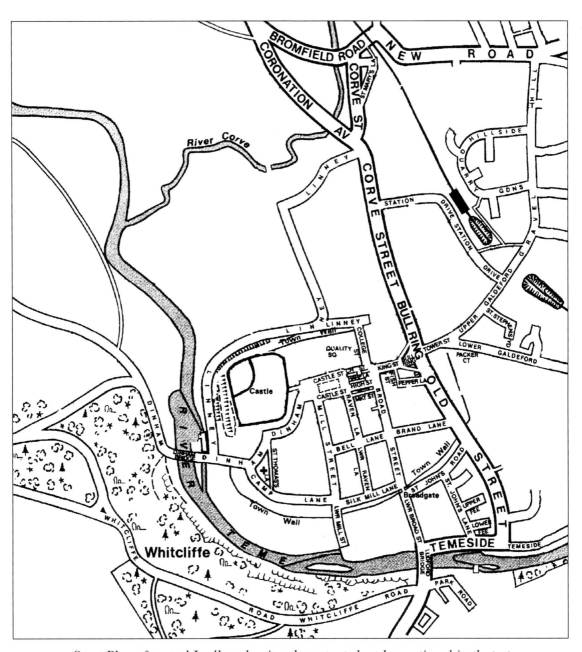

Street Plan of central Ludlow showing those streets largely mentioned in the text

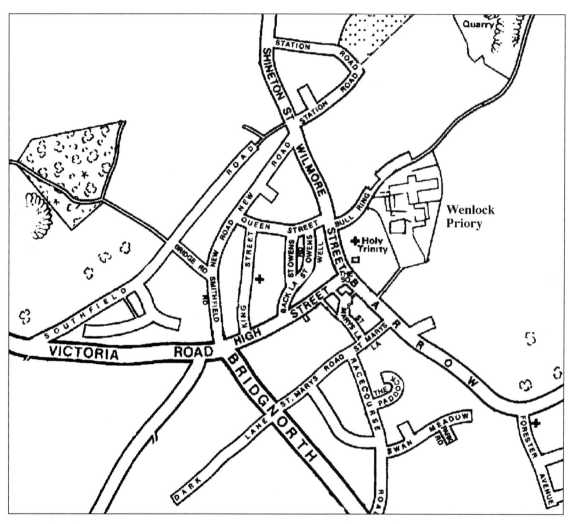

Street Plan of central Much Wenlock showing those streets largely mentioned in the text

1   Defensive Houses

Shropshire's early western border was demarcated by Offa's Dyke, the great linear bank-and-ditch earthwork raised by the Mercian king and his successors to mark the boundary between his kingdom and Wales. Following the Act of Union with Wales in 1536 the boundary was rationalised to some extent but place-name evidence, inheritance customs, language and other ethnic strands point to blurred definitions and an intermingling of races. As recently as the 1960s it was still possible to hear Welsh spoken in Shrewsbury market but it seems not to have survived the cultural shock of the demolition of the Victorian market hall. Defence against the Welsh was always of prime importance in early times and it is not surprising that the greatest concentration of defensive houses is on the western side of the county and close to the Welsh border. Iron Age hill-forts are dominant features of the whole of the Welsh Marches, virtually every prominent hill is crowned by the remains of one or more and whether these reflect strategically-placed defences or have a wider social interpretation it seems clear that defence was an integral function. The establishment of the Roman base at *Viroconium* reflects the difficulties of a conquering race when dealing with rebellious Celtic tribes and, significantly, little evidence of Roman villas has been found in Shropshire. One site, Yarchester near Much Wenlock, was discovered almost accidentally by some schoolboys in 1957 and seven other possible sites have been identified.[1]

Defensive houses in Shropshire may be divided into two main groups: blatant strongholds which can support the definition of 'castle' and houses which are intrinsically defensive, being built with thick stone walls and small windows and where the main living area is at first-floor level. Two sub-groups of the latter may be suggested: ordinary houses to which a deterrent is added, for example a moat, and longhouses where an element of defence is present in the basic concept of sheltering people and their livestock, which represented their livelihood, under one roof.

To what extent moated sites relate to defensive houses is not clear. The figure of *c.*160 recognised sites is impressive and although they can be distinguished from castles by their domestic concept the purpose of the moat should be questioned.[2] Defence against human attackers probably played little part in the majority of cases, but as a means of keeping wolves at bay even a modest moat would have been effective.[3] As a symbol of prestige and status a moat would be a desirable feature and perhaps it is significant that the majority of moated sites occur in the northern half of the county, an area which had the poorest economy at the time of Domesday and where settlement was difficult until lands were drained and assarting could take place.[4] Unless the present house on the moated site displays defensive features it is proposed to discuss it under its architectural typology rather than in its context of a moated site.

As castles are a specialised study and beyond the scope of a work on vernacular architecture it will be necessary here only to note that, like the hill-forts and the motte-and-bailey type they

Name	Date	Notes
Alberbury	1280s	1 tower remains
Bridgnorth	C.12th	Norman keep remains
Broncroft	C.14th	1 tower remains. Rest is C.19th
Clun	C.12th	Keep remains
Hawkstone	1228	Fragment of 1 tower remains (The Red Castle)
Holdgate	C.14th	1 tower remains. Rest is C.17th and C.18th
Hopton	C.12th	Norman keep remains
Lea	C.12th	Fragment of Norman keep
Ludlow	From C.12th	Extensive and substantial remains
Moreton Corbet	c.1200	Keep, gatehouse. C.16th-mansion grafted on. Now all ruinous
Myddle	1307	Fragment of stair turret remains
Ruyton	1160s	Fragment of keep
Shrawardine	C.12th	Fragment of keep
Shrewsbury	From 1280s	Extensive and substantial remains
Wattlesborough	C.12th	Norman keep remains. C.18th-house grafted on
Whittington	1220s	Gatehouse, 1 tower, other fragments

Table 1. Castles with structural remains

sometimes superceded, their distribution is concentrated along the Welsh border and, where the evidence survives, nearly all incorporate a first-floor hall. Sometimes the difference between a small castle and a defensive first-floor hall house may be negligible and the classifications in Table 2 (opposite and overleaf) should not be regarded too rigidly. Only sites which have structural remains are considered. Place-name evidence points to defence at Apley Castle, Richard's Castle, Bishop's Castle, Castle Pulverbatch and Newcastle-on-Clun. Apley Park, Charlton, Ellesmere, Hodnet, Knockin, Oswestry, Petton, Pontesbury, Rowton and Whitchurch are known to have had castles; some still display fragmentary remains, and very many smaller sites also occur.[5] The parish of Alberbury-with-Cardeston alone contains eight castle sites of 12th-century date, designed to control the valley road from Wales in the Breidden - Long Mountain gap.[6]

Acton Burnell Castle and Stokesay Castle have been deliberately omitted from the table as they are more accurately classified as fortified manor houses. The former was built by Robert Burnell in the 1280s and the latter was largely built by Laurence de Ludlow at about the same time. He had license to crennelate in 1291, but a recent intensive dendrochronological survey makes it clear that he had begun the project

Remaining 14th-century tower with later additions at Holdgate Hall

Grid Ref	Name	Date	Internal Dimensions	Notes
SJ 491125	Charlton Hall Shrewsbury	early C.14th	?	Formed a later wing to an earlier mid-C.13th (?) ground-floor hall. All now demolished.[8]
SJ 492125	Vaughan's Mansion Shrewsbury	mid-C.13th	30'9" (in truncated form) x 28'7"	Remains incorporated in The Music Hall. Part of a U-shaped complex surrounding a courtyard. Front wall is complete with moulded window frames. Roof renewed.[9]
SJ 492126	2 Pride Hill, Shrewsbury (Bennet's Hall)	mid-C.13th	length unknown x 26'10"	Remains incorporated in modern shop. Has foliated capitals to fireplace, Arched doorways to rear room. Undercroft has two arched doorways.[10]
SJ 499125	Bellstone Hall Shrewsbury	mid-C.13th	c.25' x 17'	Incorporated into a C.17th complex. Demolished 1934. Drawings show a hall or solar lit by two pointed-arched windows.[11]
SJ 495128	Shrewsbury Castle	1280s	83'3" x 27' (incl. passage)	Hall above undercroft, situated between two drum towers.
SJ 534018	Acton Burnell Castle	1280s	49' square	A fortified manor house, built by Robert Burnell. Hall probably twin-aisled, (cf. Merchant Adventurers' Hall, York.) Substantial ruined remains.[12]
SO 594920	Great Oxenbold	1247 (dendro)	43'8" x 23'	A manor of Wenlock Priory 'improved' in 1525, roof renewed, otherwise substantial remains. Has slightly vaulted undercroft and attached domestic chapel.[13]
SO 521894	The Forester's Lodge, Upper Millichope	late C.13th	30'8" x 18'0"	Traditionally the home of the head forester of a royal hunting preserve. Draw-bolted windows, nail-head ornament, roof renewed, otherwise substantial remains. Dendro dates of 1450-1 and 1633 obtained from 1st and 2nd floor ceiling beams. These are whole or half trees close-set, probably copying originals.[14]
SO 722879	Chelmarsh Hall	late C.13th or early C.14th	30'4" x 21'2"	A property of the Mortimer family. Given by them to Wigmore Abbey in 1375. Roof renewed, otherwise substantial remains.[15]

Table 2 (cont. overleaf). *Examples of First-Floor Hall Houses (excluding castle keeps)*

Grid Ref	Name	Date	Internal Dimensions	Notes
SO 507746	Ludlow Castle	late C.13th	60' x 30'6"	An addition to the castle complex by the Mortimers.
SO 511746	The Rectory, Ludlow	1313-28 (dendro)	29'6" (in truncated form) x 20'6"	May have been timber-framed above a stone undercroft. Has collar-rafter roof.[16]
SJ 643044	Abbot's House Buildwas (1)	C.13th	46'10" x 26'4"	Roof renewed but otherwise substantial remains. Features include lancet windows and nail-head ornament.[17]
SJ 643044	Abbot's House Buildwas (2)	1377 (dendro)	41'0" x 15'10"	An extension at right-angles to the above. Reasonably intact. Six-bay roof of arch-braced collar-beam construction.[18]
SO 417848	Castle Farm, Cheyney Longville (1)	late C.14th	29'7" x 14'5"	Part of an enclosed courtyard complex. Roof renewed. Has accompanying solar and other features.[19]
SO 417848	Castle Farm, Cheyney Longville (2)	late C.14th or early C.15th	24'0" x 17'0"	Possibly a second hall. This also has a solar, 9'7" x 17'0" with a traceried window. The whole complex is difficult to interpret. There may even have been a third hall. Licence to crenellate, 1395.[20]
SJ 493127	Rigg's Hall, Shrewsbury	1405-35 (dendro)	16'4" x 16'8"	Now part of the Public Library. Timber-framed above a stone undercroft. This has a crown-post roof and may have been a solar.[21]
SJ 625001	Prior's House, Much Wenlock	1425 (dendro)	20'4" x 11'0"	Building intact. This is phase 2 and may have been added as a Guest Hall. (Phase I was an aisled hall to the south of the dorter, of which the storied wing remains in the grounds.) Superb details include open timber roof, corridor, tables, wash-basins, interlocking spiral staircase, louvre position etc.[22]
SO 512746	15 King Street, Ludlow	c.1467 (dendro)	23'6" x 21'0"	Undercroft probably used as shop with hall or solar above.[23]
SO 672829	Hall Farm Stottesdon	1534-68 (dendro)	52'0" x 23'0"	Stone-walled four-bayed hall. Bays are equidistant. May have been a Court House and / or Hundred House. Roof of arch-braced collar-beam construction.[24]

Table 2 (cont.) Examples of First-Floor Hall Houses (excluding castle keeps)

earlier, grafting his design onto the remains of an existing complex. Both were powerful men. Burnell was Chancellor to Edward I and later Bishop of Bath and Wells; de Ludlow was probably one of the wealthiest wool merchants in England.[7]

First-Floor Hall Houses

Defence is an intrinsic part of the concept where the hall is located at first-floor level although, particularly in a town situation, tradition probably played an equal part. In Shrewsbury and Ludlow by the late 13th and early 14th centuries a spacious first-floor hall was an integral part of the castle and in Shrewsbury, more so than in Ludlow, it is possible to see a two-way cultural exchange between the castle and the town houses. The same probably applied to Bridgnorth and Oswestry but there the evidence is lacking. In Charlton Hall, Shrewsbury old illustrations show what is possibly a reversal of building sequence in which a ground-floor hall is superceded by a first-floor hall. Perhaps John Charlton discovered to his cost that it was impossible to live at ground level and had to resort to a more defensive pattern. Abbots and priors of monastic houses needed large halls in which to entertain important guests and, where these survive, they are found at first-floor level, apparently replacing earlier ground-floor halls. In the case of Much Wenlock Priory the earlier hall was double-aisled. Outside the towns men whose work involved danger would need a defensive house and this is well illustrated by the Forester's Lodge at Upper Millichope. Naturally, most first-floor hall houses are built of stone above stone undercrofts but it is noticeable that in Shropshire there is little evidence of vaulting in the undercrofts, and examples also occur of timber-framed chambers above stone undercrofts. These may or may not be 'halls' in the accepted sense and their defensive potential would be minimal but they are included in the table as they conform to the basic format.

The first-floor hall houses in Shrewsbury and Ludlow are discussed more fully in subsequent chapters, but it may be useful at this point to expand the description of others in the table.

Great Oxenbold

This is now a farmhouse in the parish of Monkhopton and consists of a stone-built rectangular range which has a 13th-century chapel at the eastern end and a hall above an undercroft at the western end. The hall, dendro-dated to 1247, is built on sloping land and so the undercroft only underlies part of it, and only one bay of the undercroft is accessible. Two further bays, determinable by measurement, and probably similar in form, are blocked off. The accessible bay has a vaulted appearance given by eight cambered beams of large dimensions: 1ft. 3in. wide, 1ft. 2ins. deep at the ends, 1ft. in the centre and set at intervals of 1ft. 5in. The ninth beam is a trimmer for access to a stone spiral stair which is built into the thickness of the wall. This may have served a *camera* (a private chamber) for the prior at the eastern end of the hall.

The present entrance to the undercroft is a later insertion. The original entrance into the first-floor hall, now blocked, is above it and is seen to have the same wave moulding with a fillet that decorates the jambs of the blocked original windows. Nothing remains of the original roof structure, but over the eastern part of the hall are five massive beams which simply rest on brickwork at the wall head. They are of the same dimensions as those in the undercroft and produced the same dendro date but are not so heavily cambered, and, unlike the undercroft beams which are plain, the roof beams are chamfered and brought to a grooved and stepped point in the middle. There is one similar beam in the western part of the roof and here too is a shorter beam which has a carved fleur-de-lis at the end. The beams appear to be holding the house down rather than supporting the roof.

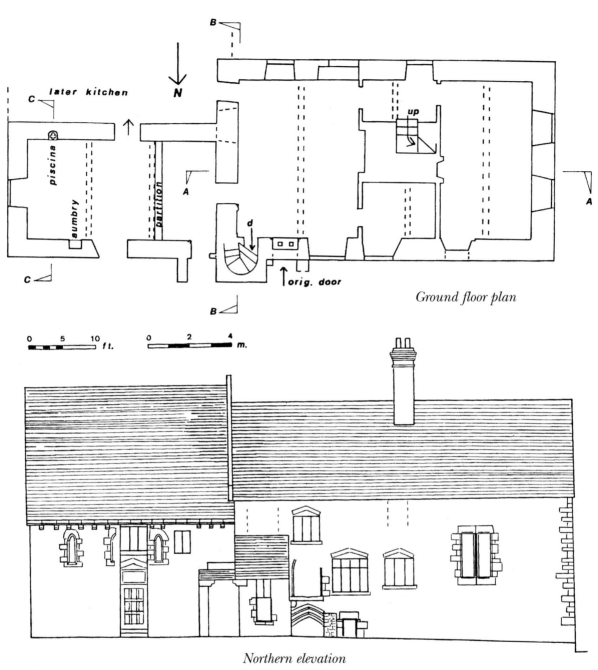

B

later kitchen

C

piscina

aumbry

partition

C

N

up

d

A

A

orig. door

B

Ground floor plan

0 5 10 ft.

0 2 4 m.

Northern elevation

Great Oxenbold,
Monkhopton

The location of the
medieval remains
in the northern elevation

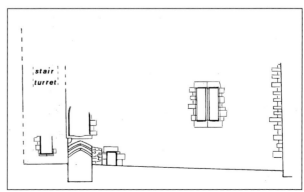

stair
turret

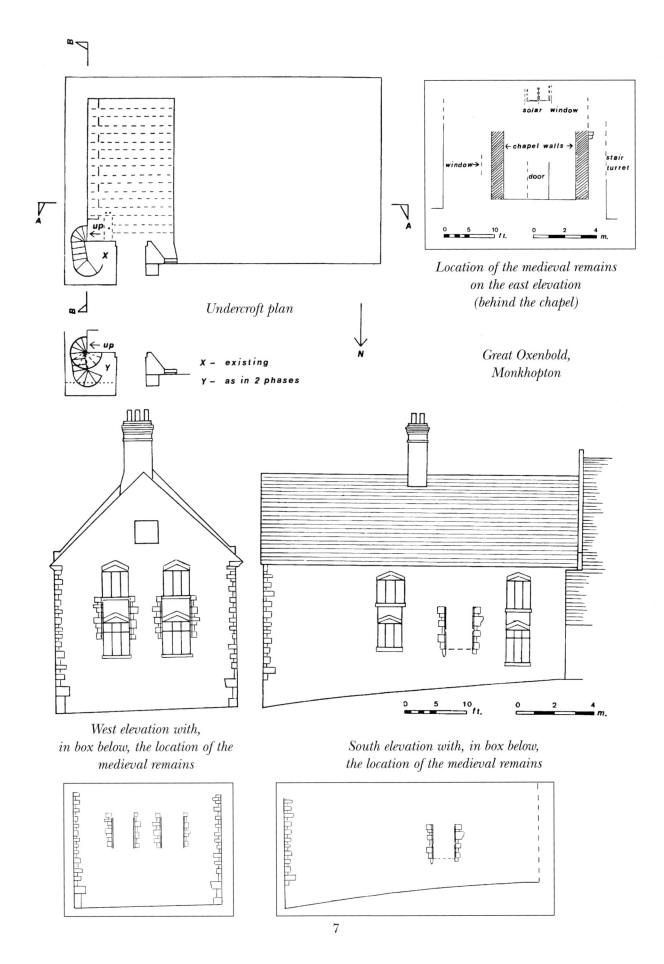

B

A

B

up

X

A

Undercroft plan

up

Y

X – existing

Y – as in 2 phases

N

solar window

← chapel walls →

window →

door

stair turret

0 5 10 ft.

0 2 4 m.

Location of the medieval remains on the east elevation (behind the chapel)

Great Oxenbold, Monkhopton

0 5 10 ft.

0 2 4 m.

West elevation with, in box below, the location of the medieval remains

South elevation with, in box below, the location of the medieval remains

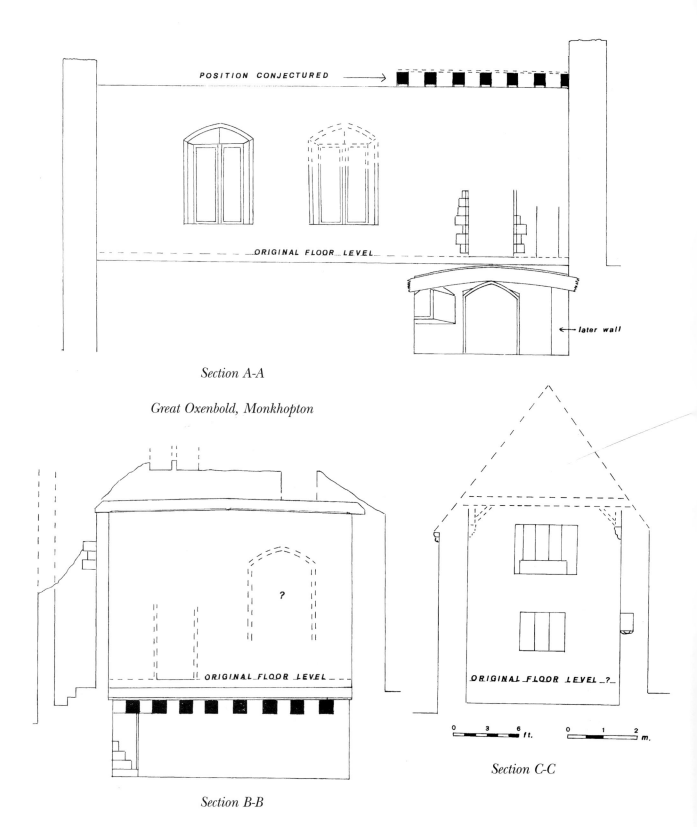

POSITION CONJECTURED →

ORIGINAL FLOOR LEVEL

← later wall

Section A-A

Great Oxenbold, Monkhopton

?

ORIGINAL FLOOR LEVEL

Section B-B

ORIGINAL FLOOR LEVEL_?_

0 3 6 ft.

0 1 2 m.

Section C-C

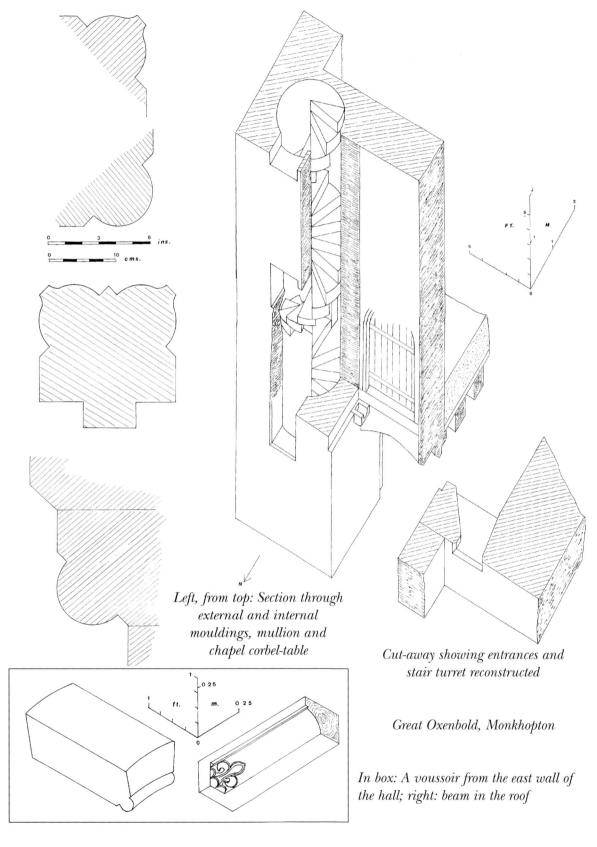

0 3 6 *ins.*

0 10 *c m s.*

Left, from top: Section through external and internal mouldings, mullion and chapel corbel-table

N

FT. M.

Cut-away showing entrances and stair turret reconstructed

Great Oxenbold, Monkhopton

In box: A voussoir from the east wall of the hall; right: beam in the roof

ft. m.

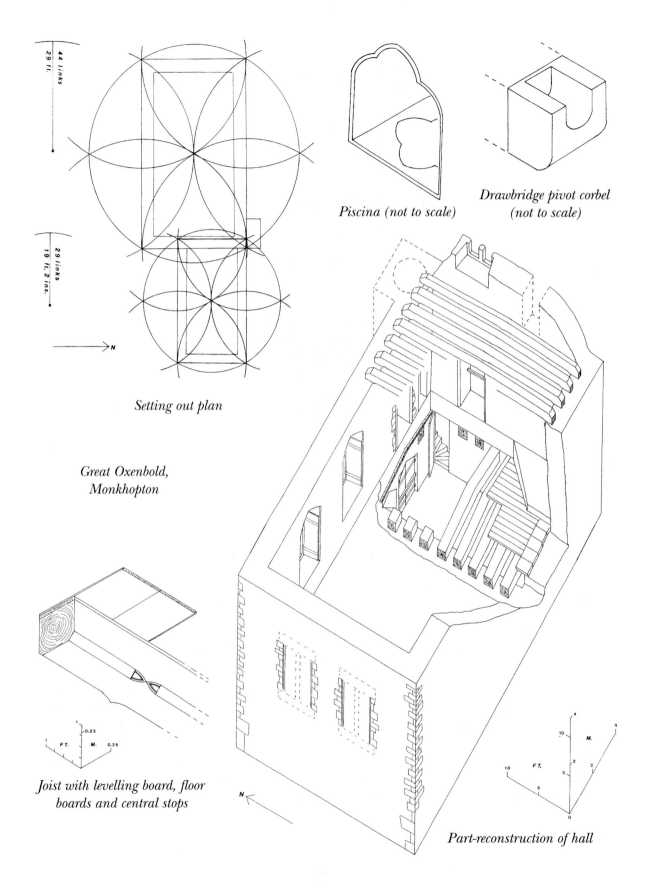

44 links
29 ft.

29 links
19 ft. 2 ins.

N

Setting out plan

Great Oxenbold,
Monkhopton

Piscina (not to scale)

Drawbridge pivot corbel
(not to scale)

Joist with levelling board, floor
boards and central stops

N

Part-reconstruction of hall

The hall must have been commissioned by Prior Humbert, the 'building prior' of Wenlock. It was he who enclosed land for a deer park here in 1251. A later prior, Roland Gosnell, said to have 'rebuilt' the hall in 1525, probably only made improvements like 'paving and glazing the great hall'.[25] The paving is probably that which underlies the present floor. The owner saw this floor when repairs were being carried out and described it as 'crazy paving laid on sand'.

The Forester's Lodge, Upper Millichope

Traditionally, the building was the home of the head forester of the district whose job it was to police the royal hunting preserves in the Long Forest and to supply venison to the priory at Much Wenlock. Such were the severity and the unpopularity of the forest laws in medieval England that the forester needed a strong house which could be defended if necessary against the king's subjects who bitterly resented what they saw as the monarch's greed and selfishness and the denial of their own liberties. With walls 6ft. thick, no access to the undercroft from ground level, windows fitted with draw-bolts and floor-joists made from whole trees the concept is certainly one of defence, but the family was not denied certain comforts. The hall was fitted with window seats and the embrasures were handsomely moulded and stopped. Externally a band of nail-head ornament was worked into the window capitals and probably the entrance door at first-floor level was similarly decorated. It is not known how the hall was heated or what the cooking and sanitary arrangements were; there is no evidence of a samson-post supporting an open hearth and it is possible that a proper chimney and garderobe were provided on the north-west wall. This is the wall which has largely been rebuilt and now provides the main access into the house at ground level. The doorway is decorated with an arch of ball-flower ornament, but it is clear that this is re-used material. It may have come from the chapel of Upper Millichope, known to have existed in 1331. The dendro dates (see above) were obtained from the floor beams and the exercise was carried out under the impression that they were coeval with the stone walls, but they proved to be later replacements. This appears to be an example of builders copying the original joisting system or as an example of extreme rural backwardness, or perhaps both. (See illustrations overleaf)

Chelmarsh Hall

Superficially Chelmarsh Hall appears to be a large Victorian mansion, but, while there is much work of this period, the shell of a U-shaped medieval stone-built complex was retained and consolidated and in all probability the overall basic size was not greatly enlarged. At the core is a first-floor hall and solar. Entrance to the hall was via a pointed-arched doorway, now blocked, which had sunk-chamfer moulding on the jambs. There is an opposing door of similar but not identical form—on the internal face it has the plain pointed-arch, but on the external face the inner plane has a rebated ogee-arch while the outer plane has the added decoration of a sunk chamfer within the ogee. This doorway must have led into a rear wing, and a matching wing to the south-west appears to consist of trussed rafters, ashlared and with braced collars. Internally the roof space of this wing is plastered over but the relevant features are discernible from outside.

The solar had a separate external entrance from a flight of steps at the north-western end of the hall block and through a Caernarvon-arched doorway, now blocked. Traces of the steps remain and other features include two blocked doorways into the undercroft, the remains of an oriel window at the dais end of the hall and evidence that there was a single-storied block projecting at right angles from the north wall of the hall which may have been a chapel. A

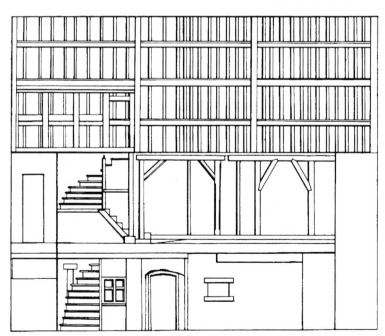

The Forester's Lodge, Upper Millichope

Above: Sketch from the south-west

Top right: Reconstruction of first-floor window on the north-east side

Centre right: Ground floor plan

Lower right: Longitudinal section of the house, looking north-west

Below: Outer view of the doorway

(none to scale)

N

12

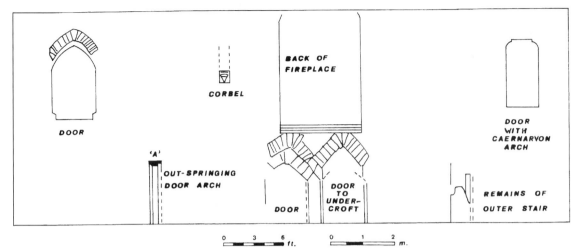

Above: West elevation of Chelmarsh Hall, whilst the photograph below shows the blocked doorway of the medieval first-floor hall

corbel on the north wall could be the mutilated remains of a mitred head which would relate to the apex of the roof, while the remains of a stone shaft, which is also sunk-chamfered and has the beginnings of a capital, suggest that here was one jamb of the entrance.

In view of its associations with the powerful Mortimer family of Wigmore and with Shropshire's own Wild Edric—the Saxon Earl of Shrewsbury from whom Ralph de Mortimer obtained possession of Chelmarsh— the site deserves to be better known.[26]

Castle Farm, Cheyney Longville[27]

This is a tantalising complex; it presents so many interesting individual features, and the overall concept of a moated and enclosed defensive courtyard site is obvious, but it is difficult to interpret the whole in an intelligible way. The present farmhouse, which is a mixture of 17th-, 18th- and 19th-century building phases, occupies most of the north side of the inner courtyard, and doubtless its construction removed vital evidence for the rest. It is tempting to imagine that members of the Cheyney family—Roger, Hugh and William—had separate first-floor hall-and-solar houses within the courtyard, but it is impossible to support this thesis either on documentary or architectural evidence. However, certain features point to at least two such structures. Hall house I on the south side of the entry has a Caernarvon-arched doorway into the presumed solar, an 'Ulenlok' or owl-door in the gable end and a distinct batter on the walls

Inner courtyard with steps giving access to hall house I

Traceried window, hall house II

Hall house I. Note the batter on the wall as it rises from the moat

Ulenlok in gable end of hall house I

Caernarvon-arched doorway giving access to solar of hall house I

Granary on graduated staddle-stones in the outer courtyard

Castle Farm, Cheyney Longueville

as they rise from the moat. Hall house II at the eastern end of the southern block has a two-light tracery-headed window to the presumed solar and a pointed-arched doorway giving access to the chamber below.

Equally tantalising is the range on the south-eastern side. This has a projection on the outer face which contains two lancet windows. All the buildings are now used either for storage or as farm buildings. Previous farming practices have also left their marks in a picturesque and instructive way. In the outer courtyard is a granary, built into the slope of the ground, which is supported on a row of staddle-stones graduated in size to take this into account, and in the inner courtyard is the trough and wheel of a 'ginny-ring' which is usually assumed to have been used for crushing cider apples. This may be so, but it had an additional function to produce rolled oats, as a frequent visitor who remembers it in action, confirmed.

The Abbot's House, Buildwas[28]
The buildings to which the public have access when visiting the ruins of Buildwas Abbey do not include the Abbot's House as this is in use by the C.E.G.B. as a social club for the workers at Ironbridge Power Station. Consequently little is known or has been written on this very interesting complex. It appears to consist of two rectangular blocks at right-angles to each other, the later one grafted on to the earlier to form a wing. Certain features of the earlier range such as the blocked doorway at first-floor level, the paired lancet windows and the decorated door-head at ground level below what would be the solar end, suggest a building date of between *c.*1180 and *c.*1280. The roof has been renewed but a few other internal features remain, including a shafted doorway with nail-head ornament at first-floor level and the remains of another at ground level.

The Abbot's House, dendro-dated to 1377
(*from Stackhouse-Acton, 1867,* The Garrisons of Shropshire during the Civil War 1642-48)

The Abbot's House, Buildwas

Top left: 13th-century first-floor hall

Above right: Hall doorway showing Caernarvon arch of 1377 within a 'Norman'-type arch

Centre left: Gable of early house with extension (right) of 1377

Bottom left: Roof of 1377

Detail of windbraces at the Abbot's House, 1377

The later range is dendro-dated to 1377 with alterations in the 15th and 16th centuries and extensions and further alterations of the 19th. Entrance into first-floor hall II was from the north side and here the doorway is well preserved as it has been protected by the later extensions. A Caernarvon-arched doorhead is set within a 13th-century outer round-headed arch supported on plain shafts of three-quarter round section which have nail-headed ornament in the moulded capitals, very similar in form to those in the shafted window at Upper Millichope. It is interesting to speculate that the Romanesque arch enclosing the Edwardian arch could be the result of the re-use of the former, taken perhaps from the original entrance to the first hall.

Inside the hall there is a lateral fireplace which also has a Caernarvon-arched surround, further emphasized by a Victorian surround of the same form. Some early encaustic tiles are set within the fireplace. Five windows light the hall, these have deep embrasures and Victorian wooden frames, but the upper lights are original and alternate between quatrefoil and trefoil in their form which appears to be a deliberate return to the plate tracery of the late 12th and 13th centuries, very like that in the porch of St. Mary's, Shrewsbury, *c.*1180.

At ground level there are the remains of a row of tall, 15th-century, pointed-arched windows inset with single-foiled shouldered frames. These continue across the end gable wall of the earlier building, and it is possible to see how the 14th-century work was integrated with the older range by the introduction of quatrefoil plate tracery above the paired lancets in the gable end. Alternatively, the latter may be original work which was copied in the later range to give an integrated appearance to the whole when viewed from the south.

The main room at ground level within the later range has a fine plastered ceiling of late 16th-century date which was probably done for Lord Powis who acquired the abbey site after the Dissolution and who then made the Abbot's House his residence. Motifs such as the portcullis and the Prince of Wales' feathers are present among stylised foliage, geometrical ribs and a central boss with the inscription 'DROIT DEV EST MAL MEV' which, translated from abbreviated old French, means 'Lawful right is ill moved'.[29]

Though now ceiled off from the hall, the roof structure is reasonably intact and consists of six bays of open arch-braced collar-beam construction. Each bay has a pair of triple-cusped windbraces which are morticed into the principal rafter and pegged through from the back of the clasped purlin. Above the purlin the scantling of the principal rafters is reduced to match that of the common rafters. When the hall remained open from first-floor level it must have been very impressive.

Hall Farm, Stottesdon

The house, dendro-dated to 1454, is situated immediately to the west of the church and consists basically of a rectangular stone-walled block. In places the walls are 4ft. thick. To this a projecting brick wing has been added on the southern lateral wall. In the roof are three identical decorative open trusses which suggest that originally the building had a four-bayed open hall at first-floor level. The purlins and principal rafters are rebated to give chamfered fillets, and where these meet a type of 'masons' mitre' is formed. The chimneystack is clearly a later insertion, but the absence of smoke-blackening in the roof supports the theory that this was an administrative rather than a wholly domestic building. Three large flat joists remain from the original flooring, the remainder has been renewed at various times and includes a good late 16th- or early 17th-century ceiling with chamfered and stopped joists in the ground-floor parlour.

West elevation

Section X-X

Hall Farm, Stottesdon

18

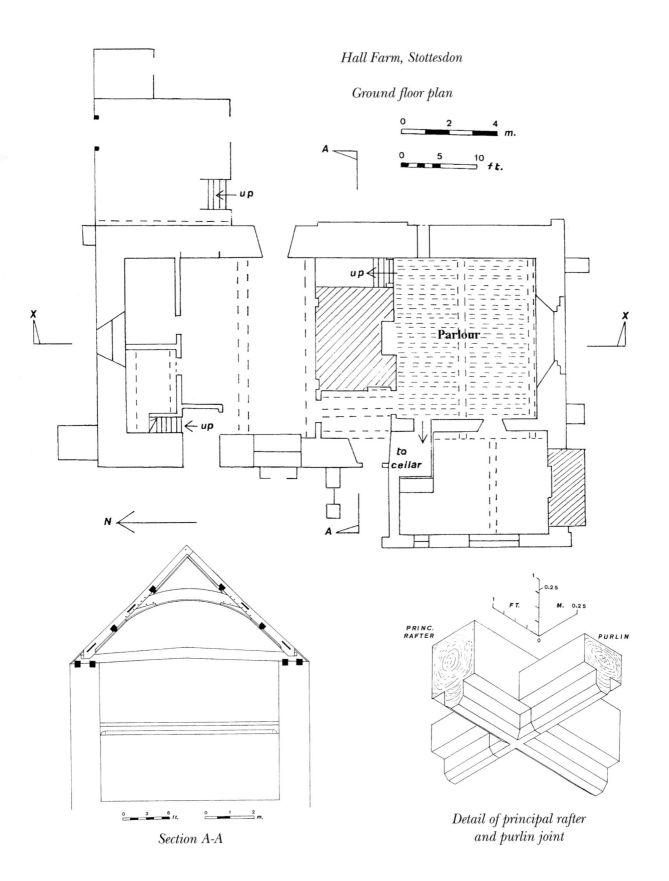

Hall Farm, Stottesdon

Ground floor plan

up

up

Parlour

to cellar

up

A

A

X

X

N

0 2 4 m.

0 5 10 ft.

0 3 6 ft.   0 1 2 m.

Section A-A

PRINC. RAFTER

PURLIN

1   0.25

1   0.25

FT.   M.   0.25

0

Detail of principal rafter and purlin joint

19

The Prior's House, Much Wenlock
Above: Unit to south of the dorter showing evidence
for aisled hall construction in the demolished range
Right: Upper gallery in the Prior's House
with doorways to the solar and hall on the right

The Prior's House, Much Wenlock

The building is better known than any of the others in this category and descriptions of it have been published in various works.[30] By no stretch of the imagination could it be described as vernacular and its lavish appointments could well have led to criticism of 'luxurious and extravagant living with a large household' on the part of the prior in the visitation of 1523.[31] It remains one of Shropshire's show-pieces, a rare and beautiful creation. One aspect which previous writers have not mentioned concerns the method of heating the hall. The present fireplace in the stack at the lower (northern) end of the hall seems to be a later contrivance, and the position of a louvre opening may be discerned where the rafters are interrupted. In the room below, formerly the kitchen, is an octagonal wooden Samson-post which has a square base and run-off stops with beading to the chamfers. It resembles an oversized displaced crown-post from southern England, occupies a relatively small area of the 7ft. square space outlined in the ceiling and appears to represent a token successor to a large stone pillar which supported the original

Hall with windows and fitted tables in the Prior's House

open hearth in the hall above. Another remarkable feature is the continuous wooden moulded and battlemented cornice along the upper gallery. It is carried over the arched and moulded stone doorways, thus adding sumptuousness to the entrances into the hall and solar. The independent roof over the gallery, the roofs over the hall, solar and apartment each produced identical dendrochronological dates of 1425. Most previous writers, not having the benefit of dendrochronology, have supported a date of *c.*1500 on account of the advanced architectural features, in particular the fenestration, but perhaps the building would be better seen as forward looking.

There are, of course, other buildings in the county where the remains are insufficient to categorise them as first-floor halls, and there is also a sub-group of medieval stone complexes where the hall was at ground level and the solar occupied its traditional position at first-floor level. Two early examples, both 13th-century aisled halls in monastic complexes, have left traces at Haughmond Abbey and at Much Wenlock Priory.[32] But the clearest and best preserved example is Stokesay Castle, where the hall is un-aisled and built from raised crucks of whole-tree form, dendro-dated to 1284-5. Profiles of an aisled form are present in each of the end walls, but these are contemporary, and are most likely to be part of the framework necessary to support the purlins and thus restrain the crucks trusses while the end stone gable walls were being built up.[33]

The same pattern of living may also be seen at Aston Eyre Manor Farm where the solar was approached from a large oriel window at the dais end of the hall and then via a spiral staircase. The oriel window occupied the full height of the building and probably had a chamber at the upper level. This represents an improvement on Stokesay where access to the solar involved an external pentice stair. The remains of Aston Eyre Manor Farm appear to be of the 14th century, and features like the oriel window in the hall and

Top: The gatehouse front to Aston Eyre Manor Farm
Below: Aston Eyre Manor Farm hall and solar

the tall pointed-arched window in the solar wing with its moulded frame and traceried head must have represented the last word in taste and elegance. It was approached via a substantial gatehouse, the arches and walls of which are incorporated into the present farmhouse. The gatehouse would provide the necessary defensive element, enabling the house to display the luxuries described above.[34] An illustration of the demolished Langley Hall shows a ground-floor timber-framed hall with a similar oriel window at the high end giving access to the stone-built solar.[35]

At Silvington Manor the present farmhouse is grafted on to the remains of a similar complex, though there is no evidence of a gatehouse. Again, the hall is at ground level and the solar at first-floor level. At present the solar is approached via an external stairway, but this is probably a modern expedient as the building is used for farm storage only. Some pointed-arched windows survive and it is clear that one in the solar had a traceried head. The floor of the solar is supported on closely-set large flat joists and there is an inscription in the gable end in artistic lower case lettering which reads 'hvfrf*m*'. The interpretation of this has so far proved elusive.

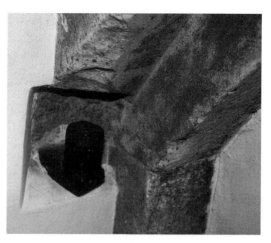

Pintle in interior of the front arch at Aston Eyre gatehouse

Gatehouses elsewhere in the county suggest that the pattern of living as exemplified at Stokesay and Aston Eyre was repeated. Some, such as the timber-framed example at Stokesay, dendrochronologically dated to 1640-1, presumably replaced an earlier defensive structure. The classical Elizabethan stone one at Madeley Court, and the delightful 17th-century essay in brickwork at Upton Cressett relate to later fashionable trends and could not be described as defensive. But others remain such as Bromfield Priory, Ashfield Hall at Much Wenlock, and at Langley Hall, or are known to have existed at Moat Farm, Stapleton; Bellaport (demolished) near Market Drayton, and High Ercall Hall, have purposeful stone-built lower stages although timber-framed superstructures were sometimes added when the need for defence had subsided. Walled towns also had the bridges and road entrances defended with strong gatehouses and although Shrewsbury and Oswestry have lost theirs, Ludlow retains its Broad Gate, and Bridgnorth its North Gate. About 50 gatehouses in the county either have greater or lesser structural remains or are known from documents or old illustrations. This number could probably be doubled by taking into account important ecclesiastic complexes and castles which must have had gatehouses as part of the concept. They seem to reflect a tradition of defence which had its origins in the 11th century, reached maturity in the 13th and 14th centuries, had become a token of fashion and prestige by the 16th century, was transmuted to timber-framing in the first half of the 17th century and abandoned after the Civil War.

About the year 1200, at the time when defence against the Welsh was a priority and seeds of the crop of first-floor halls were being sown, rather belatedly as it happens, because much of the danger had gone by the 14th century, the economic unit in the pattern of settlement in the Shropshire countryside was the hamlet. People lived in communities of between six and 12 houses, sharing plough beasts and pooling their labour. Isolated farms were unheard of, apart from monastic granges, and each hamlet had its own set of open fields and shared common land. Superimposed on this pattern were the manors, estates and ecclesiastic parishes although the latter were not yet a force for local government. The manor was the basic unit of land ownership, the manor lords holding their land under barons. Many manor lords were knights and were resident lords in their own castles, but by the 1280s, at the end of the Welsh wars, there was a significant increase in non-resident lords and many changes of ownership. This period marked the end of Anglo-Norman feudalism and of military service dues. Money rents were substituted and it is not difficult to see the change in stone-built houses from those whose prime function was defence to those where defence was minimal, lingering as a fashion, but where more attention was paid to comfort, convenience and to a display of wealth. Shropshire's collection of first-floor hall houses reflects much of its feudal history as well as its strategic border position and building practices.

Longhouses

Viewed from standpoints such as Devon, Somerset and parts of Wales where the longhouse appears to be indigenous, it may seem odd to include the type in a chapter on defensive houses, but the basic concept of housing the family and the livestock under one roof carries with it an element of defence. Cattle especially represented valuable capital, and it was cattle thieving, not land, that was the objective in raids by Welsh bandits in the 13th century and later. Therefore to have one's capital investment where it could be seen and defended if necessary, made sense. There were other advantages; feeding and watering could be done without leaving the house and the warmth generated by the animals would provide a primitive form of central heating. However, the type of building just described is the modern concept of a longhouse. It is clear from some Glebe Terriers in other areas that '*Domus Longa*' and 'Longhouse' were terms used in the 14th and 17th centuries to describe a long building which functioned as a farm building and was not part and parcel of the dwelling house.[36] As far as it has been possible to ascertain, these terms were not used to describe either the parsonage house or any of the farm buildings within its curtilage in Shropshire or Herefordshire, and it is not made clear whether the parson's cattle actually shared the same roof. In fact the evidence seems to point to the contrary. Typical entries are short and inconclusive, for example Westbury in 1801 '... parsonage house, barn, cowhouse and stable' or for Cold Weston in the same year '... a small house and cowhouse'; and more graphic entries such as for Aston Botterell in 1607 '... There is a hall house, parlour, buttery and kitchen with lofts over them, one barn of four bays with a

Detached kitchen and byre with granary over,
Lower House Farm, Cleedownton

house at the end and one stable with a loft over him, one wainhouse with a loft over him, all new builded by the new incumbent ...', or for Clun in 1604 '... one mansion house, a kitchen and house for cattle under the same roof', or for Church Stretton in 1576 and again in 1593 '... a decent house, two parlours, two butteries, five chambers, a kitchen, a boulting house, a malt chamber a stable and ox house all under one roof' strongly suggest that if the cattle shared a roof it was not that of the parson. Depending on how they are interpreted, the two latter examples may indicate that the kitchen was in a detached building which also provided housing for cattle.[37] This arrangement may still be seen at Lower House Farm, Cleedownton, in the parish of Stoke St. Milborough and is suggested at other sites where an outside kitchen can still be identified. However, for the purpose of this present study, the popular interpretation is taken of a longhouse as a communal shelter for man and beast.

No systematic search for longhouses has been done in Shropshire and Table 3 overleaf merely records those noted during general field work. Not surprisingly, the majority occur in the upland territory on the western side of the county which lies closer to Wales where they are traditional. Of course, there came a time in the life of every longhouse when it was considered undesirable to have animals in such close proximity to humans; the animals were housed elsewhere and their former quarters adapted to serve human needs, but it should be possible to work out from the way in which the plan deviates whether or not the lower end or inner room was once a byre. Other clues may come in the siting of the house—longhouses were usually on a downhill slope to assist drainage from the byre and there is often a break in the roofline between the house part and the byre. If the entrance was also shared then an extra-wide passageway may remain, perhaps up to 9ft. instead of the normal 6ft. 4in. average—cattle need a wide turning circle. Where a clearly defined passage is present the building is likely to have been a longhouse if only one opening is discernible on the low side instead of the normal two or three, and further proof may come if there are or were open panels below the first horizontal rail, through which food was pitched in to the troughs. In Shropshire the feeding walk is known as a 'byng' and sometimes the byng and the passage are dual-purpose features, but a single centrally-placed door on the low side of the passage might indicate that the byng was placed at right-angles to the passage and the cattle divided into two compartments.

There are, naturally, many examples of houses which have a byre attached to them, but they cannot be considered as classic longhouses unless there is direct access from the house part into the byre, the tell-tale feature will be a doorway, now usually blocked, between the two. Even then the byre may represent an added feature or be a rebuilding of an earlier one.

In the Welsh Folk Museum at St. Fagans are examples of reconstructed longhouses. Cilewent from Powys and Hendre'r-Ywdd Uchaf from Clwyd are particularly instructive and wonderfully evocative, and, of course, an immense debt is owed to Iorwerth Peate whose pioneering work remains the basis for all subsequent studies.[38] But Shropshire's longhouses present more problems of interpretation than the straightforward Welsh examples. The demolished Padmore in Onibury parish was probably the least

Sheppen Fields, Pulverbatch, c.1464 longhouse as seen in 1918 with the Lewis family

Padmore, Onibury. Reconstruction by S.R. Jones
(see Table 3 overleaf)

controversial example of a medieval open hall house which had a byre at the lower end and was occupied by a relatively high class yeoman-farmer family.[39] A similar example, this time of cruck construction, is the beautifully restored building known modestly as 'Ousley Barns' in Aston Eyre parish, but another, Sheppen Fields, which functioned as a long-house within living memory, could not have been built as such because the smoke-blackened open central cruck truss of the former hall now appears in the byre.[40] A house in Bitterley parish is actually named 'Longhouse' in Robert Baugh's map of 1808 and is still so called, but as the term is more likely to relate to the shape of the house rather than to a communal shelter for humans and animals, perhaps it should be seen as a true perpetuation of the *Domus Longa*. There seems to be a gap between the medieval longhouses and those which are clearly datable to the late 17th and early 18th centuries, and it is interesting that the majority of the earlier examples are cruck-built.

Carved mantel beam over inserted fireplace in the hall at Lower Spoad, Clun (see Table 3 overleaf)

Grid Ref	Parish	Name	Notes
SJ 413016	Church Pulverbatch	Sheppen Fields	*c.*1464? Cruck hall-house, with C.17th additions. Converted to longhouse. Has low-beam central truss. Property of Haughmond Abbey from C.13th to C.16th. Sloping site.[41]
SO 464794	Onibury	Padmore	C.15th box-framed hall-house of quality interpreted as having a byre at the lower end. (Dem.).[42]
SO 645949	Aston Eyre	Ousley Barns	C.15th cruck hall-house of quality with a byre at the low end. Two-bay hall with fine central truss and a solar bay at the high end.
SO 407197	Little Ness	Lower House Farm	C.15th cruck hall house of quality with a two-bay hall and possibly a two-bay byre. Floor levels now built up.
SJ 495060	Condover	Condover Court	Dendro-dated to 1445. Cruck hall-house of quality with two-bay lower end. Was one bay a byre?[43]
SJ 426076	Pontesbury	Sibberscot	C.15th cruck hall-house later used as a barn. Had low-beam truss in hall. Same louvre control as Sheppen Fields. Probably a longhouse. Was demolished, but timbers rescued and building re-erected at Brookgate Farm, Plealy.[44]
SO 326768	Clun	Timber Croft Pentre Hodre	Dendro-dated to 1465. Two-bay cruck hall with low beam. Upland site. Possible longhouse.[45] (See also Gazetteer)
SO 471879	Eaton-u-Heywood	Wolverton	Dendro-dated to 1475. Base-cruck variant. Hall-house of quality. Has one central door from passage into two-bay lower end.[46]
SO 654783	Cleobury Mortimer	Catherton Cottage	Cruck hall-house of quality, dendro-dated to 1485. Has low-beam truss in hall. 18'6" bay at low end interpreted as a byre.[47]
SJ 238260	Oswestry Rural	Bryn-y-Pentre Trefonen	C.15th cruck hall-house with C.17th additions. Good quality truss in hall. Two-bay byre.[48]
SO 468903	Eaton-u-Heywood	Hatton Farm Marshbrook	C.15th cruck hall-house with C.16th & C17th alterations. Difficult to assess but suggestive of longhouse origins. Sloping site.
SO 257820	Clun	Lower Spoad	C.15th cruck hall-house with later additions. Has byre at low end and a further cruck range at right-angles to the byre.

Table 3. Examples of Longhouses and Derivatives (in suggested chronological order)

Grid Ref	Parish	Name	Notes
SO 316758	Clun	Bryn Cambric Chapel Lawn	Upland site. Possible longhouse three cruck trusses (two from whole trees) + remains of a further truss. (See also Gazetteer)
SJ 373069	Pontesbury	Upper Farm Asterley (barn)	C.15th five-bay cruck-built, was house. Difficult to assess but suggestive of longhouse origins.[49]
SJ 431907	Church Stretton	Longmynd House Minton	C.15th cruck hall-house with C.17th and C.18th additions. Sloping site. Plan suggests byre (now removed) at low end.[50]
SO 485964	Cardington	Comley Cottage	C.15th cruck-built single-bay hall, storied bay at upper end. Box-framed byre at low end has lower roof-line.
SO 458914	Hope Bowdler	Ragdon Farm	C.15th cruck hall-house with later additions. Sloping site. Evidence from old photograph suggests byre at low end.[51]
SJ 557335	Prees	Manor Cottage	Dendro-dated to 1551-2. Two-bay cruck hall of quality. Crucks on stylobate; probable longhouse.[52]
SJ 529286	Wem	Aston Bridge Farm	C.16th cruck hall-house with lower unit at one end. Difficult to assess but suggestive of longhouse origins. Walls and truss have infill of peat.[53]
SJ 542414	Whitchurch	38 Watergate	Small town 'croglofft' cottage with suggestion of accommodation for a cow beneath. Similar to 'The Old Shop', below.[54]
SO 357831	Clunbury	26/7 Kempton	C.17th box-framed lobby-entry house with a third bay possibly a small byre with 'croglofft' above.
SO 365740	Bucknell	Old Farm	C.17th box-framed farmhouse with later alterations. Two large bays at the south (now upper) end of plan suggest longhouse origins.
SO 506951	Cardington	Honeysuckle House (renamed The Maltsters' Tap)	C.17th three-bayed box-framed byre/barn attached to remains of stone-built house-place. Original communicating door between the two. This building is distinct from the house itself.
SJ 598063	Eaton Constantine	Baxter's House	C.17th box-framed parlour crosswing replacing what was probably the byre of an earlier longhouse. Sloping site, wide passage.

Table 3. Examples of Longhouses and Derivatives (in suggested chronological order)

Grid Ref	Parish	Name	Notes
SJ 353203	Kinnerley	The White House Kynaston	C.17th box-framed house-place and parlour with byre at low end. Visual access only from houseplace to byre. Longhouse derivative.
SO 512784	Stanton Lacy	10 The Hope	C.17th box-framed longhouse of squatter origin. Direct access from house-place to byre. Cattle had separate entrance. Haystore beyond byre.
SO 548804	Hopton Cangeford	Castle Cottage	C.17th stone-built houseplace and byre built up to an earlier box-framed crosswing. Direct access from house-place to byre. Byre is at higher level. Cattle had separate entrance. Functioned in longhouse tradition within living memory.
SJ 261252	Oswestry	Gibraltar Inn Treflack Wood	C.17th longhouse derivative plan with byre and hayloft at low end. Probably had direct access from house-place to byre but evidence removed by modernisation.
SJ 553155	Upton Magna	The Old Shop Somerwood	C.17th sequence of development beginning with a box-framed single-cell unit with accommodation for a cow at one end.[55]
SJ 465298	Loppington	Old House Farm Brown Heath	C.17th box-framed addition to earlier cruck house to provide byre and hayloft. Longhouse derivative. Access was from upper-floor level of house so that the cattle could be fed from above.
SO 589822	Stoke St. Milborough	Newton Farm	C.17th stone-built longhouse derivative. Sloping site. Byre and hayloft at low end. Access was from upper-floor level of house so that the cattle could be fed from above.
SO 463834	Culmington	2 Shaw Bank	C.18th longhouse derivative. Small Two-bay stone-built cottage, one bay ceiled the other open—for livestock? Similar ones in the lane housed workers in the lime quarries.

Table 3 (cont.). Examples of Longhouses and Derivatives (in suggested chronological order)

2　Stone Houses

Shropshire's geology is extremely varied and of the 13 classic geological periods ten are represented by rock sequences.[1] The resulting richly varied scenery accompanies an equally diverse supply of building stones which, in turn, differ considerably in their quality. Some villages, such as Alberbury and Norbury, restrict their stonework to the locally quarried material while others, such as Rushbury and Cardington, draw on a number of different stones, but never from a great distance. There is a subtle difference between 'Shropshire building stone' and 'stone used for building in Shropshire'. Only one type qualifies for the former category, achieved national recognition and travelled out of the county. This is the 'Grinshill' stone, quarried at Grinshill, Yorton and Clive, about seven miles north-east of Shrewsbury. Archdeacon Plymley, writing in 1803, described Grinshill as 'superior, perhaps, to any in the kingdom'[2] but, with the exception of Grinshill and to a lesser degree Hoar Edge Grit, stone used for building in Shropshire is extremely localised and none is comparable in quality. Plymley also praised the white sandstone of Sweeny Mountain near Oswestry and gave other examples which were 'very good to build with' but none had the commercial potential of Grinshill.

While it is true that great ecclesiastic foundations and early magnates' houses, by implication defensible, were stone-built, as a material for farmhouses, later town-houses and cottages stone was not in general use probably until the 17th century. Like classicism itself, which appeared first as detailing, stone was introduced gradually for chimneys and doorcases and was frequently used for casing older timber-framed houses. Whole areas of south Shropshire such as the Corvedale and the Clun valleys, including the towns of Much Wenlock and Clun, which now have the appearance of being stone-built are, in fact, mostly timber-framed under stone exteriors.

The picture is rather different north of Shrewsbury where the exploitation of the stone coincided with the draining of meres and marshes allowing new farmhouses and cottages to be built entirely with stone, though timber-framing was still used for internal partition walls. In the parish of Myddle a farmhouse called Harmer Moss Farm, which can be identified as the 'Meare House at Harmere' which 'did stand over crosse the brooke that issueth out of Harmeare, but when the Meare was lett dry the house was removed and set by the side of the brooke' has outer walls of stone and timber-framed internal partitions.[3] In contrast, the farmhouse now known as Houlston Manor but which was originally the 'Broomhurst Farm' in the same parish, described by Richard Gough as having been built by George Chambre c.1660/70, is an example of a timber-framed house built on reclaimed land and later, c.1800, enlarged and encased in brick.[4] The parish of Great Ness which contains the Nesscliffe quarries is a good example of how the stone was used for special buildings, notably the church, in the middle ages and then abandoned because most of the houses were timber-framed. The revival of stone building came in the 19th century when it was used for bridges and cottages.

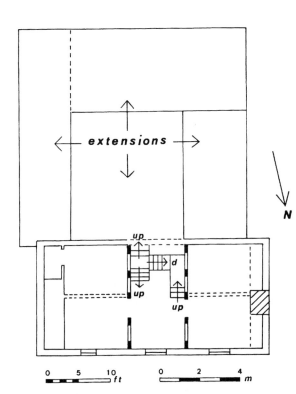

Harmer Moss Farm

First floor plan

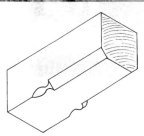

Chamfer stop
(not to scale)

The Custodian's Cottage, The Hermitage,
Bridgnorth, c.1877,
with Mr. and Mrs. Taylor

Cave Houses

The soft red sandstone around Nesscliffe and Myddle to the north of Shrewsbury, and Bridgnorth and Worfield in the south-east of the county was exploited both for building stone and by cave-dwellers. Caves, the most primitive of dwellings, were occupied well into the 20th century in Shropshire. At the Hermitage in Bridgnorth a series of caves includes the remains of a three-cell dwelling last occupied in 1928. It was well-furnished and had pictures on the walls, a cast-iron cooking range and piped water.[5] Another has historic connections with the Crown and was fitted out as a chapel.[6] Several cave-houses survive in Bridgnorth and, though now empty and barred, were once equipped with doors, windows and fire-places.

Behind the mid-19th century cottages in Railway Street is virtually a street of caves which were inhabited before the railway came and are now used as outhouses for the cottages. A painting entitled 'Lizzie's Bower', which was exhibited in the Royal Academy, depicts a notorious local prostitute outside her cave home, at present an outhouse to one of the cottages at the lower end of Railway Street.[7] The Cartway, at one time the only vehicular connection

Above left: Interior of a cave dwelling at The Hermitage during clearance
Above right: The same view in 1990

The Railway Street cave at Bridgnorth
known as 'Lizzie's Bower'

between High Town and Low Town in Bridgnorth contains many cave-houses. A 17th-century description reads 'Caves so hewn, and Shaped to the Forms of Edifices erected from the Plain, that they are rather a Rarity than a Disfigurement to the Street. On the Roof of these Caves are either gardens made without much Cost or extraordinary Art, or Pathways over them so that you may walk over the Tops of several Houses without Danger or Difficulty'.[8] Presumably vegetables could be grown in the roof gardens, indicative of a parallel life-style with Irish peasantry in their semi-underground turf huts.

Humphrey Kynaston, Shropshire's equivalent to Robin Hood, is said to have occupied one half of the well-known cave at Nesscliffe and his horse the other. His cave is hewn from an old quarry face whilst in close proximity are later 19th-century quarries which catered for the demand in a boom period for sandstone of intermediate quality. At Myddle, Gough frequently mentions people who, at various times, occupied 'the cave in Harmer Hill' as though there was only one in his day, though more are identifyable today.[9] At 'The Nest' in Myddle parish a sequence from cave to stone-built house and to the extension of the house is clearly discernible. The cave, which may be that mentioned by Gough, contains at least two chambers,

31

one of which currently serves as a wine-store but was previously a bed-recess. At the foot of the hill, within the curtilage of 'The Nest', is perhaps the cave which Gough refers to as the 'Goblin Hole'. Its position relates to Gough's description, 'There is a certain cave in the rock near this bridge (Bristle Bridge) ... and was called the Goblin Hole, and afterwards was made into a habitation, and a stone chimney built up to it ...'.[10]

The Nest, Lower Myddle,
showing the cave entrance on the left

A logical progression from living in a cave would be to utilize the rock face or the quarry face as the rear wall of the house, and an example of this practice is no.11, Lower Road, Myddle where, in addition to the rear wall, one of the lateral walls incorporates a section of natural rock. At the rear of the Mill House at Evelith in Shifnal parish are soft red sandstone caves, some of which are brick-lined and were used as bake-ovens, enabling a continuous process of wheat to flour to bread to take place on the site.

The Rock Houses of Kinver, only nine miles away from Bridgnorth, but in the neighbouring county of Staffordshire are much better known and, in their day, were more extensive, but the life-styles of the two communities must have been very similar.[11]

Grinshill Stone

Without doubt, Grinshill is the best of Shropshire's building stones. It is a Keuper sandstone of the Triassic period but it occurs in a limited area because it is a totally altered formation of the usual red sandstone, having probably been bleached by local igneous activity. Although the colours range from reddish brown to greenish grey the commonest form is pale honey-coloured when newly-quarried or cleaned and this is seen to best advantage in most of the public buildings of Shrewsbury. It is a good freestone, which means that it may be cut 'freely' in any direction without disintegrating and will yield smooth ashlar surfaces and thin joints. It has some barytes veins which are less affected by weathering than the sandstone and tend to project from the surface, particularly after some years of exposure, a feature which makes Grinshill instantly recognizable.

There is not much evidence that Grinshill was used for anything except major buildings until the 16th century, but production increased and reached its zenith in the 19th century when Yorton railway station was built to facilitate the transport of the stone. No production figures are available, but census returns show that 1861 was a year of peak production when 51 quarry workers were employed, compared with 20 in 1851.[12] One quarry remains in use today, though on a limited basis.

Buildings which employ Grinshill stone either wholly or in part range from the 13th-century Abbey Cwmhir in Radnorshire to Clive Primary School, built in 1873; from the Prime Minister's country home, Chequers, in Buckinghamshire, where it is used for dressings, to local pig-sties and cattle-troughs in north Shropshire villages, and from Aberystwyth University to the fountain which formerly graced Broseley High Street. It is thought to occur in some churches in the southern states of the U.S.A, though whether it was specifically ordered or went across the Atlantic ocean as ballast has not been established.[13]

In Shrewsbury the contrast between the locally quarried Keele Beds sandstone of the Upper Carboniferous age and the superior Grinshill is best seen in the tower of St. Julian's church where the lower stage, *c.*1200, is of Keele and the upper stage, 15th-century work, is of Grinshill. Perhaps the two buildings in Shropshire which display Grinshill at its best are St. Chad's church in Shrewsbury and Attingham Hall about three miles to the east, both 18th-century buildings and designed by the same architect, George Steuart, though it should be noted that each is basically brick-built and only faced with Grinshill. Because of its ruinous condition Moreton Corbet Hall of the 16th century illustrates this practice clearly. These examples are, of course, 'polite' buildings, and generally Grinshill was chosen for superior work because of its durability and appearance, but there are many instances of its use at vernacular and interim levels such as 'Stone Grange' in the village of Grinshill, the house to which the boys of Shrewsbury School were evacuated when epidemics were rife in the town.[14] Known to have been built for the School, when not

Moreton Corbet (1579) showing Grinshill stone facing on brick

Centre: Stone Grange, Grinshill
Lower left: Plaque on north-east porch
Lower right: Plaque on north-west porch

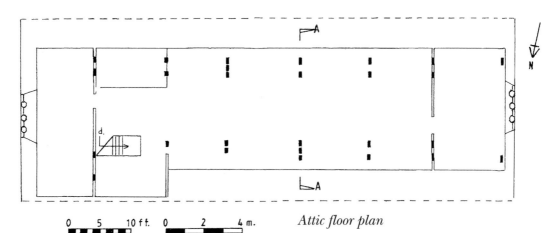

Attic floor plan

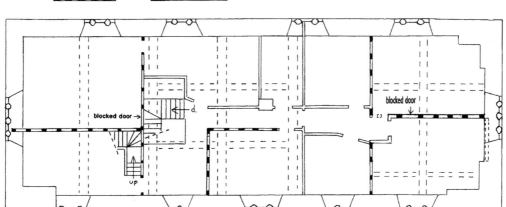

First floor plan

Stone Grange,
Grinshill

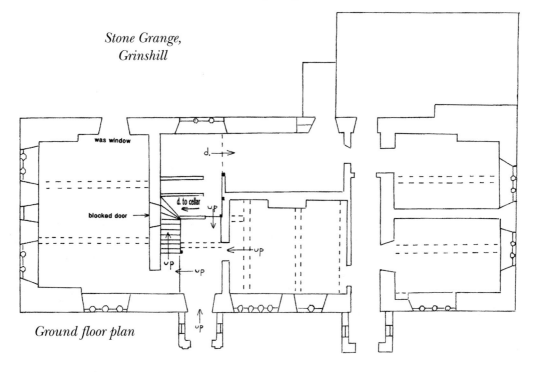

Ground floor plan

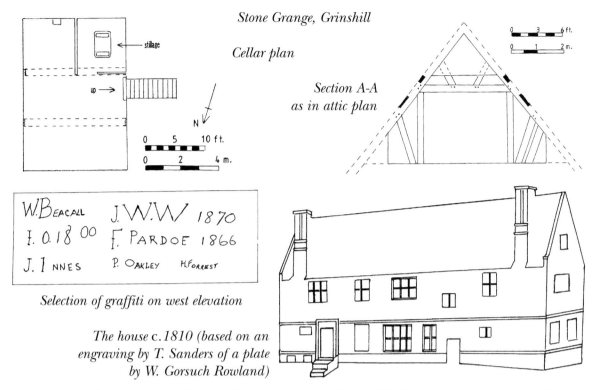

Stone Grange, Grinshill

Cellar plan

*Section A-A
as in attic plan*

0 ... 5 ... 10 ft.
0 ... 2 ... 4 m.

0 ... 3 ... 6 ft.
0 ... 1 ... 2 m.

Selection of graffiti on west elevation

*The house c.1810 (based on an
engraving by T. Sanders of a plate
by W. Gorsuch Rowland)*

in use it was let to tenants. Its two front entrances, both with later porches, one for the boys and the other for the master(s), the mass of schoolboy graffiti on the eastern wall, which relates to its use by a later private school, and the provision internally of a scholastic as opposed to a domestic hall proclaim its use and illustrate the versatility both of the plan form and the building material. Stone Grange must also be an early example, *c.*1617, of the use of corner chimneys. It has one at each corner, though the fireplaces are set on the lateral walls. It is now a private house.

In addition to complete buildings Grinshill stone was also in demand for dressings such as quoins, lintels, door-cases, window mullions, tracery, parapets, carvings and monuments; and for mundane items such as paving, curb-stones, grindstones, airfield runways, rainwater tanks, steps, boundary walls and many other items. It could be supplied in large or small blocks; among the former are the monolithic key-stones of John Gwynne's old bridge over the Severn at Atcham, built in 1769-71. The stones are 12ft. 1in. (3.69m.) in width and 5ft. 4in. (1.63m.) in height and the parapet is designed as an integral feature with the stonework, thus frustrating any 18th-century vandals' attempts to push coping-stones into the river.

Hoar Edge Grit

In terms of quality, Hoar Edge Grit comes second to Grinshill, though it was never a serious rival and its use was confined to a relatively small area around its source, the quarries along the escarpment to Lodge Hill, north-east of Lawley Hill. Of Ordovician age, it is a freestone with rounded sand grains. Its texture is rougher than that of the best Grinshill but is is durable and will take an ashlar finish. It was used in and around Cardington wherever possible, even for cottages, in preference to the very localised Chatwall sandstone from Hill End quarry to the south of the village. Examples of Hoar Edge Grit include Chatwall Hall and its neighbour, Chatwall Farm, where it is used partly to encase a timber-framed house; Willstone Farm, dated

Type	Description	Examples
Ordovician Soudley sandstone	Multi-coloured bands giving a green, brown and purple striped appearance	Houses in Hope Bowdler and in around Church Stretton. Minton House, Minton shows the stone worked to a semi-smooth finish on the front but rubble on the rear and lateral walls
Ordovician Acton Scott 'limestone'	Hard, splintery calcareous sandstone	Its use confined to the Acton Scott estate
Ordovician Stiperstones 'Quartzite'	Rough, chunky, hard sandstone, only usable as rubble	Used in and around Pontesbury, eg. The Old Rectory
Ordovician Chatwall sandstone	Dark purplish-red	Used in and around Cardington eg. 'Brookside', the base of the plinth at the Old School and intermittently at the 'Maltster's Tap'
Silurian *Pentamerus* Beds sandstone	Known locally as 'Government Rock' on account of the fossil *Pentamerus oblongus* which, when exposed is outlined as a broad arrow	Houses in Norbury, eg. Freehold Farm
Silurian Wenlock Limestone	Hard, chunky, can be worked to a semi-smooth finish	Town houses in Much Wenlock
Silurian Kenley Grit	A conglomerate	Manor Farm, Church Prees
Silurian Whitcliffe Beds	A coarse-grained siltstone	Much used in Ludlow, eg. 27 Broad St. & The Rectory in College St.
Carboniferous Limestone at Llanymenach	Quarried in large blocks, fawn coloured	At Llanymenach the 'Cross Keys' has ashlared stone on the front. The cottages at the rear are rubblestone with red-brick dressings
Carboniferous Sweeny Mountain	Limey sandstone	The Hayes, Oswestry
Carboniferous Dhustone Hard, black basalt	Hard, black basalt	The Clee Hills (coal measures sandstone), notably Titterstone Clee, were capped with a layer of volcanically-derived basalt. This was exploited for many purposes including building. Often used with other local stones. 'Dhustone' is also the name of a small industrial village on Titterstone Clee. The village of Ditton Priors displays mostly Dhustone.
Carboniferous Keele Beds	Dull red sandstone	A band stretching from the Brieddens to Haughmond Hill, including Shrewsbury where the main quarry is now a pleasure garden called 'The Dingle'. Egs. include the early buildings: castle, town walls, Vaughan's Mansion, Bennet's Hall, Rigg's Hall, Greyfriars, etc.
Permian Alberbury Breccia	A purple-brown breccia with angular grains	Houses in Alberbury and Cardeston, eg. Lower Farm, Alberbury and Keeper's Cottage in Loton Park
Permian Bridgnorth sandstone	Soft red sandstone	Used in and around Bridgnorth

Type	Description	Examples
Triassic Nesscliffe and Myddle sandstones	Soft red sandstone, acquires a 'skin' after exposure which, if broken, leads to erosion. Both display varying colours due to chemical alteration. The pickmarks left by the quarrymen appear as a herringbone pattern on the face of the stones and may also be seen on the quarry faces	The stone could only be quarried in large blocks & therefore examples, which range from Myddle church & castle to farmhouses, cottages and pigsties are all built of blocks of a relatively uniform size

Table 1 (above and opposite).
Some categories of localised stone used for building

Chatwall Farm, Cardington. Hoar Edge Grit and timber-frame

The Old School, Cardington, c.1690. The school is built of brick,
Hoar Edge Grit and Chatwall sandstone,
whilst the Master's House is of Soudley banded sandstone

1738; Langley Chapel, Gatehouse and Hall Farm.[15] Mixed with Keele sandstone it is used at Acton Burnell Castle and mixed with Chatwall it may be seen at 'The Maltster's Tap', formerly known as 'Honeysuckle House' in Cardington. One small building complex in Cardington, The Old School and Schoolhouse, displays a mixture of Hoar Edge grit, Chatwall sandstone, Soudley banded sandstone and brick.

Chatwall Sandstone

This well-known Ordovician sandstone, south-west of Chatwall, is also known as the Soudley or Horderley sand-stone depending on where it is quarried. Best seen in sunshine or after rain it has distinctive bands of green, brown and purple. Mostly the blocks are laid according to the bedding plane but often these are interspersed with blocks laid at right-angles to the plane, that is with the stripes running vertically. This is contrary to one of the basic principles of masonry, but it must be said that the buildings do not appear to be adversely affected. Hope Bowdler village is an example of where the stone is used almost exclusively and it is also found in and around Church Stretton.

Alberbury Breccia

A good example of the localised nature of Shropshire's 'stone for building' is the Alberbury Breccia of early Permian age which forms a crescent-shaped ridge, about three miles in length between Loton Park and Cardeston.[16] Like the Acton Scott 'limestone' it demonstrates how the use of a building stone was sometimes concentrated on one estate, a practice which was influenced by a number of factors but primarily the desire to make the estate self-sufficient. The breccia consists of angular fragments of Carboniferous Limestone, purple sandstone and quartz pebbles in a calcareous matrix. It is extremely hard and durable but can only be used as rubble. Dressings are usually made of brick or red sandstone. In buildings the stone is mortared, but is it used, very successfully, in Loton Park as dry-stone walling for boundaries. Perhaps the smallest and certainly the most delightful vernacular building to use the breccia is the 17th-century Keeper's Cottage in Loton Park. Sadly ruinous, it is a simple one-up, one-down dwelling but it has features of architectural quality such as the moulded doorway jambs, lintel, string-course and fireplace. A subtle effect is the use of cyma recta moulding on the string-course and cyma reversa on the doorcase. The main windows, which are identical to those at The Marsh, Barrow, have chamfered mullions which are mason-mitred, and recess-chamfered frames. On the western side are three small 'porthole' windows, a fourth has been altered. All

Soudley banded sandstone in Hope Bowdler church

Keeper's Cottage in Loton Park: Alberbury breccia with sandstone dressings

Detail of Alberbury breccia

'Government Rock' (Pentamerus *sandstone)*
at Norbury church

the dressings, including the quoins, are of the dark red sandstone which occurs in the same beds as the breccia. The remains of a wooden staircase with flat shaped balusters and a king-post roof truss are visible.[17]

Pentamerus Beds Sandstone

Another very localised 'stone for building' is the calcareous sandstone of the *Pentamerus* Beds of Lower Silurian age, quarried at Norbury, a village at the southern tip of Linley Hill, south of the Stiperstones. The predominant fossil is the large brachiopod, *Pentamerus oblongus*, which has a central dividing plate, the spondylium. This, when exposed with the two angles formed by the hinge line of the shell, resembles a broad arrow. Inevitably, the stone is known locally as 'Government Rock', and it is, perhaps, fitting that the broad arrow has roots in Shropshire; it is included in the coat of arms of Sir Henry Sidney (1529-86), one-time president of the Council in the Marches of Wales and governor of Ludlow Castle. His shield may be seen over the entrance to the castle. Weathering will often dissolve the fossils and some of the stones in Norbury church appear to be very porous and spongelike, but the durability seems to be unaffected. The stone is used exclusively in Norbury.[18]

Stone Roofing Material

Before the importation of slate from North Wales began on a commercial basis many Shropshire buildings must have been roofed with stone flags. Aesthetically, the most pleasing stone roofing material still to be seen occasionally is 'Harnage Slate'. This is a colloquial term used to describe the Ordovician shelly limestone called *Subquadrata* limestone after the

The Prior's House at Much Wenlock showing 'Harnage Slate'
*(*Subquadrata *limestone) roof and walls of Alveley sandstone*

predominant fossil which is *Orthis subquadrata*. It occurs as layers within the Hoar Edge Grit. In geological terms it is not slate and, indeed, the county has no indigenous slate. The quarries occur along the ridge from Shadwell Coppice to Grange Hill, south-east of Acton Burnell, and the stone is similar to the *Alternata* limestone so called from a similar brachiopod fossil, *Heterorthis alternata*, which is stratigraphically a little younger, appearing between the Cheney Longville Flags and the Chatwall (Soudley) sandstone at Chatwall. There is very little difference between the two in appearance and none in practical use.[19]

The earliest documentary reference to the material is in 1367 and 1368 when Robert de Harley, lord of the manor of Harley sold 'the pieres de Harnage' from the roof of his kitchen and gatehouse at Harley. Similarly, 'Harnage slates' were used extensively in Shrewsbury where they have been found in several archaeological excavations, were favoured by the influential Drapers' Company in the 15th and 16th centuries, and were specifically ordered for roofing the new Drapers' Hall in 1577 and 1580.[20] Production had ceased, probably by the mid-17th century and the quarries are overgrown, but one at Bull Hollow is occasionally re-opened to provide material for repairs to historic buildings.

Undoubtedly the most spectacular extant Harnage roof in Shropshire is that of the Prior's House at Much Wenlock, now a private house. The visual appeal of the beautifully graduated flags combined with the texture is astonishing and it is entirely appropriate that it illustrates the front cover of the late Alec Clifton-Taylor's masterpiece *The Pattern of English Building*.[21]

To support such heavy roofing material strong roof frames were required and often the difference between an originally thatched roof and one which was stone-flagged may be determined by the degree of wind-bracing and the number of purlins used. Moat House, Longnor and Penkridge Hall in the parish of Leebotwood, both timber-framed houses, are two classic examples. Moat House has three tiers of cusped windbraces and in Penkridge Hall the roof space measures only 32ft. by 16ft. (9.75m. x 4.88m.) but has 32 windbraces to resist the pressure of the wind which gusts in the gap between the Caradoc and the Lawley hills and to support the weight of the original stone roof covering.

It is difficult to determine the date range for the use of 'Harnage' stone flags as their presence on a building does not necessarily mean that they are coeval with the structure. However, the documentary reference to 1367 and the dated standing building of 1658, Manor Farm, Berrington seem to indicate a span of three hundred years and probably more. No production figures are available, and apart from Mr. Lawson's very useful short paper little has been published on the subject.[22]

Other Stone Roofing Flags
Apart from the 'Harnage Slate' which was relatively widespread in its use, there were localised pockets of suitable stone for roofing flags which were exploited. The product may survive occasionally on farmhouses or be found in abandoned heaps after removal from a roof or be reused for a totally different purpose. Sometimes fragments appear after ploughing or digging and these may be indicative of a deserted settlement.

In the Corvedale the Old Red Sandstone of the late Silurian and Devonian period produced a finely-grained micaceous greeny-grey flagstone which was much used in the locality and may have been used for roofing at the Roman city of *Viroconium*.[28] However, the Corvedale was not on an established Roman route and *Viroconium*'s roofing material probably came from the area east of Leintwardine, the Roman *Bravonium*, just over the border in the Downton Gorge area of Herefordshire, which is within the same geological grouping. Areas further south-west and the Clun Forest region are also possible sources.[29] Roofing flags in the Corvedale, with characteristic pegholes, have been unearthed on many sites, and the same applies to the Clee Hills area. The roof of Easthope Manor in the Corvedale is still partially stone-flagged and similar flags were used to cover the hall of the late medieval complex which, at present, serves as a farm building at Cottage Farm, Easthope.[30] This community probably drew on the late Silurian Aymestry Limestone, quarried locally, for its roofing requirements.

Grid Ref	Building	Date (if known)	State of Building/Roof Covering
SJ 495125	Drapers' Hall, Shrewsbury	1557 & 1580	Roof covering replaced
SJ 495128	The Schools, Shrewsbury (now Public Library)	1595	Roof covering replaced
SJ 494126	Pride Hill Chambers	16th century	From excavation. Some later reused to build an oven[23]
SJ 492128	Rigg's Hall, Shrewsbury	1595 (repairs)	Roof covering replaced. Also known from excavation[24]
SJ 492125	Lloyd's Mansion, Shrewsbury	1570	Building demolished
SJ 503125	Whitehall 'Barn' Shrewsbury		Building and roof *in situ*
SO 545928	Wilderhope Manor	*c.*1586	Building and roof *in situ* (part Harnage)
SJ 495056	Condover Hall	1587/92	Roof covering replaced
	Condover Mill		Building demolished
SJ 569023	Harnage Grange Gazebo		Building and roof *in situ*
SJ 556011	Bull Farm, Grange Hill Cound		Building and roof *in situ*
SJ 535020	Acton Burnell Castle	*c.*1280	Building mostly ruinous but some roof covering *in situ*
SJ 538001	Langley Chapel	13th century (roof covering prob. 17th century)	Building and roof *in situ*
SJ 539002	Langley Gatehouse	15th & 17th centuries	Building and roof *in situ*
SJ 527043	Pitchford Church	mostly 13th century	Building and roof *in situ*
SJ 527042	Pitchford Hall	*c.*1549/ 1551	Building and roof *in situ*
SJ 527042	Pitchford Hall, Orangery		Building and roof *in situ*
	22, Pitchford		Building demolished
SJ 549042	Old Hall Cressage	17th century	Building and roof *in situ*
	Manor House, Harley	14th century	Site unknown[25]
SJ 792069	Tong Castle		From excavations
SJ 795074	Tong College		From excavations
SJ 530068	Berrington Church Tower	15th century	Building and roof *in situ*
SJ 531067	Berrington Manor	1658	Building and roof *in situ*
SJ 625001	Prior's House, Much Wenlock	1425	Building and roof *in situ*
SO 530965	Plaish Hall, Cardington	*c.*1577	Building and roof *in situ*
SJ 695051	Madeley Court	mostly 16th century	Building and roof *in situ*[26]
	Dovecote, Eyton-on-Severn		Demolished
SJ 575062	Tithe Barn Cottage Eyton-on-Severn	17th century	Building and roof *in situ*
SJ 397190	Great Ness Church Tower	13th century & later	Roof covering replaced
SJ 458072	Old Lyth Manor ('Great Lyth') Bayston Hill	*c.*1650	Roof covering replaced. (Original flags reused as walling for farm building)
SJ 423022	Castle Pulverbatch		Fragments found during building operations
SO 745947	Hoards Park Farm Bridgnorth		Roof covering replaced
SO 767961	Rowley Farm, Worfield		Roof covering replaced
SJ 495003	Moat House, Longnor	late 14th century	Roof covering replaced
SJ 489007	Malthouse Smallholding	17th century	Roof covering replaced
SO 490977	Penkridge Hall, Leebotwood	1590	Roof covering replaced
SO 594920	Great Oxenbold Monkhopton		Building and roof *in situ* (fragments of Harnage)[27]
SJ 493210	Dovecote at Lea Hall, Pimhill	*c.*1584	Building and roof *in situ*

*Table 2. Some known examples of 'Harnage Slate' (*Subquadrata *limestone) roof covering. The table is based on a combination of Mr. Lawson's examples and the present writer's personal observations*

Quarry for roofing slabs at Corndon

*The Old Post Office at Churchstoke (Powys)
with roof of 'Corndon Slabs'*

At Castle Farm, Cheney Longville the greenish-grey Cheney Longville Flags of late Ordovician age, fashioned into roofing flags, lie disused in the farmyard, and it is clear that some of the Ludlow buildings also had stone-flagged roofs as redundant examples continue to be found in back-yards. These are probably of Downton Castle Sandstone, a Silurian rock quarried a few miles to the west of the town.

Corndon Hill to the south-west of Shrewsbury is just over the modern Shropshire border in Powys which here forms an intrusion into Shropshire to the east of Offa's Dyke. The hill itself is a large dolerite intrusion into the Hope Shales and produces a hard stone, blue-green to dark grey in colour, similar to the Clee Hill dhustone. However, on the south-western slope of the hill the altered Hope Shales on the margin of the dolerite produce finely laminated material which was extensively quarried for roofing and flooring. This must be the 'Corndon' stone referred to in the lyrical poetry of the 15th-century Welsh poet Guto'r Glyn for roofing the vicarage at Llandrinio in Montgomery-shire and, according to Owain Glyndwr's bard, Iolo Goch, for roofing Sycharth Castle, Glyndwr's stronghold base in neigh-bouring Denbighshire.[31] While plenty of evidence of quarrying remains on the hill, very few buildings now display a Corndon roof. The Old Post Office at Churchstoke appears to be the only example left of a Corndon roof in that village and there are a few fragmentary traces, mostly in outbuildings, in Priestweston. It probably had a wide distribution along the Welsh Middle Marches but little is known about it today.

3   Cruck Construction in Shropshire

The possible origins of cruck construction as seen in a national context, the survival rate, distribution and the many concomitant questions that the existence of such a form raises have provided the subject matter for a number of books and articles. With such extensive foundation material available, the aim of this chapter, after some general remarks, is to consider cruck distribution in Shropshire, the factors affecting it, how local examples conform with or differ from national trends and whether any special characteristics emerge from a county study.

Crucks seem to exert a disproportionate influence over the investigator. It is possible to become totally absorbed in tracking and analysing examples without being able to give logical reasons for their fascination. Part of the fundamental appeal must be a sub-conscious admiration of early carpenters who saw the growth pattern in certain oak trees and, with singular display of opportunism, fashioned them into trouble-free frames for houses which they probably knew would last indefinitely.

Precise definition of the word 'cruck' has caused difficulty among writers. For present purposes that given by Eric Mercer is considered most adequate: 'inclined timbers rising from ground level to an apex and serving as the trusses of a roof .... the blades may be curved or straight; they may rise from a timber sill or from a low stone base ....'.[1]

Within the category of cruck construction are many variants, and these as they relate to Shropshire will be discussed, but it is important that the general reader understands the difference between cruck-built and box-framed buildings. In cruck-framed structures the crucks themselves are load-bearing members which support the weight of the roof directly. The only essential joint is where they meet at the apex. The walls are of secondary importance, capable of replacement without the necessity of shoring up the roof or having the whole structure collapse. Box-framing, as its name implies, is a technique whereby a series of posts and beams is constructed in a boxlike form, on top of which a triangular roof is laid. The weight of the roof is more or less evenly distributed throughout the frame and the walls are an integral part of the structure. A feature of timber-framing in the West Midlands and the Welsh Marches is that the two systems frequently occur in the same building. A number of cruck-framed halls have contemporary box-framed wings, and nearly four times that number, not surprisingly, have added box-framed wings. In a few houses only the hall central truss is of cruck construction, box-framed trusses being employed at either end. Timber-framed barns, on the other hand, exemplify the dichotomy between the two techniques, being either all cruck or all box-framed. Four houses in which cruck construction is used both for the hall and the crosswing have been noted in Shropshire, though in the case of Lower Spoad the wing clearly functioned as a byre.

Theoretically, both cruck and box-framed buildings may be easily enlarged if necessary, though the cruck frame lends itself more readily to elongation by the simple addition of another pair of crucks for each requisite bay. The limitations of cruck-framing are in height

A 'Cruck Oak' (left), with drawings showing the shape and cut for an inverted cruck (top left) and standard cruck (top right)

and width, both dimensions dependent on the size of the blades which the tree yielded. It was probably these limitations which led to the disappearance of crucks from towns once the 'great re-building' was under way in the late 16th and during the 17th centuries, and to their decline and supersedure by box-framing at roughly the same time. Another factor would have been the dwindling supply of suitable trees. While box-framed houses could be fashioned from shorter lengths of timber, substantial crucks demanded specially shaped trees, the supply of which was, naturally, limited. Indeed, it is very rare today to see a living tree capable of producing a convincing cruck truss.

Under the broad category of 'Common Oak' there are two distinct species, the sessile oak (*Quercus petraea*) and the pedunculate oak (*Quercus robur*). Generally speaking, the sessile oak may be described as growing with a straight trunk and throwing off many small branches at the top; the acorn in its cup has direct contact with the branch and the undersides of the leaves are covered with minute hairs. In contrast the pedunculate oak tends to grow either with a divided trunk or with a substantial limb or limbs thrown out at intervals; the acorn cup is connected to the branch by a short stalk or peduncle and the undersides of the leaves are smooth.[2] Although hybrids are widespread and growing conditions, soil and climate determine the end product, nevertheless it is true that pedunculate oaks predominate in cruck-producing areas and sessiles in parts of the country where crucks are rare and box-framing is common, that is, the whole of eastern England, south of the Humber estuary. It is the pedunculate oak which is admirably suited for cruck construction; the natural curve of trunk and limb tailor-made for the purpose, while sessiles produce long straight timbers characteristic of the timber-framing in eastern regions. In these areas curved braces, if and when employed, are obtained from high-growing branches and have a comparatively minor function, unlike the heavy bracing of what was defined some years ago as 'the highland zone'.[3]

In Shropshire the pedunculate oak predominates. The drawings opposite show how such trees could be converted to crucks either when the cruck was to follow the natural growth of the tree, the base taken from the lower part of the trunk and the apex from the limb, or when the cruck was to be inverted, the base coming from the limb and the apex from well down the trunk. At one time the latter method was thought to be standard practice, but the theory has not been substantiated to any extent.[4] Failing scientific methods of proving whether the blade is inverted or not the only alternative is close observation of the grain, the knots and the general impression obtained. Very few Shropshire crucks suggest inversion although a clear example is at Rolly Cottage, Osbaston. Another, more questionable, is in the gable end at Condover Court. Neither of these houses is outlandish in concept and it is possible that inverted crucks are more common in the county than is thought to be the case at present.

In some parts of the country, notably where the crucks are of poorer quality, the truss blades are not matching timbers and clearly have been fashioned from two trees of roughly the same size. As a general rule this does not apply to Shropshire and even small houses and cottages at the end of the time and social scales can have trusses of matched blades obtained by sawing the tree in two longitudinally and opening the halves out with the sawn sides outside. However, there are two notable exceptions and they typify the top and bottom of the social scale, although they are very close in date. These are the great hall at Stokesay Castle, dendro-dated to 1284-5 and Cruck Cottage at Upton Magna where the internal crucks gave a dendro date of 1269.[5] Two more contrasting examples would be hard to find and they are discussed further in the chapter summarising the Shropshire Dendrochronology Project (see also illustrations on following pages).

Rolly Cottage, Kinnerley, showing (right) a possible inverted cruck

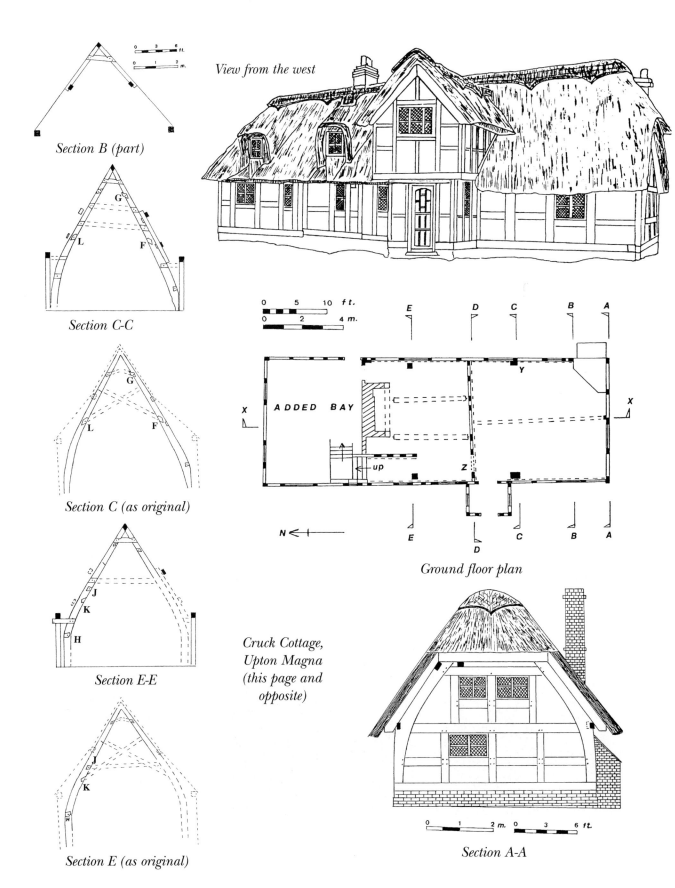

Section B (part)

Section C-C

Section C (as original)

G

L   F

Section E-E

J

K

H

Section E (as original)

J

K

H

View from the west

0   5   10   ft.
0   2   4 m.

E   D   C   B   A

X   X

ADDED BAY

up

Y

Z

N ←

E   D   C   B   A

Ground floor plan

Cruck Cottage,
Upton Magna
(this page and
opposite)

0   1   2 m. 0   3   6 ft.

Section A-A

46

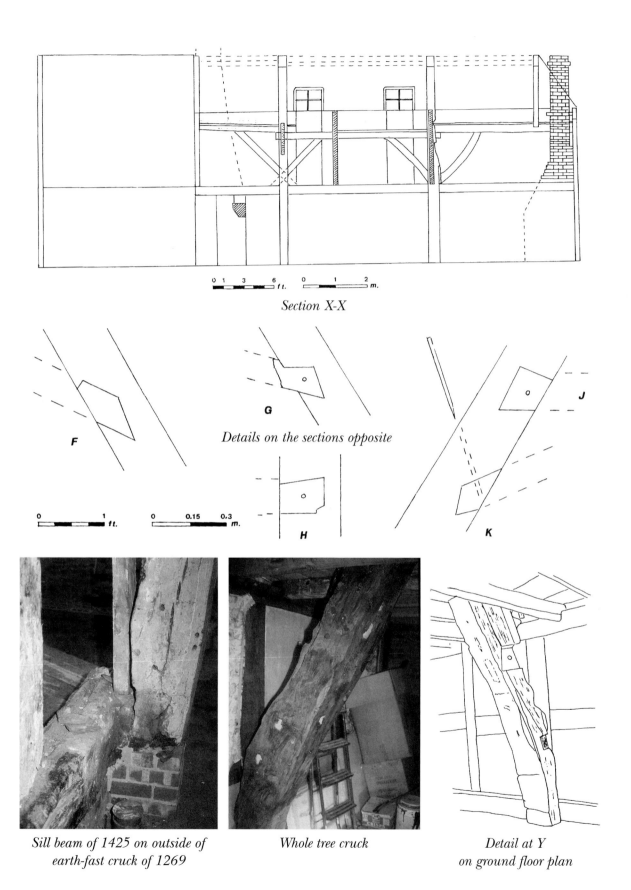

Section X-X

Details on the sections opposite

F

G

H

J

K

Sill beam of 1425 on outside of
earth-fast cruck of 1269

Whole tree cruck

Detail at Y
on ground floor plan

Raised crucks in the hall at Stokesay Castle (1285-1305)

Directional saw cuts on the central truss at Condover Court, Condover

0 ____ 1 ft.

0 ____ 0·3 m.

Where saw-marks are still discernible on cruck blades there is often a characteristic triangle formed at the elbow (see the drawing alongside). This suggests that the timber was not sawn over a saw-pit, which would indeed have been hazardous when dealing with a great curving timber, but was probably laid on trestles and sawn horizontally from one direction as far as the elbow, then turned at 90 degrees to complete the process from the other. The triangle indicates the short distance into the bend which the first directional strokes took.[6] However, there is documentary evidence that a saw-pit was employed in one case, that of Mark Tudge's house which is quoted below.

The first comprehensive survey of cruck buildings in England and Wales was published in 1973 and was based on the work of early pioneers in this field of study, with county lists compiled by local editors who were mostly members of the Vernacular Architecture Group, the body which undertook the survey under the direction of Dr. N. Alcock. The momentum engendered by this first catalogue resulted in a more extensive and exploratory survey which was published in 1981.[7] In the first list Shropshire's contribution was 94. By 1981 the total had risen to 168;

currently it stands at 273 and new discoveries are made at an average rate of five per year. In themselves these figures have significance only when related to the size of the county and to the national distribution pattern, but they show that far from being an insignificant county where crucks are concerned, as was thought at one time, Shropshire is at the heart of cruck distribution, taking a large percentage of the total of true crucks known to survive in England and Wales.

No systematic survey of cruck buildings in Shropshire has been made, and discoveries are largely a matter of chance, unlike the neighbouring county of Herefordshire which was fairly well combed for crucks by the R.C.H.M. in the course of preparation for the county volumes, although even there new examples still come to light. In Shropshire only two parishes have received detailed attention. These are Condover and Pontesbury where work in preparation for volume 8 of the Victoria County History resulted in 19 examples of cruck construction being noted.[8] In Habberley parish, which is now part of the civil parish of Pontesbury, three more were later found to be of cruck construction, and five of Pontesbury's townships yielded a further six examples, making a total of 28 for the two parishes. This concentrated effort, undertaken just before the great wave of destruction, ostensibly to rid the county of sub-standard housing, took place in the 1960s and has left an imbalance in the distribution pattern for Shropshire. Condover and Pontesbury still show the greatest density on the map (see overleaf), while areas such as the south-east corner of the county and the countryside around Ludlow are virtually blank. Pontesbury village itself fell victim to re-development and lost three examples. Condover, fortunately, lost none. Although the discrepancies thrown up by the distribution map overleaf should be borne in mind, the general trends are acceptable and conform to the national distribution pattern. The greatest concentration of crucks occurs south of the river Severn, the eastern side of the county is thinly endowed and they diminish noticeably in the Shropshire plain sweeping up to the north-eastern corner. Although further research will undoubtedly reveal hitherto unknown examples, it is unlikely to alter the general picture but merely fill in gaps which experience indicates should not be there.

Early pioneers in the study of cruck-framed buildings command a respect which is unquestioned; inspiration stems from them and in practical terms they recognized and were able to record crucks which would otherwise never have appeared on a distribution map because of the rate of subsequent demolition. In view of that it is perhaps cavilling to reflect that these people were northerners, the crucks they illustrated were typically northern and that consequently 'cruck' has become virtually synonymous with 'A-frame' which aptly describes straight inclined timbers braced by a horizontal tie-beam, the ends of which extended beyond the blades, formed the connection with the walls and supported the wall-plates. In trusses where a tie-beam was not employed then cruck 'spurs', effectively a tie-beam without its middle section, fulfilled the same purpose. Had the study of crucks commenced in Shropshire it is doubtful whether the term 'A-frame' would have been coined. The silhouette of a typical Shropshire cruck truss is more like a pair of inclined boomerangs, cruck spurs are used infrequently and are never lengthy, and the wall-plate is more likely to be supported on a step cut out of the back of the cruck where a mortice-and-tenon joint ensures its rigidity.

Cruck spurs, where they occur in Shropshire, vary considerably in the way in which they make connection with the blades. They may be secured by a morticed, tenoned and pegged joint, or crudely fashioned by a simple overlapping onto the face of the cruck with a wooden peg being driven through both timbers, and some are not strictly 'spurs' but slip-tenons, that is, short connecting pieces inserted between mortices on the edges of the blades and posts so that little of the connector is visible. In very late cruck or cruck-derived buildings spurs made

Location map of buildings in Shropshire utilising cruck construction

Whitchurch

Oswestry

Baschurch

River
Severn

Shrewsbury

Newport

Wellington

Pontesbury

Condover

Pulverbatch

Much Wenlock

Bridgnorth

Church
Stretton

Bishop's
Castle

Munslow

Stoke St. Milborough

Clun

Ludlow

Bedstone

of wrought iron are used. But the most elaborate and aesthetically pleasing spur joint is the half-lap dovetail joint. This too hardly comes into the category of 'spur' but, like the slip-tenon, simply secures the edges of both timbers; the visual effect is that of a butterfly-hinge. Examples have been noted at Bedstone Manor and at 25 Kempton in Clunbury parish. In many instances it is obvious that wallposts were thought unnecessary. The crucks were substantial members, capable of fulfilling a dual purpose and having the necessary vertical height to reach wall-plate level. Posts and spurs were thus eliminated from the start. In the cruck barn at Golding in Cound parish both inner trusses have posts to which they are connected by slip-tenons while the two outer trusses which once formed hipped gable ends have no posts. Because the crucks are of similar scantling the effect is one of intentional disproportion within the barn.

One of the undisputed advantages of building with crucks is that they have only one essential joint, that at the apex where the blades meet. On a national scale 14 different types of apex joints were noted, some being minor variations of classified types.[9] Shropshire has examples of 11 different types, and it is quite common to find variations within the same building. Towards the Welsh border the use of short king-posts is apparent, notable examples being those at Llywn-y-Go in Kinnerley parish (see p.452) and Bryn-y-Pentre in Trefonen which is now part of Oswestry Rural (see p.480). In Condover parish the universal apex joint is that classified as L2, an elaboration of the original B apex, but the difference is important. Type B is the meeting of the blades on a straight line before separating to house the ridge (see Glossary) but in L2 the joint is stabilized by a saddle immediately below the junction. The saddle is secured by morticed, tenoned and pegged joints at either end. Its use is not confined to Condover, but it tends to occur in cruck houses of good quality. Clearly it was considered to be a superior apex joint reflecting the generally high quality of the rest of the carpentry. In 25 Kempton the saddle is placed on top of the blades and is morticed, tenoned and pegged into them to form a triangular capping at the apex (see p.418). It is perhaps surprising that the most elaborate cruck truss in Shropshire, that at Bedstone Manor, should have a simple form of apex, not classified, where the blades meet on a continuous straight line and are pegged through from the side; but this cruck hall is unusual in having no ridge-beam and therefore no provision to support a ridge was necessary (see drawings p.54).

Another cruck hall-house which apparently had no ridge-beam is Ousley Barns in Aston Eyre parish and, like Bedstone Manor, the purlins are of the threaded variety associated more with box-framed buildings. A third example of a cruck hall-house with threaded purlins is 2 Ryton Grange Cottages in Condover parish.

The eastern (left) and northern elevations at Bedstone Manor (1448)

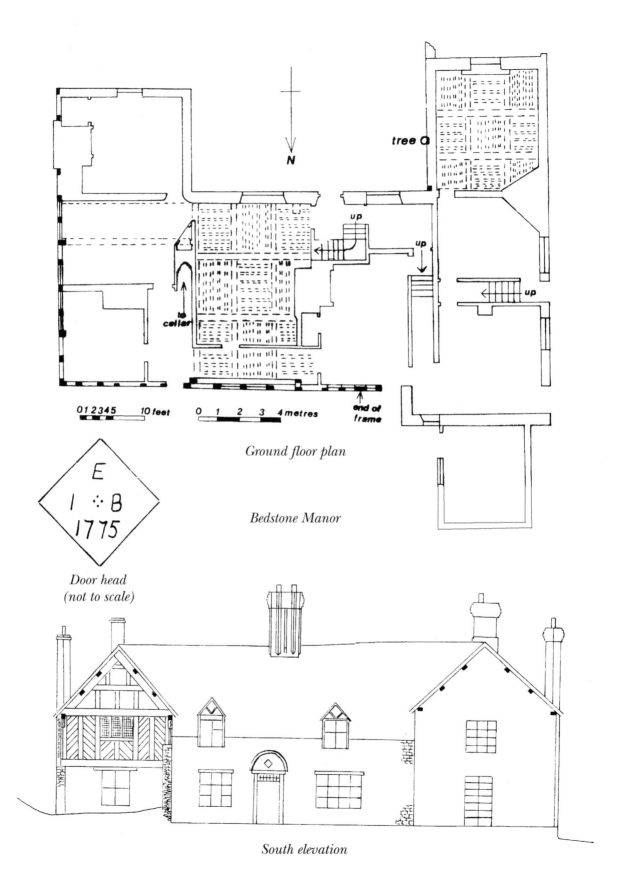

N

tree

up

up

up

to cellar

end of frame

0 1 2 3 4 5   10 feet

0   1   2   3   4 metres

Ground floor plan

E
1 ∴ B
1775

Door head
(not to scale)

Bedstone Manor

South elevation

52

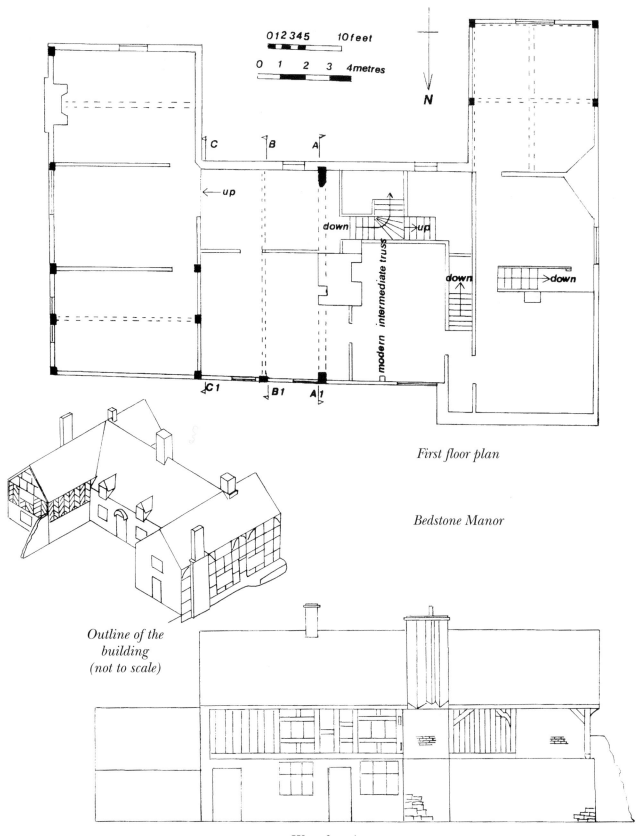

First floor plan

Bedstone Manor

Outline of the
building
(not to scale)

West elevation

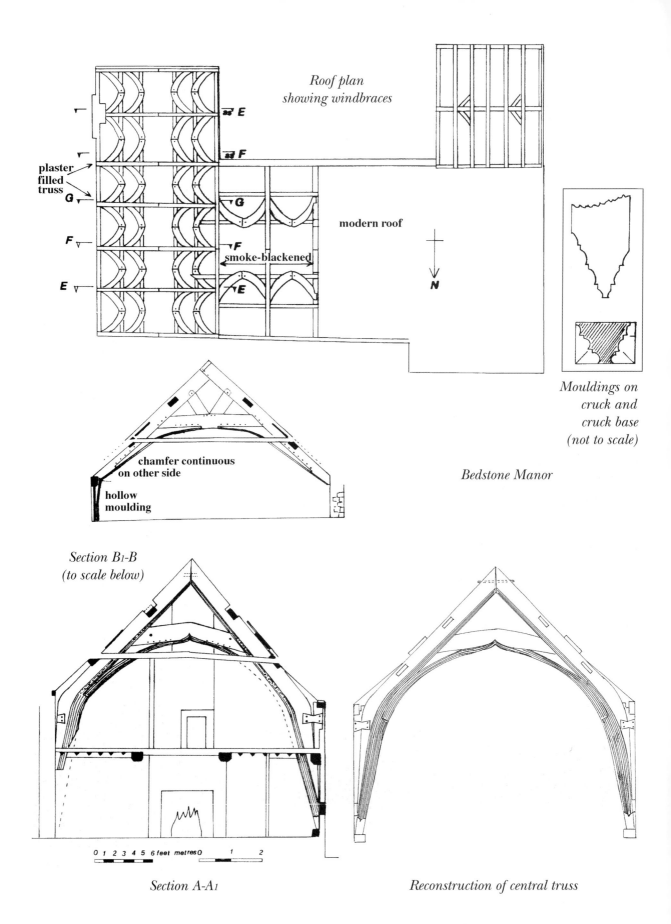

Roof plan
showing windbraces

plaster filled truss

modern roof

smoke-blackened

N

Mouldings on
cruck and
cruck base
(not to scale)

Bedstone Manor

chamfer continuous
on other side

hollow
moulding

Section B₁-B
(to scale below)

0 1 2 3 4 5 6 feet metres 0   1   2

Section A-A₁

Reconstruction of central truss

Central truss

*Detail of cruck 'spur'
on cruck/post assembly*

Ogee-arch detail on collar-beam of central truss

Chequer-board inserted ceiling

Bedstone Manor

Foot of central truss

Perhaps the most vulnerable part of a cruck is the foot, and opportunities to examine this area are rarely presented. It is usually found that the lower parts of the blades either disappear into later stone or brick walls or have been cut off and underpinned. With wall replacement being such a comparatively simple job where crucks are concerned, the feet of the blades are very vulnerable. Deep foundations were unknown and unnecessary for timber-framed houses. Theoretically the construction of a cruck truss involved a tenon at the foot of the blade engaging a mortice in the sill-beam of the side walls which, in turn, was jointed to a transverse sill-beam, the whole of the framework being supported on a low stone plinth.[10] In Shropshire, although the sill-beams may occasionally be seen, there seems to be little evidence that they were laid on stone plinths. This is generally true of the crucks in the southern part of the county. But in the north-eastern corner, in Whitchurch Urban and Whitchurch Rural respectively, are 6 Dodington and Ash Wood—both examples of where the feet of the crucks are supported on large blocks of sandstone known as 'stylobats' or 'padstones'. A further example is at Manor Cottage, Prees.[11] This practice is more frequently found in the northern counties of England and perhaps these examples show the penetration into north Shropshire of influences from Cheshire.

There is also variety in the decorative treatment of cruck blades in Shropshire. The majority are plain, some have simple chamfered edges; mouldings such as hollow, quarter-round, double-cavetto, and multi-roll-and-hollow have been noted and, where the upper parts of the blades are required to form part of a foiled decorative truss, they are cusped. At 25 Kempton the tops of the crucks are finished with inverted crow-steps (for illustrations see p.418). At first glance this appears to be a later alteration accompanying the truncation of the hall and the insertion of a stone chimneystack into what had been the central truss of the hall, but when seen from inside the house it is clear that the soffits of the crow-steps are smoke-blackened and that the later stonework has been contrived to fit the crow-steps and not *vice-versa*.

Mouldings are sometimes used to differentiate the upper bay of a hall from the lower. On the central truss at Shootrough in Cardington parish double cavetto moulding faces the upper bay while the less expensive quarter-round faces the lower bay. At Wheathall in Condover parish it is quarter-round and a plain chamfer respectively, while at Bedstone Manor the difference is subtly indicated by the use of seven rolls-and-hollows to the upper bay but only five to the lower. At 'Homeside' in Boraston parish an ogee arch is contrived by combining the curve of the arch-braces to the collar-beam on the central truss with a cutting into the collar. On the 'high' side the apex of the ogee is taken to a higher point than on the 'low' side. At Escob Farm in St. Martin's parish the central truss is chamfered only on the 'high' side, and the outstanding base-cruck at 23 Barrow Street, Much Wenlock, has evidence for a large decorative feature facing the dais end but nothing on the lower side. Unfortunately the feature has been removed. At Bradney Farm in Worfield parish a chamfer is taken to the apex saddle on the 'high' side but only as far as the collar-beam on the 'low' side, and at Lower Broughton in Lydham parish the practice extends to a box-framed hall. Here, on the collar-beam of the central truss, two nail-head/pyramid knobs face the upper bay while only one faces the lower bay.

Where cusping occurs the carpentry is as confident and the effect as pleasing as any found on box-framed trusses. Examples in cruck trusses are fewer but they occur at Llywn-y-Go in Kinnerley parish, at Catherton Cottage in Cleobury Mortimer and at Escob Farm in St. Martin's.[12]

Opinions differ regarding the theory of cruck origins and how far into antiquity cruck construction can be pushed; and it is not intended to enter into those arguments in this work. A summary of views has been published and this emphasises the diversity of thought and the wide date range suggested.[13] Where Shropshire is concerned the dates for full crucks obtained from dendrochronology range from 1269 to 1551, the bulk occurring in the 15th century and none in the 14th. The earliest known documentary reference to crucks is 1243 when the rector of Cound was given four oak trees from Cound wood to enlarge his tithe barn. This implies that the barn was cruck-built and in existence before that date. Another four oaks were for planks. ('8 *querci, viz.* 4 *ad furcas*, 4 a*d pannos*').[14] This post-dates the earliest known documentary reference to crucks in England by only 18 years. Ironically, that was in Essex, a county which produced only one cruck in the 1981 survey.[15] In 1284 the miller at Brockton in the parish of Sutton Maddock was granted a plot of land on which to build a house of six 'furcis' (cruck trusses) of 20ft., the bays each to be 14ft. The measurements are very specific and it seems that the plot was 70ft. long and 50ft. wide. At this time the word 'domus' used in the document did not necessarily refer to a dwelling house, but searches in the area have failed to reveal any remains of what must have been a large and important development.[16]

A Ludlow lease of 1296/7 refers to a tenement in Corve Street belonging to William Keterel, clearly described as being located between a cruck hall (*inter furcas aule*) and another tenement.[17] In 1272 the unfortunate Peter Gelemin was killed by a falling cruck in Ludlow. The cruck was worth 6d.[18] In 1315 the Dean and Chapter of Hereford noted that 'six wooden arches intended for a lavatory are uncovered and their timber is rotting' and that 'twelve forked timbers ... which once formed a barn' were also rotting. Forty years later the situation was the same.[19] In Wistanstow parish in 1372 the terms of a lease specified that a house with five pairs of crucks (*quino couples de forkes*) was to be erected along with a 'competent' barn.[20] Sadly, repeated probings in the parish have failed to reveal these buildings, and in Eaton-under-Heywood parish the search for Mark Tudge's 'fork' has also been fruitless.

So vivid is the description of the latter that it is worth quoting in full. It is taken from a deposition made in 1724:

> He, [Mark Tudge] has been told by his father deceased above 40 years ago that the plaintiff's great grandfather gave him a tree on Blackwood towards building his habitation in that neighbourhood and that he felled the tree on Blackwood and there made a saw-pit and sawed and squared it and carried it away and employed it in building his home without any interruption from the family of the Luttleys. Afterwards he and his father, then an ancient man were going over Blackwood and his father showed him the place and said 'Boy, here grew the tree that makes the fork that holds up the first pole of our house'.[21]

It would be good to know what Mark Tudge understood by the term 'first pole'.

In 1448 Richard Orme of Condover was accused, among other things, of placing dung at the foot of a cruck belonging to John Forster and causing it to rot. The damage was alleged to have amounted to 20 shillings.[22] Causing damage to neighbours' houses seems to have been one way of passing the time in Condover in the first half of the 15th century. Sybyl Don had a running battle with John Bedyl in the manor court. Bedyl was accused of carrying off a house belonging to Sybyl, causing her 32 shillings-worth of damage. It is not known whether the house was cruck-built, but after the dispute had occupied the court for 14 years and Bedyl had been fined 16 shillings, the very document on which the proceedings were written was later found to be forged.[23] 'Goodwife Garbot' was provided with a cruck house by Worfield parish in 1591. It was to be thatched with broom, daubed with clay and to have a boarded door. The total cost was 6 shillings.[24] A cruck cottage known as 'Bendigo', perhaps an allusion to its late 18th-century tenant, Abednego Wellings, in Berrington parish is described in the manorial survey of 1768 as 'A poor small house upon forks built by tenant but not fit to remain'. This may be the house that was first recorded in 1595.[25]

Clearly crucks were known in Shropshire in the 13th century, they probably reached the zenith of popularity during the 15th century, began to decline in the 16th century and became consigned to lesser buildings thereafter. Crucks for houses appear to have continued into the 17th century and upper crucks in farm buildings continued to be used into the 19th century. It is, perhaps, a measure of the basic practicality of the technique that has led to the re-emergence of cruck forms in the late 20th century in systems of laminated trusses which have proved suitable for such diverse buildings as public halls, swimming baths and greenhouses. Whether the impressive laminated cruck trusses in two farm buildings at Stableford Farm, Ackleton, in Worfield parish are regarded as revival or survival of the ancient technique of cruck building is an academic point; but that it was consciously chosen in the period of 'high farming' in the mid-19th century when mechanisation was in its infancy speaks volumes for the basic soundness of the system.

It is probably to the 15th and the first half of the 16th century that the majority of surviving cruck buildings in Shropshire can be dated. The large number surviving in Condover parish indicates both the favourable agricultural state of the area in pre-Reformation times and the acceptance of the cruck form as normal for prosperous yeoman-farmers' houses. Far from being a type of construction developed for men of very limited means, as was thought to be the case at one time, it is clear that crucks have acquired a vernacular character in the course of their history.[26] When the great hall of Stokesay Castle was built in the late 13th century for the wool magnate, Lawrence de Ludlow, crucks were chosen and presumably thought to be superior to other available systems. Lawrence's background was cosmopolitan. He was no rustic gaffer who happened to strike riches, neither was he a hereditary overlord hide-bound by convention and hedged about with feudal customs and dues—he was a businessman, first and foremost. His tastes would be noted, his resources envied and, where possible, his example copied.

By the mid-15th century crucks were the automatic choice for the wealthier peasantry and yeoman-farmer classes in Shropshire. In fact they appear seldom to have descended to 'cottage' level. If barns and other farm buildings are discounted, of the known remaining cruck-built dwellings in the county very few could be classed as true cottages. Although many others have a cottage-like appearance at present it is often the case that internal evidence will reveal a well-carpentered open hall with storied ends either added later or forming part of the original plan. On the other hand, it has to be borne in mind that cruck-built cottages would be wrought from poorer and thinner timbers, unlikely to survive more than three generations or be thought worth modernising, and so perhaps the overall impression of the status of crucks in Shropshire is distorted, and Lawrence de Ludlow's great hall at Stokesay and Goodwife Garbot's 6-shilling cruck cottage serve as timely reminders that they are to be found from the top to the bottom of the social scale.

Cruck Variants

The cruck family tradition includes a number of variants which, although lacking either the top or bottom sections of true crucks, are generically related. Basic definitions of the main variants are given below, followed by a summary of the extent to which they affect Shropshire.

a) Base Crucks

The blades rise from ground or near ground level only to the level of the lowest transverse member, usually a collar or collars above which the roofing technique may vary considerably. Strictly speaking, the lowest transverse member should be called a tie-beam, but in base-cruck trusses the tie element occurs at the level usually associated with collar-beams, and so confusion has arisen. As a group base-crucks have attracted much attention. It has been established that they are comparatively early in date, are associated with gentry-class housing and were designed specifically to overcome the problem of restriction in the hall caused by arcade posts of aisled halls.[27] They are usually found functioning as the central truss in a two-bay hall which has aisled trusses at either end. Halls of greater width could be achieved by using base-crucks, as the builders were not restricted by the limited span of a full cruck truss.

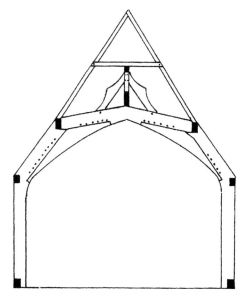

A base cruck

Not all base-crucks share the same attributes, and there is a sub-group classified as 'type W' which are really truncated true crucks and should be considered as such. In these the crucks rise to a point above the collar where they are deliberately cut off, the truss having no continuation apart from common rafters.[28] To complicate matters further, in Shropshire there is a small sub-group, as yet unclassified but belonging to the family of base-crucks, where the blades rise to a similar level on the *outside* of the collar before being terminated. The truss then continues with principal rafters, V-struts, and, in one instance, a short king-strut. This sub-group will be discussed later. The examples are in central trusses of halls of good quality and it is considered that they qualify as variants of base-crucks.

b) Upper Crucks

The blades rise from a beam at or just below eaves level.[29] For simplification those which rise to an apex and those which are truncated at the level of a high collar-beam are both included in the category of upper crucks. Although this group was one of the first variants to be noted, the majority are considered to be 18th and 19th century in date. They provided a solution to the problem of gaining headroom in the roofs of buildings where solid mass walls were used and where the sharp angle between principal rafters and tie-beam would otherwise reduce effective headroom to a zone in the middle of the roof.[30]

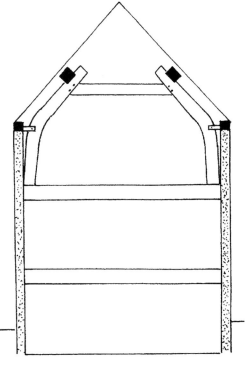

An upper cruck

c) Raised and Middle Crucks

In both these categories the blades rise from a point over half-way up a solid wall. The raised cruck blades meet at the apex while the middle cruck rises only to collar-beam level, the truss continuing with short straight timbers. When considering cruck forms generally, probably the greatest difficulty in definition lies with cruck-like forms where the principals descend insufficiently far to determine their nature.[31] Fortunately Shropshire possesses few of these. The great crucks in Stokesay hall are really in a class of their own but have been categorised as 'raised' for reasons given below.

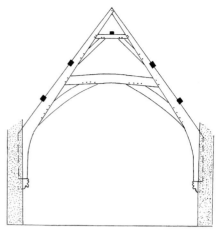

A raised cruck

d) Jointed Crucks

The blades are of cruck form, usually strongly elbowed with the rafter part and the post part contrived from separate timbers jointed at the elbow. The distribution is largely confined to Devon, Somerset and Dorset.[32] These form a distinctive group to which a similar group, classified as scarfed crucks, and found in south-west Wales, mostly in Cardiganshire and Carmarthenshire are related.[33] Neither group should be confused with the composite cruck frames of north-east Wales which, though 'jointed' in the literal sense of being morticed and tenoned, are more closely related to well-carpentered true crucks.[34] Again, perhaps it is fortunate that Shropshire adds little to the confusion.

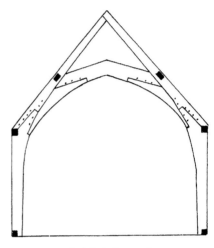

A jointed cruck

Base-Crucks in Shropshire

There can be no question that these are the most important variants, both in a national and a local context. Shropshire has seven known base-crucks, three more which are generically related and two possibles. Of the seven true base-crucks none is complete, all have suffered much mutilation and one, the Old Eagles Inn in Watergate, Whitchurch does not display features normally associated with base-crucks: double ties, aisled features, crown posts, and deep arch-bracing. The remains are indeed scanty, but the form of the truss seems to meet the criteria and the blades have a cavetto or hollow chamfer moulding on the edges, indicative of a once important building (see illustrations opposite). It is doubtful whether the Old Eagles was ever a domestic building. Its structural details suggest that its origins lie in an administrative building of some kind such as a guild hall.[35] Another example north of the Severn is Oldfields Farm in the parish of Moreton Say. This refused to produce a dendro date but is estimated to be of an early 15th-century date. Oldfields seems not to have had a crown-post roof, but otherwise it runs true to type and has the added interest of containing a 'wind-eye'. The carpentry is plain and at first it was thought that the aisled truss was the usual spere-truss, but close examination revealed that it was that rare survival: the dais end truss.[36] The fact that both the Old Eagles and Oldfields Farm are well to the north of the county may have a bearing on

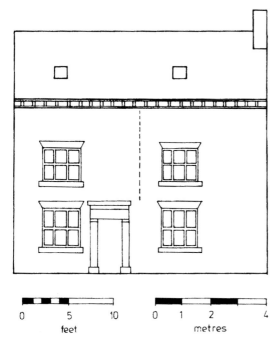

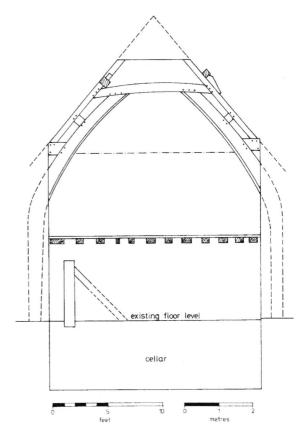

existing floor level

cellar

The Old Eagles, Watergate Street, Whitchurch
Above: The front elevation, the dotted line repre-
senting the position of the cruck shown in section
(right)

their comparative simplicity, the richest timber-framing, as noted previously, being found to the south of the river Severn.

The other five base-cruck houses each have crown-post roof construction. Plowden Hall in the parish of Lydbury North is unique in that the later insertion of a floor into the hall effec-

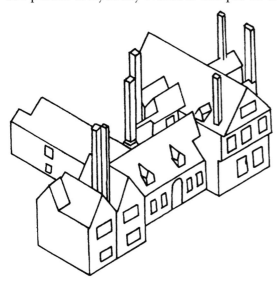

Plowden Hall
(for more illustrations see overleaf)

tively reversed the building sequence typologically. An open base-cruck hall which had aisled trusses at either end became a fully aisled building when brick piers were put in to support the floor. As all four posts were given decorative cladding, the generic class of the hall may easily be mistaken.[37] Recently the removal of plaster on the base-cruck truss has revealed that the crown-post has up-swinging braces and that the crown-post has a moulded base. These are features normally associated with the mass of crown-post roofs in southern counties.

The base-cruck truss at The Bold in Aston Botterell parish is obscure and only patient probing with skewers and a hand mirror on a string revealed the nature of the central truss. The Bold has features which include a crown-post roof, an aisled spere-truss, a dais end which

61

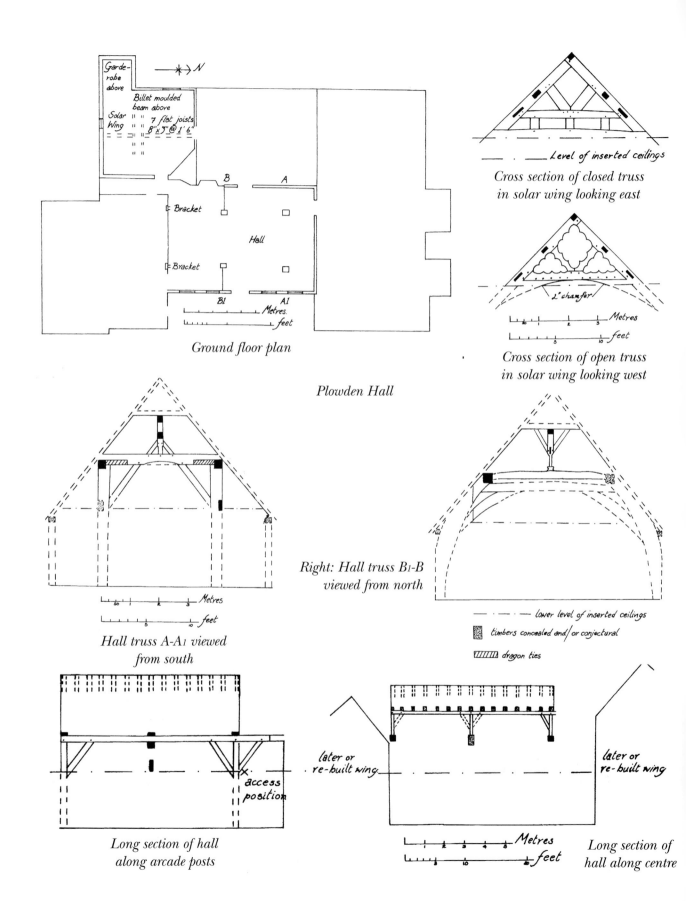

Garde-robe above

Billet moulded beam above

Solar Wing

7 flat joists 8"x3" @ 1'6"

N

B   A

Bracket

Bracket

Hall

B1   A1

Metres.

feet

Ground floor plan

Level of inserted ceilings

Cross section of closed truss
in solar wing looking east

2" chamfer

Metres

feet

Cross section of open truss
in solar wing looking west

Plowden Hall

Metres

feet

Hall truss A-A1 viewed
from south

Right: Hall truss B1-B
viewed from north

lower level of inserted ceilings

timbers concealed and/or conjectural

dragon ties

access position

Long section of hall
along arcade posts

later or re-built wing

later or re-built wing

Metres

feet

Long section of
hall along centre

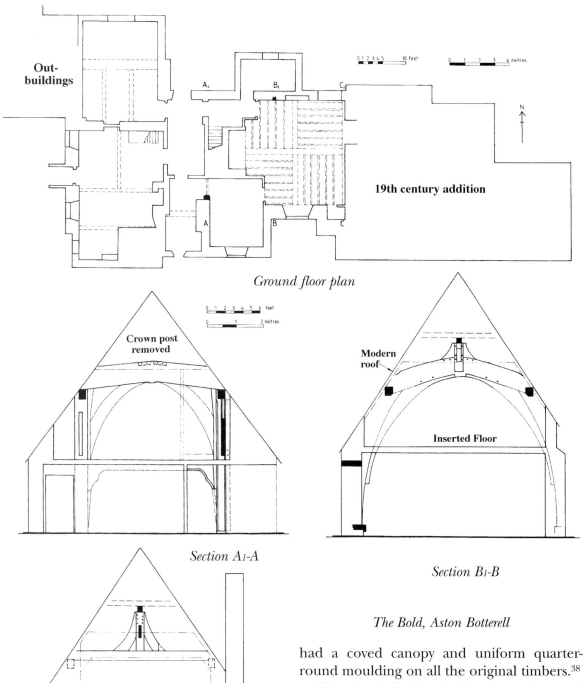

Outbuildings

19th century addition

Ground floor plan

Crown post removed

Section A₁-A

Modern roof

Inserted Floor

Section B₁-B

Inserted floor

Left: section C₁-C

The Bold, Aston Botterell

had a coved canopy and uniform quarter-round moulding on all the original timbers.[38]

Plowden Hall, The Bold in Aston Botterell and 23 Barrow Street in Much Wenlock represent the earliest base-crucks in Shropshire, their dendro dates being 1302, 1320-54 and 1327-30 respectively. The crown-post roof construction at 23 Barrow Street is determined only from archaeological evidence but the archaic form of the crown-posts and the total lack of cusping in the other two suggest early dates. The next in chronological order is High Grosvenor in Claverley parish, dendro-dated to 1375-7. Here again there is a total lack of cusping or moulding and the only decoration is a simple chamfer on the collar-purlin and on the longitudinal and lateral braces of the crown-post roof, whose form is otherwise very plain with the lateral braces rising from the transverse member in a cranked convex arch. The lower purlin is set square like the arcade plate of an aisled hall and the windbraces are also cranked. Above the present ceiling there is evidence for the louvre opening in the roof.[39]

Much Wenlock, a community which had begun as a necessary adjunct to the priory, later acquired Borough status in 1468 and continued thereafter to function as a town.[40] Though small by any standards and with a population of only 2,595 in 1988, it yields two known base-cruck houses, one mentioned above at 23 Barrow Street, the other being 15 High Street, part of which is occupied by Barclay's Bank, dendro-dated to 1408. The bank functions in a 17th-century box-framed unit on the site of what was probably the service bay of the medieval hall-house; but adjoining the business premises and at present in separate and private occupation are the remains of the two-bay base-cruck hall. In addition to the base-cruck truss its features include an aisled dais truss, crown-post roof construction, mouldings based on the ogee, cusped lateral braces to the crown-post and evidence for a louvre opening in the roof.[41]

If the plan of the hall at 15 High Street has been interpreted correctly it differs from 23 Barrow Street in its alignment to the street. The High Street example has its service end towards the street; at 23 Barrow Street the property is a reversed L-shape with what was clearly a contemporary box-framed solar wing facing the street and a base-cruck hall forming the stem. In 1983 work commenced on an extremely sympathetic and sensitive restoration of the property, revealing, among other features, what must be the finest base-cruck in the county.

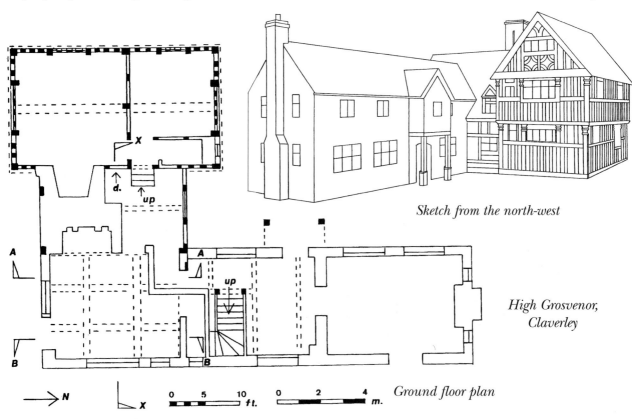

Sketch from the north-west

High Grosvenor, Claverley

Ground floor plan

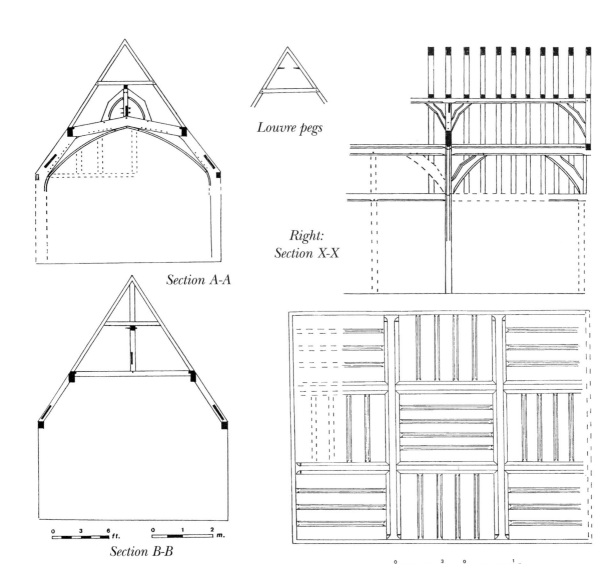

Section A-A

Louvre pegs

Right:
Section X-X

Section B-B

0 3 6 ft.   0 1 2 m.

High Grosvenor, Claverley

Above and below: Details of
inserted ceiling

0 3 ft.   0 1 m.

Panel in parlour wing
(not to scale)

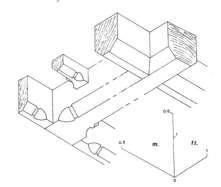

0.5   0.5   m.   ft.

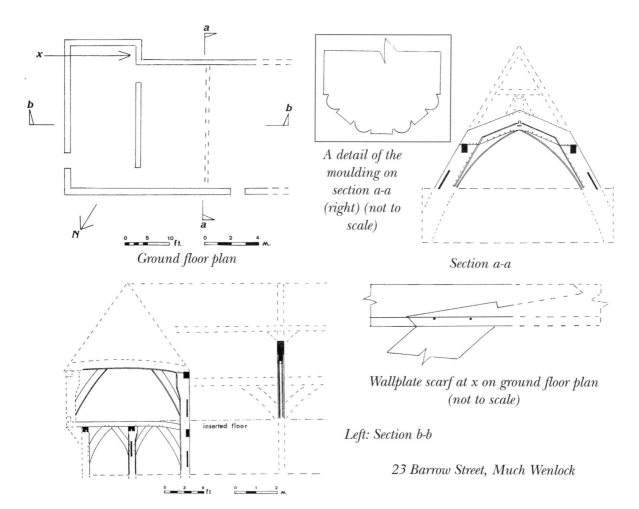

Ground floor plan

A detail of the moulding on section a-a (right) (not to scale)

Section a-a

inserted floor

Wallplate scarf at x on ground floor plan (not to scale)

Left: Section b-b

23 Barrow Street, Much Wenlock

Instead of employing a double collar, a single timber was rebated, steeply cambered and angled to surmount the base-crucks. The soffit was cut to accommodate tightly-fitting arch-braces and a decorative central boss without interrupting the profile of the arch. Unfortunately the boss had not survived. It seems clear from the evidence of the peg-holes on the upper surface of the timber that the hall had a crown-post roof originally, but it was not possible to reconstruct it and instead a king-post, flanked by two curved queen-posts has been substituted, reusing the mortices and peg-holes of the crown-post construction. A section of the lower purlin, characteristically set square like an arcade-plate, remains on the western base-cruck, indicating that generically the form of the hall is derived from those having fully-aisled construction (see section a-a above).

With the possible exception of the 'Old Eagles', the base-cruck halls of Shropshire each include at least one aisled truss, but, as already mentioned, the evidence at the 'Old Eagles' is fragmentary. Although the aisled trusses at 23 Barrow Street and High Grosvenor did not survive, the remaining structural evidence points to their inclusion in the original concept. At 15 High Street both the dais truss and, to a lesser degree, the spere-truss remain as aisled features, and at Plowden Hall there is also an almost complete aisled truss at one end of the hall and evidence for its opposite number at the other, though which was the spere-truss is difficult to say. Such evidence as there is suggests that the dais end truss was the one to become almost obliterated. At The Bold the aisled spere-truss remains although the form of the dais truss is obscured.

A Base-Cruck Variant Sub-Group

As mentioned earlier, there is in Shropshire a small group of unclassified base-cruck variants. The most complete is Wolverton Manor in the parish of Eaton-under-Heywood. Here, in the central truss of the two-bay hall, the blades just by-pass the transverse member at which point they are deliberately terminated. The truss then continues with principal rafters which have curved feet, giving an overall impression of a two-tiered cruck. Plain V-struts are incorporated in the upper structure and the house has an almost complete aisled spere-truss enriched with quarter-round moulding, double and triple-cusped windbraces over the hall, evidence of a louvre opening in the roof and many other interesting features including the finest inserted chequer-board ceiling in the county.[42]

At Cleeton Court in the parish of Cleeton St. Mary the central truss of the hall is similarly fashioned although the principal rafters are straight, the V-struts are cusped and there is a central king-strut. Where the blade receives the foot of the arch-brace the moulding on the blade is stepped back. Unfortunately the area is mostly obscured with plaster and it is impossible to determine the precise nature of the moulding, but the decorative hollow chamfer which runs parallel to the moulding continues along the collar-beam.[43]

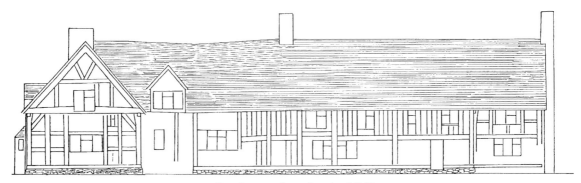

South-east elevation in 1962

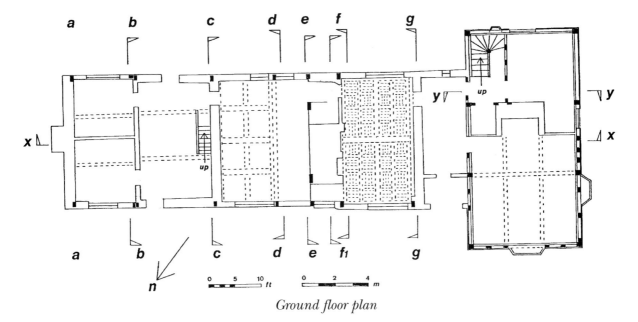

Ground floor plan

Wolverton Manor, Eaton-under-Heywood

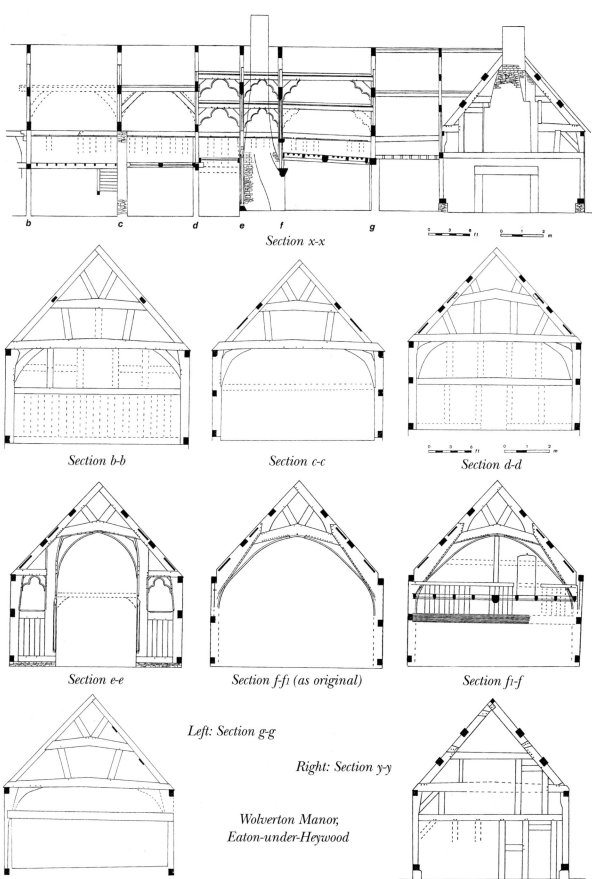

Section x-x

b c d e f   g

Section b-b   *Section c-c*   *Section d-d*

Section e-e *Section f-f₁ (as original)* *Section f₁-f*

Left: Section g-g

Right: Section y-y

Wolverton Manor,
Eaton-under-Heywood

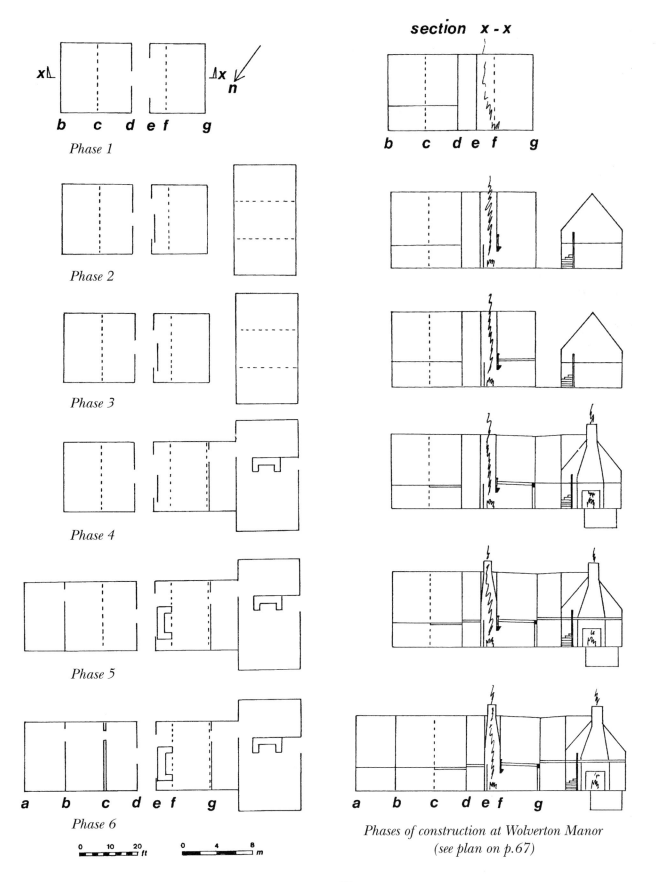

section x - x

Phase 1

Phase 2

Phase 3

Phase 4

Phase 5

Phase 6

b c d e f g

a b c d e f g

n

0 10 20 ft

0 4 8 m

Phases of construction at Wolverton Manor
(see plan on p.67)

69

'Two-tier' cruck assembly
dendro-dated to 1475

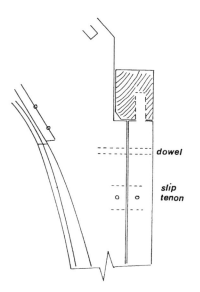

Cruck/post/wall-plate (south-east)

dowel

slip
tenon

Various details at
Wolverton Manor

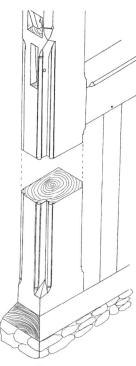

Spere post

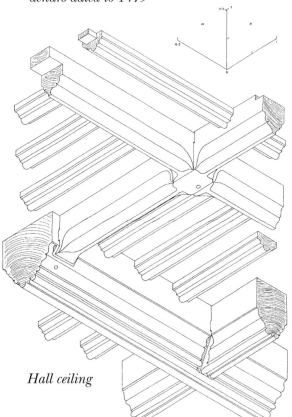

Hall ceiling

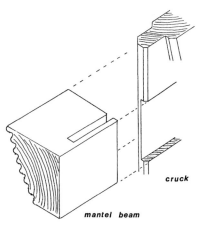

cruck

mantel beam

Mantel beam

Carving on a bench

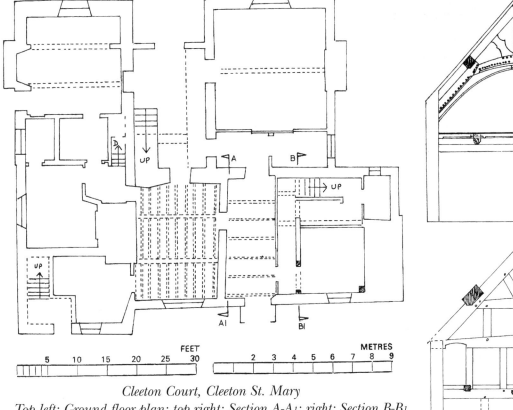

Cleeton Court, Cleeton St. Mary
Top left: Ground floor plan; top right: Section A-A₁; right: Section B-B₁

The third example in the sub-group is Lower Farm, Chorley, in Stottesdon parish where, admittedly, the evidence is scanty. While it is clear that the blades by-pass the transverse member and are then terminated, it is not possible to see what happens above that point. The blades may have been full crucks, reduced later in the course of alterations to the roof (see illustrations overleaf).

If the unclassified sub-group is accepted and included in the family of base-crucks the total for Shropshire is ten, two more than in Herefordshire. Less is known about the tenurial history of Shropshire base-cruck houses, but from what material is available and from their architectural qualities it would be fair to say that their social standing would be equal to those of the north Herefordshire group which were built by manor lords, lesser gentry or, at the very least, well-to-do farmers. The 'Old Eagles', for various reasons, may not have been a residential hall-house as such, and Lower Farm, Chorley is a doubtful candidate for the reasons given above, but the remainder form a homogeneous group in which the details may vary but whose social standing may be deduced from their structural excellence and whose date-range at present spans 1302 to 1431.

Hopes were raised when another base-cruck hall-house was reported at Lower Dairy House in Donington parish which would have given an example in the south-eastern area of the county. But on examination this turned out to be a fully box-framed structure.[44]

There are two buildings, one a farm building, once a house belonging to Cottage Farm at Easthope, and Upton Cressett Hall which retain two aisled trusses but where the vital central truss of the hall is missing. It has been suggested that these are likely to have had base-crucks,

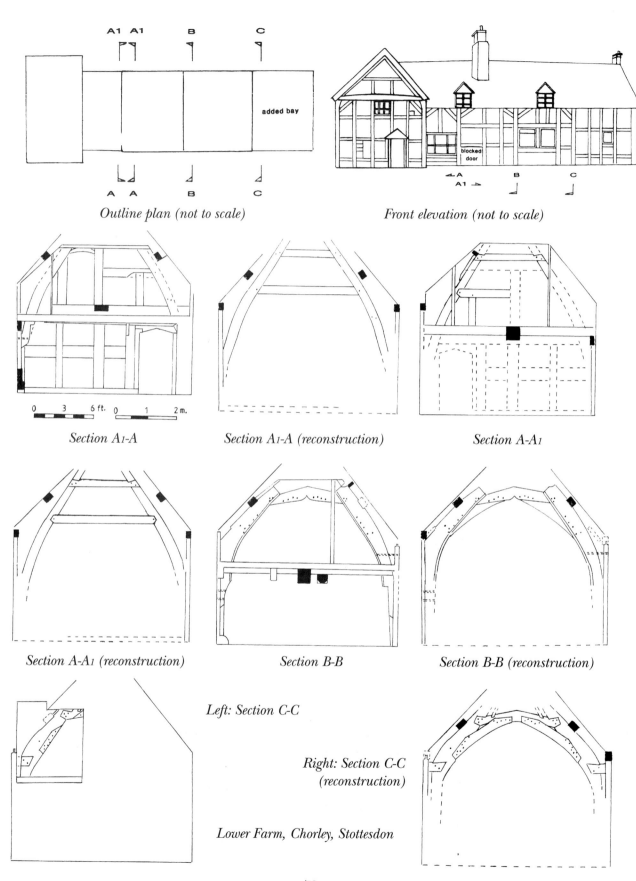

Outline plan (not to scale)

Front elevation (not to scale)

blocked door

added bay

Section A₁-A

Section A₁-A (reconstruction)

Section A-A₁

Section A-A₁ (reconstruction)

Section B-B

Section B-B (reconstruction)

Left: Section C-C

Right: Section C-C (reconstruction)

Lower Farm, Chorley, Stottesdon

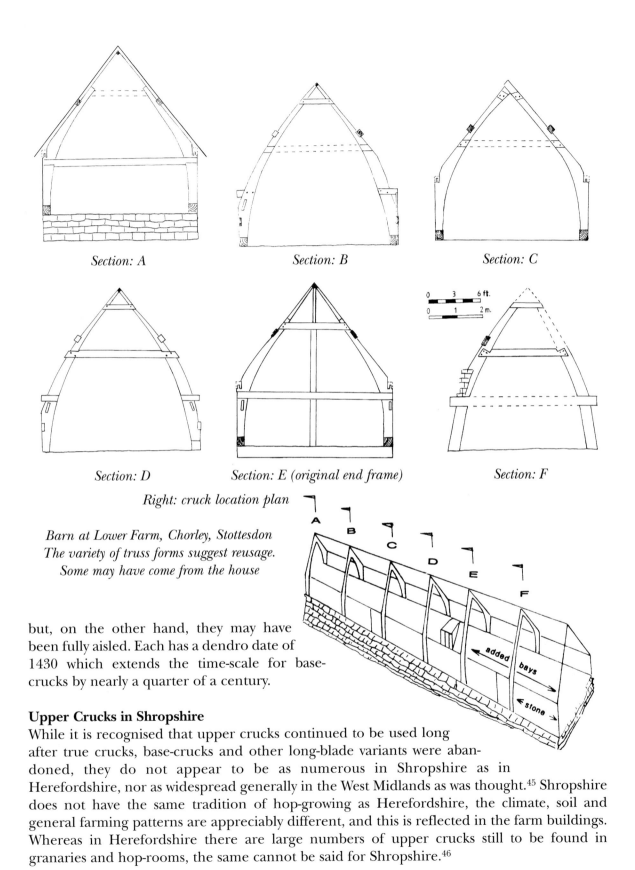

Section: A

Section: B

Section: C

Section: D

Section: E (original end frame)

Section: F

Right: cruck location plan

Barn at Lower Farm, Chorley, Stottesdon
The variety of truss forms suggest reusage.
Some may have come from the house

but, on the other hand, they may have been fully aisled. Each has a dendro date of 1430 which extends the time-scale for base-crucks by nearly a quarter of a century.

Upper Crucks in Shropshire

While it is recognised that upper crucks continued to be used long after true crucks, base-crucks and other long-blade variants were abandoned, they do not appear to be as numerous in Shropshire as in Herefordshire, nor as widespread generally in the West Midlands as was thought.[45] Shropshire does not have the same tradition of hop-growing as Herefordshire, the climate, soil and general farming patterns are appreciably different, and this is reflected in the farm buildings. Whereas in Herefordshire there are large numbers of upper crucks still to be found in granaries and hop-rooms, the same cannot be said for Shropshire.[46]

Only 39 examples of upper crucks have been noted in Shropshire. Although this may be partly a reflection of the lack of fieldwork, it is unlikely to be the whole reason. When farmhouses are examined it is common practice to take a look at the farm buildings also. Though numerically small, upper crucks have a wide distribution within the county and form the roof trusses in substantial houses, cottages, farm buildings and industrial buildings. Perhaps the example which most closely resembles the classic Herefordshire type is the rear wing at The Old Farm, Bucknell, which was probably constructed as a three-storied granary above service and store rooms, the ground floor being a semi-basement. The same farm complex also has upper crucks in one of the buildings in the courtyard complex.

There is variety in the form of upper cruck trusses in Shropshire. All the examples noted rise from a tie-beam but some, as in the wing at The Old Farm, Bucknell, terminate at collar-beam level; others, as in the courtyard building in the same farm, meet at the apex where the blades cross. At 'The Steppes', a cottage in Clee St. Margaret's parish, one blade is tenoned into the other at the apex but the blade containing the mortice continues for a further 8 inches. The form is reminiscent of that in the 'James II wing' at Ludford House, though conventional principal rafters are used there.

Top: Upper cruck at the Swan Inn malthouse, Ironbridge
Lower: Laminated crucks at Stableford Farm, Ackleton
(c.1840-60)

Mostly upper cruck trusses have wooden spurs which tie the blades to the wall-plate, but in the rear wing of the Fellmongers' Hall in Frankwell, Shrewsbury, the spurs, which are apparently original features, are made from wrought iron.

Most of the upper crucks in Shropshire are unremarkable, but a few buildings rouse more than a passing interest. The Swan Inn at Ironbridge has two semi-detached ancillary buildings which form a projecting wing to the north-west of the inn and were built as malthouses. They are well-preserved and the kiln remains at the end of the older range. Both have upper cruck trusses rising from tie-beams and meeting at the apex. Although unremarkable in themselves, because the complex is reasonably intact the trusses illustrate how this cruck form was used for industrial buildings and before malting became commercially based. The complex also gives a remarkable insight into the malting process as it was carried out in the early 19th century and the inn itself has a claim to fame, for it was the meeting place in the 1770s for the group of men who were responsible for the building of the Iron Bridge.[47]

As previously mentioned, at Stableford Farm, Ackleton, in Worfield parish are two buildings containing laminated crucks which probably date from the 1840s/60s, the period of 'high farming' in Shropshire when grain prices were high and farming was going through a period of change and innovation. Both are brick-walled buildings, the cruck trusses forming bay divisions and, in conjunction with their posts and principal rafters, supporting the roofs. Each is five-bayed. The purpose of the smaller building is unknown, but it is single-storied and uses the frames in the 'full-cruck' mode. The larger building has a storage area at ground level with an elaborate cart-entry arrangement and cast-iron pillars supporting a granary at first-floor level in which the blades are used as upper crucks. In both buildings the blades each have seven laminates, those in the granary being slightly more sophisticated with rounded edges. In both instances the crucks cross at the top and are secured to the principal rafters. The main difference lies in the method of tying the blades back. In the granary a type of wooden bridle restrains the blades and connects with the post/rafter/wall-plate assembly, while in the smaller building two spandrel struts are used, one connecting with the rafter and a longer one with the post.

Whether the buildings are regarded as 'survival' or 'revival' of a traditional method of construction is of no great moment, it merely lends emphasis to the

Stableford Farm, Ackleton
Top: Detail of crossed crucks
Lower: Detail of spur-tie

fact that it was practical and versatile and could be adapted to meet modern needs. Perhaps the surprising thing is that more examples are not known. Present-day laminated crucks may be seen in the Methodist Church Hall at Craven Arms and in the Ludlow Swimming Baths, while modern non-laminated crucks appear in the atrium to Shrewsbury Cemetery on Longden Road.

Raised Crucks and Middle Crucks in Shropshire

By a strange coincidence the only known examples of these variants in Shropshire occur in two houses, one at the top and the other at the bottom of the social scale. The raised cruck form appears in the great hall at Stokesay Castle and the middle cruck in a crude little stone-walled building which has no postal address but is located behind the old Co-op building in Bishop's Castle. It may be disputed that the great crucks at Stokesay should be classed as 'raised' but Cordingley's statement that 'Below the knee, where the blades were almost vertical, the backs fitted into shallow wall chases' fits the definition given by Mercer that 'the blades of raised crucks ... start not from ground level but from some way up the wall'.[48] Another point is that they were associated with stone walls from the start. It is difficult to say how far Lawrence de Ludlow's choice of whole-tree raised cruck construction for his hall at Stokesay influenced other magnates or inspired lesser mortals to relative expression. Nothing similar exists in Shropshire and the builder of the nearest medieval hall house, Padmore, in Onibury parish, wilfully demolished in 1980, appears to have ignored his overlord's example and opted for an entirely box-framed building.[49]

Jointed Crucks in Shropshire

As noted earlier, jointed crucks of the type common in Somerset, Dorset and Devon are virtually unknown in Shropshire. The reason is obvious—there was no need for them, an ample supply of trees capable of yielding full crucks was available.

The central truss in the hall at the White House in Aston Munslow parish has, at various times, been mistaken for a jointed cruck, but in fact it is a full cruck which is connected to the wall-post with a slip-tenon.[50] This type of junction may also be seen in the great barn, formerly a house, at Upper House Farm, Asterley, in Pontesbury parish; in the barn at Golding in Cound parish; at Wolverton Manor in Eaton-under-Heywood; and in the two cruck barns at Betchcott in Smethcott parish. J.T. Smith's drawing of the cruck blades in Stokesay could also mislead the reader into thinking that they were scarfed or jointed crucks, whereas the 'joints' are simply the result of clever surface laminations, part of the restoration programme carried out by the Allcroft family in the 1870s.[51]

A small group in Shropshire come into the category described by Commander Williams as 'extended' crucks.[52] True cruck blades, presumably not of the required length, are extended by a scarfed or jointed addition above the collar to reach the apex without disturbing the profile. Examples noted in Shropshire are at Shootrough in Cardington parish; 2 Ryton Grange cottages in Condover parish; 5 Church Street, Condover; St. Owen's Well House in Much Wenlock; Clun Farm in Clun parish; The White House in Aston Munslow; and Wolverton Manor and Ticklerton Farm in the parish of Eaton-under-Heywood. The latter is an example of an extended upper cruck.

Analysis and Conclusions

The distribution map shows a total of 273 known cruck buildings in Shropshire, but this figure is very conservative. As mentioned earlier the county has not been combed for crucks, neither have other records been trawled. What follows is based on purely personal investigations. If, from the total, certain categories such as church porches, barns, reused, upper and jointed crucks, those with short curved feet, possible crucks, unrecorded demolished, incomplete and fragmentary examples are disregarded a total of 132 is left from which useful data can be extracted. The table shows a breakdown of the figures on p.80:

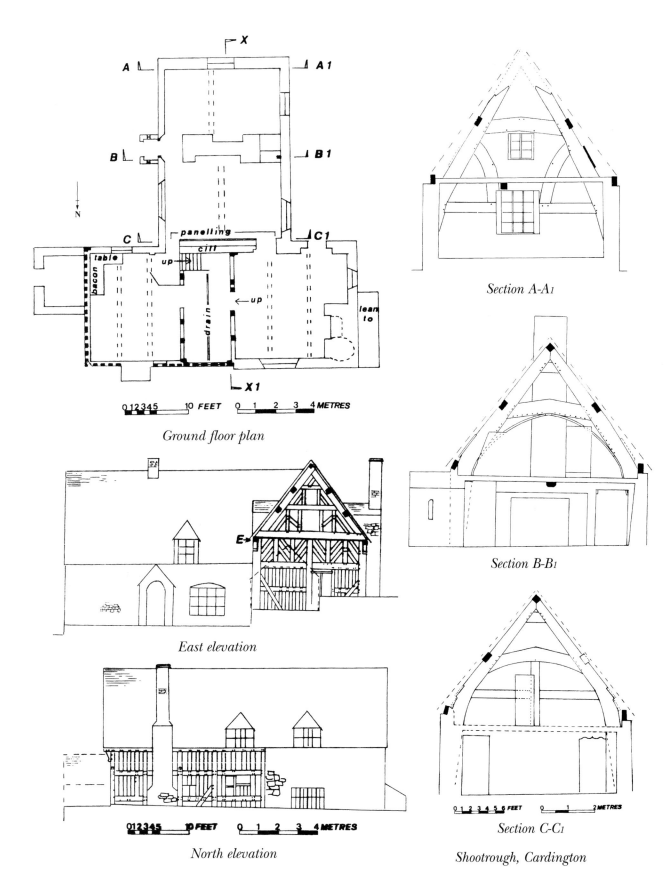

X

A 	 A1

B 	 B1

N

panelling

ciII

C 	 C1

table

bacon

up

up

drain

lean to

X1

0 1 2 3 4 5	10 FEET	0	1	2	3	4 METRES

Ground floor plan

Section A-A1

E

East elevation

Section B-B1

0 1 2 3 4 5	10 FEET	0	1	2	3	4 METRES

North elevation

0 1 2 3 4 5 6 FEET	0	1	2 METRES

Section C-C1

Shootrough, Cardington

77

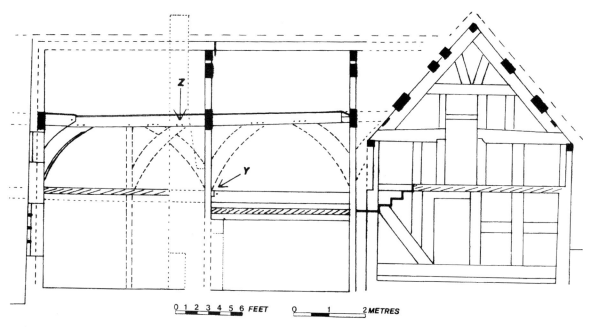

Section X-X₁

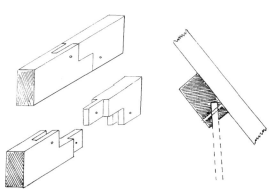

*Detail of wall-plate scarf
at Y on section X-X₁
(not to scale)*

*Spere-brace mortice
at Z on section Z-Z₁
(not to scale)*

Shootrough, Cardington

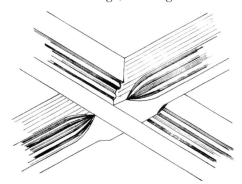

*Detail of inserted floor in hall
2 Ryton Grange Cottages, Condover (see also opposite)*

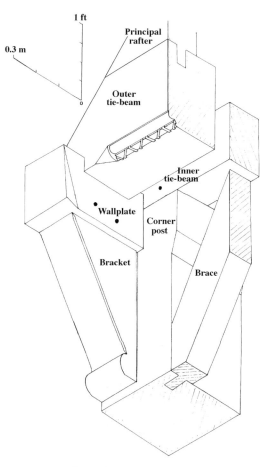

Detail at E on east elevation

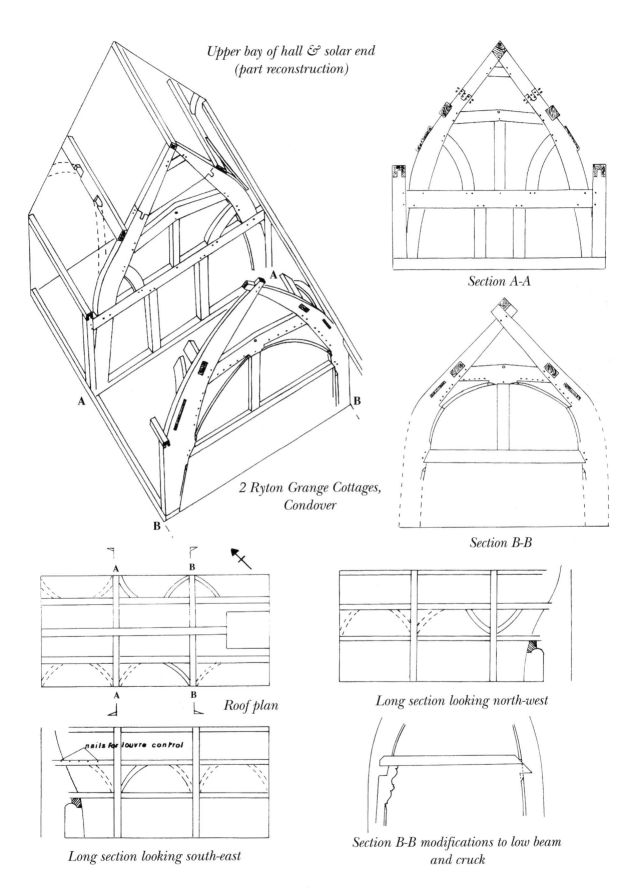

Upper bay of hall & solar end
(part reconstruction)

Section A-A

2 Ryton Grange Cottages,
Condover

Section B-B

Roof plan

Long section looking north-west

nails for louvre control

Long section looking south-east

Section B-B modifications to low beam
and cruck

79

Group	No.	% of total
Single range houses	77	58%
With added box-framed crosswing(s)	39	29%
With contemporary box-framed crosswing(s)	12	9%
With contemporary cruck crosswing	4	3%

Predictably, the single-range houses take the largest percentage, but arguably the most interesting and socially significant houses are those in the third group which have a cruck hall and a contemporary box-framed crosswing(s). Further analysis shows that these are mostly superior both in construction and social standing to the single-range houses. About 12 houses in the second group, including all except one of the base-crucks, give the impression that the later crosswing replaced either an earlier storied end or possibly a wing.

It is impossible to estimate the survival rate of Shropshire's cruck-built houses, but on the basis of current figures and what is known of their social level, it seems reasonable to suggest that the more prosperous areas in pre-Reformation times produced proportionally more houses with crosswings. This is reflected particularly in the parish of Condover where there is evidence for ten cruck houses either surviving or known to have existed. By contrast, the larger parish of Pontesbury, subject of a poorer economy and different pressures, produced more single-range houses.

Over the county as a whole the single-range cruck house is dominant and covers the whole social framework, but when houses with contemporary or added crosswings and a proportion of possible examples are added together they represent nearly the same percentage as the single-range group.

Shropshire is a cruck-biased county and perhaps it is not surprising to find the social hierarchy occupying crosswinged houses and setting the standards, and the lower orders on a diminishing scale either aiming at such a plan-form or being unable to improve their lot.

Some significance, surely, must be read into the choice of crucks by the wealthiest wool-merchant of his day, building his hall at Stokesay, even though the walls of the hall and his solar crosswing were of stone. He could have spanned his hall by a number of different methods, yet he chose crucks.

A minor point of interest is the survival in Shropshire of a number of cruck houses in a town, or perhaps where a town failed. With one exception—23 Barrow Street, Much Wenlock, a fine base-cruck house—these are single-range houses, suggesting that the crosswing plan was not considered suitable for an urban environment. The large number of crucks recorded in Whitchurch is entirely due to the perspicacity of one man, the late Geoffrey Grenville Jones Owen who made note of them before they were demolished.[53]

Dendrochronological sampling and analysis has been carried out on 29 cruck-built houses, including the two possible base-crucks. The date-range produced is 1269-1551, with the majority firmly in the 15th century. The application of dendro-dating to cruck houses is discussed further in chapter 14.

4   Box-Framed and Jettied Houses

In the previous chapter cruck-built houses were discussed at some length, partly because of the fascination that they undoubtedly hold and partly because the sheer number of surviving examples makes it clear that it was a building genre considered normal in Shropshire from the 13th century to the middle of the 16th, in variant form through to the 19th and in revival form into the 20th. But alongside was always the alternative technology, box-framing. In this the weight of the roof is spread over a series of posts and beams set in box-like form in which the outer timbers, the walls, are an integral part of the whole, unlike the walls in cruck buildings which were independent members, easily replaced.

At one time architectural historians divided non-cruck structures into two groups, 'Post-and-Truss' and 'Box-Frame'. The former employed principal rafters and trusses at bay intervals, and the bays were furnished with side purlins and windbraces. The latter did not necessarily have bay divisions and omitted principal rafters and side-purlins, linking each pair of common rafters with its own horizontal, usually a short collar-beam. Typically, 'crown-post' roofs came into this category. However, although the basic differences are fundamental, it is common practice at present to group the two under the heading of 'box-frame' and to use that term to describe timber-framed buildings which are not of cruck construction.

While cruck construction undoubtedly had its own advantages, box-framing was in many ways more versatile. Without the restrictions imposed by the length of the crucks, buildings of more stories and greater width could be built, with increased space internally. Heights of existing buildings could be extended relatively easily by taking off the roof, employing the old wall-plate as a girding-beam and adding another storey. This is evident particularly in towns such as Shrewsbury and Ludlow where pressure on space resulted in some box-framed structures rising as much as six stories. As was noted in the previous chapter, cruck buildings in towns could not be easily enlarged and this, no doubt, accounts for their virtual demise in the urban environment, although the occasional examples survive.

In the countryside it appears that box-framing was the preferred medium for houses where status was

*Timber-framed 'sky scrapers'—
houses on Mardol Head, Shrewsbury
(SRRC 6001/5326 f.99)*

81

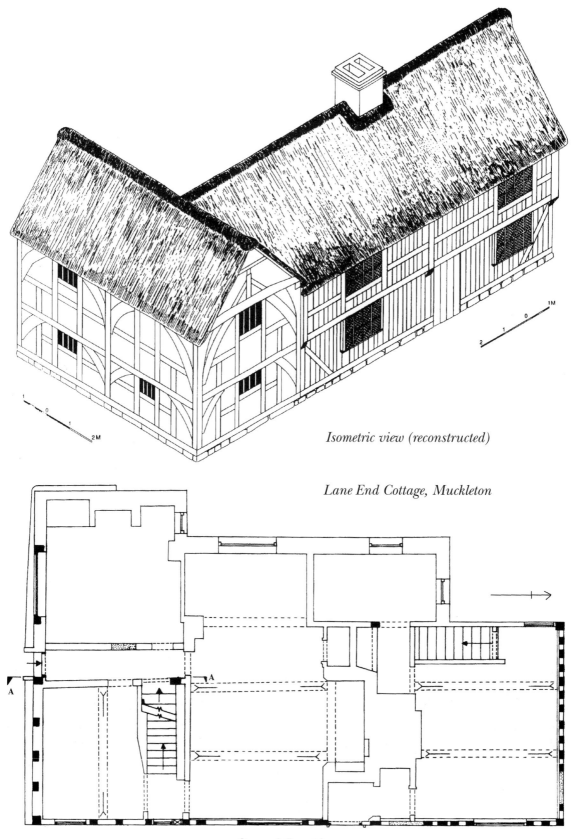

Isometric view (reconstructed)

Lane End Cottage, Muckleton

Ground floor plan

82

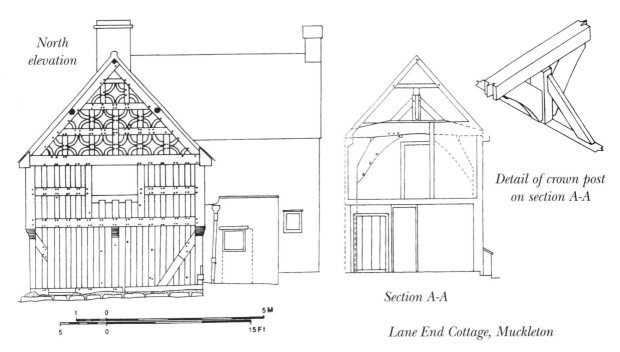

North elevation

Detail of crown post on section A-A

Section A-A

Lane End Cottage, Muckleton

important, such as manor houses. Examples such as Moat House, Longnor, Padmore in Onibury parish, Coats Farm in Rushbury, Wycherley Hall in Baschurch parish, Upper Ledwych in Bitterley parish and many others are all outstanding box-framed houses in otherwise cruck areas. But Bedstone Manor remains as the superb contradiction. Here in 1448 crucks were used uncompromisingly and at their best for the hall, and box-framing for the contemporary solar crosswing.[1]

Much can be deduced from a study of the wall-framing in box-framed houses. Not much 14th-century wall-framing survives in Shropshire but where it does it seems to indicate that large open panels with substantial bracing was favoured. The King's Head in Mardol, Shrewsbury, is a dendro-dated example of 1404, just into the 15th century, and another example in the first half of the 15th is the rear unit at 91 Frankwell.[2] Non-dated buildings in the town include the Bear Steps Hall and 3 St. Alkmund's Square. In the countryside the older part of Lane End Cottage, Muckleton, that is the large crosswing, is a clear example of 1371-2.[3] Close-studding without a mid-rail usually indicates a status-conscious builder, but the date-range is wide—over 230 years from *c.*1430 to *c.*1660—and it can be misleading, as was the case in the tiny single-celled building, Fulway Cottage at Upper Cound (see illustrations overleaf). Long thought to be of medieval date, dendrochronological sampling and analysis produced a felling date of 1603.[4]

The mid-rail is a feature which usually indicates that the close-studding is later, its hey-day coming in the second half of the 16th century. But a curious anomaly was once evident in the Abbot's House in Shrewsbury, dendro-dated to 1458, where the close-studding of the second storey had a mid-rail *applied* to the timbers at some time.[5] The witness mark is still there and a few other examples have been noted in the town. In a long-destroyed house in Bridge Street an old illustration shows shows a similar rail applied to the ground-floor framing of the cross-wing,[6] but the reason for this practice is obscure.

The second half of the 16th century and the early years of the 17th produced the most decorative framing in Shropshire. Timber, rather than brick or stone, was the medium through which new-found wealth or prosperity could best be proclaimed, and certainly it was through their houses that the Drapers' Company of Shrewsbury announced their power. The system is discussed in chapter 10.

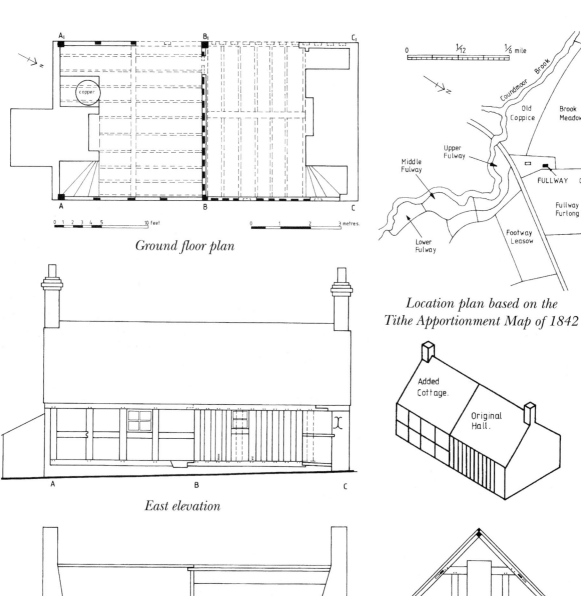

Ground floor plan

Location plan based on the
Tithe Apportionment Map of 1842

East elevation

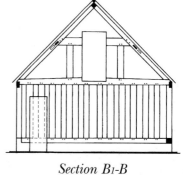

Added
Cottage.

Original
Hall.

Section B₁-B

North-south section with stacks not shown at ground floor level
so that the west wall can be seen fully

Fulway Cottage, Upper Cound

Chamfer stops on
spine beam
in southern cottage

84

This page: Penkridge Hall, Leebotwood (1590)

Chimney and garderobe chute

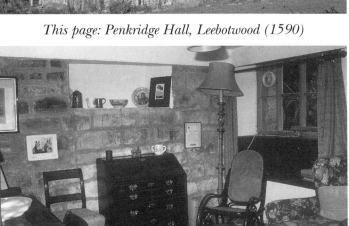

Concealed chamber to the left of the big stack in the photograph top left. It now has an inserted window

Roof space

Garderobe

Ludlow had its own school of carpentry, owing some but not all of its trends to Shrewsbury, and this too is described in the relevant chapter. Outside the towns the influence can be seen in isolated examples. One of the most rewarding examples is Penkridge Hall in Leebotwood parish. Here the Shrewsbury influence is expressed in the vine-leaf ornament on the tie-beam,

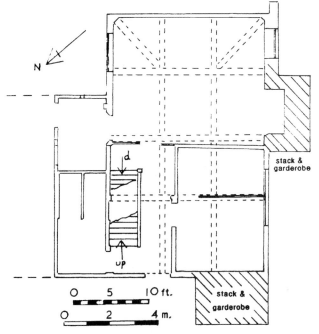

Ground floor plan

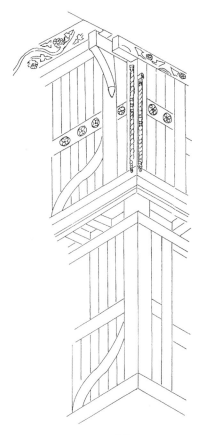

Jetty

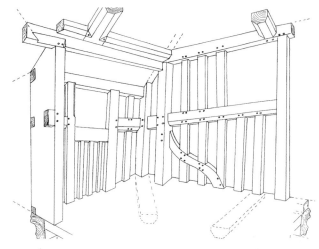

Framing in south-east upper chamber

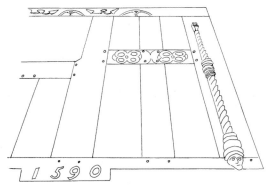

Framing on north-east return wall

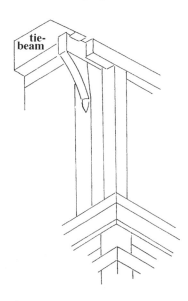

Jetty

Penkridge Hall

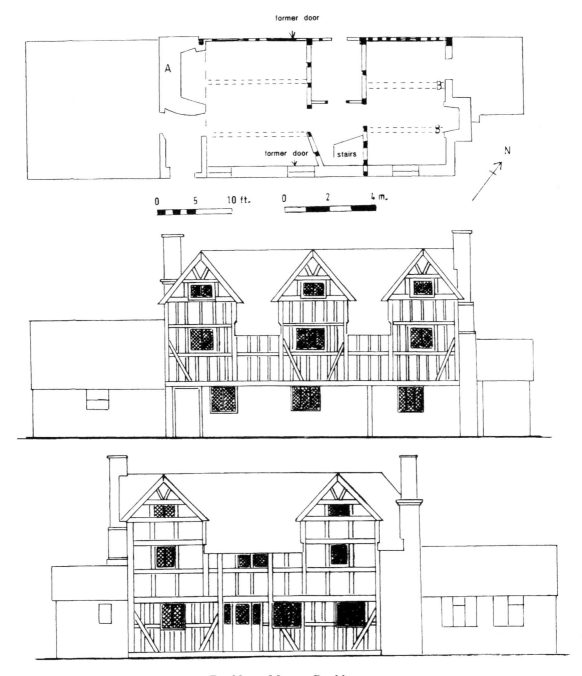

Rushbury Manor, Rushbury
Top: Ground floor plan; Centre: South-east elevation; Lower: North-west elevation

the S-braces and the sunken quatrefoils while the Ludlow influence is there in the 'lazy jetty' technique. The late Colonel Faithfull who lived in the house always insisted that there was a third school of carpentry, the 'Leebotwood School', at work in Penkridge Hall. To it belonged the rather unsuccessful staircase wing!

Square-framing, that is, framing composed of small square or nearly square panels of *c*.3ft. had always been used in rear or side walls where it could not be seen by the public. There are many examples, one of the most blatant being Rushbury Manor, but in the mid-to-late-17th

87

Comley Cottage, Cardington (2 panels)

Old Parr's Cottage, Winnington (2 panels) in 1914

The Tan House, Myddle (3 panels)

The Old Vicarage, Allscott (4 panels)

Tithe barn, Hodnet (5 panels) (1619)

Wycherley Hall, Baschurch (6 panels)

century plain square-framing came into its own right for the front walling, especially when terraces of box-framed cottages were built. A rough guide to the social standing of a square-framed house is to count the number of panels from the sill to the wallplate. Two panels high such as in Comley Cottage in Cardington, cottages at Upper Cound, and Old Parr's Cottage at The Glyn, Winnington in Wollaston parish represent the lowest rung of the social ladder, three panels as in the Tan House at Myddle, four as in The Red Lion at Myddle, The Old Vicarage

88

The east elevation of Berrington Manor (6 panels) (1608).
Note the roof of 'Harnage Slates'

at Allscott and Plaish Park Farm, five as in the Tithe Barn at Hodnet and Cross House Longden are all 'upwardly mobile' and six panels high, as in Berrington Manor, and part of Wycherley Hall represents the peak. These, of course, are a few selected examples, there are many more.

Another feature of the mid-to-late-17th century was the cut-back heads to the main corner posts. The reason for cutting back the timbers in this way is not immediately apparent and it would seem to weaken the posts, but it must have been done either so that the pattern of the framing on the front of the house could appear symmetrical, or it was seen as an up-to-date expression of the jowelled post-heads of medieval times. Cut-back heads may be seen on 15-16 Mardol and 3 School Lane, both within the river loop of Shrewsbury, and in 113-114 Frankwell where they appear internally. They tend to be rare in the countryside, but the crosswing at Coats Farm, Rushbury, has posts with jowelling at the top and sharp cutting-back lower down. Posts with jowelled feet appear to be of earlier date. The end frame of Manor Cottage, Prees, dendrodated to 1551-2 is a clear external example,[7] and several jettied buildings, such as Henry Tudor House, Wyle Cop, Shrewsbury, (1430), employ jowelled feet internally to stabilise the jetty.[8]

In timber-framed walls the spaces between the timbers, the 'interstices' have to be filled, and the panel filling varies. The commonest is 'wattle-and-daub'. Here a groove is cut in the lower crossmember and holes are bored at intervals in the underside of the upper crossmember. The groove and the holes house uprights, sharpened at one end, shaped at the other to a blunt chisel-point and sprung into the panel. They are usually of split oak but birch has

The east elevation of Coats Farm, Rushbury (to scale on plan overleaf)

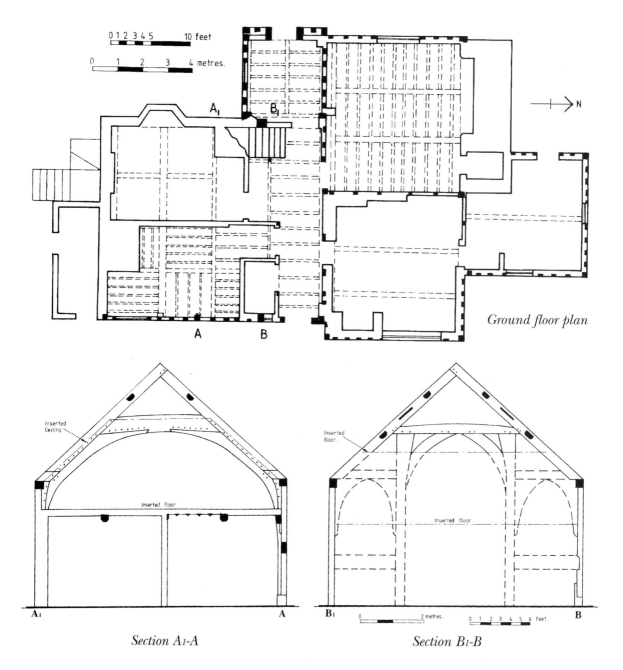

0 1 2 3 4 5   10 feet

0   1   2   3   4 metres.

N

Ground floor plan

Inserted Ceiling

Inserted floor

Inserted floor.

Inserted floor

0   2 metres.

0 1 2 3 4 5 6 feet.

Section A₁-A

Section B₁-B

Coats Farm, Rushbury

been noted. The 'wattles' are sometimes of narrow split oak laths but usually of hazel withies or other pliable wood, woven in and out of the uprights, then the 'daub' is applied to either side. Daub varies in its composition, presumably depending on what was available locally. Clay puddled with vegetable matter such as flax stalks and straw, have been noted, as has animal hair and dung. Sometimes simply mud and straw suffice. When the daub was dried out the panel would be lime-plastered on each side and finished off with a coat of white or colour wash. Where close-studding was used usually grooves were cut down the inner edges of the timbers and oak laths, tapered at each end, sprung into the grooves and daubed over.

Wattled panels in 6 Harley,
with remains of daub in the top left corner

Part of a plank-and-muntin wall at Porch House, Bishop's
Castle, with painted decoration (at A on plan overleaf)

Many framed houses at present display infilling of bricks instead of wattle-and-daub, but it is usually found that such brickwork is a later replacement. However, it is only possible to be certain if a panel can be seen without any infill. Then the grooves and stave-holes supply the evidence, but as timber-framing continued to a late date in Shropshire a few framed houses, particularly in the Baschurch area, were brick-nogged from the start.

Only three instances of 'plank-and-muntin' or 'post-and-pan' work, as it is sometimes known, have been noted in Shropshire in external walls, although a few internal screen walls or partitions are known. The term 'Post-and-pan' used to be applied to box-framed construction, but, thankfully, is now used to describe walling where the uprights (posts) are immediately adjacent to similar, usually thinner, members (pans: panels). The panels fit into grooves cut along the length of the inner edges of the posts, resulting in walls of solid wood. Two examples have been noted in Bishop's Castle. One is at the Porch House, dendro-dated to 1564/5, where the rear outer wall turns two right-angles to continue as an internal screen at the end of the hall,[9] and the other is on the opposite side of the High Street at no.25 where it forms one of the long walls running back from the street. In Castle Cottage, Clun, post-and-pan work occurs both along one internal wall and for part of the infilling for a cross-frame.

In North Shropshire a technique which does not seem to have a name has been noted in several instances.

Newholme, Loppington, showing stone
with pseudo-framing in cement render

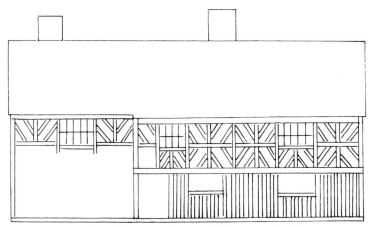

East elevation (later additions omitted)

Porch House, Bishop's Castle

Ground floor plan. The plank-and-muntin forms the west and south walls of the northern wing. 'A' shows the position in the photograph on the previous page

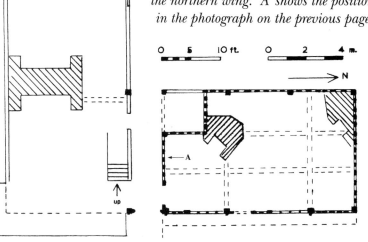

West front, Moat House, Longnor (1467)

In this the walls are given a coat of plaster externally and cement render applied to represent timber-framing. The render is worked to the appearance of weathered oak and then black-painted. It can be extremely effective.[10] Framed houses in need of renovation or brick houses needing to be disguised have all been noted, but the most startling discovery was that of 'Newholme' in Loppington parish where a stone house was given this treatment, and the pseudo-framing was five panels high.

The different roof-forms of box-framed and cruck buildings are self-evident. It is not proposed to elaborate on box-framed roofs here, constructional details will be found in chapter 5.

One house, Moat House in Longnor parish, deserves special mention. It is undoubtedly the finest box-framed house in the county. Dendro-dated to 1467 it was the manor house of the second moiety of the manor of Longnor, built by Thomas Acton who died in 1480.[11] It is thought that his is one of the carved heads that survives and that the other is one of his two wives. The house was almost destroyed in the early 1960s when it had deteriorated into two farm workers' cottages but was rescued by Mr. K.F. Rouse who undertook the first phase of restoration. Later it was bought by the present

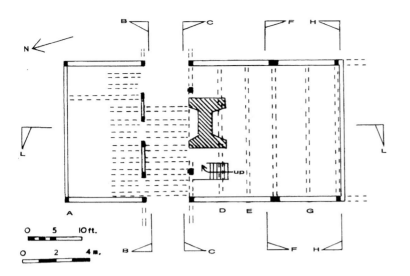

Ground floor plan

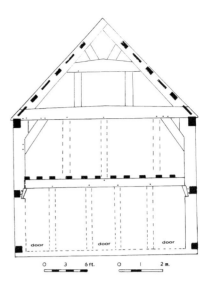

Section B-B

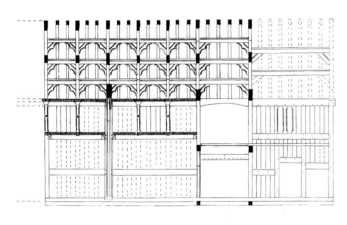

Section L-L

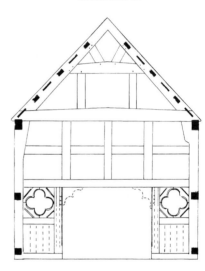

Section C-C spere truss

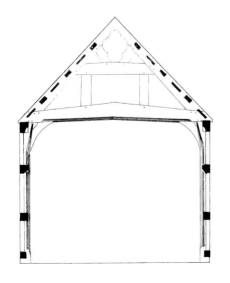

Right: Section E-E

Left: Section F-F

Moat House, Longnor

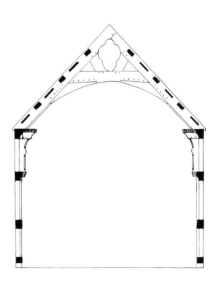

93

Triple-tiered windbraces

Screens passage and service end

Detail of roof construction

Roof construction

Detail of brattished rail and post-head

Moat House, Longnor (1467)

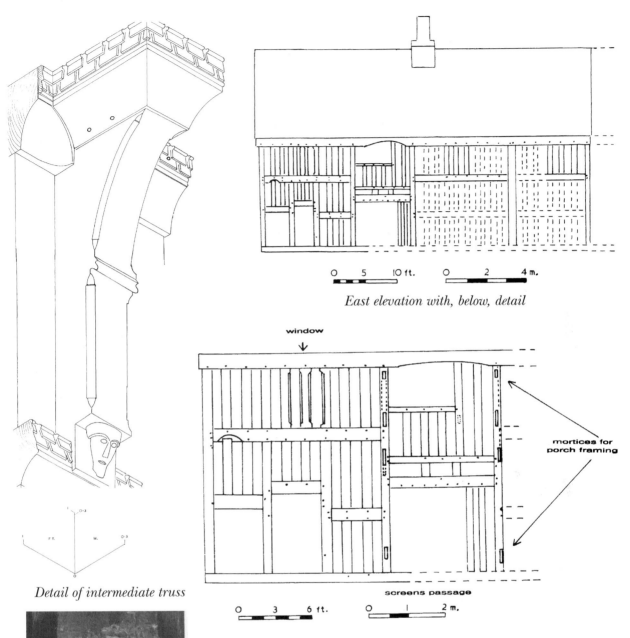

East elevation with, below, detail

window ↓

mortices for porch framing

screens passage

Detail of intermediate truss

Left: Carved head, possibly of Sir Thomas Acton.
(The holes above the head are angled to hold standards)

Moat House, Longnor

owners, Peter and Margaret Richards who initiated a comprehensive programme, among other things removing the inserted ceiling so that the full glory of the roof could be seen from the level of the inserted floor. During restoration it was discovered that the opposing doors of the former screens passage were furnished with porches, but whether these were in use at the same time is debatable. The constructional details may be appreciated from the drawings and from the 'reconstruction' painting by Noel

95

Shepherdson (reproduced on the front cover) which was done from measurements and with little 'artist's licence'. If such lavish treatment was accorded to the hall it raises the question of what standard applied to the solar. Unfortunately this was destroyed many years ago, but there is archaeological evidence that a solar wing existed.

Jetties

'Jettied' buildings are those in which the upper storey or stories are larger than, and thus over-hang, the lower. In other words, where a larger box is placed on top of a smaller one. There seems to be no single reason for this practice, but the effects are obvious and the same in all cases. More floor-space is available for use in the upper stories, and the lower stories are protected from rainwater, thus affording some shelter to pedestrians and shoppers. That the upper floor is cantilevered means that it is less likely to sag in the middle and can support greater weights. Furthermore, the main posts need not depend on the availability of long timbers, and as each floor provides a working platform for erecting its surrounding walls the need for scaffolding is eliminated—perhaps a consideration when building in cramped streets.[12] A 15th-century contract for shops in Bucklersbury, London specifies that the first floor 'shall jut (*gettabit*)', exactly describing what a jetty does for an upper storey,[13] but that such buildings were unstable is not borne out by the present writer's experience. '*Buyldynge chargydde with iotyes is parellous when it is very old*'[14] was given the lie when explosives were used to demolish a Shropshire jettied building. The net effect was to wreck the roof, the windows and the infilling, but the frame was left standing.

Most Shropshire towns display jettied buildings but they are also found in the countryside where space was not at a premium. Whether country builders were simply copying a fashion set in the town is open to question, but what is undeniable is that a jettied building has more style and appeal than an unjettied one. It also seems to provide a better vehicle for carved and applied decorations, outwardly at least.

Hewn jetty at 30 Kempton

The length of the overhang diminished with time until the jetty became a mere token, the final form being the 'hewn' jetty. This is where the corner posts are continuous timbers, fully two stories high, but are cut back at first-floor level (as shown on the picture alongside of 30 Kempton) to give an overhang of about four inches. Usually the cut-back is moulded and the moulding is carried along the bressumer. Shropshire has a number of hewn jetties. Two remain in Shrewsbury, at The Porch House in Swan Hill which has an inscribed date of 1628, and at 23 Pride Hill; and in the countryside no.30 Kempton, and Spenford House in Loppington are good examples. In the replaced hall range at Lane End Cottage, Muckleton (dated 1621) the decoration is confined to the cut-back.

Often gables are given the jetty treatment, but again, the overhang is small. In these instances the corner posts usually have carved brackets which support the ends of the projecting tie-beam of the gable. It seems clear that the jettied gable or the jettied dormer gable was intended for display and an example of the latter with the date of 1664 carved upon it may be seen at Church House, Loppington. With this, as with other examples, the date records the insertion of the dormer gable and does not relate to the basic structure.

A feature not often found in Shropshire is where the gable has a pronounced overhang and is supported with coved timbers. The later part of Providence Grove in Prees is of this type, bears the estimated date of 1611 and has much herringbone work and ornamental quatrefoils.[15] As such it relates to the Cheshire school of carpentry rather than to Shropshire, but a coved jetty survives in Shrewsbury on the long front wall of Henry Tudor House (1430).[16] Here the bressumer is moulded and there is a decorative band of brattishing on the beam which is supported by the bull-nose ended joists. The building is three stories high and the

Jettied dormer gable at Church House, Loppington (1664)

Jetty with coving at Providence Grove, Prees

coving occurs at the upper level. It is possible that the same technique was used for the lower jetty, but unfortunately this has been underbuilt. As a general rule, though, coving is a rare feature in Shropshire.

Jetties can be designed for one, two, three or four sides of a building. The simplest is one-sided where the joists of the upper floor are extended, usually, towards the front, and support a bressumer which in turn supports the upper storey. The technique is the same whether the building is set parallel to the road or is gable-end-on. To effect a jetty on two adjacent sides of a building it was normal to employ a dragon-beam. This is the term for the diagonally set beam which is taken from a convenient point on a ceiling cross-beam to the external corner post. Into the dragon-beam the projecting joists of the upper storey were tenoned on either side. The effect from inside the building is of very distinctive herringbone corners. Like the extent of the overhang, the length of the dragon-beam diminished with time. From its internal

Typical dragon-beam for corner jetty at Bockleton Court,
Stoke St. Milborough

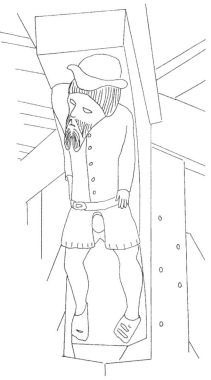

Figure on the jetty at
Blunden Hall, Bishop's Castle

measurement the longest known is 13ft. (3.96m.) in the building at the foot of the Cartway in Bridgnorth; the shortest is at The Ditches, Wem, 8ft. (2.44m.).[17] Because dragon-beams were required to support great weights they were often fashioned from fast-grown timbers and these have a wide growth-ring pattern, not helpful for dendrochronology.[18]

Sometimes the dragon-beams are decorated as is the example at Blunden Hall in Bishop's Castle, but usually the richest decoration was reserved for the corner posts. The examples on the two lower stories at the Abbot's House in Shrewsbury (1458),[19] tree trunks in themselves, are richly carved as is the one in the museum at Ludlow, thought to have come from the Palmer's Guild property, now Bodenham's, on the corner of Broad Street and King Street (1403-4).[20] Shropshire has fared badly in the attrition rate for corner posts. Of course, corners could be jettied without huge corner posts and many survive with just a bracket supporting the dragon-beam, but unques-

tionably a large no-nonsense corner post made a statement regarding the status of a building and could be breath-taking.

If a three-sided jetty was required then two dragon-beams, one at each corner were employed, and if the building was to be jettied on all four sides it would be necessary to use four dragon-beams. Single and three-sided jetties occur most frequently in Shropshire, but four-sided jetties are the most spectacular. The Tolsey in Ludlow was

Original jettied end, now an interior feature,
at Binweston Farm, Worthen

98

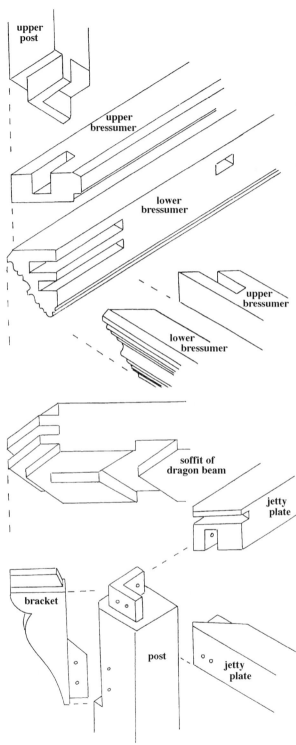

upper
post

upper
bressumer

lower
bressumer

upper
bressumer

lower
bressumer

soffit of
dragon beam

jetty
plate

bracket

post

jetty
plate

*Exploded view of jetty timbers on the west range
of Beslow Hall, Wroxeter*

such a building, and it still retains one corner post; Habberley Hall, dendro-dated to 1555, is another,[21] and The Ditches, Wem, (1612), is a late example. At Beslow Hall the west range of *c*.1580 had a four-sided jetty. Beslow was demolished in 1985.[22]

In some areas of the country, for example in parts of Surrey and Somerset, internal jetties are encountered. This is where part of an upper chamber is made to overhang the open hall. Little evidence of this practice is known in Shropshire, but at Raynald's Mansion in Much Wenlock a series of joist-ends belonging to the 1414-47 building, suggest such a situation,[23] and a development of the concept occurs at Lea Hall, Pimhill, (1584 on an overmantel), where there is no open hall but the two upper chambers in the crosswings extend slightly over the central area, supported by a row of moulded brackets. Similarly at Alkington Hall, Whitchurch, the earlier part of the house, (1572), has a slight internal jetty.[24] If a jettied building is later extended the jetty can be retained to become an internal feature. Such is the case at Binweston Farm in Worthen parish, the clues are the long dragon-beam in the older part and the square-framing of the extension.

One house-type often incorporating jetties and known as the 'Wealden' because of its concentration in south-eastern England has the hall and the two crosswings covered by a single continuous roof.[25] So distinctive is this genre that it has given rise to its own study group. Outliers have been noted in York, Weobley in Herefordshire, West Acre in Norfolk and in other lowland regions but so far no firm examples have been found in Shropshire. In the chapter on Ludlow Medieval Houses in this book the evidence for 53 Broad Street to be included in this category is given, though its alignment militates against it, but in the building once known as the 'Winter Gardens' in the Bull Ring the evidence is a little stronger. In Much Wenlock no.11 High Street has external overtones of a Wealden, but internal inspection revealed that it was built with a roof hipped on all four sides and supporting a central belvedere or lantern.

Detailed study of jetties in any particular region should begin with the article by Richard Harris.[26] In this he makes it clear that it is the treatment of the bressumer, the beam which supports the upper storey, that holds the key to the building. In Shropshire no examples of types 'b' or 'c' on his Figure 1 have been noted. This is where the bressumer is housed in a rebate on the corner post and is secured either by tenons from the post or from the bressumer itself. Examples of type 'a', however, are common. This is where the bressumer runs through under the post which usually has a jowelled foot to accommodate the tenon. The examples on Figure 2 show deep moulded bressumers, single and double, secured on the ends of the projecting floor joists and Shropshire has many examples of these. Figure 3 a) shows a type where the girding-beam runs under the post and only one of these in Shropshire, at Ashford

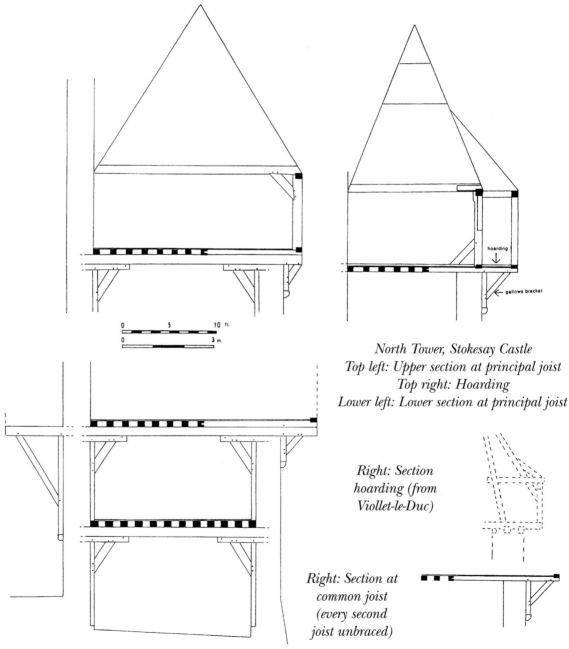

North Tower, Stokesay Castle
Top left: Upper section at principal joist
Top right: Hoarding
Lower left: Lower section at principal joist

Right: Section hoarding (from Viollet-le-Duc)

Right: Section at common joist (every second joist unbraced)

100

Bowdler, has been noted, but the county has a number of examples of b) incorporating a pendant post, and c) the hewn jetty, described above.

With the aid of the drawings and backed up by dendro-dates in some instances, the development of jetties in Shropshire may be seen to relate to the following pattern:

Group I

It may be argued that the north tower at Stokesay does not qualify as a jetty because it comes off a stone wall and its purpose was to allow a fighting platform to be formed. Nevertheless, the basic technique is valid and, as shown on the drawing, the construction bears a distinct similarity to that illustrated by Viollet-le-Duc.[27] At Stokesay a double girding-beam is employed and the common joists are set at right-angles to each other, the change in the plane coming at the midway point. Every second joist is supported by a bracket, a practice not followed in later jettying. (See drawings opposite.) The essential elements in this part of the north tower have a dendro date of 1290.[28]

Group II

This is a category not included in Richard Harris' article, but which applies to Shropshire's early jetties. In this the upper post rests entirely on the girding-beam and the bressumer is tenoned into the side of the post. Dated examples include the solar crosswing at 23 Barrow Street, Much Wenlock, of 1327-30 and The Rectory, Ludlow, of 1313-28 (see pp.141-147).[29] Some undated examples are also known, all incorporating an axial jowled post set at ground level about halfway along the side wall. This post supports the girding-beam and houses the axial-beam which supports the

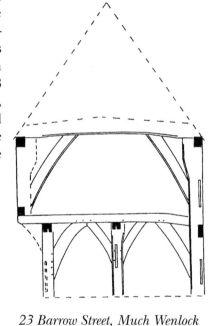

23 Barrow Street, Much Wenlock

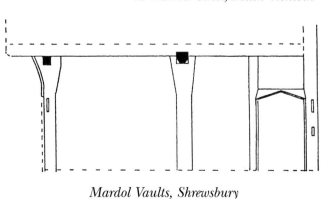

180 &182 Abbey Foregate, Shrewsbury

Mardol Vaults, Shrewsbury

101

common joists of the upper floor. At 12 Fish Street (1358-9)[30] a foot-brace strengthens the angle between the girding-beam and the upper-floor post. At The King's Head, Mardol in Shrewsbury, (1404), the bressumer is moulded and is tenoned into the post and also lapped across the front of it.[31] Possibly one of the later examples of the use of the axial post is 181-2 Abbey Foregate in Shrewsbury, and this has a roll-and-hollow moulding on the bressumer. It is likely to be of a late 15th-century date.

At the Mardol Vaults in Shrewsbury, another axial post/beam building, the end corner post at ground level is also double-jowled and the jetty-plate is clasped centrally. Adjoining buildings obscure other details. The Old Yew Tree at Ashford Bowdler is unusual in that the girding-beam runs under the post, projects a little and is finished with a curved detail.

Group III

In this group the bressumer runs under the corner post, and is supported by the girding-beam. The corner post of the upper storey is tenoned into the bressumer. At The Nag's Head in Shrewsbury (1419)[32] and at 12 King Street, Ludlow, the bressumer is extended slightly. Details at 12 King Street (no.6 in the following list) are shown in section as the corner features are obscured, but it will be seen that here the jetty-plate is supported by a smaller one, each chamfered and stopped and running through. Unusually there are no upper posts at bay intervals.

Group IV

This may be regarded as a sub-section of Group III, above. Here, as before, the bressumer runs under the corner post and is supported by the girding-beam but the bressumer is sometimes moulded. With or without the moulding this is the pattern until pendant and hewn jetties are reached. At The Great House, Corve Street, Ludlow,[33] the top third of the jetty-plate is rebated; at 106 Corve Street, Ludlow, the jetty-plate is plain but the bressumer displays an embryonic roll-and-hollow moulding. This was to become widely used in its developed form. The example at 16 King Street, demolished in 1986, is shown.

Group V

By now the pattern is established and the time-scale has moved into the 17th century. The bressumer still runs through and is supported by the girding-beam, but the joists are no longer bull-nosed and the overall dimensions are smaller. An applied bracket often takes the place of the earlier brace to support the end of the girding-beam. 14/15 Raven Lane in Ludlow is a good example and there are many others. 39 High Street, Bishop's Castle, is slightly different in that the main post has an integral jowl and the jetty-plate is housed entirely in the girding-beam.

Group VI

In this group although the bressumer still runs through and is supported by the girding-beam, the ends of the joists are tenoned into the back of the bressumer. As such they relate to Richard Harris' Group 2 where the form was apparently developed in order to be able to display a 'seamless moulding' on the front of the building and thus conceal the joist-ends.[34] Shropshire has numerous standard examples and variations on this theme. At Humphreyston Hall (1471)[35] the moulding is badly weathered and the joist-ends are visible. Here the jetty-plate is clasped in the integral jowl of the ground-floor corner post. At Church House, Highley, it is only the lower third of the girding-beam which supports the bressumer and at 12 High Street,

Much Wenlock, while the joint between the bressumer and the girding-beam is obscured it is clear that an integral jowl on the ground-floor post supports the girding-beam.

At Old Hall Farm, All Stretton, (1564),[36] and Clungunford Farm, (1591-2),[37] the bressumer and the girding-beam are almost level. An exploded view is shown of Clungunford Farm. Here the post is tenoned into both the bressumer and the girding-beam. This construction is known as the 'Clun Valley' type as it is common in the area. At 58 Church Street, Bishop's Castle, the bressumer is seated half-way down the girding-beam and an applied bracket supports the end. The Merchant's House, Corve Street, Ludlow, also has an applied bracket and here the moulding has been defaced and the joist-ends are visible.

The Abbot's House, Butcher Row, Shrewsbury, (1457),[38] has an L-shaped moulded bressumer. The girding-beam which is tenoned into the back of the bressumer has an angled soffit and the applied bracket follows the angle. A rebate is cut into the bressumer to house the end of the girding-beam. Blunden Hall at Bishop's Castle also has an L-shaped bressumer, but of a much simpler form, and an applied bracket. This construction is on the service wing, the more elaborate solar wing is shown on the drawings.

Group VII

This group, while related to Group VI in having the joist-ends tenoned into the bressumer, employs double bressumers. The practice was a hall-mark of the 'Shrewsbury School of Carpentry' so prominent in the years *c*.1560-90 in the houses of the Drapers' Company and occasionally found elsewhere. Penkridge Hall, (1590), mentioned above, is a good example of the spread of the style and because of its special interest is drawn in more detail. A further point here is what has been dubbed the 'lazy jetty'. This is where it is the penultimate post which receives the end of the tie-beam and functions as the main support. A further three possible examples of the 'lazy jetty' are known in Ludlow. Harp House in Church Street, Bishop's Castle, has the double bressumer and here the post of the upper storey overlaps the top bressumer, presumably in order to show off the cable moulding on the post. At Alcaston Manor, Acton Scott, (1557),[39] the top bressumer is flat and wide and the joists are tenoned into the back of the lower bressumer. The same applies to the Fellmongers' in Frankwell, Shrewsbury, which probably has a similar date and to 1 Fish Street also in Shrewsbury. While the gallery on the extension to Bear Steps in Shrewsbury, (1567-76),[40] is similar it has only one bressumer and the post of the upper storey cuts into the girding-beam. Some of these houses have a double-tenon in the girding-beam to engage the bressumer. Beslow in Wroxeter parish, mentioned above, was such an example and this also is shown in more detail.

At 69 Corve Street, Ludlow, the upper bressumer is smaller than the lower, perhaps indicating a change of

Jetty carving at 8 & 10 Market Place, Shifnal

103

Jetty carvings at 103/104 Corve Street, Ludlow (no.45 in the list below)

emphasis, although it is the lower one which carries the moulding. 53 Broad Street, Ludlow, has a single bressumer but this returns onto the gable and the moulding is continuous. The main post has an integral bracket and the jetty-plate is double-tenoned into it. 8-10 Market Place, Shifnal, has the double bressumer, each moulded, and an integral carved bracket.

The following table names the buildings which are simply given a number on the drawings in order to save space. The dates are either from dendrochronology or from reasonable inscriptions. It is emphasised that the examples are not necessarily tied to the groupings, but are juxtaposed where details are similar. A comprehensive survey has not been attempted; a selection only is offered:

1. 23 Barrow Street, Much Wenlock, (1320-30)
2. 12 Fish Street, Shrewsbury, (1358-9)
3. The King's Head, Mardol, Shrewsbury, (1403-4)
4. The Mardol Vaults, Shrewsbury
5. The Nag's Head, Wyle Cop, Shrewsbury, (1420-22)
6. 12 King Street, Ludlow (section)
7. The Great House, Corve Street, Ludlow
8. 106 Corve Street, Ludlow
9. 16 King Street, Ludlow, (dem. in 1986)
10. 14-15 Raven Lane, Ludlow
11. 39 High Street, Bishop's Castle
12. 180/181, Abbey Foregate, Shrewsbury
13. Humphreyston Hall, Donington, (1471)
14. Church House, Highley

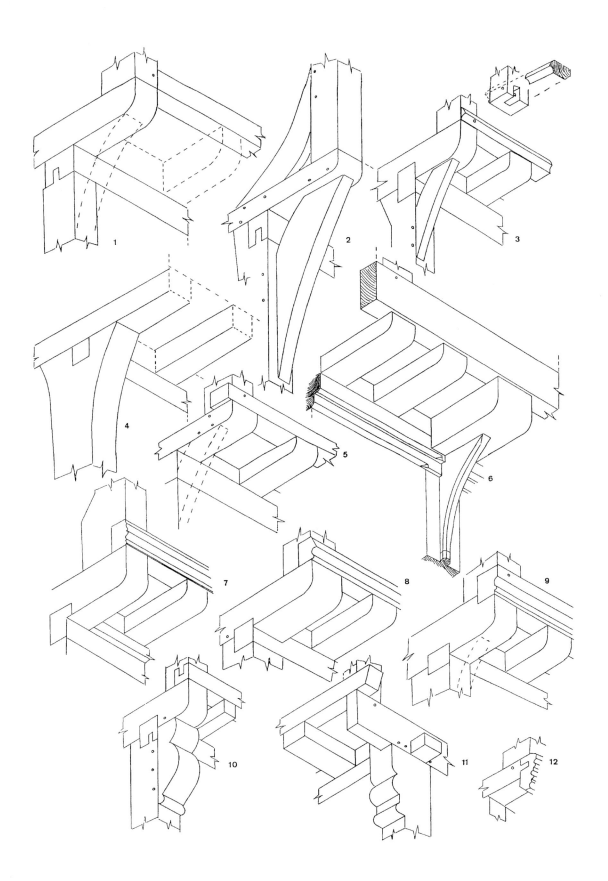

15. 12 High Street, Much Wenlock
16. The Old Yew Tree, Ashford Bowdler
17. Old Hall Farm, All Stretton, (1565)
18. Clungunford Farm, (1591-2)
19. 58 Church Street, Bishop's Castle
20. The Merchant's House, Corve Street, Ludlow
21. The Fellmongers, Frankwell, Shrewsbury
22. Bear Steps Gallery, Fish Street, Shrewsbury, (1576-7)
23. Abbot's House, Butcher Row, Shrewsbury, (1457)
24. Harp House, 26 Church Street, Bishop's Castle
25. Alcaston Manor, Acton Scott, (1557)
26. Beslow Manor, Wroxeter, (dem. 1985)
27. 1 Fish Street, Shrewsbury
28. Blunden Hall, Bishop's Castle (service wing)
29. 69 Corve Street, Ludlow
30. 53 Broad Street, Ludlow
31. 8/10 Market Place, Shifnal
32. Porch House, High Street, Bishop's Castle (section), (1564)
33. 113 Frankwell, Shrewsbury
34. 2 Dinham, Ludlow, (c.1656)
35. Dawes's Mansion, Church Street, Ludlow, (1610)
36. 14 Old Street, Ludlow
37. 40 Pride Hill, Shrewsbury
38. Ludford House, Ludlow
39. 15 Market Place, Shifnal
40. 13A Market Place, Shifnal
41. The White Lion, Market Street, Ellesmere
42. The White Hart, Sherrifhales Road, Shifnal
43. Grove Farm, Ash Parva
44. Top Farm, Knockin
45. 103/104 Corve Street, Ludlow
46. White Hart, Birch Road, Ellesmere
47. 3/4 High Street, Bridgnorth
48. The King's Head, Whitburn Street, Bridgnorth
49. Tudor Cottage, High Street, Church Stretton
50. Church Farm, More
51. Lane End Cottage, Muckleton, (1621)
52. Porch House, Swan Hill, Shrewsbury, (1628)
53. Royal Oak Farm, Bletchley, Market Drayton
54. Tudor House, Cheshire Street, Market Drayton
55. Sandbrook Vaults, Shropshire St., Market Drayton, (1653)
56. Hazlewood Farm, Darliston, (1655)
57. Claverley Vicarage
58. Henry Tudor House, Wyle Cop, Shrewsbury (2nd storey level), (1430)
59. 12 King Street, Ludlow (detail)
60. Porch House, High Street, Bishop's Castle, (1564)
61. Bishop Percy's House, Cartway, Bridgnorth, (1580)

107

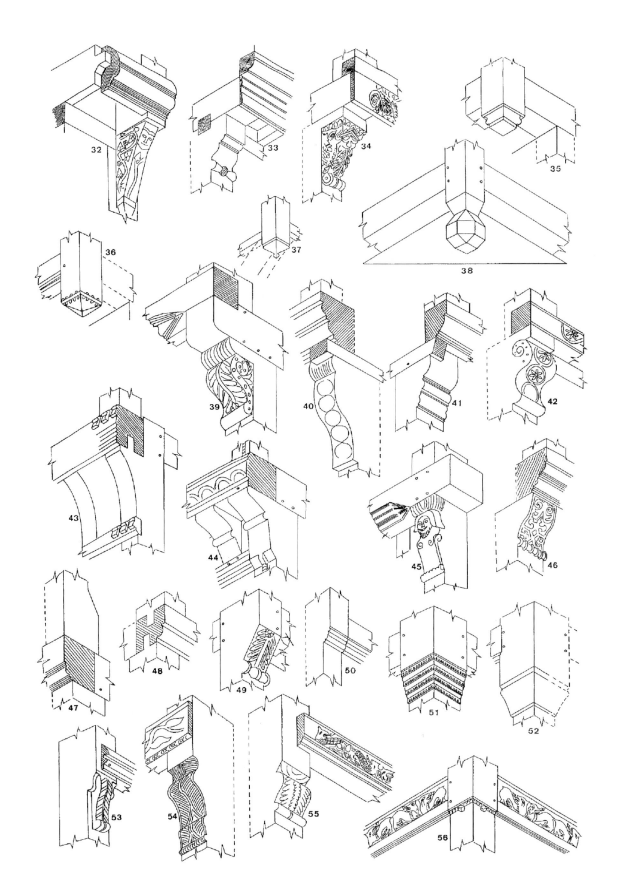

108

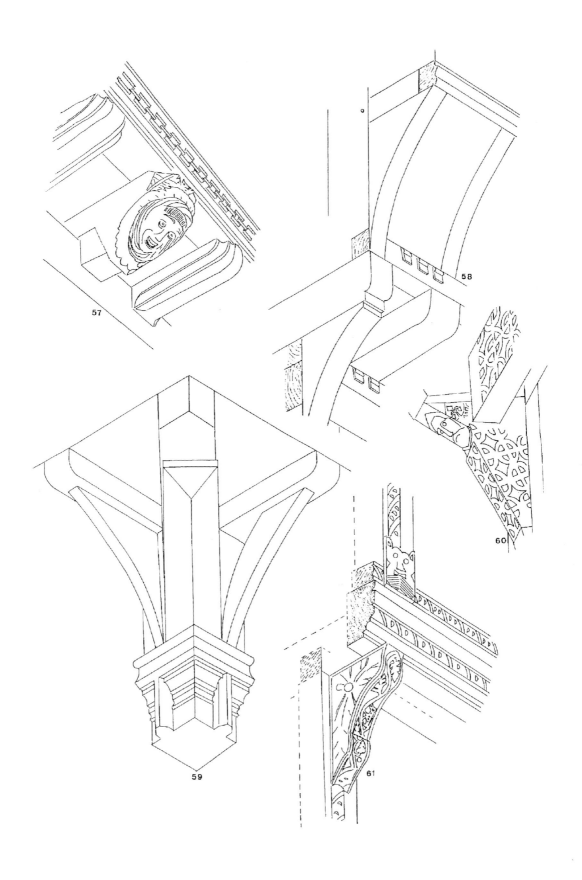

57

58

59

60

61

109

Tudor Cottage, Church Stretton (no.49 in the list above). Note roof raising and hewn jetty, of which there is a detail of the latter on the right

Special mention should be made of Crickheath Hall in Oswestry Rural parish. Here an unusual jetty occurs. It encompasses the hall and both crosswings, has no dragon-beams and the jetty plate and the bressumer are in line horizontally. Furthermore, continuous carved decoration, not moulded, occurs on the bressumer of each unit. Though badly weathered, a combination of floral and scalloped design is evident on the lower half, and traces of similar work on the upper half are discernable.

5   Roof Construction

If there is one element guaranteed to reveal the structural history of an old house, that element is the roof. It is the area that is usually left comparatively untouched once an updating exercise has ceiled it off, and present day investigators are well aware of the necessity of penetrating beyond the ceiling. Of course there are disappointments, some houses have been completely re-roofed or their vital roof components mutilated to a great extent, but an examination of the roof is essential before drawing conclusions about any structural sequence. Historic roofs may be categorised in various ways—the 'bayed' or 'unbayed' types present the obvious starting point and here, with few exceptions, Shropshire comes firmly within the bayed class in accordance with the northern and western areas of Great Britain.[1] 'Highland' and 'Lowland' are other categorical divisions that have been used.[2] 'Single Rafter' and 'Double Rafter' are terms that are, thankfully, sinking into oblivion, the expressions meaningless though the exposition is still valid. 'Cruck' and 'Box-frame' are clear divisions and relate to the concept of the building as well as to the class of roof, although hybrid examples frequently occur. In his pioneering paper on roof types Professor Cordingley listed 75 basic types which he placed within eight groups and three categories. Some have up to 16 variations.[3] Shropshire's historic roofs are reasonably predictable, always interesting and sometimes astonishingly beautiful.

Coming as Shropshire does in an intermediate zone of carpentry practice where cruck-framing was dominant in early times, but box-framing was an integral thread running through the fabric of timber-framing;[4] it is not surprising that the county produces a variety of roof types. Unbayed roofs, that is where the coupled rafters are of uniform scantling throughout the roof and have no longitudinal stiffening in the form of purlins or ridge-pieces, are virtually unknown at vernacular level. The northern transept of Wistanstow church is an ecclesiastic example of the type and this, incidentally, produced Shropshire's earliest dendrochronological date, 1192-1226.[5] The roof over the nave at Church Stretton's parish church is also of this form and another church, the delightful little chapel-of-ease at Pradoe in the parish of Ruyton-XI-Towns—the work of the Victorian architect, M. Rohde Hawkins in 1866—is a Gothic pastiche of mid-13th-century design. Here the roof is unbayed, coming off stone walls. It may be classified as a six-canted, ashlared, scissor-braced roof. The thrust is taken uniformly on the wall-plates and the stability of the roof relies on stone gable walls, careful jointing of the rafters into the wall-plates and the sheer weight of each roof-truss. As such it is alien to Shropshire but is the clearest and most accessible example of the southern unbayed system.

Only two, possibly three, domestic examples of the unbayed roof are known in the county. One is at The Rectory in College Street, Ludlow. Here, in the main range, the roof comes off a stone wall, although the upper storey may have been timber-framed like the contemporary cart-entry crosswing. The roofs of both the main range and the cart-entry crosswing may be classed as **collar-rafter roofs**, the rafters are of uniform scantling, each pair is coupled at the top and triangulated with its own collar-beam and there is neither ridge nor side purlins. A dendro date of 1313-28 was obtained.[6] The second example is over the solar at Stokesay Castle, built by the great wool magnate Laurence de Ludlow and dendro-dated to 1289.[7] In the latter case all the jointing is by mortice-and-tenon whereas at such an early date notched-lap joints could legitimately be expected. One which may come into the category is over the south-west wing at Chelmarsh Hall. Internal access is not possible at present, but externally the collars can be seen projecting from the wall, each supporting a common rafter secured by a peg to the collar.

Pradoe Chapel roof of 1860 in mid-13th-century style

The bayed roof system is usually closely related to the main trusses which mark the normal bay divisions within the house, though this is not inevitable. However, in box-framed structures the roof bays are usually demarcated by the use of principal rafters, that is, rafters which are considerably larger than

Collar-rafter roof in The Rectory, Ludlow

the common rafters in the same roof. In cruck-framed structures the upper parts of the blades serve this purpose. Often the crucks will have common rafters attached to the backs of the blades and blocking pieces are used to facilitate the alignment of the rafters, but in the better cruck roofs the blades themselves are fashioned so precisely that rafters at bay intervals are unnecessary. Similarly, below wall-plate level, the lower parts of the better crucks perform the function of posts, obviating the need for these components.

The intermediary nature of Shropshire is further emphasised by the intrusion of 'lowland' elements into the ethnic 'highland' tradition. For example, the use of a ridge-purlin has the strongest associations with the north and west and most of the later Shropshire roofs, from about the late 17th century onwards, employ this component. However, in earlier buildings the rafters are coupled at the top, and there is neither provision nor need for a ridge purlin. Where a Shropshire roof incorporates elements of 'lowland' culture or otherwise exemplifies a convergence of type it has been found that the building is usually a comparatively early one.

Purlins

As side purlins are common features in the majority of roofs their study can be rewarding and they can help in an overall understanding of the building. In medieval open halls the purlins are an integral part of the framing and may be decorated accordingly. In floored buildings, if the lower edges of the purlins are chamfered and have decorative 'stops' at bay intervals this is a safe indication that the roof space was intended for use.

a) Trenched Purlins

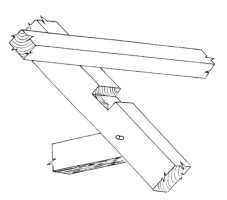

In the older text-books and architectural papers these were called 'Through' purlins, but the term is misleading. 'Trenched' is a better description as the purlin lies in a trench specially cut for it on the back of the principal rafter or the cruck as the case may be. They are usually associated with cruck construction[8] although, such is the effect of the strong cruck tradition in Shropshire, that it is not uncommon to find them used in box-framed buildings and remaining long after cruck-building has died out. The medieval examples are usually flat in section, and twice as long as they are deep whereas the 17th-century variety are square, requiring a deeper trench.

Trenched purlin

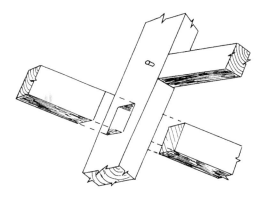

*Tenoned or threaded purlin, with an example (right) in cruck construction at
2 Ryton Grange Cottages, Condover*

b) Tenoned Purlins

Similarly, these used to be called 'Butt' purlins because they appeared to butt up to the principal rafter. In fact they may pass straight through it, when they are better described as 'threaded', or be tenoned into its side.[9] They are normally associated with box-framing although four important cruck-framed houses in Shropshire have tenoned purlins as part of the original concept. These are The White House at Aston Munslow;[10] 2 Ryton Grange Cottages, Condover; Bedstone Manor; and Stokesay Castle.[11] The use of threaded purlins appears to die out after c.1600 though the tenoned purlins continue.

c) Clasped Purlins

Alternatively, these are sometimes described as 'trapped' purlins. This technique involves housing the purlin between the end of the collar-beam and the principal rafter. A suitable amount of timber is cut from the end of the collar on the upper edge and this is matched by

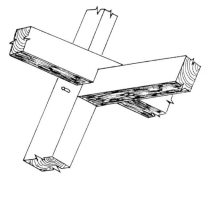

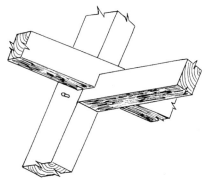

Above left: Clasped purlin with diminished principal rafter
Above right: An example in the Abbot's House, Buildwas, 1377
Left: Clasped purlin with undiminished principal rafter

an opening cut from the inner face of the principal rafter. The purlin then fits into the aperture and is effectively 'clasped' between the two. Sometimes, particularly in the earlier roofs, the reduction of the principal rafter continues to the apex so that the scantling above the purlin is the same as that of the common rafters. The 14th-century roof over the Abbot's Hall at Buildwas is a good example of this practice. In the 15th century, however, the principal rafter was not reduced and sometimes an alternative method which involved clasping the purlin between the principal rafter and the end of a raking queen-strut was used. The use of clasped purlins had largely ceased by *c.*1550.

d) Straddled Purlins

These are not common but may occasionally be found in late 16th-century or early 17th-century buildings. This technique involved cutting a 'trench' from the outer edge of the principal rafter and a similar one from the inner face of the purlin which then fitted over the principal rafter. Where this occurs the scantling of both members is the same and a very neat join with no protruding parts is achieved.

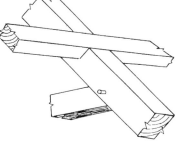

Straddled purlin

Historic Roof Types in Shropshire

Apart from the basic distinctions mentioned earlier, Shropshire's historic roofs may be divided into further categories. A noticeable absentee is the early **king-post roof**, where a central vertical strut rises to the ridge. This, in vernacular buildings, is a northern characteristic and is only found in Shropshire in association with 18th-century agricultural improvements. Once adopted, however, it remained the standard roofing truss for barns and other farm buildings until after the Second World War. Its course from wooden trusses with a bolt-screw in the junction between the base of the king-strut and the tie-beam, enabling the joint to be tightened if

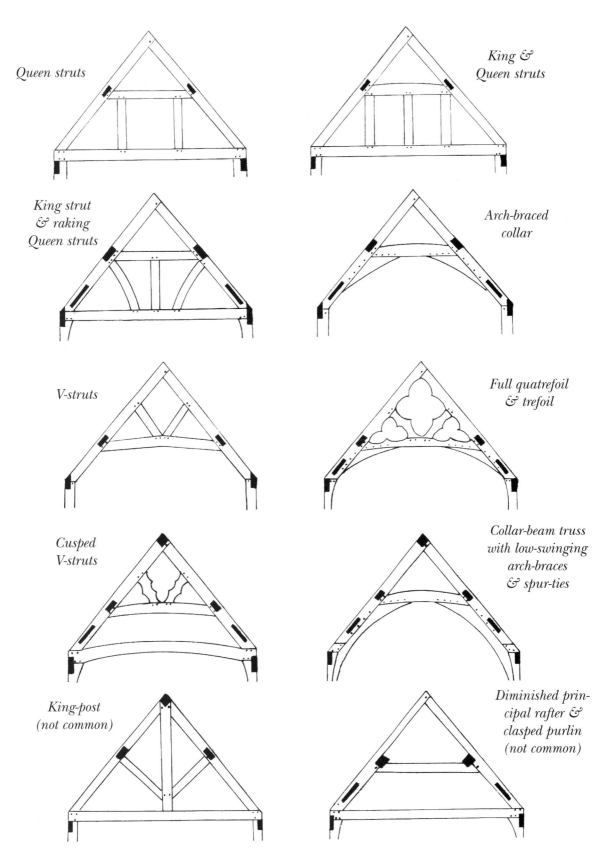

Queen struts

*King &
Queen struts*

*King strut
& raking
Queen struts*

*Arch-braced
collar*

V-struts

*Full quatrefoil
& trefoil*

*Cusped
V-struts*

*Collar-beam truss
with low-swinging
arch-braces
& spur-ties*

*King-post
(not common)*

*Diminished prin-
cipal rafter &
clasped purlin
(not common)*

Some Shropshire roof types (excluding crown-posts and crucks)

necessary, to all-metal trusses may easily be traced. It may be argued that there is an historic precedent in the form of the 'Type G' cruck apex joint where the blades meet on a king-post rising from a collar or yolk.[12] About a dozen examples of these are known, the most striking ones being near the Welsh border. It is very doubtful that these had any influence on the agricultural king-post truss which seems to have evolved independently and on a national basis.

Type 'G' apex with blades meeting on king posts, Llwyn-y-Go, Maesbrook, Kinnerley

a) The Crown-post Roof (Table 1 opposite) In this type of roof construction a centrally-placed vertical timber, known as a crown-post, is set between the tie-beam and a higher collar-beam. It supports what is usually the only longitudinal member, the collar-purlin, or, as it is sometimes called, the crown-plate. Lateral and longitudinal braces to the crown-post itself are used and in some areas of the country side purlins may also occur, but no examples of the latter practice have been noted in Shropshire.

Twenty-nine crown-post roofs are known to exist or to have existed in Shropshire and the break-down is shown in Table 1. Doubtless more remain to be discovered. The distribution is mainly south of the river Severn with the greatest concentration in Shrewsbury and, as will be seen from the table, no two are exactly alike. All the available examples have been sampled for dendrochronolgy and the results show that there is a compact date-range from *c*.1300 to 1431. There is no reason to think that the undated examples would not fit into this range. Because a precise date cannot be ascribed to some, they may not fit exactly into the table as shown, but there can only be slight discrepancies.

Crown-posts are usually positioned at bay intervals and, in Shropshire, are comparatively short plain timbers with lateral braces *down-swinging* from the head, or near the head, of the crown-post to the tie-beam. In these respects they differ from the majority of crown-posts to be found in abundance in southern England. These are much taller, have decorative details and are braced laterally with *up-swinging* braces to the collar.

It was hoped that the heights of the crown-posts would form a pattern within the chronology, but this is not so; the heights vary throughout from 1ft. 6ins to 6ft. Most are rectangular and plain, the only variations are those of cruciform, T-shape or octagonal form. All are down-braced to the tie with the exceptions of those at 3/4 Broad Street, Ludlow, and those on the the central truss at Plowden Hall which are up-braced to the collar. The Nag's Head hall in Shrewsbury has both forms in the same truss.

Crown-post roof with six-way bracing at the Nag's Head, Wyle Cop, Shrewsbury

Grid Ref	Address	Type of Building	Length	Section	Connection to collar-purlin	Long. Braces	Lateral Braces	Associated Features	Dating
SO 454935	Buck's Head, Church Stretton	Urban, secular, timber-framed	3'	Rectangular, plain	Collar-purlin over-rides crown-post	Plain, curved	Down-braced to tie, concave, plain, extend from middle of crown-post	Roof is in crosswing, hall rebuilt	1287-1321 (dendro)
SO 375866	Plowden Hall, Lydbury North	Manor House	3'6" on end truss; 4' on central truss	Rectangular, plain on end truss; rectangular moulded at base on central truss	Collar-purlin over-rides crown-posts	Plain, square section	Down-braced to tie, plain, square section, straight on end truss; Up-braced to collar, plain, square section, straight on central truss	Base-cruck hall	1302 (dendro)
SJ 613114	Leaton Grange, Wrockwardine	Rural, secular, timber-framed	3'8"	Rectangular, plain	Collar-purlin over-rides crown-post	Plain, curved	Down-braced to tie, plain, concave	Roof is in crosswing, hall rebuilt. Hipped end with cusped longitudinal brace	after 1313 (dendro)
SO 642848	The Bold, Aston Botterell	Rural, secular, timber-framed	1'6", extending to 2'6"	Octagonal, 10' square with 4" chamfers	Collar-purlin over-rides crown-post	Curved, chamfered, extend below top of tie-beam	Down-braced to tie, plain, concave, extend from head of crown-post	Base-cruck hall, crown-post extends down tie-beam	1320-1354 (dendro)
SO 623999	23 Barrow St., Much Wenlock	Urban, secular, timber-framed	c.2'	Rectangular			Down-braced to tie	Base-cruck hall	1327-30 (dendro)
SJ 616053	Home Farm, Leighton	Rural, secular, timber-framed	4'3"	Rectangular, plain	Crown-post clasps collar-purlin	Cusped on outer edge	Down-braced to tie, plain, concave, extend from middle of crown-post	Roof is in crosswing, hall rebuilt	1358 (dendro)
SO 512746	3/4 Broad St., Ludlow	Urban, secular, timber-framed	5'2" and 5'5"	Rectangular, chamfered	Collar-purlin over-rides crown-post	missing	Up-braced to collar-rafter, slightly curved, chamfered on one truss	Ground floor may have had through access for the public	1358 (dendro)
SJ 493124	12 & 12A Fish St., Shrewsbury	Urban, secular, timber-framed	4'8"	Rectangular, plain, jowelled head	Crown-post clasps collar-purlin	Cusped on both edges	Down-braced to tie, plain, concave, extend from head of crown-post but not uniformly	Housing for collar-purlin is not central in crown-post head	1358-9 (dendro)

Table 1. Crown-post roofs, the shaded columns giving the details of the crown-posts (continued overleaf)

Grid Ref	Address	Type of Building	Length	Section	Connection to collar-purlin	Long Braces	Lateral Braces	Associated Features	Dating
SJ 493126	The Old Mansion, St. Mary's St., Shrewsbury	Urban, secular, timber-framed	6' on central truss, 7' on two others	Rectangular, plain	Collar-purlin over-rides crown-post	missing	Down-braced to tie, plain, concave, extend $^3/_4$-way up crown-post	Central truss has soulaces. Arch-braces from tie to post form ogee with laterals to crown-post	1366 (dendro)
SO 594213	Lane End Cottage, Muckleton	Rural, secular, timber-framed	2'7½"	Rectangular, plain	Collar-purlin over-rides crown-post	Plain, curved	Down-braced to tie, straight, extend from near head of crown-post	Roof is in crosswing, evidence of 3 trusses, hall rebuilt in 1621	1371-2 (dendro)
SO 771936	High Grosvenor, Claverley	Rural, secular, timber-framed	3'1" and 4'1"	Rectangular, plain	Collar-purlin over-rides crown-post	Plain, curved, chamfered	Down-braced to tie, plain, convex cranked, extend from head of crown-post	Base-cruck hall, cranked windbraces	1375-7 (dendro)
SO 543102	Home Farm, Attingham	Rural, secular, timber-framed	6'	Rectangular, plain	Crown-post clasps collar-purlin	Plain, curved	Down-braced to tie, plain, concave, extend from near head of crown-post	Roof is in crosswing, hall is rebuilt	1385-6 (dendro)
SO 453984	39 Woolstaston	Rural, secular, timber-framed	3'	Rectangular, plain	Crown-post clasps collar-purlin	Plain, straight	Down-braced to tie, plain	Roof is in crosswing to a contemporary cruck-built hall	1398 (dendro)
SO 512746	1 Broad St., Ludlow (Bodenham's)	Urban, secular, commercial, timber-framed	4'4"	Rectangular, plain, double jowelled head	Crown-post clasps collar-purlin	Plain, curved	Down-braced to tie, plain, convex, extend from head of crown-post	1st and 2nd floors are jettied	1403-4 (dendro)
SJ 623001	15 High St., Much Wenlock	Urban, secular, timber-framed	3'6"	Cruciform, plain	Crown-post clasps collar-purlin	Cusped on outer edge, extend below top of tie-beam	Down-braced to tie, cusped, extend from head of crown-post	Base-cruck hall, limb of crown-post extends down tie-beam	1407-8 (dendro)
SJ 494128	Rigg's Hall, Castle Gates, Shrewsbury (A)	Urban, secular, timber-framed above stone	3'4" extending to 4'4"	T-shaped	Crown-post clasps collar-purlin	Plain, curved, extend below top of tie-beam	Down-braced to tie, cusped, extend from head of crown-post	Limb of crown-post extends low down tie-beam. Thought to be solar	1405-35 (dendro)
SJ 494128	Rigg's Hall, Castle Gates, Shrewsbury (B)	Urban, secular, timber-framed	3'10"	Rectangular, plain	Crown-post clasps collar-purlin	missing	Down-braced to tie, plain, straight, extend from head of crown-post	Thought to relate to hall of above	1413-43 (dendro)
SJ 493125	Nag's Head hall, Wyle Cop, Shrewsbury	Urban, secular, timber-framed	3'7½" extending to 4'1½"	Cruciform, plain	Crown-post clasps collar-purlin	Cusped, extend below top of tie-beam	Down-braced to tie, cusped; up-braced to collar-rafter, cusped	Limb of crown-post extends down tie-beam	1420 (dendro)

Grid ref	Location	Type	Height	Plan	Collar-purlin	Crown-post profile	Braces	Notes	Date
SJ 482124	The Lion Tap, Barracks Passage, Wyle Cop, S'bury	Urban, secular, timber-framed	5' ext. to 5'6"	Cruciform, plain	Crown-post clasps collar-purlin	Plain, curved, extend below top of tie-beam	Down-braced to tie, plain, concave, extend from head of crown-post	Limb of crown-post extends down tie-beam, 1st & 2nd floors jettied	1423-6 (dendro)
SJ 506952	The Barracks, Cardington	Rural, secular, timber-framed	2'8"	Rectangular, plain	Crown-post clasps collar-purlin	Plain, curved, extend below top of tie-beam	Down-braced to tie, cusped, extend from head of crown-post	Large, curved wall-braces	1425-6 (dendro)
SJ 565953	Cottage Farm, Easthope (now farm building)	Rural, secular, timber-framed	2'6"	Rectangular, plain	Crown-post clasps collar-purlin	Plain, curved, unilateral	none	2 aisled trusses	1430 (dendro)
SO 653925	Upton Cresset Hall	Rural, manor house	2'4"	Cruciform, plain	Crown-post clasps collar-purlin	Curved, chamfered, moulded at base, extend b'low top of tie-beam	Down-braced to tie, cusped	2 aisled trusses, ¼+ round moulding on arch-braces; billet moulding on arcade plate	1431 (dendro)

The following was sampled for dendrochronolgy but with unsatisfactory results

Grid ref	Location	Type	Height	Plan	Collar-purlin	Crown-post profile	Braces	Notes	Date
SJ 493124	Bear Steps Hall, Shrewsbury	Urban, secular, timber-framed	3'7"	Rectangular, plain	Crown-post clasps collar-purlin	Plain, curved	Down-braced to tie, plain, slightly concave, extend from head of crown-post	Hall abuts 12/12A Fish St., Shrewsbury (above)	

The following are known from archaeological evidence only

Grid ref	Location	Type	Height	Plan	Collar-purlin	Crown-post profile	Braces	Notes	Date
SJ493127	Church Farm Café, S'bury (demolished)	Urban, secular, timber-framed	c.5'	Rectangular, plain, straddles tie-beam	Crown-post clasps collar-purlin	Cusped on outer edge	Down-braced to tie, cusped on outer edge, ogee-arched on inner edge, extend from head of crown-post	Associated vertical struts between tie and collar-rafter; one either side of crown-post, cusped on inner edge, ogee-arched on outer edge	
SJ 494124	Corner of Dogpole/Wyle Cop, S'bury (demolished)	Urban, secular, timber-framed	c.5'	Rectangular, plain	Crown-post clasps collar-purlin	Not known	Down-braced to tie, plain, straight, extend from head of crown-post	See SRC photo no.535. This shows demolition in progress, crown-post truss exposed. (Mallinson photo)	
SJ 623001	14 High St., Much Wenlock	Urban, secular, timber-framed	6'	Rectangular, plain	Crown-post clasps collar-purlin	Plain, curved	Down-braced to tie, plain, concave, extend from near head of crown-post		
SJ 527043	Pitchford Hall	Rural, secular, timber-framed	?	?	?	?	Down-braced to tie	Evidence is on two trusses in west wing	
SJ 577392	Grove Farm, Ash Parva	Rural, secular, timber-framed	?	?	?	?	Down-braced to tie	Evidence is on tie-beam in east wing	
SO 625998	29 Barrow St. Much Wenlock	Urban, secular, timber-framed	c.2'3" ext. to 3'	Cruciform plan	Crown-post clasps collar-purlin	?	Down-braced to tie, plain, curved	Info. from L. Walrond, July 1956	

Table 1. Crown-post roofs, the shaded columns giving the details of the crown-posts (continued)

Only three have any form of decoration. On two, The Bold in Aston Botterell parish and 3/4 Broad Street, Ludlow, the decoration is merely a simple chamfer on each visible arris, but on the recently-exposed crown-post of the central base-cruck truss at Plowden Hall the post diminishes in width at the junction of the up-swinging laterals and expands at the foot into a simple moulding. As such it relates more to the crown-posts of southern England and is allied, as they are, to aisled trusses at either end. The chart shows that the three are early examples in Shropshire (and are illustrated on this page).[13]

It was thought advisable to juxtapose the two Rigg's Hall examples as, clearly, one building programme was involved here. This means that 15 High Street, Much Wenlock, is slightly out of sequence. At Rigg's Hall the solar is unusual in having a combination of crown-post and arch-braced collar-beam roof construction. The chamber is timber-framed above a stone-walled ground-floor unit and the arch-braced collar-beam truss functions as the central truss. It seems to have been incorporated as a means of freeing the central area from intrusive crown-posts, perhaps a first step towards the total demise of this historic roof-form. Aesthetically it must have been considered more pleasing. It was cleverly contrived by threading the collar-purlin through the collar-beam, but as this left only about one inch of supporting timber below the aperture the result seems more related to the social concept of the building rather than to structural considerations.[14] Rigg's Hall is now part of the Public Library complex.

As shown on the table, three of the Shrewsbury buildings, including Rigg's Hall, display cruciform or T-section crown-posts. By this means it is possible

Crown-post assembly (1320-54) at The Bold, Aston Botterell

Crown-post at 3/4 Broad Street, Ludlow (1358)

Crown-post on spere truss (1302) at Plowden Hall

to extend the limb of the crown-post down the tie-beam. This facilitates the use of a larger longitudinal brace and also increases the stability of the joint. At the ill-fated Church Farm Café, described below, the same straddled effect was achieved without the use of limbs, though there the housing for the longitudinal brace was confined to the crown-post, and the straddling merely allowed a larger wooden peg to be used for the mortice-and-tenon joint. Unless the extended limb was pegged back to the tie-beam there was little point in its incorporation except for aesthetic reasons. The cruciform and multi-angled crown-post is known in other areas, but the extended limb appears to be a Shrewsbury speciality. It would seem that crown-post roofing was standard in the county town throughout the 15th century, at least for buildings of substance.

It is always worth noting the way in which the collar-purlin is supported. With the exception of 12/12A Fish Street, Shrewsbury, which interrupts the sequence, those before 1375 have the collar-purlin over-riding the crown-post while those after 1375 clasp the collar-purlin, the crown-post itself being jowelled out for the purpose.

Cusping enters the equation in 1358-9, at 12/12A Fish Street, but does not appear again until 1408 in 15 High Street, Much Wenlock. Thereafter it is to be expected and can occur on the lateral or the longitudinal braces and sometimes both. In one superb example in Church Farm Café, Castle Street, Shrewsbury, the lateral braces were cusped on the outer edge and ogee-arched on the inner. The exuberance was carried further by the introduction of vertical struts immediately alongside the braces. These were cusped on the inner edges and ogee-arched on the outer ones. The longitudinal braces were also cusped, but on the outer edges only. All this richness was lost when the building was destroyed in the 1960s to make way for chain-store development (see illustration on p.247). Cottage Farm, Easthope, is a maverick example in its paucity of bracing and is in startling contrast to the richness of the other house which contains two aisled trusses, Upton Cressett Hall. Each was built at the same time.

Above: Crown-post assembly at 1 Broad Street, Ludlow (Bodenham's) 1404 and, right, at Rigg's Hall, Shrewsbury (1405-35)

Most of the down-swinging lateral braces describe a concave curve, whether cusped or not. However, in two examples the lateral braces are convex and, as such, seem to relate more to those in York city[15] and also, perhaps to the the older roofs in southern England. High Grosvenor in Claverley parish is one example and here both the windbraces and the lateral braces to the crown-post are canted;[16] the other is at 1 Broad Street, Ludlow.[17]

Crown-post assembly at Upton Cressett (1431)

When attempting a relationship between Shropshire crown-post roofs and those in other counties questions arise which are not easily answered. Why, for instance, are only two domestic examples known in the whole of Wales? Both these, Llai Hall in Denbighshire and the barn at Basingwerk Abbey in Flintshire are significantly close to Shropshire.[18] Why was the form not favoured for Shropshire churches? Only one has been noted, at Stottesdon, and that hardly counts as it is a 19th-century insertion and totally at variance with local tradition. Conversely, why was it popular for upper-class dwellings for so long? This, perhaps, may be answered simplistically at least. It was structurally stable, there was less danger of the rafters racking as their position was regulated indirectly by the longitudinal stiffening provided by the collar-purlin, it could cover a wide span, in multiple units if necessary, and it could be decorated to a greater or lesser degree or left plain. Why, then, did its popularity decline in Shropshire when it continued to be used extensively at vernacular level in the south? Was it simply a fashion which had run its course? It would always have been in competition with crucks in Shropshire, and the arch-braced collar-beam roof, whether in conjunction with crucks or not, gave a desirable 'vaulted' appearance and lent itself to more elaborate forms of decoration. Perhaps, too, the simple triangulation of the principal-raftered roof made carpentry at vernacular level less costly.

While it seems clear that the crown-post roof in Shropshire was superseded by the principal-raftered tie-and-collar-beam roof with a central king-strut and flanking queen-struts it is not easy to suggest the roof-type that preceded it. There is little evidence for scissor-braced roofs and none for early king-strut roofs or parallel-rafters, but Shropshire is unfortunate in having no early ecclesiastic or military buildings with any trace of original roofing. Some evidence of scissor-bracing remains in Cruck Cottage, Upton Magna, dendro-dated to 1269, but that is about all (illustration on p.46).[19] The county has neither a cathedral nor a university, the remaining early first-floor halls in Shrewsbury have all been re-roofed and evidence for the aisled hall is scanty indeed. In counties where such buildings survive the accompanying documentary evidence, though not proof, can provide useful guidance in establishing a chronology. It seems, therefore, in Shropshire that the crown-post roof is the second or third earliest *surviving* non-cruck type, the first two being the **scissor-braced** and the **collar-rafter roof**.

From the number of firm dates given in Table 2 on pp.125-6 it will be noted that none is earlier than the late 13th century, although, of course, the table cannot account for the attrition rate. Roughly half are attributable to the 14th century and half to the first half of the 15th. As a general rule it may be safe to say that crown-post roofs with straight bracing are the earliest, and that the large scantling, down-bracing and short crown-posts found in all the examples point to an early typological date when set in a national context. Some pioneering papers and regional studies in southern England help in the understanding of the problems[20] but the most recent comprehensive view is contained in Eric Mercer's *English Vernacular Houses*.[21] From this scholarly study it may be deduced that crown-post roof construction was once standard practice for men of means in England in the 13th and 14th centuries over the area south of the Mersey and Humber and that the reason why it appears localised in the south-east today is that other areas, including Shropshire, adopted different roof forms at an early date while the south-east continued to use and develop it at vernacular level. Nationally it had a run of about three hundred years, from the 13th to the 16th centuries. Perhaps, when the form became obsolete in Shropshire, a vestige of it was retained in the central strut of the side-purlin tie-and-collar-beam truss. Though not structurally necessary it was reminiscent of the central support which the crown-post had provided.

b) The Hammer-Beam Roof

Although a total of 15 churches with hammer-beam roofs seems impressive for the county the earliest are post-1450 and the finest are 16th- and 17th-century in date.[22] As a type, domestic examples are rare. Arguably the most beautiful of roof-forms, the hammer-beam concept evolved from the desire to dispense with the arcade posts of aisled halls and thus create more

Plaish Hall, from The Castles and Old Mansions of Shropshire *by Mrs. Stackhouse-Acton*

freedom of movement at ground level. Put simply, the basic aisled structure moved upwards.[23] With significantly few exceptions, Shropshire is devoid of aisled halls and it is, therefore, not surprising that hammer-beam roofs are also rare. One at Vaughan's Mansion in Shrewsbury, now part of the Music Hall complex, was drawn by J.C. Buckler in the early 19th century (see p.216). It was destroyed by fire in 1917 but copied in the rebuilding. Mr. Smith describes it as displaying a mixture of influences, '... Its principal rafters and heavy purlins with their massive cusped windbraces, ten to a bay, stem from the western school of collar-beam roofs; the tiny hammer-beams and posts and the delicate arch-braced cambered collar might come straight from a Suffolk church'.[24] However, Buckler's drawing shows the roof sitting uneasily on the stone walls then, as it does now in the post-fire version, and it seems unlikely that it is the original roofing of the 13th-century first-floor hall. It may have come from another building entirely.

Plaish Hall in Cardington parish had a form of hammer-beam roof when it was built in the late 16th century. This very interesting house must have been the last open hall of any size to be built in Shropshire and is perhaps an early conscious use of brick. Mrs. Stackhouse-Acton's drawing of the hall, made *c*.1868 (shown on previous page), shows the hall still open although it received an inserted floor towards the end of the 19th century.[25] The hammer-beams were then reused as support posts for the new staircase and the flat balusters which surmounted the screen at the lower end of the hall were reused as stair balusters. High Ercall Hall has roof trusses in the west-facing range, which employ straight braces connecting the feet of the arch-braces to the stone walls at a point well below wall-plate level. As such they may be seen to be acting as false hammer-beams. A total of three, none of which is a classic hammer-beam roof, hardly points to this as an ethnic roof form in Shropshire.

c) The Principal-Raftered Tie and Arch-braced Collar-beam Roof

This title, though cumbersome, aptly describes the indigenous Shropshire roof-form as applied to box-framed houses and to many churches and other buildings where they come off stone walls. Mr. Smith makes the point that as a western type they are numerous and because the mode of construction has always seemed so simple and obvious they have received less attention than more complicated types.[26] The Shropshire roofs, in general, conform to the basic concept of having threaded or tenoned side purlins and no ridge-piece; the main interest lies in the rhythm of the trusses—the number and type of variations that occur in the treatment of the arch-braces; the degree and form of decoration, whether or not stub-ties are employed; the number and type of purlins; the form and treatment of the windbraces; and similar details. Table 2 opposite sets out the non-ecclesiastic examples, personally known to the writer, which can be dated to pre-Reformation times. There must be many others.

The rhythm of the trusses in the larger halls is one tie-beam truss to two arch-braced collar-beam trusses. Usually the latter are intermediate trusses, that is, they come off the wall-plate. Where the arch-braced collar-beam truss forms the central truss of a two-bayed hall then it will have posts forming the sub-structure.

Deep-swinging arch-brace at Coats Farm, Rushbury (1486)

Grid Ref.	Parish	Name	Notes
SO 705976	Astley Abbotts	Colemore Farm	Two-bay open hall, deep arch-braces
SO 702968	Astley Abbotts	Great Binnall	Two-bay open hall, deep arch-braces, cusping giving quatrefoil design. Dendro-dated 1460[31]
SO 613842	Aston Botterell	The Manor House	Four-bay open hall, quatrefoiled cusped windbraces
SO 511865	Aston Munslow	Lower Farm	Two-bay open hall, deep arch-braces, stub-ties, cusped V-struts on central truss
SO 554793	Bitterley	Upper Ledwyche	Six-bay open hall, rhythmic trusses, no cusping. jowelled & battlemented posts. Dendro-dated 1463[32]
SJ 643044	Buildwas	Abbey House	Six-bay open first-floor hall truncated principals, clasped purlins, cusped wind-braces. Dendro-dated 1377
SJ 425045	Church Pulverbatch	Walleybourne	Three or four-bay open hall, cusping on principals, V-struts & collar-beam[33]
SO 565953	Easthope	Farm building (was House) at Cottage Farm	In 2-bay parlour wing, cusping on V-struts & wind-braces. Hall largely gone. Dendro-dated 1454[34]
SJ 494002	Longnor	Moat House	?-bay open hall, rhythmic trusses, jowelled & battle-mented posts, cusping on principals, V-struts & windbraces (three tiers). Hall truncated five half-bays remain. Dendro-dated 1467[35]
SO 512745	Ludlow	53 Broad Street	Two-bay hall, no cusping possibly a 'Wealden'[36]
SO 512745	Ludlow	10 Broad Street	Six-bay range, probably an inn, 'newly-built' 1439 no cusping[37]
SO 513746	Ludlow	15 King Street	Two-bay hall, deep-swinging arch-braces, no cusping Dendro-dated 1467[38]
SO 510745	Ludlow	The Guildhall, Mill Street	Eight-bay hall, prob. ten orig. Alternate intermediates have arch-braced collars, cusping on V-struts & windbraces. Main trusses have cusped V-struts either side of central king-strut between tie & collar. Fully aisled building. Dendro-dated 1411[39]
SO 375866	Lydbury North	Plowden Hall	In three-bay solar wing, cusping on principals, V-struts & collar-beam. Dendro-dated 1454[40]
SO 314905	Lydham	Lower Broughton	Two-bay open hall. Upper & lower bays distin-guished by decoration

Table 2. Principal-Raftered Tie and Arch-braced Collar-beam Roofs. c.1350-1530

Grid Ref.	Parish	Name	Notes
SJ 623002	Much Wenlock	Brookhouse Farm	Two-bay hall, no cusping
SJ 746188	Newport	1 High Street (The Guildhall)	Two-bay hall, deep-swinging arch-braces, stub-ties, quatre-foil cusped & pierced wind-braces. Dendro-dated 1487[41]
SO 464794	Onibury	Padmore	Two-bay hall, deep-swinging arch-braces, stub-ties, carved capitals. (demolished)[42]
SJ 547043	Pitchford	Pitchford Hall	Two trusses in west wing have evidence for arch-braced collars supporting crown-posts
SO 525925	Rushbury	Coats Farm	Two-bay hall, deep-swinging arch-braces. Dendro-dated 1486
SJ 494128	Shrewsbury	Rigg's Hall	Two-bay solar(?), deepswinging arch-braces, crown-posts in end trusses.[44] Dendro-dated 1405-35
SJ 494128	Shrewsbury	The Council House	In solar wing, cusped windbraces (two tiers). Dendro-dated 1465-75[45]
SJ 547043	Shrewsbury	14 Mardol (Old White Hart)	Arch-braced collar-beam truss in solar in rear unit
SO 672829	Stottesdon	Hall Farm	Four-bay first-floor hall, former court/hundred house (?). Dendro-dated 1454[46]
SO 656924	Upton Cressett	Upton Cressett Hall	In four-bay solar wing, clasped purlins. Dendro-dated 1428-30[47]
SJ 322244	West Felton	St. Winifred's Well House	Two-bay former chapel over holy well. Cusping on trusses & windbraces. Dendro-dated 1478-82[48]
SJ 540418	Whitchurch	High Street Garage	In remains of solar(?) wing. King-post in end truss[49]
SJ 543416	Whitchurch	The Olde Shoppe, 23 High Street	In solar wing, cusped windbraces[50]

Table 2 (cont.). Principal-Raftered Tie and Arch-braced Collar-beam Roofs. c.1350-1530

In open trusses deep-swinging arch-braces, spanning the angle between the post and the collar-beam and by-passing the wall-plate, are uncommon in Shropshire, though abundant elsewhere in England and Wales. At Rigg's Hall in Shrewsbury they spring from the post-head,[27] but at Lower Farm, Aston Munslow; 15 King Street, Ludlow; Coats Farm in Rushbury parish; 1 High Street, Newport (The Guildhall); Colemore Farm and Great Binnall in Astley Abbotts; and Padmore in Onibury parish (demolished)[28] they reach a depth below wall-plate level. These are unusual examples, comprising 30% of the known total; normally they brace the angle between the principal rafters and the collar-beam. All arch-braces may be decorated by means of a simple chamfer or be more elaborated moulded, but moulded arch-braces are more often found in cruck-built halls.

Possible evidence for Wealden construction (the juxtaposition of the two main posts and the fact that only the wall-plate, brace and post are original timbers) at 53 Broad Street, Ludlow (see Table 2)

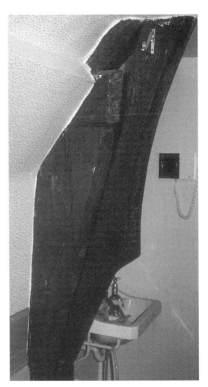

Deep-swinging arch-brace at Newport's Guildhall (1486)

Padmore, Onibury. Reconstruction by S.R. Jones

A 'stub-tie' is, in effect, a truncated tie-beam and performs the same function as a 'spur' in a cruck building, that is to 'tie' the brace (or cruck) back to the wall-plate. In box-framed buildings they over-ride the wall-plates and can therefore be considered part of the roof structure. Again, they are not common in Shropshire. The examples quoted above, with the exceptions of Rigg's Hall; 15 King Street, Ludlow; Colemore Farm; Lower House Farm, Aston Munslow; and Great Binnall are the only known ones, although, as a type, the truss with deep arch-braces and stub-ties is widely distributed in the central midlands.[29] In fact, the numbers are fewer than the distribution suggests.

Windbraces are the diagonally-set roof members found between the principal rafters and the side purlins. The same definition applies to cruck buildings where the blade may perform the same function as the principal rafter. Windbraces are used to improve the stability of the

Central truss at Upper Lake, Westbury.
Note the inset windbrace on left (1546)

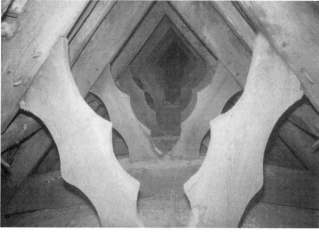

Guildhall roof at Ludlow (1411)

Solar roof at Plowden Hall (1454)

roof by providing resistance to the wind and they normally occur in pairs. Depending on the age, form and size of the building they can be plain, nicked, chamfered, curved, cusped, cusped and pierced, ogee-arched, cranked and straight; they can be single, double and triple-tiered and form either half or complete quatrefoils. Normally they brace the angle in a concave curve, are tenoned into the sides of the principal rafters and are either tenoned into the soffit of the purlin, notch-lapped or simply pegged through from the back of it. Sometimes they are seated on the back of the principal rafter and pegged through, and occasionally they are overlapped on the back of the purlin when the pair can be secured with a single peg. A curious deviation at 2 Ryton Grange Cottages in Condover parish, where two of the windbraces, one on either side of the hall end cruck truss describe a convex curve. As they appear to be original members, and there is no reason why they should not have been set in the conventional way, the 'drunken carpenter' or 'hapless apprentice' syndrome is perhaps applicable. Whatever the reason, the hall must have worn a lop-sided look, not entirely pleasing, perhaps, to whoever paid for it.

At Affcott Manor in Wistanstow parish, although only one windbrace of the open roof of the hall remains, it is clear that each bay had a pair which were seated on the wall-plate towards the centre of bay, and secured to the back of the principal rafter, passing the purlin on the outside. This deviation in form must have given a curious 'inverted' look to the windbracing. At Upper Lake in Westbury parish the windbraces are inset on the wall-plate and tenoned into the purlin, another unusual arrangement but one which was noted in the nearby Upper House Farm, Asterley, in what is now a farm building but is

The roof at Bettws-y-Crwyn church

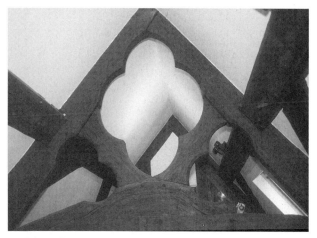

Central truss apex at Great Binnall, Astley Abbots
(1460) (see Table 3 on following pages)

thought to have been a longhouse. Upper Lake has been dendro-dated to 1546.[30]

Cusping is the commonest form of decoration found in Shropshire roofs and it was used confidently and enthusiastically on tie-beams, collar-beams, principal rafters, windbraces and V-struts. The practice was also occasionally extended to crucks. The effect can be breathtaking and experienced investigators have been silenced at their first encounter with the roof of the Palmers' Guildhall in Ludlow (illustration opposite). Many other roofs have cusped detailing in one form or another but it is those in which the cusping on the principal rafters, V-struts and the collar-beam form a full quatrefoil flanked either by two trefoils or two mouchettes which are the most spectacular. Plowden Hall's multi-cusping in the solar wing is also breathtaking (illustration opposite). Although the church roof at Bettwys-y-Crwyn is an ecclesiastic building, it is taken as the criterion on account of its perfection and its accessibility. Table 3 overleaf shows where cusping occurs in Shropshire vernacular roofs, but for the sake of completion cusped braces in outer walls and speres are also included. As the table shows, the most popular candidates for cusping were the windbraces, followed by the V-struts, whilst the dendro-dated examples make it clear that the practice was at its height during the 15th century.

Roof of Manor Farm, Aston Botterell
(see Table 3 on following pages)

Name	Braces in outer walls	Laterals in crown-post roof	Longs. in crown-post roof	Crucks	Speres	Princ. rafters	Wind braces	V-Struts	Tie/Collar	Full effect	Date
Leaton Grange, Wrockwardine			*(hip)								after 1313
The Bold, Aston Botterell					*						1320-54
12a, Fish St. Shrewsbury	*		*								1358-9
King's Head, Shrewsbury	*	*									1404
Rigg's Hall, Shrewsbury	*	*	*								1405-35
15 High St, Much Wenlock			*								1408 (Barclay's Bank)
Palmer's Guildhall, Ludlow							*	*			1411 (+ braces to king-post)
Nag's Head Hall, Shrewsbury	*	*	*		*						1419
Nag's Head, Shrewsbury							*				1419 (if contemp.)
Prior's Ho. Much Wenlock							*				1425
Henry Tudor Ho., Shrewsbury	*						*				1430
Upton Cressett, Hall		*									1431
Chapel, Halston, Whittington						*	*	*	*	*	1437
32 Broad St, Ludlow							*	*			1439 (from doc. source)
Condover Court							*				1445
Barnaby House, Ludlow						*	*	*			1450-1
Plowden Hall (Solar)							*	*	*	*	1454 (multi-cusps)
Cottage Farm, Easthope							*				1454 (crosswing)
Great Binnall, Astley Abbots						*	*	*	*	*	1460 (mouchettes)
Moat House, Longnor						*	*	*		*	1467 (quatrefoils)
Council House, Shrewsbury								*			1472 (solar)
25 Kempton, Clunbury				*							1474 (crow-stepping)
Wolverton, Eaton-u-Heywood					*		*				1475 (hall)
St. Winifred's Well, West Felton						*	*	*		*	1478 (mouchettes)
Catherton Cottage				*				*	*	*	1485
Newport Guildhall							*				1487 (quatrefoil)
Brookgate Farm, Plealy					*	*	*	*			1490
Council House, Shrewsbury							*	*	*		1550-1 (hall)
Market Hall, Shrewsbury							*	*	*	*	1596 (1 only, ? reused)

Table 3. Examples of Cusping (continued below)

Table 3. Examples of Cusping

Name	Braces in outer walls	Laterals in crown-post roof	Longs. in crown-post roof	Crucks	Speres	Princ. rafters	Wind braces	V-Struts	Tie/ Collar	Full effect	
The following are undated examples:											
Bettws-y-Crwyn Church						*	*	*	*	*	This is the criterion
Er 'w 'r Escob, St. Martin's				*		*		*	*	*	
Trebert, Llanvair Waterdine				*				*	*	*	(On arch-braces)
Llwyn-y-Go, Maesbrook				*		*	*				(also on king-post)
Old Hall, Claverley						*	*				(ogee also on w/braces)
Church Farm Café, Shrewsbury		*									(Dem. + ogee)
Vaughan's Mansion, S'bury			*				*				(copy of origs. Quatre)
19 Mardol, S'bury (Mac Fish)							*				(demolished)
Walleybourne, Ch. Pulverbatch						*		*	*	*	(mouchettes)
The Barracks, Cardington		*									
Church Ho. Much Wenlock	*										
111-12, Frankwell, S'bury	*										
The Bull, Ludlow							*				(quatrefoil)
Manor Fm, Aston Botterell							*				(quatrefoil)
Abbot's House, Buildwas							*				
Wycherley Hall, Baschurch							*				
Cleeton Court, Bitterley								*			
Old School Ho., Condover								*			
21-3 High St., Whitchurch							*				

One example which does not fit into any of the above categories is at Blunden Hall, Bishop's Castle where the external bracket on the corner of the parlour wing is strongly cusped. This has the decorative male figure on the front (see p.98). Another is at the Old Vicarage Cottage, Sutton Maddock, where the lower panels in the dais truss are strongly cusped, and the third is 11 Mardol where cusping occurs on the barge-boards which appear to be early, that is, not 19th century.

131

Cruck Roofs

These are an integral part of the concept of cruck framing and are discussed in chapter 3.

Roof Coverings

a) Slate

Before the development of railways in the 19th century allowed the importation of Welsh slates on a large scale the choice of roof covering in Shropshire was largely between thatch, stone tiles or hand-made clay tiles. Welsh slates, probably from Glynceiriog, were brought via the Severn to roof Tern Hall in 1701 and doubtless they were used in Shrewsbury around that time, but it was not until 1857 that a company was formed to exploit the slate on a commercial basis. Tern Hall was later engulfed by Attingham Hall in the 1780s but not before some rebuilding in the 1750s had also employed both Welsh slaters and their native product.[51]

One economical method of using Welsh slates, though not to be be recommended, was what came to be known as the 'Hit and Miss' type of roofing. In this the slates were not closed up, but were set apart from each other, saving about one-third of the normal quantity. Unfortunately it increased the potential for the slates to slip. The practice seems to have been confined to farm buildings.

b) Thatch

It is not known when thatched roofs were first forbidden in the major towns. In Shrewsbury a bye-law of 1706 ordered that '... no houses or other buildings hereafter to be built shall be thatcht with Broome Straw or other combustible matter ...' but this is probably a reiteration of an earlier order.[52] The records usually specify broom; wheat straw was probably not used very much until the late 18th century and reeds would be unknown except, perhaps, in the vicinity of the larger lakes and meres. At present there is little thatch in the county although there

Thatched cottages at Badger

is now one resident master-thatcher and some renewal of thatched roofs is, fortunately, taking place. When times were hard and funds would not stretch to re-thatching the usual practice was to clap corrugated iron over the old thatch, but current comparative affluence means that these buildings are prime targets for restoration.

c) Stone Tiles

These are discussed in chapter 2 on stone-built houses.

d) Clay Tiles

As with thatch, roofs with old, hand-made, clay tiles are not common nowadays, but clay roofing tiles were made in vast quantities in Coalbrookdale in the 19th century. They were a

Polychrome roof tiles at a warehouse, Ironbridge

lucrative by-product of coal mining and although by the mid-19th century the clay industries were concentrated in several large brick and tile works, earlier scattered tileries associated with coal, lime and brick production were commonplace.[53] Clay was being dug for tiles in 1497 in Easthope and Thomas le Tyler was a tenant of Easthope mill in 1413.[54] Bricks and tiles were made in Broseley from the 16th to the 20th century[55] and it is recorded that tiles were being made at Horton in 1681, and in 1738 St. John Charlton paid for the making of 17,000 tiles at Apley.[56] In 1772 Thomas Botfield's Old Park Iron Works supplied 7,500 roofing tiles to the Horsehay ironworks,[57] but the best quality tiles came from Broseley and even today a roof of Broseley 'Rosemarys', 'Irons', 'Crowns' and 'Coalports' is regarded with awe and affection. Some measure of the importance of roofing tiles comes from two detailed probate inventories.

Roof of Harnage Tiles at the Old Hall, Cressage

When William Langley, a cleric from Wellington, died in 1689 his 'Brick and Tyle crests and Gutters' were worth £10. This represented 6% of the total value of £161 16s. 2d. Only his silver plate and desperate debts were worth more. William Cheshire of Admaston, described as a 'gent' who died in 1725 or 1726 had 'Six thousand of Tyle' worth £3.[58] Many of the old records and, unfortunately, some modern histories do not make distinction between roofing tiles and floor tiles and between clay tiles, stone roofing slabs and wooden shingles and so care is needed with interpretation.

It is dismal to have to record that no distinctive roof-ridge cresting tiles seem to have survived in Shropshire. The writer possesses an old hand-made one from Phoenix Place in Shrewsbury, given to her by the owner, in which the workman has pinched up the ridge with finger and thumb in three places, but this hardly compares with the delightful equestrian example held in the museum at Totnes in Devonshire.

e) Clay Slurry

A roof of unbaked clay seems to be a contradiction in terms but one was discovered at the 'Rose and Crown' in Church Street, Ludlow in 1982. At present it is contained within a later, tiled roof which relates to an enlargement of the building on the north side of the courtyard, but it is clear that the slurry originally functioned as an effective covering. Some special glutinous quality must be present in the clay for it to withstand the weather. The only other clay slurry roof in the area, known to the writer, is at Overton Hall, Malpas, which is just over the border in Cheshire. Here it was used to cover that part of the solar roof which adjoined the hall and thus would never have been exposed to the weather.[59]

Clay-slurry roof covering at Overton Hall, Malpas, Cheshire

f) Pantiles

Modern housing estates display numerous examples of pantiled roofs, but in historic terms they are virtually unknown in Shropshire. In Rowley's House Museum in Shrewsbury are examples of both main types of Roman roofing from Wroxeter: the flat tiles (*tegulae*) which, when used by themselves, were given pointed ends, and plain rectangular tiles in conjunction with rounded ones (*imbrices*). It is from the latter combination that pantiles seem to have developed. In the Town Hall at Bishop's Castle a painting of the castle of *c.*1800 includes two small ancillary buildings in the inner bailey clearly depicted with pantiles, but how much 'artist's licence' needs to be taken into consideration is impossible to tell.

g) Oak Shingles

By their nature early oak shingled roofs are unlikely to have survived, and to the best of the writer's knowledge no documents make specific mention of them, which is not to say that they were unknown in Shropshire. One building, at present used as the Christian Youth Centre in Neen Savage, retains its roof of oak shingles and this is a single-storied all-wood hut.

Apart from interesting structural details, old roofs are capable of providing surprises of many kinds. Some encountered by the writer include a bag of sovereigns secreted by an ancestor of the householder, skeletons of cats, numerous old shoes, a family bible and a complete set of Tudor star-shaped chimneys. It is always a pleasure to restore lost family treasures to the owners; skeletons and old shoes are a different matter. Shoes were often left as a 'good luck' talisman when a roof was ceiled off, sometimes they belonged to adults and sometimes to children. It is said that live cats were also ceiled off for the same reason. The forgotten chimneystacks were a complete surprise to the owner who did not realise that her 18th-century farmhouse was simply an enlargement and encapsulation of an Elizabethan timber-framed house.

6   Ludlow Houses: The Medieval Period

Ludlow's origins, like Shrewsbury's, lie outside the town, but there the similarity ends. Ludlow does not feature in the *Domesday Book* but is a classic example of a planned town of the 12th century. It is likely that such a prime site was exploited before this time and there are several lines of reasoning to support this view. However, these are not the concern of this study and it seems appropriate to take the link between the new town and the manor of Stanton Lacy as a starting point.

Stanton was one of the rewards enjoyed by the de Lacy family following the Norman Conquest and it was in the south-west corner of that manor that the de Lacy family began to build a castle between 1086 and 1094.[1] At least, that is the account that is now generally accepted, although other versions attribute the founding of Ludlow Castle to another Norman war lord, Roger de Montgomery, the Earl of Shrewsbury.[2] However, it seems indisputable that the castle was the *raison d'être* for the planning of a town which was primarily intended as a servicing agency for the border stronghold. How that planning was implemented is open to debate[3]—whether the grid-iron plan was a single concept from the start, or developed in planned stages. The town's architecture can do little to resolve the issue, but what an attraction the new town must have been to people whose business it was to serve the castle, to skilled artisans and traders and to rootless and landless would-be settlers. Here, for the sum of one shilling a year, a burgage plot, often 33ft. wide, could be rented. This provided sufficient room to build a house, make a living and grow food for the family, secure in the knowledge that there was a fortress handy if Welsh bandits or other insurgents became too bold.[4]

Such a prospect could hardly fail, and yet there is evidence to show that not all the burgage plots were taken up and that the projected town plan covered a much larger area than that which was walled in the 13th century.[5] Nevertheless, the community thrived and by

Saxon doorway with pellets and pilasters, church of St. Peter, Stanton Lacy

1199 was in a position to rebuild the church.[6] Later, when the town walls were built, there were seven gates giving access to the town but only one, the Broad Gate, has survived in recognisable form. The original width of the High Street may be gauged from a point outside the entrance to the castle, but towards the eastern end encroachments of markets and subsidiary streets have resulted in a distorted plan and some very narrow passageways.

Late 13th-century Great Hall and service block at Ludlow Castle

Prosperity in the 13th, 14th and 15th centuries came from a number of factors. Wool was produced and marketed, and indeed, Laurence de Ludlow, who was granted licence to crennelate his manor at Stokesay in 1291 and whose grandson established the Carmelite Friary in Corve Street in 1350, was probably the wealthiest wool merchant of England in his time.[7] The river Teme which curves round Ludlow is fast-flowing and would have powered corn and woollen mills alike. Cloth manufacture was the basis of Ludlow's economy until *c*.1600.[8] Politics played a greater part in Ludlow's fortunes than in most provincial towns. The lordship had passed through marriage in the 14th century from the de Lacy family to the powerful Mortimers of Wigmore, and Edward IV, whose grandmother was the last of the Mortimers, rewarded the town for its loyalty to the Yorkist cause in the Wars of the Roses by granting it borough status.[9] This set the royal seal of approval on Ludlow and was to affect its future in many ways. Agriculture also played a large part, and Ludlow's situation made it a centre for the production, marketing and distribution of produce of all kinds. Most of these points are common ingredients in the mixture of most towns but Ludlow had another component, one which guaranteed success—the Palmers' Guild.

The Palmers' Guild began about 1250 as a kind of 'Friendly Society' but quickly became geared to religion which was regarded in the same way as a modern 'consumer durable'; saving the soul was the target, and this was best done by making a pilgrimage to the Holy Land. (A window in the Guild's own chapel in the parish church, that of St. John the Evangelist, depicts a legend that attributes the foundation of the Guild to Edward the Confessor.)[10] Inevitably as membership grew and, indeed, extended nationwide, the Guild's role changed and its earlier ideals became submerged beneath its commercial enterprises. Property had been a key factor in the Guild's finances from early times; it owned, built and was endowed with shops, houses and rents. It had its own Guildhall in Mill Street and maintained its own College of Priests in College Street. It controlled Hosier's Almshouses and the Grammar School and by 1550, shortly before it was dissolved and its possessions granted to the Corporation, it owned 241 town properties and drew rents from 63 others.[11]

Such a powerful influence was bound to affect the architecture, and it is interesting to note that in Shrewsbury a similar influence, the Drapers' Company, left its mark on the town. This, however, had a different constitution and reached its peak in the late 16th century, after the Palmers' Guild had been dissolved. Shrewsbury's early domestic architecture had been along different lines, but there was a time in the mid-15th century when the two communities were building framed houses in a similar way.

Ludlow Houses up to *c*.1500

In the late 13th or early 14th century the Genevilles and Mortimers added the Great Hall block to the castle. As at Shrewsbury and at much the same time, this was a stone-built hall at first-floor level above an undercroft; but whereas in Shrewsbury smaller halls of the same form occurred in the town it is not easy to see a similar two-way influence at work in Ludlow. The only hint of such a life-style occurs at The Rectory, College Street, described below and at 18 Castle Street where demolition in 1995 revealed traces of a medieval undercroft. At the Castle Lodge, outside the castle gate, the stonework contains a moulded doorway which may represent the original entrance into a ground-floor hall. The roll moulding with a fillet suggests a 13th-century date.

As Ludlow's medieval houses form such a distinctive group it is possible to list them individually, but to suggest a chronological sequence unless supported by dendrochronology is to

St. John's House

The Broadgate

invite disaster. Apart from other considerations their features are unlikely to be confined to one building phase. It is not proposed to discuss early ecclesiastic buildings or those within the castle complex.

St. John's House[12]

Although largely rebuilt in the 16th century, fragments of 13th-century work, probably relating to the early years of the Hospital of St. John are incorporated into the house. Most noticeable is the arch in the gable end which overlooks Ludford Bridge. Though severely remodelled and mostly obscured on the outside, remains of shafts with typical Early English plain semi-circular capitals are visible internally.

The Broadgate[13]

Though basically a military and non-vernacular building the Broadgate was converted to domestic use once the need for defence had gone. Stylistically it relates to the 1280s and although licence to 'enclose the town'

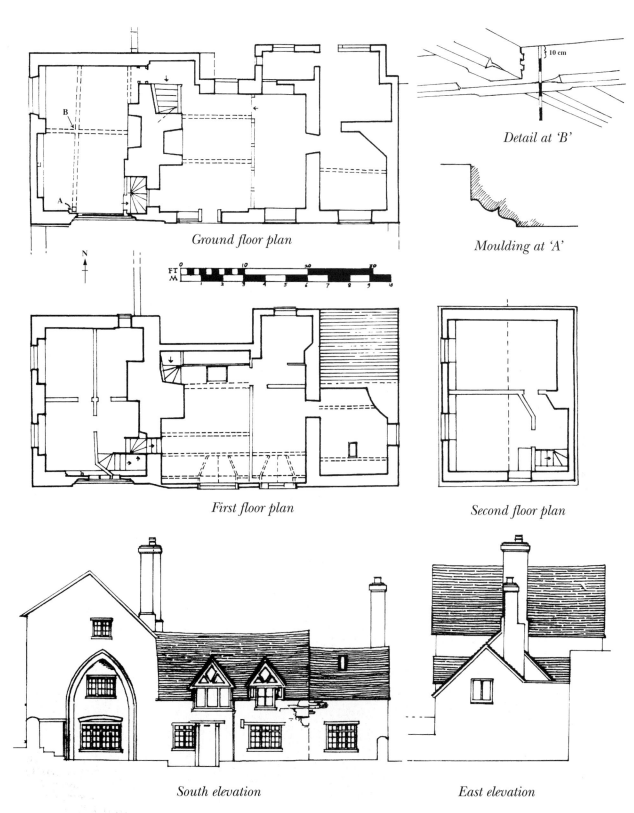

Detail at 'B'

Moulding at 'A'

Ground floor plan

First floor plan

Second floor plan

South elevation

East elevation

St. John's House (this page and opposite above)

138

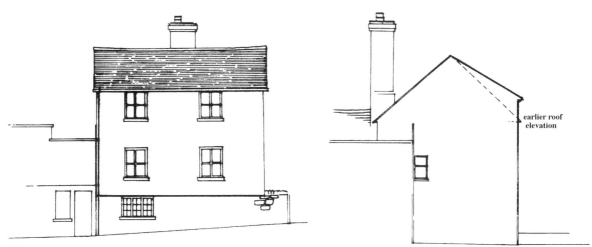

West elevation   *North elevation*

with walls had been granted in 1233, it is probable that building did not commence until after 1260.[14] Many reminders of the Broadgate's defensive origins remain today including the two tall three-storied semi-circular towers with their shooting-slot windows, the arched gateway and the portcullis housing. It forms a striking closure to the south end of Broad Street. Much of its present charm relates to the fusion of the medieval work with that of the 17th and 18th centuries which will be described later.

Barnaby House[15]

Traditionally this building was a staging post for pilgrims on their way to visit the holy well of St. Winifred in north Wales. Thomas Barnaby was Cofferer (Treasurer) to Edward IV, (1461-1483) but some structural details of this stone mansion relate to a late 13th- or early 14th-century date, noticeably the Caernarvon-arched door and windows (restored) to the west of the later chimney stack. The door jambs

Barnaby House, Mill Street with, below, part of its roof dating from 1450-51

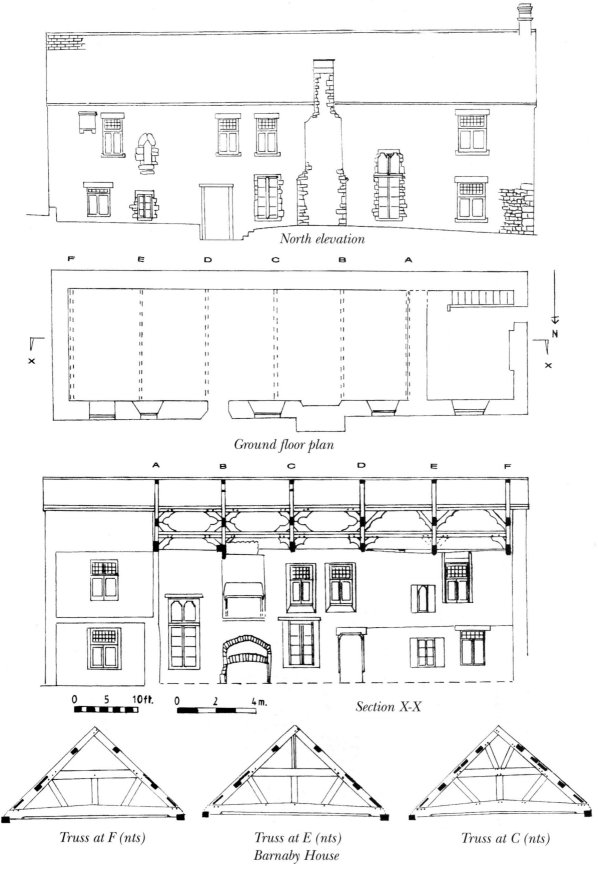

North elevation

Ground floor plan

Section X-X

0 5 10ft.

0 2 4 m.

Truss at F (nts)

Truss at E (nts)

Truss at C (nts)

Barnaby House

Barnaby House when in use as a school gymnasium

have three-quarter round moulding, again suggestive of this date. The open timber roof of five bays appears to sit uneasily on the stone walls and clearly came from another building entirely. Its style also suggests a date later than the walling, and dendrochronological sampling and analysis produced a date of 1450-51. It is of tie-and-collar-beam construction with a king-strut and raking queen-struts in each truss. Two of the trusses have V-struts above the collar. The tie-beams fit well over the wall-head but only single wall-plates on the outer edge of the wall-head are used. There is no ridge-purlin and the side purlins are threaded through the principals. The windbraces vary with two tiers in each slope and for the most part they are cusped members, a double tier to each slope, but in three bays the upper tier is both cusped and set upwards to form a wide quatrefoil pattern. At one time the whole of the interior was gutted to serve as the gymnasium to Ludlow College, formerly the Grammar School, but floors have been re-instated and the building is no longer a gymnasium. The west end, which probably represents the siting of the solar bay, contains a well-preserved Elizabethan wall-painting in an upper room. This is probably co-eval with the arched doorway which gave access from the solar bay into the hall. The painting is described in chapter 13.

The Rectory, College Street[16]

As it stands, The Rectory consists of three distinct units, two of which, the northern range and the crosswing, have been dendro-dated to 1313-28. The crosswing was a large, timber-framed, two-bayed, cart entrance with an upper chamber which was jettied at either end. The wall-plate has the remains of a stop-splayed scarf joint with two edge-pegs and the rafters have rafter holes. The northern range, which is set parallel to the street, has a stone-walled undercroft at ground level with an open-roofed chamber above. Each unit has a collar-rafter roof, that is,

The Rectory

each pair of rafters is triangulated with its own collar-beam and there are no principals or side purlins. The framing of the third unit, which is also set parallel to the street to the south of the cart-entry, is of 16th-century form with the ground-floor room containing a double-chamfered spine-beam with double-pyramid stops. An unusual feature of this unit is the second floor which has been framed with wide joists and window openings, but never finished, remaining as a very large and inaccessible roof-space.

Datestone
(not to scale)

West elevation

0 1 2 3 4 5   10 *feet*   0   1   2   3   4 *metres*

East elevation

The Rectory, College Street

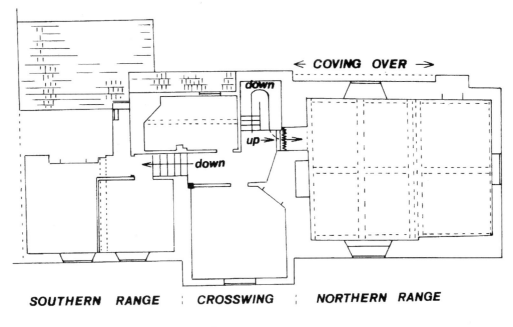

SOUTHERN RANGE | CROSSWING | NORTHERN RANGE

0 1 2 3 4 5   10 *feet*   0   1   2   3   4 *metres*

First floor plan

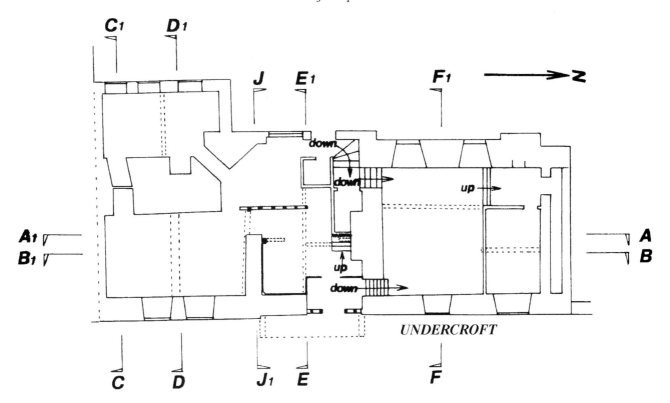

Ground floor plan

The Rectory, College Street

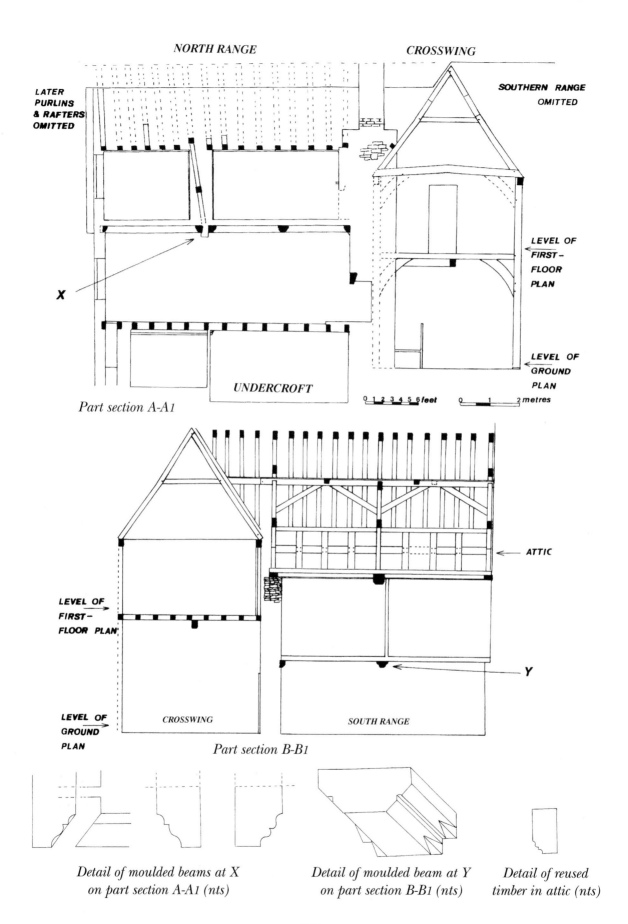

NORTH RANGE

CROSSWING

LATER
PURLINS
& RAFTERS
OMITTED

SOUTHERN RANGE
OMITTED

X

UNDERCROFT

LEVEL OF
FIRST –
FLOOR
PLAN

LEVEL OF
GROUND
PLAN

0 1 2 3 4 5 6 feet

0   1   2 metres

Part section A-A1

ATTIC

LEVEL OF
FIRST –
FLOOR PLAN

LEVEL OF
GROUND
PLAN

CROSSWING

SOUTH RANGE

Y

Part section B-B1

*Detail of moulded beams at X
on part section A-A1 (nts)*

*Detail of moulded beam at Y
on part section B-B1 (nts)*

*Detail of reused
timber in attic (nts)*

144

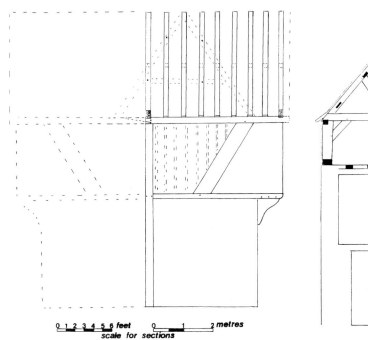

Section J-J₁ (crosswing) (conjectural reconstruction)

Section C-C₁ (south range)

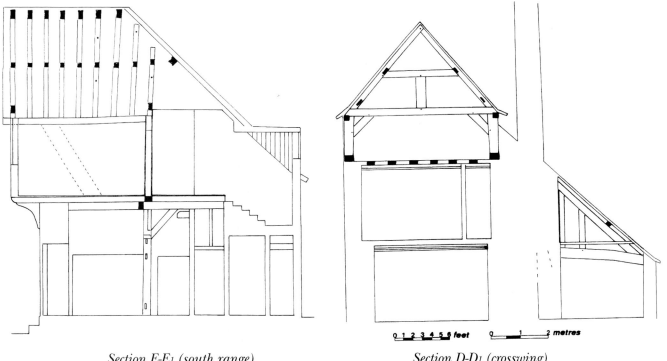

Section E-E₁ (south range)

Section D-D₁ (crosswing)

The Rectory, College Street (this page and opposite)

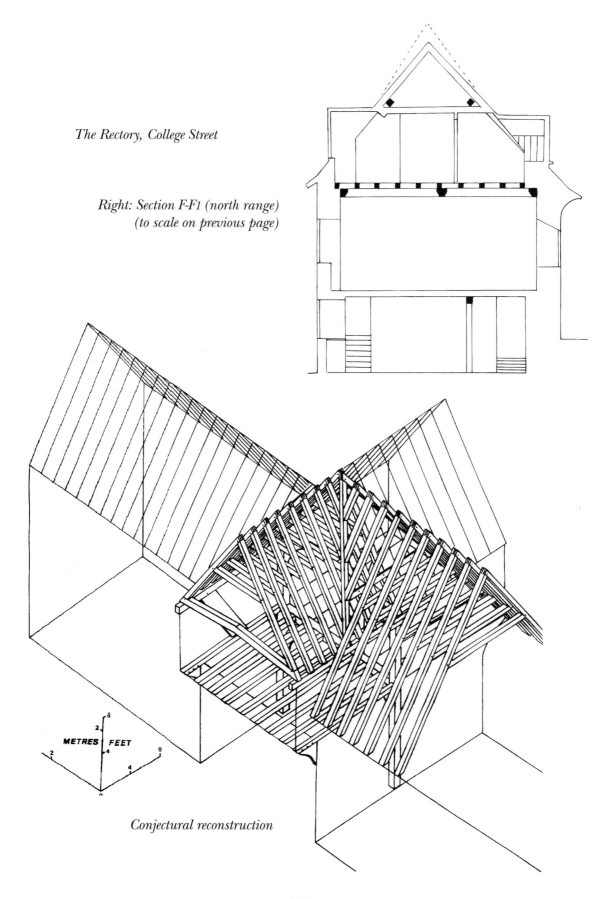

The Rectory, College Street

Right: Section F-F1 (north range)
(to scale on previous page)

METRES FEET

Conjectural reconstruction

146

3/4 Broad Street[17]

This building represents the original termination of Broad Street before the encroachment of 1 Broad Street/20 King Street effectively narrowed King Street (see below). It was stripped out in 1988 and interpreted as being of two bays and three stories, with the ground floor open to admit through traffic, and a chamber above. Though later fitted with a side-purlin roof, two original crown-post trusses remain. These are unusual for Shropshire in that they have up-swinging lateral braces. Normally lateral braces are set in a down-swinging arc onto the tie-beam. The crown-posts are plain and un-jowelled and support the collar-purlins. They have a narrow chamfer on each visible arris. It is clear that the crown-post roof once continued to the south into what is now 5 Broad Street. The superstructure was not jettied although later filling in of the ground floor and the addition of a third story has given a jettied appearance to the front. The eastern (rear) elevation had large open panels with substantial wall-braces whereas the front was close-studded.

3-4 Broad Street, with first floor plan below

A dendro date of 1358-60 was obtained. It may have been a public building of some kind.

The College of Priests, College Street[18]

Adjoining The Rectory and partly interwoven with it is the building which was re-adapted in 1874 to serve as the town's cottage hospital until 1985 and was then altered again to form part of a modern sheltered housing complex. In the courtyard at the rear is a wall which contains the remains of the priests' cells.

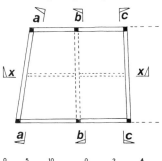

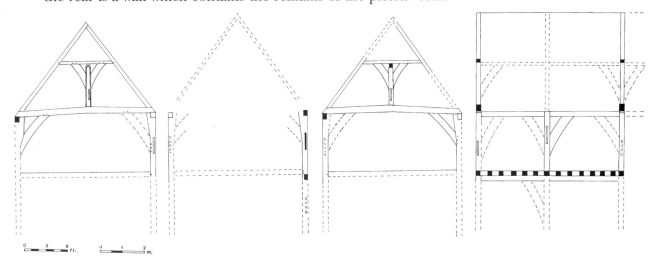

Section a-a   *Section b-b*   *Section c-c*   *Section x-x*

3-4 Broad Street

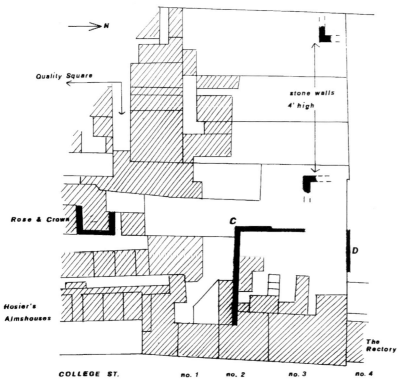

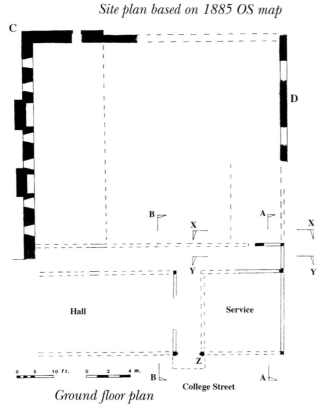

Site plan based on 1885 OS map

Ground floor plan

The Priests' College

They are on two levels and are planned so that two priests each shared a heated sitting-room but had separate unheated sleeping chambers. One or two of the fireplace lintels are re-used grave slabs. There were 10 priests at the height of the Palmers Guild's activities. For many years it was thought that the outline of the cells was all that survived of the College but during the most recent alterations several features in the street-facing range were uncovered which proved that some of the 1393-4 building phase remained and that possibly the 'great chamber' which was added in 1446-7 can be identified. A moulded beam, thought to have come from the spere-truss, was dendro-dated to 1393. Most rewarding of all was the discovery that the entrance door, so Victorian looking, was a re-cutting and re-siting of the original and that the doorposts had carved wooden capitals. Apart from those at Padmore which occurred on the central truss of the hall[19] these are the only known wooden capitals in Shropshire. Decorative post-heads have been noted in only two buildings: Moat House, Longnor and Upper Ledwyche in Bitterley parish. All four buildings are in south Shropshire.

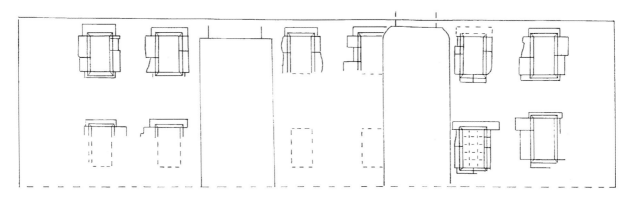

Exterior of the south wall

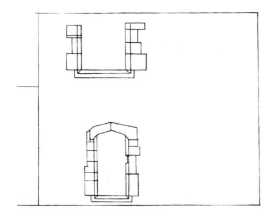

Exterior of the west wall

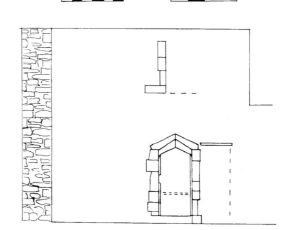

Interior of the west wall

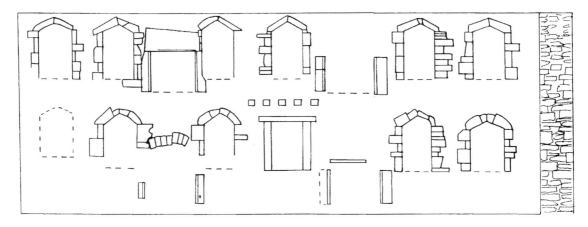

Interior of the south wall

The Priests' College

149

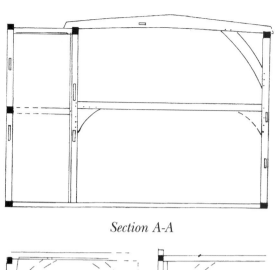

Section A-A

Section B-B

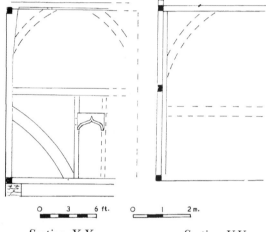

Section X-X   *Section Y-Y*

Capital on door post at Z on ground floor plan (with its own scale)

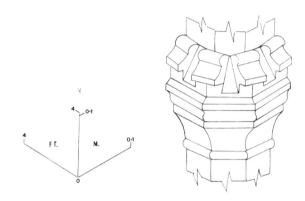

The Priests' College

Re-cut medieval doorway

Remains of priests' cells

20 King Street/1 Broad Street ('Bodenham's')

A three-storied, box-framed and jettied corner property with a double-pile plan and crown-post roof construction. It has been dendro-dated to 1404 and stands as a remarkable example of speculative building and street encroachment by the Palmers' Guild to provide four lock-up shops with chambers above, the chambers intended for occupation by a higher strata of society than the shopkeepers. The roof structure incorporates lateral braces to the crown-posts set down-swinging in a convex arc, a type more familiar in York with which Ludlow had trading connections. The crown-posts are jowelled at the head to clasp the collar purlin and on one a splayed scarf with a sallied abutment-joint on the collar-purlin is cleverly contrived to allow the central tenon on the crown-post to act as a key to secure both halves of the joint. Further security comes from the crown-post's extended 'ears' which continue up into the tenon joint of the collar where they are pegged. Bull-nosed joists define the jetties; the basic framing consists of rectangular panels divided by a horizontal rail with struts set in lozenge fashion. After the account of 1978 was published[20] a decorative corner-post was found abandoned in the garden of the cottage hospital. Its style and measurements suggest that it could have come from the Bodenham's building. It is now in Ludlow museum.

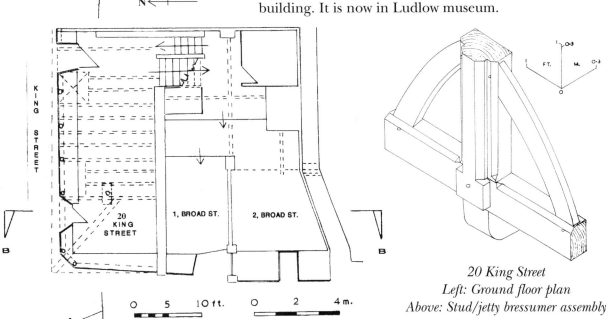

20 King Street, 'Bodenham's'

20 King Street
Left: Ground floor plan
Above: Stud/jetty bressumer assembly

151

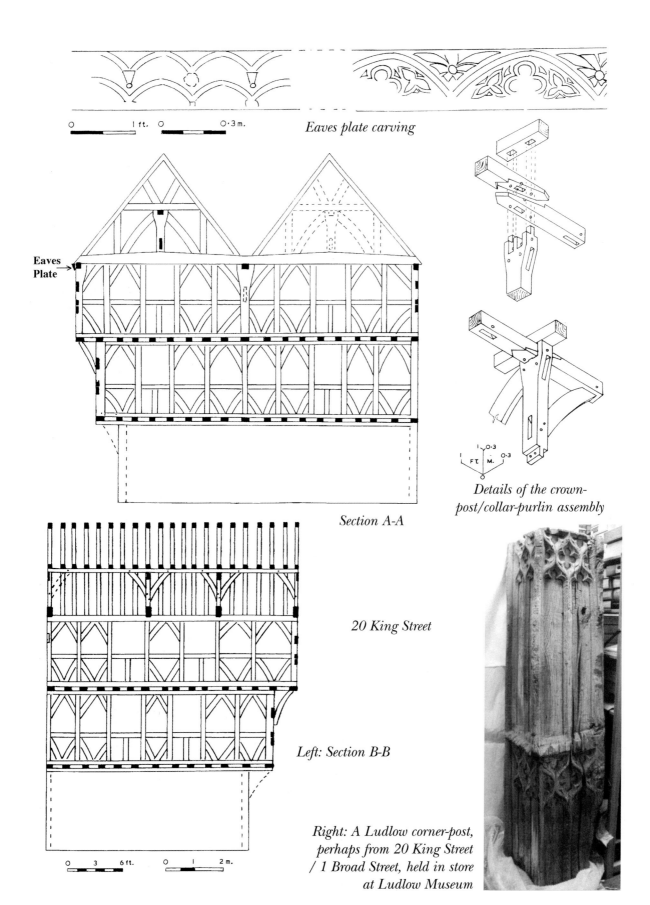

Eaves plate carving

Eaves
Plate

Section A-A

Details of the crown-
post/collar-purlin assembly

20 King Street

Left: Section B-B

Right: A Ludlow corner-post,
perhaps from 20 King Street
/ 1 Broad Street, held in store
at Ludlow Museum

The Guildhall[21]

The Mill Street façade is entirely of the 1768 remodelling which was done by the Shrewsbury architect Thomas Farnolls Pritchard who was commissioned to create municipal law courts from whatever was left of the Palmers' Guild medieval headquarters. Pritchard succeeded in producing a clever disguise while retaining the original fully aisled form and most of the plan of the earlier timber-framed building. He left the roof trusses intact, merely ceiling the intermediate trusses over. The rhythm of the trusses is one tie-beam truss to two arch-braced collar-beam intermediaries. Access to the upper stages of the roof is difficult but the sight of eight unbroken bays each with cusped decoration on substantial timbers is breathtaking. The body of the hall also had a wealth of ornament from carved wooden bosses to triple-roll moulding and broach stops on the arcade posts. It is the only fully aisled secular building as yet identified in Shropshire although there is fragmentary archaeological evidence for a handful of others. It is, perhaps, significant that in the Palmers' window in St. John's chapel in the parish church Palmers are seen, fully robed and perhaps at their pentecostal feast, being entertained by a harpist in a building which appears to have aisled construction. The dendro date for the Guildhall is 1411, but it is known that the Guild maintained an earlier hall on the site.

Panel of the Palmers' Guild window in St. Laurence's church showing feasting in aisled area

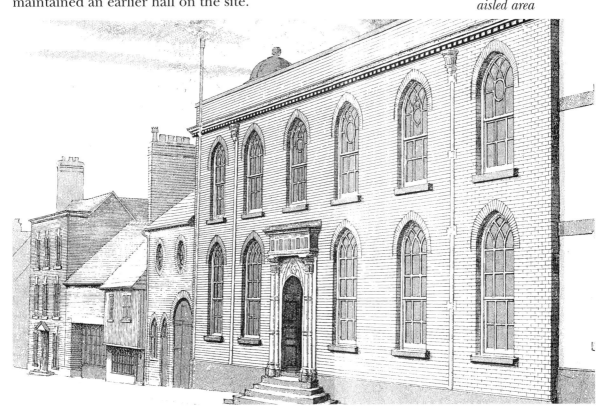

The Guildhall, Mill Street, as drawn by Noel Shepherdson in 1979

Rear view of the Guildhall, as drawn by Noel Shepherdson in 1981

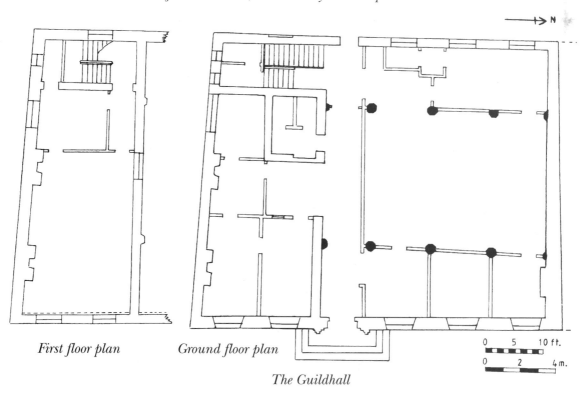

First floor plan   *Ground floor plan*

The Guildhall

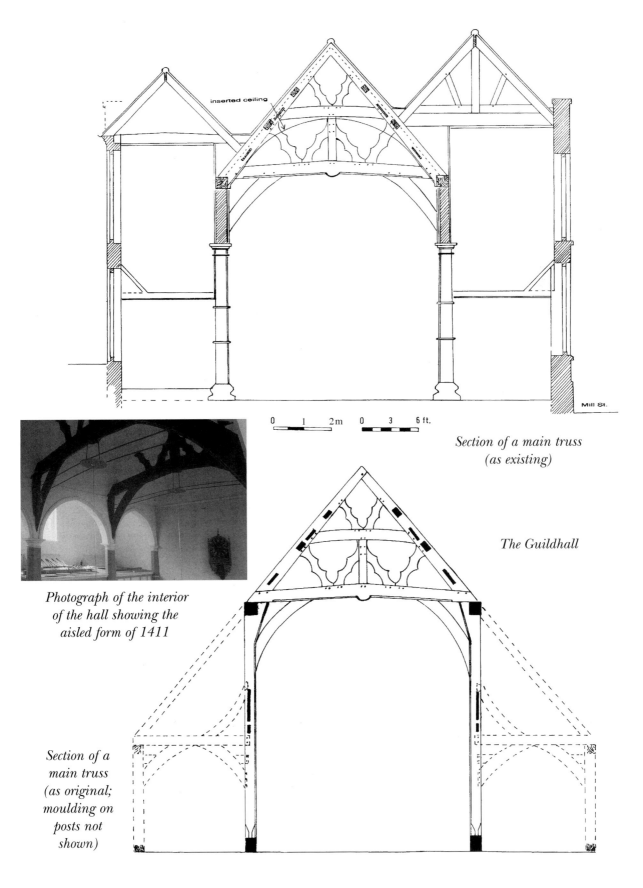

inserted ceiling

Mill St.

Section of a main truss
(as existing)

The Guildhall

Photograph of the interior
of the hall showing the
aisled form of 1411

Section of a
main truss
(as original;
moulding on
posts not
shown)

0   1   2m   0   3   6 ft.

155

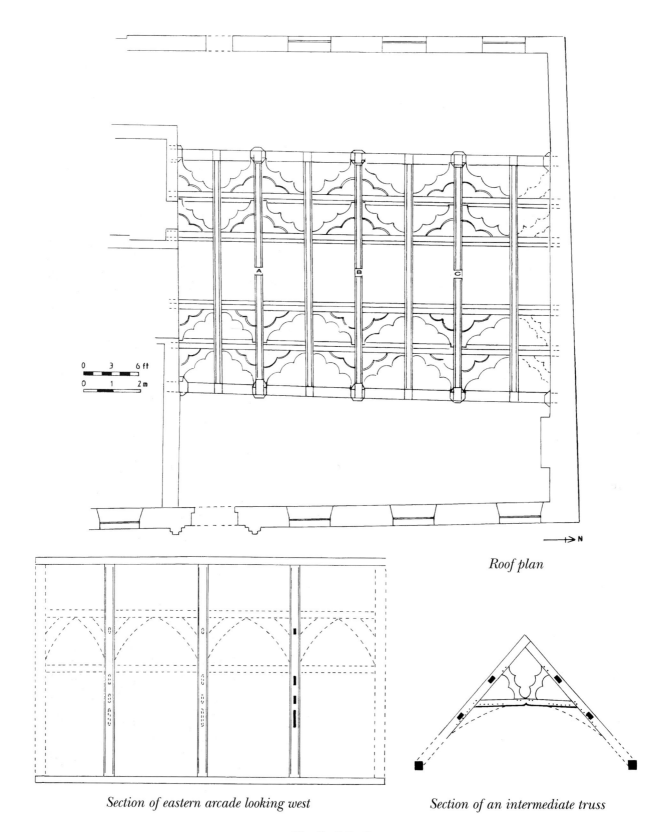

Roof plan

Section of eastern arcade looking west

Section of an intermediate truss

The Guildhall

156

Bosses dating from 1411 on tie-beams at The Guildhall

14-15 King Street[22]

The sub-division of 14-15 King Street has resulted in a complicated pattern of tenure, but if the block is regarded as a two-bayed, box-framed structure of double-pile form the building sequence may be followed. The rear unit of no.15 has been dendro-dated to 1467 and records show that it was a freehold property. It is set partially underground in a manner reminiscent of a medieval undercrofted building. A chimneystack was later inserted into the undercroft, but the intersecting spine-beams are chamfered and stopped in such a way as to suggest that originally a large samson-post or pillar supported an open hearth in the chamber above. That the upper chamber was an open hall is suggested by the arch-braced collar-beam construction of the central truss. In this the arch-braces swing low below wall-plate level. Present also are jowelled posts and two tiers of plain curved windbraces. When seen some years ago smoke-blackening was present on the roof timbers.

14-15 King Street

The front unit of no.15 is an addition of 1476 (dendro-dated). This is also timber-framed and was jettied at the upper level. The jetty has since been removed. It also has jowelled posts, though these are less pronounced than those in the rear unit. The roof is of tie, collar and raking queen-strut construction. Records show that the unit was Palmers' Guild property.

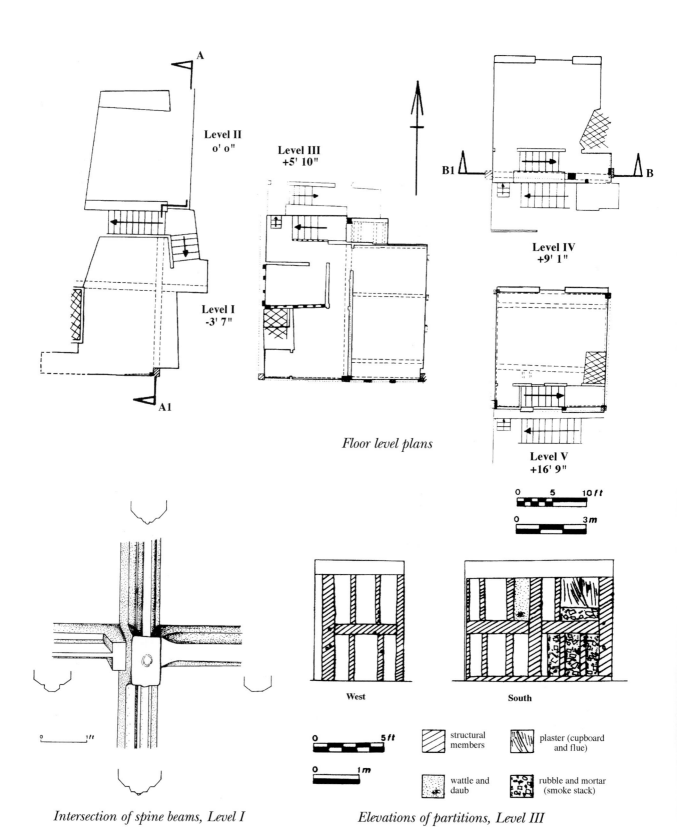

Level II
0' 0"

Level III
+5' 10"

Level I
-3' 7"

A

A1

B1

B

Level IV
+9' 1"

Level V
+16' 9"

Floor level plans

0   5   10 ft

0   3 m

0   1 ft

West

South

0   5 ft

0   1 m

structural
members

plaster (cupboard
and flue)

wattle and
daub

rubble and mortar
(smoke stack)

Intersection of spine beams, Level I

Elevations of partitions, Level III

15 King Street

158

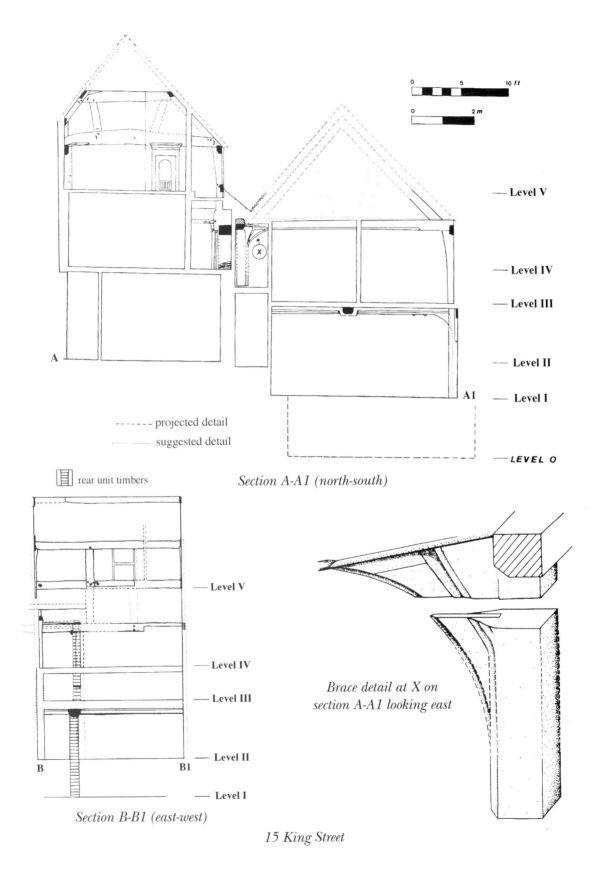

0   5   10 *ft*

0   2 *m*

— Level V

— Level IV

— Level III

— Level II

A1   — Level I

A

------- projected detail

·············· suggested detail

— **LEVEL O**

rear unit timbers

Section A-A1 (north-south)

— Level V

— Level IV

— Level III

— Level II

B   B1

— Level I

Section B-B1 (east-west)

*Brace detail at X on
section A-A1 looking east*

15 King Street

159

The block is particularly interesting for its development sequence. It is known that the south side of King Street represents the colonisation of an originally wide High Street which ran as a spine along the ridge from the castle to Old Street. Temporary market stalls became incorporated into permanent structures encroaching onto the street, which had taken place by 1330.[23] In 1459 Ludlow was 'sacked' by the Lancastrian armies during the Wars of the Roses, and although the extent of the destruction is not known it is possible that the dates obtained for 14-15 represent re-building after the conflict and in anticipation of peace under Edward IV who always had Ludlow's interests at heart.

In 1986 only determined protest from concerned parties and monetary compensation to the developers saved this historic building from modernisation which would have destroyed its nature completely.

16 King Street

Unfortunately, in 1986 the price paid to the developers for retaining 15 King Street involved a 'trade-off' in the form of a *carte blanche* to gut the interior of no.16 which had many surviving medieval features, and was probably of about the same date as no.15—1467. Consisting of a ground-floor shop with a cellar below and a two-bayed chamber above which was jettied over the street, the structure was set gable-end on. The cellar had massive chamfered spine beams above which were laid large flat joists. The posts of the central truss were jowelled and had a chamfered T-section, similar to those found in the Palmers' Guild College of Priests. The truss had knee-braces and, unusually, the pegs were set within the chamfer on the posts. The roof trusses consisted of cambered tie-beams, collar-beams and raking queen-struts; the central truss had V-struts above the collar, but there was no sign of smoke-blackening and the method of heating the chamber was not apparent. There were also good 17th-century features which are described later.

The Grammar School (now Ludlow College)[24]

The complete form of a medieval three-part plan of open hall with screens passage, solar and service ends is discernible beneath later alterations. The building was probably built by Sir Hugh Cheyney of Cheyney Longville, five times M.P. for Shropshire in the late 14th century. It

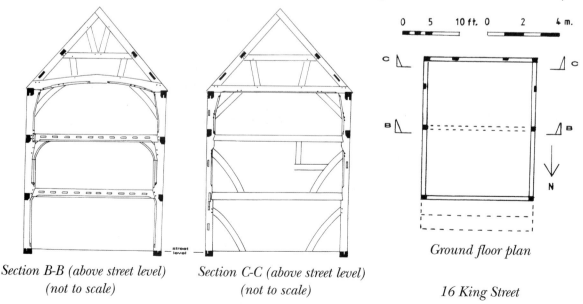

Section B-B (above street level)
(not to scale)

Section C-C (above street level)
(not to scale)

Ground floor plan

16 King Street

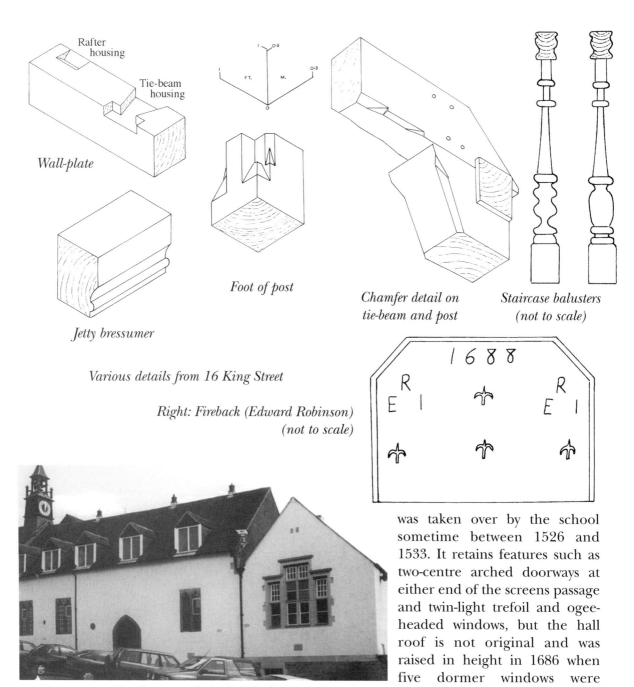

Rafter housing

Tie-beam housing

Wall-plate

Foot of post

Jetty bressumer

Various details from 16 King Street

Right: Fireback (Edward Robinson)
(not to scale)

Chamfer detail on
tie-beam and post

Staircase balusters
(not to scale)

1 6 8 8
E^R I   E^R I

The Grammar School, Mill Street

was taken over by the school sometime between 1526 and 1533. It retains features such as two-centre arched doorways at either end of the screens passage and twin-light trefoil and ogee-headed windows, but the hall roof is not original and was raised in height in 1686 when five dormer windows were inserted.

The Tolsey[25]

Still occupying an island site at the entrance to the town at the top of Old Street this early 15th-century building originally consisted of a courthouse chamber and two other rooms jettied on all four sides above an open ground floor. The four diagonal dragon beams are still *in situ* but only one carved corner post has survived. The Tolsey was where market tolls were paid and disputes were settled in the 'Pie Powder' court (from the French *pieds poudres*, dusty feet), that is 'before the dust was shaken from the feet'. The courtroom has been identified as the west-ernmost bay of the upper storey on account of fragmentary wall-painting and an upper

The Tolsey

moulded wall-plate above a lower one which is chamfered; details not present in the other bays. On the north-east corner is an example of the odd practice noticed elsewhere in Ludlow of giving structural primacy to the penultimate post rather than to the end post, a technical quirk which has been dubbed the 'lazy jetty'. In Louise Rayner's 19th-century painting of the Bull Ring the Tolsey is shown completely bricked over.

32 Broad Street[26]

Behind the 18th-century façade fragments of a medieval hall house are concealed. In a cupboard at first-floor level is a deeply cusped and chamfered windbrace, mortices for a lower tier of windbraces and timbers relating to a transverse truss. The unit was set parallel to the street and is described as 'newly-built' in a Palmers' Guild rental of 1431.

The following six buildings form a loosely-knit group, the common denominator being the survival of a medieval range at the rear of a later street-facing unit:

10 Broad Street[27]

Behind the street-facing block is a range running at right angles and consisting of eight bays arranged in the manner of a medieval inn with stables below and chambers above. Four of the bays are open and have clear evidence of a louvre opening and smoke-blackened timbers indi-

10 Broad Street. A 'with fire' bay

cating that travellers could hire rooms 'with fire' or 'without fire' according to the scale of charges. The open trusses with the louvres have arch-braced collar-beams and the closed trusses have tie-beams, collar-beams and queen struts. There are clasped purlins and plain curved windbraces throughout, but, apart from simple chamfers on the collars and arch-braces, nothing decorative. The block is described as 'newly-built' in a Palmers' Guild rental of 1439.

The courtyard at the Bull Hotel

53 Broad Street with, centre above,
the interior of the hall range

The Bull Hotel,
The Bull Ring[28]

Although masked by a late 18th-century façade, the earliest building phase that can be identified is the street-facing unit which contains remains of a 14th-century timber-framed structure of four bays, each 8ft. long, thus approximating to a standard 33ft. burgage plot. Its roof had two tiers of cusped windbraces each forming a pattern of quatrefoils. In the 15th century the building was extended by an eight-bayed jettied wing at the rear, which incorporated a gallery on the courtyard side. Like 10 Broad Street this also consists of a mixture of open smoke-blackened bays and closed clean bays, indicating a similar use as an inn range with stables below the chambers. In the 17th century a further timber-framed unit was constructed over the entrance and at this time it is possible that a complete courtyard plan existed, comparable with the New Inn at Gloucester and other well-known examples.

53 Broad Street[29]

Behind a 17th-century three-bayed timber-framed unit is a well-preserved two-bay medieval hall which has a central truss of arched-braced collar-beam construction, tenoned purlins, large plain curved windbraces and evidence of a louvre opening. To the east a closed truss demarcates the end of the hall and above wall-plate level this consists of the usual tie-beam, collar-beam, central king-strut and raking queen-posts arrangement. However, less than 3 feet in from the post at the southern end of the truss is another post into which the brace and floor beam are tenoned. Coupled with the fact that only the wall-plate, brace and post on the long southern wall are original timbers the

163

question arises of whether the house comes into the category of 'Wealden house' or is another example of the Ludlow 'lazy jetty' technique. In the 17th century unit an overmantel in the northern room, painted with the royal arms of James I, c.1620, is seen as a sycophantic expression by one of the new landowners during Ludlow's second wave of prosperity, after the demise of the Palmers' Guild and the decline of the cloth trade.

5 Old Street[30]

At the rear, at right-angles to the street-facing block, are two bays of an earlier building, perhaps 15th century in date. Here a transverse truss has typical Ludlovian tie-and-collarbeam construction with raking queen posts and clasped purlins. Once the Red Lion Inn, the front unit has lavishly moulded ceiling beams, described in the next chapter.

Kingston Place, King Street[31]

Between 1351 and 1436 five shops were amalgamated to form a prestigious block with 'solars, chambers and kitchens', the property of a rich burgess who bequeathed it to the Palmers' Guild. Although much altered since, two shops—nos.7 and 8—may be identified, and part of the old solar range remains at the rear. In 1576 the block was rebuilt for Thomas Hankey, and this is followed up in the next chapter.

40 Broad Street[32]

A three-storied 18th-century frontage, four bays wide and with a parapet roof faces Broad Street, but behind it is a range at right-angles containing large curved windbraces and smoke-blackened rafters. Since the description of the details was published in 1979, recent stripping out has revealed that the trimming back and chamfering of the principal rafters was a later alteration to create head-room for an attic door and had no connection with a louvre. This unit formed a link between two parallel ranges, the whole complex having 15th-century origins. In the Palmers' Guild rental of 1439 the rent was 13s. 4d., the highest of any Guild property in Broad Street. A close link with the Guild was the discovery of a fossilised palm leaf behind a purlin, indicative perhaps of someone's pilgrimage to the Holy Land.

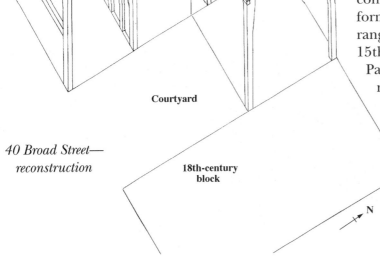

smoke-blackened bay

smoke-blackened rafters

Courtyard

40 Broad Street— reconstruction

18th-century block

N

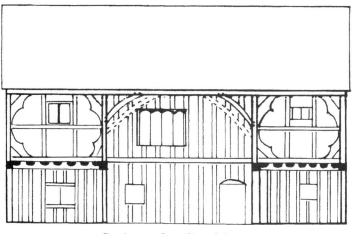

Conjectured medieval frontage

1980 frontage (neither to scale)

Frontage in 2002

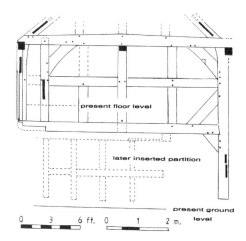

Above: frame at 'A' drawn during 1981 remodelling

12 & 13 The Bull Ring

12 & 13 The Bull Ring[33]

During a recent re-fronting exercise this property, which adjoins the Bull Hotel, was found to contain similar constructional details to 53 Broad Street and The Tolsey, suggestive of either a Wealden form or the use of the 'lazy jetty'.

27 The Bull Ring (Emporos)

Set gable-end on to the street this five-bayed timber-framed range, probably *c*.1450, is difficult to interpret. The framing is very heavy and includes jowelled corner-posts and undivided close studding on the street façade. A side passage is an integral feature and shows a continuation of the large flat joists which are present in the first three bays. In all the bays the windbraces are large curved members and those in the street-facing bay are chamfered. A later range at the rear could represent the rebuilding of a service bay at right-angles to the main block. The building can be seen as having a combination of domestic and

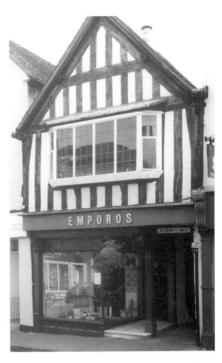

*Above: the High Street looking east
with No.8 (Fosters) after 'restoration'
Right: 27 The Bull Ring*

commercial uses, but any assessment of the relationship and function of the bays can only be conjectural.

8 High Street

Two dragon-beams, large flat joists, a corner post with its tension brace, window recesses in a bressumer and two ogee-headed doorways are some of the details uncovered when the building was renovated in 1979. These indicate that it was originally jettied on three sides and was two stories high. It is at the end of one of the rows associated with mid-15th century market colonisation which effectively reduced the width of the High Street. Unfortunately, instead of restoring the 15th-century form, the refurbishment programme resulted in the loss or disguise of all the interesting features and the exposure of additional timbering which was never meant to be seen.

Lane's Hospital

Lane's Hospital, Old Street

The building, part stone and part timber-framed, is set at the corner of Old Street and St. John's Lane, and incorporates part of a tower belonging to the town wall at the Old Gate entrance. There are two distinct parts. The range which is set parallel to St. John's Lane is four-bayed and the two eastern bays have an open roof of tie-and-collar-beam construction with clasped purlins, raking queen-struts and large plain curved windbraces. This would have been open from first-floor level. The other unit faces Old Street and is mostly 16th and 17th century in its detail (see later).

166

Roof of 15th-century range at Lane's Hospital

112 Corve Street, 'The Great House'

62 Corve Street showing two (blocked) service doorways on the right

112 Corve Street (The Great House)[34]

Although fragments of an earlier structure have been identified on the site and documentary sources record a hall house on the site from 1270 onwards, the bulk of the Great House probably dates from between 1430 and 1450. This includes the jettied frontage where the two-part plan of hall with screens passage and service end with solar above is evident. A cart-entry was driven right through the service end at a later date and the roof was rebuilt to a four-bay design instead of following the three-bay division of the lower storey. Both stories display uninterrupted close-studding, typical of the early 15th century, and the bressumer retains evidence of moulding. The joist-ends are bull-nosed and empty mortices indicate the position of brackets for oriel windows, one to light the solar and the other the chamber over the hall. These have been replaced by modern windows. The original entrance is marked by a lintel over the modern window to the right of the cart-entry. The Great House was sympathetically restored in 1977/8.

62 Corve Street

Perhaps built at about the same time as the Great House, this property was similar in form with a continuous jetty along the front, close-studding and bull-nosed joists. However, the solar to the south was housed in a bay which formed an extension to the plan and is now part of the adjoining property; the moulded beam over the hall in no.62 continues through the partition. As at The Great House, the entrance has been changed, the original screens passage position is marked by the two large joists between the modern bay windows. Similarly, the roof has been altered, this time to create a third storey. Internally the two service doorways into the buttery and pantry are present, though blocked, and details of the carpentry associated with the screen at the dais end of the hall now appear in the wall on the left of the passage. These include jowelled posts with roll-moulding, broach stops and angle braces.

64, 65 and part of 66 Corve Street (The 'Unicorn')

Though much altered, the 'Unicorn' has a similar form to 'The Great House'. It is a four-bayed, timber-framed structure of two stories, having a continuous jetty towards the street. The upper storey displays close studding without a mid-rail and the bressumer has a moulding similar to that on the wall-plate at St. Winifred's Well House at Woolston. The total width of the frontage is 49ft. 6ins.; exactly one-and-a-half burgess plots.

106/7 Corve Street

It is difficult to reconstruct the original plan of this property as it has been drastically altered, re-roofed and re-built. However, features such as the large curved wall-bracing and jetty on the exterior, and cambered tie-beams and large flat joists in the interior of the two northern bays which are set gable-end on to the street suggest the survival of a wing of a mid-to-late 15th-century house.

The Rose and Crown, Church Street

This is a good example of a courtyard-plan house on a three-perch wide plot. A good run of references from 1480 show a mercer's house at the rear with two shops facing the street, one of which survives in part as 7 Church Street.[35] Even so it is difficult to interpret the individual units and almost impossible to make sense of the plan. In a rear stone wall is part of a 13th-century two-light mullioned window with trefoil heads which may indicate that the building was associated with the nearby College of Priests belonging to the Palmers' Guild, or it may have come from another structure entirely. However, this unit is unique in having a roof covering of clay slurry over closely-spaced laths. It is enclosed by a later roof

Top: window at rear of the Rose and Crown with, below, the inn itself

and so not visible from outside. The roof structure consists of tie-and collar-beam trusses with queen-posts, probably dating from the mid-15th century. Forming the eastern flank of the courtyard is a timber-framed range which terminates with a cruck truss at the southern end. The blades are largely obscured and mutilated but a high cambered collar-beam is visible and the purlins are clasped between the blade and the collar—a detail not normally found in cruck construction. At bay intervals there are two further trusses to the north, but these are of box-frame construction, the northernmost one having shaped knee-braces between the post and the tie-beam. The western side of the courtyard has been largely rebuilt. The form of this complex invites questions which its complicated assembly of parts makes extremely difficult to answer.

The Bull Ring Tavern[36]

At present the Tavern consists of two distinct units. The two-bayed, twin-gabled eastern unit is entirely of the 17th century and is described in its context in the next chapter, but the western unit, which is also two-bayed, has structural evidence which suggests that a two-bayed framed and jettied house of three stories which had its roof-line parallel to the street and dated from c.1500 was re-modelled in the late 16th century and given large twin dormer-gables in the 17th century. The external evidence lies in the jetty plate which supports the third storey. The plate is surmounted by another which projects slightly and is chamfered and stopped. Above this are the projecting bull-nosed joists and the bressumer of the third storey. Similar constructional details may be seen in the long side wall of 12 King Street, described below. Internally a transverse frame dividing the two bays seems to relate to the same late 15th-century building phase. The details include large curved tension braces and a splayed foot to the jetty post at first-floor level, very similar to the form of construction found at Henry Tudor House, Wyle Cop, Shrewsbury. Documents show that this part of the Bull Ring Tavern was an inn in 1482.

12 King Street[37]

Situated at the corner of King Street and Taylor's Lane the property has a two-bayed, two-storied unit set parallel to King Street, and a three-bayed range at right-angles to it which has a continuous jetty along the Taylor's Lane frontage. Here the bay divisions are marked by enlarged joists and the double jetty plate, similar to that on the Bull Ring Tavern, described above, may be seen. At the southern end is a fine carved corner post with a moulded capital. The post is 14ins. (0.36m) square in section and is cut to overlap the sole-plate which is set on a stone plinth. Two dragon beams indicate that the whole block was jettied on the three exposed sides. In 1986 partial stripping out of the King Street unit revealed remains of two transverse frames set about 3 feet apart. One frame had chamfered and moulded posts with broach stops, a chamfered beam and knee-braces, probably repre-

*Corner-post and jetty
at 12 King Street*

senting the equivalent of a spere truss at the low end of the hall. With the large curved wind-braces and flat joists which were also revealed at this time, and the features noted in the Taylor's Lane wing, the documentary date of 1492 seems appropriate for the construction; here there is no sign of buildings on two levels as found in the older King Street properties.

12 Mill Street

Occupying a position on the corner of Mill Street and Bell Lane this little building gives the impression of having once been part of a larger complex, and it could mark the end of 15th-century timber-framing or be a transitional form of the early 16th century before the 'great rebuilding', described in the next chapter, began. It is a two-storied unit and has close-studding without a mid-rail on both elevations and on both stories. The corner post is not quite in alignment with the roof truss in the gable end, but this may be a result of ancient structural distortion. Although there is no jetty the juxtaposition of the penultimate post and the end corner post is reminiscent of the 'lazy jetty' technique, noted in other buildings. All the visible joints are secured by single pegs, which may be another indication of its comparatively early date.

Summary of the Medieval Buildings

The period up to c.1500 covers the first wave of prosperity in Ludlow's economic history which, if not entirely due to the Palmers' Guild, was developed and sustained by its activities. The number and nature of surviving medieval buildings reflect the picture of a thriving community; compact, self-contained but by no means insular. As in Shrewsbury the earliest permanent buildings were either wholly or partially of stone, but once the need for defence had diminished, timber-framing became the natural medium for all but the gentry class. However, it is interesting to note that John Hosier, a rich merchant and benefactor to the Palmers' Guild, chose to build his almshouses in stone. Founded in 1462, the year before his death, they were rebuilt in brick in 1758 but sections of stone walling remain at the back and particularly on the northern side. Some but not all is re-used material, and it is worth remembering that Thomas Farnolls Pritchard, the architect chosen for the 18th-century design, was adept at grafting new work onto old, as his Guildhall in Mill Street testifies. Hosier's scheme was far more ambitious than the equivalent Drapers' Company almshouses of a few years earlier in Shrewsbury.[38]

Hosier's Almshouses of 1462, rebuilt in 1758

The town was well equipped to cater for travellers, as the two long inn ranges testify, and doubtless there were others, in addition to guest chambers provided in the castle for the nobility. At this time the framed buildings were mostly two stories high and there seems to have been space to set them either parallel to the street or gable-end on, depending on how many burgage plots were leased. Some suggest that a courtyard plan was adopted and others were clearly straightforward encroachments to take advantage of the best trading positions.

In 1459 the Lancastrian forces laid waste to the town after the 'battle' of Ludford Bridge, but it is a mistake to think that everything was flattened then or even that the majority of the framed buildings post-date the attack; the list shows clearly that this was not so.

Before the Corporation took over the Guildhall in 1552 the only public building, apart from the castle, where litigation could take place, was the Tolsey; and this seems to be confirmed by the features found in the upper room which, for a short time at least, would have had a sweeping view up to the castle.

As in any successful town, box-framing was preferred to cruck construction as a rule, and it is possible to see the tie-and-collar-beam with raking queen-posts assembly as a standard form of construction. Jetties were executed with confidence and there are examples of buildings jettied on one, two, three or all four sides, the earlier ones incorporating the use of bull-nosed joists.

Detail of Hosier's Almshouses

Although The Great House and The Unicorn are the only early examples to incorporate a moulded bressumer, these became popular in the 17th century. Cusping was used lavishly on the more prestigious buildings and, presumably, on others where taste and pocket decreed; elsewhere simple chamfers sufficed.

Only two examples of crown-post roofing have been discovered in Ludlow and neither can be said to be typical of the Shropshire genre. The side-purlin roof, with its variations, was the type most favoured, and the way in which it is brought to perfection in the Guildhall reflects the trend. Perhaps the crown-post roofs represent a phase of experimentation to improve on the collar-rafter roof of which The Rectory is a striking, if the only surviving, example. Generally speaking the carpentry was strong, purposeful but not ostentatious. Except for the bosses in the Guildhall roof there was none of the imagery which was to become a hallmark of Ludlow's carpentry later on.

One of the unanswered questions is whether or not the 'Wealden' form reached Ludlow. This is where a recessed hall between two jettied cross-wings is linked by a 'flying wall-plate' and the three units are covered by a roof in a single plane. The style can be seen in Weobley in the neighbouring county of Herefordshire and it is possible that it was adopted in Ludlow. On the other hand it should not be confused with the 'lazy jetty' technique which seems to have been a Ludlovian peculiarity. The best example of the latter occurs at Penkridge Hall near Leebotwood, where two schools of carpentry, Shrewsbury's and Ludlow's, seem to meet in a building of the late 16th century.

The transition from the open hall to the two-storied hall is well illustrated by The Great House and by 62 Corve Street. Both may represent re-building after the Lancastrian raid, but this is not necessarily so. Elsewhere in the town are examples of early timber-framing such as those mentioned above which form a loosely-knit group, the large flat joists at 1 Old Street, upper crucks in a back building at 5 Broad Street and two further upper cruck trusses at 139a Corve Street. Exploration has also yielded glimpses of fragmentary roof trusses, jetties, posts and other early features in numerous buildings. These have not been included in the list as it is either too difficult to put them into a comprehensive account or, as in the case of the upper crucks, their dating is too problematical. Doubtless much remains to be discovered. There are numerous examples of the re-use of timbers but not in the early buildings, here first-hand oak was the medium. Nothing obvious in the way of external painting or wash has been noted, unlike Shrewsbury where red ochre was freely used.

Inns are notoriously difficult to analyse. In one respect they are buildings which are likely to retain early features but they are also subject to frequent changes, and the Rose and Crown is a good example of how alternate rebuilding can result in an accumulation of parts which have no coherence, structurally speaking, but present an overall exercise in planning which cries out for investigation.

The work of the Ludlow Historical Research Group aims to bring together as many aspects as possible, and the fusion of documentary research and architectural investigation must be the best way to approach local history. The way in which facts are presented and analysed, particularly in Research Paper 3, 'Broad Street', is exemplary and has provided a basis for the greater understanding not only of Ludlow's vernacular architecture but that of the county as a whole. While it remains true that one should always be cautious about ascribing a standing building, or parts thereof, to a documentary date, the consistency of these factors when applied to buildings associated with the Palmers' Guild cannot be co-incidental. There comes a point when the relationship must be accepted.

7   Ludlow Houses: The Post-Medieval Period

16th-Century Houses

In Ludlow, as in Shrewsbury and Bridgnorth, the first half of the 16th century appears to be almost devoid of datable houses. Shropshire's three foremost towns featured in an Act of Parliament of 1535 aimed at dealing with decaying houses and the hazards they caused. The many 'pittes, cellers and vaultes lienge open and uncovered, very perillous for people to go by in the night, without jeoperdie of life' are described where 'in times past have been beautiful dwelling houses, there well inhabited'.[1] Although, following the generally prosperous 14th and 15th centuries, Ludlow's economy was at a low level, the town had resources which helped it to withstand such reversals. Its political connections and the close involvement it had with royalty had led, among other things, to the choice of Ludlow Castle as the headquarters of the Council in the Marches of Wales when it became obvious that Wales and the Welsh Marches could not be controlled from Westminster. It had its origins in 'The Prince's Council' set up in 1471 to administer the estates of the Prince of Wales, the infant son of Edward IV, but neither the prince nor his younger brother survived incarceration in the Tower of London, and the Council lapsed. It was revived by Henry VII and put on a formal basis in 1501 when Prince Arthur, newly married to Catherine of Aragon, was sent to Ludlow as the nominal ruler of Wales. Five months later the prince was dead, but the Council continued and by 1525 its authority was considerably strengthened. It governed the whole of Wales and five border counties. It was a peripatetic body, but Ludlow was the power base and continued as such until the disruption of the Civil War. The Council was not formally abolished until 1689.[2]

Such then is the background against which Ludlow's architecture of the second half of the 16th and the early years of the 17th century should be seen. The legacy of the first wave of prosperity, described in the preceding chapter, stood the merchant class in good stead; there was a stock of good quality timber-framed houses and shops in a well laid-out town, in some ways too successful for its own good, judging by the number of encroachments that had taken place. Onto this basis was then grafted the houses of officials of the court—lawyers, executives and clerks. Not for nothing has Ludlow been described as a 'bureaucratic anthill' at this time.[3]

One of the earliest examples of the connection between the Council and housing for one of its officials is the Feathers Hotel—not in its present form, it must be stressed, that is the result of extensive re-modelling in 1619 and will be discussed later, but documentary evidence shows that Thomas Hackluyt became Clerk to the Council in 1528 and that he had a house on the site of the Feathers. Encapsulated within the present structure is a transverse truss belonging to an earlier frame which relates to a two-storied jettied house. This may have been the Hackluyt house, and over the doorway of the present Writing Room is a plaster shield combining the arms of the Hackluyt and Fox families who were connected by marriage.[4]

Outline drawing of the façade showing elements which may date from before 1619, though most of the woodwork has subsequently been replaced

View of a House in Ludlow' by John Clayton (d.1861), published in Timber Framed Edifices of the West Midlands *(1846)*

Outline showing some of the elements which were completely replaced in 1969-70, the detail being closely copied

The overmantel in the King James I Lounge

The Feathers, Ludlow

The Hackluyt / Fox shield

The façade today

The Reader's House
Left: porch dated 1616; above: the rear elevation

Another building which can be ascribed to the early part of the first of Ludlow's 'great rebuilds' is The Reader's House[5] which is situated on the eastern side of the churchyard and belonged to the Palmers' Guild although it seems to have had close connections with the Council. Surviving building accounts of 1550 point to a remodelling of an existing stone-built house at that date. The mid-16th-century framework can only be seen from the rear where it is obviously grafted onto earlier stone walls. The new work was in square-framing, with diagonal braces marking the bay divisions; and of two stories, the upper storey jettied over the lower, each storey being three panels high. It was probably jettied on three sides, but the continuation to the north has been lost in later development. The moulding on the bressumer is distinctive, consisting of a triple-ovolo-and-quirk form. It is a great pity that the plan is not complete because it seems to suggest an early appearance of the modern concept of an entrance hall containing the staircase, as opposed to the older traditional one of a screens passage. If so, this is an important milestone in plan development.

The Sidney apartments (1581) at the castle

Fragments of plaster decoration and fireplaces of this period remain and some of the panelling seems to belong to this phase. It must have been at this time also that the entrance was changed from the Bull Ring side to the churchyard side. Later alterations are described below.

Probably the best known President of the Council was Sir Henry Sidney (1560-86) and his additions to the castle mark both an important phase in Ludlow's history and the launch of another great wave of building activity. The Sidney apartments are located to the east of the keep. They consist of a block which is stone-built, fully three-storied, with two end gablets on either side and a rear hexagonal stair turret. The block was added in 1581 and incorporates an older arched entrance over which the arms of the Sidney family, surmounted by the royal arms, are framed in an aedicule incorporating classical pilasters and a curiously provincial pediment. The Latin inscription has been interpreted as Sidney's contrived and diplomatic

Castle Lodge

way of expressing his disappointment at not being given higher office, literally 'to ungrateful men these stones do speak'.[6] For 'ungrateful men' read 'an ungrateful Queen'. Though now ruinous the building compares well with the drawings done in 1765 when it was only just beginning to deteriorate.[7] There are 11 main mullioned and transomed windows and these exhibit the sunk chamfer moulding rather than the ovolo moulding which was becoming fashionable at that time.

Many additions and improvements to the castle took place during Sir Henry's presidency, as the building accounts show.[8] Some remain, for example the double-flued chimney which was inserted into one of the windows of the great hall in 1580, some of the alterations to St. Peter's chapel when it became a courthouse, the expanded stone parts of Castle Lodge near the entrance, by Thomas Sackford, Sir Henry's steward and accountant, and the stable block to the west of the entrance from the outer bailey; others have vanished, although their form may be known from illustrations. Sometimes details will evoke more of the spirit of Elizabethan times than whole buildings. One example is a fireplace in Castle Lodge which has a charac-

teristic flattened arch, moulding which is expressed in stone in the jambs and continues across the wooden lintel—possibly the earliest example of this popular Shropshire fireplace design—and the skilfully contrived recessed cross in the brickwork which would normally have been hidden by an iron fireback. Strangely, only one complete example of the popular Elizabethan star-shaped brick chimneystack remains in Ludlow and this is at the castle where a set of three was added to

Castle Lodge fireplace.
Note the recessed cross in the brickwork (outlined in black)

the Pendover Tower. Another remains in fragmentary form at 72 Corve Street—'The Tan House'—where it relates to a building dated 1661. This building is significant in the development of Ludlow's domestic architecture and will be described later. The 16th- and 17th-century memorials in St. Laurence's church are outside the scope of this study but they also reflect the importance of the town in the Elizabethan age. One is to Sir Henry's own daughter, Ambrosia, and the others are mostly connected with officers of the Council in the Marches. The Townsend tomb incorporates one of the few examples of true classical detail to be found in Ludlow.

By this time the street pattern with its encroachments was set, although constructional details of the properties on the north side of the Bull Ring and The Shelde suggest that some open market stalls were still to be metamorphosed into permanent structures. The influx of families whose livelihood depended on the Council was absorbed by the existing housing stock, although, naturally, there was much re-furbishing, alteration and rebuilding. One example of how officials' families were integrated into the town is Kingston's Place in King Street, a medieval complex, described in the previous chapter, which was rebuilt in 1576 by Thomas Hankey, Steward of the Council.[9] The plaque bearing the Sidney coat of arms which previously adorned the outside wall of the upper storey is preserved in the museum. The property has been almost completely rebuilt in modern times. Thomas Churchyard, (*c.*1520-1604), the Shrewsbury poet, describes 'a fayre house by the gate of the making of Justice Walter' and 'a fayre house of Maister Sackford which he did build' and 'a fayre house that Maister Secretarie Fox did bestowe great charges on' and Mr. Townsend too 'hath a fayre house at St. Austins once a friarie'. Churchyard was so impressed with all this that his introductory verse to 'Lodloe Towne, Church and Castle' closes with the couplet 'On every side thereof fayre houses are, That makes a shew, to please both mynd and eye'.[10]

One person determined to 'make a shew' was 'Secretarie Fox'. This was Charles Fox, a lawyer and local landowner with estates at Caynham and Bromfield.[11] Aptly described as a 'gifted pluralist'[12] he was ambitious and quite ruthless, managing to secure for himself, between 1558 and 1565, key posts with the Council, combining the offices of Secretary and Clerk and acquiring a partnership in the clerkship of the Signet, a lucrative office involving the application of the official seal to all orders, writs and processes of the Council. Payment had to be made each time it was used. In addition to his country estates and investments he had a town house in Ludlow which has been identified as that enclosing the courtyard now known as Quality Square. Here, not only did he use bricks as the main constructional medium but he incorporated a long gallery at first-floor level on the western side which overlooked the courtyard. At least, this seems to be the logical explanation for the fact that the ceiling beams are each purposefully chamfered and stopped but have no provision for partitions between the bays, that the windows are placed on the courtyard side only and that a fireplace was placed in what was the centre of the wall opposite the

Entrance to Quality Square,
the site of Charles Fox's house

windows. There is a tenuous link between Fox's long gallery in Ludlow and that of the very similar one at St. Fagan's Castle, now the core of the National Museum of Wales. The link is the Herbert family of Oakley Park, Bromfield, near Ludlow. The daughter of Dr. John Gibbon, who had built St. Fagan's between 1560 and 1580 married into the Herbert family from whom the Earl of Plymouth, the present owner of Oakley Park and donor of St. Fagan's, is descended. Fox's grand-daughter also married into the Herbert family, continuing the association which probably began when, following the Dissolution, Fox acquired the buildings, lands and hunting park belonging to Bromfield Priory and grafted his country house onto the church, incorporating the chancel as part of the plan. Fragments of this house remain and it is interesting to note that Fox favoured the use of sunk-chamfer window mouldings at Bromfield and that these also occur at St. Fagan's. It is a great pity that Fox's fenestration does not survive in his town house for it may have provided another architectural link, and it is sobering to reflect that Fox, the Shropshire whizz-kid of his day, was able to influence the form of St. Fagan's Castle, now an important National Monument. The essay in brick-work may be seen in the south-west corner corner of Quality Square and must represent the earliest to survive in the town; the bricks are narrow and set in English bond in thick mortar.[13]

Late 16th-century brickwork on Charles Fox's house, Quality Square

The sites of the other 'fayre houses' noted by Churchyard are also known. Thomas Sackford's has been mentioned. Mr. Justice Walter's occupied five burgage plots on the corner of Broad Street and Silk Mill Lane, just within the Broad Gate, but in the 18th century this was rebuilt as three houses, nos.35, 36 and 37 Broad Street, the Dunne family of Gatley Park being responsible for nos.35 and 36 in 1756.[14] Robert Townsend was granted the site of the Austin Friars in Lower Galdeford in 1547, but nothing now remains of his house.[15] There were others, of course, in this period of re-development, although perhaps not as many as might be expected; and unfortunately insufficient evidence remains which would enable conclusions as to plan and size to be drawn.

Part of 'Secretarie Fox's' Long Gallery

In many cases it is even impossible to know what materials were used, be they stone, brick or timber. In the analysis of the Broad Street houses, only four have positive documentary dates and these include the remodelling of St. John's house following the Dissolution and Mr. Justice

Properties on the south side of the Bull Ring.
The Bull Ring Tavern's east wing is the two left-hand bays, the west wing the two middle bays, and no.45 the two right-hand bays

Walter's 'Fayre House' already mentioned.[16]

Perhaps the properties on the southern side of the Bull Ring give at least some indication of the Elizabethan townscape as manifested in Ludlow, but although these form a homogenous group of timber-framed houses they have a wide date range and owe their aesthetic appeal to the 17th century's predilection for twin-gabled frontages. The western unit of the Bull Ring Tavern has close-studding with a mid-rail on both the second and third stories, but, as shown in the previous chapter, the evidence suggests that this relates to a late 16th-century remodelling of an earlier house. The eastern unit of the Bull Ring Tavern, again three-storied, twin-gabled and jettied appears to represent a complete re-building of the early 17th century and will be put into its context later. The other prominent building in the group is 45 The Bull Ring, once the Bear Inn, which adjoins the western unit of the Bull Ring Tavern. Here again appearances are deceptive. The twin-gabled upper storey is an addition of the 17th century to what was basically a three-storied, two-bayed jettied house of the first half of the 16th century, which had a roof line parallel to the street and with close-studding but without the mid-rail to the third storey. Its form may be determined by examining the method of adding the fourth storey, and this will be discussed later.

From the little evidence which survives it is possible to suggest that Elizabethan town houses in Ludlow, at least those alongside a street, were mostly timber-framed, usually jettied, of two or three stories, with roofs set parallel to the street and consisting of two or three bays, depending on the number of burgess plots they occupied. Close-studding with a mid-rail was the preferred design for the upper stories, and most of them had little ornamentation. An illustration of the White Horse Inn,

Arms of Elizabeth I at Lane's Hospital

The White Horse Inn from an old postcard

Moulded ceiling beams at 5 Old Street

demolished in 1840, which stood at the top of Mill Street on the eastern side, shows a relatively unaltered example of this genre.[17] But the pattern of framing to the lower stories of all the houses is largely unknown. What little evidence survives suggests that it was similar to the upper storey. External decoration seems to have been strictly a matter of personal preference and, presumably, the ability to pay. Much would depend on whether the building was intended for owner-occupation or was built as speculation.

Lane's House in Old Street, the older parts of which were noted in the previous chapter, has a plaster frieze and the arms of Elizabeth I in the main ground-floor room of the twin-gabled block which fronts onto Old Street, but, apart from fragmentary sections of internal trusses, the building owes most of its present appearance to 17th-century re-modelling. 5 Old Street also retains an ornamental ceiling in the main ground-floor room; here the beams are richly moulded, the spine-beams with a combination of roll-and-hollow and ogee-and-quarter-circle and the herring-bone joists with a double ogee.[18] In what is now nos.40 and 43 Lower Broad Street richly moulded floor joists suggest that at least part of a late 16th-century house survived the otherwise extensive destruction in the suburb during the Civil War.

Here and there it is possible to identify timber-framed houses, thinly disguised under roughcast, plaster, or other material which were probably built in the second half of the 16th century or earlier. 12 and 13 Brand Lane are two clear examples. Both are now three-storied

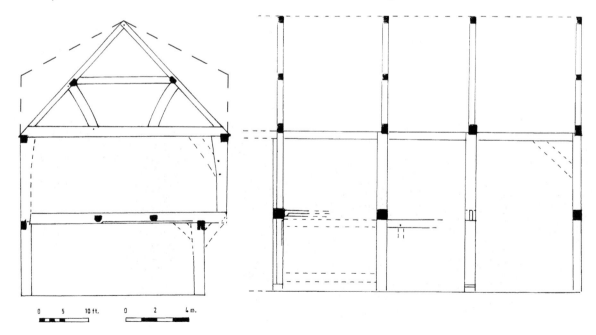

13 Brand Lane. Sections A-A (left) and X-X , as located on the ground floor plan opposite above

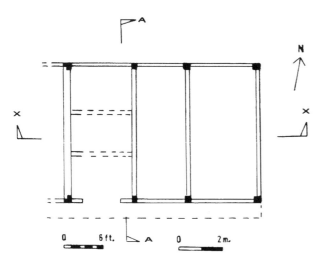

and jettied although now completely rendered over. In Raven Lane nos.16-19A is a block which is covered with weatherboarding, but the form of a three-bayed, two-storied late 16th-century house is discernible. This had a continuous jetty across the three bays. A later passageway has been driven through the property to give access to back buildings, and this has left exposed a spine-beam decorated with double-ogee moulding. A third storey was added in the 17th century. An old photograph of 16 High Street shows the timber frame of a three-storied jettied house briefly exposed before being replaced by a Victorian frontage of four stories. The third storey of the framed house had close-studding divided by a mid-rail, a form as popular in Ludlow as it was in Shrewsbury.[19]

On a few houses of this period the framing remains exposed or has had later cladding removed. 16 Tower Street presents a two-bayed, two-storied frontage, but it is clear that this was once a longer building, probably extending eastwards by a further bay. Again the upper storey displays close-studding with a mid-rail, but the form is austere with no carved brackets or decoration of any kind on the exterior although substantial ceiling beams with chamfers and stops are visible within the present shop at ground level. Tamberlaine House, adjacent to the Buttercross, in its present form is a single-bayed, three-storied structure with attics, but the 'gable-end on' appearance is deceptive; the roof-line actually runs parallel to the street. Like 16 Tower

Tamberlaine House. Left: front elevation; right: detail of carved bracket and 'tied bundle' motif

181

Street, Tamberlaine House displays close-studding with a mid-rail on the second storey. The third storey is similar but has been largely rebuilt. However, unlike 16 Tower Street and most of the others noted above, Tamberlaine House is greatly enriched with carving, and because the rear of the property was open to view from Church Street, that too is jettied and decorated, though not as lavishly as the front. It is worthwhile studying the carving as similar work is found on two other buildings in Ludlow. On the rear elevation the fascia board which masks the ends of the joists is

Matching carpenters' assembly marks at the rear of Tamberlaine House

an original feature. The carving incorporates swirling stylised foliage and what are sometimes described as 'tied bundles'—like shocks of corn bound in the middle. The brackets which support the jetty are carved, the eastern one incorporating a side half-face similar to that found at 2 Dinham where 'tied bundles' and stylised foliage also occur. The work is so similar that the same wood carver may be suspected. Clear scribed carpenters' marks are another feature of the rear elevation.[20] On the front elevation the fascia board is either an addition or, more probably, a replacement. One of the brackets incorporates a dolphin motif with an arrow-shaped tongue, and a similar one occurs on 45 The Bull Ring. The name of the house is derived from Tamberlaine Davies, a mercer, (1620-85) whose baptism apparently commemorated 'Tamberlaine', a work by Christopher Marlowe (1564-93) which established his reputation as a dramatist. Success appears to have been bestowed with the name because when Tamberlaine Davies died his inventory registered movable goods worth £854 14s. 4d.[21]

At the northern or lower end of Corve Street the centre of the leather trade—particularly tanning and glove-making—was located. This was an industry which arose after the Civil War and after the abolition of the Council in the Marches when Ludlow needed a new life-line to revive its fortunes. However, the timber-framed houses on the western side have features which appear to span a date range from the 15th to the 17th centuries. The earlier ones, such as the 'Unicorn' (now nos.64, 65 and part of 66) and no.62, each described in the previous chapter, consisted of four and three bays respectively, set parallel to the street; but where the plan form can still be deduced, the 16th- and

46-58 Lower Corve Street—part of the glovemaking area

Above: A glover's house at 38 Lower Corve Street.
Note the louvred top storey for skin drying
Right: The Glover's House, 101 Corve Street, reputedly
where the firm of Dents' Gloves originated

17th-century houses were smaller, consisting of one large bay and one smaller bay in line. No.48 may be considered typical; here the house is two-storied and jettied, the bays measuring 11ft. (3.35m.) and 8ft. 4ins. (2.54m.) in width. The upper storey displays close-studding with a mid-rail and originally the three main joists were supported by brackets. At no.50 the 'gable-end on' appearance is deceptive; it is the result of a re-modelling in the 17th century of an earlier parallel roof form. The division of the earlier form into one large bay 14ft. (4.27m.) wide and one smaller bay 10ft. 6ins. (3.20m.) is marked by a large projecting joist which, in turn, relates to a 15th-century joisting system. The tie-beam rests on a horizontal timber, once the wall-plate of the earlier building. Included in the 17th-century remodelling is typical lozenge-within-lozenge work to the second storey and cusped and spiked lozenges to the attic gable, and there are mortices relating to an oriel window in the larger of the two bays. As remodelled, no.50 is likely to have been the house of a prosperous glover or tanner.[22]

The famous gloving firm of Dent's reputedly had its origins at 101 Corve Street, a building that documents describe as 'newly erected' in 1592.[23] It is basically a two-bayed, two-storied timber-

Charles Fox's almshouses (1593)

framed house, although later re-modelling has given it a brick façade. However, the 1592 reference may relate to a rear brick-built wing in English bonding which has numerous windows, two of which still display ovolo moulding and wide glazing bars. If so, this little building ranks with Charles Fox's town house in Quality Square as an example of the earliest brickwork found in Ludlow. Fox's own foundation of almshouses, dated 1593, remains in Corve Street and has been very little altered.

Not much is known about other houses of the late 16th century and of course the homes of the lower classes have left no trace.

An oligarchy such as the Council in the Marches was bound to be open to abuse and corruption, in the latter years its credibility was increasingly questioned and its powers restricted. It was in decline by the early years of the 17th century, considerably weakened by the Long Parliament and officially abolished in 1689.[24]

17th-Century Houses

Although Ludlow's wealth of 17th-century timber-framed houses gives an overall impression of a massive rebuilding programme in the second half of the century, following the Civil War (1642-46), that may not be entirely true. Like many old market towns Ludlow was garrisoned for the King, but surrendered to the Parliamentarians in 1646. Certainly the Civil War had a marked effect on some parts of the town; the suburbs particularly suffered from the activities of both attackers and defenders, the southern suburbs were burned by a Parliamentary army and much of the northern suburb of Corve Street below Corve Gate was destroyed by the Royalist defenders seeking to clear their lines of fire, although clearly some of the houses survived. However, if the Civil War is regarded as an interruption and not a watershed it is possible to suggest a chronology of steady building activity throughout the century. Future research may prove some of the suggested dates wrong, but it is hoped that the following may provide a basic framework for comparative studies.

If the building account of 1703 for 17 Broad Street has been interpreted correctly, the timber-framed rear wing must be 'the new building' which was to be left when the street-facing block, described as 'very ruinous' in 1570, was rebuilt. Everything is relative, and compared with the main block doubtless it would seem 'new' although by 1703 it would have been over one hundred years old. It has been reasoned that it was built c.1600 for Richard Bailey, a wealthy member of the Corporation, and consisted of an upper chamber in plain square-framing above what is possibly an older ground-floor storey, now bricked. The chamber was heated and had a pleasant view overlooking the garden.[25] A similar wing, also in square-framing, has been noted at 32 Broad Street,[26] and in a slightly different concept is St. John's Cottage in St. John's Road. This single-cell cottage retains its square-framing of two panels high and has an end out-built stack. It was entered from the north-east corner of the

*'The New Building' (c.1590)
at the rear of 17 Broad Street*

side wall, away from the stack. Original rafters with cusped ends are visible under the eaves and the timbers display chiselled carpenters' marks. It stands outside the town wall, but is a remarkable survival in a busy town.

Perhaps the earliest example of how plain square-framing could be varied to give a more striking appearance is the upper storey of Castle Lodge, mentioned above. Here, in what is assumed to be an addition of *c.*1604 by Robert Berry, who held an impor-

St. John's Cottage

tant post in the Council in the Marches and was Member of Parliament for Ludlow, the jettied upper storey has the eastern half in triple lozenge-within-lozenge work and the western half in the more sober close-studding with mid-rail.[27] The bressumers to each half are also different. Both begin with an ogee, but the western unit then has a double billet design while the eastern unit finishes with three square steps. It is unlikely that two different building phases are represented, probably a clash of taste is perpetuated. Perhaps it is an early expression of the 'male' and 'female' divisions of a house so evident in the internal decoration of the great 18th-century mansion at Attingham.

At about the same time the street-facing unit at 53 Broad Street must have been added to the medieval complex at the rear, described in the previous chapter. The new block has a central entrance into a passage with a parlour and shop on either side at the front and a buttery and a kitchen behind. It is three-storied, continuously jettied at each level, but the lower bressumer with its double-ovolo-and-quirk moulding protrudes further than the upper one which has a single ovolo with brattishing. The pattern of the framing probably set the fashion for most of 17th-century Ludlow: plain close-studding to the ground floor, close-studding with a mid-rail for the second story and lozenge-within-lozenge work for the third storey. Carved brackets with scrolls are a prominent feature and the doorcase combines ovolo moulding with an outer sunken channel. The original windows on the ground floor were wider than the present ones and projected to the jetty line; the evidence of alternate diamond and rectangular impressions left when the mullions were removed remain as witness marks. The same form applied to the second storey windows, although these were not so large. In the front parlour—the northern room—the fireplace lintel has the Arms of James I painted on it. This has been interpreted as a sycophantic gesture by Robert Saunders, an ambitious ironmonger and three times Bailiff who was responsible for building the new block and who represented a new class of merchant, one rising from comparatively humble origins. His panelled parlour has been described as 'the most complete Jacobean room' in Broad Street.[28]

Lozenge work was strictly for street situations, where it would create the greatest impression. For an enclosed courtyard, as at the Bull Hotel, plain not-so-close-studding with a mid-rail sufficed on both stories for the addition over the entry, although billet moulding and ornamental brackets provided some decoration. The structure, though clearly not unsafe, appears to have no visible means of support, no joists nor bressumer.

Ventilated panel and cornice   Valentine Dawes's panel

'1610 Valentine Dawes'
10 Church Street

By 1610 the first houses with inscribed 17th-century dates were appearing. 10 Church Street has '1610 Valentine Dawes' carved on a bressumer at the rear. This seems to indicate a complete re-build on the site, pre-dating the remodelling of the Feathers, and perhaps setting a standard that discouraged emulation for this is a double-pile plan with two full stories plus attics in each unit. The block is set with the twin gable-ends facing the street and there is a continuous jetty across each unit. Doubtless the same applied to the rear, but here later encroachments have obscured the form, and over the whole building most of the timbering is concealed beneath plaster. However, the inscribed bressumer have double-ovolo-and-quirk moulding and pendants which must relate to extended storey posts. Dawes and Saunders clearly rivalled each other as trend-setters. Internally the Dawes house is no less impressive in its detail. The main room upstairs, probably known as the 'great chamber', is completely panelled in contemporary fashion and one section again incorporates Dawes's initials with that of his wife and what is possibly a merchant's mark. The same room has a dentilated cornice with a band of guilloche moulding below, a panelled ceiling, a ventilated panel which possibly has a spiral staircase concealed behind it, and carving depicting teasels. Dawes was a rich mercer, patronised by Sir Charles Fox of Oakly Park.

In Ludford, a separate parish to the south of Ludlow just across Ludford bridge, is the Old Bell House, so called because it was once a public house of that name. It has a date on the porch which is invariably quoted as 1614, but which is more likely to be 1674. The porch is an addition to the house and does not indicate the original entrance. However, the house probably dates from the first quarter of the 17th century and as such is contemporary with the others described above. But Ludford is a country setting and the house reflects the continuation of the 'hall-and-crosswing' plan of medieval times, though the hall, of course, is no longer open. There is a shallow jetty both on the front and on the eastern side which faces the old road leading up from the ford and the mill and which then continued eastwards to Leominster and Hereford. The bressumer has ovolo-quirk-and-ogee moulding. In typical fashion the showy

timbering appears on the elevations most noticeable; both the front and the eastern side have close-studding with a mid-rail to the ground floor and lozenge-within-lozenge work to the second storey, while the back and the western side have plain square-framing. Elaborate chimneystacks are a prominent feature. That serving the front parlour in the crosswing is out-built in stone and has nine columns of nibbed brickwork for the shafts; the two service chimneys in the range running back from the parlour have recessed brick panels, and the stack serving the hall and the parlour behind it has rectangular brick shafts with star-shaped caps. The original entrance was at the lower end of the hall. Its position is marked externally by a tension brace and the blocked opening to the west of it. Internally a short spere or screen remains *in situ.* Fragments of wall-paintings remain in the hall, but on the fireplace of the upper chamber in the crosswing the paintings are clearer, with bands of swirling concentric circles which may represent huge roses, and some guilloche work. The style is very similar to that found at Churchyard Farm, Neenton, about 12 miles to the north-east of Ludlow.[29]

The date 1616 is inscribed on the tie-beam of the timber-framed porch at the Reader's House, mentioned above. Three-storied porches are not common and on

This page: The Old Bell, Ludford (1674). Top: From the south-west; centre: From the south-east; bottom: The Great Chamber, remodelled by Basil Stallybrass in 1909

187

this example each storey is jettied. Close-studding occurs on the second storey and herring-bone work on the third. There is a wealth of carving on the door surround, bargeboards, tie-beam and brackets, and among the motifs Catherine Wheels are prominent. Ovolo-moulded windows with mullions and transoms are another distinctive feature. At the rear of the house the added third storey and large dormer-gable with herring-bone work probably also date from 1616 and it seems likely that at this time the entrance position was changed so that the house was entered from the churchyard. Thomas Kay, the man responsible for these changes, was chaplain to the Council in the Marches and probably wanted easy access to the church. 'Reader' was an 18th-century office of the church, performed by one of the curates.[30]

An ambitious property on the corner of Broad Street and Market Street also relates to c.1616. The Broad Street frontage now has a plain 'Georgianised' façade, three stories high and five bays wide with an overhanging eaves cornice which returns for a short distance into Market Street where the timber-framing has recently been restored. Here the second and third stories each display square-framing and there is an attic level, again square-framed, although distortion has largely obscured the design. The whole block was probably jettied at each level, there are carved brackets with scrolls and, unusually, pentice boards emphasising the storey levels. A lease of 1619 describes the property as 'recently built' for a corviser (shoemaker) named Edward Colbatch. Like some of the Shrewsbury corner properties it was probably a speculative venture.[31]

Dodmore Manor (demolished), from Parkinson and Olde, 1904

Dodmore Manor on the northern outskirts of the town, now demolished, was equally ambitious, had a similar double-pile form to Valentine Dawes's house described above, and was built about nine years afterwards. Fully three-storied and jettied at each level Dodmore incorporated lozenge-within-lozenge work to the second storey and square-framing to the third. A noticeable feature was a raised diamond within a larger diamond inset on three of the panels at the front. This device is also encountered on Sherer's Mansion, Wyle Cop, Shrewsbury (demolished) and on the Feathers Hotel where it is expressed as raised heads. All three houses were occupied by officers of the Council in the Marches; Dodmore became the home of Richard Fisher, an apothecary and brother-in-law to Rees Jones, an attorney at the Council, who remodelled the Feathers in 1619.[32]

The Feathers Hotel, in its present form, has rightly been described as a prodigy building. The total effect is of a sum greater than its parts. Its fame is world-wide and it must be one of the most photographed buildings in England. It comes as a surprise, therefore, to learn that it has only been an inn since 1670 and that very little original timbering remains on the front—successive restoration programmes have replaced most of it, although there is no reason to

A panel of the ceiling in the Great Chamber at the Feathers

doubt that the older work has always been faithfully copied. The asymmetrical appearance is partly the result of grafting Rees Jones's façade onto an earlier frame and partly because the northernmost gable originally incorporated the porch entrance at ground level and was treated rather differently from the other two gables. The façade shows almost every conceivable decorative motif: ovolo-moulded windows, lozenge-within-lozenge, plain lozenge work, cusped and spiked lozenges, classical blank arches, cablemoulding, carving of all kinds, brackets, pendants, finials, egg-and-dart moulding, stiff leaves, raised heads, grotesques, dolphins etc. Among all this the three ostrich feathers of the Prince of Wales, after whom the building is named, are not easily distinguished. They occur on the collar-beams of the gables, but the unusual thickness of the spikes on the cusped lozenges was to enable the 'feathers' motif to appear as fletching on each arrow or spike, and these appear in abundance on the third storey. Almost all the decorative features can be found on other Ludlow buildings of this time, but only at the Feathers do they come together as though in a great virtuoso concerto, played 'allegro vivace', to continue the musical allegory. Parts of the interior are equally lavish. The great chamber, now known as the James I lounge, has an elaborate plastered ceiling, is fully panelled and has a richly carved overmantel incorporating the arms of James I. All these and a full architectural and tenurial account are covered in depth in the published history of the Feathers.[33]

The Feathers was a major remodelling exercise. Elsewhere updating was on a more modest scale. At 45 The Bull Ring, mentioned above, a jettied fourth storey with twin gables was added to an earlier building. The addition incorporated not-so-close-studding with a mid-rail, and cusped lozenges and V-struts in the gables. On the western side of the building the original jowelled post/tie-beam/wall-plate assembly may be seen and it is clear that the earlier building had a parallel roof-line. By the 1630s the building had become the Bear Inn, so perhaps the addition was made sometime in the 1620s. One of the carved brackets on the earlier part has a dolphin and tongue motif, similar to that on Tamberlaine House. Internally the stairs to the top story have shaped and pierced flat balusters.[34]

Flat balusters of the 17th-century staircase at 45 The Bull Ring

Similarly, and about the same time, twin dormer-gables were added to the western unit of the adjoining property, The Bull Ring Tavern, the earlier part of which is described above. On these the carved brackets are integral with the angle posts; the barge-boards, pendants and window frames are original, the latter having ovolo moulding. Remains of mullions suggest that the first glazed panels were not fixed, but tied to the mullions with lead ties, and it is possible that the present lead cames and ties represent the original portable panels, later adapted to become fixtures. The eastern unit, by contrast, appears to represent a complete re-building of c.1620. This is fully three-storied with continuous jetties at each level, and twin gables which do not incorporate dormers. The second storey displays close-studding with a mid-rail, the third storey has plain lozenge work, and each gable has a cusped and spiked lozenge and a triangle, similarly treated, above the collar-beam. Again the brackets are integral with the angle posts. On the second storey the studs on either side of the central stud are chamfered. This raises the question of whether there was a form of continuous lighting here. On the other hand it may simply be a subtle form of decoration. The conventional jetty technique employed on this unit is in marked contrast to that of the fourth storey of 45 The Bull Ring, mentioned above, which demonstrates that the latter was an addition.

The Shelde (Brigg's Shoes),
showing consolidation of open market stalls

It was probably while this extensive rebuilding and improvement programme was under way on the southern side of the Bull Ring that a decision was made to convert the open market stalls of 'The Shelde' on the northern side into permanent structures on their island site, thus consolidating the encroachment and creating future traffic hazards. Now all part of the Bull Ring, the shoe shop, which does not have a postal number, has external timbers on the western unit which appear to be mostly of the 19th century, but some internal details, in particular the transverse tie-beam, suggest that the western unit is slightly earlier than the eastern unit which has more original work visible. Both units are only two-storied but have attics in the gables. Again, on the eastern unit, not-so-close-studding with a mid-rail is a feature of the second storey and cusped and beaded lozenge work appears in the gable. Strangely, the gable timbers and those of the upper storey are separated by a 3-inch gap, so that the tie-beam is, in effect, two distinct timbers, the soffit of the upper beam carrying a chamfer. What constructional crisis caused this peculiarity can only be conjectured.

While the Bull Ring quarter was being remodelled, there was no respite either for the northern part of Broad Street. On the western side early 17th-century work affecting nos.53 and 68/9 has been described. Opposite, there was an attempt to unify a group of buildings of assorted ages which led to the creation of the Butterwalk, or, as it was known then, 'the Penthouse', a covered way or 'piazza' intended to shelter pedestrians and protect shop fronts, but which was quickly encroached upon by opportunist traders. The encroachments have since been removed, and the wooden supporting posts were replaced in 1795 by cast iron pillars, leaving the Butterwalk to rank with that of another cloth town, Totnes in Devon, as a civic amenity. At the same time the whole group was 'standardised' by order of the Corporation.[35] Presumably this included plastering over the fronts to disguise the timber frames. When Louise Rayner painted her watercolour of the Buttercross the buildings on the eastern side are shown still clad with stucco, that is with the exception of no.2 where the stucco

The Butterwalk

had been removed, the timber-frame restored and some elaborate Victorian woodwork, dated 1871, had been added.[36] The other buildings had to wait another 50 years before some of their frames were revealed, and as late as 1984 a golden opportunity to restore the frontage of no.10 was missed. This would have been a valuable exercise, as, like no.53 opposite, it is known that a medieval range lies behind the later front unit.

When buildings have been in turn timbered, enlarged, stuccoed, de-plastered, restored and modernised it is often difficult to sort out a plausible building sequence, particularly as some of the finer points of Victorian work can be hard to distinguish from that of the 17th century. In Broad Street the following are considered to display mainly timberwork of *c*.1620, although, of course, there are earlier and later pockets within the group. No.13 is basically a single-bayed and three-storied building with a parallel roof, but the large dormer-gable with its louvred window gives a 'gable-end-on' appearance. Both the second and third stories display lozenge-within-lozenge work, and irregular cusped and beaded lozenge work appears below the third

Carved faces at 13 Broad Street

storey window. The building was originally jettied at each level. A form of brattishing appears on the barge-boards, the tie-beam and the bressumer of the second storey which may be compared with that on no.53, opposite. But the most endearing features are the carved brackets; four of them have faces where the imagery seems to hark back to that of the medieval misericords in the church.

No.9 is the much-restored former Angel Hotel, recorded in 1551 as an inn.[37] This frontage is perhaps the most difficult to analyse. The ground floor and second storey appear to be co-eval and display not-so-close-studding with a mid-rail and lozenge-within-lozenge work respectively. This is acceptable as c.1620; but the third storey, though with similar but less regular lozenge work, appears to be a later addition. The shallow-pitched roof, end chimneys, and the flowing design of the carving on the bressumer of the un-jettied third storey raises the question of whether the third storey, complete with its timber-frame, is attributable to the 18th century. And were the distinctive bow windows of the second storey added at the same time or are they pure Regency work? It would be interesting to know whether an 18th-century landlord regarded the prevailing taste for plain plaster fronts as decadent and struck a blow for tradition. If so, this part of the Angel must rank as one of the last examples of timber-framing in Shropshire, certainly at this social level. Perhaps the idea of a landlord with traditional taste is not completely fanciful. There are tenurial and family links between the Angel and the Feathers, the link being the Jones family, who, after Rees's extravaganza at the Feathers, described above, took up residence at the Sheet, then a country house with its own estate to the east of the town. They were still there in the 18th century when Thomas Jones became owner and landlord of the Angel. He is recorded as such from 1713 or earlier until 1731.[38] He would be familiar with his illustrious ancestor's example and may have inherited his affinity with timber, although clearly unable to match his exuberant use of it.

No.8 Broad Street still has its timbers concealed with roughcast. Three brackets protrude, each surmounted by a firemark. The brackets could support the wall-plate of a two-storied building or the bressumer of three-storied one. On no.7 the third storey is clearly an addition, but the framing of the second storey is rectangular and probably relates to the early 17th-century rebuilding programme as does its neighbour, no.6 with whom it shares a roof-line. No.5 has a slightly higher roof-line but the framing is similar although the northern unit appears to have been largely rebuilt. Oriel windows, perhaps as less expensive versions of those at the Angel, are a unifying feature of the Butterwalk properties, and another is a horizontal rail which runs between the southern unit of no.5 and the Angel. This was probably a wall-plate when the buildings were two-storied. Confirmatory evidence is suggested by the protruding brackets on the plastered front of no.8.

Elsewhere in the town early 17th-century features have been noted. For example, in Corve Street no.139 retains an ovolo-moulded window internally, and no.168 contains framing relating to the same period. The remodelling of no.50 has been described above, and in nos.46/47 the same division into two bays, one larger than the other, may be seen. Here the second storey is square-framed, two panels high and plain, although an arched window-head interrupts the pattern. Possibly these cottages formed the service end of a larger house which had already gone when Coronation Avenue was constructed.

On the corner of Bell Lane and Lower Raven Lane a property which was sadly mutilated has recently been restored as a private house. It is two-bayed, timber-framed, two-storied and jettied towards Bell Lane. The eastern bay retains lozenge-within-lozenge work, and a carved bracket remains which has three shields upon it. But the bressumer, with its combination of ogee, ovolo and double quirk bears resemblance to those noted at Castle Lodge (1604), 10

*The corner of Bell Lane and
Lower Raven Lane after restoration*

The Lecturer's House, Old Street

Church Street (1610) and Lane's House (1621), all of which are based on the ogee and ovolo.

Lane's House in Old Street was extensively remodelled in 1621, as the carved date on the southern dormer gable indicates. The lozenge-within-lozenge work on the second storey is probably co-eval and is echoed by the herringbone-work on the northern dormer gable which was given less lavish treatment than the southern one. On the latter, and on the oriel window below it, the decoration includes billet, ovolo, guilloche and cable moulding, classical blank arches, leaf decoration and the initials E.G. Both oriel windows have ovolo moulding on the mullions and transoms and the carved brackets incorporate what appear to be Tudor roses. Thomas Lane was a prominent figure in Ludlow society and was a kinsman of Sir Job Charlton of Ludford. After his death in 1674 his trustees converted the house, formerly owned by Lane, into a Workhouse and a House of Correction. After 1833 it became an almshouse, and is now a private house.[39]

Another framed house in Old Street is the Lecturer's House. This has an inscribed date of 1611, but, in typical misleading fashion, this dates the appointment of Thomas Kay to the post of Town Preacher. Records show that the house was rebuilt by the Corporation later in 1622 at a cost of £26 7s. 9d. Given that the stone for the foundations and the clay for the tiling and bricks were from Corporation-owned land, and thus free, and that most of the internal framing is re-used material, such a small sum could only represent a remodelling, although the lobby-entry plan with the hall on one side of the stack and a smaller parlour on the other marked an important advance in planning.[40] The lozenge-within-lozenge work on the front elevation is disturbed by twin double-height bay windows which are, in turn, surmounted by large dormer gables displaying beaded cusped lozenge work. This raises the question of whether the fenestration has been completely changed since 1622 and whether the dormer gables have also been added.

An indication that brick as a constructional medium had arrived in Ludlow before the Civil War comes from the Bull Ring, where no.46 was distinguished by the name 'The Brick House' in 1633.[41] The standing building on the site is a four-storied 18th-century structure of three bays and has a parapet roof, plat-bands and segmental-headed sash windows. It seems to represent a complete rebuilding since 1633 and the top storey is little more than a deep façade.

14/15 Raven Lane (right) with (left) its 17th-century 'Dirty Gertie'
and (centre) the late 20th-century 'Busty Brenda'

After the Civil War it seems that Ludlow carpenters simply picked up where they had left off, continuing to build framed and jettied houses, often three stories high and with gables to the street, employing the same decorative designs which they frequently brought together in a dazzling display, and adding touches of humour in the form of carved brackets with figures or faces which had no trace of solemnity. A typical example is 14/15 Raven Lane, which has recently been restored, although, as usual, the ground floor framework had long since departed. A word of warning may be timely. The bracket figure of a nude female on the third storey at the junction of the twin gables is a finishing touch added at the end of the modern restoration, and the one below it on the second storey, though older, may not be *in situ*; it partly conceals an empty mortice on the stud. It is difficult to suggest a use for a mortice in such a position unless it secured a hanging sign board or something similar.

Others in Raven Lane, if stripped of their cladding, would reveal a similar design. In Corve Street nos.103/4—The Tudor Guest House—has had the third storey either added or remodelled since it too was rebuilt after the Civil War. This house has a central chimney but was not designed to have a lobby-entry. Entrance was via a side passage at the southern end. No less than nine carved brackets with faces feature on the front elevation. As time went on the jetties usually became smaller. This trend can be seen in the High Street where no.3 is dated 1651 on a bracket. This has a parallel roof line and is three stories high, but its neighbour, no.2 is four-storied and is set gable-end on. The addition of Regency bow windows has destroyed much of its impact although the carved bressumers and brackets command attention. At no.4 (see drawings overleaf), which has been restored recently, the front is not jettied at all although the rear is, but over the ground floor only. The property is four stories high and displays the familiar exuberance in the pattern of the framing on the front although the rear, which over-

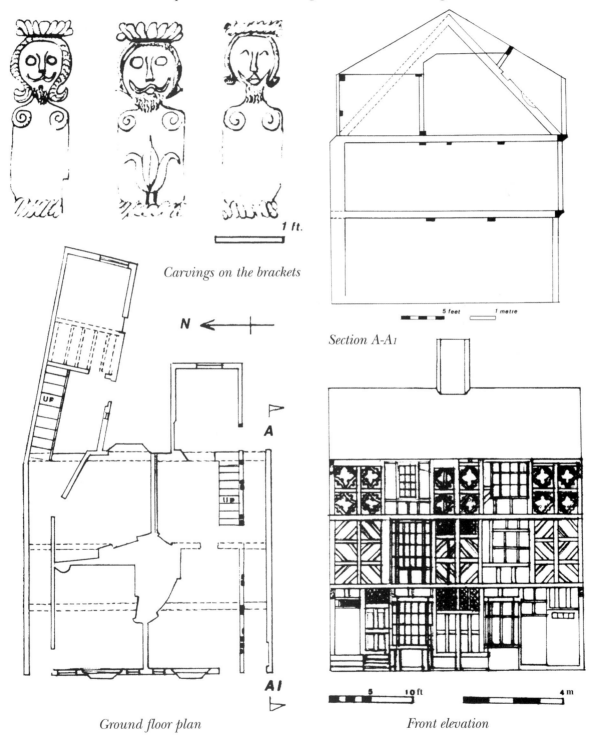

Carvings on the brackets

1 ft.

Section A-A₁

5 feet   1 metre

N ←

Ground floor plan

Front elevation

Tudor Guest House, Lower Corve Street

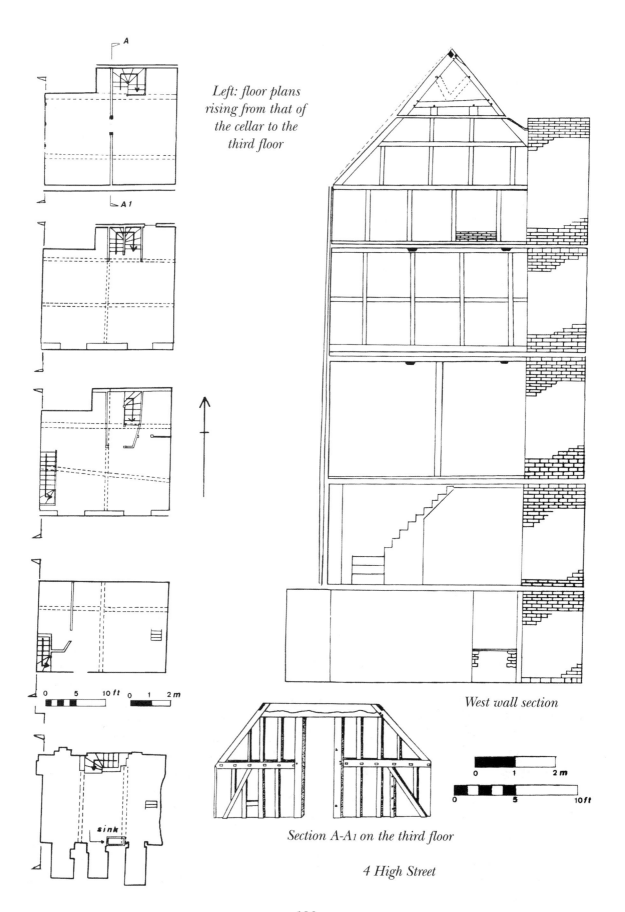

Left: floor plans rising from that of the cellar to the third floor

West wall section

Section A-A1 on the third floor

4 High Street

sink

0 5 10 ft   0 1 2 m

0 1 2 m

0 5 10 ft

196

South façade, 4 High Street

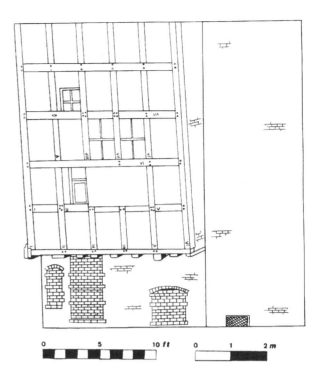

North façade, 4 High Street

North-west elevation of 2 Dinham from Antient Domestick Architecture *by Dollman & Jobbins c.1890*

looks Harp Lane, has plain square-framing. Although the fourth storey gives the impression of having been added, there is no structural evidence of this either internally or externally. Perhaps the absence of the jetty at the front marks the beginning of the end of traditional framing in Ludlow at this social level.

Still jettied, though with a noticeably smaller overhang, is 2 Dinham. This house is similar to those in Raven Lane, noted above, and is quoted from documentary sources as having being rebuilt in 1654, following damage during the Civil War.[42] However, there are many puzzling features, not least that the position of a ceiling boss in the ground floor room of the southern bay suggests that the house was once three bays wide instead of the present two; and the existing

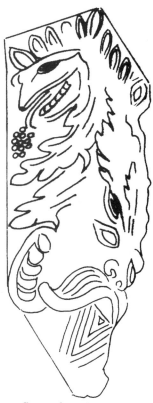

Carved brackets at 2 Dinham

pattern of the lozenge work on the second storey also tends to confirm that it continued further to the south-west. As mentioned earlier, the carving on the fascia board which masks the joists of the jetty incorporates the same 'tied bundles' and leaf scrolls which were noted on Tamberlaine House, and similar half faces are carved on the brackets on either side of what was an original doorway on the front elevation. Other brackets depict heraldic beasts, a full face which, though smaller and cruder, may be compared with that on the north-west corner of the jettied gatehouse at Stokesay Castle, and scroll work with foliage. Other details, including the little cusps at the top of the bargeboards, also occur on the gatehouse and are referred to in the following chapter. It is possible that the post-Civil War 'rebuilding' was an exercise that involved reducing the structure to two bays, and adding a third storey with twin dormer gables to what was left. The house was Corporation property in 1654 and was leased to Ralph Goodwin of Eyton, Herefordshire, a former M.P. for Ludlow. It has the unsupported tradition that the poet John Milton (1608-74) stayed here, although it is well known that his masque 'Comus' received its first performance at Ludlow Castle in 1634.

In the glovers and tanners' area at the northern end of Corve Street, no.69 was probably the home of Thomas Powys, a prosperous tanner.[43] It appears to date to *c.*1650-60 and although some of the details are echoed in the town centre properties its overall form is different. A full three bays wide it is only two stories high but has three separate tall dormer windows in the roof. Both the ground floor and the upper storey have close-studding with a mid-rail, and it is clear that the bulk of the capital outlay was spent on creating an impressive—if old-fashioned—front; the back has simple square-framing, four panels high. On the front the bressumer is, curiously, surmounted by another. The upper one is plain, but the smaller, lower one has a double-stepped moulding on the soffit, and the joists are tenoned into it. Another curious feature is the bracket at the northern end; it is integral with the post but is twice as wide as the joist which it supports. If the structure is considered to be backward-looking, the same cannot be said for the plan. The stairs are contained within a central entrance hall, and a central stack has a parlour on one side and kitchen on the other. A passageway at the southern end, once a wide cart-entry, gives access to the rear where the remains of a timber-framed wing at the northern end suggest that the ground floor was open, possibly for storage and to accommodate wagons, whilst the staff and apprentices had their living quarters above. The river Corve, which would be used in the course of leather working, forms the property boundary on the western side.

Another example of post-Civil War rebuilding, though less impressive, is 136 Corve Street. This occupies only half a burgage plot, but, like no.69, has a central entrance and a timber-framed wing at the rear. Similarly, Richard Collier's house at 68 Lower Broad Street was rebuilt on a half burgage plot. He was a mason and his inventory taken after his death in 1672 shows that his house contained a hall and parlour at ground level, a great chamber and a back room upstairs, a cellar and a cockloft.[44] On other houses in Lower Broad Street, certainly on the western side, the same plan may be discerned, and each house was probably jettied towards the street, and had a lobby entry associated with the end chimney. The passages to the rear, contained within the structures, are later insertions.

'The Tan House' at 72 Corve Street is dated 1661 and bears the initials of Edward Brampton.[45] Here the end lobby entry plan is evident when the interior is examined. The present entrance is a later insertion. In this part of Corve Street alterations to the boundaries have resulted in some interlocking of properties, but it is likely that Edward Brampton's house occupied a full burgage plot originally. He too would have had a hall and a parlour at ground level, though set in line parallel to the street. Square-framing,

69 Corve Street
Top: Front of c.1660; lower: Rear elevation

136 Corve Street, half-size burgage plot

probably three panels high in each storey, was used for the front and the rear, but the evidence of the internal chamfered beams which extend to the building line suggest that the house was not jettied. As mentioned earlier, the stack at the Tan House had star-shaped shafts. There is no evidence that this was left over from an earlier building, although the possibility should be borne in mind, but is a reminder of how popular this form of chimney was and of how late its use continued.

Rear of Edward Brampton's House, 72 Corve Street (1661). Note the remains of star-shaped shafts on the chimneystack

Late timber-framing may be seen in Dinham, where, in addition to the problematic no. 2, described above, nos.13 and 14 are also representative. Perhaps because Dinham was neither an industrial nor artisan area, the framing is more decorative, and lozenge-within-lozenge work predominates. Both buildings are two-and-a-half stories high and each has a shallow jetty. No.13 has a parallel roof line but a full-width dormer-gable gives a gable-end on appearance. Cusped lozenges and herringbone work occur in the dormer-gable, and cusped and spiked lozenges

13-14 Dinham

are used to give added interest to the second storey. No.14 also has a parallel roof-line but twin dormer gables are used instead of the single one at no.13. Again spiked lozenges and herring-bone work are featured and the bargeboards incorporate carved quatrefoils. It is a pity that the decorative fronts of the brackets have been mutilated.

These houses are the last to display showy framing, at least, where it is still visible. Elsewhere in the town timber-framing continued to be used although the frontages were later disguised. The Elephant and Castle at 15 The Bull Ring was reputedly built *c*.1662;[46] a plot in the former town ditch outside the walls in Lower Broadgate was leased to William Woodall in 1664 'upon condition of building',[47] this is now the Wheatsheaf; and in 1677 at 18 Castle Street Thomas Crumpe, a lawyer at the Council in the Marches, rebuilt the hall range of the property known as 'The House with the Leaden Porch'.[48] Unfortunately the porch disappeared many years ago and only the date, Crumpe's initials and that of his wife Mary remained on the front. The whole hall structure was demolished in 1995, revealing traces of a medieval undercroft below. The ground-floor storey was stone-built but the walls reduced to timber-framed dimensions in the upper storey. A room at the rear had a large 'Yorkshire' horizontal sliding sash window.

Perhaps the last visible examples of timber-framing are at 10 Lower Raven Lane, where plain square-framing is preserved in the upper storey, and in cottages in Dinham beyond no.19. These incorporate reused timbers and may have been converted from a barn. No.19, though brick-fronted, has a late timber-framed side wall which is visible from the rear of no.17. From this vantage point it is possible to see an earlier building line with fragments of stone walls and a pitched floor. This may be medieval, suggesting that Dinham was originally much wider than at present. There are probably many more examples of late timber-framing awaiting discovery in Ludlow, but it would would be fair to say that after the late 17th century brick held sway.

A cast iron fireback, dated 1668 and bearing the initials of Edward Robinson, a bookseller, was found at 16 King Street. He was taxed on three hearths in 1672.[49] The good staircase in his house with its turned balusters, wide hand-rail and string was probably co-eval. Unfortunately, both were ripped out when the property was redeveloped in 1986. The misfortune is compounded because there are in the town few dated or datable fittings remaining which relate to the 17th century. 27 Broad Street has a similar staircase which pre-dates the elegant 18th-century one in the entrance hall, and at Castle Lodge a cast iron fireback dated 1630 and bearing the initials 'K W E' is thought to be *in situ* and to accompany the fire surround. Some, such as the panelling at 53 Broad Street, 10 Church Street, and the Feathers have been mentioned, but these are all early 17th-century examples. The later type of panelling, with carpenters' mitres at all four corners, has been noted only in a room at the Broadgate. Here the panels are raised and fielded and the one over

10 Lower Raven Lane

*Edward Robinson's fireback of 1688
at 16 King Street*

Fireback of 1630 at Castle Lodge

the fireplace has a bolection-moulded surround, but the work could relate to the early 18th century, particularly as the panels are large and rectangular. There is a good bolection-moulded fireplace at 39 Broad Street and the same room has some early 17th-century moulding on a plaster panelled ceiling. These features were retained when the house was extensively remodelled in the 18th century. The 17th-century ceiling plasterwork at the Feathers has been mentioned; this, of course, is exceptionally decorative, elsewhere plainer plaster

Late 17th-century panelling at the Broadgate

panelled ceilings with moulded surrounds to the panels have been noted, for example at the Reader's house and at 6 Tower Street. But the only known 17th-century wall paintings occur at the Old Bell in Ludford, although in 1985, while the building was being re-furbished, a stencilled pattern in blue-grey paint was noted in the building on the south side of the Feathers. The better-preserved painting at Barnaby House dates from the late 16th century. Several windows with wooden ovolo-moulded mullions and transoms survive. One which cannot be seen from outside is in the rear wall of the James I lounge at the Feathers and another, as noted above, is at 139 Corve Street.

Documentary sources and architectural evidence combine to suggest that the period from c.1580 to 1642 saw a major rebuilding programme in Ludlow. There was a brief hiatus caused by the Civil War and its aftermath, but building resumed fairly quickly and timber-framing continued to be popular until the 1670s and later. For much of this time it would be in competition with brick, and towards the end of the period it is clear that second-hand timber was being used for internal work and continued to be used for roof trusses well into the 18th century.

The order in which the buildings are described above may not be chronologically correct in all cases, and it is impossible to assess how many others have since been rebuilt, but it is hoped that a reasoned sequence has been postulated. The first quarter of the 17th century saw the style being set with two-storied houses having close-studding divided by a mid-rail to the ground floor and either similar or lozenge-within-lozenge work above. When three-storied houses were built or a third storey added then cusped or cusped and spiked lozenge work was used in the upper stages. Ludlow carpenters made lozenge work something of a local hallmark, but their treatment of carved brackets and of imagery generally was entirely their own. Square-framing was usually confined to parts of the house that were not open to public view, to service ends, cottages or to very late framing.

Many houses made full use of the roof space as attics and therefore structural features tend to be obscured, but it is curious that no straight windbraces of the type associated with the 17th century have been noted. Roof trusses of this time are otherwise unremarkable, usually consisting of principal rafters, tenoned purlins, a ridge purlin, tie-beam, collar beam, queen-struts and V-struts above the collar. The overall impression is that the second 'great rebuild' from c.1700-80 eclipsed most of what had gone before, and left Ludlow with a 'Georgian' reputation. But that is another matter and beyond the scope of this present work.

8   Stokesay Castle Gatehouse & Ludford House

Two buildings, both outside Ludlow, clearly have cultural links with the town and are significant structures in their own right. They are therefore treated separately as an appendix to the Ludlow chapters. One, the Gatehouse at Stokesay Castle is entirely of its time; the other, Ludford House, is a true 'gothic' complex which has simply grown and been altered over the centuries and may be seen as a superb example of piecemeal development. Because every constructional phase has interesting points and its tenurial history is reasonably well documented Ludford House is described in some detail.

Stokesay Castle Gatehouse

Most descriptions of the Gatehouse refer to it as 'Tudor' or, more daringly, as 'Elizabethan'. Others push the dating into the 1620-25 Jacobean period but recent dendrochronological sampling and analysis, commissioned by English Heritage, has produced a felling date of 1639-40, just as the Civil War was beginning.[1] This raises questions about its function during that conflict. Assuming that it replaced an earlier stone-built entrance to the complex the first point to consider is how a pretty timber-framed structure could possibly function as part of a defensive curtain wall; as such it resembles a dropped stitch in a row of knitting. Times would have to be very settled indeed before such a conceit would be feasible. Secondly, given that

Stokesay Castle Gatehouse—the outer face (1639-40)

Stokesay was involved in the Civil War, was taken over by the Parliamentarian side and played a key role thereafter, is it possible that such a vulnerable component could emerge unscathed? Surely it is more likely to be in Sir Samuel Baldwin's time after the war that it replaced a more defensive structure. The Baldwin family held Stokesay on a long lease from about 1630 and it is probably because of their concern for the complex and in particular the influence wielded by Sir Samuel that Stokesay was

Stokesay Castle Gatehouse
Top left: The inner face from the south tower
Top right: 'Adam'; lower right: 'Eve'
Carved corner brackets: lower left: 'Neptune'; lower centre: Serpents

Scalloped bargeboards, cf. 2 Dinham, Ludlow

*Apex of lintel on inner face,
with flower head motif*

Fireplace in upper chamber

not reduced to rubble after the war. Apart from the practicalities of the situation, when seen in conjunction with some of the Ludlow carpentry school as described in the preceding chapter, the felling date and the architectural details suggest that perhaps the timbers were cut in 1639-40 but then stored during hostilities.

The building is timber-framed on a stone plinth, basically two-storied but with a large dormer-gable on either side forming architectural rather than lighting features. The wide entrance is centrally placed and the roof is pierced by an axial chimney-stack on the northern side of the dormer-gables. The brick shafts are star-shaped but any decorative capping that they had has been removed. The outbuilt stack on the southern side is a later addition. It is, of course, the carved decorations, the symbolism, the pattern of the framing and the fact that the building is jettied on all four sides that make the Gatehouse particularly interesting.

On the ground floor close-studding with a mid-rail is used consistently. The upper storey is square-framed with plain lozenge work, and in order to maintain uniformity of panel size on all four sides the wall-plates and the tie-beams are jointed so that the latter fits over the former with no protrusion. This is a refinement rarely seen and only one other example has been noted in Shropshire, although that is in a medieval building, the Old Hall at Claverley. The dormer-gables display cusped and spiked lozenge work within square-framing. Taken together the pattern of the framing is typical of the mid-to-late 17th-century work seen in Ludlow and there are marked similarities between the gatehouse and 2 Dinham in Ludlow, particularly with regard to the treatment of the bargeboards on the dormer-gables. The carving is similar, both have cusping at the apex and were furnished with finials and pendants. The Gatehouse has lost its finials and pendants but the fixing points remain exposed. 2 Dinham, it will be remembered, was remodelled, if not rebuilt in 1656, following the Civil War. The classical blank arches below the windows of the upper storey are found on a number of Shropshire buildings of the 17th century. Two dated ones may be quoted: Castle Gatehouse in Shrewsbury (1620) and Berrington Manor (1658).

However, it is the imagery of the carvings which attracts most attention. They are particularly delightful and not really repetitive. The most elaborate corner brackets are those on the northern (approach) side. One is of a Neptune-like figure with a stylised beard similar to the ceremonial beard seen in Egyptian iconography. He is flanked by dolphins. The other is of serpents with barbed tongues and tails. On the eastern side over the entrance are the figures of Adam and Eve and these are repeated in a smaller form higher up. On the lintel a tree (of knowledge?) occupies the centre and is flanked by an oak tree and a fig tree. On the inner face of the Gatehouse the post-heads on either side of the entrance are carved with figures, one male and one female. These are flanked by 'temptation' motifs. The lintel has foliage, dolphins and a central flower head. Some of the other carvings are badly weathered, but is it obvious that the craftsman was skilled in working in the triple-facet genre, and the overall theme appears to be the triumph of good over evil, with dolphins symbolic of love. Bounty and blessings are also suggested and it is interesting to speculate that the figures on the post-heads may represent Sir Samuel and his lady. The appearance of the flower head in such a prominent position in the centre of the lintel raises the question of whether the Gatehouse is the work of John Abel, the well-known Herefordshire carpenter. The flower-head was part of his 'signature' which he used throughout his career.[2] The dolphin motif also occurs on the Feathers Hotel in Ludlow, another building with which Abel's name is linked, although it must be stressed, purely on stylistic and not documentary evidence; and on Tamberlaine House, 45 the Bull Ring, Sandbrook Vaults in Market Drayton (dated 1653) and Hazlewood Farm, Darliston (dated 1655).

Ludford House

The river Teme forms the boundary between Ludlow and Ludford and formerly divided Shropshire from Herefordshire. Until 1901 Ludford was in Herefordshire.[3] Originally the road to Leominster made a left turn after the bridge and passed in front of the entrance to the church, the almshouses, Ludford House, the Old Bell, the ford and the mill before looping back to join the present line further to the south. The present road from Ludlow to Leominster takes traffic past what was the back of Ludford House where all that can be seen is a high forbidding stone wall, four huge out-built chimneystacks and a gateway beneath a timber-framed upper storey. Perhaps it is a combination of these factors which has led to its relative obscurity, but a descriptive account of Ludford House was written in 1949 and, more recently, it featured in an authoritative account of the life and work of the Shrewsbury architect Thomas Farnolls Pritchard (1723-1777).[4]

As mentioned above, the house consists of many different building periods. There are extensive out-buildings and the complex is partially sub-divided into separate dwellings at present, but a coherent picture of the development can be formed. The exterior is described first. Much of it is in timber-framing above a ground-floor storey of stone and the genre provides a linking theme throughout. The western range with the four large stacks is said to contain evidence of medieval construction, but has so far proved inaccessible. However, on the frontage of the northern range, which can be seen from the churchyard, the concept of a medieval three-part plan hall-house is discernible. Part of this range is known as 'St. Giles' House'. The name is significant. A hospital for lepers was in existence in Ludford by the early 13th century. It soon became an almshouse known as St. Giles' House and belonged to St.

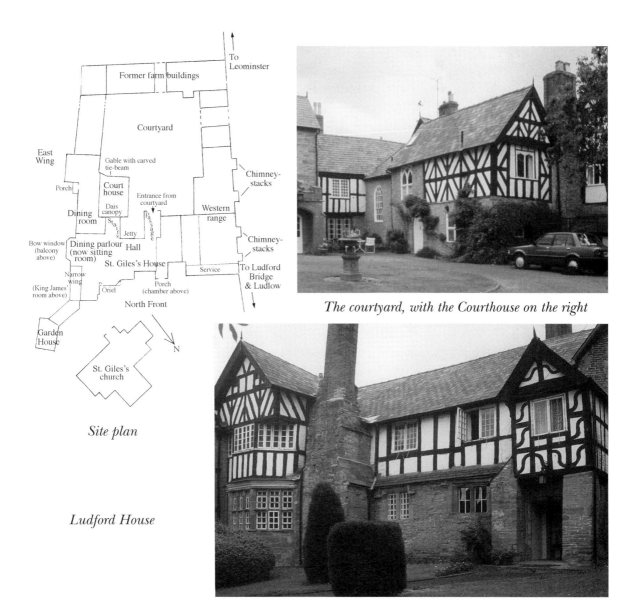

Site plan

Ludford House

The courtyard, with the Courthouse on the right

North front, St. Giles' House

East wing, remodelled in 1761 by Thomas Farnolls Pritchard

John's Hospital across the river on the town side. The present almshouses to the north-east of St. Giles' church probably owe their origins to William Foxe and his wife Jane in the middle of the 16th century, although they were rebuilt *c.*1672 and are now known as 'Sir Job Charlton's Hospital'.[5]

The Northern Range

A doorway with double-ogee moulding is set within the stonework of the ground-floor storey of St. Giles' House. It appears to be *in situ* and is probably of an early 15th-century date. If it did give access to a screens passage this has been lost in later alterations, and although there is an opposing doorway on the southern (courtyard) side they are not in line and in any case the block to which the latter relates is a later addition. Similar moulding may be seen on a door surround contained within the block known as the 'garden room' in the north-east corner of the plan, but is is possible that this has been brought in from elsewhere. It is a blocked opening which would lead beneath the churchyard and its width has been narrowed. Perhaps significantly, similar moulding may be seen on the remains of St. John's Hospital overlooking Ludford Bridge on the town side. The site of the medieval St. Giles' Leper Hospital is unknown but the moulded doorway on St. Giles' House may relate to its period as an almshouse, and the one in the garden room may also have belonged to it.

Above the doorway of St. Giles' House is a timber-framed projecting porch chamber. The framework includes S-braces, a jettied pediment, carved bargeboards, brackets, a finial and a pendant in the form of a carved mask. The carvings may be compared with some in Ludlow, and the thought arises that perhaps this is an early expression of the exuberance that distinguished the later Ludlow school of carpentry described in the previous chapter.

To the west of the doorway in St. Giles' House is a stone-built crosswing which would correspond to the service wing of the medieval plan. This contains a window with stone mullions and a transom and has sunk-chamfer mouldings. Possibly this relates to the late 16th-century phase. The 'hall' unit to the east of the doorway has unremarkable timber-framing set above and recessed from the medieval stonework. A pentice roof compensates for the difference in the wall thicknesses. Two windows which once lit the hall have drip-moulds and labels. Their rebated stone frames suggest a late 16th-century date, although they may be earlier. Further to the east is what could be described as a 17th-century up-dating of a dais-end oriel window, and a large out-built stone chimneystack, also of 17th-century form occupies the re-entrant angle. The timber-framed upper stage of the oriel has pendants similar in form to those at Valentine Dawes' house in Church Street, Ludlow, which is dated 1610 and described in the preceding chapter. Beyond the oriel is a stone-built unit which now forms the return on the eastern side of the plan and continues as the courtyard boundary on that side, but which probably originated as the solar end of the medieval plan.

The Eastern Range

The northernmost part of the eastern range is occupied by a block known as the 'James II' range because, according to tradition, he stayed at Ludford House in 1686 and occupied a bedroom in that range. It consists of rectangular timber-framing over the stonework which contains the garden room, and the gable end has scalloped barge-boards which appear to be of late 16th- or early 17th-century date. The unit continues along the eastern side with work largely attributable to Thomas Farnolls Pritchard in the 1760s. Of outstanding interest, whether or not of Pritchard's design, is the balcony window above the bay window. This will be described later. In his remodelling, Pritchard preserved the framing-above-stone theme, introducing sash windows along the length of the wing and a porch to shelter the access door to the garden. The porch is of brickwork rendered over to resemble stone and is classical in its design with an arch, pilasters with ionic caps, bands of egg-and-dart moulding and an entablature incorporating a dentilated cornice. It closely resembles the porch at 49/50 Broad Street, Ludlow, which also contains work in the Pritchard genre and was the town house of the Baldwin family of Corvedale.[6]

Beyond the porch the upper story of a projecting wing is supported on posts. This marks the end of the domestic range but the building line continues for some distance and an opening in the wall gives access to the courtyard and to the range of farm building on the southern side of the plan, thus completing the rectangular form. Again, the framing-above-stone theme is repeated on the southern range. In the courtyard it becomes clear that the north-eastern angle of the quadrangle has been filled in with further construction. A range in the north-west corner, now entirely of stone on the exterior, has carved bargeboards with a design similar though not identical to that on the bargeboards of the north porch. This range contains the entrance porch which gives access to the present hall range, and this is slightly jettied, again with framing-above-stone. The moulding on the bressumer is an unusual combination of ogee and half-rounds separated by a straight flat chamfer. The unit on the eastern side, framing-above-stone like so much else at Ludford House, is a self-contained unit which, for reasons which will be given below, is possibly the long-lost Courthouse. Although bold lozenge-within-lozenge work is used on the walls, stylistically the building owes something to the Shrewsbury school of carpentry; the carving on the tie-beam uses the vine and vine-leaf motif and is very similar to that found on a number of Shrewsbury town houses of the late 16th or early 17th centuries, particularly that on the tie-beam of the porch which once graced Shrewsbury School headmaster's house, Rigg's Hall, and is dated 1589.[7]

The Interior

As the Courthouse is a relatively independent structure it may be helpful to begin the description of the interior of Ludford House with the reasons for suspecting that this little ancillary building is that which was used as a courthouse. The reasons are three-fold: architectural, historical and tenurial. Within the body of the house, in the upper level of that area where the northern wall of the supposed courthouse meets a linking block, is a feature which, if stripped of various accretions, would be seen as a dais canopy. A slender post with a moulded capital supports braces which, in turn, support a moulded canopy. It is not a structural component, its decoration is in the classical mould and its form, or something very similar, may be seen illustrated in judicial scenes of the late 16th century.[8] Historically and tenurially it is known that there was a courthouse in Ludford, that in 1586 Edward Foxe owned Ludford House and in that year a sum was paid 'for reparations of the house in Ludford, of the gaol delivery, to Mr Foxe'.[9]

Near the same upper area there is evidence that the Courthouse was added to an existing wing which ran at right-angles. Concealed within the present roof space is an earlier gable-end which has braces supporting a protruding wall-plate, rafters with cusped ends and empty mortices for side wall-bracing. This feature is weathered, but beyond it is the unweathered framing of the northern gable of the courthouse.

Nothing remains of any medieval hall structure at Ludford House although vestiges of such a plan are apparent. The present entrance from the courtyard leads into a long vestibule and a wider passage. The entrance porch, door and vestibule have Pritchard attributes and he may have worked on the remodelling of the passage. The present hall is approached through a choice of two double doors in the eastern wall of the passage and it is tempting to see in these, overtones of the aisled form of a medieval spere-truss, but it is clear that the hall was completely remodelled about the middle of the 17th century. The wall panelling and the panelled ceiling with its moulded beams are all of this time as is the fireplace which is served by the out-built stack on the north elevation. At what would have been the dais end of the hall the effect of the oriel window has been lost as the hall was curtailed at that point and the window area used to create a small room approached from an open archway in the passage which is clearly attributable to Pritchard. Contained within the passage is an elegant staircase, the details of which are specified in Pritchard's estimate. It is similar to the staircase at 27 Broad Street where he was responsible for remodelling the house for Somerset Davies.[10] Each has a ramped and moulded handrail, turned balusters grouped three to each tread, and each is lit by a multi-paned window with an arched head.

Other rooms in the east wing display clear evidence of Pritchard's hand. The present dining room contains the 'Italian white and Vein'd Chimny peice with a Dressing of proper ornaments' of the estimate. This, like the documented one at 27 Broad Street has an eared surround and an overmantel with flowing stylised foliage, deeply undercut in typical fashion. Other Pritchard touches are evident in the pelmets and windows, but the vine decoration on the soffits of the ceiling beams belongs to an earlier age and could be contemporary with the hall ceiling, though there the decoration on the soffits, if it existed, has been removed. The fireplace in the dining room is backed by one in the present sitting room which is the 'dining parlour' in the estimate. Here the 'Bow Window' is a prominent feature but as Pritchard was to 'new Set the Chimny peice' it is difficult to decide whether the Jacobean overmantel belonged to the room before 1761. Perhaps Pritchard simply added the two oval medallions. In another ground-

Fireplace in the dining room by Thomas Farnolls Pritchard

Dining room ceiling with late 16th-century plasterwork

Detail of pomegranate ceiling in 'King James' Bedroom'

floor room in the east wing, beyond the present dining room, is a fireplace which also has Pritchard characteristics. This is a fairly recent acquisition by the present owner and it is a happy coincidence that it came from 49/50 Broad Street, mentioned above.

Perhaps the most impressive piece of 18th-century work at Ludford House is the balcony window above the 'Bow Window' of the estimate. This is not mentioned in the estimate but it is so typical of Pritchard's style that either it was an afterthought on Sir Francis' part or there is another estimate which is missing. In Pritchard's own notebook there is a sketch for a 'Chimney frame for the Liberary at Croft Castle' which he apparently used again for the French windows of the balcony at Ludford House. The similarity is striking, and at Ludford House he used all his favourite

Balcony window in the east wing by Thomas Farnolls Pritchard

'gothick' devices to great effect—the triple-cluster banded pilasters, quatrefoils, crockets, trefoil-heads, ogee and roll mouldings; and he designed an ingenious opening so that when the leaves were closed the rhythm of the grouped pilasters was not disturbed.

If the ceiling of the present dining room with its vine-leaf decoration is noteworthy, the panelled ceiling of 'King James' bedroom' is more so. The room has been subdivided but the

Roof of James II wing

ceiling beams are undisturbed and have an impressive flowing design of pomegranates in applied plaster-work. As usual the pomegranates are depicted with the skin peeled back and the seeds showing.

Over the 'King James' wing the roof is unusually steep and narrow. This is partly due to the fact that the ridge-piece is not supported in the usual way; one of the principal rafters on each truss is cut so that is about 1ft. (0.3m.) longer than the other. This makes the tie, collar and queen-post construction unusually cramped. It is difficult to see what advantage this was intended to give, but the form is consistent throughout the three bays. The remainder of the house appears to have been re-roofed, probably in the 18th century. Nothing remains of any medieval roof structure, but the floor at attic level has narrow joists with double tenons and diminished haunches. As such it probably relates to the early 17th century and may be compared with those at Wolverton Manor (crosswing), Rowley's Mansion in Shrewsbury, The Porch House at Bishop's Castle and Brereton Hall in Cheshire.

The Tenurial History

The history of Ludford House is inextricably bound up with with that of the parish and that of the Hospital of St. John. Very little is known about the leper hospital of St. Giles which seems to have become part of the endowment of St. John's Hospital as early as *c.*1330.[11] Up to this date the site was in the ownership of the Ludford family, from then until the Reformation it was held by St. John's Hospital. At the Reformation it was acquired by the entrepreneurial Foxe family who held and occupied it until 1638 when it was sold to the Charlton family. Sir Job Charlton, followed by his heirs, continued to own and occupy the house until 1920 when it was sold to Mr. H.E. Whitaker. It is now owned and occupied by Mr. D.F.A. Nicholson. Until the 17th century it was known as 'St. Gile's [*sic*] House', and part of it is still known as such.

| **Phase 1** | **Phase 2** | **Phase 3** | **Phase 4** |
St. John's Hospital (1330-1537)	*Edward Foxe (1546-1635)*	*Sir Job Charlton (1614-1697)*	*Sir Francis Charlton (1701-1784)*
C.15th doorway with double-ogee moulding under north porch	North porch	remodelling of dais window on north range (cf. Val. Dawes 1610)	remodelling of east wing, inc. porch (cf. 49/50 Broad St.)
some stonework on north range?	sunk-chamfer window on north range (cf. Sidney Apartments, Foxe house at Bromfield, St. Fagan's, (Glam.)	remodelling of hall int.	porch and vestibule on courtyard side
form of north range	James II wing with tall roof		curtailment of hall and oriel window
doorway in garden room	remodelling of hall range inc. jettied wall to courtyard		remodelling of parlour (now dining room) and room adjoining
	the courthouse inc. dais canopy		staircase and passage balcony chamber and window
	dormer gable predating court house		remodelling of Jacobean over-mantel
	dining room ceiling with vine motif		(All these by T.F. Pritchard 1761)
	James II room with pomegranate motif		
	courtyard range		
	re-roofing inc. use of double-tenon floor joists		

Table of suggested architectural phases

9   Shrewsbury Houses: The Medieval Period

Although in the 14th century Shropshire as a county was rated only 29th in the scale of wealth and, by analogy, importance, Shrewsbury, the county town, came 7th in the league of prosperous towns. This was in 1334 when the figure was based on taxation records. By 1377 it had dropped to 17th and, though there were fluctuations, it continued to lose its position until in 1801, by the yardstick of the census return, it was 24th.[1] Some indication of its early dominance is given in the Domesday entry when five churches and 252 houses on the peninsula site are mentioned, and the conversion of St. Peter's into an abbey by Earl Roger is recorded as being in progress.[2] St. Peter's lay outside the river loop in what is now regarded as a suburb of Shrewsbury—Abbey Foregate. But after the establishment of Roger's abbey there in the 1080s the Foregate functioned as a separate manor with its own charters, courts, fairs, customs and privileges. One of the privileges granted to the abbey was the monopoly of grinding corn at the abbey's mills. This rankled with the burgesses of the peninsula and led to acrimony and conflict, not fully reconciled, presumably, until the abbey was dissolved in 1540.[3]

However, the origins and early history of Shrewsbury are not the prime concern of this work, and to go into much detail would be superfluous. The work of the 19th-century historians Owen and Blakeway was so scholarly that future writers have always been able to use the two classic volumes as a ready-made database. But Shrewsbury's geographical position within a great horseshoe loop of the river Severn, its royal connections and its proximity to the Welsh border with a defensive potential real and implied obviously has a bearing on the type and form of its buildings and the way in which they developed. That an urban power-base followed the establishment of a military base at Roman *Viroconium*, four miles downstream to the east is an undisputed fact. The extensive ruins are still there. Historians also agree that the appendix '*Cornoviorum*' indicates that the tribesmen who occupied the hill-fort on the Wrekin were subjected to Roman integration policy.[4] Whether or not the British '*Pengwern*' was the forerunner of the Saxon '*Scrobbesbyrig*' which became 'Shrewsbury' is another matter, but it would be surprising if such a prime site was not exploited in pre-Roman times and even more surprising if, after *Viroconium* was finally abandoned in the 5th century, its role was not eventually assumed by *Scrobbesbyrig*.

It is a mistake to think that all of Shrewsbury 'standeth on a Rocky Hill of stone' to quote the 16th-century traveller and historian Leland. Shifting sand, gravel, marshy ground and crumbling cliffs also make up the site and cause problems, the latest of which was shown to be its inability to withstand an earthquake measuring 5.2 on the Richter scale on 2 April 1990. The epicentre was at Guilden Down about two miles north of Clun which suffered no ill effects at all, but few buildings in Shrewsbury, over 30 miles away, escaped damage of some kind and the town centre was closed for two days for safety reasons.

From early times the underlying soft dull red Carboniferous Keele Beds sandstone was quarried to provide building stone for the town and it is clear that material from the Roman city was recycled in some of the major buildings.[5] But it is with a distinctive group of stone-built houses dating from the 13th and 14th centuries that this study commences. Some have substantial physical remains, others are known from drawings and some are inferred from documentary references. All are contained within the defensive town walls, and two at least actually use the stub of the wall as foundations. As

The inner face of Shrewsbury Castle

a group they have a common denominator in that the hall, the main living area, is at first-floor level above an undercroft. The castle, as rebuilt in the 1280s, also adopted this form, but it is likely that some of the first-floor hall houses in the town antedate the Edwardian castle and take their style from cultures arriving with the Norman conquistadors, the most influential of whom, in Shropshire, was Roger de Montgomery, a kinsman of William the Conqueror. Roger received vast areas of England as a reward for his services, including Shrewsbury and most of Shropshire. He was created the first Earl of Shrewsbury and was responsible for building the earlier castle which caused the inhabitants of the town so much aggravation, destroying as it did, 51 existing houses.[6]

Stone-built First-floor Hall Houses

2 Pride Hill

To generations of Salopians this building was known variously as Bennet's Hall or The Old Mint; the latter on account of the belief that the travelling Royal Mint was housed in the property during the Civil War, the former because a deed of 1378 exists which refers to 'A tenement formerly called Benneteshalle opposite the Hey-strete'. The deed is in the Cartulary of Haughmond Abbey, but recent work on the Cartulary has established that Bennet's Hall stood on the adjoining site, 1 Pride Hill, now occupied by Lloyd's Bank. Even so, 2 Pride Hill, according to the tenurial history, seems to have been all part of the same holding, at one time the property of the powerful Ludlow family of Stokesay Castle fame whose wealth derived from wool.[7]

North-west view of 2 Pride Hill, traced from an undated sketch by J. Buckler (Bod. MS Top. Salop C2 f.12)

Carved capital on fireplace jamb at 2 Pride Hill

Whatever the origins, the medieval remains of a first-floor hall house are now incorporated into a modern shop and are beautifully exposed. A transverse wall containing the fireplace and two flanking doorways divided the hall from a smaller room behind. The fireplace had a wood and plaster smoke hood or 'fumbrell' similar to those whose profiles remain at Stokesay in the north tower and at Moreton Corbet in the solar tower; both relating to stone jambs and capitals of *c*.1200. It is, perhaps, the jamb capitals of the fireplace at 2 Pride Hill which are the property's chief architectural features. The left one is well preserved and is a remarkably fine piece of stone carving with deeply undercut foliage, suggesting a date of *c*.1250-1260 (see illustration on rear cover).[8]

The springing for the arch of the entrance door is on the long left-hand wall and so access to the hall would have been from a passage and a flight of steps down the left side of the property which was set gable-end on to Pride Hill. Two arches of the undercroft are preserved at the lower level and these are also contained within the transverse wall. The doorway to the right of the fireplace has more elaborate treatment than that to the left and consists of an arch within an arch, the left jamb doing double duty as a jamb for the fireplace.

The plan deviates from the normal lay-out of a medieval hall house but perhaps boundary restrictions and the exigencies of the site dictated the unusual positions of the main features. The rear gable wall was briefly exposed in 1986 during the construction of the Pride Hill Shopping Centre.[9]

Vaughan's Mansion

This was a larger complex than 2 Pride Hill, but of a similar date. It occupied a site on the western side of the Square. The remains are incorporated into the Music Hall, whilst the first-floor hall is used as the lounge/bar. Old illustrations show the complex to have been U-shaped, with the buildings grouped around a courtyard.[10] The whole of the front wall of the hall is intact and, within the Music Hall, a section of it is visible behind a plastic sheet. Particularly interesting are the two stone window frames complete with three-quarter round moulding, the timber screen, though much restored, at the upper or 'dais' end of the

Vaughan's Mansion from the courtyard in 1780
(SRRC 6001/5326 f.5)

215

Top: Vaughan's Mansion from College Hill (SRRC 6001/200 p.284)
Lower: From the corner of Swan Hill / College Hill
(SRRC 6001/200 p.290)
Below: Roof as drawn by J. Buckler in 1821

hall and the pointed-arched doorway on the rear wall which gave access onto College Hill. Such a rear doorway is an unusual feature to find in a hall of this kind but, again, perhaps the lie of the land made this extra exit desirable.

Viewed from The Square, a service wing occupied the left side of the plot, then came the hall with its roof set parallel to The Square and its entrance at the lower or service end approached from a flight of steps, next was a small linking block and, at right angles, another small unit and a larger range which was, presumably, the solar wing. The latter had yet another wing which had its gable towards Swan Hill. This probably housed a private chapel. Much of the stonework of the solar wing may be seen from Swan Hill. A tie-beam bearing a shield with the initials M.R.M. and the date 1620 has recently been uncovered on the gable facing Market Street. This could relate to a member of the Mytton family who are known to have occupied Vaughan's Mansion after it passed to them through marriage with the Vaughans in the 14th century.[11] The 17th-century date probably indicates a remodelling of the solar at that time. It is said that the cellars below the service wing were adapted at one time to house debtors awaiting trial in the courtroom above the Market Hall in The Square, but documentary evidence seems to be lacking.

Judging from Buckler's drawing of the roof as he saw it in 1821 the present roof is a faithful copy of the one which

Charlton Hall
Top left: As it appeared in 1818 (SRRC 6001/5326 f.10)
Centre: Mid-13th century, as drawn by
J. Buckler in 1821
Lower: The rear of the Hall, c.1325,
as it appeared in 1818 (SRRC 6001/5326 f.9)
Top right: With mid-16th century addition,
as drawn by J. Buckler in 1821

was destroyed by fire in 1917. It is basically a hammer-beam roof, though the hammer-beams are light. delicate timbers; but the heavy side purlins and fully-foiled cusped and pierced windbraces are more typically Welsh border style carpentry. However, the roof sits uncomfortably on the stone walls and is unlikely, even in the pre-fire version, to be original. Whole roofs were often brought in from other buildings, when necessary, perhaps during a refurbishing programme. Its original form was more likely to have been of the crown-post type.

Charlton Hall

Unfortunately, little survives of this complex which occupied the corner of Market Street and Shoplatch.

Drawings made by John Buckler, the architect and topographical artist, in 1821, suggest that it was the largest and most imposing of this group of buildings and included a hall at first-floor level to which the building licence of 1325, granted to Sir John de Charleton, probably relates.[12] However, the drawings show the remains of what was possibly a large ground-floor hall at right-angles to the other. Sir John de Charleton of Apley Castle near Wellington married Hawis, a Welsh princess of the Powis dynasty, and they are recorded as donors of the east window in St. Mary's church sometime

217

between 1332 and 1353.[13] It is possible, though conjectural, that Sir John began in Shrewsbury by building a ground-floor hall, found life at this level was untenable and was obliged to resort to building a more defensive house. The first-floor hall block appears to have been remodelled in the 15th century to become a great chamber block, but still with the remains of the ground-floor hall attached to it.[14]

Old Salopians remember the site of the first-floor hall house as occupied by the Theatre Royal, and at the rear of the building is a substantial stretch of medieval stonework which must relate to Charlton Hall. Unfortunately, any distinctive features have been removed. A measure of the theatre's former glory remains in the decorative plaster-work on the frontage although the top storey which displays the plaster swags must relate to an enlargement and remodelling after 1834.[15]

Others in this group include:

Bellstone Hall

On the site of the Morris Hall in Bellstone. Both Buckler and Owen show this with 16th- or 17th-century additions to an older chamber, probably a solar, over an undercroft. Two beautiful lancet windows lighted the chamber which, in Owen's time, was 'a very handsome drawing room'. He describes 'its unusual loftiness and the sharp gothic arch of the roof'. Presumably in 1808 it still had its open timber roof.[16]

West view of Bellstone Hall by J. Buckler in 1823

Shute's Place

This was a large complex which occupied the north-west corner of The Square. Parts of it are incorporated into the 'Hole in the Wall' public house, but it is difficult to interpret them. In Drayton's Passage stood what was probably the private chapel of Shute's Place. An old illustration shows that it had an elaborately moulded arched doorway at ground level and a note on the drawing states that it was 'formerly owned by the monks of Haughmond whose property it was before the Dissolution'.[17] The upper storey later

Chapel (?) at Shute's Place (SRRC 6001/5326 f.1)

became the printing works of Adnitt and Naunton where, by custom and in the belief that they worked in a consecrated building, the staff refrained from swearing. It is now all part of the Hole in the Wall.

The Shearmen's Hall, 2 Milk Street

The site is now occupied by solicitors' offices. Significantly, the Shearmen, an important guild of woolmen, had a stone-built first-floor hall for their headquarters, but nothing remains of the old structure. Owen describes several 14th-century-styled windows, an octagonal stone chimney and a spacious vault, and Buckler's drawing of 1821 confirms this.[18]

Cole's Hall

This was located on the south side of Hill's Lane. It had a pointed-arched doorway at ground level and may have been a private chapel serving another large complex. It was demolished in 1934.[19]

South-east side of Shearmen's Hall,
as drawn by J. Buckler in 1821

North-east view of Cole's Hall,
(Bod. MS Top. Salop C2, f.20)

17 St. Mary's Street incorporating
'The Loggerheads' in Church Street

The properties described above are the better known examples in the group; others such as Stury's Hall and Burgh's Hall may be deduced from documentary sources. Burgh's Hall probably occupied a large area between High Street and Fish Street to the south of the old Cross Keys Inn on the corner of Grope Lane. Sir John Burgh was a major figure in Shropshire and the Welsh Marches during the 15th century and he held various properties in Shrewsbury. Extensive portions of a sandstone wall probably belonging to Burgh's Hall have recently been examined.[20]

Some properties such as that on the corner of Church Street and St. Mary's Street, part of which is occupied by the Loggerheads Inn, have the dimensions and give the overall impression of the siting of similar first-floor halls. Fragments of dressed stonework often come to light during excavations and renovations. In the cellars of 14 and 15 Pride Hill are a pointed-arched doorway and a shouldered or 'Caernarvon'-arched doorway respectively. These appear to belong to a very large stone complex whose property boundary, though not the structure, probably relates to the 11th or 12th century.[21] The cellar of The Yorkshire House in St. Mary's Place has walls of dressed stonework identical to that in the early 13th-century work in St. Mary's church. The site, so close to the church, was probably part of the church's ancillary buildings, perhaps part of its college, although this was thought to be in St. Mary's Street, opposite the churchyard.[22]

Company guilds other than the Shearmen also had their trade halls. The Mercers, Taylors and Weavers each had a hall but although the sites are known nothing remains of the buildings.[23] Less wealthy guilds would have to rent a room somewhere. The most powerful guild, that of the Drapers, rebuilt their hall in the late 16th century, and that building is described in the following chapter.

In addition to those hall houses which were entirely stone-built, some had stone undercrofts and timber-framed superstructures. Two have been fully recorded recently:[24]

Rigg's Hall, Castle Gates

Incorporated into the Library building the part that contains the most interesting surviving details is probably a solar unit above a stone undercroft. It has crown-post roof construction at each end and a central truss of open arch-braced collar-beam form. This is an unusual combination although a similar example occurs in the north-west wing of Gawsworth Hall in Cheshire.[25] Cusping is used freely at Rigg's Hall, internally on the down-swinging braces to the crown-posts and externally on the angle-braces of the framework. During restoration in the early 1980s it was found that red ochre had been used as a wash both inside and outside. Rigg's Hall is one example where the stump of the town wall was used as the foundation of a late medieval house. The whole Library complex, for hundreds of years the home of Shrewsbury School, is a mixture of buildings dating from the 13th to the 19th centuries. A dendro date of 1405-35 was obtained for the solar block and 1413-43 for what was probably a contemporary hall block at right-angles which is also of crown-post roof construction, though much plainer. Documentary evidence points to the complex being built for David Holebatch, a prominent lawyer and bailiff of Shrewsbury in 1412-13. He had been granted leave to build on the site in 1401-2.[26]

Interior of Rigg's Hall after restoration

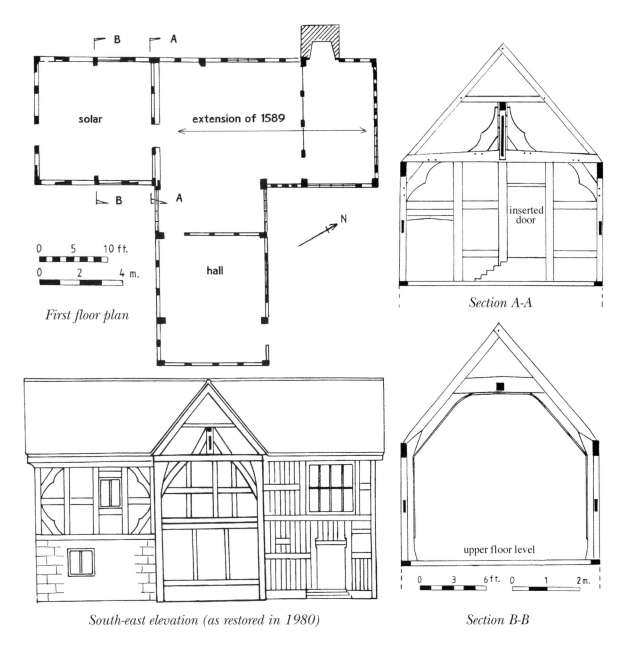

B   A

solar   extension of 1589

B   A

0   5   10 ft.

0   2   4 m.

First floor plan

hall

N

inserted
door

Section A-A

upper floor level

0   3   6 ft.   0   1   2 m.

South-east elevation (as restored in 1980)

Section B-B

Rigg's Hall

11 Pride Hill

At present this is a fast-food outlet. The property incorporates the remains of a 14th-century house which had two timber-framed stories above the stone undercroft and also utilised the stump of the town wall for its foundation. Surviving features include an ogee-headed window, a flight of steps from the level of Pride Hill running along the western side of the plot and giving access to the terrace in front of the house, the garderobe tower and a wool merchant's trade mark on the jamb of a window.[27] The trade mark is based on the '4' symbol, thought to be derived from the *Agnus Dei*, and is similar to others used by known wool merchants.[28]

There may have been others having a combination of stone undercroft and timber-framed superstructure. J.H. Parker describes a framed house 'in the High Street, the lower storey of

Garderobe tower   *Ogee window*   *Merchant's mark*

11 Pride Hill

which is half underground and vaulted in the manner usual in the fourteenth [century]'.[29] So far, however, this has eluded searches and he may have confused High Street with Pride Hill.

Building behind the Barge Inn, 45 Wyle Cop

This was demolished in the 1930s. It was described as stone-built, 14th century in date and measuring 40ft. x 20ft. It had a fireplace in the upper storey and 'massive oak principals carrying the roof'.[30] The description suggests another first-floor hall house with a stone under-croft and a timber-framed superstructure.

In the Haughmond Cartulary there are 128 entries relating to properties in Shrewsbury, including the suburbs, in which the abbey had an interest. Only one, Roger Reyner's house, is specifically described as 'stone-built' and, of course, its form is not mentioned, but it would be surprising if some did not have a hall at first-floor level. There are two entries each relating to '2 shops with their appurtenances and superstructure' which suggest stone-built ground floors with timber-framed upper stories, and one other simply as '4 shops and their solars'. The dates range between 1200 and 1294.[31] Apart from the Cartulary there are references to 'shops and solars' in numerous medieval deeds relating to Shrewsbury.[32] In these the position of the hall, assuming one was provided, is conjectural. But it suggests that the shops were not 'lock-up' shops and that the shopkeepers lived over them, unlike the situation which pertained to some fully timber-framed structures later on.

A recent detailed study of taxation records for Shrewsbury between 1297 and 1332 reveals that the town enjoyed really solid commercial prosperity in those early days. Merchants dealt in wool, cloth, spices, furs and other luxury goods and had connections with London. Their houses would, naturally, reflect their wealth, and judging from their taxable assets they lived in some style, had tapestried walls, wore jewellery, ate well and were conscious of their obligations to royalty when the monarch spent time at the castle. Wool was the dominant factor, Shrewsbury had advantageous trading privileges, was a major entrepôt for borderland wool and home to the man who has been described as 'probably the most famous merchant of the day', Nicholas de Ludlowe, who died in 1279. His two sons John and Laurence were also highly successful. Laurence was able to rebuild Stokesay Castle and John's son was reckoned to be the richest inhabitant of Shrewsbury by quite a margin and held that position throughout the period under study.[33]

Timber-framed Hall Houses

With such a solid background, secure on its peninsula site, guarded by a strong castle and town walls, and with the Welsh threat in decline Shrewsbury's wealthier inhabitants could afford to change the concept of living above an undercroft in a semi-fortified stone house to the cheaper and more convenient form of an entirely timber-framed house where the hall could be sited at ground level. From c.1350 to c.1500 there was great spate of such construction and it seems that the crown-post roof was the type most favoured. In these the support comes from a centrally-placed upright (the crown-post) which has lateral and longitudinal bracing; there are usually no side purlins. A number remain in the town and make an interesting study. No two are alike but they all conform to a local pattern of having down-swinging lateral braces, sometimes cusped. Often the crown-posts are of cruciform or T-section so that they straddle the tie-beam and enable a very firm joint to be made. These framed houses were of 'box-frame' construction but the alternative technology of 'cruck-frame' was probably also used. At present only three of the latter type are known in Shrewsbury and they occur in the suburbs. As pressure on space increased the cruck houses were not as easily enlarged as the box-frames and this could be the reason why they are no longer seen within the loop of the river. Shortage of space in the expanding town was another reason for the number of 'double-pile' or 'tandem' houses that were built, where a twin unit was part of the original plan or was added to an existing house to increase the accommodation. The primary double-pile houses may be recognised by the way in which the two units are joined with a post whose head is thickened on both sides, known as a double-jowl post.

The following descriptive list includes examples of the town's great wealth of 14th- and 15th-century timber-framed houses. It is not exhaustive, and much more remains to be discovered:

12a Butcher Row/12 Fish Street, and Bear Steps Hall

The range of 12a Butcher Row and 12 Fish Street, which effectively closes Butcher Row in the heart of the medieval town, is the earliest scientifically-dated timber-framed building in Shrewsbury. It is a domestic range which has a decorative crown-post roof. Originally its jettied frontage, with up-and-down cusped bracing echoing the cusped longitudinal bracing to the crown-posts, overlooked St. Alkmund's churchyard and the then market place. It is dendro-dated to 1358-9.

Later, Bear Steps Hall, with a crown-post roof of plainer form, was added as a tandem block, obliterating the outlook of the older building. The new hall, which refused to produce a felling-date despite promising samples, was probably designed as an administrative building of some kind. It was later extended as a storied range towards Fish Street and this produced a felling-date of 1576-7. The balcony was probably added very shortly afterwards. Structurally it is not an integral part of the extension, but it produced a similar felling-date range.

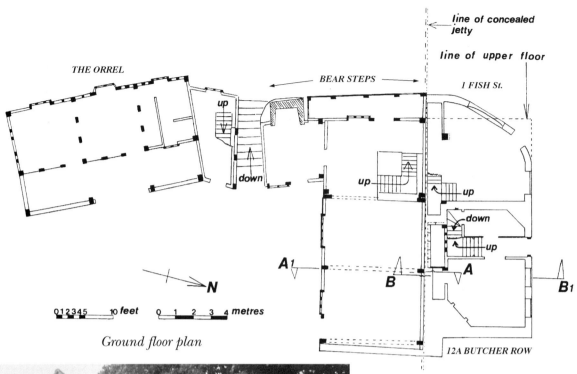

THE ORREL

BEAR STEPS

line of concealed jetty

line of upper floor

1 FISH St.

up

down

up

up

up

down

up

A₁

B

A

B₁

N

0 1 2 3 4 5   10 feet   0 1 2 3 4 metres

Ground floor plan

12A BUTCHER ROW

The Bear Steps complex as seen from St. Alkmund's churchyard to the north-east

Left: 12A Butcher Row / 1 Fish Street

Right: Section A-A₁

The Orrel, Bear Steps, 1 Fish Street and 12A Butcher Row

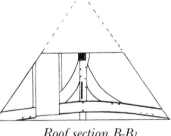

Roof section B-B₁

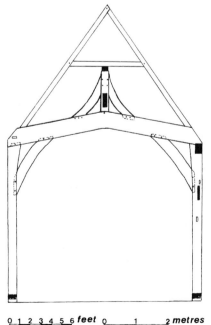

0 1 2 3 4 5 6 feet   0   1   2 metres

224

Fish Street with Bear Steps complex on the left

The 'Orrel', a framed range with shops at two levels, is part of the complex and is linked to the hall by a small unit which contains two fireplaces of Grinshill stone. The 'Orrel' is dendro-dated to 1601. The steps which led to the 'Bear' inn on the corner of Fish Street and Grope lane, another framed and jettied medieval building, run below the linking block.

In 1968 the whole complex was saved by the Civic Society from complete demolition by the borough council, restored and handed back to the Corporation.[34]

The Old Mansion, St. Mary's Street

The only approach to this building is from a narrow passage leading off St. Mary's Street. It has an unprepossessing brick frontage of three stories and uncharacteristic frontal chimneystacks. Inside, the block divides into four phases of building and a fifth may be added if the stone undercroft with its spiral staircase is accepted as a remnant of a yet earlier phase. There is a curious feature in the upper part of the long walls of the undercroft: battered panels divided as though to provide lighting. It is clear that this could only work if the stonework once continued to a higher level. Furthermore, the present superstructure does not exactly fit onto the perimeters of the undercroft and it is therefore suggested that the undercroft belonged to a 13th-century hall house which preceded the timber-framed open-hall house, parts of which remain and are dendro-dated to 1366.

Of this phase three crown-post roof trusses remain, delineating a two-bay hall. One soulace, a straight brace between the rafter and the collar-beam, was found, but there was evidence for more in all the other common-rafter couples. Very few soulaced roofs are known in Shropshire, and this one suggests an outside influence combined with a strong local tradition. The lower braces between the principal posts and the tie-beam are arched, producing a perfect ogee when allied with the lateral down-swinging concave braces to the

The Old Mansion, St. Mary's Street

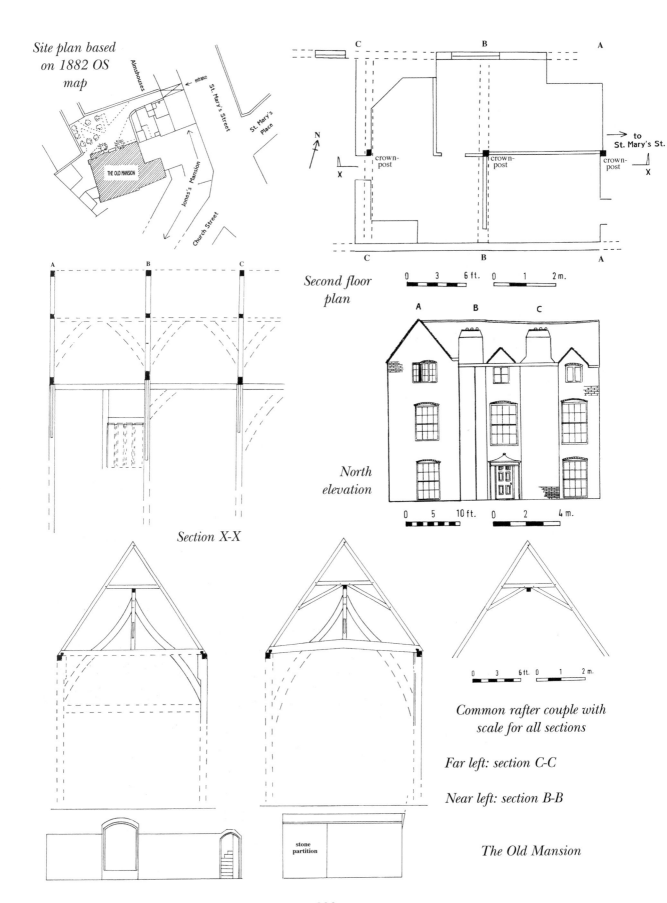

Site plan based on 1882 OS map

Second floor plan

0   3   6 ft.   0   1   2 m.

Section X-X

North elevation

0   5   10 ft.   0   2   4 m.

0   3   6 ft.   0   1   2 m.

Common rafter couple with scale for all sections

Far left: section C-C

Near left: section B-B

The Old Mansion

226

*Thomas Jones' staircase
in the Old Mansion*

crown-posts. The timbers are smoke-blackened and there is slight evidence for a louvre.

The hall range was later extended in two directions and later still a close-studded range with twin gables was added, filling in the south-west corner of the plot. This contains a superb open-well staircase with wide treads, carved finials and carved flat balusters. A felling-date range of 1615-49 was obtained for these features including an ovolo-moulded mullioned window.[35]

Although there is some controversy regarding the actual location of 'Jones' Mansion' it is generally thought to be the Old Mansion. 'Jones' Mansion' is mentioned frequently by historians and shown on the 1882 and subsequent O.S. maps. Thomas Jones was the first Mayor of Shrewsbury, having previously served as Bailiff and Sheriff for the county. His mayoralty occurred in 1638, and he is reputed to have acted as host to Prince Rupert, then known as Prince Robert, in 1642 during the Civil War.[36] A plaque at the stairhead gives the dates of Jones' civic appointments and was certainly there in 1808 when it was noted by the antiquary H. Owen of Owen and Blakeway fame.[37]

111/112 Frankwell

These appear to be two semi-detached houses of early 15th-century date, each having a two-bay frontage with cusped up and down bracing and a side passage. That belonging to no.111 still has its wooden 'Caernarvon'-arched doorway. The large dormer gable and the smaller dormer windows are later additions.

The King's Head, Mardol

A double-pile house, it originally had twin gables facing the street. The double-jowl post is a prominent feature of the frontage, and from this a

111/112 Frankwell

wall-plate, which still bears the seatings of the rafters on either side, runs back. On the soffit of the northern side of this plate are stave holes which have rounded corners, noticed elsewhere in Shropshire as an early feature. It is possible that both units had crown-post roofs. When the roof was realigned to give the appearance of a building set parallel to the street the original tie-beams became a wall-plate. Jettied at two levels and with large flat joists and (restored) trac-eried windows, the building has cusped decoration and open framing on the exterior. Bull-nosed joists are exposed on the upper storey but concealed with coving on the lower story. The

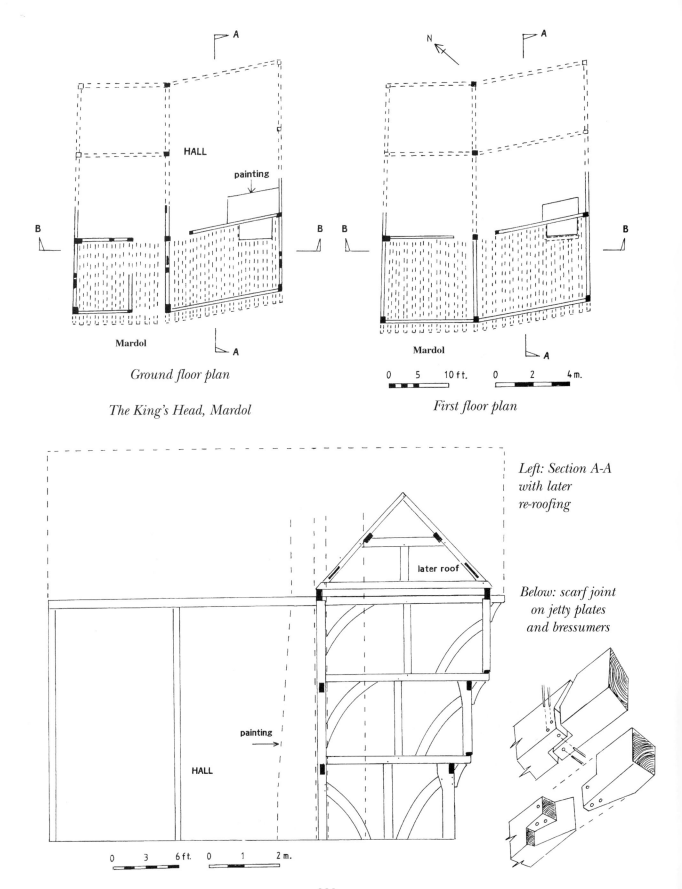

Ground floor plan

The King's Head, Mardol

First floor plan

0   5   10 ft.   0   2   4 m.

Left: Section A-A
with later
re-roofing

Below: scarf joint
on jetty plates
and bressumers

HALL

painting

Mardol

HALL

painting

later roof

0   3   6 ft.   0   1   2 m.

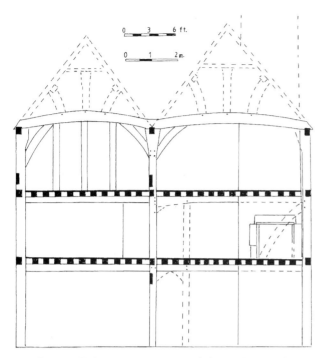

Section B-B *(reconstruction of the earlier roof)*

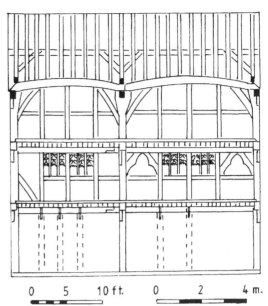

South-west, street, elevation
(reconstruction with roof rebuilt at 90°

Outline of painting on chimneystack (Last Supper and Annunciation)

The King's Head, Mardol

original building is dendro-dated to 1404, the year following the battle of Shrewsbury.[38] The two rear 'wings' are simply continuations of the original gable-end units, but they had their roof-lines lowered in the remodelling.

Recently a wallpainting on a chimneybreast at ground level was uncovered. It has three sections or 'registers'; centrally a depiction of the Last Supper, above is a symbolic lion, and below is the Annunciation with the figures of Mary, the angel Gabriel, the dove, the lily-pot and the 'Ave Maria' scroll—all familiar motifs in Annunciation scenes. The painting

The King's Head, Mardol (1404)

probably belongs to the period *c*.1450-1520 and has some similarities with that of the Last Judgement in Cound church.[39] There is also painting on the reverse side of the chimney, though this is not pictorial and is applied with stencils (for more on these paintings see pp.323-5). The chimney is located in the southern rear 'wing' which suggests that this unit was an open hall at the time of the remodelling. The fact that the chimney is brick-built indicates an early use of brick in the town.

12-14 Mardol

Currently subdivided into three commercial premises, this was originally a three-storied double-pile block bounded by Hill's Lane. The street-facing range was jettied at two levels and probably housed shops with chambers above. The end of the moulded bressumer where it butts up to the drainpipe of the adjoining premises, itself an encroachment, is visible from the street. The rear block has a smaller span but accommodated living quarters, presumably for the merchant

Evidence for a smoke louvre in rear unit of 13 Mardol—the short horizontal is a 'trimmer' defining the area of the louvre, and the small rafter on the right is part of the later infilling

12-14 Mardol

or landlord who owned the block. A two-bay solar of arch-braced collar-beam construction is sited at the end nearest Hill's Lane, each bay measuring 8ft. 9ins. (2.67m.). A single-bay hall which measures 9ft. 10ins. (3m.) is located in the same plane next to the solar. This contains evidence for a smoke louvre. The fire itself must have been placed at second-floor level, a not impossible situation as other open hearths at upper-floor levels have been noted. The wind-bracing continues into no.12, suggesting that its rear unit functioned as the service end.

92 Frankwell

At the southern end of no.14 it is possible to identify a cross passage running through the front and rear units, suggesting that although the block had a commercial use it was also a home, and the family probably had use of the chambers over the shops. A curious detail of the framing is the way in which the ends of the collar-beams are raised to accommodate clasped purlins.

11 Mardol

Although this is a separate building from 12-14 and has been modernised to a much greater degree, it contains a few interesting features: cusped barge-boards on the western gable, a wheel hoist in the rear wing, lime pebble-dash on the internal partition wall of the front unit, later wallpapered over, and a drain-head at the rear with the date 1700 and the initials JP.

92 Frankwell

Exposed in the gable wall is the central truss of a two-bay cruck-framed hall house. The house was truncated when Drinkwater Street was driven through it in 1882.[40]

St. Chad's Almshouses (SRRC 6001/5326 f.50)

St. Chad's Almshouses (demolished) These stood on the south side of the cemetery, projecting into the street now known as Belmont. They were founded in 1409 and must have been taken down soon after 1808. Originally 13 in number, they had been reduced to five by that date. An old watercolour shows them to have been single-cell dwellings, and in the gable end a very substantial box-framed truss is shown. This has a tie-beam and a collar-beam, with a central king-strut between the two. One corner post is illustrated and this has a thickened head and a tension brace. The details are compatible with a building date of 1409.[41]

Above: Carved ogee-arched doorhead at the Nag's Head hall
Far left: The Nag's Head (1421)
Left: Remains of the Nag's Head hall (1419)

The Nag's Head

The Nag's Head hall, Wyle Cop

At the rear of the public house are the remains of a hall house which had a crown-post roof with six-way bracing. The screens passage, three service doorways with ogee-heads and the whole of the spere-truss remain. There is rich decoration in the form of cusping and billet-moulding. Old photographs show that the hall was two-bayed, had cusped braces in the wall-frame and extended as far as the inner town wall, which means that the solar was located above the service end, a common arrangement in town houses on cramped sites. The house was located between the inner and the outer town wall and is dendro-dated to 1421. The Nag's Head itself, which is contained within the street-facing range, appears to be part of the same building programme, the same felling-date was established for a corner post linking the two buildings.[42] The street-facing range has a deep front jetty and cusped windbraces in a side-purlin roof. Recent repair work revealed that the upper storey had panels with up-and-down cusped bracing similar to that noted in 111/112 Frankwell, Rigg's Hall and 12A Butcher Row.

Clive House, College Hill

The remains of a medieval hall house are incorporated into an 18th-century town house which was leased to Lord Clive when he was M.P. for Shrewsbury. What appear to be two service doorways in the screens passage

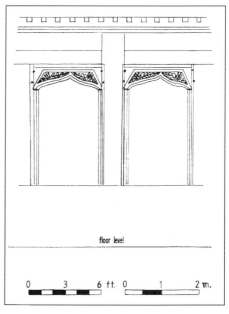

Clive House, College Hill
Ornamental doors as
indicated on the plan on.p.235

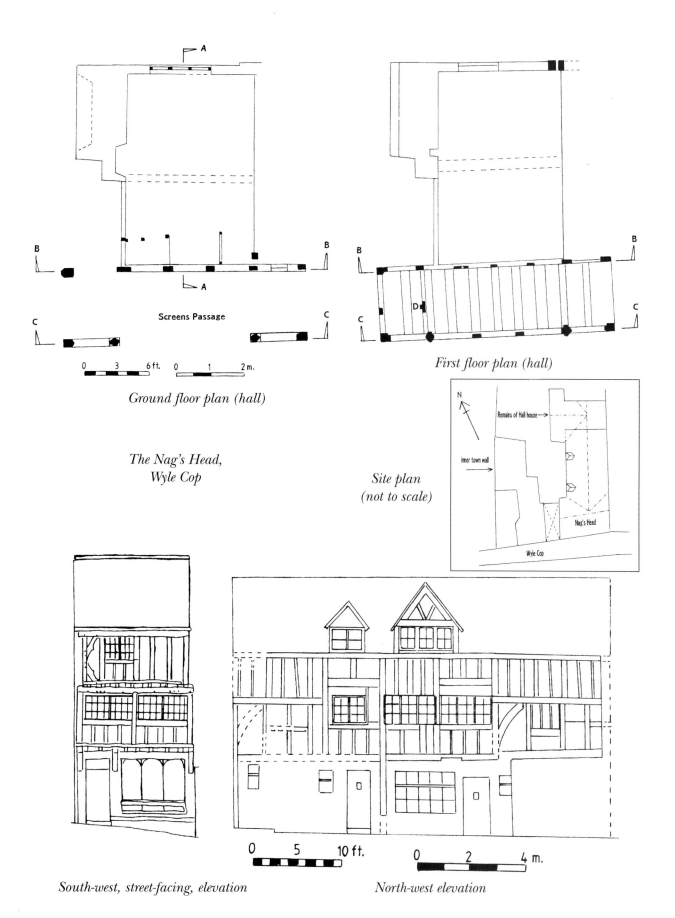

A

B   B

C   C

Screens Passage

B   B

D

C   C

0   3   6 ft.   0   1   2 m.

Ground floor plan (hall)

First floor plan (hall)

The Nag's Head,
Wyle Cop

N

Remains of Hall house →

inner town wall →

Nag's Head

Wyle Cop

Site plan
(not to scale)

0   5   10 ft.   0   2   4 m.

South-west, street-facing, elevation

North-west elevation

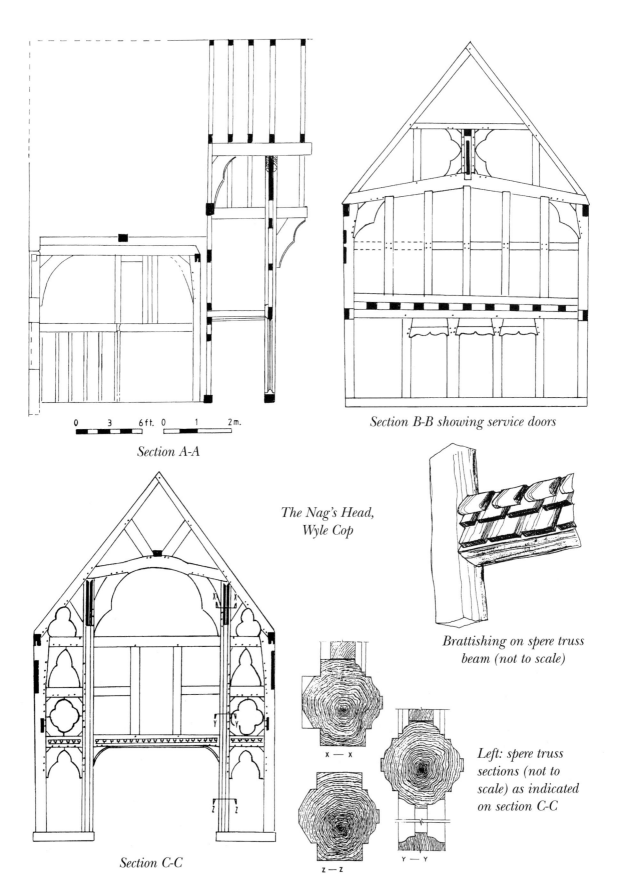

Section A-A

0   3   6ft. 0   1   2m.

Section B-B showing service doors

The Nag's Head,
Wyle Cop

Brattishing on spere truss
beam (not to scale)

Section C-C

X — X

Z — Z

Y — Y

Left: spere truss
sections (not to
scale) as indicated
on section C-C

234

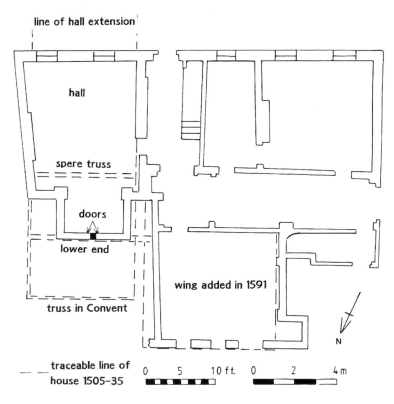

line of hall extension

hall

spere truss

doors

lower end

truss in Convent

wing added in 1591

N

_ _ traceable line of
house 1505-35

0   5   10 ft.   0   2   4 m

Ground floor plan

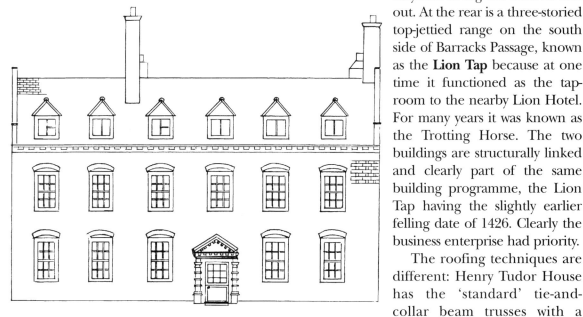

South elevation (not to scale)

Clive House, College Hill

of the old house are preserved in the drawing room, but they may be insertions. However, they have carved and moulded door-cases, the carving similar to that over an internal upper door in the Nag's Head hall. The relative position of the spere-truss has also been established.

Henry Tudor House, Wyle Cop
Reputedly where Henry VII stayed on his way to the battle of Bosworth in 1485, this is an imposing block, dendro-dated to 1430-31. It is jettied at two levels and has a wide cart-entry dividing the building into domestic and commercial halves. External decoration includes cusping, moulding and (restored) traceried windows. Over the entry is a projecting bay window, perhaps for the tallyman to log the carts in and out. At the rear is a three-storied top-jettied range on the south side of Barracks Passage, known as the **Lion Tap** because at one time it functioned as the tap-room to the nearby Lion Hotel. For many years it was known as the Trotting Horse. The two buildings are structurally linked and clearly part of the same building programme, the Lion Tap having the slightly earlier felling date of 1426. Clearly the business enterprise had priority.

The roofing techniques are different: Henry Tudor House has the 'standard' tie-and-collar beam trusses with a central king-strut and curved queen-struts and cusped wind-braces echoing the cusping on

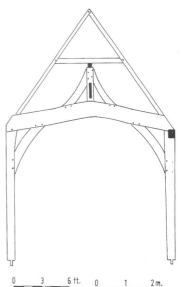

Above left: Henry Tudor House (1430)
Above right: the Lion Tap, Barracks Passage, of 1426
Lower right: typical crown-post truss (as original)
in the Lion Tap, Barracks Passage

the external timbers, while the Lion Tap, has crown-post roof construction. The crown-posts, at 5ft. (1.52m.) tall, are above average height for Shropshire. They are cruciform in plan, the limbs extending the crown-posts by 6ins. (0.15m.) in typical Salopian fashion. Also typical are the down-swinging lateral braces and the way in which crown-post clasps the collar-purlin. At some time the building was altered and side-purlins were introduced together with angle-braces between the tie-beams and the principal rafters. This may have been done in or shortly after 1599 (felling-date) when the end gable wall was rebuilt.

Henry Tudor House and the Lion Tap were probably built for Hugh Wygan, M.P. for Shrewsbury, as a commercial invest-ment. In 1429, shortly after completion, it was sold to the brewer, Nicholas Clement. It was in the possession of Nicholas Waring, a merchant, in 1474. During the 15th century the Lion Tap was used as a brewhouse and evidence of this activity remained in the building until recently. At one time it was part of the estate of the Gibbons family.[43]

On the street front the lower unit on the south side, known as **Davey's**, also had a jettied front and was probably an integral part of Henry Tudor House. It has a tandem block at the

Ogee-headed doorway in Compasses Passage

rear which is distinguished by a deeply-cut, ogee-headed doorway. This feature is visible from Compasses Passage.

Mytton's Mansion, 66/67 Wyle Cop

This is a similar range to Henry Tudor House though less elaborate and having a smaller, though well moulded and coved entrance passageway which would admit a donkey train but not large carts. Again, jettied at two levels with exposed bull-nosed joists and another tallyman's(?) window over the entry. Reputedly, this was the home of Thomas Mytton, county sheriff, whose task it was to deal with the Earl of Richmond, later Henry VII, when he demanded entry to Shrewsbury in 1485.

Range incorporating Mytton's Mansion behind and to the left of the car

The Drapers' Almshouses

(demolished)

In 1444 Degury Watur, one of the wardens of the Drapers' Guild, founded the almshouses which stood on the south-western boundary of St. Mary's churchyard. These, like St. Chad's almshouses (p.231), were single-cell dwellings and in 1808 they numbered 16. An illustration by P. Vandyke Browne, a part-time drawing master at Shrewsbury School, shows each of them with a tall front chimney, probably added in the 17th century. They were taken down in 1825 and replaced by a row on the opposite side of the street. These, in turn, were demolished in the 1960s, the present almshouses being in Salter's Lane, Longden Coleham.[44]

The Booth Hall, The Square

(demolished)

Like its predecessor this was some-times called the Guildhall, and closed The Square on the north-eastern side. Built in 1452, it was an

The Drapers' Almshouses (SRRC 6001/5326 f.56)

The Booth Hall (Guildhall) as drawn in 1774. The Shelds is the timber-framed range on the left, the arch in the centre of the picture probably leads to the covered passage, and the shops and courtroom are to the left of the tower (SRRC 6001/200 p.189)

L-shaped timber-framed building which gave access to The Square through a covered passage. The main block housed shops at ground level and a large courtroom above. Other rooms were contained in the wing, and there was also a three-storied strong stone tower, built in 1490 and known as the 'Exchequer tower' which held the town records, charters, money and other valuables. The complex was taken down in 1783 and replaced with John Hiram Haycock's Shirehall which was confined to the south-eastern side, hitherto an open space with the town's pond.[45]

The Shelds (demolished)
Many market towns had a row of stalls (Latin *selda*, stall) which began as temporary structures, were later consolidated and often finished as quite elaborate buildings. Shrewsbury's *seldae*, known as the Shelds, were on the north-western side of The Square, opposite the Booth Hall. They were described as 'two-storied timber tenements of a very simple type' and, in their final stage, are shown in old illustrations of the Booth Hall.[46]

The Abbot's House

The Abbot's House
Situated on the corner of Butcher Row and Fish Street, this is one of Shrewsbury's 'showpieces'—a fine L-shaped timber-framed block, dendro-dated to a felling date of 1458, jettied at two levels, and with a row of (restored) butchers' shop windows at ground level.[47] Much of the fabric is original, for example the carved corner posts which support the jetties,

Abbot's House, Butcher Row c.1820. Drawing by J.Buckler, engraved by J.C. Varrall (SRRC B2487)

the moulded bressumers, the close-studding to the second storey and some of the framing to the third storey; decorative details such as the carved interlaced arches on the tie-beam and the knopped colonettes on the Butcher Row frontage. One oriel window on the north-east wall of the crosswing appears to retain its original form and has a moulded bracket and head. Three-quarters of the way along the Butcher Row frontage there is a wide cart-entry giving access to the rear of the property.

Above the shops are chambers which may or may not have related directly to the shops, but at third-storey level the space in both ranges was designed for single occupation. The roof structure is uniform in having tie-and-collar-beam trusses with straight queen-posts. The tie-beams are cambered, there are plain curved windbraces and the posts have thickened heads. Large tension braces are present, and they alternate between front and rear posts in every other bay. Of the four bays over the Butcher Row frontage the two northern ones remain open and there is a communicating door between them and the two southern bays.

The crosswing has the same structural form. At third-storey level it consists of two bays subdivided by intermediate trusses into four half-bays. The dimensions of the main timbers are massive, the head of a post on the central truss measures 2ft. (0.61m.) across.

The site had belonged to the Abbot of Lilleshall since the 12th century,[48] and while it may be doubted that the abbot would be content with his town lodging over a row of butchers' shops, the top storey could have provided him with spacious accommodation sufficiently removed from the trade at street level.

An entry in the bailiff's accounts for 1459 indicates that probably by April of that year the site had been prepared and the frame was pre-fabricated and ready for assembly ('*sufficacio*').

A ceremony was held at which the abbot, his carpenter—whose name is not recorded—and some of the town dignitaries were present. Wine circulated and the carpenter received a bonus of 20 pence. The time-lag between the felling date of the timbers and the time when the frame was ready for erection, that is about 12 months, gives a useful reference. The following is a transcript and translation of the entry in the Bailiff's accounts:

Et in den' solut' carpentar' abbatis de Lylleshill pro regardo
ill' dat' in sufficacione domus sue in le Fyschstrete.. xxd
Et in vino dat' dicto abbati eodem tempore pro honestate ville .... xiiijd

And in pence paid to the carpenter of the abbot of Lilleshall for his reward,
given at the *sufficacio* of his house in Fish Street 20d
And in wine given to the said abbot at the same time for the good reputation of the town 14d

Of course, everything turns on the meaning of the word '*sufficacio*' and this is capable of more than one interpretation, but the one mentioned above is that favoured, rather than 'laying a foundation for' or describing a topping out ceremony. The phrase *pro honestate ville* ('for the good reputation of the town') is frequently used in the accounts whenever a distinguished person, such as the Abbot of Lilleshall is concerned. In medieval times Fish Street and Butcher Row were interchangeable names.[49]

Left and above: 2 Milk Street
The view above is of the rear (1566 and 1655)
with the shop on the left of the photograph (1466)

2 Milk Street
This is a multi-phased complex occupying the site next to the old Shearmens' Hall from which it is divided by an entry which at present leads to the hostelry known as the 'Old Post Office Inn'. The oldest part is at the rear and this has close-studding in the upper storey which is jettied. Bull-nosed joists and a bressumer with quarter-round and cavetto moulding support the jetty. Below this is the remains of a moulded shop window and door, in detail very similar to that which survives at the Abbot's House and there is some slight evidence for a further window towards Milk

Street. The felling date of 1467 is only 11 years after that for the Abbot's House. This section retains its original roof structure and this too is similar to that at the Abbot's House except that a central king-strut is positioned between the queen-struts. Similarly, there is a single tier of plain curved windbraces and no smoke-blackening.

The second phase of the development has a felling date of 1566. This was when whoever occupied the Milk Street frontage had it rebuilt to provide a two-storied range, jettied towards the street, and perhaps with two large oriel windows. But in or about 1655 (felling date) the roof was removed and a large half-storey was added. Included in the remodelling were three large gables each with decorative motifs. Internally the new roof structure employed a curious form of upper-cruck-with-spur, but only in one bay at the front at the northern end. At the rear the raised section was framed with diamond-patterning within square panels.

The block, which includes 3 Milk Street, is known to historians as 'Proude's Mansion'. George Proude was a wealthy draper and the felling-date of 1566 accords well with the 1568 date usually quoted for it. What is uncertain is the relationship between the older part at the rear, and the later street-facing range with its vertical extension, but the chronology of the three parts is now quite clear.[50]

The Council House
Built within the outer bailey of the castle, this was the headquarters of the historic Council in the Marches of Wales when it sat at Shrewsbury. Its base was Ludlow Castle. Formed during Edward IV's reign, ratified by Henry VII and finally abolished in 1689, it was both a judicial and administrative body that virtually governed Wales and the border counties to the east of Offa's Dyke. Although the house has extensions of the 17th century and later, the older part consists of two units, a solar crosswing, dendro-dated to 1465-75, which has a roof of tie-and-collar-beam construction with one open arch-braced collar-beam truss and another of the standard Shrewsbury closed-truss form, and a hall range of 1501 where the roof-line is higher. Each range has two tiers of cusped windbraces, those in the hall being of less robust form and having a V-shaped nick cut in the back edge. It seems clear that the hall range was designed to make use of of the roof space as it has a fully-framed floor at attic level and a framed door giving access from the older crosswing which was, presumably, floored across at this time. The hall was truncated at some time and subdivisions of the whole complex has led to difficulties of interpretation, but the felling-date of 1501 coincides with a deed dated 18 September 1500 which specifies a transfer from Elizabeth Kynaston to Peter Newton.[51] Peter Newton was

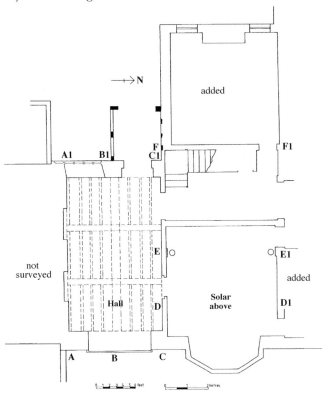

Ground floor plan of the Council House

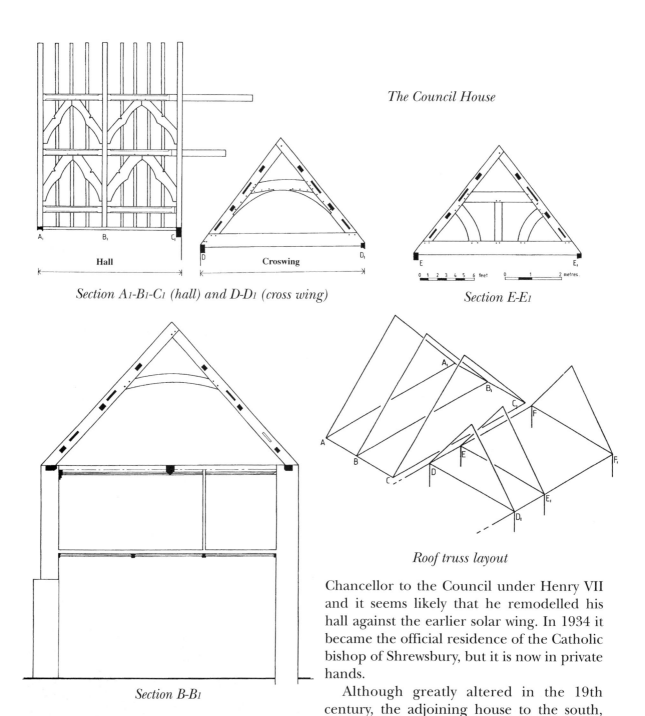

The Council House

Section A₁-B₁-C₁ (hall) and D-D₁ (cross wing)

Section E-E₁

Hall

Croswing

Roof truss layout

Section B-B₁

Chancellor to the Council under Henry VII and it seems likely that he remodelled his hall against the earlier solar wing. In 1934 it became the official residence of the Catholic bishop of Shrewsbury, but it is now in private hands.

Although greatly altered in the 19th century, the adjoining house to the south, Courtyard Cottage, contains many features relating to the Council including plasterwork designs in what would have been the Council Chamber at first-floor level.

18/19 and 20/21 Abbey Foregate

These two properties each contain three cruck trusses and are adjacent to each other with only a 6ins. space between. They probably belonged to the abbey, but their function is unknown. Dendro dates of 1408 for 18/19 and 1430-31 for 20/21 have been obtained.[52] They may once have formed part of a terrace of crucks, perhaps similar to that identified in Barrow Street, Much Wenlock.[53]

St. Chad's Parochial School, Bridge St. (demolished)

The name refers to a building of 1838-9, but an old photograph shows a medieval timber-framed open truss in the half-demolished building. This had either been brought in and reused in the Victorian building or the new building was grafted onto the skeleton of a much older one. The latter is the more likely explanation. The truss had deep-swinging arch-braces to a collar beam, a central boss of some kind, short struts in the spandrels, and principal rafters which crossed at the apex, an unusual feature in box-framed construction. These features were visible from first-floor level but they probably related to a fully-framed two-bay hall, open from ground level.[54]

30 Wyle Cop (Tanner's Wine Lodge, formerly the 'Unicorn')

In about 1890 this large timber-framed block was reconstructed, retaining some of its earlier design. The front elevation now presents a mixture of styles, but in the room above the square-headed entry is part of a 15th-century framed truss which has characteristic jowelled heads to the posts and a massive tie-beam supported by deep curving arch-braces.

The Golden Cross, Princess Street

Jettied towards the street and along Sextry Shut, now known as Golden Cross Passage, this building always had connections with Old St. Chad's church. It is reputed to have been the Sacristy and to have provided lodgings for the Sacristan and other personnel. Until it was removed in 1794, there was an overhead covered passageway which gave access to the church. Stylistically the framework suggests a date in the second half of the 15th century, but a stone doorway in the shut (covered passage) may be a relic from an earlier building.[55]

18/19 and 20/21 Abbey Foregate, a cruck range of 1408 and 1430

15th-century timbers in 30 Wyle Cop

The Golden Cross

51/52 Mardol, *c.*1500

Jettied at two levels towards Mardol, both upper stories have close-spaced vertical timbers without a middle rail. A building of similar date at the rear has a roof of tie-and-collar-beam construction, with a central king-strut and curved queen-posts supporting the clasped purlin. This is similar to the form at Henry Tudor House, although the Mardol building has plain curved windbraces while those at Henry Tudor House are cusped.

62 Mardol

62 Mardol, *c.*1500

A large double-pile house, jettied towards Mardol and with a continuous jetty along Rousehill, this building has a double-jowl post similar to that on the King's Head. The gable end of the rear unit has been altered, but its original roof line may still be seen.[56]

27 Mardol, *c.*1500

This is a four-bay two-storied structure set gable-end on to Mardol and jettied towards the street. The timbers are all verticals and there is no decorative work.

1 Fish Street (Wesley House), *c.*1500.

Another double-pile house, the front is jettied although at present the jetty is obscured and the façade is stuccoed. The rear unit displays open framing with large curved braces to each storey, and the roof is of tie-and-collar-beam construction with straight queen-struts, clasped purlins and large straight windbraces. At ground level and seen from the passage a

27 Mardol

Rear view of 1 Fish Street

178-182 Abbey Foregate

Double-jowel post in wall of 181/2 Abbey Foregate

The Olde House, Dogpole

jowled post marks the division between the units, large curving tension braces on either side confirming that the two units are contemporary.

181-2 Abbey Foregate, *c.*1500
This is a similar double-pile framed house, jettied towards the street and employing clasped purlins in the roof construction. It too has an axial jowled post with flanking braces, the difference lies in the form of the double-pile. Wesley House has parallel roof lines while the two units of 182 Abbey Foregate are accommodated under one ridge. The axial jowled post truss is not weathered and therefore it must have been erected against an existing building, though not the present one. The pegging is from west to east, which tends to support this theory, and the use of such posts in conjunction with a street-facing jetty raises interesting questions regarding the use of jetties. Though not relevant to the building, it is interesting to note an attempt to create a pattern of a bow or a butterfly in the cobbles in front of the premises. This is not a common practice in Shropshire, and is the only example known to the author.

The above examples are the more obvious, but there are remains of others of this period where the details are concealed or tucked away behind later frontages, and in the spate of destruction in the 1950s and '60s Shrewsbury lost, among other medieval treasures, what was probably the finest of its crown-post roofed hall houses at **8a Castle Street**, the old Church Farm Café. This had cusped and ogee-arched detail in its roof.[57] The middle section of the **Lion Hotel** on Wyle cop has a 15th-century roof, and **The Olde House** on Dogpole has evidence of a

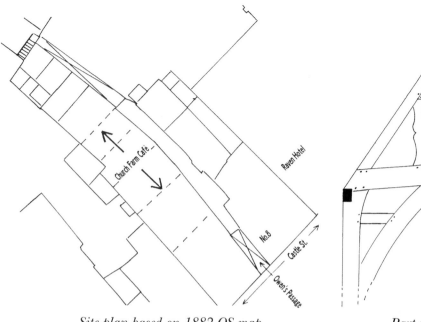

Site plan based on 1882 OS map

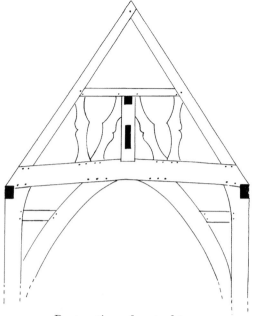

*Part-section of central truss
(not to scale)*

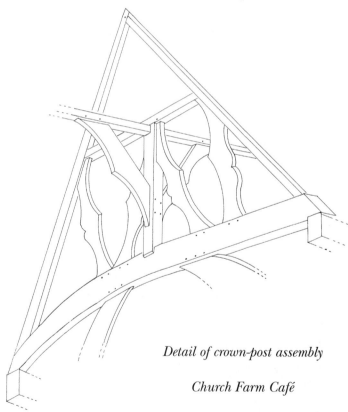

Detail of crown-post assembly

Church Farm Café

jettied front towards the street and fragments of cusped bracing. It is difficult to place this house in a given category because at least six different building phases are present and each is significant. Some of the later features will be described in the appropriate sections.

When, in 1953, J.T. Smith wrote 'Shrewsbury: topography and architecture' for his M.A. thesis he was fortunate to be able to examine and leave a valuable record of many buildings which have since been demolished.[58] These included the Church Farm Café, mentioned above, 160-1 Abbey Foregate which had large curved wall braces, the old Gullet Inn in Hill's Lane which had 15th-century bracing in the wall frame and upper crucks in the roof, and 19 Mardol which old Salopians remember as 'Macfisheries'. The latter had cusped wind-braces and Smith was able to identify a hall and a solar at first-floor level, both with an open roof structure.

It is equally frustrating to read accounts of Shrewsbury buildings by earlier writers such as H.E. Forrest, (1935), and J.B. Blakeway, (1905). The latter in particular had such a sense of the stability of things that it is sometimes difficult to work out exactly where some of the buildings were located.[59] The buildings that Blakeway knew included 'a large old timber tenement with a kind of corridore [*sic*] or piazza in front, of considerable antiquity ...'. This was in Ox Lane, now St. Mary's Street, and seems to have been of a form otherwise unknown in Shrewsbury. In addition he gives tantalising glimpses of, or documentary references to, buildings with names like Romboldsham Hall, Schildeshall in Romboldesham, Sir John Burgh's Hall in High Street (see above), Lord Talbots' inn (mansion) on Dogpole, Hord's Hall in Romboldesham (for which there is a good description), John de Ludlow's Hall in Candle Lane, Betton's Mansion in Wyle Cop (where the rear part contained the foundation of a defensive tower), and stone houses in Romboldesham belonging to Roger Reyner and Juliana de Linlaye. The Bent Stone House (Bellstone Hall) had another stone house adjoining, but the latter must refer to the 16th- or 17th-century additions mentioned above. Finally, Blakeway's description of Jones' Mansion compounds the problem of its location which is posed by Smith's interpretation of Owen's account. If Blakeway is correct there were *two* houses: a stone house and a wooden house on the corner of Church Street off St. Mary's Street. The wooden house must have been an ancestor of the Prince Rupert Hotel and the Old Mansion block, but whether the stone house is represented by the block containing the Loggerheads, mentioned above, is not clear. The medieval houses were owned by Agnes de Hibernia in the late 13th century, and she, in the spirit of her time, gave them to Haughmond Abbey in exchange for masses for the salvation of her soul and those of her family.[60]

Three 15th-century shops at 22-25 Frankwell (demolished in 1982)

It seems reasonably clear that Shrewsbury's wealth in medieval times found expression in the numerous 'shops and solars' and 'halls' revealed by the documents. Whether the stone halls were all at first-floor level is doubtful, bearing in mind Buckler's drawing of Charlton Hall, but the present-day remains of Vaughan's mansion and 2 Pride Hill strongly suggest this arrangement. In the spate of timber-framed construction which followed the stone the hall often seems to have continued at first-floor level. Jettying was popular and this encouraged the retention of the first-floor hall or chamber which could have an open roof. Until 1982, when they were wilfully destroyed, it was still possible to see how three medieval shops functioned in Frankwell. Nos.22-

25 comprised a block of three 15th-century timber-framed shops, each with a chamber above which was jettied towards the street. They were served by a detached rear block which may have been a workshop, a communal kitchen, or both, the approach to which was via a passageway at the end of the block. Smith, in his thesis, castigates an authority which 'can boast of having destroyed one medieval house (Bellstone Hall) and the remains of another (Cole Hall) in the same year (1934) without bothering to record either'. Sadly, the situation became even worse, but a movement mostly led by private enterprise and supported by a growing awareness of the amenity value of historic buildings has brought some pockets of excellent restoration work to the town.

In a description of Shrewsbury in 1926 allowance has to be made for vaguely drawn date boundaries and perhaps some exaggeration, but it shows the impact that the town had on one author, and how greatly it has suffered since. After describing first-floor hall houses with stone ground floors and timber-framed superstructures in French towns such as Cluny, St. Antonin and Amiens, the writer goes on to say '... our own country will supply us with an abundance of examples of houses, both of timber and stone, of the fifteenth century. Nowhere perhaps, are there better examples than at Shrewsbury, where they are so numerous in some parts, for example in the High Street and in Butcher Row, as to give a very good notion of the picturesque effect of a whole street - of a whole town of them'.[61]

10   Shrewsbury Houses: The 16th & 17th Centuries

16th-Century Houses

Shrewsbury's prosperity in medieval times was based on solid commercial enterprise, helped by a fortuitous geographical siting, royal interest and little in the way of competition. As the previous chapter has shown, these factors gave rise to a spate of building which culminated in the late 15th century with splendid timber-framed structures, many of which remain. There was probably an overspill into the early 16th century, but by 1535 the town was in decline and featured in the same Act of Parliament to deal with failing towns that included Ludlow and Bridgnorth.[1] Buildings were in decay, pedestrians were in danger of falling into open pits and cellars and the scene is reminiscent of a bombed city in wartime. Henry VIII's accession to the throne in 1509 came at a time when the country was at peace and he himself was to declare official peace with Wales in 1536. But these trends were not reflected in growth and expansion in Shrewsbury, and, as in Ludlow, it is difficult to date any buildings to the first half of the 16th century. An assessment of the Lay Subsidy return of 1525 comments that there was 'exceptionally severe marketing contraction between 1450 and 1500' and that the Welsh cloth trade 'had yet to create the substantial personal fortunes encountered in later decades ...'.[2]

Regarding the development of timber-framing in Shrewsbury, virtually the whole of Henry's reign is blank. But shortly after his death signs of improvement in the town's fortunes can be detected. 1552 was a year of consequence for Shrewsbury. It saw the founding of Shrewsbury School by Edward VI and the provision of a piped pure water supply from wells at Broadwell, near Nobold. The latter enterprise was no mean feat of engineering and was begun when Sir Adam Mytton and Roger Lewis were bailiffs. Such was the scheme's success that Shrewsbury continued to receive its drinking water from Conduit Head, as it is known, until 1935, and the system continued in limited use until 1947. Only minor modifications were ever necessary, such as the replacement of the old wooden pipes with those made first of lead and later of cast-iron. At Conduit Head, now a Visitors' Centre, the little building which houses the stone collecting tank still stands. That it could be the building of 1578 at first seems incredible, but the documentary

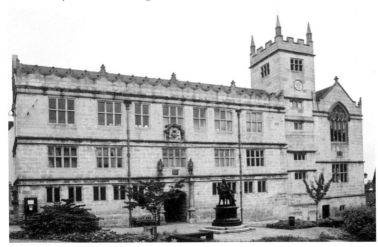

Shrewsbury School, Castle Gates, founded 1552 (now the library)

The Head of The Conduit

The collecting tank for the well water was covered in 1578. From here the pipeline ran the 2 miles into town. A contemporary manuscript records this event:

"The olde heade of the conduit leadinge into Shrewsbury was made new agayne with stone and covered with tymber…one house of lime or stone of mason's works, covered with good 'branned' tile or slate, 12 feet long and 9 feet broad, 6 foot high from ground to roof."

Conduit Head (left)
and (above) the information displayed

evidence for that year is clear: '… the old head of the conflit … made a newe again with stone and coveryd with tymber because that the origynall wat' [water] before was open …'.[3] Certainly its stone walls and remarkably heavy roof trusses, which would not be out of place in a cathedral, are testimony to the fact that it was built to last.

The rising fortunes of the Drapers' Company, especially in the second half of the century, ushered in another building boom when timber-framing was again favoured by the Company and others who sought to copy the style. These houses may be identified by certain 'hallmarks' of a school of carpenters who worked almost exclusively in Shrewsbury. Very few others bearing such hallmarks are known in the county, but the largest and most imposing of these, Pitchford Hall, is a country house and appears to be the prototype. This was the work of John Sandford in 1549 for the Ottley family. He came from a family of carpenters and at least three of his sons followed the same trade.[4] Doubtless, other carpenters copied what was clearly a popular method of using timber-framing to display ornamentation, and, by analogy, wealth, in a way that was both eye-catching and tasteful. The 'hallmarks' of this local Elizabethan school of carpentry are curved S-braces, sunken quatrefoils, cable-moulded pilasters sometimes terminating in carved heads, and carved vine-leaves and fruit on tie-beams and bargeboards. The vine as a symbol of good living in every sense appears to be rooted in biblical times. Psalm 128, verse 3: 'Thy wife shall be as a fruitful vine by the sides of thy house; thy children like olive plants round thy table'. Viniculture was a common practice, even in north Shropshire, if the number of times that 'Vineyard' occurring in street, field and house names is an indication, though the English climate was never conducive to olive growing. The cable moulding and quatrefoil motifs represent clear continuation of their use in in medieval ornamentation, but the popularity of the vine may have come about through increasing familiarity with translations of the Bible and the use of the book of Common Prayer.

The following is a descriptive list of the more obvious of these late 16th- and early 17th-century framed houses, but not all are highly ornamented. That was an advantage of the system; the client had no need to pay for frills that he did not want:

Gibbon's Mansion, *c.*1570, (demolished)
Located behind 19 Wyle Cop this may be regarded as a transitional type in framing, form and plan. It was three-storied, jettied at both main floor levels and each storey had close-studding divided by a middle rail. S-braces were incorporated, but none of the other decorative motifs. A model of the house is in Rowley's House museum.[5]

250

Additions to **Charlton Hall** (demolished)

Buckler's drawing (top right on p.217) shows that a jettied 16th-century range was added to the medieval remains. This appears to have been of a similar transitional type, with S-braces and a high second storey.[6]

The Rev. Wm. Gorsuch Rowland's house, **Abbey Foregate** (demolished)

Buckler's drawing shows this to have been a large two-storied, framed and jettied house with S-braces and close-studding divided by a middle rail to each storey. Two large pointed gables at the eastern end were probably additions of the 17th century. It appears to have been another transitional house.[7]

The following group of buildings marks the end of the transitional phase and takes the development into the mature Elizabethan period:

Proude's Mansion, 2 Milk Street

The earlier part of this building (1467) is described in the preceding chapter (see p.219, which also has an illustration of the frontage). The block fronting Milk Street has a dendro date of 1566, coinciding with the date usually quoted for it of 1568, when it is described as George Proude's 'new house now building'. This was a jettied two-storied building with rectangular framing that had a half-storey added in 1655 (dendro date). This was when the prominent triple gables appeared with star panels and spikes at the apex, and ornamental blind arched windows flanking the main attic windows. A peculiar form of upper-cruck was used as part of the roof-raising exercise. At the rear, the raised section has diamond-bracing between the studs. In a drawing dated 1821 two large box-oriels at first-floor level are shown. George Proude was a draper and a bailiff of the town in 1569.[8]

Lloyd's Mansion, The Square

Lloyd's Mansion
(demolished in 1930)
This stood in The Square on the corner of Princess Street. Built in 1570 for David Lloyd, a member of the Drapers' Company and three times a bailiff, it was the earliest dated example of the decorated style and included all the hallmarks mentioned above. It was a large two-storied property, probably partly speculative building, sub-tenanted as well as owner-occupied.[9]

Above: the old String of Horses, Frankwell

*Above: Drapers' Hall
extension dated 1582
(SRRC 6001/5326 f.35)*

*Left: Side view of Drapers' Hall
showing out-built stack
and jettied garderobe*

The String of Horses, Frankwell

A property on the corner of New Street and Frankwell, dated 1576 and very similar in form and style to Lloyd's Mansion. It was removed to Avoncroft museum in 1970 where part of it has been re-erected at the entrance.[10]

The Drapers' Hall, St. Mary's Place, 1576-82

This is probably the second guild hall of the Drapers' Company and was framed by a Welsh carpenter, Roger Smyth. His building has been much restored and enlarged, but the hall, at ground level at the front, retains its dais and is still used by the Company for meetings. At present the interior walls of the hall are panelled to their full height, but the records of the Company show that at first only the lower half was wainscotted, the upper half being hung with 'antiques'—probably meaning painted cloths. An inserted Grinshill stone fireplace in the hall is dated 1658 and it was probably at this time that the room was fully panelled. One piece of

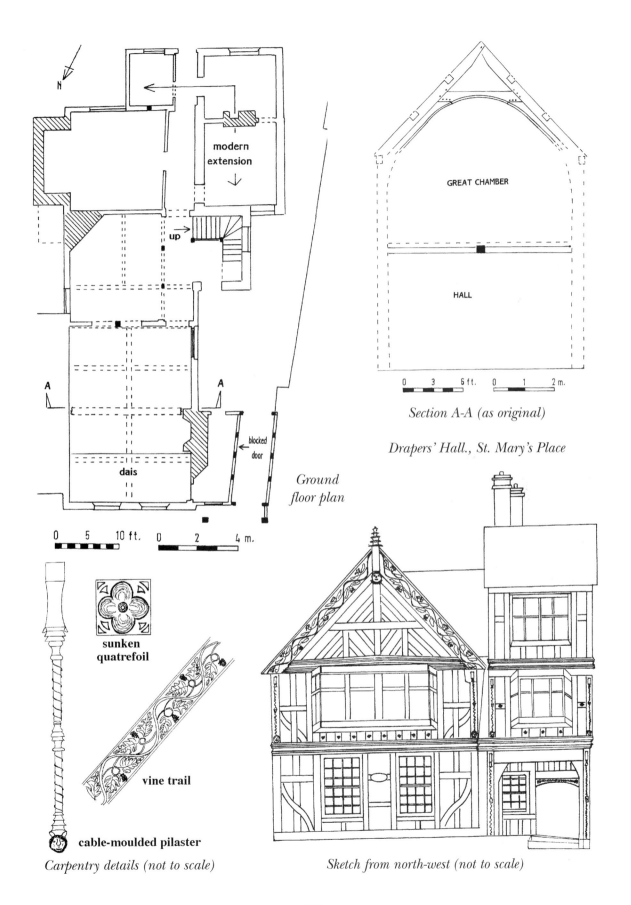

modern
extension

N

up

A   A

blocked
door

dais

Ground
floor plan

0   5   10 ft.   0   2   4 m.

sunken
quatrefoil

vine trail

cable-moulded pilaster

Carpentry details (not to scale)

GREAT CHAMBER

HALL

0   3   6 ft.   0   1   2 m.

Section A-A (as original)

Drapers' Hall., St. Mary's Place

Sketch from north-west (not to scale)

253

panelling is dated 1579 and was therefore part of a screen of wainscot bought from Guillaume (Gyllan) Wisbeche in that year for 15s.[11] Above the hall is the great chamber which was open to the roof as its central truss with an arch-braced collar-beam testifies. The service rooms are located behind the hall in the traditional position.

Ireland's Mansion

Ireland's Mansion, High Street, *c*.1575
This is easily the most ambitious house in this group—four stories high and four units wide; symmetrical, but including canted and rectangular bay windows. It has S-braces, and carved bargeboards and tie-beams, the latter bearing the arms of the Ireland family. Otherwise it relies for effect on timbers which are plain and straight. The accommodation divides into one large central house, which incorporates the two rectangular bays, and two flanking tenements each with its own entrance and canted bay—it is therefore another instance of speculative building. Cable moulding is applied to the rectangular bays only, suggesting that this was the part occupied by the owner. There are two entrances at present, but Buckler's drawing of 1821 shows a third (central) doorway which served the main section.[12] The Irelands were a long-established family of mercers and officeholders in Shrewsbury, and two brothers, Thomas and Robert, were each involved with property speculation, Thomas as the acquisitor of the manor of Albrighton after the Dissolution and Robert as the builder of the Shrewsbury house.[13]

William Weale's House as engraved by J. Barnett from a drawing by J.C. Buckler (SRRC 6001/5326 f.84)

William Weale's House (demolished)
There is some confusion over the siting of this house, but according to Forrest it was Weale who was responsible for the beautiful double oriel window above an archway in a house at the foot of Wyle Cop, adjacent to the English Bridge on the northern side. The double oriel was in the rear of the premises and had the same canted form as those in the flanking bays of Ireland's Mansion (above). The house was dated 1575. A fine drawing by Buckler was used by Owen and Blakeway.[14]

Later, the front part of the house must have been completely rebuilt by William Jones, alderman and

254

draper, and five times a bailiff. (He was the father of Thomas Jones who built the other 'Jones' Mansion' which later became the 'Prince Rupert'.) It seems to have been a three-storied house with continuous jetties on the street elevation, and unbroken at eaves level by dormers or gables. Owen gives perhaps the most complete description of it and emphasises that the principal apartments were towards the street.[15] It is difficult to date, and its non-gabled form suggests that it could belong to the 'transitional' group of buildings, described above. But some of the decorative details on the front are similar to those on Sherer's Mansion, a house of the first quarter of the 17th century, which is described later.

15/16 High Street with, below, its previous life as the Cross Keys Inn. This illustration shows the street frontage, plastered over, without the gable and projecting window but with a two-storied porch (SRRC 6001.5326 f.19)

15/16 High Street,
corner of Grope Lane

Although the date plaque of 1575 is modern, the suggested year is reasonable. The upper storey is framed in small square panels each containing a star pattern, a form of decorative work that became very popular and was used with the other hallmarks. The projection at the south end is the upper storey to a former two-storied porch entrance. Other houses in the town are known to have had porches which encroached onto the pavement, but they were cleared away under later Street Improvement Acts. The property was an inn from 1786 until the early years of the present century.[16] Recently it has been beautifully restored and given carved beams with motifs based on modern political and environmental issues.[17]

17 High Street,
on the other side of Grope Lane

Badly restored, but probably of the same date as the above. It bears some of the hallmarks but employs herringbone work in place of star patterning.

The Plough Inn, The Square

Of a similar date as 15/16 High Street and with all the hallmarks, but the third storey is an addition of 1898, remarkably well done and an object lesson in architectural good manners. An account of the alterations described the new timbers as 'oiled, thus showing the natural grain of the oak'. The deplorable practice of painting framed buildings black-and-white came later, although in 1759, in a reference to work at Edward Elisha's house, now Henry Tudor House,[18] an entry in Gibbons' account book reads '...pd whiting and blacking front about 7s'.[18]

Perche's Mansion, Pride Hill, dated 1581

This appears to be a large U-shaped complex which has been so much sub-divided and altered that interpretation is difficult. It contains two plaster ceilings. The date may refer to alterations and

The Plough, The Square. The top storey was added in 1898

additions made in 1581, but the style of the framing of the long flanking wall of the eastern wing, now exposed in Windsor Place, is compatible with that date.

Rigg's Hall, within the Public Library complex

An extension to the late medieval work was made in 1589, to provide accommodation for the headmaster, then newly married, when Shrewsbury School was still housed on the site. The framework includes close-spaced verticals, S-braces and carved bargeboards with vine trails. The porch, which was removed at some time, had a tie-beam with similar carved vines, the date and the inscription 'DOMUS ARCHIPAEDAGOGI'. The tie-beam survives and is kept at the Kingsland site to which the school moved in 1876.[19]

The Fellmongers, Frankwell, *c.*1590

This building epitomizes the activities of the Drapers' Company and is symbolic of the source of Shrewsbury's wealth. The street-facing range has no domestic concept but may be described as a wool and skin processing plant above a row of small shops. The block is three stories high and has close-studding divided by a middle rail on each of the upper stories. There is a wide cart-entry at ground level and it is not difficult to imagine the well-lighted upper jettied storey filled with weaving looms. Some of the windows are ovolo-moulded and glazed, but one still displays its form of a

Extension of 1589 to Rigg's Hall

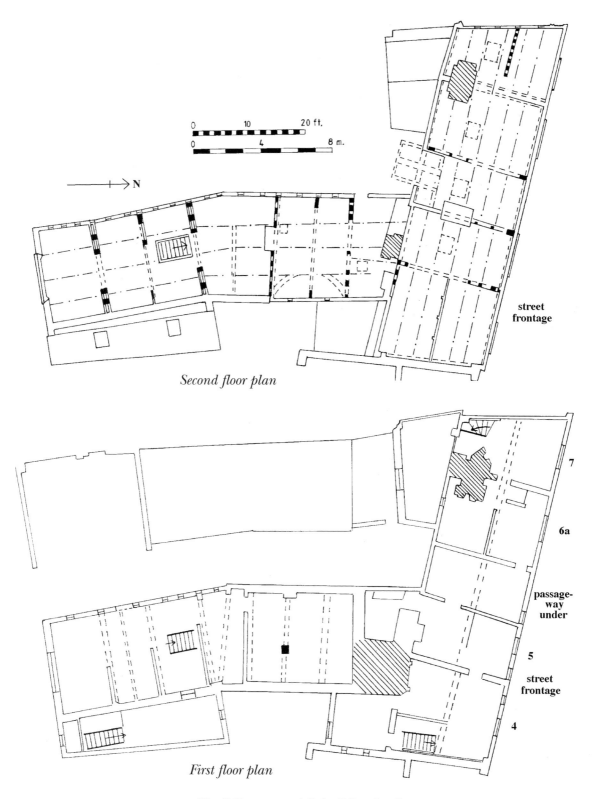

Second floor plan

street
frontage

7

6a

passage-
way
under

5

street
frontage

4

First floor plan

The Fellmongers, 4,5,6a,7 Frankwell

257

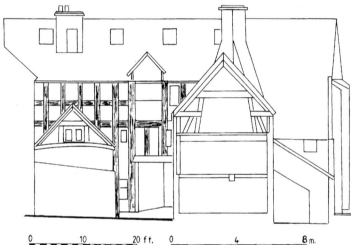

Top: north elevation of The Fellmongers
Above: part of the south elevation

Rowley's House

block of wood, pivoted at the top and simply closing a gap in the framework. A rear range makes use of upper crucks for its roof construction and these have iron spurs as ties to the wall-plate; an interesting use of cast iron at this date.

Rowley's House, Barker Street

This large three-storied framed structure is probably of a similar date to the Fellmongers' and functioned in much the same way under William Rowley, a draper who settled in the town before 1594 when he was admitted as a burgess.[20] Only the part adjoining his brick mansion, built *c.*1618, contains domestic details and it seems likely that he expanded a relatively modest Elizabethan house to provide storage and workshops for his enterprise.

Owen's Mansion, High Street, dated 1592

Opposite to Ireland's Mansion, though more modest in scale. It is reduced to a façade but it shows Elizabethan town architecture at its best and displays a richly decorated front with all the hallmarks plus finials and pendants on the two purely ornamental gables above the oriel windows in the top storey. Three stories high and jettied at two levels, the ground floor has the inevitable modern shop frontages; the first floor has a pattern of close-studding divided by a middle rail, with S-braces marking the bay divisions, and the second floor has three bands of star patterning, with sunken quatrefoils and cable moulding. The finials are in the form of figures. Doubtless they

have been renewed at various times, but silhouetted against the sky they give the building a crowning touch. The plaque bearing the date and the reference to 'Richard Owen the elder, gent' was discovered in the building *c*.1870, and originally was probably over a front porch. The Owen family, like the Irelands, were prominent members of the community in Shrewsbury.[21]

22 High Street, dated 1598
Presumably an extension to the above. However, there is a marked debasement in the style, with outsize dormer gables and wavy herringbone work in place of the close-studding. Immediately below eaves level is a row of flat baluster work which became a popular device in the 17th century, beginning in a squat form but becoming taller as time went on. This could be their first appearance.

Merevale (demolished), dated 1601
This house stood just outside the river loop in Abbey Foregate, on what is now the car park to the Wakeman school. Though the main timberwork was plain, the building displayed all the hallmarks and was L-shaped, with a two-storied jettied unit set gable-end on to the street. The roof-spaces in both units were fully floored and lit by gable-end windows. It seems to have represented the latest dated example in this group.

Merevale

Other 16th-Century Houses

The town has many examples of late medieval and Elizabethan timber-framed houses which have been disguised by a later brick 'skin' or have been plastered over. Two clear examples of the Elizabethan period are **no.4 Belmont** where the 'skin' has been removed from the gable end, exposing the timbers on which there is an extremely well-preserved set of carpenters' assembly marks; and **21-23 Claremont Hill** which has S-braces and striking evidence of later roof raising. In 1990 it was discovered that the range running back from no.4 Belmont contained a late open hall at ground level which had renaissance-style wallpaintings at its high end, very similar to those in Barnaby House, Ludlow, thought to be c.1580.

4 Belmont at the corner of Belmont and Belmont Bank

In 1985, following a fire in Market Street which destroyed Talbot Chambers, it was found that the part adjoining the Music Hall had been an encased Elizabethan framed house which had cable moulding.

Kingston House in St. Alkmund's Square owes its curious appearance to the fact that it is a brick-cased timber-framed house; the belvedere is the result of adding a room at the top, and has nothing to do with lighting the stairs.

21-23 Claremont Hill.
Note the S-braces,
roof raising and brick 'skin'

Allowing for the fact that it is difficult to know what is the attrition rate for timber-framed Elizabethan buildings in Shrewsbury, and assuming, perhaps dangerously, that what is left is reasonably typical, it is possible to make an analysis of them and to draw certain conclusions. The majority (64%) were two-storied, but many had attics in the roof space. This contrasts with the transitional phase before the mature Elizabethan where, in the larger houses, two bold jetties with moulded bressumers facilitated three stories. 28% of the later ones were three-storied, but only one (Ireland's) was four-storied. Purely functional buildings, such as the

Kingston House, St. Alkmund's Square

Fellmongers' and Rowley's House were three-storied. Carved decoration, not surprisingly, depended on taste and pocket. It was available for those who wanted it and could pay for it. Nearly 43% of the surviving examples have the full treatment, over 28% have limited decoration and over 14% are plain.

In most cases it is only possible to guess how the interiors were planned, but there are a few indications. Shops tended to be small and there were often spacious living quarters above them which were probably occupied, not by the shopkeeper, but by a higher strata of society, perhaps by whoever commissioned the building. Halls, or the Elizabethan equivalent of them are found at ground level and at first-floor level, have much more privacy. Kitchens are no longer housed in a detached building, whilst the roof space is utilised for attics or cocklofts if it is not open over a great chamber. Chimneys are an integral part of the plan and were often built to serve two back-to-back fireplaces. This is well illustrated by the building in Abbey Foregate which for a time was the Park Hotel. Though plastered over at present, its timber-framed and jettied form is unmistakable.

In 1557 the building which was variously known as the Booth Hall or the Guildhall and which closed the Square on the northern side, was enlarged '... and especially the nether hall next adoiyning to the Escheker was newly beutyfied both with waynscetts and glasse windows and a chymney and also sylyd overhedde for the assembly of the aldermen and counsell ...'. When Sir Henry Sidney, in his office as President of the Council in the Marches of Wales visited Shrewsbury in the same year he gave the building a name '... and namyd it the Chamber of Concorde and so to be named for ever'.[22] Unfortunately it was demolished in 1783. If the connotations of the name evoke a sense of *dèja vu* in present times it is to be hoped that the consequences are not the same.

So far only timber-framed buildings have been considered, and it is clear that at this time timber had lost none of its popularity, indeed it is significant that the wealthy and powerful Drapers deliberately chose timber. They must have considered it the medium best suited for the ornamentation which would display their wealth. Brick had yet to make much impact, although one brick-built house which is shown on the 1882 Ordnance Survey map as '**attached**

Above: 'New Ship' inn yard in 1895 with the Downes family and
Sam Gittins, the brewer, on the right (courtesy of Walter Downes)
Right: demolition taking place in 1934

to the New Ship Inn' had English bond brickwork and stone-mullioned windows and probably pre-dated Rowley's House.[23] This house was lost in the demolition programme of the 1930s. Brick as a building medium seems to have been used more for details such as chimneys. Two superb chimneystacks were introduced at the **Olde House, Dogpole**—both have tall triple-clustered star-shaped shafts with decorative capping. One fireplace in the summer parlour at the rear has a carved overmantel bearing the name Robert Sego and the date 1553. It is a fine piece of classical design, advanced for its time and correct in every detail. Sego appears in Shrewsbury *c.*1548 when he was admitted to the Guild of Carpenters. In 1560 he was made a Freeman of the town.[24] There is no record of him living at the Olde House and, as it is unlikely that he would be allowed to display his name so prominently on an artifact paid

Top: Robert Sego's overmantel in the Olde House, Dogpole
Above: Jacobean overmantel in the same property

for by a client, its provenance remains a mystery. Another fireplace in the front room at ground level has a pattern of stylised foliage painted on the brickwork of the overmantel, and a painted design on the mantel-beam incorporates a crown, pomegranates, and Tudor roses. It is a tradition of the house that the young Princess Mary, the daughter of Henry VIII and Catherine of Aragon, came to the Olde House in the charge of a courtier named Rocke, whose house it was. The symbols relate to Catherine's personal badge (pomegranate), her royal status (crown) and a royal badge of England (the bicolour rose). Later, when it was foolhardy to display Catherine's emblems, the beam was concealed behind a Jacobean overmantel.

A painting (see opposite) which belongs to the house shows a formal rear garden relating to the adjoining house, then known as the **Mansion House**, but which has since been demolished. It includes figures in Jacobean dress. The garden front of the Olde House appears incidentally and is clearly that which preceded an 18th-century façade, but the Tudor chimneys are unmistakable. Both gardens are shown running down to the inner town wall, as they still do.

Stone, as a building medium, was not used apart from public buildings in Elizabethan times, and then it was the best white Grinshill sandstone that was favoured. Although in 1567 'two fayre houses' had been built in The Square to house the corn market, and three others were added to them in 1571 these, presumably of timber-framing, were demolished in 1596

Old painting of the garden at the Mansion House

and the stone **Market Hall**, a joint venture between the Corporation and the Drapers' Company, took their place.[25] In this the upper room was used for the sale of cloth, while corn was sold in the open area below. The building is thought to be the work of Walter Hancock, a master mason from Much Wenlock.[26] Its classical design, incorporating open arches supported by Doric pillars was thought by Owen to be 'one of the most spacious and magnificent structures of its kind in the kingdom', and certainly its fabric and proportions, perfect for the setting, are in marked contrast to those of the unsympathetic modern development on the southern side of The Square. Curiously, there are two backward-looking elements in Hancock's building: the use of cusped windbraces in the roof structure and window mullions in which the ovolo moulding is not fully developed—an embryonic ovolo, even though the mature form had reached Shropshire by the 1570s.

Market Hall of 1596

Another good public building from these times is **Shrewsbury School**. The tower and the west wing, which housed the chapel on the ground floor and the library and dormitories above, were begun in 1595 under the headship of John Meighen for whom Rigg's Hall was extended. The south wing followed, being completed in 1620. The parapet of this unit is very similar to that on Hancock's Market Hall and may be the work of his son who appears to have continued the business after his father's death in 1599.[27]

The Dissolution of the monasteries and friaries in the 1530s and '40s would have released a supply of cheap building stone, but only one large house appears to have been generated— **Whitehall** in Monkmoor Road, a building really in a class of its own. Built in 1578-82 by Richard Prynce, a wealthy lawyer and a Freeman of the town, it has its own gatehouse, and is a multi-gabled almost square double-piled plan house of advanced design. It was still being white-washed in 1808; tradition says that this was done to disguise the origin of the stones. There is a brick-built dovecote which retains its revolving ladder (potence) in the grounds, and a stable-

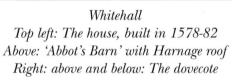

Whitehall
Top left: The house, built in 1578-82
Above: 'Abbot's Barn' with Harnage roof
Right: above and below: The dovecote

block, '**Abbot's Barn**', which is the only building in Shrewsbury to retain a 'Harnage slate' roof.[28] Whitehall, like the Market Hall, has embryonic ovolo-moulded window mullions. Until recently the house was used by the Department of Social Security, but it has been badly treated and its future is uncertain.

The stone wing added to **Bellstone Hall** in Elizabethan times by Edward Owen, an alderman and draper, was built of red sandstone and therefore may also have represented a recycling of the abbey stones.[29]

Although the few stone buildings of this time help to bridge the gap between the demise of timber-framing and the adoption of brick for whole houses, they really do no more than emphasise the difference between the thinking of institutions and exceptionally powerful men, and of the ordinary businessman in the town. It seems that, until forced by circumstances

E.P. Owen's engraving of the High Street in 1822

to change over to brick, the average Salopian simply continued to use timber, stamping his individuality on his house by whatever means he chose. One building, which was situated on the corner of High Street and Pride Hill, was illustrated by several reputable artists, including Buckler who even made a detailed drawing of an unusual ovoid bow window in the gable end and showed the pegholes and joints. It stretches credulity to the utmost, but all the illustrations show a jettied building which appears to have overhangs between the storey levels. Only slightly less fascinating is the building on the opposite corner which had a tall star-shaped chimneystack, very similar to those which survive at The Olde House, Dogpole.[30]

17th-Century Houses

The suburb of Frankwell, located to the north-west across the Welsh Bridge, in historic times always regarded itself as independent of Shrewsbury. For many years it bore the tag of the 'Little Borough'. To some extent this independence is reflected in its buildings. A group of framed buildings, each set parallel to the road in uncompromising fashion, are planned on a two-unit basis with a smaller service bay and a larger in-line hall-and-parlour range. Probably they all had shops at ground level. However, the earliest dendro-dated property in this 17th-century group does not conform to the Frankwell ethos:

165 Frankwell, built in 1601-2

165 Frankwell

Dendro-dated to 1603 this is a square block which was given an improved trading position when the Welsh bridge was realigned in the 1790s. Although containing much 20th-century work, it is notable for its over-sized scantling which includes two spine-beams with lambs' tongue stops and a bressumer with triple ovolo-and-quirk moulding. The roof is of principal rafter and queen-post form. Included in the 20th-century remodelling is the framed and jettied gable on the northern side.[31]

127 Frankwell

This is perhaps the prototype of the Frankwell ethos. Dendro-dated 1610, it seems to have set a pattern for Frankwell, both in its plan-form and its rejection of the excesses of decoration popular in the centre of Shrewsbury. Perhaps, in its way, it may be seen as the start of a return to plainer framing. S-braces mark the division of the house into two unequal parts, one clearly superior to the other. The front is jettied at two levels and the vertical timbers are divided by a middle rail. The windows are provided with a dropped sill and are not simply a gap in the framework. The ground floor seems to have consisted of small shops, and the large room at first-floor level on the right-hand side was clearly the 'great chamber'. This has the remains of a fine, plastered ceiling, though of a later date than the framing. The roof is of queen-post construction with trenched purlins.[32]

127 Frankwell (1610)

Council House Gatehouse and two finials (1620) (see opposite and p.270)

104/107 Frankwell
A smaller version of no.127. No.9 Frankwell (demolished) was similar.

The Porch House, Swan Hill (1628)

*Centre: the front of St. Alkmund's Vicarage
with, lower, the rear of the building*

14 Frankwell (demolished)
This was also similar. Photographs show this to have had a two-bayed frontage with close-studding and a mid-rail to the first floor, S-braces and an added top storey.[33]

133/4 Frankwell
Similar, but with added dormer gables.

Shrewsbury centre
As the first half of the 16th century appears almost devoid of datable houses, similarly the first half of the 17th century produced little in the way of dated houses which have survived. The two dendro-dated houses in Frankwell, described above, go some way towards bridging the gap but housing needs must have been largely satisfied by the boom in Elizabethan times and so, while other towns entered a great building phase in the run-up to the Civil War, Shrewsbury had something of a respite from such activities. There are only two examples of framed houses with inscribed dates of this period: the **Gatehouse to the Council House**, 1620, on Castle Gates and the **Porch House**, 1628, on Swan Hill, although it is possible to suggest others from their stylistic evidence.

Rowley's Mansion, adjoining Rowley's House and dated 1618 on a fireplace, is brick-built and is commonly thought to represent the introduction of brick into the town but, as previously mentioned, a house in the New Ship Inn yard (demolished) probably predated it.

Another early brick house, likely to be of a similar date to Rowley's Mansion, is **St. Alkmund's Vicarage**. The frontage has timberwork applied in Victorian times when the appearance of timber-framing was enjoying a revival, but the back retains early brickwork of different bonds.

Thorne's Hall (demolished) was also an early brick house of *c*.1620. On the rear elevation there were two wings with straight gables, forming a U-shaped plan, but between them were two large curvilinear gables and a smaller central one of the same form over a porch, giving the house an E-shape. It stood in Castle Street and was demolished in 1920 to make way for a Co-operative store. Some excellent photographs of the rear view and some of the internal

Rear view of Thorne's Hall

rooms were published at this time. Reputedly it was the birthplace of Mrs. Fitzherbert, the morganatic wife of George IV.[34]

Sherer's Mansion (demolished), *c*.1620

This large three-storied, jettied and triple-gabled framed house stood at the foot of Wyle Cop. In it the jetties were supported partly by carved brackets and partly by applied rectangular bay windows which effectively doubled the overhang. It displayed classical blank arches under the windows of the central bay, some star patterning and diamond panels containing raised heads. It is unlikely to have been built by the Thomas Sherer (d.1598) who was clerk to the Council in the Marches of Wales, but it is very similar in appearance to the Feathers Hotel in Ludlow

Sherer's Mansion, Wyle Cop

which was remodelled in 1619 by Rees Jones, an attorney at the Council. The Feathers has raised heads and it is interesting to note that another house in the county, Dodmore (demolished) near Ludlow also had raised decoration in the panels. Dodmore had connections with the Council as it was occupied by Rees Jones' brother-in-law. The illustration of Sherer's Mansion by Buckler shows that Jones' Mansion, (above), near the English Bridge also had raised decoration in diamond-shaped panels.[35]

113/114 Frankwell, *c.*1620

At first glance the two units appear to be a pair of semi-detached houses with a communal entrance passage through the middle but, in fact, the passage divides one house into two distinct parts, a residential side on the left and a commercial side on the right. The former has a small jettied chamber at the rear, which overlooks a courtyard, and generally displays more attention to detail. When built, it was perhaps regarded as an up-to-date version of Henry Tudor House and functioned in much the same way, except that the passage would not have admitted carts. The front has a unified appearance and the treatment of the windows is strikingly different from Sherer's Mansion; in the latter the projecting windows were 'applied' to the frame, here they are an integral part of it and give a 'wrap-around' effect. Other contrasts include the use of flat balusters, closely-spaced plain timbers with two rails to the upper storey and a single star panel in each gable. There is extensive use of ovolo moulding and the doorcase has 'pyramid' stops. Internally a feature occurs which became widely used both internally and externally in the latter half of the the century: sharply cut-back heads to the posts. There is a marked difference in the treatment of the attics—the commercial side is bare, unplastered and has no fireplace, whereas the residential side is plastered, has a fireplace and is provided with a whitewashed hempen screen.[36]

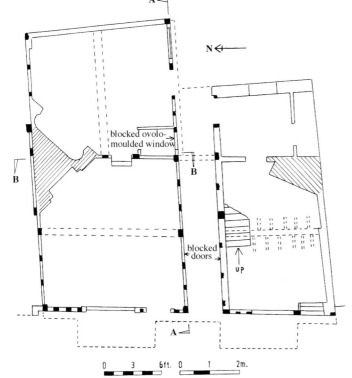

113/114 Frankwell, frontage and ground floor plan (as in 1982)

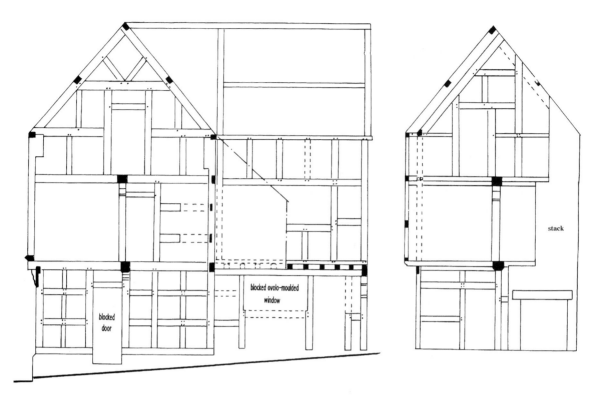

113/114 Frankwell. Left: Section A-A; right: Section B-B (both as in 1982)

The Gatehouse to the Council House, 1620

This is a delightful example of flamboyant Jacobean framing, richly carved and with finials, ovolo-moulded windows, classical blank arches and flat balusters (see illustrations on p.266). On the front elevation the panels display heart-shaped motifs, a design which was popular in other framed buildings of the 17th century. The rear elevation has star patterning over the entrance, but the remainder is plain square-framing although an old watercolour shows cusped lozenge work in all the panels.[37]

Porch House, Swan Hill, 1628

Compared with the Gatehouse (above) Porch House is more sober and has the appearance of a farmhouse translated to a town position. The doorcase has carved ornamentation but the porch, from which the house is named, has been removed and the timbering is otherwise plain with square panelling to the upper storey and close-studding with a dropped rail to the ground floor. The three gables are an echo of larger triple-gabled town houses, but it has one feature which is rare in the town, though fairly common in the county—the 'hewn' jetty. In ordinary jettied buildings the stories are framed separately and consist, in effect, of larger boxes on top of smaller boxes; but as time went on the jetty became smaller until the overhang was no more than four or five inches. This was achieved by simply reducing the scantling of the full-length corner posts by that amount at storey height, but, of course, as at Porch House, the hewn jetty would normally only be used on two-storied buildings. Another example of the hewn jetty may be seen at 23 Pride Hill.

15/16 Mardol

15/16 Mardol, *c.*1620

In 1988 this property underwent an excellent restoration programme when later accretions were removed from the front and the twin-gabled form was reinstated. The previously concealed frontage displays heart-shaped panels and flat baluster studs as well as star panelling and some plain diamond panels. Like 114/15 Frankwell (above), this property has ovolo-moulded windows and in many ways it is a smaller version of it. It also has a cut-back head to the post, but this time it is visible on the exterior. The building has a remarkable tilt which has been faithfully reinstated. The tilt occurs not because the frame has warped, but because it was deliberately fashioned to follow the warping of the frame of the adjacent property. This suggests that it represents an encroachment onto Hill's Lane, effectively narrowing the entrance to that thoroughfare.

The Prince Rupert Hotel, Church Street

Originally this house had a return to St. Mary's Street but the courtyard has been filled in with later buildings. The wing which formed the return was a separate property called The Old Mansion, described on p.225, but it is now absorbed into the hotel. It is this part which contains the grand Jacobean staircase. Of open well design it has a moulded handrail and shaped balusters descending to a string. The newel posts are continued upwards as carved finials. The Prince Rupert was entirely brick-cased at one time and has had so much restoration that interpretation is difficult, but surviving details suggest an early 17th-century date. Reputedly it was the house of Thomas Jones, a lawyer, who became Shrewsbury's first mayor in 1639. It was a royalist 'safe house', sheltering Prince Rupert and the duke of York in 1642.[38]

The Dun Cow, Abbey Foregate

An inn which has framework of the first half of the 17th century. The building has had at least two phases of concealment by plaster. Much supposition and many legends are attached to this building, but the model of the cow over the entrance is striking despite recent attempts to turn it into a Friesian.

Left: the Dun Cow

46 Pride Hill (demolished)   *40 Pride Hill*

As far as it is possible to tell, the above are nearly all houses of one build, but it is clear that many people were refurbishing and enlarging older houses in the first half of the century. Several instances of roof raising to gain another storey or more height in the upper storey may be seen, of which 27 Wyle Cop and 2 Milk Street, described above, are good examples.

In Pride Hill, Castle Street and Butcher Row it was as though fashion dictated that old two-storied buildings could best be up-dated by adding a projecting three-storied central gable-dormer unit which could be decorated *à la mode*. Old pictures of Pride Hill show several of these *in situ*, but only two remain: **29 Castle Street** and **40 Pride Hill** which also displays the heart motif. One which was demolished in the 1880s, **46 Pride Hill**, had every possible piece of dating criteria, from the sunken quatrefoils of the late 16th century to the intricate decoration of the late 17th century. The building even had a frieze of gambolling lambs, symbolic thanksgiving to the source of the original wealth from wool which built the house—the pictorial equivalent of the text which the rich wool merchant John Barton of Holme-by-Newark had, a century and a half earlier, inscribed on a window of his manor house: 'I thank the Lord and ever shall, It is the sheep hath paid for all'. The fact that when Buckler made his drawing of 46 Pride Hill the premises were occupied by Mr. Jones, the butcher, is coincidental.[39]

During the second half of the century, after the Civil War, there was another burst of building activity which has left little evidence today. Old illustrations show long vanished timber-framing in all the main streets. A remarkable group stood on the site of the new Market Hall (see illustration opposite); taking into account the number of times that roof raising took place one of these, which probably began as a three-storied jettied house, ended by being six stories high. Another was four stories high in its own right, whilst a further example on the corner of Shoplatch was a brick-built house, probably contemporary with the Guildhall (Newport House) but with two classical architraves to full length windows at first-floor level.[40]

As a building practice jettying died out before the Civil War, but it lingered as a feature in the 'hewn jetty' houses.

The Boar's Head, Belle Vue Road, Coleham, *c.*1650

Basically this is a timber-framed building, but the walls have largely been rebuilt in brick and a complete wing has been added at the rear and a large gable at the front.

*T. Shotter-Boys' painting of Mardol Head,
demolished to make way for the erection of the Victorian market hall*

Some square-framing remains on the rear elevation. Only the roof retains features of interest; it is four-bayed, but only two of the trusses are identical. These were of tie-and-collar-beam construction with straight queen-struts, but the collars have been cut through to provide doorways, presumably to increase accommodation when the building became an inn in 1780.[341] One good windbrace survives; this is plain, curved, double-pegged and tenoned into the principal rafter and into the purlin. Chiselled carpenters' marks feature prominently on the truss at the southern end.

The King's Arms, Claremont Street (demolished)

This was lost in the same demolition programme that removed the houses described above. It was a three-storied timber-framed house, with twin gables and flat baluster work, but its chief feature was a projecting canted oriel window supported on columns which effectively provided an entrance porch. In the 18th century it is said to have been the home of James Millington, founder of Millington's Hospital in Frankwell, a charity school for 20 poor boys, 20 poor girls and cottage homes for 12 poor old people.[42]

*The King's Arms in Claremont Street,
now demolished*

164/5/6 Abbey Foregate

Old House, Barker Street (demolished)
Another 17th-century framed house which had a two-storied porch with carved columns. This was drawn by Buckler in 1821.[43]

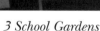

3 School Gardens

3 School Gardens
Extant maps of the area show that this was built between 1640 and 1670. It is probably one of the latest examples of flamboyant framing. Here, the cut-back heads are part of the external pattern. In his thesis John Smith comments that it is 'reminiscent of the Jacobean taste in pulpits'.[44]

Another Old House, now demolished, which stood opposite the Abbey National School in Abbey Foregate (SRRC 6001/5326 f.105)

164/5/6 Abbey Foregate
This may represent a terrace of four box-framed houses. They are two-storied, but full use is made of the roof space, each house having a dormer window set wholly in the roof. The chimneys pierce the front slope of the roof and the framing is plain, squared and four panels high, showing a return to plain framing and simple form.

178-80 Abbey Foregate
No.178 is a square-framed rectangular block with a 'thrown-out' wing facing the street at the eastern end. The wing is also timber-framed but it has been brick-faced at the front, with fake timbers painted on. The framing is four panels high, and there are straight tension braces and angle braces. The posts are plain and straight,

and although the panels are at present infilled with brick they were probably of wattle-and-daub originally. No.180 is now in separate occupation, but is the westernmost bay of the block. It has a type of upper cruck roof truss. From the ground floor of no.180 the double-jowl post relating to the adjoining older property (nos.181-2), mentioned in the previous chapter, may be seen.

3 St. Mary's Place (The Verger's House)
This also represents a late and simple form which seems to indicate that timber-framing was on its way out. The panels are rectangular and the gable end includes cut-back heads to the posts and some poor timbers which would have been concealed from view by the shut (covered pedestrian passageway) which once abutted the building.

The Guildhall
An important brick house of 1696 in Dogpole, The Guildhall, not to be confused with the earlier Guildhall or Booth Hall in the Square, closes the 17th century and introduces the elegant Georgian houses of the 18th century which, in their way, were to transform Shrewsbury into a fashionable social centre for the gentry class and those who aspired to it. The Guildhall was the town house of the newly-created first Earl of Bradford, Sir Francis Newport, and his coronet decorates the portal. The house is typical of those which were designed at this time to be comfortable, fashionable and manageable. Outwardly symmetry was paramount; internally, as at the Guildhall, the plan could be anything but symmetrical. The right-hand side at ground-floor level consists of one full-length room containing two bolection-moulded fireplaces, and similar moulding occurs on the panelling. There is a similar room above it. The rear of the entrance hall contains a fine staircase with twisted balusters descending to a string. Two external features occur at the Guildhall which were to be forbidden by law in London houses a few years later because they were thought to constitute a fire hazard: window frames flush with the brickwork and an overhanging eaves cornice. The hipped roof, the raised brick quoins and plat band all add to the 'Queen Anne' look and only two features detract from its correctness: the

The Guildhall (1696)

The staircase at the Guildhall

275

Castle Gates House

porch, which was added in the 19th century, and the Welsh slates for the roof covering. Originally it would probably have had a covering of hand-made clay tiles. The earl was an early conservationist, for instead of destroying the timber-framed house which occupied the site, he had it removed to the foot of the castle drive where it survives in an altered form as Castle Gates House.[45]

11   Much Wenlock Houses

The decision to allocate a separate chapter to Much Wenlock was taken partly because the number of entries would have made the Gazetteer top-heavy, but mostly because of the unique nature of the place. Visitors frequently refer to it as a village—and are swiftly corrected by the inhabitants. It functions as a town and has all the trappings of a town, but the impression is given that it 'belongs in spirit wholly to the past'.[1] By 1247 it had the status of a borough and remained so until 1948.[2] The establishment of a double monastery there before 690 doubtless gave it a kick-start and it had no less a personage than St. Milburga herself as abbess.[3] The parish church of Holy Trinity was probably a minster by 901 and was rebuilt in the early 12th century to serve the community which had grown up as an adjunct to the great religious house.[4] In this respect it may be compared with Ludlow town which grew up to serve the castle.

Much Wenlock's hey-day was certainly in the medieval era. It maintained its *status quo* in Tudor times, but certain factors seem to have ensured that the 'Age of Enlightenment' in the 18th century and subsequent waves of architectural fashion in Victorian and post-Second-World-War eras largely passed it by. While it is true that frontages have been modernised with brick, stone or plaster facings it is also true that behind most of the façades a much older building remains, usually timber-framed.

It is proposed to describe the buildings in chronological order as far as possible. Obviously, only those known to the author are included, and the views expressed are personal ones.

55/57 Sheinton Street (Bastard Hall)

So-called from the name of the family most closely connected with it.[5] The building is mostly stone built, but with the upper storey displaying close-studding. At the rear of no.55 the profile of what appears to have been an aisled hall occurs in the stonework. This would have stretched eastwards, that is at right angles to the street-facing unit. In the latter the rear wall contains two arched openings and there is springing for a third, strongly suggestive of

55/57 Sheinton Street

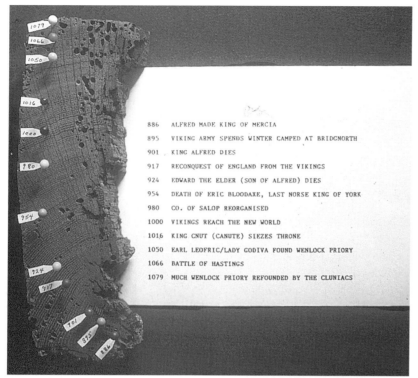

886   ALFRED MADE KING OF MERCIA

895   VIKING ARMY SPENDS WINTER CAMPED AT BRIDGNORTH

901   KING ALFRED DIES

917   RECONQUEST OF ENGLAND FROM THE VIKINGS

924   EDWARD THE ELDER (SON OF ALFRED) DIES

954   DEATH OF ERIC BLOODAXE, LAST NORSE KING OF YORK

980   CO. OF SALOP REORGANISED

1000   VIKINGS REACH THE NEW WORLD

1016   KING CNUT (CANUTE) SIEZES THRONE

1050   EARL LEOFRIC/LADY GODIVA FOUND WENLOCK PRIORY

1066   BATTLE OF HASTINGS

1079   MUCH WENLOCK PRIORY REFOUNDED BY THE CLUNIACS

55 Sheinton Street
Above left: Timber with dendro
dating of historic events; above right:
Post and pad construction;
lower right: Stone arches

service doorways. In the southern of the two rooms in the street-facing unit is a large samson-post, octagonal in section, bead-moulded and dendro-dated to 1255-1289. This supports a bolster or pad, similarly dated, which in turn supports two axial beams, the provenance tree growing in 881. The floor structure supported by the beams consists of flat 5-inch thick planks, set transversely, above which is a solid masonry floor, 6 inches thick. The window lintel on the front wall also produced a similar 13th-century date, and a corbelled chimney is outlined on the rear wall. Possibly this served a solar above the masonry floor.[6]

No.57 has fewer remains, and the garden was the location for a Channel 4 'Time-Team' programme in 1993. In an upper rear room is a beam, moulded on one side and with ten mortices on the soffit, each with a peg-hole. It is probably a re-used bressumer and has been dendro-dated to 1474-1507.[7]

In the 18th century 'Bastard Hall' was used as a gaol.[8]

23 Barrow Street
('Cruck Antiques')

This building was threatened with demolition some years ago. Its form was apparent, but it had lain empty and derelict for some time and was declared dangerous largely because of repeated arson attacks by vandals. However, once its importance was made known to the authorities, it was reprieved, listed and carefully restored.

Dendro-dated 1327-30 this L-shaped property has a box-framed solar crosswing facing the street and a base-cruck hall at right-angles to it. Both units are contemporary.[9] The central truss of the hall is especially fine, with double roll-and-fillet moulding on the arch-braces joining a hollow chamfer on the base-crucks. The tie-beam is steeply cambered and so shaped and chamfer-rebated that it fits over the base-crucks as though giving added height to them. Witness marks on the upper face indicate that a central boss of some kind faced the dais end—another example of the social differentia-

23 Barrow Street with, immediately above, its base cruck truss after restoration

tion between the hall bays. Empty pegholes suggest that the hall had a crown-post roof; it now has side-purlins and, sensibly, no attempt was made to 'reconstruct' the crown-post roof in the recent refurbishment programme.

The length of the lower bay cannot be determined and it is not known whether there was a spere-truss, cross passage and service end beyond the hall, although this is most likely. In its moulding details and probably in its roofing form it closely resembles The Bold in Aston Botterell parish which has a similar dendro date, 1320-1354.

The two-bayed crosswing was formerly jettied towards the street and the posts have thickened heads. At ground level there is a central axial jowled post, originally supporting an axial floor beam which in turn supported the jetty joists. This feature, while effectively giving a 'double-pile' concept to the ground floor, is not repeated above and clearly relates to the method of flooring. This raises questions concerning the validity of the theory that jettying was a means of counteracting the sagging floor problem in early framed buildings.[10] On the wall-plate of the rear wall is a scarf joint of the type known as a stop-splayed scarf with under-squinted butts and four face-pegs. It probably had a transverse key, but this part is obscured.[11] Nothing of the original roof structure remains.

15 High Street, (Barclays Bank)

Dendro-dated 1407-8, this building incorporates a two-bay hall of base-cruck construction which has a crown-post roof. One aisled truss (section A-A), that at the dais end of the hall, is reasonably intact and there are the remains of another at the opposite end of the hall. The service end of the house has been replaced by a 17th-century box-framed unit, currently in use as the bank. Spurs with slip-tenons effect the connection between the posts and the base-crucks which have an ogee moulding that continues into the arch-braces. The soffit of the tie-beam has a more elaborate version of the same moulding. The crown post has cusped lateral braces which down-swing to the

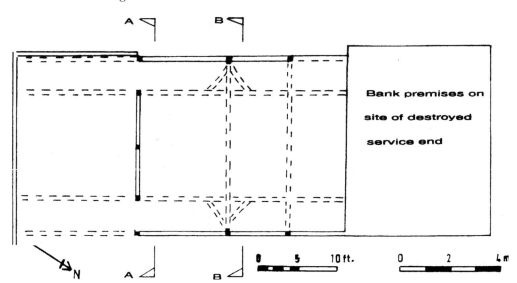

15 High Street. Top: Viewed from the south-east. The base-cruck and crown-post unit is to the rear of the bank; middle: Aisled truss at dais end of hall; lower: Ground floor plan

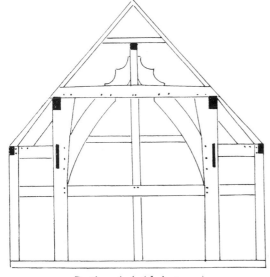

Section A-A (dais truss)

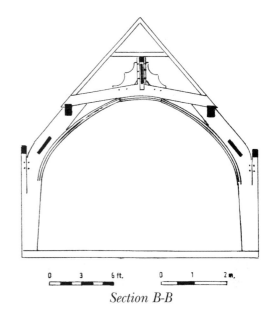

Section B-B

15 High Street

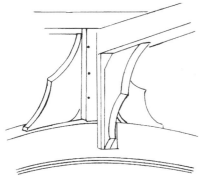

Sketch showing crown-post assembly on truss B

tie-beam, and the sole remaining longitudinal brace is similarly cusped. The position of the louvre is discernible through the trimming of the roof timbers immediately to the upper end of the open truss. The hall has an inserted ceiling above with a floor of lime plaster laid over oak laths.[12]

This property marks a kind of watershed—it is the last dated base-cruck and the first where cusping is used with any degree of conviction, at least as an internal feature.

14 High Street

Situated next to the above, but separated from it by a contrived yard, no.14 also has crown-post roof construction, although only the tie-beam, the lower part of the crown post and the start of the longitudinal brace are visible below the inserted ceiling. The remains of the collar purlin may be seen in the exposed gable end.

Raynald's Mansion, High Street

Although thoroughly disguised by the 1682 triple-gabled frontage, at least five building phases are evident. Phase 1 is a hall-house, dendro dated 1414-1447, in which the north-east bay was jettied into the

Raynald's Mansion. The 1642 frontage conceals a hall-house of 1414-1447

281

Raynald's Mansion
Left: staircase of c.1620; above: medieval frame of 1414-47

hall, forming an internal jetty. The eight oversailing joists are very large and evenly spaced. If the hall was two-bayed then it and the north-east bay would have occupied the whole plot. The hall may have had a canopy over the dais.

In the 16th century the hall was rebuilt to a 27ft. (8.23m.) width, making the width twice the length. The original rafters, windbraces and purlins were reused, the hall remained open and had an open hearth and a floored bay to the south. The front was subsequently re-modelled to give a three-storied, triple-gabled façade. Probably to this phase or the next belong the two internal doors with ovolo-moulded frames and the staircase which has square newel posts and shaped flat balusters. Finally each of the three bays was given two-storied projecting bay windows and a continuous pentice roof. This phase relates to the 1682 date (John and Mary Raynalds) inscribed on the north-east bay. The bays were eventually connected by small balconies, probably in the 19th century.[13]

St. Owen's Well House (1416)

St. Owen's Well House
Dendro-dated to 1416, this is basically a two-bayed cruck-built house, with a later addition of a boxframed bay. One of the bays was an open hall while the bay nearest the road appears to have been a small solar above two service rooms. A cross passage separated the service rooms and the hall while a contemporary ogee-headed doorway led from the solar above giving access to the hall, presumably via a stair-

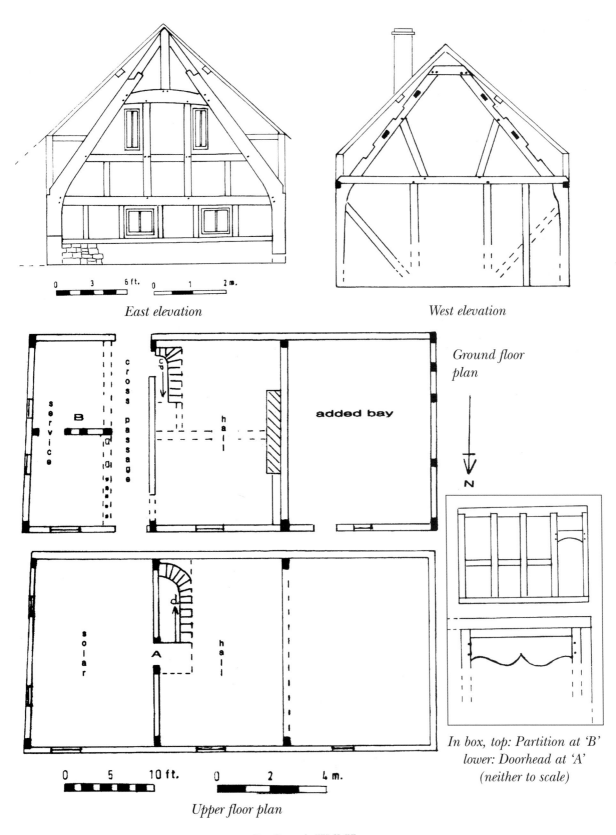

East elevation

West elevation

Ground floor plan

cross passage

service

B

c p

hall

added bay

N

solar

A

hall

In box, top: Partition at 'B'
lower: Doorhead at 'A'
(neither to scale)

0   3   6 ft.   0   1   2 m.

0   5   10 ft.   0   2   4 m.

Upper floor plan

St. Owen's Well House

283

case. In 1546 William Corvehill, a priest serving the Guild of Our Lady, was living in the block. He was a 'jack-of-all-trades', an 'expert in geometry, making of organs, clocks and chimes, carving and masonry, weaving of silk and painting, a bell-founder and maker of frames for bells'. He died later that year and was buried in a grave of his own design in the Lady chapel of the parish church.[14]

Brook House Farm

It is difficult to know where to place this property chronologically. Occupying the corner of Sheinton Street and Queen Street, at least four building phases can be identified. Dendro-dating of the timber-framed unit was not successful, but a two-bayed box-framed open hall can be identified and this has some timbering exposed on the rear wall. However, it is clear that at the front the hall was built up against a stone wall relating to an earlier building of *c.*1300. The Queen Street elevation contains a two-centred arch doorway and the wall itself is 2ft. 4ins. (0.71m.) thick. The central truss of the framed open hall is reasonably intact and provision was made for a low beam.[15] There was no need for a wall-plate on the south side because the older stone wall had its own wall-plate and this would continue to provide the necessary seating for the rafters. The tie-beam is shaped, chamfered and rebated and the posts are T-shaped, the whole composition carefully designed with the arch-braces to give the effect of double-cham-fering along the full length. The hall received an inserted ceiling, but this was done in two stages and the large central chimneystack then served as a pivot for the whole house. It was large enough to allow a pantry/store to be cut into it at ground level.

At sometime in the 18th century the Sheinton Street end of the house, which was either a service end or a byre, was replaced with an up-to-date brick-built unit with a three-bayed symmetrical frontage. This unit had excess fenestration but no doorway originally, and is only one room deep.

Brook House Farm is a fine example of an almost extinct concept—a working farm in a viable town. The buildings of the inner fold yard form a delightful and wholly uncontrived

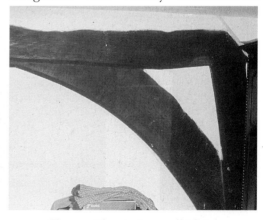

The Sheinton Street frontage in shadow, with Queen Street to the left

Truss with missing wall-plate

Brook House Farm

*The inner fold yard at Brook House Farm with timber-framed barn and stableblock
in Wenlock limestone*

composition of local vernacular building materials and style. There is no uniformity—this was never a 'model farm'—each building was erected to serve a specific purpose as and when required. Viewed anticlockwise the group includes a wash-house, kitchen, bakehouse and dairy in the first block, then a granary with a large semi-underground brick-vaulted structure below used at one time to store barrels of beer for two family-connected public houses, but it may have been an ice-house originally, possibly supplying ice to the Priory. Next comes brick-built stables, stone-built stables, a box-framed three-bay barn with pig-sties at the gable end, then a stone-built cowshed/ stableblock with a bothy over and a further cow-shed. Doves were accommodated in the gable end of the house and the pump was in the middle of the yard.

Interior of ice-house at Brook House Farm

Timber, brick and local Wenlock Limestone are the materials used for the farm buildings, as they are for the house. Where limestone is employed it is mostly as rubble, roughly coursed, but in the stone stableblock it is given a surface dressing which, though far from ashlar work, has the effect of distin-guishing the stables from the byres.

remains of arch

0 5 10 ft.   0 2 4 m.

South elevation   *East elevation with out-built stack*

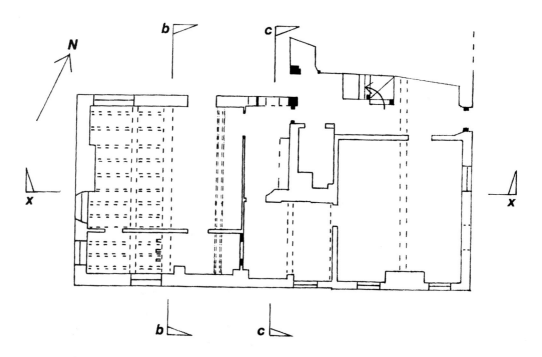

Ground floor plan

Brook House Farm (this page and opposite)

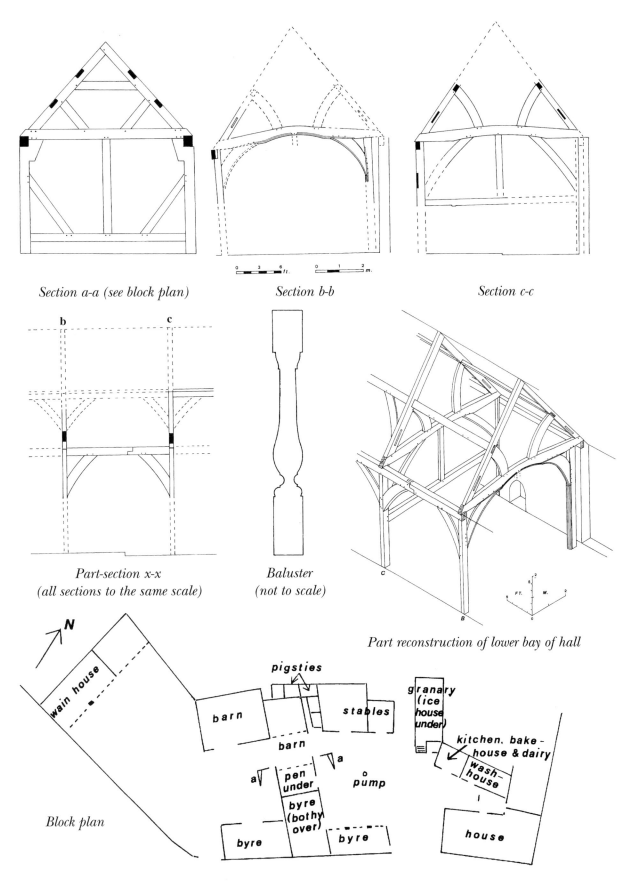

Section a-a (see block plan)   *Section b-b*   *Section c-c*

Part-section x-x
(all sections to the same scale)

Baluster
(not to scale)

Part reconstruction of lower bay of hall

Block plan

wain house

pigsties

barn

stables

barn

granary
(ice
house
under)

kitchen, bake-
house & dairy

wash-
house

pen
under

pump

byre
(bothy
over)

byre

byre

house

The Prior's House

Though strictly not vernacular this well-known building is included because its dendro date of 1425 conflicts with every other published estimate, all of which favour about 75 years later. So surprising was the dendro date, which was the same for the hall roof, solar, apartment and the upper gallery, that it was double-checked. The advanced form of the traceried windows and the two-storied gallery surely reflect the fashion-consciousness of the Cluniac order, as evinced by the mother house in Burgundy, and perhaps the ambitions of the Prior, John Stafford, at the time. Stafford seems to have been a colourful character, to say the least.[16]

The timber-vaulted roof of the first-floor hall is very elaborate, with trefoiled ornament, brattishing, cusping and carving. There are overtones of crown-post roof construction with the inclusion of a collar-purlin, but this is accompanied by open arched-braced collar-beams. That it functioned as a hall is evinced by an open hearth supported by a massive stone pillar with a louvre above. The solar and the north apartment which flank the hall are unbayed and of plainer form. The hall was

Oxenbold-type window on the first-floor hall range to south of the dorter in Much Wenlock Priory

provided with built-in window seats and tables and also hand wash-basins. A double-helix staircase at the lower end was clearly intended for use by the lower orders. The Prior would have had easier access.

Within the grounds of the Prior's Hall the east side of the block to the south of the dorter range has two windows and a blocked door in the upper floor which are identical in form to those at Great Oxenbold in Monkhopton parish, known to have been the property of Wenlock Priory and built *c.*1247.[17] On the west side there remains the profile of an aisled hall with carved corbels to support the arcade plates. The same wall contains two blocked doorways at ground level. These have Caernarvon-arched heads and may relate to a later alteration.

25-28 Barrow Street

Though undistinguished externally, this range of buildings is so far unique in the corpus of cruck construction, being a five-bayed terrace, hipped at either end and with each

25-28 Barrow Street—the cruck terrace, built in 1435

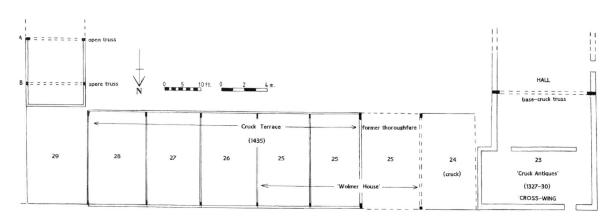

Above: Block plan of medieval houses (numbers 23 to 29) on south side of Barrow Street
Left: upper section of cruck truss in 25 Barrow Street

bay forming a separate cell, open to the roof and heated by an open hearth. In view of the dendro date, 1435, it seems likely that the row was built as medieval almshouses. Hugh Wolmer left money in his will of 1485 to maintain four almshouses, but these were on the opposite side of the road. 25-28 can be identified as five which pre-date Wolmer's death. While there may be other interpretations of the row, that of almshouses in the one favoured at present.[18]

24 Barrow Street

Infilling the space between the base-cruck house (no.23) and the cruck terrace (nos.25-28), no.24 is also of cruck construction although it is not a continuation of either of its neighbours. A three-bayed brick and stone outbuilding has a timber-framed and brick-nogged upper storey. The north-east bay is three-storied with a brick-vaulted basement. The central bay was a cow-house with tying for four or five cows, each tethered by means of an iron ring running freely along a square-sectioned iron upright set into the floor and anchored to the sill of the feeding-trough. There are no high partitions. Clearly the complex belonged to an early 19th century cow-keeper who must have supplied milk to the townspeople. The dairy still has its setlas (a raised platform on which dairy vessels were kept).

Setlas in former dairy at 24 Barrow Street

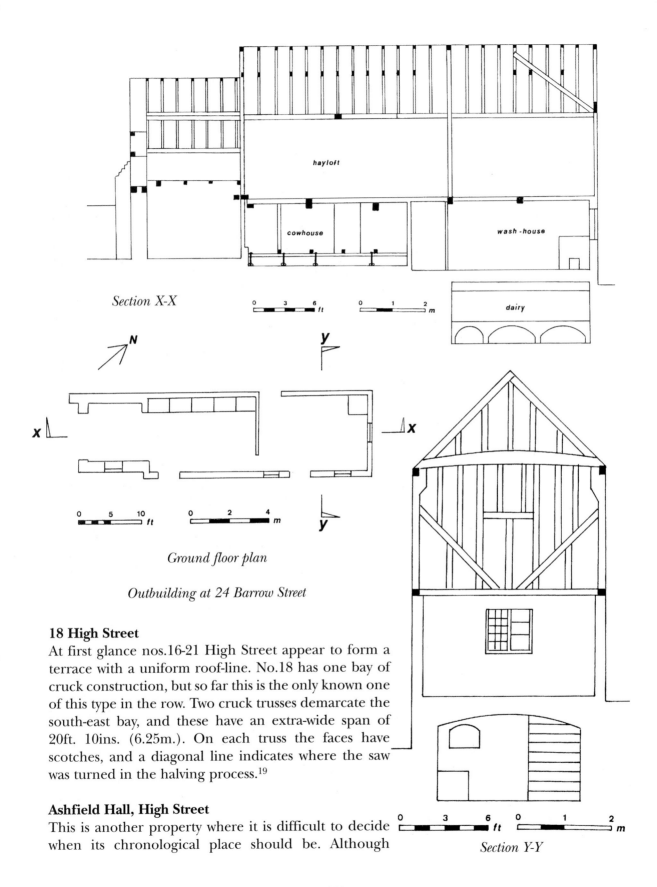

Section X-X

hayloft

cowhouse

wash-house

dairy

N

y

x

x

y

Ground floor plan

Outbuilding at 24 Barrow Street

Section Y-Y

18 High Street

At first glance nos.16-21 High Street appear to form a terrace with a uniform roof-line. No.18 has one bay of cruck construction, but so far this is the only known one of this type in the row. Two cruck trusses demarcate the south-east bay, and these have an extra-wide span of 20ft. 10ins. (6.25m.). On each truss the faces have scotches, and a diagonal line indicates where the saw was turned in the halving process.[19]

Ashfield Hall, High Street

This is another property where it is difficult to decide when its chronological place should be. Although reduced in size, it is one of Wenlock's many important medieval named halls, part stone, part timber-framed and incorporating a 15th-century stone archway. Traditionally it was the site of St. John's hospital, founded in the 13th century for 'lost and naked beggars'. High Street was formerly 'Spittle Street', the name derived from the hospital. An upper room incorporates a recess in a thick stone wall in which a 'Caernarvon' arch is worked, but the stones may be reused. Later features include 'Tudor'-style chimneystacks, fine panelling and a labelled cheese room.

The Ashfield family, connected with Wenlock since the 14th century, seem to have been in occupation until after the Dissolution when it was bought by the Lawley family who also purchased the Priory. Dr. W.P. Brookes bought it *c.*1853. Among other benefactions he founded the 'Wenlock Olympics', now regarded as the forerunner of the modern Olympic Games.[20]

Top: Ashfield Hall with 'Wenlock House' on the left
Lower: Rear of Ashfield Hall with labelled cheese room

'Wenlock House', 48 High Street

Adjoining Ashfield Hall to the north, the three-bayed front unit is built from local limestone, but an area near the conjunction with Ashfield Hall is of red sandstone. It has a dummy window in the upper storey which was meant to balance the elevation. The front unit is probably of early-to-mid 18th-century date, but a rear range at right angles encapsulates the remains of a box-framed hall-house of the 15th century. Two trusses remain; each with jowelled heads to the posts and large arch-braces supporting the tie-beam and the floor-beam. On the end truss the soffit of the tie-beam is cut to continue the chamfered arch formed by the braces, suggesting that this was perhaps the central truss of a two-bay hall. The roof has been renewed but remaining evidence points to it having been of a central king-post form flanked by raking queen-struts.

Above: 15th-century truss in the rear range
of Wenlock House, High Street
Right: Exposed truss with jowelled post-heads
and cusped braces at Church House, Barrow Street

Church House, Barrow Street

A notable feature of this much altered house is the framing in the exposed gable where the posts have jowelled heads, and cusped braces support the tiebeam. Cusping rarely occurs on external angle-braces and it is suggested that the house has been truncated and that this truss was once an internal division.

Roof of Talbot Hotel, High Street

The Talbot Hotel, High Street

Basically this is a four-bayed and two-storied box-framed house. The roof trusses have cambered tie-beams, collar-beams and a central strut flanked by two raking queen-posts, and there are threaded purlins and curved windbraces. The roof timbers are clean, clearly this was a floored building. A date in the second half of the 15th century is suggested. One of the town's principal hostelries, the county quarter sessions met by adjournment here in 1697.[21] The malthouse at the rear is dated 1762.

12 High Street

The recently uncovered timbering on the frontage is complemented by an internal transverse truss which has jowelled heads to the main posts, a cambered tie-beam and a roof structure consisting of a central king-strut, two raking queen-posts and a collar-beam. The property seems to have been two-bayed and two-storied with the roof line set parallel to the street. A date of *c*.1450 is suggested.

11 High Street

This property was drastically altered in the 1960s and now has overtones of the 'Wealden' house form, but this is illusory. It is actually a rectangular block, and at eaves level are four dragon beams, one at each corner. These do not relate to a jettied third storey but to a pyramidal roof-form which had a central raised lantern or belvedere. This is deduced from the form of the internal roof structure. The question arises regarding the nature and function of such a building in the middle of the High Street, and no satisfactory answer suggests itself.

11 High Street

1 of 4 dragon-beams at 11 High Street

Corner of Barrow Street and St. Mary's Street

In medieval times this would have been a key point in the town. The visible timbers in the gable end of the St. Mary's Street building suggest a late 15th-century date and excavations on the empty corner site revealed what was thought to be the order of a jettied building.

The Guildhall

Like other Shropshire towns there is little evidence in Much Wenlock of building activity in the first half of

The Guildhall

the 16th century. The impact of the Guildhall, the building which dominates the T-junction made by High Street, Wilmore Street and Barrow Street, must have been considerable, and however much it was changed in later years it seems that the bulk of it was built by the carpenter Richard Dawley *c*.1540—the one notable exception to the opening statement. Dawley's Guildhall was built over an open market place and was probably roofed with wooden shingles as the Bailiff's account for 1540-1 includes an item of 1 shilling and 6 pence for 'carriage of shingles for the Court House'. There is a difference of opinion regarding the chronology of the parts but the Parish Register contains the entry 'On 23rd and 24th September 1577 was reared the house over the prison house'. This can only be the two bays at the north end, now used as the Committee room. In 1676 it was necessary to lath and plaster the prison house 'to keepe out the smoake and nesty smell' which was affecting the 'Election House' (Committee room). Its pattern of close-studding with a mid-rail follows through to the main block and to the extension which was made at the south end in 1868. The latter forms the present entrance bay with a 'retiring room' above. The Guildhall still serves Much Wenlock well. Markets and fairs are held in the traditional open area, and Council and public meetings are held in the Committee room and Court room above.[22]

14 Callaughton

Although located about 1½ miles from the town, this house is within the parish of Much Wenlock. Historically, Callaughton was a dependency of Wenlock Priory. No.14 is a stone-clad two-storied and two-bayed house with a lobby entry. It presents an asymmetrical front elevation because it was remodelled around two internal timber-framed trusses at right-angles to each

other. In one, all the timbers were of primary use and produced a dendro date of 1569-70. A chequer-board ceiling is a feature of the main room.[23]

Internal framing of 1569-70 (left) at 14 Callaughton (right)

294

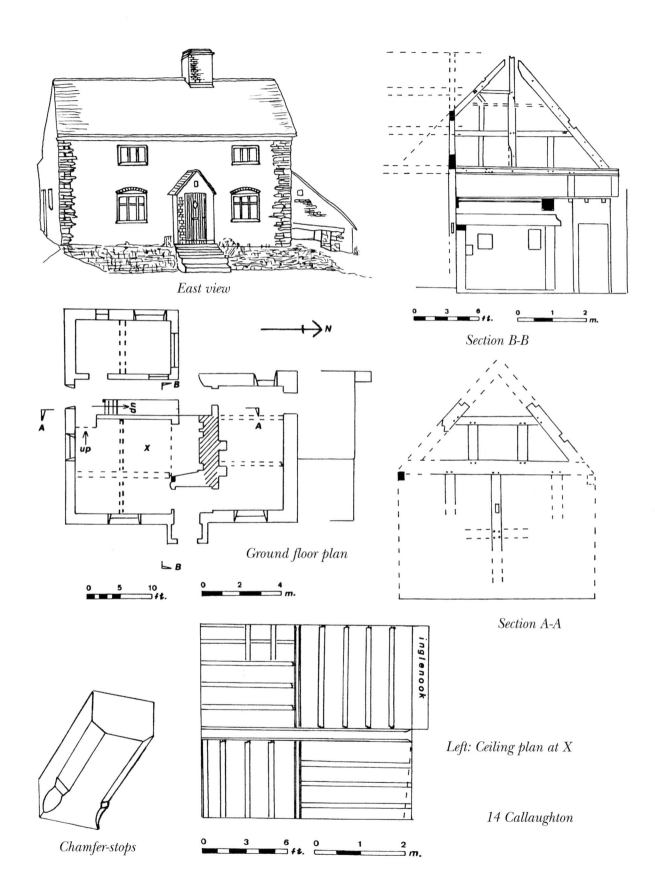

East view

Section B-B

Ground floor plan

Section A-A

Left: Ceiling plan at X

14 Callaughton

Chamfer-stops

295

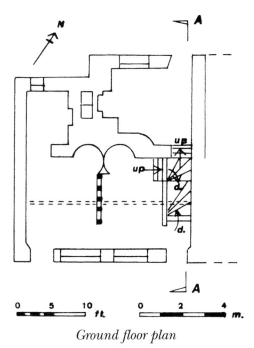

Ground floor plan

53 High Street

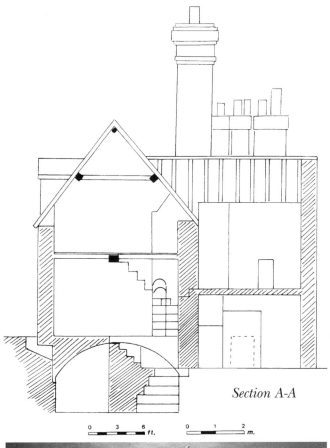

Section A-A

Stone-vaulted cellar at 53 High Street

53 High Street

This property is another which is difficult to date. Stone-built but roughcast over, it is basically three-up and two-down, but was probably built as a four-bayed block adjoining Raynald's Mansion. It now interlocks with its neighbour, no.54—the east upper room of 53 is above the shop in no.54. Each of the two ground-floor rooms of no.53 has an internal corner fireplace and these back onto one another (see ground floor plan above). They are large and imposing but not identical. There are curious floor levels. The eastern unit has steps down to a vaulted cellar and to a rear kitchen which is a later addition. The two units are divided by a timber-framed partition. The property seems dominated by the profusion of chimneystacks. It was once divided into two cottages.

The Malthouse Café, High Street

Now brick-cased, this appears to be a box-framed property of the mid-17th century. There is a shaped doorhead in the attic, and the roof structure is of queen-post construction with post-and-pad reinforcement at one end. Clearly malting was carried on here—a winch remains in the roof and a malting floor partly survives. The windows are horizontal sliding sashes, perhaps of late 18th-century date.

Above: 1 Smithfield Road
Right: staircase (?1693) at 61 High Street

1 Smithfield Road

A huge outbuilt chimneystack attached to this small single-storied stone cottage suggests squatter origins on the edge of the town, but it is not known whether this can be substantiated.

61 High Street

This double-fronted, plain, Victorian-looking shop bears a date plaque, NIR 1693 which could well date the distinctive staircase with its wide moulded hand-rail, shaped flat balusters, deep string and square newel-posts, moulded and fitted with carved finials.

29 Barrow Street

The street frontage presents a pretty 'Regency'-type cottage appearance with its twin bow windows each of 24 panes. The rear is dominated by a large added brick-built wing which itself

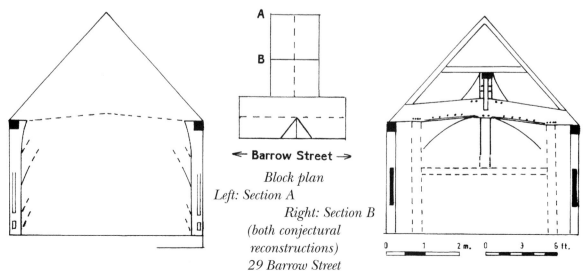

Block plan
Left: Section A
Right: Section B
(both conjectural
reconstructions)
29 Barrow Street

← **Barrow Street** →

297

has an extension. In the attic there is a gypsum floor, thought perhaps to be connected with malting. Some years ago medieval timbers, including a crown-post roof construction, a spere-truss and large curved windbraces were noted, but are no longer visible.

The Old Malthouse, Bourton Road

This was part of a maltings and allied industrial complex which, in 1985, underwent conversion. It is a two-bayed building set back from and at right-angles to the road. It has side walls of limestone and gable walls of brick and was probably a granary. The central truss has an upper-cruck truss rising from a tie-beam which rests on a brick transverse wall. The kiln was sited in front of the building. A few perforated malting tiles survive.

5 Bourton Road

Sadly this dwelling was gutted by fire in 1985. Once two stone-walled adjoining cottages occupying a road-side position—they may have had squatters' origins. The western cottage was one-and-a-half-bayed (one-and-a-half-down, one-up) and the eastern cottage was one-down, one-up. Each had large outbuilt chimneystacks at the rear and an external privy and pig-sty. The cottages were divided transversely by an upper-cruck truss which came off a brick wall.

Comment

The above inventory of buildings is not a comprehensive survey and doubtless many more historic and architectural gems await discovery. For an area of *c.*200 square yards in a town with a population of under 2,500 to be able to produce two base-cruck hall houses and evidence of a third, evidence of an aisled hall, a terrace of full-crucks and three others of cruck construction, four crown-post roofs, a building where the construction tree was growing in the time of Alfred the Great, the nationally known Prior's Hall, one building jettied all round and two with upper-crucks—is surely remarkable, at least by Shropshire standards. In vernacular terms it is a ready-made teaching aid. All this is in addition to the spectacular ruins of a great priory and the architectural glories of a parish church where a remarkable Norman west front is preserved by a later 12th-century tower.

In just a casual walk around the town there are many features which cannot fail to impress. The local Wenlock Limestone is much in evidence. Sometimes it is used in a raw chunky state, sometimes worked to a rough ashlar and occasionally as in Dr. Penny's Corn Market and Library worked to a smoother finish. There are windows with 'gothick' ogee-arches and pointed heads, chequered brickwork, a working farm, exposed crucks, alleyways called 'shuts', a pleasing row of almshouses and much more. In 1914 H.E. Forrest published his book *The Old Houses of Wenlock* which devotes 15 pages to the town itself. A pioneering work, it remains the basis of all subsequent studies.

12 The Transitional House in Shropshire

The transition from the fully developed three-part plan medieval house with its clearly defined solar and service ends or wings, screens passage and open hall to what may be called the 'early modern' house, fully floored, with a central entrance and displaying symmetry to a greater or lesser degree was, in Shropshire, no sudden event. Like classicism itself it came by a series of steps. Just as there is no example of an Inigo Jones-type house suddenly arriving in the Shropshire countryside, neither was there an overnight change from a medieval-style living pattern to one offering more privacy and where class distinction was even more pronounced.

Two houses in particular seem to terminate the old style and anticipate the new: Blunden Hall in Bishop's Castle (see drawings overleaf) and New Hall in Eaton-under-Heywood (see drawings pp.300-304). Each has the fully-developed H-plan with a floored hall, and is timber-framed. Other houses acquired this culminating form but the two mentioned are single-phased. On a smaller scale Aston House Farm in Wem parish is a good example (see drawings on p.306). This shows the hall, floored, but just beginning to lose its importance, and flanked by service and parlour crosswings.

Blunden Hall, Bishop's Castle

New Hall, Eaton-under-Heywood

Aston House Farm, Wem

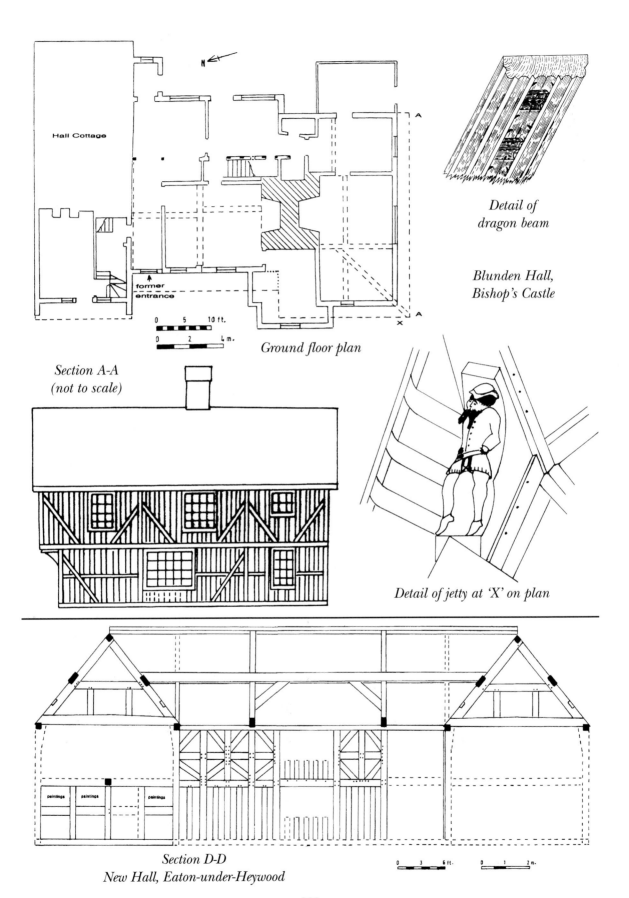

Hall Cottage

N

A

former
entrance

X

A

0   5   10 ft.

0   2   4 m.

Ground floor plan

*Detail of
dragon beam*

*Blunden Hall,
Bishop's Castle*

*Section A-A
(not to scale)*

Detail of jetty at 'X' on plan

paintings   paintings   paintings

0   3   6 ft.   0   1   2 m.

*Section D-D
New Hall, Eaton-under-Heywood*

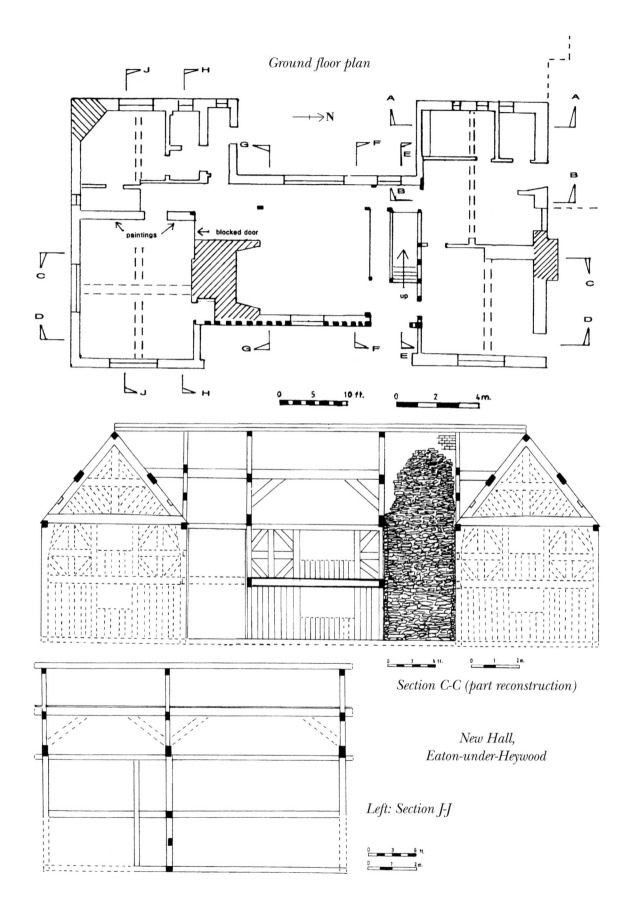

Ground floor plan

→N

paintings ← blocked door

up

0   5   10 ft.

0   2   4 m.

Section C-C (part reconstruction)

New Hall,
Eaton-under-Heywood

Left: Section J-J

0   3   6 ft.

0   1   2 m.

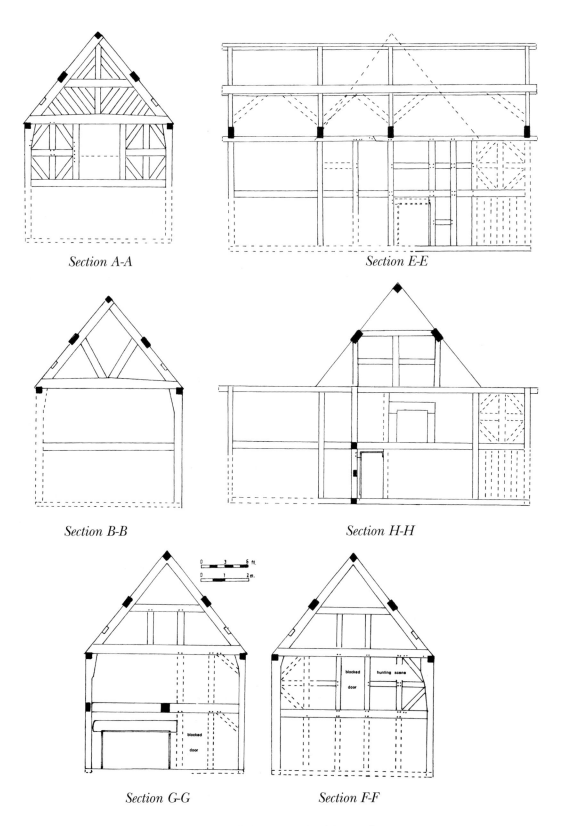

Section A-A

Section E-E

Section B-B

Section H-H

Section G-G

Section F-F

New Hall, Eaton-under-Heywood

7ft. 4ins.

3ft. 9ins.

Paintings at New Hall, Eaton-under-Heywood
Top: in the Great Chamber; bottom: in ground-floor parlour

Paintings at New Hall, Eaton-under-Heywood
Left: on the 'Jenks Post'; right: detail of huntsman

The changes, gradual as they were, began in the 16th century, but not in the early part. It has been noted previously that virtually the whole of Henry VIII's reign is a blank as far as new building in Shropshire is concerned. Dendrochronological sampling and analysis confirms this. From a total of 182 workable dates obtained by this method only seven relate to Henry's reign, and of these one is a reused wall-plate, one is a replacement cruck-truss and one is a reused cruck in a farm building. Of the remaining four only two—the hall at Abcott Manor and Upper Lake in Westbury parish—can be considered as single entities. The other two are wings added to older halls and in the case of Newport's Guildhall the timbers for the added wing were felled only a year before Henry died.[1] Plaish Hall, the single example previously thought to be of *c.*1540 on account of the HR cipher on the parlour ceiling is now known to be of *c.*1577 and the painted ceiling to be a piece of late 19th- or early 20th-century antiquarianism.[2]

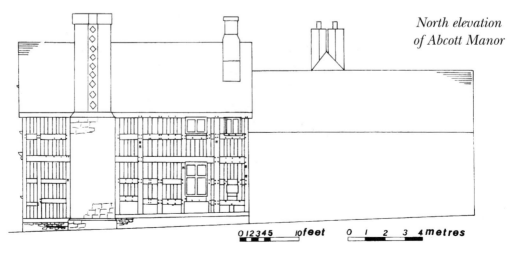

North elevation
of Abcott Manor

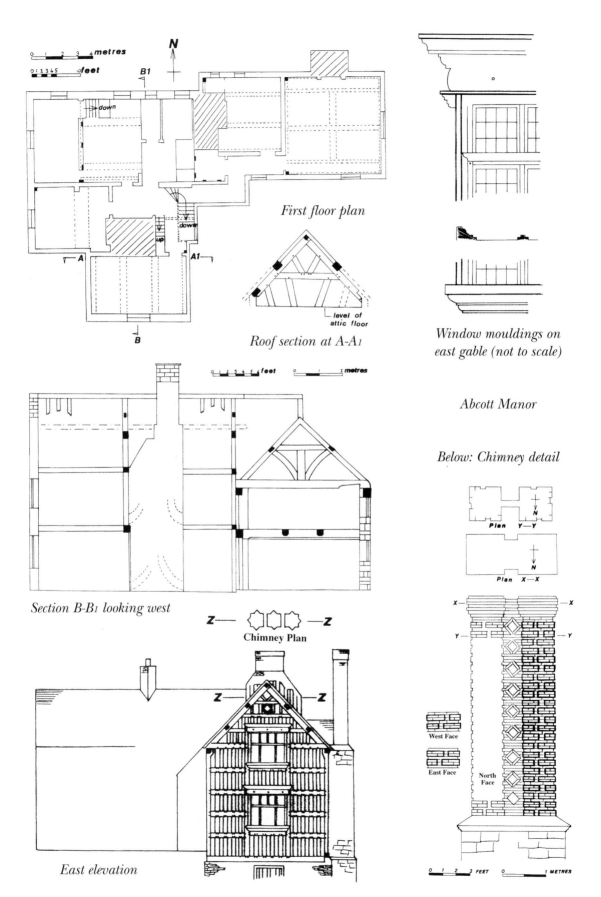

First floor plan

Roof section at A-A1

level of
attic floor

Window mouldings on
east gable (not to scale)

Abcott Manor

Below: Chimney detail

Plan Y—Y

Plan X—X

Section B-B1 looking west

Chimney Plan

West Face

East Face

North Face

East elevation

305

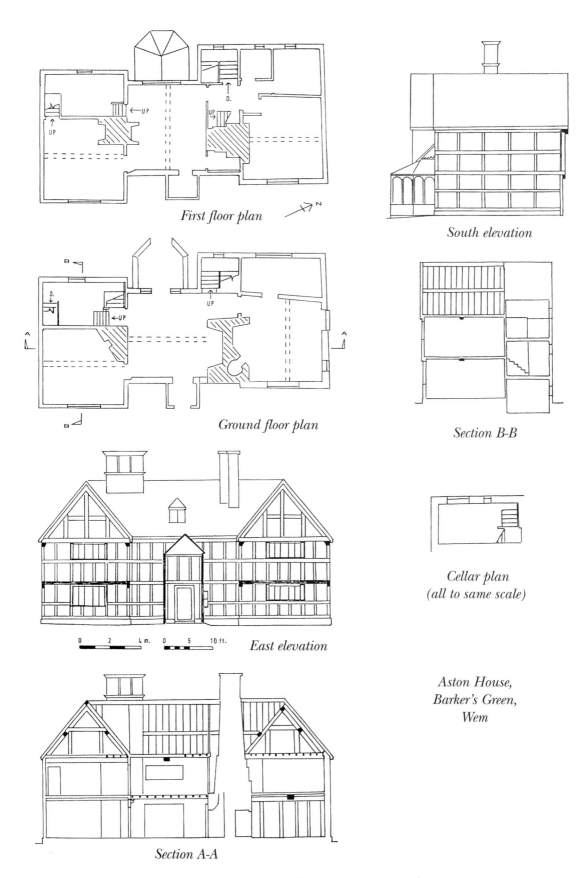

First floor plan

South elevation

Ground floor plan

Section B-B

East elevation

*Cellar plan
(all to same scale)*

Section A-A

*Aston House,
Barker's Green,
Wem*

Plaish Hall, Cardington

Ash Wood, Ash, Whitchurch (1550)

Manor Cottage, Prees (1553-4)

It may be argued that dendrochronology presents a lop-sided view of affairs, and, doubtless, improvements and alterations to houses were being carried out during this time. But, on the evidence available at present, no major building works were undertaken and confidence seems to be lacking until after the turn of the half-century. Even then little new building occurred until Elizabeth I's reign when an up-turn in the fortunes of the Drapers' Company in Shrewsbury sparked off a boom in building activity, the results of which survive in many cases and are datable from sources other than dendrochronology. Two vernacular buildings in north Shropshire, Ash Wood in Ash and Manor Cottage in Prees, have felling dates of 1550 and 1553/4 respectively. Each is cruck-built. Ashwood was built with a single-bay open hall and was subsequently altered, but Manor Cottage, built with a two-bay open hall and a byre at the lower end, is comparatively unchanged. Each emphasises the persistence of tradition in Shropshire, how late the practice of cruck building continued, and how reluctant people were to abandon the open hall.[3] Indeed, Plaish Hall, mentioned above, although in the forefront of brick construction, was entirely medieval in its plan-form, and incorporated an open hall with a hammer-beam roof.

However, changes were on the way and the first of these seems to have been concerned with the management of the open hearth. Where previously control of the louvre must have been something of a hit-or-miss affair, judging by the evidence remaining in a number of houses, the introduction of a purpose-built smoke-hood to duct the smoke through the roof and into the open air, heralded the first of these changes. Manor Cottage and

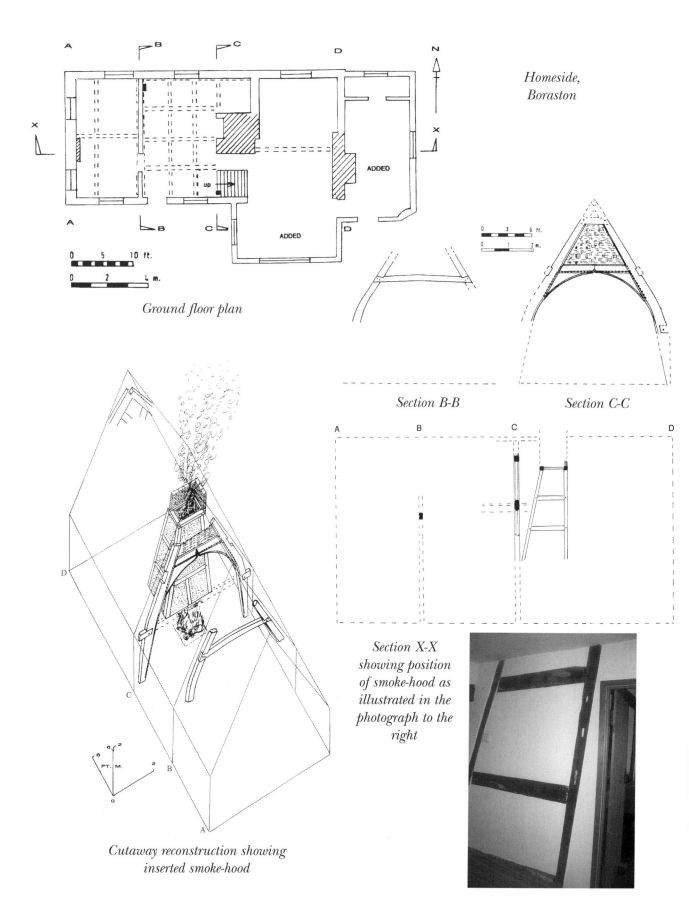

Homeside, Boraston

0 5 10 ft.

0 2 4 m.

Ground floor plan

0 3 6 ft.

0 1 2 m.

Section B-B

Section C-C

Section X-X showing position of smoke-hood as illustrated in the photograph to the right

Cutaway reconstruction showing inserted smoke-hood

Homeside, Boraston

Ashwood were each built with a smoke-hood; at Habberley Hall (1555), a building jettied on all four sides, a central smoke extractor was built[4] and at Wolverton in Eaton-under-Heywood a smoke-hood was inserted into the lower bay of the hall sometime between 1557 and 1589, the most likely date being 1570.[5] At Homeside in Boraston parish (see opposite) the smoke-hood survives with a brick-built chimney inside it, and here there is clear evidence that the smoke-hood was topped with a brick projection and that later the whole wattle-and-daub 'gathering' was lined with brickwork. At the Old Shop in Somerwood in Upton Magna parish it was possible to trace the development of a small single-celled cottage with an open hearth at one end and accommodation for a cow at the other, to its present form of desirable residence (see drawings on this page). Phase two in this development included the replacement of the open hearth by a smoke-hood or 'fumbrell' which survives to the present day.[6]

Of course, this is not to say that smoke control was not possible in earlier times. There is plenty of evidence in magnates' houses such as Stokesay, Moreton Corbet, and various castles for stone fireplaces which must have

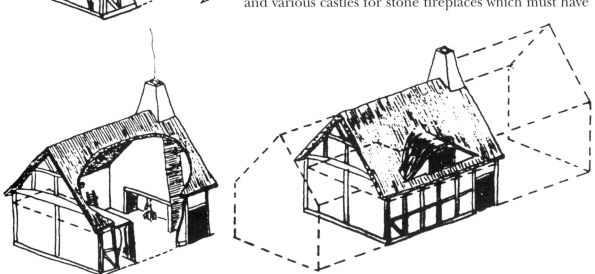

The Old Shop, Somerwood, Upton Magna
Top left: phase 1; lower left: phase 2 with the addition of the smoke-hood;
lower right: phases 3 and 4, phase 4 being indicated by the dotted lines

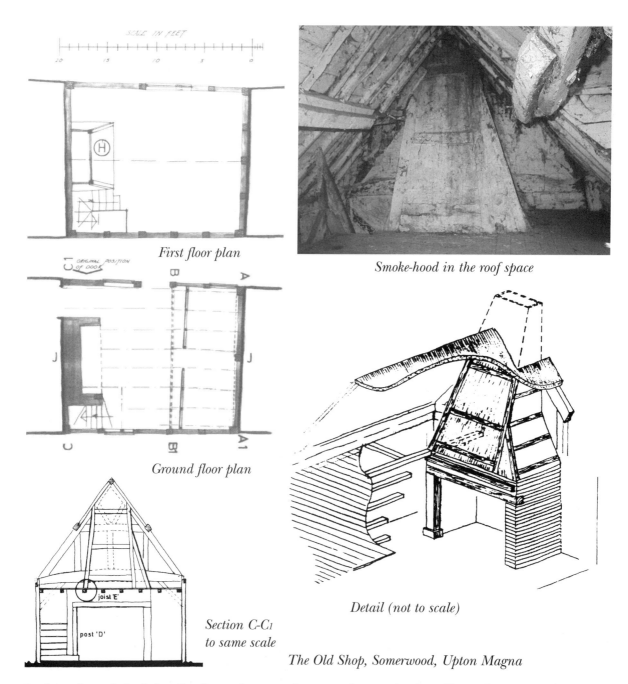

First floor plan

Smoke-hood in the roof space

Ground floor plan

Detail (not to scale)

Section C-C₁
to same scale

The Old Shop, Somerwood, Upton Magna

had wattle-and-daub hoods above them, and one such remains in a Shrewsbury town house, 2 Pride Hill, which has an estimated date of 1250-60.[7] A curious anomaly is the lack of evidence for main fireplaces at Acton Burnell, which, like Stokesay, was a defensible manor house rather than a castle.[8] But these are supra-vernacular houses and this work is mainly concerned with houses at a lower social level.

Having improved the heating arrangements and general visibility in the open hall, it seems that thoughts turned firstly to replacing smoke-hoods with chimneys built with either brick or stone and then, quickly, to flooring over the open hall, thus getting two or more rooms where previously there was only one.

The Isle, Bicton—a 'back-to-front' house

When chimneystacks were inserted their siting is interesting. Frequently they were placed where the hearth had always been, and this often accounts for the absence of louvre details in old roofs. Often they were sited not far away from the original open hearth, sometimes backing onto the the spere-truss, sometimes in the screens passage, occasionally against the rear wall, but never against the front wall. Frontal chimneys are not a feature of Shropshire houses and when they do occur they can nearly always be shown to be either very late and uncomfortable additions or they are indicating that the house is now back to front. The Isle at Bicton is a good example of the latter as is The Orchards in Ditton Priors, though on a smaller scale. Plaish Hall was built with a rear wall chimneystack serving the hall and this, with those for the parlours, forms a distinctive feature of the house, but it must be emphasised that Plaish was a magnate's house.[9] Corner chimneys, where they can be shown to be insertions, are usually later, and normally they are associated with newly-built houses of the 17th century.

With the insertion of the brick or stone chimneystack it was a small step to the flooring over of the hall. But in many cases it is possible to detect an interim phase when the upper bay of the hall was floored across but all or part of the lower bay was left open, presumably because the smoke-hood continued in use. The evidence for a two-stage development can usually be found in the difference in the treatment of the spine-beam and in the sizes and forms of the joists. Often in Shropshire the inserted ceiling which naturally accompanied the flooring over of the hall was a thing of beauty, not simply a utilitarian feature. Probably the most striking example is that at Wolverton. Here there is a main axial beam, a transverse beam and secondary intersecting beams which divide the area into squares. Within the squares are set joists in chequerboard fashion. All the components have a moulding based on the cyma and the area is defined by perimeter beams, similarly moulded. The timbers were too fragile to sample by dendrochronology, but the date of 1570 is suggested by analogy with other features which were sampled.[10] An inserted ceiling of almost identical form is found at The Hyde in the parish of Ditton Priors. Here the inserted chimneystack occupies the whole of the lower bay of the hall and has three star-shaped shafts with continuous star capping. The

Inserted chequerboard ceiling at The Hyde, Ditton Priors

Hyde is otherwise a humbler dwelling than Wolverton and is box-framed throughout in contrast to Wolverton's two-tier cruck and spere-truss construction with cusping.

Fifteen further chequerboarded ceilings, not as elaborate as the two already quoted, but pleasing nevertheless, occur elsewhere in Shropshire, and doubtless there are more. Some have ascribed felling dates: Bedstone Manor is *c.*1560, High Grosvenor in Claverly parish is 1566-1610, and 14 Callaughton in Much Wenlock parish is 1569-70. By analogy it seems reasonable to suggest that the second half of the 16th century was the heyday for these chequerboarded, counter-changed or cross-joisted ceilings.[11]

If the inserted chimneystack was sited in the screens passage or, if there was no demarcation at the lower end of the hall, in the cross passage, it altered the pattern of access into the house and gave rise to the lobby-entry or baffle-entry as it is sometimes called because on entering the house a person would be faced with the 'baffle' of the side wall of the stack and could turn left or right but not progress further along the passage as was previously the case. Obviously, access was restricted to two rooms only; the stairs, necessary now to reach the newly acquired room over the hall, were usually placed at the rear of the stack, filling what was left of the old screens passage, and to reach the stairs it was necessary to pass through one of the two rooms. The central entrance hall which gave access to all the ground-floor rooms and to the staircase was still a thing of the future. But despite the restrictions of the lobby-entry it seems to have been a popular feature and many houses were adapted accordingly. In a few instances in Shropshire examples of a dog-wheel have been found in the side wall of the stack instead of the more common place above the fireplace. Siting the source of power for the roasting-spit here would have the advantage of keeping the dog cooler, and if it was a hot day and he required more ventilation it would be a simple matter to open the front door. Whether humanity was a consideration is not known. The best example is at Eudon George in Chetton parish.

New houses were built incorporating the lobby-entry and with this it became possible to plan a symmetrically-fronted house of two stories. The 'early modern' house had arrived. A house called The Ditches in Wem parish is the supreme example of the new thinking. It has a date of 1612 engraved on the door-latch and although this seems a curious place for a date, it accords well with every feature: fully two-storied, jettied on all four sides, three-bayed with the central bay occupied by the chimneystack, a central two-storied porch and close-studding with a middle rail forming the pattern of framing at either level. The casement windows have ovolo moulding as does the Grinshill-stone parlour fireplace. The ceilings in both ground-floor rooms are partly chequerboarded and the roof has two tiers of purlins and straight windbraces. The room on the northern side of the stack was the kitchen or 'houseplace' and the other was the parlour, a plan repeated frequently around this time.[12]

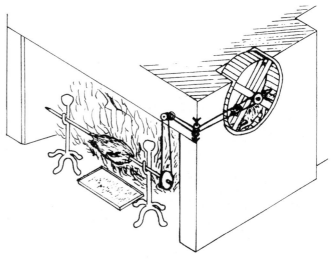

Conjectural reconstruction of dog-wheel housing at Eudon George, Chetton

The Ditches may be regarded as a trend-setter, or perhaps as a catalyst inasmuch as other houses changed their

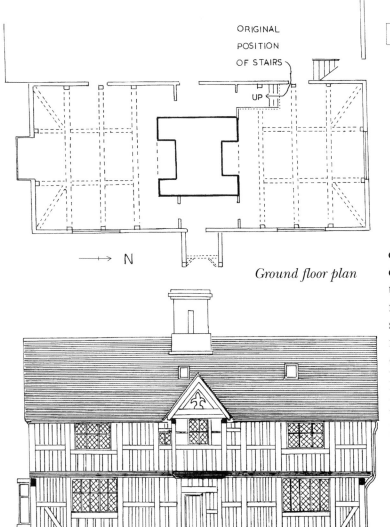

ORIGINAL
POSITION
OF STAIRS

UP

→ N

Ground floor plan

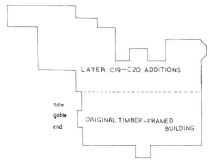

LATER C19—C20 ADDITIONS

new
gable
end

ORIGINAL TIMBER-FRAMED
BUILDING

Outline plan of building

The Ditches, Wem

East elevation

North elevation

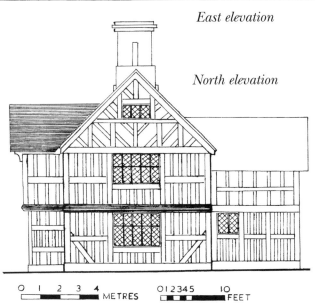

0 1 2 3 4 METRES   0 1 2 3 4 5 10 FEET

existing form to keep up to date, adopting the twin or triple-gabled approach as the next fashion. Examples abound such as Cherrington Manor near Newport (see illustrations on following pages), Coppice Farm in Pulverbatch, Home Farm, Sandford in West Felton which was brick-clad, Arleston Manor (see photograph on p.318), Rushbury Manor (see photograph on p.318) and many others. Town houses developed the gable-fronted trend earlier, and Owen's Mansion in High Street, Shrewsbury, (1592), though only a shell, remains a superb example of Elizabethan domestic architecture at least in its two upper stories as seen from the street. Sherer's Mansion at the bottom of Wyle Cop in Shrewsbury was the text-book example of the style: timber-framed, triple-gabled, jettied at two levels, with applied projecting windows, moulded bressumers, brackets and much ornament. Sadly this house was demolished, but Ludlow retains a building which had tenurial links with Sherer's Mansion—the Feathers. This seems to have assumed much of its present spectacular appearance *c.*1619. It was the culmination of the trend, better examples would be hard to find.[13]

313

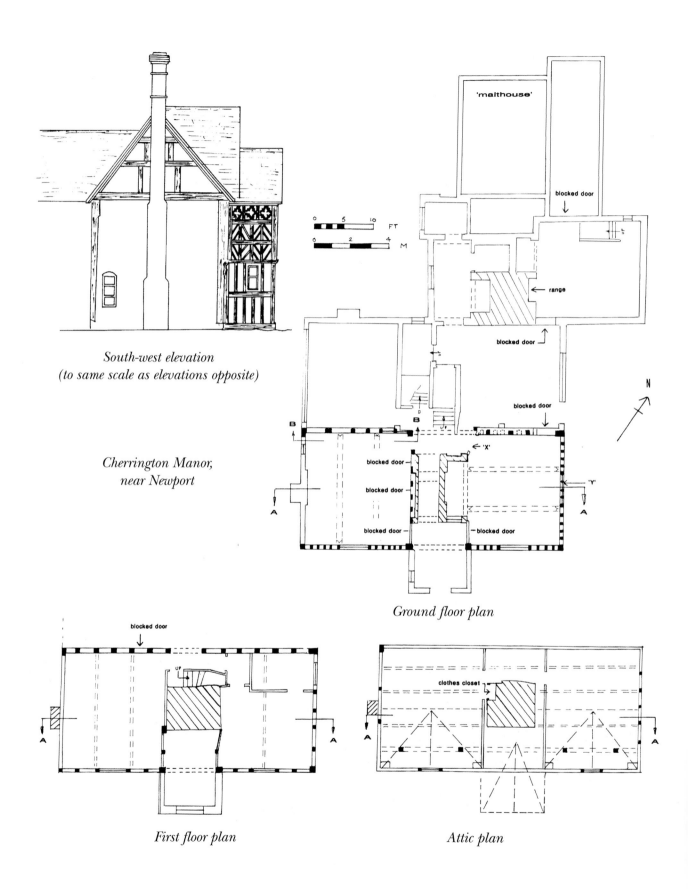

South-west elevation
(to same scale as elevations opposite)

Cherrington Manor,
near Newport

'malthouse'

blocked door

range

blocked door

blocked door

'X'

blocked door

blocked door

'Y'

blocked door

blocked door

Ground floor plan

blocked door

First floor plan

clothes closet

Attic plan

314

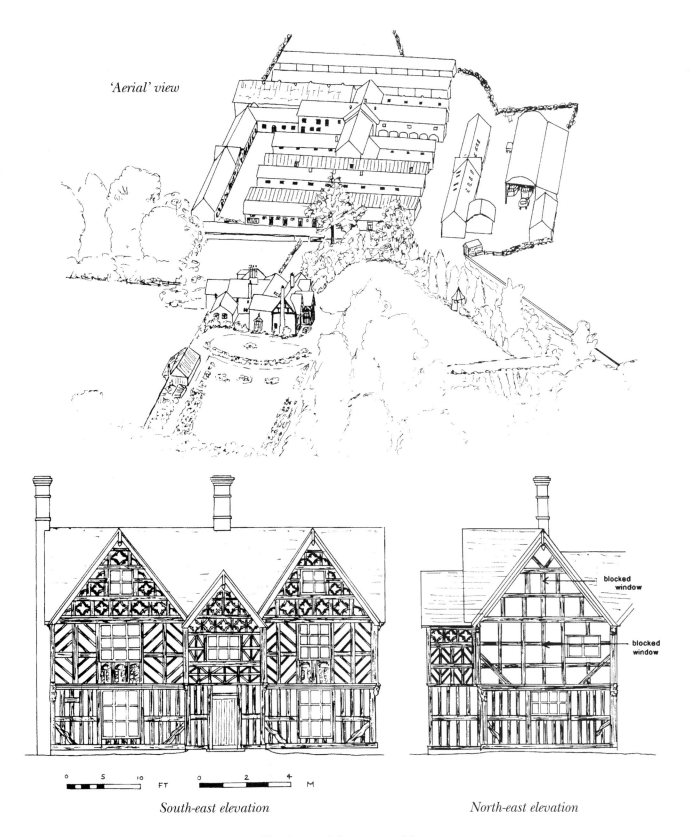

'Aerial' view

blocked window

blocked window

0	5	10		0	2	4	
		FT				M	

South-east elevation

North-east elevation

Cherrington Manor, near Newport

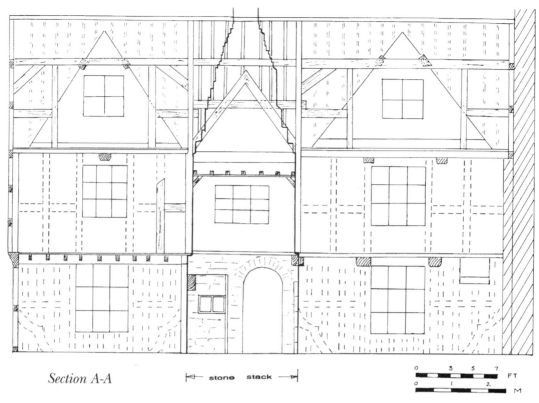

Section A-A   ⟵ stone   stack ⟶

0 3 5 7 FT
0   1   2. M

Cherrington Manor, near Newport

*Far left and near left: middle and lower
panel, respectively, in door shown
at 'x' on ground floor plan
(both to scale shown)
Below: bracket to east corner post on
south-east elevation
(not to scale)*

0 1 3 IN
0 3 4 8 CM

North window panel on south-east elevation

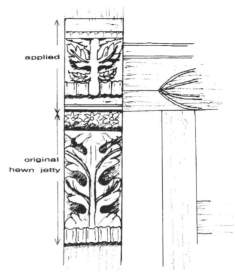

applied

original
hewn jetty

*Details to south corner post on
south-east elevation*

*South window panel on south east
elevation*

*Left: Details of south side
porch brackets*

*Right: Details of east side
porch brackets*

*(none of the drawings
on this page are to scale)*

Cherrington Manor, near Newport

Arleston Manor—twin-gabled

Rushbury Manor—triple-gabled

Cross House, Longden

The progression from the lobby-entry arrangement to the central entrance hall plan is more difficult to demonstrate, and it may have come about in a subtle way. If the T-shaped house is accepted as a desirable form, and there can be little doubt that this was the case in Shropshire, and if it had acquired a lobby-entry such as at Cross House in Longden, Eudon George in Chetton (see drawings opposite and overleaf), or Brookgate Farm, Plealy in Pontesbury, to give but a few examples, access to the second room in the crosswing was only possible through the first. Similarly, the stairs could only be accessed by going through the parlour(s) on one side or the hall/kitchen on the other. The great step forward was to bring the stairs into the entrance area and to relocate the chimneystack to the end wall. This was a major undertaking in a lobby-entry house, but new houses could be built to this plan and in Whitchurch there are two houses, Ellesmere House in Dodington (see photograph overleaf) and Barkhill House in Barkhill where the front and rear walls are timber-framed, but the gable walls which accommodate the chimneystacks are of brick. The entrance in both examples is centrally placed and opens into an entrance hall which contains the staircase and gives access to all the ground-floor rooms.[14] A late 17th-century date is suggested for these houses and this marks the arrival of the really modern house whose plan is still considered the most desirable today.

318

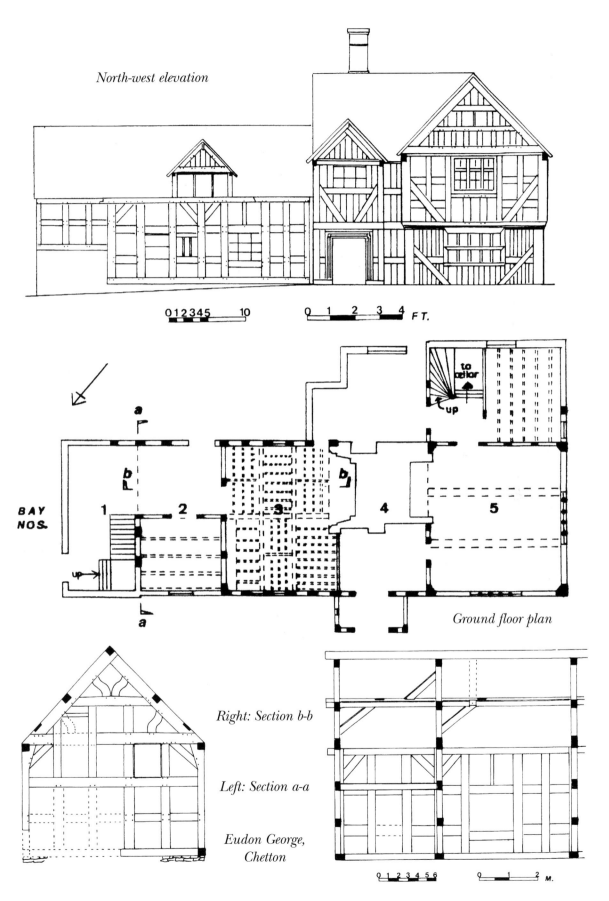

North-west elevation

0 1 2 3 4 5   10

0   1   2   3   4   FT.

BAY NOS.

1   2   3   4   5

to cellar

up

up

a   *b*   *b*   *a*

Ground floor plan

Right: Section b-b

Left: Section a-a

Eudon George, Chetton

0 1 2 3 4 5 6   0   1   2   M.

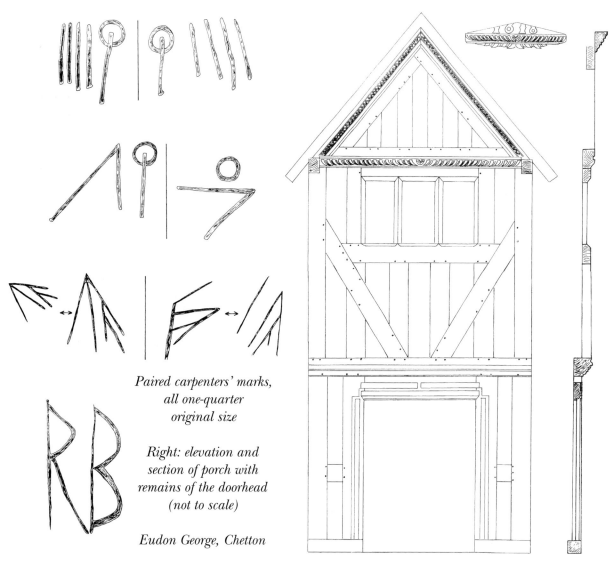

*Paired carpenters' marks,
all one-quarter
original size*

*Right: elevation and
section of porch with
remains of the doorhead
(not to scale)*

Eudon George, Chetton

In south Shropshire Lower House Farm, Cleedownton, in Stoke St. Milborough parish (see illustrations opposite) illustrates the forward thinking in a truly rural area. Almost square in plan, it has stone outer walls, timber-framed partition walls, is three stories high and has attics. Only two bays wide, it has a central entrance which leads into the main room, but from here the stairs are accessed as are the three other ground-floor rooms. Its plan, there-fore, mirrors the plan at Whitehall in Shrewsbury (1578-83) built for

Ellesmere House, Dodington, Whitchurch (after restoration)

320

Lower House Farm, Cleedownton

Richard Prince, a magnate, which is regarded as if not the first, then a very early example of the double-pile plan and *avant garde* in its conception.[15] Admittedly there is probably a century's time lapse between the two, but this only emphasises the gulf at this time between the 'polite' and the 'vernacular'.

Staircase at Barkhill House, Whitchurch

From this arrangement it is only a small step to planning a proper entrance hall.

In Shrewsbury the house known as the Guildhall in Dogpole which was built as the town house of the Newport family in *c.*1696 neatly closes the 17th century and ushers in the 18th. Brick-built, hip-roofed, five-bayed, two-storied and very dignified it has a perfectly symmetrical front but, like a handful of others in the county, internal symmetry was absent. The Ditches of nearly one hundred years earlier displayed more harmony.

The 'transitional house', therefore, was a developing embryo with a gestatory period of about one hundred and fifty years. But this is not to say that all the phases were as neatly

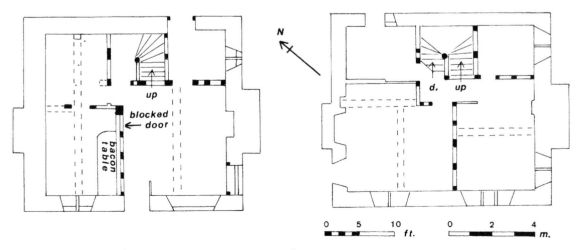

Lower House Farm, Cleedownton, Stoke St. Milborough
Left: Ground floor plan; right: First floor plan

ordered as the text perhaps suggests. In a lecture given at a seminar in Birmingham University in May 1985 Eric Mercer said 'Builders of vernacular houses seem to have been a very open-minded lot, some of them well able to think up answers to new problems without having to wait for somebody else from somewhere else to find a solution for them; men, that is, capable in practice of jumping some of the phases in a development which has to be envisaged in theory'. From that it follows that present-day thinking needs to be as flexible as that of our fore-fathers, which, often it is not.

13   Painted Decorations in Shropshire Houses

A consequence of the post-war improvements in education, the conservation movement and the current comparative affluence of property owners, is that when buildings are stripped out as part of a restoration programme the uncovering is done with more care, and hitherto unsuspected features are not so easily lost as in previous decades. A case in point is the number of examples of early painted decorations that have been revealed in Shropshire houses. These range from simple and sometimes crude designs painted on walls and beams to elaborate events or scenery. As churches have layers of whitewash removed from their internal walls so earlier paintings are revealed, although nothing to equal the spectacular mural depicting the battle between the Virtues and the Vices at All Saints, Claverley, discovered at the turn of the 20th century and thought to date from the late 12th, has emerged. But this chapter is concerned only with known domestic examples.

No tapestries are known to have survived in the county, but there is a remarkable example of the 'poor man's tapestry'—a set of painted cloths—in Munslow Farm. By their nature these wall hangings were never very durable, and few examples have survived nationally, making this Shropshire set extremely important. Almost equally rare is the set of the 'Nine Worthies' at Great Binnall in the parish of Astley Abbotts, and the possibility of two further sets within the complex of Wenlock Priory almost smacks of a Shropshire monopoly. To these, though in a different context, can be added the stock of 40 sets once held by the 16th-century Shrewsbury bookseller, Roger Ward.

The discovery of the tripartite religious painting, technically a 'fresco' as the colours were applied to damp, freshly-laid plaster, at the King's Head in Shrewsbury was undoubtedly the most important archaeological discovery of its type in 1987 and brings home the message of how easily it could have been lost had the repair work not been entrusted to a firm of architects experienced in dealing sensitively with old buildings. By the same token it is distressing to contemplate the number of paintings that have been lost. All the examples described below have been seen by the author, but because of the variety in subject matter, media, type, age and condition it has proved impossible to tabulate them in any meaningful way, and therefore they are grouped under broad headings and in a very conjectural chronological order.

Freehand painting applied to walls, panels, timbers and fireplaces

The King's Head, Mardol, Shrewsbury
In 1987, during restoration work a remarkable fresco was discovered on a brick chimneystack located at the junction between the main block, which is set parallel to the street, and a rear hall range at right-angles to it. The stack had had another flue constructed against it and this

meant that the painting had suffered mutilation and the effects of heat but had still been preserved. When fully exposed, cleaned and conserved it was seen to consist of three 'registers'; at the top is a lion *couchant*, the middle register depicts the Last Supper, and at the bottom is the Annunciation. The lion may represent St. Mark's symbol; the other three Evangelists' symbols may have occupied the space above, but these have not survived. The Last Supper is remarkably well preserved, although the Christ figure has suffered most (see illustration p.229). The apostles are seated behind the table and Judas stands in front of it with his hand in the dish. ('He that dippeth his hand with me in the dish, the same shall betray me'; Matthew 26, 23). Included is a very rare feature in Last Supper depictions—St. Paul on Christ's left, holding a sword, the instrument of his martyrdom. St. Peter with his keys is thought to be the figure on Christ's right. Details of the table, cutlery, dishes and food are all very clear. The Annunciation scene shows Mary with her hands raised, Gabriel with wings outstretched and between them the lily pot, lilies being symbolic of Mary's purity. Linking the three elements is a scroll with gothic lettering. In Annunciation scenes this is usually the

*Fresco on chimneystack
in the King's Head*

opening verse of the Latin prayer which begins *Ave, Maria, gratia plena; Dominus tecum: benedicta to in mulieribus, et benedictus fructus ventris tui, Jesus.* The lettering in the painting is too badly worn to be deciphered but is likely to be the conventional text. There is also a flying dove with the host in its beak. Though close to Mary's head this relates to the Last Supper scene.[1]

The artwork is executed in black outline on a background of red ochre, the foundation being a coating of lime plaster on the brickwork. A range of pigments was used to emphasise

Detail of Apostles' heads

the objects and figures, predominately white, but with traces of blue and orange. The importance of the painting lies not only in the quality of the artwork and the unusual features, but in its rarity value. Of the number of surviving pre-Reformation paintings known nationally, probably less than 5% occur in non-secular buildings. It has proved difficult to date but is thought to belong to the period *c.*1450-1520. The framework of the building has been dendro-dated to 1404.[2] The nearest comparative

on north wall of crosswing ← ——————— → ← on door-posts →

0 ——————— 1 ft.

0 ——————— 0·3 m.

Painted studs at Church Farm, Withington

painting is that of the Last Judgement in Cound church, but there are marked similarities with the Last Supper painting at Savigny in the maritime département of Manche in north-west France, thought to date from *c*.1300.

Its discovery also has implications for the use of bricks in Shropshire—until now thought to be no earlier than the mid-16th century—for the nature of the site of the King's Head, and for the function of the room in which it was found. More artwork was discovered on the reverse of the stack. This was a stencilled pattern and is described under the next group heading.

Church Farm, Withington
In this farmhouse there are paintings in the ground-floor room of the crosswing, on the studs and the door-posts. Flowers, fruit and foliage are depicted in white on a black background.

Alcaston Manor
This is a house of several different builds. The oldest surviving unit is the north-western jettied crosswing and this has been dendro-dated to 1556.[3] Historically the manor court was held in the upper chamber, which had its own external entrance, but the paintings are in the ground-floor room. They occur on the joists and the dragon-beam in vertical bands of stylised foliage and are very fragmentary. Some variety is introduced with at least one joist having guilloche work instead of foliage. The medium is black distemper for the background with white imposed design work.

The Olde House, Dogpole, Shrewsbury
Above the fireplace in the ground-floor, street-facing parlour is a fireplace lintel or mantel-beam which bears painted emblems of a crown flanked by two pomegranates and two Tudor roses. These are executed in vivid reds and gold and outlined in black or dark grey. On the brickwork of the chimney above is a design incorporating ancanthus leaves and flowers. These are also outlined in black and have blues, greys and shades of brown predominating.

Traditionally the house was visited by the Princess Mary, daughter of Henry VIII and Catherine of Aragon, when a child under the guardianship of Anthony Rocke, the owner of the house and one of Catherine's retainers. Although there is no documentary proof that such a visit or visits took place the symbols certainly relate to Catherine of Aragon and the pomegranate, the incorruptible fruit, is shown with the skin peeled back, exposing the seeds. Significantly, the lintel is concealed underneath a

Overmantel raised to show paintings at The Olde House

carved Jacobean panel. It was discovered in the mid-19th century, and the then owner had the later panel hinged so that it could be lifted up to expose the paintings. Perhaps it was considered a judicious move to conceal the earlier painting once the Reformation had taken place. It is believed that similar paintings on canvas remain beneath the panelling in the room.[4]

Painted post at Newport's Guildhall

The Guildhall, Newport

The restoration of this building has uncovered four hitherto concealed examples of painted decoration. The earliest occurs on a post in the eastern street-facing bay. The post is a support for an inserted floor. The painting is unlikely to have been executed after the alterations and therefore must relate to an unknown provenance. It is a design of a thick stem carrying a Tudor rose and clusters of fruit, probably pomegranates, foliage and flowing ribbons. At the top there is hint of classical design in a capital which has a band of guilloche-type ornament below it. Surmounting the capital is a strong ancanthus leaf motif. The painting is done in white outline on a black or dark grey background and may have been intended to commemorate Henry VIII's marriage to Catherine of Aragon, for the pomegranate was one of Catherine's symbols. However, this marriage took place in 1509 and the painting is stylistically similar to others in Shropshire which appear to relate to the later 16th century. The other paintings in the Guildhall are described under their appropriate headings.

New Hall, Eaton-under-Heywood

Here a hunting scene is executed across two panels and a stud in the chamber above the hall. Mostly outlined in dark grey on white, there are traces of colour, notably in the blood of the stag which has been brought down by the hounds and is receiving the *coup-de-grâce* from the huntsman's spear. The lines and movement are flowing and vigorous, trees and foliage are shown, as are features which may have local significance such as the fresh-water mussels still to be found in the Byne brook

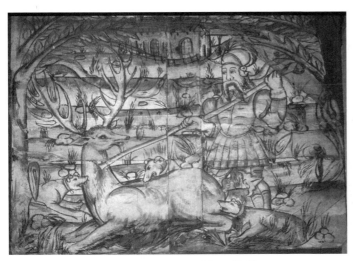

Hunting scene at New Hall

Figures on the left-hand panel in the parlour at New Hall

*Musician and monkey on the right-hand panel
in the parlour at New Hall*

which borders the property, and the building at the top which may represent the parish church, a local castle or even a previous house on the site. The huntsman is shown wearing a square-necked full long-sleeved waisted tunic with a pleated skirt, chausses with knee-shields, gauntlets and a helmet with an adjustable peak. He has a forked beard and full moustache. The costume suggests a date in the first half of the 16th century, but the house itself is more likely to date from nearer 1600.

At ground-floor level the great parlour has paintings across the wall which divides that room from the adjoining small parlour. Unfortunately an inserted doorway has removed some of the paintings but the remainder seem to depict scenes of jollity. The left hand panel consists of three figures—two female and one male—in Elizabethan costume. The central female figure holds a lute, the lady on her right holds a rose in one hand and offers a different kind of flower to the musician with the other. The male figure is less well preserved but he wears a doublet and pouched hose, and has his hands on his hips. The quality of this painting has been described as 'uneven', with the ruffs crudely done but the faces and hands delicately drawn.[5] Elsewhere on this side of the doorway fragments of human figures remain.

On the other side of the doorway the remaining, right-hand panel shows a male hand-bell ringer, a male figure playing a stringed instrument with a bow, the lower half of a large bird, and, most puzzling of all, what seems to be a monkey or an ape-like creature of some kind. The head is very vigorously painted in a darker colour than the human flesh tones and it seems to be applauding or perhaps beating time to the music. In the lower half of the same panel is a hare and some kind of 'Renaissance-type' foliated frieze or border.

At first-floor level is a post with paintwork at the top. This depicts an oval medallion with the initials F F and I I (J J in the consonantal form of the time) picked out in dark blue or black. This may relate to the Francis and Frances Jenckes for whom it is thought the house was built. Curiously, the post is in the service wing, but it may have been moved.

Barnaby House, Mill Street, Ludlow

Barnaby House, now part of Ludlow College, is a medieval stone building which borders Silkmill Lane. The wallpainting is contained within the westernmost bay which probably represents the later addition of a solar block at that end. Access to the block is through the 3ft. thick wall which was formerly the gable end of the medieval range. The painting is in the upper room and is protected by a door inserted into the panelling in the south-east corner. It is executed in black distemper on a limewashed wall. The wall has an uneven surface, the stones were roughly dressed and only the mortar of the jointing spread out to form a base, meaning that the coat of limewash is very thin. A description by Henry T. Weyman (of *circa* 1913) hangs by the painting, and in the text Weyman states that fragments of the design occur on the other walls of the room, but are now covered over. It is difficult to assess the overall design but a description written in 1936 gives an indication of the complete work: 'Only a small fragment of the frieze remains, of slight depth and ornamented with a succession of simple swags. It is divided from the "filling" by a narrow band of strapwork with eyelet holes. The "filling" is divided by ornate pilasters into long panels in which are two roundels, each of which is supported by amorini, and beneath by a curious ornament consisting of the upper portion of

a human figure tailing off into two acanthus sheaths terminating in a scroll of foliage. Each roundel contains a shield with charges; one is probably a dragon, another is the double-headed eagle'.[6] It seems generally agreed that a mid-16th century date is applicable. It may be compared with a recent discovery in 4 Belmont, described below.

Full length panel at Barnaby House   *Detail at Barnaby House*

4 Belmont, Shrewsbury

The painting occurs on what appears to have been the high end of a late open hall bordering Belmont Bank. It is very fragmentary, but stylistically it is remarkably similar to the example at Barnaby House. The medium is the same, black distemper on a limewashed wall, although the surface is smooth plaster, and classical pilasters, free-flowing arabesques and foliage are included. A mid-to-late-16th-century date is suggested. At right-angles to the open hall is a timber-framed storied block of the same date which has had its front façade altered by the addition of an 18th-century brick 'skin'.

Whitehall, Shrewsbury

This was the mansion built by Richard Prince in 1582 using stones from the dissolved abbey. The paintings are on the two side walls in a small upper room. They are in panels, each measuring 2ft. 9ins. square and in three different designs, arranged symmetrically. They have a smooth black background with designs in white with some shading. Each panel incorporates swirling arabesques, fleur-de-lis and a classical concept. Some are frescoes, others are on canvas stretched across the timber studs. They have been retouched and are now behind glass. Another small room is said to have had similar treatment.

Harp House, Church St., Bishop's Castle

The painting occurs on a panel of the timber-frame in the ground-floor room of a crosswing which was added to an earlier cruck-framed range in the late 16th century. It is not in good condition but appears to be a pictorial representation of two figures, male and female, in Elizabethan costume. The lady's dress is clearest, with a deep-pointed bodice, buttoned down

the front, puffed sleeves with padded shoulders, and wide-spreading skirts. The man appears to be wearing trunk-hose and gartered stockings. The panel is bordered with a scalloped design and there are traces of flowers and foliage. The painting is executed in black outline on a plaster skim, so thin that in many places the wattle-and-daub of the infill shows through. It is known that the room contains more panel paintings, but these have been emulsioned over.[7]

The Porch House, High Street, Bishop's Castle

Here the paintings appear on a plank-and-muntin screen at the passage end of the hall in a storied hall house of 1564.[8] The design is of three-dimensional chequerboarding below a border of triangles. Although the border is carried across all the uprights, the chequerboarding appears to have been confined to the planks, where the black distemper is applied directly to the wood, but there are traces of a different, perhaps free-flowing design, on the muntins, and here the wood has had a skim of plaster or limewash to provide the base for the paintwork. The work on the screen could be contemporary with the timber-framing of the house, but there is a wallpainting in an added unit which is described later.

Painted decoration on a plank-and-muntin screen at Porch House, Bishop's Castle

Room with paintings at 45 Muxton Lane, Lilleshall

Detail of painting on framework at 45 Muxton Lane, Lilleshall

45 Muxton Lane, Lilleshall

In modern terms this building would be classed as a cottage, but its framing is substantial and suggests that it was once part of a larger, important structure. The main ground-floor room of the cottage contains fragments of paintings and a text. The paintings are done on linen cloth which was stretched across the framework and the panels, but at present the panels are white-washed over. There is a frieze which includes a type of guilloche banding and this runs all around the headbeam. The text appears over the communicating door and in gothic lettering the words '... not as a drinker but in ...' can be deciphered. Where the design on the studs can be seen the artwork is of superior quality to most of the examples quoted in this category. Included are a pegasus with a naked female figure astride and a full-length male figure armed with a scimitar-like sword. The background is black and the designs are mostly in black and white but with touches of orange, red and blue. The room must have presented a vivid impact when first decorated. The paintings are difficult to date but a late 16th- to early 17th-century date appears appropriate.

The Tolsey, Ludlow

This timber-framed building, jettied on all four sides and once completely open at ground level, was where tolls were collected and the day-to-day administration of the markets was carried out in the 16th and 17th centuries.[9] The court of Pie-Powder, a summary hearing of market disputes, was also held here and the courtroom is thought to be the west-facing room at upper level. Here the wall-plate is moulded and on the transverse partition truss there are wallpaintings; features which appear to distinguish this room. The paintings are very faint, some foliage is discernible, but it is impossible to determine the exact nature. The building appears to be of late 16th-century date and the paintings are probably contemporary.

Penkridge Hall, Leebotwood

The design occurs on a main post at the stairhead. It is very fragmentary, but appears to have been of intertwining foliage executed in a flowing and vigorous style. Traces of red ochre are present. The house is dated 1590 and the painting is likely to be coeval.

The Old Bell, Ludford

At one time an inn on the old road from Ludlow to Leominster, this box-framed house of the late 16th/early 17th century has a 'hall-and-crosswing' T-shaped plan, the hall being always a two-storied unit. Two sets of paintings occur—one, very fragmentary, on a stud at the side of the hall fireplace, and the other in the upper front room of the crosswing. The painting in the hall is an outline in black distemper, directly onto the wood, of flowing stylised ancanthus leaves while that in the upper room is more sophisticated. On the side of the chimneystack and across the overmantel the surface is plastered and carries a pattern of horizontal banding. There are five bands; the central band has an elongated guilloche-type pattern, while the flanking ones have swirling concentric circles which may represent roses. The overmantel is not in such good condition, but appears to have a more random design of fruit, flowers and foliage. Like the hall painting, the work is carried out in black distemper.

17 and 19 Watergate, Whitchurch[10]

In very poor structural condition at the time of writing, these two shops with chambers above are part of a larger complex which incorporates 21 and 23. The deeds of the property make it clear that the block is a long-lost timber-framed inn called the Raven. The paintings occur in the first-floor, street-facing chambers of 17 and 19. Though fragmentary, certain patterns and motifs can be discerned and the more complete and typical sections have been copied. In 19, one particular stud has a zig-zag pattern of framework with sprays of flowers and leaves. The flowers include a stylistic five-petalled type of daisy or fritillary, mulberries carefully depicted and showing the natural hang of the fruit, and clove-pinks, otherwise gillyflowers. The latter are not the familiar modern wallflowers, but correctly clovepinks, which, as the name implies, gave a flavouring of cloves in cookery and also to wine.[11] Mulberries were used as fruit and also for dyeing and sweetening. The paintings are carried out in the appropriate colours, mostly pink, blue and orange against a dark background. On the stud in question the design appears to join a horizontal frieze which probably encompassed the room.

Reconstruction by P. Gates of a painting at 19 Watergate

Reconstruction by P. Gates of a painting at 17 Watergate

In the equivalent room in 17 the paintings are even more fragmentary, but occur on the studs and on the plaster of the interstices. A different design is used in this room, one which includes classical arches and columns, but the occasional gillyflower is included and is identical to its counterpart in 19. The building has been dendrochronologically dated to 1625 and the paintings are thought to be not much later. It was normal for important chambers of inns to be decorated with paintings and these illustrate the point. Only one other example of wallpainting is known in Whitchurch (see below). A description of the stencilled decoration at 60 High Street is included in the appropriate section.

Reconstruction by P. Gates of a painting at 19 Watergate

28 Watergate, Whitchurch

Almost opposite the old Raven, no.28 is basically a two-bayed, box-framed structure, dendro-dated to 1597. The southern bay was open but the northern bay, clearly the 'parlour' end, was floored. In the ground-floor room one wall retains vestiges of wallpaintings which appear to be of a stylised floral pattern combined with lozenge-shaped banding. They extend across the panels and the studs on a thin plaster skim, the pigments being indigo, natural ochre and charcoal. They are thought not to be contemporary with the building and to have been renewed several times. At a later date, Prussian blue was used—a pigment not invented until 1704.[12]

Painting in parlour wing at High Grosvenor

High Grosvenor, Claverley

The painting is in the main ground-floor room of a prestigious box-framed and jettied parlour wing which replaced the service end of a medieval base-cruck hall, *c*.1600. All four walls were known to have been decorated, but only one section of the painting remains. This shows a free-flowing pattern of foliage, black on white, with some fruit and perhaps seed-heads. A band of guilloche-type decoration is set in the upper half of the panel and above that is what appears to be lovers' knot. Some of the motifs are picked out in an orange colour. Others, such as the lovers' knot and some of the fruit are in a fawn colour. The condition of the painting has deteriorated towards the right-hand side and the top band has been almost obliterated, but the quality of the work is unmistakable. It has a different sentience from any other Shropshire painting, but it is difficult to pin-point the reason for it.[13]

Sutton Court Farm, Diddlebury

In a parlour wing very similar to that at High Grosvenor, except that it is jettied only towards the front, there are paintings in the main rooms at either level. Although they are all in a fragmentary state, that in the ground-floor room occurs on the partition wall between the main room and the lesser (rear) room and also on the rail of the front wall. On the rail the design is a simple repetitive arabesque while on the partition wall a seemingly random freehand design covers the studs and the rails. The panels were probably similarly treated, but the infilling has been renewed. The decoration is carried out in black distemper on a cream background, but it is difficult to work out the motifs except to note that there appear to be flowers and foliage. In the chamber above the design on the tie-beam is slightly clearer. Here there is

a double black line border, top and bottom with oblique hatching. The body of the design is difficult to describe. There are some motifs with a geometrical theme, some *fleur-de-lis,* arabesques and general swirls. Again a cream background was used, with black distemper for the motifs.

The Court House, Aston-on-Clun

Taken from an upper room, but when seen was lying on the cellar floor, is a panel from a timber-framed wall which has a table of yearly dates on it. They range from *c*.1594 to *c*.1610, and the dates divisible by four are given a symbol. The wording on either side of the table was badly damaged when the panel was removed but on the left-hand side 'Almanack, Easter and Lepe Year' can be discerned, while on the right is 'Feb when shall be'. It appears to be a calendar for working out when Easter and leap years occur. It is painted in black directly onto the plaster, and it is probably only part of a much more extensive exercise.

Almanack at The Court House, Aston-on-Clun

Shootrough Farm, Cardington

During recent years this former hill farm has undergone complete refurbishment which has resulted in the discovery of two different sets of wall paintings. The room at the eastern end of the box-framed crosswing, which was added *c*.1600 and later became a dairy, seems to have been originally designed as a heated parlour. Across the main transverse beam in the end wall was a design of a serpent with its head at one end of the beam and the tail at the other, its undulations covering the length of the beam. All the posts, studs and panels in the room were

decorated with various motifs, some geometrical in a pattern of vertical and horizontal close coils, some straight lines and some free-flowing guilloche-type border-work. They were not in good condition and it is difficult to describe them accurately, but it was clear that the medium was a black distemper painted directly onto the wood or onto the plaster panels for the outline, with quite a bright red ochre used freely for infill. The room must have been very vivid and lively when first

Painting on dais screen at Shootrough

decorated. Unfortunately these paintings were obliterated soon after discovery but further discoveries were made later behind panelling at the dais end of the hall and these have been preserved. The panels in the framing had been removed when alterations were made many years ago, what remained was a pattern on the beams and studs carried out in yellow ochre on a black background. But traces of bright blue and red ochre were also present. The design across the main horizontal beam was of a diamond-pointed outline, not dissimilar to the undulations of the serpent, mentioned above, and in each division was a multi-petalled flower-head. As only half the flower-head occurred in each part it seems reasonable to conclude that they were completed on the missing panels. Two studs remained and the painting on these showed clearly that the design had been applied after the frame had settled and tilted to one side. A vertical line dividing two sections of the design was intended to 'correct' the tilt visually. On one part the motifs included pomegranates, foliage, some tied bundles and what appeared to be a *fleur-de-lis*. The design was washed over with red ochre and seems to have formed a wide border to the two missing panels, the only remains of which showed a design of foliage done in yellow ochre on a black background. This occupied the other part of the studs. It is possible that both sets of paintings are contemporary, but those in the parlour were done with more skill and sophistication. They could date from 1609 when the parlour crosswing was added.[14]

Painting at Hilltop

Hilltop, Great Ryton, Condover

Hilltop is smaller than Shootrough, described above, but a similar development occurred whereby a lavishly decorated box-framed parlour crosswing was added *c*.1600. Many layers of wallpaper and paint have recently been stripped away to reveal that each of the four rooms in the new unit was fully decorated over all the studs and panels and on each wall with an intricate pattern of free-flowing arabesques, flowers and foliage. Some of the horizontals and the verticals which have been exposed carry a diamond-pointed frieze with flower-heads in the divisions, very similar to that at Shootrough. The paintings are outlined in black on a white limewashed background and in some places it is apparent that the timbers had a thin layer of plaster applied to them before receiving the paintwork. No traces of bright colours have yet been exposed, but they may be present. Every care is being taken to preserve these paintings.

Aston Hall Farm, Aston, Little Wenlock

A fragment of a painted partition wall survives in the attic of this farmhouse, presumably the capital messuage of the Newport family's Aston estate.[15] The free-flowing design is similar to those at Hilltop, described above, with flowers and foliage outlined in black distemper on a thin plaster skim over the wattle-and-daub. There are traces of bright red and other pigments. It is probably of similar date to that at Hilltop.

Cottage Farm, Easthope

The building in question is currently in use as a farm building belonging to Cottage Farm, but was a fine hall house with a spere-truss and a crown-post roof. It has been dendro-dated to 1430.[16] The painting is very fragmentary and occurs on one beam only. It is a free-flowing design of flowers and foliage, executed in black distemper directly onto the timber.

Middle Farm, Betchcott, Smethcott

Here the painting occurs on a windbrace which appears to be a reused timber, but its provenance is unknown. The design is carried out in black distemper directly onto the wood. At some time it was whitewashed over, but it is now visible. Obviously part of a larger scheme, the design is basically geometric, incorporating numerous *fleur-de-lis* and some random motifs.

Cruckmeole Old Hall, Pontesbury

Painting at Cruckmeole Old Hall, Pontesbury

Piecemeal development has resulted in a house of many parts. The wallpainting occurs in a unit of early 17th-century square-framing, but only a small section is exposed. The painting covers the panel, the stud and the rail. It is a pattern of stylised acanthus leaves above a diamond-pointed border. The medium is black on white, but there are hints of colour, badly faded.

The Guildhall, Newport

The second example at the Guildhall is fragmentary and occurs on a stud in the north wall of the second bay, which was concealed by a cupboard until recently. Here there is a design of flowing lines in a beige colour on a dark red background, reminiscent of slip-ware work in pottery.

Woundale Farm, Claverley

A close-studded partition wall at the end of one of the ground-floor rooms has traces of paintings on the verticals. Some of the motifs resemble enlarged molar teeth. They occur several times and are set in different positions. A flower-petal motif is also discernible. These features are picked out in an orange colour. They are painted directly onto the timber and presumably occurred also on the interstices. The timber-framed house is dated *c.*1600.

Painting at Glebe Farm, Munslow

Glebe Farm, Munslow

Contained within a panel of a timber-framed wall formerly concealed by later plasterwork is a painting of a cavalier-type figure wearing a patterned or embroidered jacket or doublet open at the neck to reveal a collared shirt. He has long curling hair, a small pointed beard and a curled moustache. In his right hand he holds a long-stemmed clay pipe and in his left a drinking-vessel. The painting is vigorous in black outline on a limewashed smooth surface. It appears to date from the time of Charles I (1625-49), but may be later. It could represent propaganda either for the Royalist cause ('see what a jolly set of fellows we are') or for the Puritan movement ('look at this sinner, drinking and smoking his life away'.)

53 Broad Street, Ludlow

On a plastered overmantel in the northernmost of the two street-facing rooms the arms of James I is painted. This occupies the central position and is flanked by two others of unknown origin. The predominance of the royal arms is thought to be a sycophantic expression by the owner, Robert Saunders, a member of a *nouveaux riches* family of the era.[17] The colours are bold: blue, red, green and gold.

Detail of bird at Plas Gwynne, Market Drayton

Plas Gwynne, Shropshire Street, Market Drayton

The paintings occur in an upper rear room. They are carried across the close-studding, mid-rail and panels and are exposed on two walls, but are thought to have been lost on the others. Though not in good condition, elements of a hunting scene are discernible, the clearest being a large ostrich-like bird, perhaps a crane. There are also a tree, stag, doe, hound, foliage and perhaps a horse. A 16-inch deep border across the top has stylised horizontal batons and foliage, a band of guilloche-type motifs and upper and lower margins of simple strokes. The medium is black distemper outlining on a grey base, with some crude shading and white emphasis. The house dates from the 1660s and the painting is likely to be contemporary.

Detail of border and stag's head at Plas Gwynne

Churchyard Farm, Neenton

The farmhouse has a two-storied hall and crosswing plan with a continuous jetty and dates from the early 17th century. The paintings, recently exposed, cover the walls in the great chamber, that is, the upper room of the crosswing. The design is boldly executed in black distemper directly onto the plaster of the panels and across the studs. It consists of stylised acanthus leaves springing in four sections from a central cusped lozenge. As such it is very similar to that at Petsey, described below. As at Petsey it also has a guilloche-type border, but it has, in addition, a painted frieze of wheat-ear design on the top rail. A vivid orange colour is used as background infill.

Petsey, Stoke-on-Tern

This box-framed and jettied farmhouse is dated 1634 on the porch. In the ground-floor parlour are two well-preserved painted panels now protected by specially made doors. Their form suggests that the whole room was once so decorated. Each panel has a guilloche-type border, and at the centre of each panel is a small cusped lozenge. From the cusps the panel is then quartered, the outline swirling round with a pattern of stylised acanthus leaves, some hatching and terminating in beasts' heads with protruding tongues in profile. They may represent leopards or lionesses. The work is skilfully done in bold brushwork in black distemper on limewashed plaster. It covers the studs as well as the panels.

Detail of painting at Churchyard Farm, Neenton

Paintings exposed at Petsey, Stoke-on-Tern

Detail of painting at Petsey

14 The Critt, Shrawardine

At present divided into three cottages, nos.12, 13 and 14, The Critt once comprised a cruck-built hall house of traditional three unit plan. The paintings, though fragmentary, occur in no.14, which, if the interpretation is correct, would be the solar end. Here on the inner face of the closed end truss the two main verticals are decorated with stylised acanthus leaves and flower-heads. The paintings are executed in black distemper directly onto the timber. The design is bold and skilfully done, with introduced colours of orange, green and blue. There is some hatching, reminiscent of that at Petsey (above). A similar design also occurs on a rail in the side wall of the room.

Lea House, Lea Cross, Pontesbury

Some of the joists in the west wing bear traces of a crude guilloche-type pattern executed in black distemper directly onto the timber. The chamfer and the faces of the joists bear a crude stylised leaf design. The wing has medieval origins, but the joists are part of a 17th-century programme of alterations.

Chevron decoration at Newport's Guildhall

The Guildhall, Newport

The third example at the Guildhall occurs in what is now called The Chevron Room. This is at ground level in the northern extension which has been dendro-dated to 1546.[18] Here the joists are lavishly decorated with chevrons; some are in a bold black on the natural wood, some have a beige background and others are in black and orange on a pale background. The effect is still striking.

The White House, Stanwardine, Baschurch

Though much altered and enlarged, the house is basically a box-framed, two-bay structure of the early 17th century. The painting occurs on an internal truss and was meant to be viewed from first-floor level. It is mostly obscured by the inserted chimneystack, and only a fragment is visible. Executed in black distemper on plaster, it appears to have been confined to the panels in the timber-frame and does not extend across the studs. There is a clearly defined border containing tear-drops or leaves, and with a mitred corner, but the design within the panel is too badly damaged to describe accurately. Overall, it seems to resemble that in a house called Mossgate in Pilling, Lancs., which bears a date of 163?.[19]

Stokesay Castle

Surprisingly, there are very few examples of wall decoration at Stokesay Castle which, of course, would be more accurately described as a fortified manor house. The only area where any positive design can be discerned is on the wall in the well room at the base of the north tower, and even here the paintwork is fragmentary. It is carried out in red ochre directly onto the plaster, and consists of a random design of simple swirling stem and leaf outlines. It may be part of a post-Civil War refurbishment programme carried out during the occupancy of Sir Samuel Baldwin.

Hall Farm, Wall-under-Heywood, Rushbury Here the paintings were uncovered when alterations were carried out in the 1960s in a ground-floor room in the eastern crosswing of this H-shaped hall house, where the hall is of cruck construction. In what was clearly a best parlour, the paintings consisted of a geometrical pattern of squares with mitred corners. Each square was outlined with two triple bands of paintwork separated by a gap, and at the centre was a diamond shape. There was a border of crude arabesques. The design was carried over the studs, rails and panels, and covered the four walls. The strongly-mitred corners would have produced a three-dimensional effect.

Around the top, on the girding-beam was a text, doubtless of a biblical nature, but it proved impossible to decipher the lettering. All the work was done in red ochre directly onto the wood or plaster and suggested a date perhaps in the first half of the 17th century. The paintings were not left on view.

The Bache, Sidbury

This is a farmhouse where there is little cohesion between the various units that make up the complex. A date of 1680 occurs on some internal plasterwork and this date could well apply to the main staircase. It could also apply to the painting over the fireplace in one of the upper rooms. It depicts a biblical scene, the sacrifice of Isaac by Abraham. Though the artwork is unsophisticated, the subject matter is vigorously portrayed and bright red touches are included in the garments. The angel is particularly homely, only her large wings distinguishing her from an ordinary housewife of the time. The painting is not in good condition.

Painting on overmantel at The Bache, Sidbury

The Porch House, High Street, Bishop's Castle

At the rear of the timber-framed range are two 18th-century extensions and the rear of the crosswing. In one of the extensions is a wall-painting which may be a pictorial representation of the castle itself as it appeared in the 18th century. It

Castle painting at Porch House, Bishop's Castle

is skilfully done, in black distemper on a plastered wall and is similar to a painting which hangs in the Town Hall although it has fewer castellations and the keep and towers are not in identical positions. Unfortunately, application of whitewash to the wall has caused damage to the painting.[20]

The Broadgate, Ludlow

Panoramic painting at the Broadgate, Ludlow

Panoramic views of Ludlow are plentiful, but they are mostly movable works of art. At the Broadgate on the overmantel of a rear bedroom is a view painted directly onto the plasterwork. Included in the scene is the castle, the castle walks, old Dinham bridge, castle mills, the mill-race and the weir. The artist is unknown, but the painting must date from between 1772, when the castle walks were laid out, and 1794 when the old bridge was improved to take wheeled vehicles. The bridge as depicted pre-dates the alterations and is shown as a single-track pack-horse type.[21] No bright colours are used and perspectives are a little strange, but the different textures and a sense of atmosphere are well conveyed.

15 and 15A Holly Road, Little Dawley

This property was demolished in 1985. Originally a cruck-built house of medieval origin, overtaken by the industrial development of the Shropshire coalfield, at one time an inn, partly a shop, and reduced eventually to cottage status, the building had undergone more vicissitudes than most. Two types of wall decoration were noted in the part that had been an inn. One was very crude, consisting of loops, horizontal lines and circles in black distemper applied to a head-beam. The other was more sophisticated, and is described under 'Stencilled Decoration', below.

The Nag's Head, Wyle Cop, Shrewsbury

Basically a jettied medieval building, the street-facing room of the third storey contains an 18th-century corner cupboard with scalloped shelves. At a later date a door was added, the inner face of which is decorated with a depiction of what appears to be the god Neptune. A full-length bearded figure, he holds a trident pointing downwards and has a wild expression exaggerated by empty eye sockets. Curiously, although the torso and feet are male, the over-long legs are female. Painted with a dark background, the colours are sombre and, at present, not enhanced by the amount of nicotine staining.

'Neptune' at the Nag's Head, Shrewsbury

'Judas' painting on overmantel at 4 Castle Square, Ludlow

Drawing at the Old Hall, The Isle, Bicton

Detail of nursery mural at The Old Hall, The Isle, Bicton

4 Castle Square, Ludlow

A chamber at first-floor level contains a panelled and painted ceiling with depictions of mainly biblical scenes, together with a small section in the centre of the fireplace lintel portraying Judas after the betrayal. The whole room has painted mural decorations, but these are concealed at present. As at the Nag's Head, Shrewsbury, (see above) the colours are sombre and the background dark. The effect of such work to modern eyes is extremely depressing.

The Isle, Bicton

The timber-framed house in which the mural decorations occur is the forerunner of the present main house. Strangely, there are two decorated rooms— one at ground-floor level has a rural scene with a man scything, another drinking from a pot, two female figures gathering the corn, various other figures, trees, a church and other buildings. The artwork is carried out with a thick lead pencil directly onto the plastered wall. It may be compared with some pencil sketches by 'G.L.S' dated *c.*1849.[22] The other room is at first-floor level and was probably a nursery. Here there is a wide band of painted decoration with nursery-type motifs, simple buildings, teddy-bears and 'Noddy'. It is clearly much later than that in the lower room but skilfully done and for that reason worthy of inclusion in this survey.

Combination of Freehand and Stencilled Designs

Paintings at Halfway House, Eardington

Halfway House Inn, Eardington

The inn is a former farmhouse, stone-walled but with timber-framed internal partitions and dating from *c*.1620. During restoration work in 1992 wallpaintings were discovered in a ground-floor rear room which probably originated as a parlour. On a thin plaster skim, tinted pink and carried over the studs and the panels is a diaper pattern executed in a double outline of black distempered blotches. These are stencilled, but superimposed on the diapers and not necessarily respecting their limits are freehand flower-heads and leaves of differing designs. These incorporate tints of orange and green. The panels are full length (6ft. x 1ft. 2in.) and it is thought that the whole room was decorated. The paintings are now preserved behind sliding glass panels. Only one other example is known where freehand and stencil are used in the same painting, and thus it may be regarded as an excellent example of the transition between the two techniques.

Detail of stencilling at Church Farm, More

Church Farm, More

Here the freehand painting takes the form of a border around the door and is carried upwards to underline the purlin. The room is a bedroom in an extension to the northern timber-framed unit, and each wall is stencilled with a repetitive design of a temple-like building with a porch. There are water, trees and swans. Four colours are used: a pale grey overall wash, grey-green ochre for the main features and black and white for emphasis. The whole effect is more elaborate than any other known example in the county. The border is a series of circles surrounded by dots with a top line of leaves and three horizontal bands between the circles. Compared with the stencilling the hand-work is crude. A date in the late 18th century is suggested.

Stencilled Decoration

Stencilling at Mill House, Boraston

*Stencilling at The Gate House,
Orleton Hall, Wrockwardine*

The Guildhall, Newport

In this, the fourth example at the Guildhall, each joist of the floor which was inserted into the easternmost of the two central open bays of the hall bears simple stencilled decoration in the form of a row of six-petalled flower-heads set at intervals of 1ft. The pattern is executed in black distemper directly onto the joists.

Mill House, Boraston

This is basically a 17th-century square-framed and L-shaped house. The painting occurs in the room above the parlour where stencilled decoration on one wall was uncovered in 1985. It is thought that the whole room was similarly treated. The painting is applied to the panels only and is in black distemper on a white plaster skim. The pattern consists of alternate vertical bands of triple flower-heads with leaves and an undulating leaf motif with a smaller flower-head in each drop. It is good quality work and compares well with that at the Gatehouse at Orleton Hall (see below).

The Gatehouse, Orleton Hall, Wrockwardine

The original form of the Gatehouse was that of a timber-framed structure, jettied on all four sides. As such it is likely to pre-date the 1588 date thought to relate to a rebuilding at that time.[23] The date of 1766 on one of the chimneystacks could indicate a remodelling in the 18th century which included the application of stencilled decoration in an upper room. It is in good condition and is a particularly fine example, executed in olive green paint on a white plastered background. Two different designs are used in alternating vertical bands; one has flower-heads and leaves, the other has similar leaves and what appear to be stylised barley heads. The small fireplace is bordered with a geometrical design, also stencilled and in the same colour.

15 and 15A Holly Road, Little Dawley

This building contained two types of painted wall decoration. The freehand example has been described on p.340. The second type consisted of alternate bands of stencilled designs, one a stylised triple-leaf pattern, the other alternate blocks of dots and blotches. A blue-green distemper was used for the leaves and for background to the blotches, and black for the dots and blotches and for an added hand-applied touching to the leaves. What made this paintwork unusual was that the bands were set horizontally instead of vertically, and appeared to be confined to the upper part of the wall.

The King's Head, Mardol, Shrewsbury

The artwork on the street-facing side of the chimneystack is not comparable with the earlier work, described above. Here it occurs at second-storey level on the jamb and chimney breast. The jamb is of stone, plastered over, but the chimneystack itself is brick-built, the bricks measuring on average 9in. x 2in. The stencilling is crude, in two patterns, one measuring 5in. x 7in. in red and the other 4in. x 6in. in black. Both are on a cream background and suggest vaguely heraldic motifs.

60 High Street, Whitchurch

Both sides of the High Street have evidence for street encroachment, and at no.60 the encroachment bay contains stencilled wall decoration in the form of a repetitive pattern of flower-heads, leaves and acorns contained within swirling arabesques. The design is carried across the studs and panels of a partition wall and the colouring is petrol-blue and black on a yellow ochre background. As such it is very similar to that at 12 Friar Street, Worcester, which is described as a 'pre-neoclassical floral design copying wood-block printed wallpaper'.[24] A date of 1740-50 is suggested for the Worcester example. The Whitchurch example could be contemporary with the encroachment, c.1760.

Stencilling at The King's Head, Mardol, Shrewsbury

Stencilling in attic room at 60 High Street, Whitchurch

Plaish Hall, Cardington

The ceiling in the 'oak parlour', that is, the southern ground-floor room of the east wing is divided into squares by broad flat moulded wooden ribs with a pendant boss at each intersection. Each square has a border of elaborate 'antique' scroll-work and a central shield bearing

Ceiling in parlour, Plaish Hall, Cardington

either a royal (Tudor) device or a heraldic crest and is flanked with the initials HR (*Henricus Rex*). The background is pale blue; much of the design, including the royal monograms, is outlined in a rusty-red shade, with darker blue, black and gilt used to highlight individual features. Until recently it was assumed that the ceiling was an authentic piece of artwork dating from the 1540s, but recent research points to it being commissioned by a 19th-century owner with antiquarian tastes.[25] It is uncertain whether the painting is entirely done with stencils—it may have involved a mixture of woodblock and stencils. It is certainly not freehand work.

Derelict Cottage in Stoney Stretton

Basically a 17th-century two-up and two-down timber-framed cottage with an attached byre and hayloft, the living room/kitchen has the remains of stencilled decoration on all four walls. One panel is well preserved and shows a pattern of oak leaves and acorns in black distemper on a background of red ochre. Later wallpapering concealed the paintings.

147 Abbey Foregate, Shrewsbury

At one time covering the walls in a back bedroom at second-storey level, the stencilling has been left as circles within the present decoration scheme. Probably of 19th-century date the pattern is of green leaves, life-sized and similar to those of a crab-apple tree, depicted in triple clusters with surrounding bursts of miniature leaves. The scheme was finished with a top border and the background is chalky white. The house probably dates from *c.*1780.

Depictions of the Nine Worthies

Great Binnall, Astley Abbots

The original form of the house is that of a medieval timber-framed open hall with a solar end. The dais end of the hall is marked by a coved canopy which has a battlemented rail at the base of the coved section. Above the rail nine separate vertical timbers follow the curve, each painted with a head-and-shoulders figure. The set is the traditional one of three characters from the 'classical' or pagan world of Troy, Greece and Rome, three from the old Testament and three from the Christian early medieval world; from left to right: Hector, Alexander, Julius Caesar, Joshua, King David, Judas Maccabeus, King Arthur of England, Charlemagne and Godfrey de Bouillon, the leader of the French faction in the first crusade who was proclaimed king of Jerusalem, a title which he rejected. The common factor is their fame as soldiers and

Above: Dais at Great Binnall, Astley Abbots, with nine worthies with,
top left, a detail of Alexander the Great and, lower left, of David

their strong connections with Jerusalem. Much has been written on the subject of the Nine Worthies and the cult of chivalry, and much more remains to be understood. It is not proposed to pursue the origins and spread of the cult in this book, merely to remark that the Great Binnall set is probably of 17th-century date and represents a late provincial expression of a literary, dramatic and decorative theme once popular right across western Europe. The professional quality of the artwork, though not first rate, is competent and vigorous, with prominent black, red and gilt colouring used effectively. The paintings are done directly onto the boards which are nailed to the coving. They appear to have once formed a continuous frieze and were probably acquired from elsewhere, although it is strange that the curve of the coving exactly matches that of the painted boards.

The Prior's Hall, Much Wenlock

At present the wall at the southern (dais) end of hall is blank, but a drawing by John Buckler dated 23 June 1820 shows what appear to be nine full-length figures forming a wall decoration at that end.[26] The primary purpose of the drawing was to show the roof structure; the window embrasures with their built-in tables form a secondary feature, and the nine worthies, if such they are, seem to have been put in almost as a casual afterthought to relieve a blank wall. But Buckler is noted for his accuracy and is unlikely to have drawn something from his imagination.

There is yet a further reference to a set of the nine worthies at the priory. Although they were described as being 'over the cloister at Wenlock Abbey, with mottoes' and numbering seven, not nine, the reference is clearly to a set of the worthies.[27] This is quoted 61 years later by a 19th-century writer who refers to them as being 'pourtrayed [*sic*] on the walls of the Cloister ...'.[28] It could be that the term 'cloister' was being used loosely, and that what was really meant was the prior's hall. However, it must be admitted that the cloister and the hall are totally unconnected, a long way apart, structurally incompatible and in separate ownership, then as now. At present there is no trace of the worthies in the cloister, but much has happened to the priory ruins since Gough's time and the possibility that a cloistral set existed should not be discounted.

Buckler's drawing of The Prior's Hall, Much Wenlock, 23 June 1820

Roger Ward's Bookshop, Shrewsbury
In 1585 this bookseller had numerous pictures for sale and had, apparently, converted a woodcut originating from Gyles Godet, a refugee from religious persecution in France, from 'a genealogie of all the kynges of England' to the Nine Worthies. He added text explaining the moral lesson to be drawn from each character.[29] The inventory of his goods includes 40 sets of the Nine Worthies.[30]

Painted Cloths[31]

It is stating the obvious to say that if a householder could afford tapestries to hang on his walls, then that is what he would do, rather than buy the cheap imitation that was available in the form of the painted cloth. But that is only a half-truth. There is documentary evidence to show that 'poor men's tapestries' were used in the houses of men of means, and were hung in important rooms.[32] Tapestries and cloths were multi-purpose artifacts: they were decorative, they provided some insulation from draughts and they could be used to tell a story in pictures, depict an event and commemorate whatever was thought worth recording. Because tapestries were more durable they lasted longer. But, to the best of the writer's knowledge, no tapestries have survived in Shropshire, whereas a set of painted cloths remains in a Shropshire farmhouse. In view of the low survival rate of these objects, this is remarkable.

'Hangings' in probate inventories relating to gentry houses are likely to have been tapestries; painted cloths, on the other hand, are often described as such and they occur fairly frequently in the Whitchurch inventories of 1535-1650.[33] Strangely, they do not seem to feature very much in those of the Telford area.[34] In Shrewsbury an item in the Drapers' Company papers specifies that the lessee, Andrew Lewes, was 'to halfe waynscott the hall - with benches - myter and cipher joint, and to paynte the rest upon cloth with Antick [antique] work'. He was also 'to syle the hall and great chamber and to colour the posts and wier trees with greene'. The work was to be completed by Lady Day 1577/8.[35] The painted cloths did not stay in the

Cloths room at Munslow Farm

hall. They are recorded in 1653/4 in the chamber over the porch and were described as 'old' in 1664, by which time they had been moved to 'the passage to the kitchen chamber'.[36] None has survived.

The 'painted cloth shelter or screen' which was at one time fixed over the the seats for the bailiffs and council at the Guildhall in Ludlow and had the king's arms painted over the bailiffs' seat, likewise has not survived.[37]

At Munslow Farm (SJ 524874) the situation is very different. Here, in the upper room of a small brick-built parlour block of *c.*1660/70 which was added to an older farmhouse, is a set of eight painted cloths, still mainly in the setting for which they were designed. Alterations in the brickwork show that the fenestration has been reduced, and at present all the windows on the rear elevation are blocked. It seems likely, therefore, that the cloths on the front and rear walls have either been moved around or that the windows were blocked in order that cloths could be added to the rear wall. Framed, but not glazed, the cloths at present occupy the space above the panelled wainscotting on three walls. The fourth wall, that opposite the fireplace and containing the doorway, is blank, but the form of the panelling suggests that a large cloth was displayed on each side of the doorway. On each side of the fireplace is a large cloth; that on the right depicts a scene with trees and stylised foliage, a row of poplars, a church with an apsed end and a steeple, a river and a waterfall (see lower illustration overleaf). This cloth is in good condition. In the others the condition varies. Some are reasonably intact, others are worn, faded and torn. The cloth to the left of the fireplace is in fairly good condition and depicts similar stylised foliage, a church with a tower, a river and a water conduit within a classical domed and arched building (see illustration alongside). Three of the cloths on the rear wall have similar trees, foliage and water features (see upper illustration overleaf) and a fourth depicts a huntsman among the trees (see illustration alongside). He is clean-shaven and wears a wide-brimmed hat, a belted jerkin, breeches and a shirt with long full sleeves. In his right hand he

Detail of two cloths at Munslow Farm, showing a huntsman among some trees on the left, and a rural scene with a church, river and water conduit on the right

carries a lance and with his left he is pointing forwards. Behind him is a building, possibly a hunting lodge, but this is simply outlined with a gable end and two windows. One cloth on the front wall is in poor condition, but depicts similar trees and foliage and has a river with a bridge and a building with a crow-stepped gable, a large circular opening in the middle of the gable and three rectangular openings below (see illustration below). The eighth is in very poor condition, and it is difficult to determine the motifs, but it seems to contain an animal, perhaps a hare, in the design.

The cloths are of a canvas-type linen, known locally as 'hurden',[38] and the distemper colours used are mostly blue-grey for the background with the trees in beige, the foliage in a deeper blue-grey and outlined in black. Water is silver-white and buildings are white and brown with details picked out in black.

There is a ninth cloth, also in a wooden frame, which is in excellent condition. It is held separately by the owner and may have been made at a slightly later date, perhaps to replace a damaged one or to add to the collection. Though similar in size, design, style and colouring, the cloth is a finer hemp-linen, there is less detail and the foliage is less rounded.

Detail of a cloth at Munslow Farm, one of the three on the rear wall

None of the motifs depicted on the cloths reflect local buildings or scenery. Though clearly made to order, it is suggested that they were, perhaps, made by Flemish craftsmen domiciled in England. Certainly, the architecture, the water treatment and the arboreal style are reminiscent of Flanders. The techniques employed, particularly the effects of shading, seem to owe as much to embroidered hangings as to tapestry work. The cloths are similar in style to those noted at Jenkyn Place, Bentley, Hants.,[39] and have been used as models by Birmingham's City Museums and Art Gallery department for the new ones at Blakesley Hall, Yardley, Birmingham.[40]

Details of two cloths at Munslow Farm. On the left is one of a row of poplars with a church, river and waterfall, to the right one that includes a building with a crow-stepped gable

As mentioned above, the painted cloths seem to have been made for the room, though, in view of the alterations to the fenestration, perhaps not immediately. The little parlour block is two-storied, with brickwork in a type of Flemish stretcher bond: two rows of stretchers and a row of headers and stretchers. The original windows were round-headed with brick voussoirs. There are two brick plat-bands, an out-built chimneystack and an external entrance door in the north-east corner. This gives immediate access to the staircase which has simple moulded nosing to the treads, a string, a square panelled newel-post, turned balusters with twisted cable effect and a wide moulded handrail. The fireplace in the cloths room has bolection moulding on the surround and an overmantel consisting of eight carved panels with different motifs, divided and bordered. While it forms a unified piece of carpentry it gives the impression of having been acquired from elsewhere. The window in the ground-floor room is interesting for the survival of its horizontal sliding shutters.

It is emphasised that the above examples do not form a comprehensive survey of Shropshire wall decorations. Many more are known to exist, but only those seen by the author or known by her to have existed are included here.[41]

14   Dendrochronology in Shropshire: A Summary

Begun in the 1990s with grant money from various sources, the dendrochronolgy project was born out the frustration caused by having to rely on estimated building dates. Other factors were also involved, but the project gained momentum and at the present time 182 workable dates have been obtained ranging from 1192 to 1824. 117 buildings have been sampled, some having more than one building phase. Each building was carefully chosen for its potential contribution to the knowledge of how timber-framing developed in Shropshire, whether there was an obvious evolutionary pattern and what trends could be perceived within such a pattern. The sampling results were put into the form of a 'star-chart' (see following pages) so that in addition to pin-pointing the date of individual buildings, their place in the overall development could be seen.[1]

It is considered that the results are sufficient to justify using the project as the basis of a summary of timber-framing in the county. The dates are those when the trees were felled, but there is sufficient documentary and other evidence to show that there was usually very little difference between the time of felling and that of building. The timbers were worked in a green state and the frame would season as it stood. While documentary dates are important, they can be misleading and reliance on them is fraught with danger, whereas there can be little argument with a scientifically obtained date.

One rather surprising and pleasing conclusion is how often an inscribed date tallies with the dendro date. In only one case, that of the Guildhall in Newport, is the proclaimed date nonsensical, and here it is believed that the date-plaque was obtained from another building entirely.

It is hoped that the preceding chapters have shown that Shropshire is a county rich in timber-framing, abounding in crucks, containing key features such as crown-post roofs, quarter-round and other mouldings, decorative carvings, jettying, close-studding and much more. It is also geographically strategically placed on the Welsh Marches, forming at the same time a boundary and a link with Wales, and a meeting point between the distinctive style of the Cheshire framing to the north and that of the Hereford/Worcester area to the south.

Only 'relevant' dates are included in the list, for if every sample which yielded a date or a date range was included, the exercise would become very cumbersome and partly defeat its own object. For example, at Stokesay Castle 67 dates were obtained from 122 samples but only nine entries are in the chart. In choosing the entries I took the advice of the dendrochronol-ogist and have shown what we both consider to be the important phases. Similarly, on a smaller scale, ten samples were taken at Bradney Farm at Worfield, but only one felling date, the crucial one, is listed. At the Bear Steps complex in Shrewsbury nine samples were taken in the hall, but, although the ring-growth pattern was good and the sapwood was present, none would match with a site-master (a chronology built up from overlapping ring-widths in given areas against which new samples can be cross-dated) and so no felling date at all could be released. The provenance of the Bear Steps Hall timbers, therefore, is a mystery.[2] In every case the full table is published in the appropriate volume of *Vernacular Architecture*.[3]

Name	Hall	Spere Truss	Cont. Wing	Base Cruck	Cruck	Crown Post	Close Studding	C'ping	M'ding	Date
Wistanstow church, N. Transept										1192-1226 (com.-raft. roof, soulaces, single wall-plate)
Great Oxenbold, Monkhopton	*								*	1247 (½-round moulding, chamfer with groove, stone walls)
55 Sheinton St, M. Wen. (Pad above S.P.)									*	1247-90 (no sapwood)
55 Sheinton St, M. Wen. (Samson Post)										1254-99 (no sapwood, bead moulding, tree growing in 881)
Stokesay Castle (Solar u'croft)										1261-64 (earliest dated feature in Stokesay complex)
Stokesay Castle (joists in S. Passage)										1262
Cruck Cottage, Upton Magna					*					1269 (notched-lap joints, earthfast, scissor-braced)
Stokesay Castle (North Tower, u'croft)										1280-1304
Stokesay Castle (Hall)	*		*	*						1284-5 (raised cruck/comp. roof, stone walls, tracery winds.)
Buck's Head, Church Stretton						*				1287-1321 (crosswing, dragon-ties, boss, hall gone)
Stokesay Castle (North Tower, 1st. floor)										1287 (middle part, brace to floor)
Stokesay Castle (Solar roof)										1289 (com.-raft. roof, soulaces, m&t joints, off hall corbels)
Stokesay Castle (North Tower, 2nd. floor)										1290
Plowden Hall, Lydbury North	*				*	*				1302 (tree growing in 977, dragon-ties, cent. truss different)
The Rectory, Ludlow			*							1313-28 (collar-rafter roof, 1st-fl. hall, wing roof similar)
Leaton Grange, Wrock. (Solar wing)		?						*	*	after 1313 (hipped ends)
The Bold, Aston Botterell		*	*		*	*		*	*	1320-54 (short chamf. crown-post, bead m'ding elsewhere)
23 Barrow St, M. Wen.		?	*		*	*				1327-30 (bead moulding on crucks & arch-braces, deep tie)
Clungunford Church, Chancel										1329
Clungunford Church, Nave										1338-9
Aston Eyre, Gatehouse										1341-52 (stone-built detached entrance to manor house)
St. Mary's church, Westbury										1342 (north aisle)
Home Farm, Leighton (Solar wing)						*		*		1358 (hall range replaced)
3/4 Broad St, Ludlow						*	*	*		1358 (? not domestic, 170 rings, up-swinging laterals)
12A Butcher Row/ 12 Fish St, S'bury										1358-9 (jettied range of ?shops overlooking market place)
Abbey, S'bury, Bellchamber floor										1365-95 (single timber)
Old Mansion, St. Mary's St, S'bury	*					*				1366 (built over earlier undercroft, soulaces)
Lane End Cottage, Muckleton, Shawbury						*				1371-2 (in crosswing; hall rebuilt 1621)
Abbot's House, Buildwas	*									1377 (1st.-fl. hall, triple cusped w'braces. Diminished p.r.s)
High Grosvenor, Claverley	*			*				*		1375-77 (lateral braces - convex)
Abbey, S'bury, Tower roof										1380-95 (original timbers)
Home Farm, Attingham						*				1385-6 (lateral braces - concave. 3-bay roof)
All Forces Club, Low Town, B'north	*	*								1392-1422 (? a warehouse, close to river, private door)
Palmers' Guild College, Ludlow	*		*						*	1393 (roll, ogee, billet, cavetto on spere, decor. doorpost)
38/39 Woolstaston (Crosswing)						*				1398-9 (short plain crown-posts)
38/39 Woolstaston (Hall)	*		*	*					*	1399-1400 (¼-round moulding, low beam)
1 Broad St, Ludlow (Bodenham's)			*							1404 (3-stor'd, jettied, db-pile, encroach., Palmers' Guild)
The King's Head, S'bury	*							*	*	1404 (3-stor'd, jettied, db-pile. ¼-round, wallpaintings)

Name	Hall	Spere Truss	Cont. Wing	Base Cruck	Cruck	Crown Post	Close Studding	C'ping	M'ding	Date
Rigg's Hall, S'bury	?	*	*			*		*	*	1405-35 (solar ab've stone u'croft. Open arch-br. cent. truss)
Barclay's Bank, 15 High St, M. Wen.	*	*		*		*		*	*	1408 (ogee moulding, cusping on all braces to crown-post)
18/19 Abbey Foregate, S'bury					*					1408 (? part of a terrace of crucks)
Palmers' Guildhall, Ludlow	*	*	*			*		*	*	1411 (fully aisled hall, bosses, Palmers' Guild property)
Rigg's Hall, S'bury	?									1413-43 (short straight laterals. Prob. contemp. with above)
Raynald's Mansion, M. Wen.	*								*	1414-47 (ogee d'hd, 2-stor'd, later encaps. in extn. of 1682)
St. Owen's Well House, M. Wen.	*				*					1415 (single-bay hall, ogee-head to solar door)
Nag's Head hall, S'bury	*	*				*		*	*	1419 (hall gone, ogee-hd. drs, 1/4-round/ogee, 6-way brac.)
Shootrough, Cardington	*				*				*	1422 (1/4-round & cavetto on central truss, ogee doorhead)
The Lion Tap, S'bury	*					*				1423-26 (tall crown-posts, jettied rear range—?indust. use)
Prior's Hall, M. Wen.	*								*	1425 (1st-fl. hall, st. walls, trac. winds, 2 stor'd gall'y)
Prior's Solar, M. Wen.										1425 (traceried windows, unbayed roof)
Prior's Apartment, M. Wen.										1425 (single-bay, traceried windows)
The Barracks, Cardington	*				*	*		*	*	1425-6 (jowelled posts, lge wall braces, [crosswing rebuilt])
Cruck Cottage, U. Magna (phase 2)	*				*		*			1425-6 (remod. of earl. build, crucks added, roof changed)
Henry Tudor House, S'bury	*									1430 (3-storied, jettied, traceried windows, street-facing)
Cottage Farm, Easthope	*	*		?	*	*	*		*	1430 (unilat. bracing, 2 aisled trusses, now farm building)
20/21 Abbey Foregate, S'bury	*				*					1430 (? part of a terrace of crucks)
Upton Cressett (Hall)	*	?		?		*	*	*	*	1431 (short crown-post, 2 aisled trusses, 1/4-round moulding)
Upton Cressett (Solar wing)			*							1429-31 (clasped purlins, arch-br. collar/queen-post roof)
25-28 Barrow St, M. Wen.	*				*					1435 (cruck terrace, hipped ends, 5 single-cells - ?almshses)
The Chapel, Halston, Whittington							*	*	*	1437 (cusping in roof, spandrels carved, chapel refit. C.18)
Condover Court, Condover	*		*		*					1445 (cusping on windbraces only, 2 louvres)
91 Frankwell, S'bury										1447 (2-bay rear unit with large wall braces)
Bedstone Manor, Bedstone	*		*		*				*	1448 (moulded crucks, ogee detail, very fine hall)
Barnaby House, Ludlow	*							*		1450-51 (5-bay tie/collar roof, reused on C.13 stone shell)
Foresters' Lodge, Upper Millichope	*						*			1450-51 (ins. 1st fl. ceil. in stone 1st-fl. hall)
Cottage Farm, Easthope (Crosswing)										1454 (cusping on windbraces only, now farm building)
Hall Farm, Stottesdon	*									1454 (4 equid. bays, poss. remodelling of 1st-fl. hall)
Plowden Hall, Lydbury N. (Solar Wing)							*		*	1454 (2 bay solar, lavish cusping)
Homeside, Boraston	*				*				*	1457 (ogee on brace/collar, later fumbrell in situ)
Abbot's House, S'bury							*		*	1457 (shops/jettied rooms ab., dec. ext., frame ready 1459)
Great Binnall, Astley Abbots	*		*				*	*	*	1460 (dais end has 9 Worthies, cusping is 1/4-round-m'lded)
Upper Ledwych, Bitterley	*		*					*		1463 (6-bay roof, jowelled/battlemented posts)
Timber Croft, Pentre Hodre, Clun	*				*					1465 (2-bay hall, low beam, hewing mark)
2 Milk Street, S'bury							*	*	*	1466 (shop(s)/jettied rooms above, 1/4-rd/cavetto m'ding)
Moat House, Longnor	*	*							*	1467 (lavish cusp., arch-brac.coll./queen-post roof, v. fine)

Name	Hall	Spere Truss	Cont. Wing	Base Cruck	Cruck	Crown Post	Close Studding	C'ping	M'ding	Date
14-16 King St., Ludlow, (rear unit)	*									1467 (1st-fl. hall, cent. truss, arch-braced. Freehold prop.)
19-21 Drayton Road, Hodnet	*		*							1467 (single-bay hall with croggloft, 2-stor'd wing)
Providence Grove, Prees										1468 (joists of 2-bay floored hall, remodelled later)
Manor Farm, Aston Eyre, joists in Solar			*						*	1469-71 (? reused. Complex changed hands in 1469)
Humphreyston Hall, Donington	*								*	1471 (jettied, spere-beam, gt. chamber over hall)
Council House, S'bury, Solar wing						*			*	1472 (Council in the Marches. Cusped windbraces)
25 Kempton, Clunbury	*	?		*					*	1474 (crow-stepped crucks to cent. truss, p'haps cruck spere)
Wolverton, Eaton-u-Heywood (Hall)	*	*					*	*	*	1475 (2-tier cruck, cusping on windbraces & spere-truss)
14-16 King St., Ludlow (front unit)	*						*	*		1476 (jettied, street encroach. by Palmers' Guild)
St. Winifred's Well, West Felton	*							*	*	1478-82 (timber-fram'd chapel, lavish cusping)
Catherton Cottage, Cleo'y Mortimer	*			*			*		*	1485 (1½-bayed hall, chamf. & stopped wall-plate, l'house)
Coats Farm, Rushbury	*				*					1486 (low-swinging arch-braces; spurs, ends changed)
Bradney Farm, Worfield	*				*					1486 (chamf'd crucks, arch-brs, 2-bay hall, louvre mechnsm)
Newport Guildhall (Hall)	*						*	*	*	1487 (cusp/pierced quatrefoil w'braces, cavetto mouldings)
57 Sheinton St, M. Wen. (reused beam)								*	*	late C.15 (was bressumer; no sapwood)
Brookgate Farm, Pleaty	*	*		*			*	*	*	1490 (elab. spere-t. with boss, close-stud. in dais screen)
Clunbury Church, Nave roof										1494-5 (arch-br: collars, V-struts, ashlar pieces)
Upton Cressett Hall (ext. to solar wing)										1498 (6-bay queen-post roof)
Council House, S'bury (Hall)	*			*			*		*	1501 (rebuild of hall for Peter Newton, Council in Marches)
Meeson Farm, Bolas Magna	*	*								1502 (low-beam, notched-lap joints)
Clive House, S'bury, older part	*	*								1504 (poss. part of college of St. Chad's)
Corner of Bridge St/Cartway, B'north										1506 (floor joist only - not indicative of building)
The Bold, Aston Botterell										1508 (term. post-quem, from one dais corbel (?))
Great Oxenbold, Monkhopton										1510-45 (reused wall-plate)
Clungunford Church										1513-17
Brookgate Farm, Pleaty (wing 1)				*			*			1533-81 (added at rear of original solar end)
38/39 Woolstaston (added/replaced truss)			*	*						1537 (closed truss at end of hall)
Cherrington Man. Reused cruck in farm bld.)					*					1537-57
Abcott Manor, Clungunford	*	*								1541 (crosswing is 1547)
Upper Lake, Westbury	*			*			*		*	1545-6 (2-bay hall, triang. wall-pl., added C.17 box-fr. unit)
Newport Guildhall (added range)										1546 (2 bays, king-strut roof, at right-angles to orig.)
Abbot's House, Buildwas									*	1547 (earlier phase than above, but with rebuilt roof)
Great Binnall, Astley Abbots, ins. ceiling)										c.1550 (ranges 1506 & 1529-54, elab. roll moulding, boss)
Ashwood, Ash	*				*					1550 (single-bay hall, crucks on stylobates)
Manor Cottage, Prees	*			*			*			1551-2 (stylobates, site of manor house, longhouse?)
Habberley Hall										1555 (jettied all round, central smoke extractor)
Park Farm, Alkington, Whitchurch										1556 (box-frame, later brick-clad)
Alcaston Manor, Crosswing (Courthouse)										1557 (jettied; upper fl. entrance. Paintings in lower floor)

Name	Hall	Spere Truss	Cont. Wing	Base Cruck	Cruck	Crown Post	Close Studding	C'ping	M'ding	Date
Wolverton, Eaton-u-Heywood (smoke-hood)										1557-89 (inserted into lower bay of hall)
Bedstone Manor, Bedstone (crossing)									*	1560 (with cable moulding and other dec. features)
Bedstone Manor, Bedstone (Ins. hall ceiling)								*		1560 (chequerboard joists set diagonally)
Newport Guildhall (inserted screen)										1562 (inserted at lower end of hall)
60 High St, Whitchurch										1563-97 (crosswing, hall gone, 3 others similar)
Porch House, Bishop's Castle		*					*			1564 (2-stor.hall, jettied. Lozenges. Plank/muntin ext. wall)
Old Hall Farm, All Stretton (Crosswing)										1564 (jettied, 2-bay, service wing)
2 Milk St, S'bury										1566 (remodelling of front rage)
High Grosvenor, Claverley (inserted ceiling)										1566-1610 (in hall, chequerboad joists, chamf'd & stopped)
Ightfield Hall Farm, Barn										1567 (6-bay, box-fr. some reused crucks, sq. panels, 4 high)
Bear Steps, S'bury (balcony)										1567-80 (added to hall extn. as part of same programme)
14 Callaughton, M. Wen.										1569-70 (stone-clad, much altered, chequerboard ceiling)
Leaton Grange, Wrock. (repair phase)										1570-1600 (corner post & tie-beam replaced)
Wolverton, Eaton-u-Heywood										1570 (inserted kitchen ceiling)
Rowton Grange, Clungunford (Hall range)							*			1571-2 (2-storied hall, cambered ties, longhouse origins?)
Alkington Hall, Whitchurch (S.W. quarter)										1572 (box-framed remnant of earlier build)
Oldfields, M. Say (rebuild. of E. end)										1573 (hall is base-cruck but undatable)
Detton Hall, Neen Savage (Crosswing)								*		1575-6 (2-bay jettied wing to vanished range)
Bear Steps, S'bury (extension to hall)									*	1576-7 (side-purl./wind-br. add. to undated crown-post hall)
Stokesay Castle (N. Tower alterations)										1578 (ovolo-moulded project. window in top of tower)
Wolverton, Eaton-u-Heywood (Crosswing)										1581 (add. beyond upper bay of hall, incorp. reused crucks)
Bank Farm, Aston Piggott, Westbury (Barn)							*			1591 (term. post-quem, reused t'bers c.1700, box-fr. L-shape)
Alkington Hall, Whitchurch (main part)										1591 (dble-pile, brick, door-post & purlin from same tree)
Clive House, S'bury (added unit)										1591 (service wing)
Clungunford Farm, Clungunford										1591-2 (jettied crossing)
Manor Farm, Aston Eyre, Gatehouse										1596-1616 (timber-framed extension to stone original)
28 Watergate, Whitchurch		*								1597 2-cell, floored parlour, ogee d'head, paint's, window)
Church Farm, Clungunford (Crosswing)										1598 (smoke blackening in both bays)
Rowton Grange, Clungunford (Crosswing)										1599
Lion Tap, S'bury (rebuilt gable end)								*		1600 (term. post-quem, jettied 4 sides, wallpaintings)
High Grosvenor, Claverley (crosswing)										1601 (block of shops/chambers at 2 levels cf. Chester Rows)
Bear Steps, S'bury, The Orrel									*	1603 (corner property, triple ovolo & quirk on bressumer)
165 Frank-well, S'bury (Ashley's)										1603 (single cell, very close-studding all round)
Fulway Cottage, Cound			*							1606-7 (additions to earlier stonework)
Langley Gatehouse										1607-41
Madeley Court, Brewhouse (beam)										1607-8 (relates to later insertion or replacement)
Bear Steps, S'bury (axial beam in hall)					*					1608 (3 raised crucks, whole trees)
High Ercall Hall										

Name	Hall	Spere Truss	Cont. Wing	Base Cruck	Cruck	Crown Post	Close Studding	C'ping	M'ding	Date
Shootrough, Cardington (Crosswing)									*	1609 (box-fr. 1½-bays, wallpaintings, jettied gable)
127 Frankwell, S'bury							*		*	1609 (3-stor. gr-fl shops, jettied, S-braces, mid-rail)
Brookgate Farm, Plealy (Wing II)									*	1612 (square framing, ovolo-moulded window)
Manor Fam, Aston Eyre (Barn)										1612-13 (timber-framed with some stud-and-panel)
Ashwood, Ash (inserted ceiling)									*	1620 (spine–beam soffit moulded w. double cavetto & fillet)
Detton Hall, Neen Savage (Hall range)										1625-59 (2-storied, 2-bay hall, entrance & staircase)
17-23 Watergate, Whitchurch							*			1625 (formerly Raven Inn, wallpaintings, one build)
Clungunford Farm, Clungunford										1628-9 (2-storied hall. Oldest tree, 355 rings)
Old Hall Farm, All Stretton										1630 (lobby-entry, queen–posts, fireplaces in both attics)
Old Mansion, St. Mary's St, S'bury							*		*	c.1631 (rear range with elab. s'case & ovolo-mould window)
Forester's Lodge, Upper Millichope										1633 (ins. ground-fl. ceiling, using whole or ½-trees)
Cherrington Manor							*		*	1635 (mixed framing patt's, hewn jetty, carv's, ogee mould)
Meeson Hall, Bolas Magna										1637 (intern. tie-beams, gentleman's residence, stone-built)
Fulway Cottage, Cound (inserted ceiling)										1640
Stokesay Castle (Gatehouse)							*	*	*	1640 (jettied on 4 sides, elab. carvings, cusped lozenges)
Stokesay Castle (ceiling in S. Tower)								*	*	1640-1 (beam moulding based on ogee)
Abbey, S'bury, Tower roof										1641 (present roof)
Meeson Hall, Bolas Magna										1644 (2 timber-framed rear service wings)
Sycamore Cottage, Clungunford										1652
Bird on the Rock, Clungunford										1653
2 Milk St, S'bury				*						1655 (roof raising using 1 upper cruck)
Golding Hall, Cound							*			1660 (gentleman's residence, [Langley's], later brick-clad)
Golding Hall, Cound (Crosswing)										1666 (brick-built, datestone of 1668 - Thomas Langley)
Abbey, S'bury, (Bellchamber floor)										c.1667 (underpinning)
Abbot's House, Buildwas (staircase)										1687-1717 (in W. block. Splat balusters)
Alcaston Manor (Cellar)										1704
Bell Inn, Alveley (Granary)										1753-4 (box-frame truss in upper floor)
Detton Hall, Neen Savage (purlins in hall)				*						1789-90 (introduced during a refurbishment programme)
Bell Inn, Alveley (Granary)										c.1824 (2 upper cruck trusses in extension)

Shropshire Dendrochronolgy 'Star Chart' as at 1 December 2002

How Dendrochronology Works (*by* Daniel Miles)

Until relatively recently, radiocarbon dating was the only known scientific method of dating wooden objects. Although usually successful, dates produced would have a range of plus or minus 20 years at best, and at worst could span two centuries or more. In addition only the actual rings sampled for Carbon 14 analysis were dated—the tree may well have continued to live for decades or even a century or more afterwards. In the 1970s a new scientific method of dating buildings was developed—dendrochronology.

The way dendrochronology works is relatively simple. As a tree grows, it puts on a new growth or tree-ring every year, just under the bark. Trees grow at different rates according to the weather in any given year: a wider ring in a favourable year and a narrower ring in an unfavourable year. Over a period of time there will be a sequence of wider and narrower tree-rings reflecting the climate pattern. In effect, the span of years during which a tree has lived will be represented by a unique fingerprint, which can be detected in other trees growing over the same period in the same vicinity.

To obtain this fingerprint, a radial section of timber from the pith or centre of the tree out to the bark edge is required. The most common and least intrusive method of obtaining this is by taking cores from a number of timbers within a building. This is done by using a 16mm outside diameter coring bit which produces a 12mm diameter core. These core bits are specially manufactured for the purpose and have hardened steel teeth necessary to cut through timber hardened by centuries of seasoning. Where samples have been taken from visible timbers in the habitable areas of buildings, the resulting hole is plugged with a ramin dowel, stained and distressed to match the surrounding surface. The cores selected should have a sequence of tree-rings of at least 50, and ideally 100 years. Ideally, too, they should retain the final ring at the bark edge: that is, the last ring that was grown in the year in which the tree was felled. Therefore, the best samples are from large, slow-grown timbers, without distortions, and with bark edge remaining. Slices are obviously much more useful, but rarely obtainable without causing severe distress to the buildings, not to mention the owners. Other sampling techniques might involve photography and direct *in situ* measurements with a graticule, but these are not often used for a variety of practical reasons.

Once the samples are obtained, and are thoroughly dry, they are then sanded on a bench-mounted belt sander, or linisher, using 60 to 1200 grit abrasive paper, and cleaned with compressed air to allow the ring boundaries to be clearly distinguished. They are then measured under a x10/x30 microscope correct to a precision of 0.01mm. Thus each ring or year is represented by its measurement which is arranged as a series of ring-width indices within a data set, with the earliest ring being placed at the beginning of the series, and the latest or outermost ring concluding the data set.

Whilst the principle behind tree-ring dating is a simple one, the determination of what is an actual match is much more involved. When an undated sample or site sequence is compared against a dated sequence, known as a reference chronology, an indication of how *good* the match is must be determined. Although it is almost impossible to define a visual match, computer comparisons can be accurately quantified. Whilst it may not be the best statistical indicator, Students (a pseudonym for W.S. Gosset) *t*-value has been widely used amongst British dendrochronologists. The cross-correlation algorithms most commonly used and published are derived from Baillie and Pilchers CROS (short for cross-matching) programme.[4]

Statistically, *t*-values over 3.5 should be considered to be significant, although in reality it is common to find demonstrably spurious *t*-values of 4 and 5 because more than one matching position is indicated as similar patterns of tree-rings could be found repeated within a sequence of years. For this reason, dendrochronologists prefer to see some t-value ranges of 5, 6, or higher, and for these to be well replicated from different, independent chronologies with local and regional chronologies well represented. To give some idea of how good a match can be expected, two timbers from the same parent tree will often give a t-value of 10 or higher. Users of dates also need to assess their validity critically. They should not have great faith in a date supported by a handful of t-values of 3s with one or two 4s, nor should they be entirely satisfied with a single high match of 5 or 6. Examples of spurious t-values in excess of 7 have been noted, so it is essential that matches with reference chronologies are well replicated, and that this is confirmed with visual matches between the two graphs (see below).

In reality, the probability of a particular date being valid is itself a statistical measure depending on the t-values. Consideration must also be given to the length of the sequence being dated as well as those of the reference chronologies. A sample with 30 or 40 years growth is likely to match with high t-values at varying positions, whereas a sample with 100 consecutive rings is much more likely to match significantly at only one unique position. Samples with ring counts as low as 50 may *occasionally* be dated, but only if the matches are very strong, clear and well replicated, with no other significant matching positions. Here, it is essential for intra-site matching when dealing with such short sequences. Consideration should also be given to evaluating the reference chronology against which the samples have been matched: those with well-replicated components which are geographically near to the sampling site are given more weight than an individual site or sample from the opposite end of the country.

It is general practice to cross-match samples from within the same building phase to each other first, combining them into a site master, before comparing with the reference chronologies. This has the advantage of averaging out the 'noise' of individual trees and the resulting mean is much more likely to obtain higher t-values and stronger visual matches. Thus, after measurement, the ring-width series for each sample is plotted as a graph of width against year on log-linear graph paper or similar graphic display. The graph or curve for each sample is then compared visually with others in the group and those found satisfactory and consistent are averaged to form a mean curve for the site or phase. This mean curve and any unmatched individual sequences are then compared against dated reference chronologies to obtain an absolute calendar date for each sequence. Sometimes, especially in urban situations, timbers may have come from different sources and fail to match each other, thus making the compilation of a site master difficult. In this situation samples must then be compared individually with the reference chronologies.

Therefore, when cross-matching samples between each other, or against reference chronologies, a combination of both visual matching and a process of qualified statistical comparison by computer is used. In the Shropshire project ring-width series were compared on an IBM compatible computer for statistical cross-matching using a variant of the Belfast CROS programme.[5]

A precise felling date is only achievable when the last growth ring beneath the bark is present. However, when some of the outer sapwood rings have been removed through decay or conversion, it is still possible to ascribe a felling-date range within a 95% confidence limit. In 1992, a local sapwood estimate of 11-45 rings was produced for the Shropshire area, based on 47 timbers with sapwood complete to the bark edge.[6] This was a reduction of about 25% from the standard sapwood estimate of 10-55 years in use at the time.[7] By 1993 even the 11-45 year estimate was thought to be slightly broad, but it was intended to continue to use it to the conclusion of the project when all the sapwood data collected would be reassessed and a new, narrower one produced. However, the project continued to be extended year after year, and by 1997 a nationwide study of sapwood produced a new estimate of 11-41 years for Wales and the border counties, including Shropshire.[8]

When even some of the outer heartwood rings as well as the sapwood has been removed from the sample, then only a *terminus post quem* or 'felled after' date can be given. This is the least useful interpretation of a dated sample and is calculated by adding the minimum number of sapwood rings (11) to the last measured or counted heartwood ring.

Here was the answer to the building historian's dream—if the outermost ring was present, an absolute dating process accurate to a single year, if not the season the tree was felled. It should be noted, however, that tree-ring dating can not always be successfully applied. Timbers, for example, may be too fast-grown with fewer, complacent rings (i.e. where there is little variety in the ring sequence), or come from slower grown trees with distorted ring sequences due to pollarding or other damage. In neither case are they generally datable. Most historic roofs and timber-framed buildings were made from oak, which is the most suitable species for successful tree-ring analysis. Although elm and beech can also be dated and matched with the oak chronologies, elm in particular can often contain distorted and fast-grown rings making routine dating difficult.

It must be remembered that dendrochronology can only provide the date or date-range when the tree was felled. However, it is known from numerous documentary sources that oak was used 'green', or unseasoned. This means that construction probably took place in the year of felling or within a year or two thereafter. If a group of five or ten timbers from a building, preferably of different types, all were felled within the same year, then it is most likely that the actual *construction* of the building would have taken place during that or the following year.

Open Halls

The chart shows that the open hall spanned the years 1247-1603, effectively finishing *c.*1550. Of course, this is not to say that there were not earlier and later examples. With over 160 castles and moated sites in the county still identifiable, and 41 known religious and allied houses, many must have contained open halls, most of which would have been at first-floor level, but the project was concerned with halls of a vernacular or slightly superior class and the proven run of over 300 years emphasises that the open hall must have been the most popular feature ever included within the concept of English architecture. Fifty-two buildings with an identifiable open hall were sampled. Only one, Ludlow Guildhall, built for the powerful Palmers' Guild in 1411 was a fully-aisled structure, and it remains the only standing and recognisable aisled hall in the county, although a handful of others may be postulated. This is not surprising; Shropshire is a cruck-biased county, and national distribution maps of the two types shows a clear demographic division.[9] However, a kind of marriage between the cruck and the aisle may be observed in the reconstruction drawings of the two cruck trusses at Cruck Cottage, Upton Magna (see pp.46-7). When sampled, the internal crucks in this building were the earliest standing crucks in Europe, but they have since been supplanted by those at The Royal George in Cottingham, Northamptonshire, of 1262.[10] Perhaps their form—allied notched-lap joints and earth-fast construction—will help to push back the barriers of knowledge regarding the techniques of early cruck building. The building was remodelled in 1424/6 when a further cruck-truss was introduced, the walls realigned and the original apexes altered.

Of the 52 open halls one (Upper Ledwyche) was six-bayed, one was five-bayed (All Forces Club, Low Town, Bridgnorth, thought to have been a warehouse), two (Stokesay and Stottesdon Hall Farm) were four-bayed, three (The Guildhall and Barnaby House, Ludlow and The Prior's House at Much Wenlock) were three-bayed; 30 were two-bayed, one was 1½-bayed and there were seven single-bayed halls. In seven cases the number of bays could not be ascertained. Two-bayed halls, therefore, represent nearly 60% of the total, but this is unlikely to be a true reflection of the stock of hall houses countywide; the two-bayed hall is considered normal for Shropshire and the true percentage must be higher.

Once the initial shock of discovering that the bulk of the open halls related to the 15th century, rather than the mid-to-late-14th as had previously been thought, had been absorbed, the dating became comparatively predictable. Over 62% belonged to the 15th century and were spread evenly throughout it. Only nine had felling dates of the 14th century; one early survivor, Great Oxenbold,[11] was dated 1247 and there were two in the northern half of the county, close together in terms of distance and date which produced felling dates of 1550 and 1551. One small maverick hall, Fulway Cottage, well-carpentered with very close vertical studding and thought by many people to be of medieval date, produced a felling date of 1603. A curious anomaly was observed at Brookgate Farm, Plealy, where a single-bayed, cruck-built hall, of no great architectural merit, contained an elaborate spere-truss, richly decorated with cusping, moulding and a carved boss. The dates on both components were carefully checked, and there was no doubt regarding their contemporaneity.

Including Brookgate Farm, nearly 27% of the halls examined had spere-trusses. This is also probably not a true reflection; more are known to exist in the county. In three further examples it appeared that the spere-truss was missing, and in general terms it seems to have been a vulnerable feature. Usually the spere-truss took the expected form of a tri-partite arrangement giving an aisled form with soaring spere-posts, but at Moat House, Longnor, the finest of the box-framed halls, a continuous low rail is set over diminutive spere-posts which are devoid of decoration. Of the five base-cruck halls sampled three had their spere-trusses intact, and in total 14 spere-trusses were noted with a span of nearly 200 years. Although the physical remains were not always present, it is a fair assumption to say that all the base-cruck halls would have had a spere-truss at the lower end. The earlier spere-trusses were without cusped decoration, but at The Bold (1320-54) cusping makes its first appearance in a secular building, and, perhaps significantly, it occurs there only in the spere-truss, the status symbol.[12]

Contemporary Ranges and Crosswings

Although 16 buildings were shown to have a contemporary range or crosswing, three of these relate to commercial town properties. At 1 Broad Street, Ludlow,[13] the wing takes the form of a shorter parallel range, giving a double-pile plan-form; in another—The King's Head, Mardol, Shrewsbury—the double-pile plan-form is repeated, but with a ground-floor hall in addition; while in the third—The Abbot's House in Shrewsbury—the crosswing occupies the corner of the street and is part of the concept as a whole.[14] The other examples are all clearly solar crosswings accompanying an open hall, although some are in a town setting. No examples of contemporary service wings were found, and none are suspected. Where original service accommodation can be identified, it occurs at the lower end of a hall range, as for example, at Moat House, Longnor. At Bedstone Manor the finest of the cruck hall houses, a service wing was added at the lower end in 1560, probably replacing a service end and bringing the complex to a fully developed H-shape, a trend that has been observed elsewhere in the county.

Base-crucks and Full-crucks

Shropshire lies at the heart of cruck country and it was, therefore, of great importance to obtain firm dates for as many key buildings as possible within the genre. It was vital to cover as many base-crucks as possible as these buildings exercise an overwhelming influence within the study of cruck-building. Seven proven examples of base-crucks remain in Shropshire, and there are two further possibilities. We were able to sample them all, including the doubtful ones, although one had fast-grown timber which would not date, and in another case the timbers looked unpromising and the money ran out before it could be sampled. Significantly, both these were in north Shropshire; the examples south of the Severn all produced firm dates. The date range of the latter is 1302-1408, virtually the whole of the 14th century, although if the possibilities are included the range extends to 1431.

Each has a crown-post roof construction. This is in direct contrast to the neighbouring county of Herefordshire where none of the base-cruck halls has crown-post roofing. The double tie-beam feature, normally associated with base-crucks, occurs only in Plowden Hall, the earliest of the group;[15] the remainder have a single tie, usually of substantial scantling. That at 23 Barrow Street, Much Wenlock, measures 3ft. (0.9m.) at the centre. But all the other associated features such as the square-set lower purlins and deep arch-bracing to the tie are present in all cases. The quality of the carpentry fully justifies the reasoning that base-cruck halls were built by men of means who would regard the form of their hall as a status symbol, but whether it is seen as a modification of the migrant aisled hall in a westerly direction is open to question. With only one standing aisled hall in the county, the question of whether base-crucks are chronologically and typologically later than aisled halls is not answered by our project, but, for the record, Shropshire's solitary surviving aisled hall (1411) coincides with the last-built base-cruck (1408). Another curious and probably irrelevant statistic is that, notwithstanding its premature appearance at The Bold and in a small homogeneous group in Shrewsbury, cusping commences when base-crucks finish, the two features merging in Barclay's Bank, Much Wenlock, in 1408.

With the current total of known cruck buildings in the county approaching 300, sampling had to be carefully targeted, and, with a very small percentage of the whole likely to be covered, difficult decisions had to be made. For example, the village of Condover boasts ten surviving houses of cruck construction, most of them displaying similar characteristics such as type L2 apexes,[16] sturdy plain blades and no cruck spurs, the wallplate being supported on a step cut from the back of the blade. It was thought that expenditure should be limited to one building, and that this would provide a peg on which to hang the rest. Condover Court was chosen as the most complete example and the date of 1445 obtained for it throws much light on the study of crucks as a whole. Overall, the date range for full crucks in Shropshire is 1269 to 1551, but the 1269 example must be regarded as an isolated survivor as far as the project is concerned, and its impact is discussed later. The other early cruck hall at Stokesay of 1284-5 is, of course, a gentry-type building in a raised-cruck genre and it remains the earliest ground-floor hall in the county.[17] Incidentally, Cruck Cottage and Stokesay, so close together in date but at opposite ends of the social scale, are almost the only buildings where whole trees were employed to make the crucks. The evidence supplied by the majority of those surviving suggests that cruck construction was at its height throughout the 15th century. Significantly, the two late examples of 1550 and 1551/2, though fully within the cruck tradition, are in the north of the county where it has been our experience that late dates are to be expected. Here too it was noted that the crucks sometimes sat on stylobates or padstones, whereas in south Shropshire invariably they are tenoned into the sill-beam.[18]

14th-century crucks are almost entirely missing, the All Forces Club in Bridgnorth (1392-1422) being a marginal exception. Of course, this is not to say that they were never built or that they have not survived, but it must be admitted that it was salutary to learn that those previously thought to be of 14th-century date were firmly rooted in the 15th. But as we were only able to sample less than 10% of the known total in the county it is too early to draw positive conclusions from the study, only a perceived trend.

Condover Court seems to exemplify the comparative wealth of copyhold tenants in pre-Reformation times. Though the largest and most complete of the Condover group, it is typical in its detailing: finely wrought blades, each pair obtained from a single tree, sawn on one side, adzed-dressed on the other; L2 type apex joints with the central truss having a cambered collar-beam with arch-braces tailored to form a perfect arch. Some form of decoration is usually included within this group—in this case there is cusping on the windbraces. Condover Court is a little unusual in having two service bays and two louvres for smoke extraction, but in its two-bay hall form with a contemporary solar crosswing forming an L-shaped plan it can be said to be typical not only of Condover, but also of much of Shropshire's cruck-building tradition. It is outclassed, it must be admitted, by Bedstone Manor (1448), where the central truss has moulded crucks and arch-braces incorporating seven rolls-and-hollows facing the dais end and five facing the service end. In addition the collar-beam of the central truss is carpentered to form an impressive ogee-arch. The contemporary solar crosswing has six half-bays and contains the remains of wallpaintings. It must surely rank among the most impressive of cruck-built hall houses on a national basis and certainly represents the apogee of cruck development in Shropshire.

However, cruck construction had clearly been at a high aesthetic level for half a century at least, because the blades in the central truss at 38/39 Woolstaston (1399/1400) are decorated on each arris with quarter-round moulding which is also carried onto the arch-braces. This house also has a contemporary crosswing, and it can be demonstrated that the crosswing, with its crown-post roof, was built first. The same sequence was observed in both Condover Court and Manor Farm, Bedstone.

Wolverton in Eaton-under-Heywood (1475) was chosen for dendrodating partly for its surviving medieval features and partly because its central cruck truss exhibits a two-tiered form. The blades rise to a level just above the collar-beam where they are deliberately terminated and a principal rafter with curved feet takes the truss to the apex. Two others are known in the county, although in those the rafters are straight. Wolverton posed a problem of definition. It exhibits characteristics of base-cruck construction, but its late date puts it well outside the known date range.[19]

In some cases the social difference between the upper and lower bays of the hall is expressed on the central truss. As has already been stated, at Manor Farm, Bedstone, (1448), seven rolls-and-hollows face the dais end, but only five occur on the low side. At Shootrough, Cardington (1422) a double cavetto moulding faces the dais end while the less expensive quarter-round is used on the low side. At Bradney Farm, Worfield, (1486), a chamfer reaches the apex on the dais side but is only taken as far as the collar-beam on the low side. Other examples for which dating was not obtained are known in the county, but, of course, mouldings are not the only medium through which the differences could be detected. Usually the sawn side of the tree, flush-jointing and carpenters' assembly marks face the dais, and, if evidence for a smoke-louvre remains, it will usually be found in the lower bay of the hall.

It was particularly pleasing to obtain a firm date for the only known terrace of crucks in Britain—25-28 Barrow Street, Much Wenlock (1435)—and although this does not prove that they represent a row of almshouses which pre-date the death of Hugh Wolmer, a local bene-factor, at least it does nothing to disprove the hypothesis. But the date of 1415 for the little single-bayed St. Owen's Well House in the same town rules out the notion that it may have been built by the priest, William Corvehill; it pre-dates his death by 131 years. With such cruel spikes are dendrochronological mantraps baited. However, the same exercise confirmed that the deep ogee-headed doorway which must have given access to a tiny floored solar at first-floor level, was a contemporary feature.[20]

19-21 Drayton Road, Hodnet (1467) was chosen as a reasonably complete example of a single-bay cruck-built hall with a contemporary, box-famed crosswing, but on a much smaller scale and at a lower social level than the examples quoted above. It was probably furnished with a croglofft at the lower end, in the manner of many Welsh houses, and seems to emphasise that the Shropshire cruck-building tradition was as strong in the lower social echelons as in the higher, and in use at the same time. For slightly different reasons Catherton Cottage (1485) was chosen. Here the hall was $1^{1}/_{2}$-bayed, and there were indications of a longhouse form, but the central truss was decorated with cusping on the upper parts of the blades which, with cusped V-struts above the collar-beam formed a full quatrefoil flanked by two trefoils—a very carefully thought-out design, and one which occurs in larger and more prestigious buildings. It may have been the home of an early iron-master, and again it demonstrates the cultural correlation between the cruck tradition, longhouse form, the desire for aesthetic satisfaction and being fortunate enough to have the means to achieve it.[21]

As mentioned earlier, Brookgate Farm (1490) posed an interesting problem regarding the relationship between a single-bayed cruck-built open hall of utilitarian design and an elaborate spere-truss with cusping, moulding, jowelled spere posts of unusual form and a carved central boss. The prime objective was to determine whether the two elements were contemporary, and this proved to be the case. Perhaps it can be used to emphasise the freedom of choice enjoyed by the builder. That may be considered too simplistic, but all other reasoning collapses in the light of the dating evidence. The house is also a good example of the way in which the function of the ends could be changed. It was clear that the original service end was replaced with a square-framed parlour wing in 1620, while the solar end was redesigned as a kitchen. Such change overs have been noted elsewhere in Shropshire.

It must be admitted that Cruck Cottage, Upton Magna, was initially chosen as a possible example of a small late cruck—a type that was, at the time, missing from our survey. Only marginally was this objective achieved as the crucks in the end gable produced a felling date of 1424/26. It was known that the feet of the two internal pairs of crucks by-passed the sill-beam on the inside and disappeared into the ground, but because they were rough-hewn timbers, each from a single tree, and littered with empty mortices and other joint-housing, it had been assumed that they represented reused blades. However, when they were sampled, carefully measured and allowances were made for slumping, the startling discovery was made that they were *in situ*, were probably earth-fast originally, had scissor-bracing and notched-lap joints and dated to 1269. Moreover, the roof-line, when drawn out, showed a distinct inclination to change its angle at eaves level and thus adopt the form of an aisled structure. Though not identical in form and clearly of a much later date, the barn at Bolderstone in south Yorkshire, noted by Addy, is a useful comparison, incorporating as it does, the cruck and the aisle.[22] The end gable crucks were introduced as part of a remodelling scheme in 1424/26, and at the same time the older crucks were given new apex joints. As mentioned earlier, this little dwelling bears comparison with the great hall at Stokesay Castle in some respects.

Crown-post Roofs

Shropshire has a total of 29 known crown-post roofs which either survive or have left structural evidence for their existence. This includes two demolished examples in Shrewsbury known from photographic evidence. The chart on pp.117-119 gives details of their construction and date range. Generally they conform to a distinctive style. It was important to obtain firm dates for as many as possible in order to make comparisons with areas where they are more numerous and also to discover whether a pattern of development could be detected within the county. South-east England contains by far the bulk of crown-post roofs and it is in this area that the form continued to be used at vernacular level long after it was abandoned as a gentry-type elsewhere.[23] Therefore where they survive in Shropshire they tend to be early and are usually associated with substantial houses.

The vexed question of whether the medieval builders regarded crown-posts as being in tension or compression is not answered by our survey. But it is clear that they knew exactly what they were doing—nowhere had any joint failed.

We successfully sampled 22 buildings and these appear on the 'star-chart' as a ly-knit group occurring between 1287 and 1431, spanning virtually one and a half centuries. Shropshire crown-posts are invariably plain and comparatively short. Only one (The Bold) has any form of embellishment and then only in the form of a plain chamfer on each arris. Lateral support usually takes the form of down-swinging braces in a concave arc, only occasionally convex. Sometimes the lateral braces are cusped, and occasionally the longitudinal braces are also cusped. Only one, that at Cottage Farm, Easthope, in a building which was a house but is currently in use as a farm building, has unilateral bracing to the crown-posts. This and Upton Cressett Hall each have two aisled trusses, but in both cases the vital central truss of the hall has not survived. They are shown in the chart as possible base-cruck halls but,

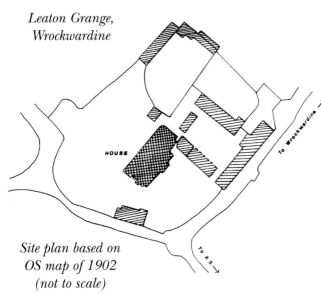

*Leaton Grange,
Wrockwardine*

*Site plan based on
OS map of 1902
(not to scale)*

*South-east elevation
(not to scale)*

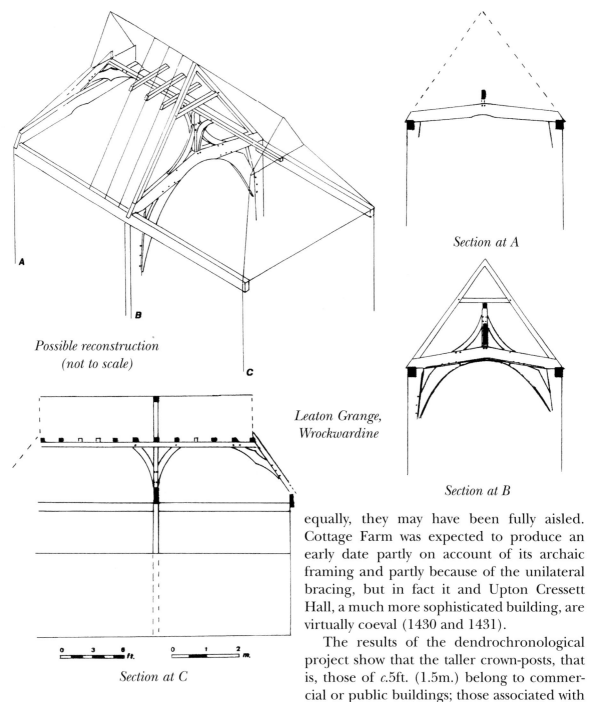

*Possible reconstruction
(not to scale)*

Section at A

*Leaton Grange,
Wrockwardine*

Section at B

Section at C

equally, they may have been fully aisled. Cottage Farm was expected to produce an early date partly on account of its archaic framing and partly because of the unilateral bracing, but in fact it and Upton Cressett Hall, a much more sophisticated building, are virtually coeval (1430 and 1431).

The results of the dendrochronological project show that the taller crown-posts, that is, those of *c.*5ft. (1.5m.) belong to commercial or public buildings; those associated with purely domestic buildings range from 2ft. 4ins. (0.7m.) to 4ft. (1.2m.). The average height is *c.*3ft. (0.9m.) Curiously, the shortest—at Upton Cressett (2ft. 4in. or 0.7m.)—is the latest built (1431), but this is not to say that they became shorter as time went on, the heights vary throughout the date range.

One crown-post roof, that at Leaton Grange, Wrockwardine, would only yield a felling date of after 1313. This is unfortunate, as it is associated with an unusual hipped end to the building where a straight longitudinal brace has an additional cusped brace springing from it.

365

In Shrewsbury there was a trend to make the crown-posts of cruciform shape and to extend the front and back limbs over the tie-beam, thus straddling it. This resulted in a very firm joint, providing the limbs were pegged back into the tie-beam—which was not always the case. We were able to sample the three surviving examples in the town itself—Rigg's Hall (1405-35), the Nag's Head hall (1420), and the Lion Tap (1423-6)—but it seems that the practice did not commence in Shrewsbury as one of the buildings where it occurs is The Bold (1320) in Aston Botterell parish in south Shropshire and the other is Barclay's Bank, Much Wenlock (1408).[24] Only two examples of straddling have been noted outside Shrewsbury. It would be interesting to know why some of the Shrewsbury builders adopted it with such enthusiasm in the early years of the 15th century. Not all did; in crown-post roof design there was as much individuality in Shrewsbury as in the county as a whole.

The cusping at The Bold—and this admittedly is in embryonic form—does not occur on the crown-post truss. Cusping seems to make a positive introduction in a full-blown form on the lateral braces to the crown-post at Barclay's Bank, Much Wenlock, right at the start of cusping itself. From then on it is to be expected in domestic buildings of any pretensions, but cusping as a topic is discussed more fully below.

One building, Plowden Hall (1302), stands out. On the aisled truss at the lower end, presumably the spere-truss, the crown-post, which is 3ft. 6in. (1.07m.) in length, is severely plain and the lateral braces are short and straight, bracing the angle between the crown-post and the tie-beam. There appears to be a similar truss at the upper (dais) end, but this is obscured with plaster. However, the central truss, which is of base-cruck construction, has recently had its plaster removed, revealing a crown-post 6in. (0.15m.) taller than the other, and with a simply-moulded base. It also has upswinging braces to the collar-beam. This rhythm of down-swingers on the outer trusses and up-swingers on the central truss is a feature of southern counties where the dating seems to be later.

As mentioned earlier, base-crucks are almost invariably associated with crown-post roofs in Shropshire. All that we were able to sample had this characteristic, as did the two possibilities.

On a human note, an interesting discovery was made at the Buck's Head, Church Stretton (1287-1321), which has a crown-post roof of typical Salopian form, and also has dragon-ties similar to those noted at Plowden Hall. The building was erected as a town house or inn of the Botfield family and was occupied by a John who was known as John o' th' Inn. This inevitably became corrupted to 'Thynne' and it was John's great-grandson and namesake who built the Wiltshire Renaissance mansion, Longleat, in the 1550s/60s. The family crest is a *reindeer or* (gold reindeer) and the hall at Longleat is liberally furnished with bucks' heads.[25]

Close-studding

Solely on the basis of the evidence supplied by the chart, this feature makes a tentative appearance in 1430 in Henry Tudor House in Shrewsbury, and then after 1454, when it was used in the solar wing at Plowden Hall, it gained popularity and has a virtually uninterrupted run until the end of the 15th century. It was still used sporadically until 1660, the last dated example being Golding Hall, a substantial house. While the majority of close-studded houses clearly relate to families in the upper income bracket, one or two do not. The most surprising example was Fulway Cottage at Cound (1603) which is a very small single-bayed open hall house. Here the vertical studs are wider than the interstices. Manor Cottage, Prees (1551/2), also provides a salutary lesson. Here the close-studding occurs in the floored end, whereas the open hall, which is of cruck construction, is square-framed. As Manor Cottage is one of the few examples where the wall-framing can be shown to be contemporary with the crucks, the lesson learned here is that uninterrupted verticals are not necessarily indicative of an open hall. A few other examples are known in the county.

Cusping

Long thought to be an early feature, which had died out by the beginning of the 15th century, our project has shown that in Shropshire cusping became fashionable in secular buildings at the beginning of the 15th century (The King's Head, Mardol, Shrewsbury, 1404) and continued as a popular concept to the end of the century. It returned as a decorative feature in lozenge work in the late 16th to early 17th centuries. As mentioned earlier, The Bold (1320-54), has a form of embryonic cusping in the braces of the spere-truss, but then, apart from 12A Butcher Row/12 Fish St, Shrewsbury (1358-9), there is gap until it appears in a mature form perhaps as much as a century later. However, the gap is probably misleading. It is known that other (undated) buildings in Shrewsbury have similar forms of cusping on their frontages, and they are all distinctive with up-and-down cusped braces forming quatrefoils. Though too early to say definitely, it is possible that this piece of trend-setting in Shrewsbury marked the beginning of the fashion. It is clear that once established, it was used with enthusiasm, and sometimes with spectacular effects. In Ludlow's Guildhall (1411), it is a unforgettable experience to look through the opulent display of the cusped V-struts and windbraces of the medieval roof bays as they fade into the distance.[26] Similarly, the view of the roof of the Guildhall, Newport (1487), with its quatrefoil pattern of cusped windbraces which are pierced and chamfered, is breathtaking. At Moat House, Longnor (1467), there are three tiers of cusped windbraces in the roof and the effect reaches a spectacular climax with the cusping on the V-struts allied with cusping on the tops of the principal rafters to form a quatrefoiled apex. Cusping also occurs on the spere-truss. Visitors invariably gasp at the sheer beauty of the framing at Moat House. The solar wing at Plowden Hall (1454), has what can only be described as an exuberance of cusping, and the effect is similar. These are all high class buildings, but cusping is also found in modest houses, and has become a kind of watershed when estimating the date of buildings without the benefit of dendrochronology. The question usually asked is 'does it have cusping, and if not, why not?' It is a pertinent question, well illustrated by the case of Bedstone Manor (1448). Here, in a building which has a wealth of carpentry detail, moulded crucks and ogee form, there is no cusping, and this at a time when it was at the zenith of its popularity.

Mouldings

Within the parameters of our survey, it seemed important to establish firm dates for the various types of mouldings where they occur. Stone mouldings are more easily dated as such examples found in churches often have a documentary building date. Wooden mouldings pose more problems, and it appears that the chart, though necessarily not comprehensive, at least helps to establish certain trends. The moulding at Great Oxenbold, admittedly, occurs in the stone fabric and is half-round. This was to be expected, half-round moulding being common in the 13th century. The earliest date for a wooden moulding in Shropshire is 1254-99, and this relates to a well-preserved samson-post in 59 Sheinton Street, Much Wenlock. This is octagonal and has a moulded head and base. The moulding at the head relates to the chamfers which result in the octagonal form, and consists of two bands of bead moulding at what is, in effect, the run-off to the chamfer. As the run-off is in two parts, the beads are about 6in. (0.15m.)

apart. The base is simpler, the chamfer runs off into a simple stop, returning the octagon to square section, but in two stages.

At The Bold (1320-54) the mouldings are consistent throughout the house on those timbers which are chamfered. On them the chamfer is moulded along its length with two beads separated by a fillet. The exception is the crown-post itself which has a plain chamfer on the four arrises.

At 23 Barrow Street (1327-30) the mouldings on the base-crucks continue along the arch-braces to the collar. They are identical to those at The Bold and, of course, the date range is close and both are base-cruck hall houses.

The Palmers' Guild College in Ludlow (1393) must have been a lavishly decorated building, reflecting the wealth and importance of this institution. Only fragments of the complex remain, but when a beam of the spere-truss was rescued and sampled it was seen to have a combination of roll, ogee, billet and cavetto moulding, while an original doorpost, embedded in later walling, was seen to have a carved capital with battlemented ornament.

Quarter-round moulding seems to make its appearance in a fullblown form at 38/39 Woolstaston (1399/1400) where it appears on both edges of the cruck blades, continues along the arch-braces to the collar, and is also present on all arrises of the central strut which is set between the collar-beam and the low-beam. An added bonus at Woolstaston was that a firm date was obtained for one of the enigmatic 'low-beam' examples.[27] Quarter-round was superseded by ovolo moulding which first appears in the chart in 1578 at Stokesay Castle. This accords with observations generally in the county and there are examples of an 'embryonic' ovolo in the windows of two stone-built important buildings in Shrewsbury—Whitehall (1578-82) and the Market Hall (1596). Neither has been dendro-dated, but the documentary evidence is reasonably certain.

Conclusions

That our survey was worthwhile is indisputable and, depending on funding, it will continue. Although, inevitably, it has raised more questions than it has answered and it is clear that there are many gaps still to be filled in, everyone involved knows much more about Shropshire timber-framing than they did previously. Some cherished beliefs must now be jettisoned—for example the Prior's house at Much Wenlock is dated 75 years earlier than architectural historians like to think; cruck-building has its flowering in the 15th century, not the 14th; and close-studding does not appear until the early 15th century, by which time crown-post roof structure had ceased. The Abbot's House in Shrewsbury, which has 'c.1450' painted on its signboard and features in many textbooks, is closer in date to local thinking than to external academic dogmatism.

At Stokesay it is clear that Laurence of Ludlow's building programme was well advanced before he obtained royal permission for it in 1291. Only the undercroft of the solar suggests that an earlier building on the site pre-dates his activities there. His was a continuous building sequence, and his hall was cruck-built from the start and not a later adaptation of an aisled structure.[28] Also at Stokesay, the date for the Gatehouse (1640) suggests that the Civil War interrupted a programme of renewal and that the timbers were stored until hostilities ceased. Certainly the oft-quoted date of c.1620 or even earlier cannot be sustained, and the same applies to the ceiling in the south tower. Until recently the roof structure of the solar was unknown territory to most people and Cordingley's curious omission of it in his account together with his description of a 'jagged line' which seems to imply that all above it was rebuilt after the Civil War, added to the frustration. All is now made clear. The solar roof is a sans-purlin collar-rafter roof of 1289; clearly part of the main building programme. Each truss has soulaces and on the northern side the wall-plate is supported by stone corbels which were purposefully incorporated into the masonry of the end wall of the hall. On the southern side the rafters are longer, ashlar pieces and sole-plates being employed to triangulate the angle at the wallhead. Curiously, the single wall-plate is embedded centrally in the masonry wall below the sole-plate and the triangle is filled with rubble masonry. It is interesting that all the joints are morticed and tenoned; at that date notched-lap joints might be expected. It is good that, thanks to English Heritage, the building history of this internationally important complex can now be correctly charted.

It was never intended to include churches in the project, but when English Heritage offered us the chance to sample the north transept of Wistanstow church, it would have been foolish to refuse. As a result it gave the earliest date of all, justified Christopher Currie's inclusion of it in his paper on Archaic Roofs and made an interesting comparison with the solar roof at Stokesay.[29] The two are only about half a century apart in date. After Wistanstow it seemed a natural progression to sample the timber-framed chapel at Halston which, though very different, had the controversial outcome described below. The chapel at St. Winifred's Well was more predictable, its cusping indicating what we had more or less expected. There are many other church roofs in Shropshire which would benefit from dendrochronolgy, if future funding allows.

Although, numerically, Shropshire cannot match Somerset for identifiable church houses,[30] it is very probable that Hall Farm, Stottesdon (1534-68), comes within that category. It is situated next to the church and the layout of the hall at first-floor level suggests a communal rather than a private domestic role.

One fact emerged which confirmed what this researcher had previously thought: that there was a remarkable paucity of new building in the first half of the 16th century when Henry VIII reigned. Alterations, additions and updating were being carried out but there is only one example of a newly-built house at that time: Upper Lake in Westbury parish, (1545-6).

In addition to the instances quoted other surprises resulted, among which was that at Upper Millichope where the stonework has 13th-century features. Two new floors were inserted, one in 1450 at second-floor level and the other in 1633 at first-floor level. In each case the workmen used whole or half trees roughly squared and set very close together copying what must have been the flooring technique employed originally. This was a case where we set out to find the original building date and ended with completely different data.[31] Another surprise was that the little timber-framed chapel at Halston dated to 1437. The carved spandrels include the Bear and Ragged staff, symbol of the powerful Neville family with whom the Mytton family of Halston had intermarried in 1552.[32]

Inscribed dates as opposed to dendro dates make an interesting study. Our survey highlighted only one glaring anomaly: the Guildhall at Newport which has an admittedly applied date of 1615, whereas the dendro dates for the three phases are 1487, 1546 and 1562. In five other cases the dendro dates match the inscribed or ascribed dates. Perhaps a little more suspension of disbelief is called for in the future. In three cases it was pleasing to be able to match the dendro dates with documentary dates. Laurence of Ludlow's 'license to crenellate' in 1291 obviously relates to his whole building programme and not just to the south tower. The description of junketings in Shrewsbury when the frame of the Abbot's House was ready for erection is documented in the borough bailiffs' accounts for 1459.[33] Peter Newton's acquisition of the Council House in Shrewsbury, documented in a deed of 1500, accords well with the dendro date, indicating that he added the present hall to an existing solar crosswing of 1472 to serve the needs of the Council in the Marches.[34] The dates obtained for buildings in Ludlow, though not specifically documented, reflect what is known of the activities of the Palmers' Guild at the appropriate times. Although the date of the roof of Barnaby House, (1450-1), does not help with the provenance, it cannot have come from any great distance and thus emphasises the wealth and importance of Ludlow at that time. The date of 1247 for Great Oxenbold, the earliest, of the domestic buildings, comes neatly within the priorship of Humbert, known to have been a 'building prior'.

An element of local pride may, perhaps, be forgiven. Though entirely fortuitous, it is pleasing to be able to record Shropshire as possessing the second earliest known cruck building in Europe (Cruck Cottage, Upton Magna). In addition, the county has the only known cruck terrace (25-28 Barrow Street, Much Wenlock), structural timber from a tree which was growing in 881 at the time of Alfred the Great (59 Sheinton Street, Much Wenlock), the humble ancestor of Longleat (The Buck's Head, Church Stretton), which also has the earliest crown-post roof in the county and the earliest scientifically dated timber-framed building (12A Butcher Row/12 Fish Street) in Shrewsbury. That there are so many firm dates with little or no time-span is due to two factors: the slow growth pattern of the oaks, particularly those south of the Severn, and the expertise of the dendrochronologists.

Finally, in attempting this summary at all, the writer is driven to the conclusion that if humans were meant to study vernacular buildings they would not have been given the power of rational thought.

Gazetteer

The following brief notes are of some of the more interesting houses which have received little or no mention in the text. All have been seen externally and internally by the author. They are grouped under parish headings. It is not a comprehensive survey; many more remain on file, and for descriptions of the larger houses in the county readers are referred to Pevsner's *Shropshire* and to Eric Mercer's forthcoming volume on Architecture in Shropshire.

Acton Burnell

The Croft (SJ 532018)
Behind 'The Croft' is a timber-framed building which belonged to the old Rectory and probably functioned as a stable/coach-house unit with accommodation for outdoor staff. Though 19th century in date it was built mostly with re-used timbers but in traditional fashion and with a 'hall and crosswing' format. It represents the last phase of timber-framing in Shropshire.

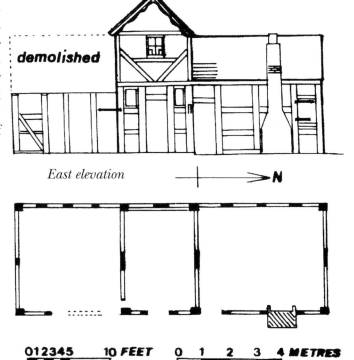

East elevation

Isometric projection (not to scale)

Ground floor plan

The Croft, Acton Burnell

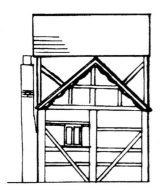

The Croft, Acton Burnell,
above and right.
Above: north elevation
(to scale on previous page)

Acton Round

Manor House (SO 636956)
Reputedly built by Francis Smith of Warwick for Sir Whitmore Acton as a dower house to Aldenham Park *c.*1713. This building has fine brickwork which includes 'aprons' to the windows—a Smith motif. It is two-storied, with seven bays and a hipped roof with a pedimented three-bay centre. The centre bay of the attic floor has a gypsum plaster floor; the rest are boarded. Bolection moulded fireplaces—rather plain—and a good staircase.

Acton Scott

The Old Post Office, Marshbrook (SO 444898)
One of a pair of semi-detached dwellings, the pair constructed to give the appearance of a timber-framed 'hall and crosswing' complex with the upper storey of the crosswing jettied. The rear wall is of stone and the framing, although 17th century in style is not done with traditional methods. The complex is probably an essay in 19th-century 'cottage orné' by the Acton estate.

The Moat (SO 459872)
A house much altered since 1913. Then is was of double-pile form with parallel roof ridges. Now it has a hipped roof and is entered at first-floor level through what had been a window. Basically built of Flemish bond brickwork, with vitrified headers. The bricks are narrow and have wide mortar joints; they could be reused. A window in the stone cellar has ovolo moulding. In 1980 a severe remodelling took place and Spanish-style extensions were added. The moat probably relates to an earlier house on the site.[1]

Left: Alcaston Manor, Acton Scott, in 1999 (after restoration)

Alcaston Manor (SO 458872)

A classic example of piecemeal development, the hall range and west crosswing are dendro-dated to 1557. The upper chamber in the crosswing served as the manor courtroom and had its own external door with an ogee head. Cable-moulding is present and the lower chamber has traces of wallpaintings which are described in chapter 13. Reputedly built by Humphrey Hill who died here in 1585. An old drawing shows five main units, at present there are four.[2]

Admaston

Admaston Farm (SJ 633132)

A box-framed, hall-and-crosswing farmhouse of *c.*1630 with square-framing to the hall (four panels high) and close-studding and jettying to the parlour crosswing. A projecting timber-framed, single-storied wing at the rear of the hall may be the original kitchen. The corner fireplace in the parlour has double-ovolo-and-quirk moulding on the lintel. The jambs are modern.

Alberbury-with-Cardeston

Wattlesborough Hall
(SJ 355126)

Now a farmhouse, but clearly the older part was built as a late 12th-century castle to control the valley between the Brieddens and the Long Mountain. A large square tower has original windows with draw-bars. The second phase is probably 14th century and includes a window with cusped tracery and a carved stone head in the south-west corner.[3]

Hall and castle at Wattlesborough (drawn by Sir B. Leighton)

Allscott

The Old Vicarage (SJ 613130)

A two-bayed, two-storied house, square-framed, brick-nogged and with a central stack. It probably represents a 17th-century re-modelling of a much earlier house, but with no attempt to make it T-shaped. An internal partition at the side of the staircase incorporates re-used medieval timbers and one external post on the rear wall has a swollen head and is probably another remnant of the earlier house.

Alveley

The Bell (SO 760845)

Known chiefly for the collection of sculpted 12th-century stones of the 'Herefordshire School' built into its walls, the house and the 'malthouse' each contain upper crucks. Those in the malthouse are dendro-dated to 1824 when the building was extended.[4]

Upper floor of 'granary', The Bell

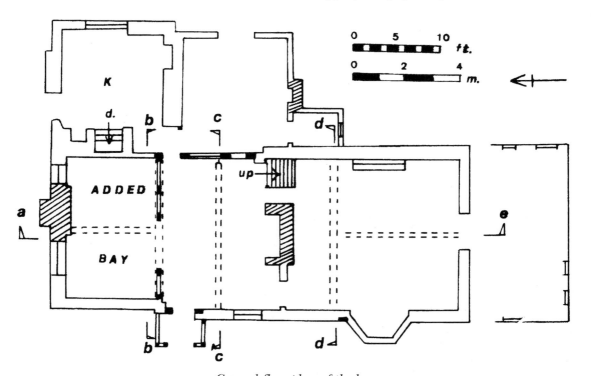

Ground floor plan of the house

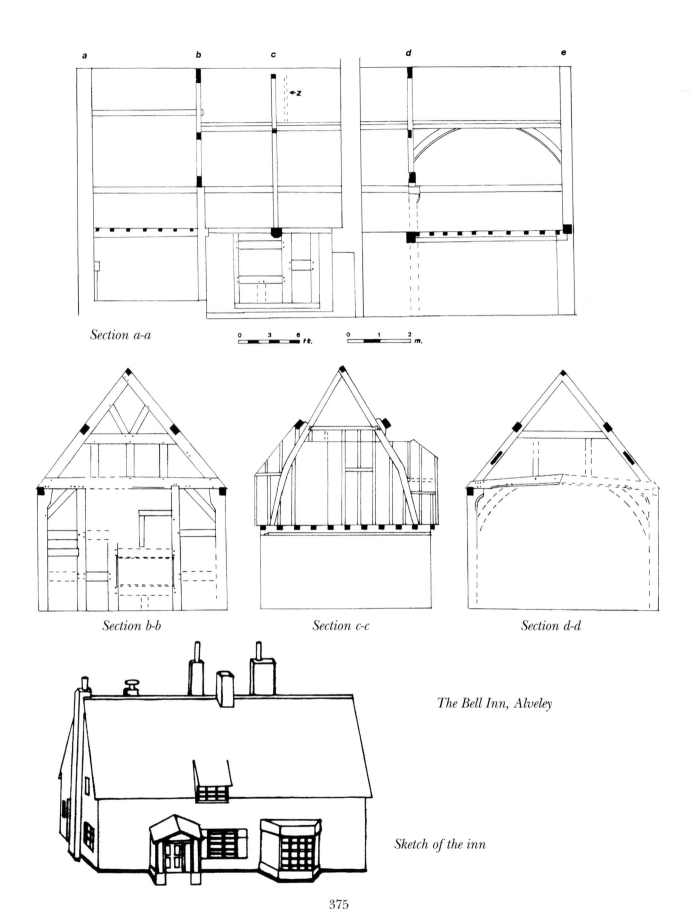

Section a-a

0 3 6 ft.   0 1 2 m.

Section b-b   Section c-c   Section d-d

a   b   c   d   e

←z

The Bell Inn, Alveley

Sketch of the inn

375

Carving no.1 at the Bell Inn

Carving no.3 at the Bell Inn

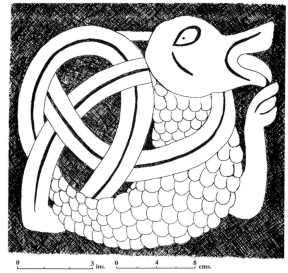

*Carving no.6
at the Bell Inn*

Carving no.4 at the Bell Inn

Carving no.12 at the Bell Inn

Carving no.13 at the Bell Inn (not to scale)

Carvings at the Bell Inn, Alveley

Carving no.2 at the Bell Inn

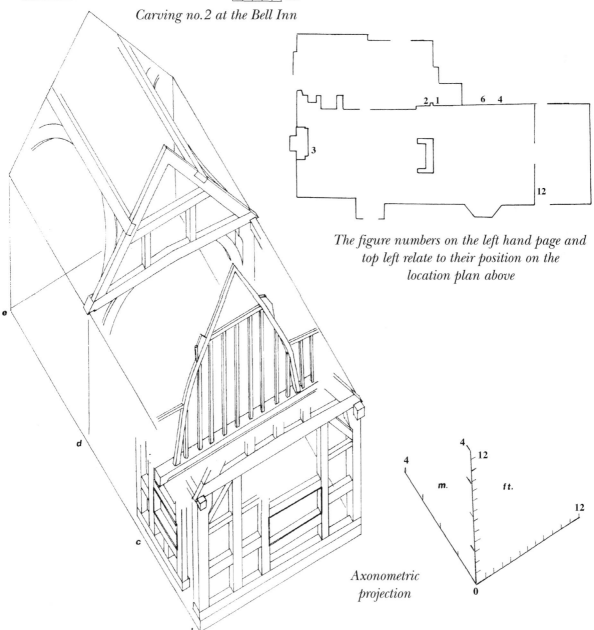

The figure numbers on the left hand page and top left relate to their position on the location plan above

Axonometric projection

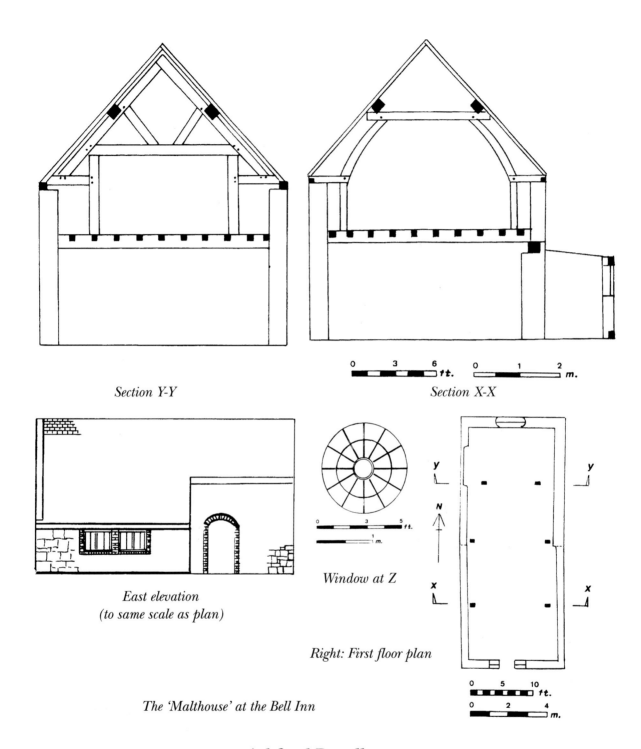

Section Y-Y

Section X-X

*East elevation
(to same scale as plan)*

Window at Z

Right: First floor plan

The 'Malthouse' at the Bell Inn

Ashford Bowdler

Manor Farm (SO 517706)

A farmhouse of *c.*1800. The brickwork on the east wing has English bond in the lower stages which changes to Flemish higher up. The 'hall' range has a bond of three rows of headers and one of stretchers which does not seem to have a name. At the rear is a detached kitchen with bake oven, copper etc. There is also a pump and a cider house.

Astley Abbots

Colemore Farm (SO 705976)

Derelict in 1989. A two-storied, box-framed, isolated farmhouse of three bays comprising a two-bay hall and a bay at the upper end of the hall. It contains a wattle-and-daub smoke-hood (fumbrell). Low-swinging arch-braces to the central truss descend to a T-section post.

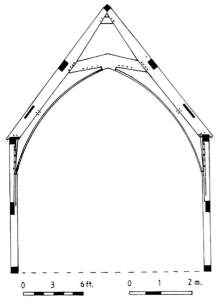

Section A-A

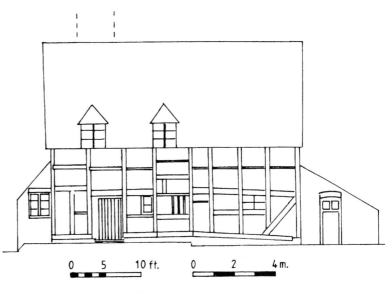

North elevation

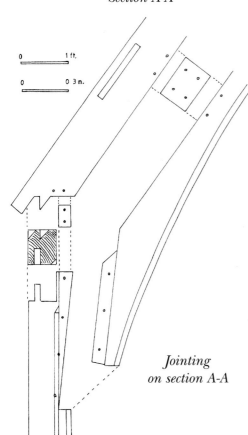

*Jointing
on section A-A*

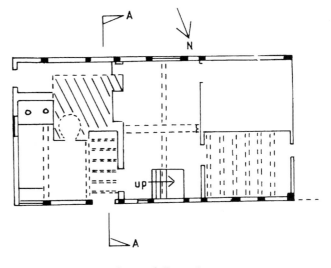

Ground floor plan

Colemore Farm, Astley Abbots

Dunvall Hall (SO 701962)

A U-shaped house of late 16th- to early 17th-century date, almost symmetrical and with a mixture of close-studding and lozenge work and large out-built stacks with star-shaped shafts. On the decorative panels of the solar and service wings the spikes point upwards and downwards respectively—differentiating the social classes and perhaps indicating their eventual destination.

Dunvall Hall, Astley Abbots

Hoard's Park Farm (SO 715946)

Basically this is a large, timber-framed, T-shaped building, but with many additions. At the south end there is evidence of a jettied crosswing with moulded ceiling beams including a dragon-beam. The matching one was lost when the west end was altered. This part is probably mid-16th century. In the late 17th century the whole house was bricked over and extended to the north. An outshut and a large out-built chimneystack were added on the east side along with an additional storey to provide a gallery. This is unlikely to have been a 'long gallery' although it has similarities with other known ones. On the east side what appears to be a buttress to the stack is a flue serving one of the bedrooms. There are interesting fireplaces and some good Maws' floor tiles in the hall and one panelled room in the crosswing. Good farm buildings including what was perhaps a gatehouse with close-studding, but latterly was used as a granary. It was later extended and used as a drift-house. A later granary was built and this has steps and an open shelter below.

Great Binnal (SO 702968)

Known chiefly for its set of 'Nine Worthies' paintings, this building is remarkable for its surviving coved dais end, moulded beams and the carved boss of the inserted ceiling, along with the form of the central truss of the hall. The latter has extended post-heads which accommodate low-swinging arch-braces, a cambered collar-beam cusped to form mouchettes flanking full quatrefoiling on the V-struts and principal rafters. Dendro-dated to 1460.[5]

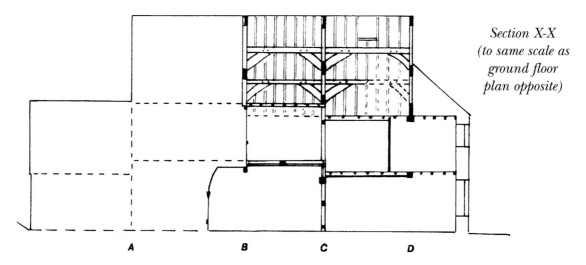

Section X-X (to same scale as ground floor plan opposite)

A   B   C   D

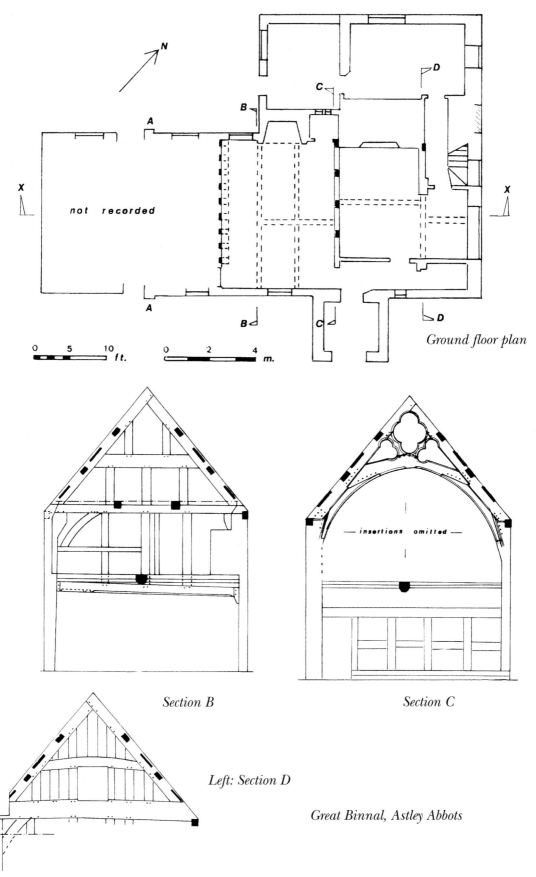

not recorded

N

Ground floor plan

0 5 10
ft.

0 2 4
m.

Section B

Section C

insertions omitted

Left: Section D

Great Binnal, Astley Abbots

Aston Botterell

The Manor House (SO 613842)

A complicated house, part of which incorporates four bays of an open hall with cusped wind-braces forming foil-patterning. One room at first-floor level has plasterwork of 1576 (dated). The frieze is known as the 'Botterell frieze' as the faces on it are said to be those of the family. The initials A.B and W.B. appear.

Ford Farm, Burwarton (SO 651848)

An L-shaped, box-framed farmhouse, brick-clad with a mixture of bonding which includes rat-trap and monk bond. The parlour wing has a large out-built stone stack with twin brick star-shaped shafts.

Aston Munslow

The White House (SO 510866)

A full report of this cruck-built hall house with 16th and 18th century additions has been published.[6]

Lower House Farm (SO 511865)

Unlike its neighbour, The White House (above), Lower House Farm is entirely box-framed. It is a classic medieval hall house and was either T-shaped or H-shaped. The central truss is particularly interesting as it has deep-swinging arch-braces and spur-ties. Cusping is present on the V-struts above the collar. The position of the smoke louvre is discernible, as is the spere-truss. There is an inserted chequer-board ceiling in the hall.

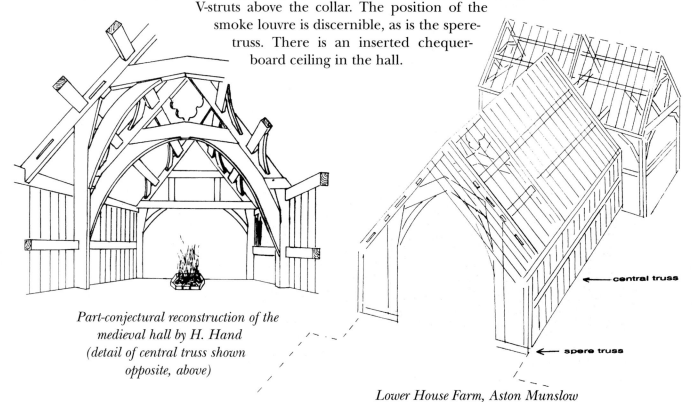

Part-conjectural reconstruction of the medieval hall by H. Hand (detail of central truss shown opposite, above)

central truss

spere truss

Lower House Farm, Aston Munslow

Detail of central truss
Lower House Farm, Aston Munslow

Aston Hall (SO 508866)

Built of Corvedale stone with ashlar dressings this H-shaped house has a symmetrical frontage, two rear wings and a two-storied central porch. The hall is also two-storied and the wings two-and-a-half-storied. Three large chimneystacks are of small bricks and star-shaped. Basically the house seems to be *c*.1660s/70s, but fragments of an earlier house are incorporated. Some timber-framing shows on the exterior of the north-west wing beyond the stonework. It has a design of fairly close studding with continuous posts marking the bay divisions and a mid-rail occurs on the upper storey. However, the internal timbers on the opposing wall are much heavier, with large jowelled posts. The difference indicates the two phases, and the roof structure is similarly echoed. Bolection moulding is a strong feature in the house and one ground-floor room is fully panelled. The hall has a fireplace set on the skew and this has a fire-back with the initials CER and the date 1637. As at Dunvall Hall the social order is expressed, this time with the treatment of the staircases. The terraced gardens are a feature, apparently laid out when the house was remodelled. There is some early brickwork in the boundary walls, that on the north-east boundary incorporates some diaper work. On this side are two three-seater privies. The stable block is notable. The property was held by the Smith family from 1492 to *c*.1914. It was clearly an 'upper bracket' house, just on the edge of gentry status.

Aston Hall

Three-seater privy at Aston Hall

Barrow

The Marsh (SO 642995)

The present farmhouse is a double-pile, three-bayed, three-storied house, mostly brick-built in Flemish bond. The date 1799 and 'J. Jenks' appears on a coping-stone on an outbuilding, and this could also relate to the house. Within the curtilage is a late 16th-century stone-built house, now used as a grain store. It is remarkable for its profusion of windows and doorways. The main doorway in the gable end has an arched doorhead. The windows—12 on the east side wall—have recessed chamfers on the frames and the mullions are mason-mitred. The reason for the profusion of openings is not known. At the south end are the remains of a star-shaped stack.

Baschurch

Stanwardine-in-the-Wood (SJ 428278)

A Corbet house of 1560-88, probably replacing that on a nearby moated site, and with similarities to the main seat at Moreton Corbet. The central (porch) bay is faced with Grinshill stone, the rest is English bond brickwork with stone dressings. The house was probably intended to be triple-gabled and symmetrical, but was not completed as such. There are ovolo-moulded windows in the west wing, and straight-chamfered ones in the east(service) wing. There was possibly a gallery over the hall. The internal arrangements are not symmetrical.[7]

Wycherley Hall (SJ 418273)

A large multi-phased timber-framed house, the oldest part of which is the western south-facing gable. Completely encapsulated in this is a two-bay structure which has one tier of cusped wind-braces in the remains of a central truss with an arch-braced tie-beam with V-struts above. A framed partition to the north appears to be a later insertion, but it continues above the level of the inserted ceiling and its purpose is unknown. The original roof timbers in the west gable are smoke-blackened. At right angles to this early unit is a two-storied jettied and square-framed range which may have been added as a porch entrance to the earlier house. Extensions seem to have occurred at generation intervals and the house is now very complex.

Cartref, Baschurch

'Cartref', Weston Lullingfields (SJ 425259)

This is a 'transplanted' house, the late owner having boyhood memories of helping his father to move the timbers on a cart from its previous site. Basically box-framed one-and-a-half–bays, raised from one storey to two and extended. A cannon ball was lodged under the threshold for luck.[8]

Milford Hall (SJ 419209)

A T-shaped, box-framed farm-house with square framing to the two-bay hall range and close-studding set in a pattern of small rectangles to the parlour wing (cf. Abcott Manor, Clungunford). Continuous posts at bay intervals to the hall suggests that it was built as an open hall and floored over later. This is confirmed by the internal supports. Great and small parlours in the crosswing. Ovolo moulding and other decorative motifs. The stone stack, with star-shaped brick shafts, is at

Milford Hall, Baschurch

the junction of the two units. This was in position when the wing was built. The house is probably a replacement for the nearby cruck range called Milford Cottages.

Bayston Hill

Grove Cottage (SJ 479083)

An extended 17th-century squatter's cottage, originally one-up, one-down, partly timber-framed, with a large out-built stack and a thatched roof. The transverse beam in the house-place is probably reused, but it bears ritual charm marks and initials which relate to a previous owner and tenant.[9]

Lower Bayston (SJ 491080)

Basically an L-shaped farmhouse of *c.*1650s with a later south wing making a U-shaped frontage. There is a jettied gable on the north wing, but no evidence that the lower stage was jettied or that there was an open hall. Square framing where not brick-cased. The building has some ritual charm marks on the fireplaces in the hall and crosswing, and good carpenters' marks, scribed, not chiselled. There is a baffle-entry at the rear, and an internal square-framed partition between the hall and the north wing.

Great Lyth (SJ 455072)

An early brick house of *c.*1668. U-shaped, English bond, decorative string-course, narrow hand-made bricks.[10]

Cherry Tree Cottage, Hookagate (SJ 464090)

A box-framed, single-cell cottage with out-built brick stack. It is mainly of reused timbers and the floor and stairs are inserted. Probably a 17th-century squatter's cottage associated with local coal mining.

Berrington

Betton Grange (SJ 509093)

A two-storied, brick-walled farmhouse, much altered and probably originally timber-framed. Totally enclosed in the present roof space is a pair of star-shaped brick chimney-shafts rising from a square plinth. They are capped with corbelled tiles which are surmounted with more brickwork. Clearly they are a remnant of the earlier house.

Berrington Manor
with, below, central truss in old solar wing

Berrington Manor (SJ 531067)

The main range is a box-framed L-shaped structure, square-framed and dated 1658 with the initials R.B. (Richard Blakeway) and M.B. over the door. The parlour wing gable has an inbuilt porch with a lobby-entry. The hall was served by a square stair turret at the rear and has a large dormer gable and classical blank arches under the first-floor window. There are internal sliding shutters to the ground-floor window. The hall is jettied and the wing has a hewn jetty. To the west is an earlier wing, presumably the solar wing to the hall which was demolished to make way for the 1658 build. The solar has a fine central truss with plain curved windbraces and deep arch-braces to a canted collar-beam. Its function changed to a service wing when the new block was built. Each wing has a star-shaped 'Tudor' brick stack. The 1658 block is covered with 'Harnage slates'. The farm buildings include a polygonal ginny-ring.

Bicton

The Isle (SJ 459168)

A promontory site similar to that of Shrewsbury, but only ever occupied by one family—the Sandfords. The present house is brick-built and three-storied. The two large frontal stacks suggest that the house has been 'turned' and this is supported by scroll-work and other details on the 'back' with a plaque bearing the date 1749 and the initials SHE. It is probable that Thomas Farnolls Pritchard, the Shrewsbury architect worked here; several features suggest his hand. Nearby is an earlier house, timber-framed and said to date from 1450 but difficult to assess. Most remarkable are two wall decorations, described in chapter 13. Within the site is a moated mound on which the vanished chapel of Up Rossall is said to have stood and a stone capital, elaborately carved with rams-head (?) ornament. Its provenance is unknown, but by tradition it came from a demolished market hall in Shrewsbury.

Bishop's Castle

The House on Crutches (SO 323890)

So called because two wooden posts support an upper storey, creating a covered passageway for pedestrians and giving the impression of an incredible jetty. The overhang is simply an ingenious extension to a box-framed medieval house which has eccentric details such as short queen-struts, foot-jowelling on a main post and staggered mortice-and-tenon housing on another.[11]

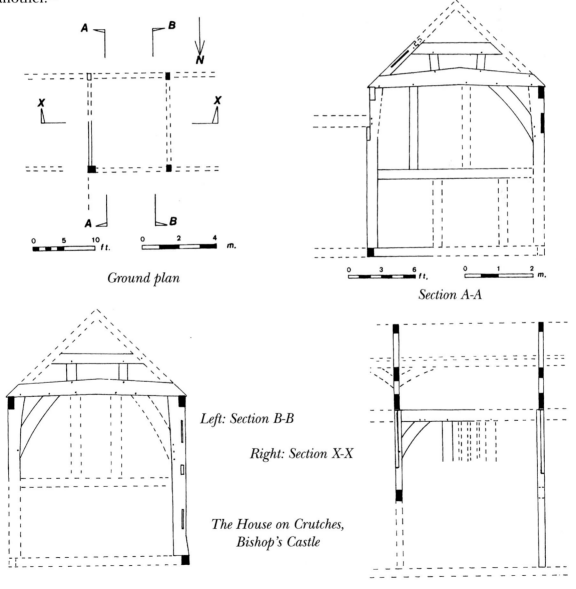

Ground plan

Section A-A

Left: Section B-B

Right: Section X-X

*The House on Crutches,
Bishop's Castle*

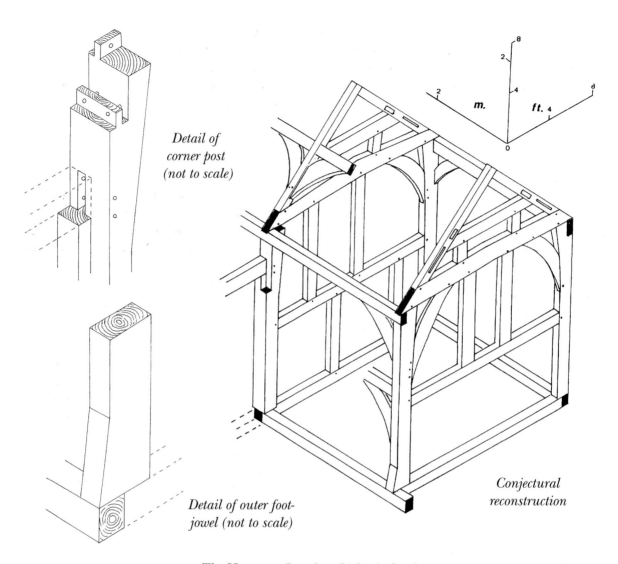

Detail of
corner post
(not to scale)

Detail of outer foot-
jowel (not to scale)

Conjectural
reconstruction

The House on Crutches, Bishop's Castle

Porch House (SO 324889)

A box-framed town house dendro-dated to 1564. The porch is dated 161?. The building is basically L-shaped, consisting of a two-storied hall, a cross-passage and an ambitious crosswing which had its own external staircase. It has some elaborate carvings and some eccentric features, e.g. the hall seems to have been unheated, but was decorated with paintings, the screen at the high end of the hall is next to the passage, and plank-and-muntin work continues from the screen to form the rear wall, making in effect an external wall of solid wood.[12]

25 High Street (SO 324889)

Known as 'The Old Pharmacy' this house also has a (side) wall of plank-and-muntin work. On both sides of the central stack are large fireplace lintels with an extraordinary number of burn marks. These are thought to date from when the property was an inn, and wiping the red-hot poker used for mulling ale on the beams was responsible for the marks. They are not thought to be rush-taper marks.[13]

27 High Street (SO 324888)

This property incorporates the remains of a box-framed hall-house of *c.*1550, set gable-end on to the street, with a gable jetty and herringbone work. The plan is that of a great chamber with an intermediate truss and an open hall behind it. There is no evidence that the chamber was floored, but this could have been removed. The hall is smoke-blackened. A further bay to the east represents street encroachment and there is an additional bay to the west.[14]

Harp House, Church Street (SO 323885)

T-shaped and timber-framed, the stem of the T is set parallel to the street and contains a cruck truss fashioned from whole trees. Part of the house was replaced by a jettied crosswing in the late 16th century. This has a moulded bressumer, herring-bone work in the upper storey and remains of cable moulding. The ground-floor room contains a wallpainting described in chapter 13.[15]

Swallow Bank Cottage, Colebatch

Swallow Beck Cottage, Colebatch (SO 319871)

Outstanding for its steep stone-flagged roof and huge chimneystack, this single-bayed cottage is all that remains of a substantial cruck hall-house, possibly Colebatch manor house. The original arch-braced central truss of the hall now serves as the gable next to the added stack, a situation noted in a few other instances.[16]

Bitterley

Crow Leasowes Farm (SO 548785)

A farmhouse with an elaborate front elevation in brick of the (?) mid-17th century. This encapsulates one-and-a-half bays of a box-framed structure. The Rouse-Boughton estate added a stone wing *c.*1808. It is remarkable for the model farm layout of 1863 by Rouse-Boughton containing a railway with turntables to serve the cattle-feeding complex, of which one truck survives. A cider mill with a granary over is located in front of the house.[17]

Right:
South-east elevation

Crow Leasowes Farm,
Bitterley

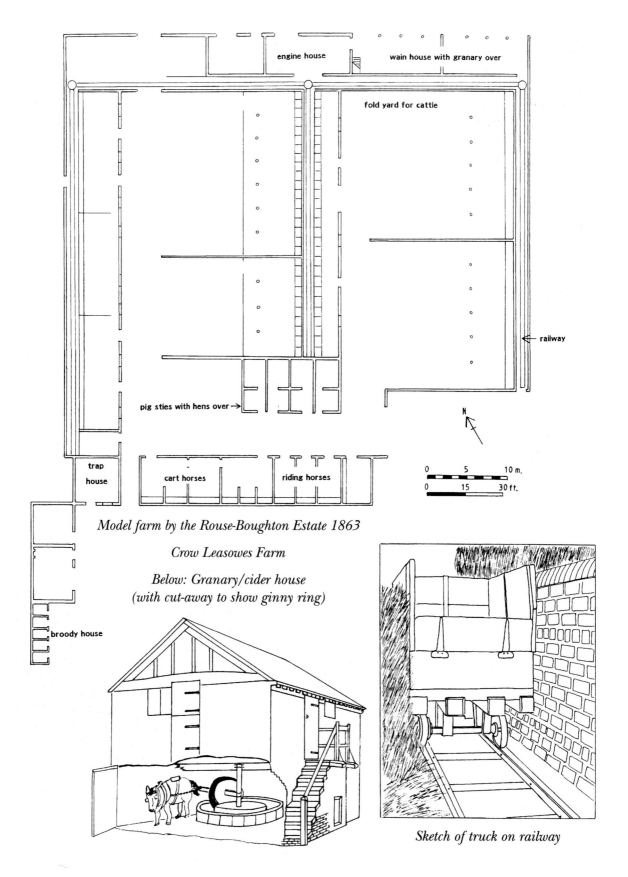

engine house

wain house with granary over

fold yard for cattle

railway

pig sties with hens over →

N

0   5   10 m.

0   15   30 ft.

trap
house

cart horses   riding horses

Model farm by the Rouse-Boughton Estate 1863

Crow Leasowes Farm

Below: Granary/cider house
(with cut-away to show ginny ring)

broody house

Sketch of truck on railway

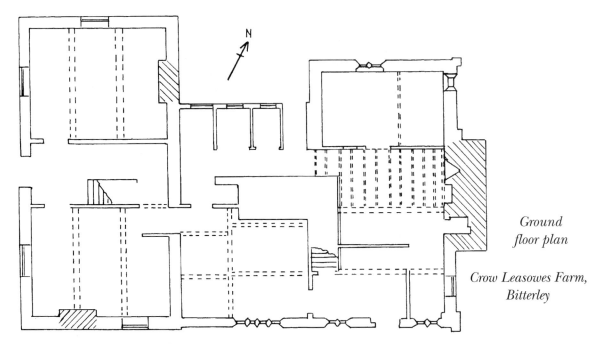

*Ground
floor plan*

*Crow Leasowes Farm,
Bitterley*

Upper Ledwyche (SO 554793)

A four-bay, two-and-a-half-storied brick frontage by the Rouse-Boughton estate was applied in 1860 to an older stone-walled house which was probably originally timber-framed. The stone is part Dhustone and part local sandstone. There is a large 'Tudor' brick star-shaped stack at the rear. The roof is six-bayed with a rhythm of one tie-beam truss to two arch-braced collar-beam trusses. No cusping, plain windbraces, but the heads of the posts are jowelled and crenellated. There is evidence for a projecting crosswing. Dendro-dated to 1460-1. Elements of a model farm lay-out remain.[18]

The Long House (SO 567762)

So called on Baugh's map of Shropshire 1808, the term is descriptive of the shape of the house rather than implying the traditional function of communal shelter for humans and animals. There are three domestic units in line, the earliest of which is a

Upper Ledwyche, and roof trusses in the north-east section

two-bay, one-and-a-half-storied structure of the late 17th century, and although it has a byre built up to it a solid wall divides the two. Later extensions were made until the whole complex, including the farm buildings, assumed a half-courtyard lay-out. All of stone and brick.

Bitterley Court (SO 572773)

Basically a 17th-century house, H-shaped by 1769 and altered by Thomas Farnolls Pritchard. There are some fine interior details. It has associations with the Walcot and Littleton families.[19] The 'dragon frieze' in the hall is similar to the bressummer at the Sandford Vaults in Market Drayton and to the date-plaque at Hazlewood Farm at Darliston in Prees parish.

Hall Farm, Snitton (SO 557754)

A moated site. The house is box-framed of hall and crosswing form, late 16th or early 17th

Overmantel in oak room at Bitterley Court

century with ovolo and triple-ovolo-and quirk mouldings. The stack is centrally placed at the junction of the hall and crosswing and has very tall brick star-shaped shafts.

Lower Court Farm (SO 561775)

A large stone and brick-built house, basically L-shaped but with many additions and largely remodelled by the Rouse-Boughton family in the late 19th century. Earlier features include a plaque stating 'Erected by Thomas Hopton Esq and his wife, daughter to Adam Luttley Esq 1602'. The shield above displays the Luttley coat of arms and above that are three heads, a man, a woman and a horse. To the left of the shield is a blocked multi-light window with ovolo moulding. One large out-built stone stack has three tall brick star-shaped shafts. Internally there is some close studding and square-framing. The cellar has an elaborate chequer-board ceiling with moulded beams and joists but may have been moved from an upper room. However it appears to be an integral part of the structure and as such is inexplicable.

Quarry Farm, Middleton (SO 539773)

A T-shaped farmhouse of three distinct units. The middle unit has the remains of an elaborate ceiling with moulded beams and is probably of late 16th-century date. The crosswing was added in the 17th century, replacing part of the older structure. It has square framing, four panels high, and a brick stack with two tall shafts, set diagonally. To the north of the house is a barn containing a cruck truss which may represent the remains of an earlier house. The barn was extended by the Rouse-Boughton family in 1868, a date worked into the roofing slates.

Cleeton Court, Cleeton St. Mary (SO 606795)

A U-shaped stone-clad house which encapsulates a medieval timber-framed house of considerable interest, particularly regarding the form of the central truss of the hall. This may be seen as either a form of base-cruck or as a deviant of a full-cruck. As at 'Wolverton' the blades pass the ends of the collar where they are deliberately truncated, the truss continuing with principal rafters.[20]

Bolas Magna

Meeson Hall (SJ 658207)
An E-shaped triple gabled house of red sandstone. The rear courtyard has two timber-framed service wings. A Jacobean overmantel in a front room is dated 1639 and the service wings and the roof structure are dendro-dated 1644. Elaborate drainage system. An impressive gentleman's residence, it was the country seat of the Tayleur family who had a town house in Shrewsbury.[21]

Meeson Farm (SJ 654207)
An unpromising exterior masks the remains of a cruck-built hall house dendro-dated to 1502. The central truss has a low beam and notched-lap joints. Other features include a good inserted ceiling with broach-stops and inglenook cupboards with carved doors.

Meeson Hall

Rear courtyard with timber-framed service wing at Meeson Hall

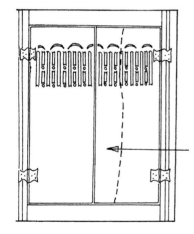

Meeson Farm, Bolas Magna

The unpromising exterior

INCHES

CM

Left: Details of cupboard doors in the inglenook. The arrow indicates a missing portion

393

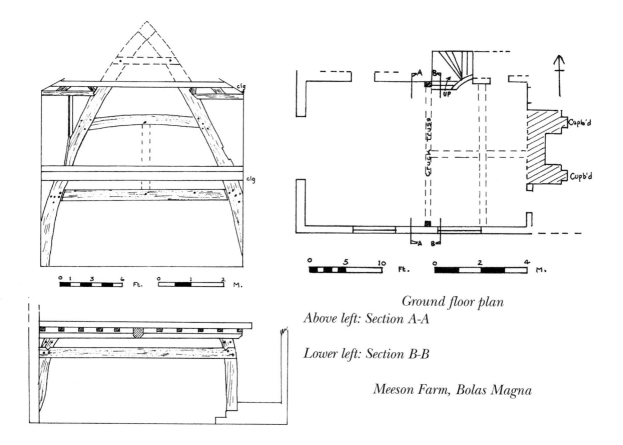

Ground floor plan

Above left: Section A-A

Lower left: Section B-B

Meeson Farm, Bolas Magna

Bridgnorth

42 Riverside (SO 738931)
Situated on the corner of Riverside and Cartway, the house is unremarkable apart from features at attic level. Here there are three pairs of truncated upper trusses, two pairs in Cartway and one at right angles in Riverside. Where they meet they are joined by a 'yoke-and-cushion' arrangement, the cushion supporting the end of the hip-rafter which makes the third component of this juncture. Where the hip-rafters meet at the apex one rafter is halved and bird-mouthed over the other. The floor-joists are secured by bare-faced lap-dovetail joints.

Bishop Percy's House (SO 738931)
One of Bridgnorth's 'show pieces' in Cartway, it is a three-bayed, box-framed, two-and-a-half-storied building with three large dormer gables. It has decorative framing with S-braces and cusped lozenge work. The entrance at the west end leads into a through passage while an added wing at the rear contains the staircase which winds around a central pillar. In the

Bishop Percy's House

394

main ground-floor room is an inscription above what was the fireplace: EXCEPT THE LORD BUILD THE HOWSE THE LABOURERS THEREOF PREVAIL NOT. ERECTED BY R.FOR. 1580. Richard Forster was barge-master, but the house takes it name from being the birth-place of Thomas Percy (1729-1811), antiquary, poet, friend of Dr. Johnson and churchman who became Dean of Carlisle and Bishop of Dromore, Co. Down.

Overmantel at Bishop Percy's House

15 Bridge Street (SO 719930)
Situated on the corner of Cartway and disguised by its 19th-century exterior, this is an early-to-mid 15th-century timber-framed building, jettied along two sides. The dragon-beam measures c.13ft. (3.96m.). The jowelled posts and projecting joists remain along the Cartway frontage, but can only be seen from inside. It compares with the Bodenham building in Ludlow and the Abbot's House in Shrewsbury.

The Crown Hotel, High Street (SO 716933)
Once a coaching inn, now much altered and incorporating other buildings. Inside the inn sections of a plaster frieze remain. A cockpit at the rear was transferred to Avoncroft Museum.

British Legion Club, Low Town (SO 719930)
Set gable-end on to the street and close to the river this is probably a medieval warehouse. An ogee-headed doorway in the side wall probably gave access for the owner. Cruck-built and dendro-dated to 1392-1422.[22]

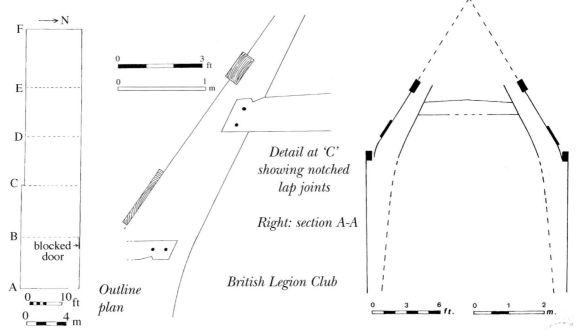

Detail at 'C' showing notched lap joints

Right: section A-A

British Legion Club

Outline plan

48, 49 and Coney Villa, Friars' St. (SO 719935)
These houses display good examples of chequerboard brickwork on their front elevations but are plain on the back and sides.

Bromfield

The Gatehouse (SO 482768)
The gatehouse to the former priory has a lower stage that is stone-built with a two-centred arched entrance. This is probably early 14th century, but the upper stage is timber-framed, three-bayed, with close studding and long straight tension bracing and is probably mid-15th century.

Remains of Fox's House
(SO 513742)
The ruins of Charles Fox's house are attached to the south side of the church. Fox was Secretary to the Council in the Marches and acquired the priory after the Dissolution. He incorporated the chancel into his house, but this was restored to the church in 1658. The house had mullioned and transomed windows with sunk chamfers, very similar to those in the Sidney apartments at Ludlow Castle.

Remains of Fox's House at Bromfield.
Notice the sunk chamfers in the windows

Brompton and Rhiston

The Lack (SO 265938)
A box-framed, two-storied farmhouse, jettied on three sides, with herring-bone work in the upper storey and close-studding with a mid-rail to the lower. The plan is that of a lobby-entry with one internal stack, a style dominant in neighbouring Montgomeryshire.[23]

Broseley

Rowton Farm, Dovecote (SJ 699014)
A rectangular brick-built structure with a pitched roof, the dovecote, though ruinous, retains its nesting-boxes which are of shaped and fired blocks except in the upper stages where they are unfired. Composed of reddish clay and chopped straw known as 'clay bat' they are not easily distinguished from the fired ones. Was this an experiment or deliberate defrauding by the contractor?[24]

Bucknell

Old Farm (SO 356740)

A courtyard-type farm lay-out with a drift-house entry. The 17th-century box-framed farmhouse with additions probably has longhouse origins. A motte to the south-east was converted to an ice-house.

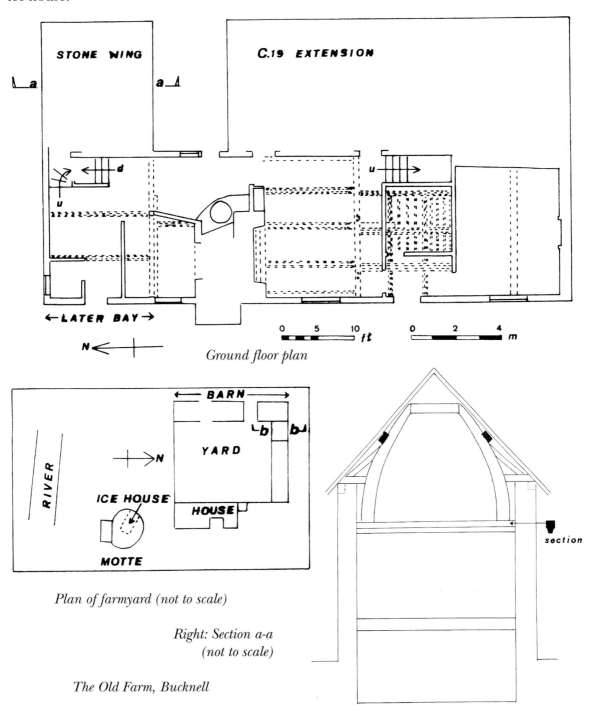

Ground floor plan

Plan of farmyard (not to scale)

Right: Section a-a
(not to scale)

The Old Farm, Bucknell

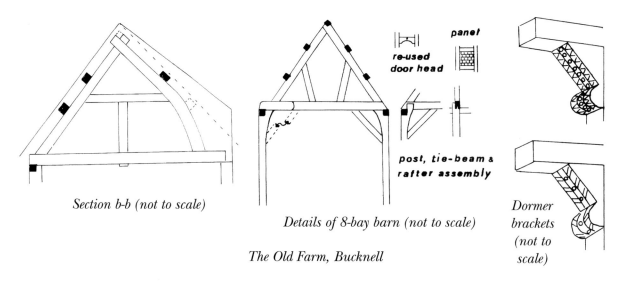

Section b-b (not to scale)

panel

re-used door head

post, tie-beam & rafter assembly

Details of 8-bay barn (not to scale)

The Old Farm, Bucknell

Dormer brackets (not to scale)

Burlton

Hatchett's Farm (SJ 458261)

An L-shaped farmhouse, apparently of two building phases. The earliest part is the unit at the east end. This is timber-framed and was presumably given a brick 'skin' when the house was enlarged by a complete suite of rooms to the west which incorporated a lobby-entry. Included in this phase is the rear stair wing. At the rear a stable adjoins the western end of the house. This has a men's room over it which is approached via a flight of outside steps. The farm was clearly geared to cheese production. A number of very large cheese presses survived in the rear kitchen in 1971.

Burwarton

Yew Tree Cottage (SO 611837)

A one-up, one-down cottage/smallholding, stone-built with an end entry. The stack was on the opposite gable. A bay added next to the stack was the brew-house which contains an old range, bakeoven and boiler. The main room has an internal sliding shutter to the window. The smallholding was 15 acres.

Burwarton Farm (SO 618850)

Built of Dhustone, this house has a three-storied stone porch. From the second storey a spiral staircase with oak treads gives access to the roof space. The house has a cellar which contains a reused datestone of 162?. One tie-beam is virtually S-shaped, but is unlikely to be a reused cruck.

Burwarton Farm

2 Banbury Lane (SO 608836)

Built mostly of Dhustone, this is a two-storied, two-bayed house with a large out-built gable stack heating one room only. It probably began as a single-celled squatter's cottage before the enclosure of Loughton Common.

Cardington

The Barracks (SO 506952)

A house of two main builds, the older part is set gable-end on to the road and incorporates two surviving bays of a medieval timber-framed hall house which had a crown-post roof. The wall framing incorporates two large curved braces. The stack has three 'Tudor' brick shafts and probably occupies the position of the screens passage. Beyond it is the second build, a box-framed crosswing of the early-mid 17th century. This was jettied at each end. The bressumers have ovolo moulding and carved brackets. A later stone bay of Hoar Edge Grit was added to the gable-end of the earlier build. Opposite the house is an old smithy which has a woodblock floor.

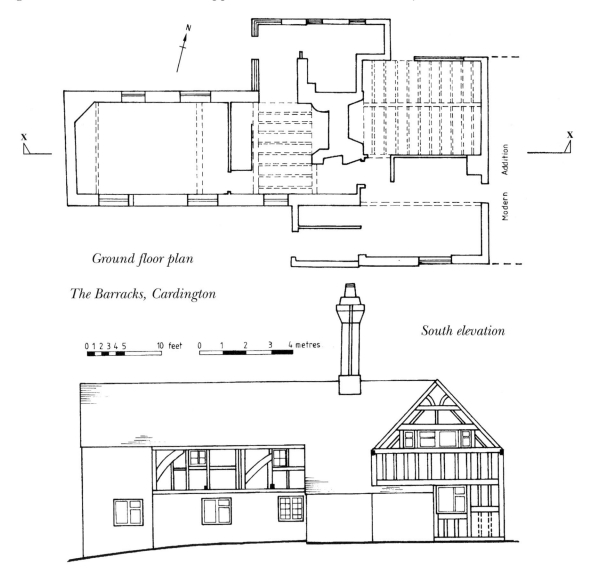

Ground floor plan

The Barracks, Cardington

0 1 2 3 4 5   10 feet   0   1   2   3   4 metres

South elevation

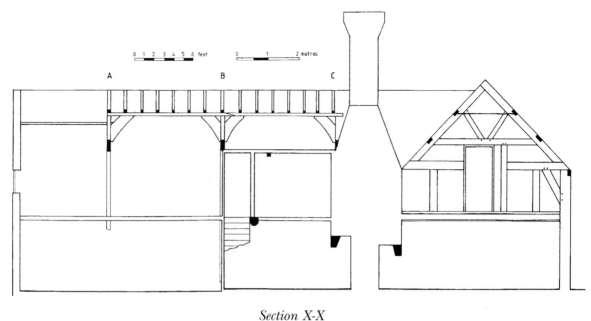

Section X-X

The Barracks, Cardington

The Old School (SO 505952)

Two units form this complex. The old school is basically a brick building of *c.*1690 which has a base plinth of local Chatwall stone from Hill End quarry, and an upper plinth, quoins and plat-band of Hoar Edge Grit. Attached to it is is the schoolmaster's house of Soudley banded sandstone.

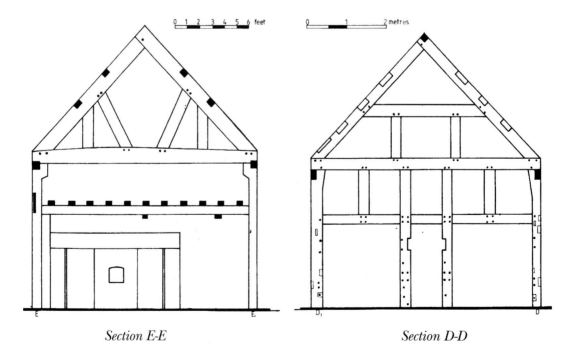

Section E-E   *Section D-D*

The Maltster's Tap, Cardington

The Maltster's Tap (SO 506951)

Formerly called 'Honeysuckle House', the present house is basically L-shaped, two-storied and stone-built apart from the gable in the wing which is timber-framed in the upper storey. To the left of the house is a building which was probably its precursor. This appears to have been a longhouse. It consists of a three-bay barn, box-framed and clad with weatherboarding, and one surviving bay of domestic form, stone-built, and containing a large stone chimneystack. There cannot be much difference in the dating of the present house and the longhouse. Possibly they functioned independently although they were either joined or part of the longhouse was taken down to make room for the new house.

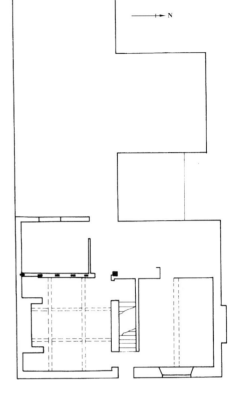

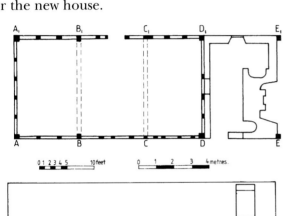

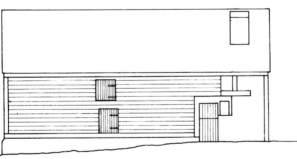

Longhouse: Ground floor plan and east elevation

House: Ground floor plan and east elevation

The house with remains of the longhouse on the left

401

Shootrough (SO 490964)

A T-shaped farmhouse with stone, timber-frame and brick visible externally. Within the stem of the T is a two-bayed cruck-built hall; this has a central truss in which the social difference between the upper and lower bays is made clear by double-cavetto moulding on the upper side and quarter-round on the lower. An ogee-arched doorhead gave access to the solar and fixing points for a high seat occur on the dais wall. The solar has been replaced by a parlour/dairy/kitchen crosswing which forms the bar of the T. In the kitchen in addition to the bread-oven is a portable cloam oven—shouldered, flat-topped and heated by coals heaped around it in the hearth. Usually these are made of clay, but this example is in cast iron. There are many other interesting features including scarf-jointing on the wall-plate, the framing pattern on the gable wall of the crosswing, the lobby-entry formed by the insertion of a stack into the hall, lath-and-plaster infilling of the frame of the crosswing, scissored windbraces in the lower bay of the hall, the possibility of a spere-type screen, and a set of goosepens outside the kitchen door. The wealth of the wallpainting is described in chapter 13. Dendro-dating for the hall range is 1422, for the crosswing 1609.[25]

Plaish Park Farm (SO 530964)

This was the Home Farm to Plaish Hall. The name was changed when the present occupiers moved from the original Park Farm (SO 520968). In a wall of the house a pair of brass nut-crackers was found embedded, presumably originally placed there to ward off ill luck. In the range of farm buildings is the granary, a two-bayed, timber-framed building which may be a moved building called the 'Ffat-oxe-house' which is described at length in a contract of 1689.[26]

Willstone Farm (SO 499946)

A five-bayed, two-storied farmhouse built of Hoar Edge Grit with a symmetrical front and end chimneys. The dressings are of a different stone. The 12-light sash windows are flat-headed with key-stones. A plaque bearing the names John and Eliz. Sheppard, a crest, decoration and the date 1738 is above the front door.

Chatwall Farm (SO 513975)

A U-shaped farmhouse with Hoar Edge Grit casing on timber-framing. The symmetrical front is of mid-to-late 17th century with a bolection-moulded entrance and pedimented doorway. There are stone-mullioned windows and roundels (ovals) in the gables. In the 'chapel room' the fireplace has a semi-circular stone chimneypiece incorporating a carved head and wings. It is weathered and may have functioned previously as an external feature.

Chelmarsh

Woodlands (SO 711889)

A large house, stone-faced, probably built for the Whitmore family. Many features have Thomas Farnolls Pritchard characteristics although the house does not feature in his day-book. The fireplace that he designed for Samuel Egerton of Tatton Hall is very similar to that in the rear sitting room, even to the 'Dove Marble'. Another is similar to that for the 'Purple Room' at Condover Hall. Alterations c.1800 were done by Smallman of Shrewsbury. His work is easily distinguished from Pritchard's.

Chelmarsh Hall (SO 722879)

In Victorian times the complex was remodelled, making a cohesive whole from a number of medieval and later parts. Some evidence for an aisled hall remains on the west side and at right angles to this is a stone-built block where the openings suggest either a first-floor hall or a chamber block of the 14th century. It has an internal cross-passage where the opposing door has an ogee-headed and rebated inner face and a sunk-chamfered outer face. The latter is not weathered and must have connected with a further medieval block. A matching range appears to have a sans-purlin roof of collar-rafter form. The roof is ceiled at present—the evidence is external. There are many other early features in addition to 16th- and 17th-century work. Also noteworthy are the Victorian additions and alterations.

Cherrington Manor

Cherrington Manor (SO 666203)
A box-framed, triple-gabled farmhouse, dated 1635, and confirmed by dendro-dating. It has true 'magpie' framing with close-studding, lozenge work and square panels with cusped and spiked lozenges. A curious kneeling figure supports a corner jetty. The house was added to an earlier structure, now gone. The porch is a 19th-century brick addition with applied timbers which opens into what was a lobby entry, cut through to gain access to a later staircase.

Reputedly this is 'the house that Jack built', possibly because it featured in some of the illustrated editions of the rhyme and also because of the couplet referring to the 'malt which lay in the house'. A malthouse is located at the rear of the manor.[27]

Chetton

Bush House Farm (SO 653904)
A box-framed, brick-cased, H-plan house but with non-projecting wings. A two-bay open hall with a chimney bay gives an elongated appearance to the hall (cf. Earnwood Farm, Kinlet).

Eudon George (SO 687889)
In the attic was found a loose board bearing the date 1618. Clearly this came from the two-storied porch and indicates when this and the prestigious close-studded and jettied crosswing was added to an earlier range which contained an open hall. At the same time a large stack was built to serve both units, creating a lobby-entry and incorporating a dog-wheel housed in the side of the stack to provide power to turn the spit in the hall. The hall received an inserted ceiling in two stages. At first the half-bay nearest the hearth was left open. The initials RB are scratched in the framework of the great parlour and there are some interesting carpenters' marks and decorative details.

Chirbury

School House (SO 262984)
Box-framed and dated 1675 with small rectangular panels and straight tension braces. Added porch and a large dormer gable.

Heightley Farm Barns (SO 271988)
Two timber-framed barns, one of ten bays and the other of three. Windbraces in the larger barn are of cusped quatrefoil design, suggesting that they are reused from an ecclesiastical building. The smaller barn has close-studding and elaborate carved brackets. This was probably a house. A ginny-ring was once attached to one of the barns.

Forge and Wheelwright's Shop (SO 262985)
In 1987 the complex was due for refurbishment. It was relatively intact, and was recorded as an example of a rural industry no longer in demand.

Interior of wheelwright's shop at Chirbury

Church Pulverbatch

Walleybourne Farm (SJ 425045)
A medieval hall house, box-framed and now brick-cased with added crosswing. The central truss and the spere-truss each have a steeply-cambered collar-beam with quatrefoil cusping and lateral 'mouchettes' (cf. Great Binnall in Astley Abbots).[28]

White Horse Inn (SJ 424024)
A farmhouse until the 19th century, the structure is unusual for having two cruck ranges at right angles to each other (cf. Crowther's House at Easthope, Clun Farm at Clun and Lower Spoad in Clun parish).[29]

Sheppen Fields (SJ 425011)
Adjacent to the present farmhouse is its predecessor, a cruck-built longhouse, *c.*1464, with an added crosswing. In use as a longhouse until the 1920s, it is particularly interesting for the inclusion of a low beam which has chamfering, moulding and a central upright with holes for transverse rods (cf. Sibberscot barn, Pontesbury).[30]

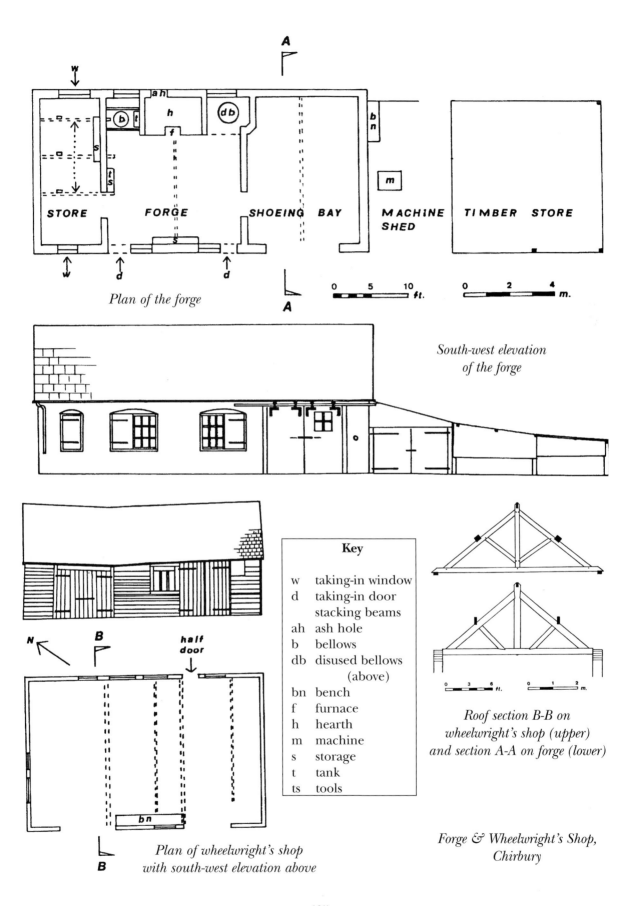

A
A

w

STORE **FORGE** **SHOEING BAY** **MACHINE SHED** **TIMBER STORE**

ah
h
b
t
db
f
s
ts
s
bn
m

w
d
d

A
A

0 5 10 ft.
0 2 4 m.

Plan of the forge

South-west elevation of the forge

o

B
N
B
half door

bn

B
B

Plan of wheelwright's shop with south-west elevation above

Key

w taking-in window
d taking-in door
   stacking beams
ah ash hole
b bellows
db disused bellows (above)
bn bench
f furnace
h hearth
m machine
s storage
t tank
ts tools

Roof section B-B on wheelwright's shop (upper) and section A-A on forge (lower)

0 3 6 ft.
0 1 2 m.

Forge & Wheelwright's Shop, Chirbury

405

Church Stretton

Longmynd House, Minton
(SO 431907)

A house of three units on the west side of the village green is built into the slope of the hill. Two cruck trusses remain—one is visible, the other was the central truss of a two-bay hall. The middle unit is box-framed and now stone-clad. Its spine-beam has ovolo moulding. The third unit is a stone-built crosswing. The house probably began as a longhouse with the byre, now demolished, at the lower end beyond the exposed cruck.

Longmynd House

The Buck's Head (SO 453936)

Bordering on the churchyard and High Street, the inn displays piecemeal development. The oldest part produced the earliest dendro-dated crown-post, 1287-1321. It also has dragon ties and a central boss. This unit is enclosed in diaper brickwork.[31]

The Malthouse, Little Stretton (SO 444915)

Complete T-shaped box-framed house with through-passage plan. The hall has had its roof raised and a floor inserted. There is a flattened ogee-arched doorway into the crosswing which has an ulenlok in its rear gable. The cellar has a cobbled floor.

Claverley

Old Hall (SO 794935)

This is basically a box-framed, two-bay open hall, sub-divided by intermediate trusses into four halfbays. Each half-bay has a pair of cusped and ogee windbraces and the intermediates have arch-braced collar-beams. There are clasped purlins and quarter-round moulding on the wall-plate, main tiebeam truss and the mid-rail. It was probably an administrative hall of some kind, late 14th/early 15th century, which was later extended and converted to cottages.

High Grosvenor (SO 771936)

A house of at least six major building phases. Apart from the interest of the base-cruck trussed hall and the wallpaintings in the parlour wing which are described in chapter 13, the inserted ceiling in the hall is of interest, having a chequerboard design with diminished haunch joints to the spine-beams. Squared or mitred soffit shoulders are used, depending on their position, the mitres occurring in the central area. The name is derived from the family of 'Gravenor' and on a map of 1613 the house is called 'Height Gravenor'. The dendro date of the hall is 1375-7 and the inserted ceiling 1566-1610.[32]

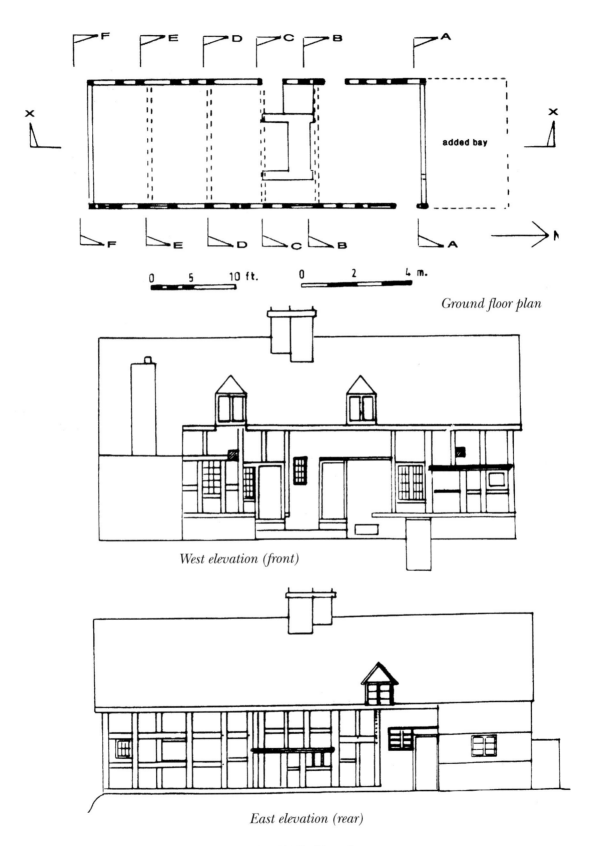

Ground floor plan

West elevation (front)

East elevation (rear)

Old Hall, Claverley

407

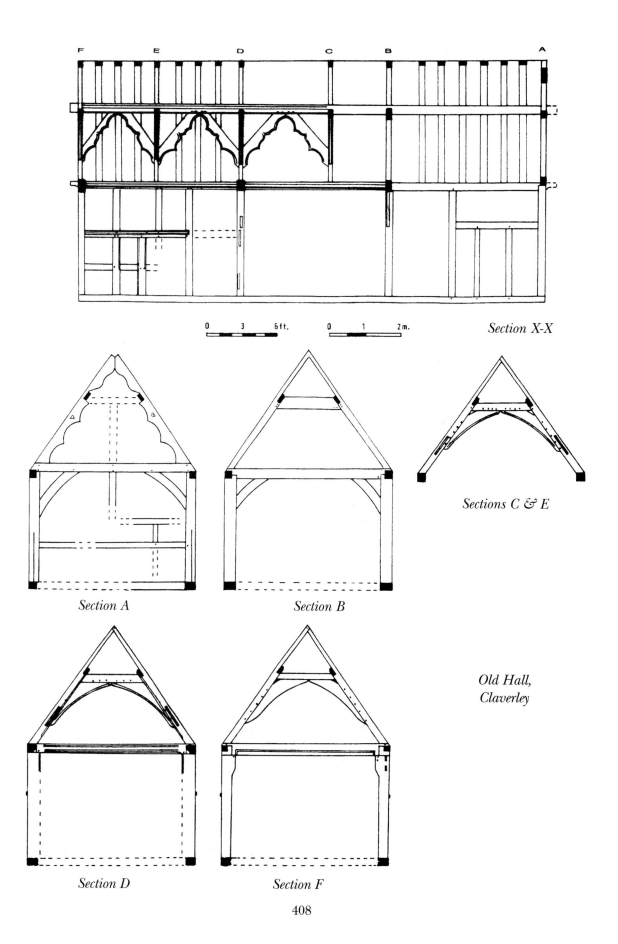

F E D C B A

Section X-X

0 3 6 ft.

0 1 2 m.

Section A

Section B

Sections C & E

Section D

Section F

Old Hall,
Claverley

408

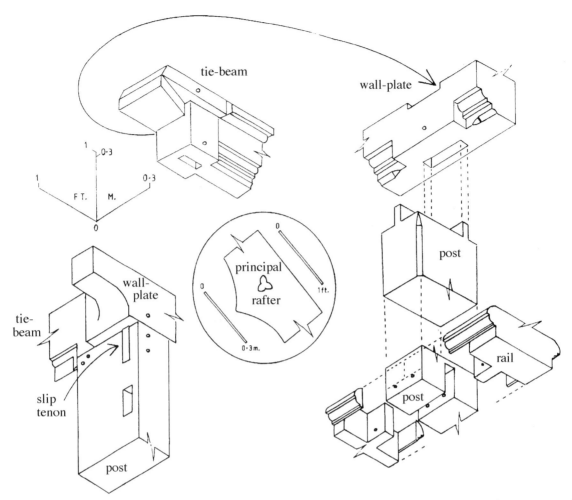

Left: Detail at truss F; top and right: Detail at truss D; within centre circle: Detail of wind-eye in truss A

Old Hall, Claverley

Clee St. Margaret

Yeld Farm (SO 568838)
Derelict in 1994, and I think still so, this is a rare example of a mid-17th century squatter's cottage, one-up, two-down, with a thatched roof and an out-built stack that may have incorporated a garderobe. The larger of the downstairs rooms was for animals and had sleeping accommodation above. It was built of Clee Hills sandstone flags and lime mortar.

Yeld Farm, Clee St. Margaret

409

Lower Brook House (SO 563844)

A stone-walled former farmhouse consisting of two adjoining ranges built at different levels. There are strong suggestions that the lower unit was part of a longhouse and that the upper range was a later addition built to provide a houseplace, parlour and dairy. The lower range contains one cruck truss.

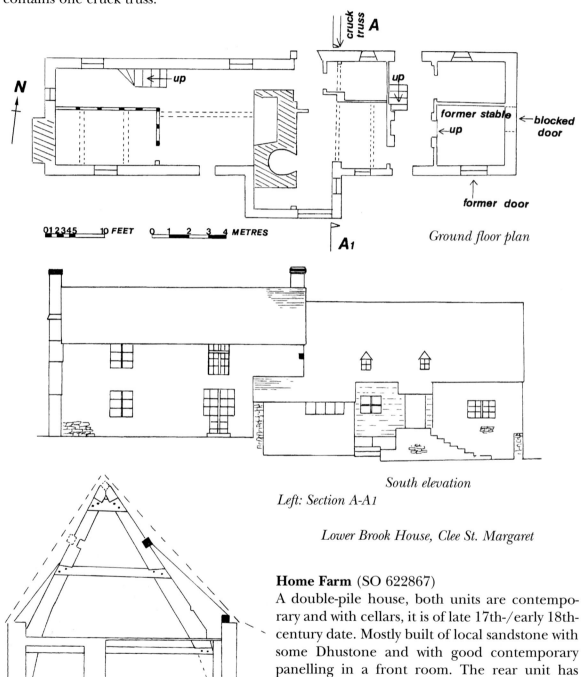

Ground floor plan

South elevation

Left: Section A-A1

Lower Brook House, Clee St. Margaret

Home Farm (SO 622867)

A double-pile house, both units are contemporary and with cellars, it is of late 17th-/early 18th-century date. Mostly built of local sandstone with some Dhustone and with good contemporary panelling in a front room. The rear unit has grain storage facilities in the attic and an intake door. Each unit has two industrial king-post trusses in wood and without screw tightening.

410

Cleobury North

Charlcotte Farm (SO 634862)
Basically of hall-and-crosswing form, the house incorporates several phases, but the outstanding feature is the plaster ceiling in a ground-floor room. Containing pomegranate trails with the seeds showing, strapwork and large bosses, the work is comparable with that at Ludford House.

Cleobury Mortimer

Catherton Cottage (SO 654783)
A cruck-built hall house, probably with longhouse origins which is dendro-dated to 1485. The central truss has cusped decoration and a low beam. The arch-braces each have two non-structural pegs, the purpose of which is not clear.[33]

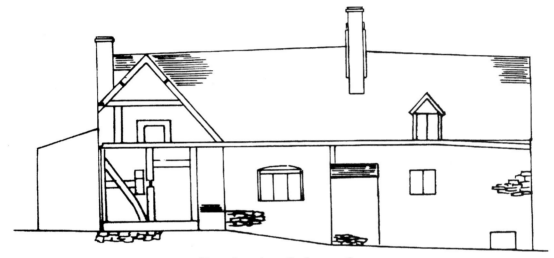

East elevation, Catherton Cottage

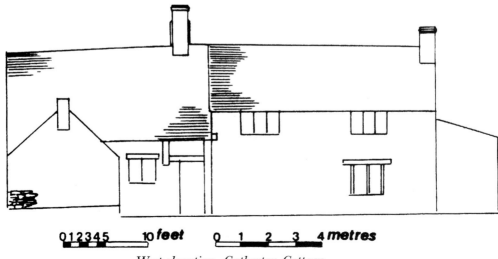

West elevation, Catherton Cottage

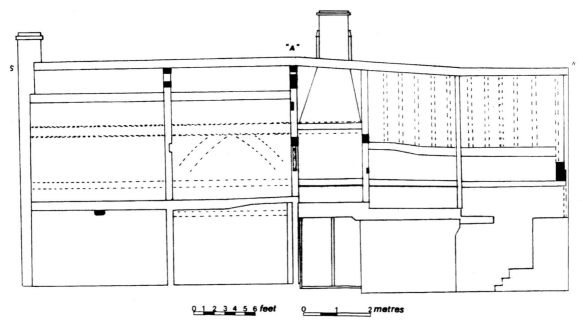

Long section looking west

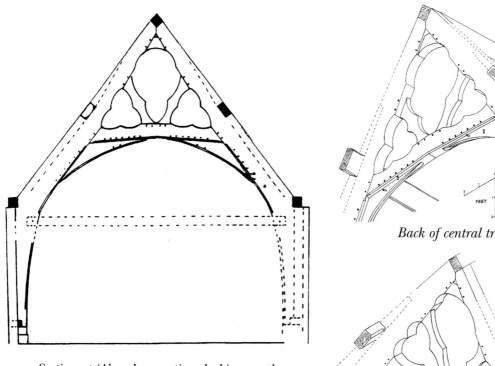

Section at 'A' on long section, looking north

Catherton Cottage,
Cleobury Mortimer

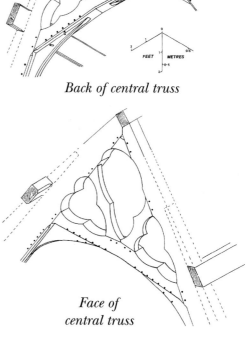

Back of central truss

Face of
central truss

Clun

Castle Cottage (SO 300808)

A cruciform-plan house, box-framed but stuccoed over with a two-bay open hall, service bay and three-bay crosswing of *c*.1500. Hall bays are smoke-blackened. The truss at the upper end of the hall has an infill of post-and-pan work and this is repeated in a truss in the crosswing.

Clun Farm (SO 304808)

An L-shaped farmhouse, both units are probably cruck-trussed and contemporary. It was later clad in stone and a brick extension added to form a T-shaped plan. The brickwork is in rat-trap bond. The cruck truss, at the division of the hall and crosswing, is extended by means of a scarf-joint and the apex is pegged through from the side. The central truss was originally arch-braced.

2 & 3 Little Hospital (SO 303811)

Two cottages which may have been part of a cruck-framed terrace. No.1 has a canopied bread-oven.

The Bryn Cottage, Clun

The Bryn Cottage (SO 294854)

The cottage is a stone-walled L-shaped building with a stone-flagged roof, a two-storied porch and some timber-framed internal partitions, and is dated to 1653. There is a chequer-board ceiling in the wing, with a bacon-cratch and spit-rack in the rear room. The front room has no front window, but one side window is latticed and has a drip-mould. The cellar under the wing is approached from both outside and inside. It contains a one-and-a-half–storied hall with a large central chimney and one added chimney to the right of the porch. A cheese press survives. This building is a well-preserved example, both of plan-type and detailing.

Lower Spoad (SO 257820)

This was a cruck-built longhouse with a further two-bay cruck range built at right-angles to the byre. There is a 17th-century box-framed addition with a garderobe. The large inserted stack has a carved overmantel vividly depicting a hunting scene.[34]

413

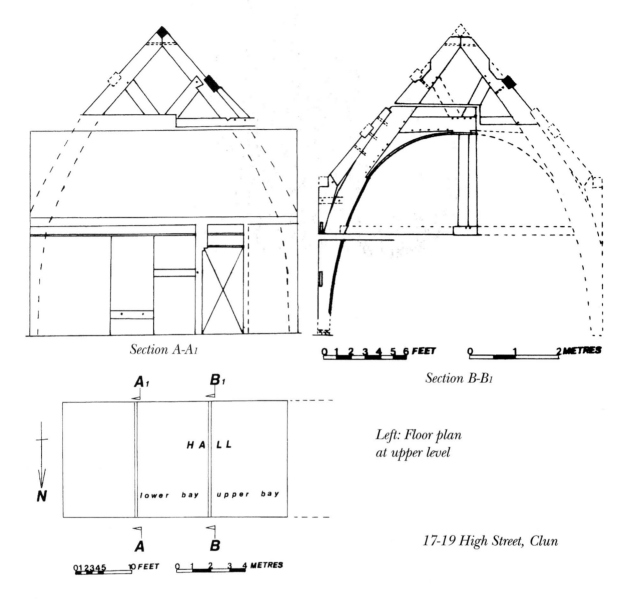

Section A-A₁

Section B-B₁

A₁   B₁

H A L L

lower bay   upper bay

N

A   B

0 1 2 3 4 5   10 FEET   0 1   2   3   4 METRES

0 1 2 3 4 5 6 FEET   0   1   2 METRES

Left: Floor plan
at upper level

17-19 High Street, Clun

17 & 19 High Street (SO 303808)
The building incorporates the remains of a cruck structure with a low-beam.[35]

Timber Croft, Pentre Hodre (SO 326768)
This is an upland ex-farmhouse, possibly with longhouse origins. It was cruck-built with the central truss incorporating a low-beam. The chamfer treatment differentiates the upper and lower bays. One blade carries a 'hewing-mark'. It has been dendro-dated to 1465.[36]

Bryn Cambric, Chapel Lawn (SO 316758)
This is another upland ex-farmhouse, possibly with longhouse origins and cruck-built. Two pairs of crucks are from whole trees, whilst one pair is from split oak. It has a good inserted chequerboard ceiling. The lobby-entry is created by the insertion of a large chimneystack. According to a sale catalogue of 1914 'Trewithpint' (9d.) and 'Meal rent' (5s.) are to be paid every other year to the Earl of Powis.[37]

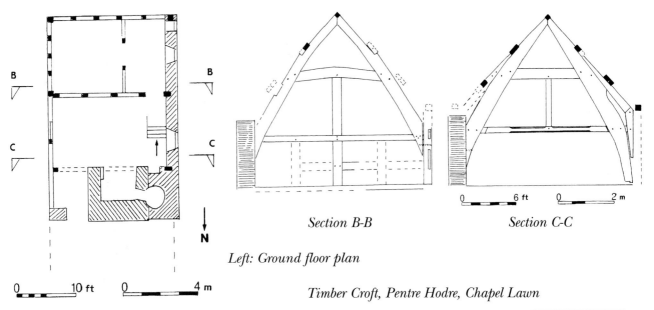

Section B-B   Section C-C

Left: Ground floor plan

0 — 10 ft   0 — 4 m

Timber Croft, Pentre Hodre, Chapel Lawn

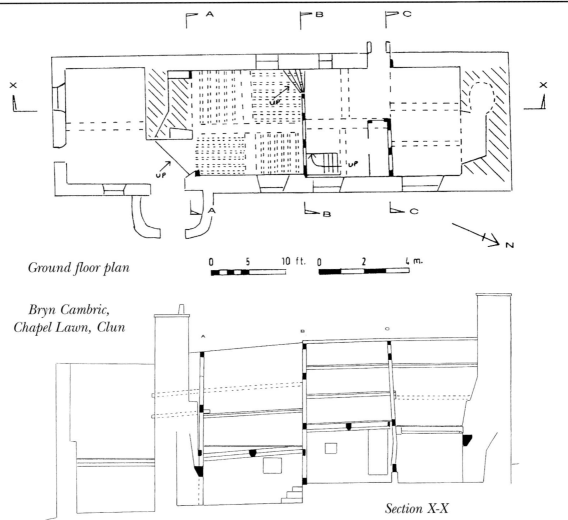

Ground floor plan   0 — 5 — 10 ft.   0 — 2 — 4 m.

Bryn Cambric,
Chapel Lawn, Clun

Section X-X

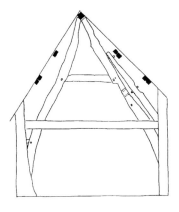

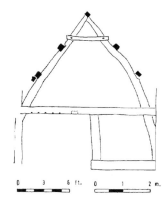

Section A-A   Section B-B   Section C-C

Bryn Cambric, Chapel Lawn

Pen-y-wern (SO 306788)
Stone-built three-unit farmhouse, unusually tall for the area. Dated 1747, but this relates to extensions at the front. Basically a late 17th-century plan of a lobby-entry floored houseplace flanked by an unheated room on one side and a dairy with a rear heated parlour behind it. 'Wet' cellar with access from the dairy.[38]

Bryn Cambric, Chapel Lawn

Field Farm, Purlogue (SO 285771)
The complex consists of two semi-detached smallholdings, one older than the other. The older possibly has longhouse origins. It has a three-room plan, but the middle room at ground floor level is blocked off. The end room has a fine chequerboard ceiling. A panelled door in the upper storey is dated 1635.[39]

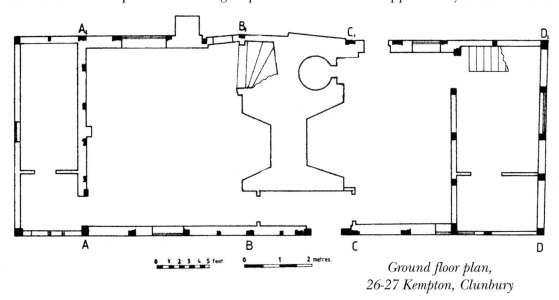

Ground floor plan,
26-27 Kempton, Clunbury

416

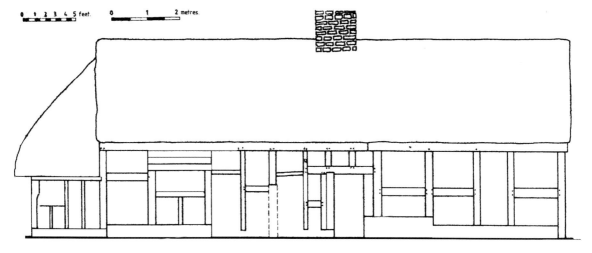

North elevation, 26-27 Kempton, Clunbury

Clunbury

26-27 Kempton (SO 357831)
A classic lobby-entry, one-and-a-half-storied, three-bay, 17th-century, box-framed farmhouse, now cottage. Houseplace and parlour on either side of the stack and a dairy occupying the third bay beyond the houseplace. A stone spiral stair on the opposite side of the stack from the entrance rises from the parlour.[40]

28, 29, 30 Kempton (SO 356829)
A hall-and-service range (28-29) with a parlour wing (30). Mid-to-late 17th century with a hewn jetty and close-studding to the parlour wing and square framing to the remainder.[41]

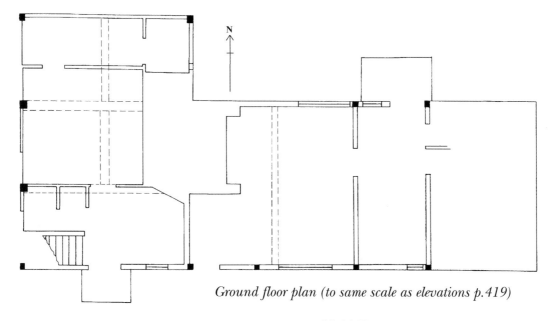

Ground floor plan (to same scale as elevations p.419)

28-29 Kempton

417

25 Kempton (SO 375831)

What was the central truss of a cruck hall-house is now exposed in the gable and a large stack has been added as part of the later infill. The crucks are crow-stepped at the top and there are small 'butterfly-hinge' spurs. Dendro-dated to 1474. Possibly a cruck spere-truss.[42]

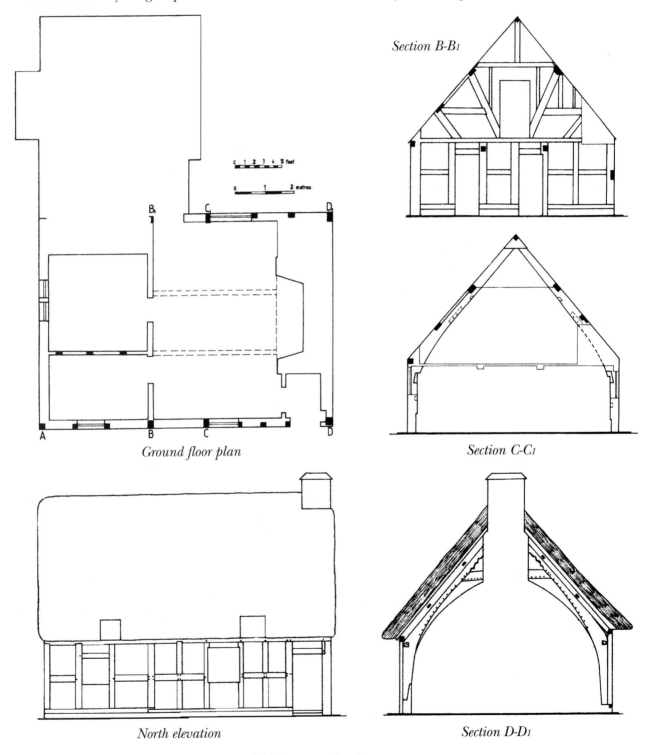

Ground floor plan

Section B-B₁

Section C-C₁

North elevation

Section D-D₁

25 Kempton, Clunbury

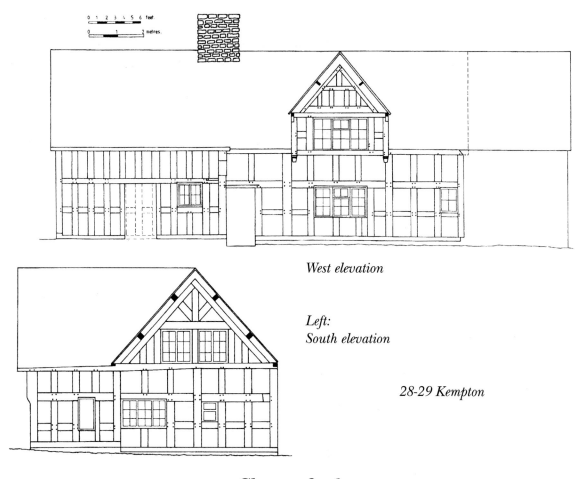

West elevation

Left:
South elevation

28-29 Kempton

Clungunford

Abcott Manor (SO 392787)
A manor house complex of stone, brick and timber-frame. The framed unit is an added two-bayed parlour wing with four rails to wall-plate level giving a pattern of small rectangles. Ovolo moulding in the cellar window. The unit has a complex out-built stack in stone with twin brick shafts, ribbed, with open zig-zag brickwork between them. The great chamber has an elaborate plastered ceiling with pomegranates, scrolls, heraldic beasts, strapwork and plain oval bosses. Once the property of the Prynce family of Whitehall, Shrewsbury.[43]

Clungunford Farm (SO 397787)
An H-shaped farmhouse of which the box-framed and jettied north wing is the oldest part. The joists are tenoned into the back of the bressumer and are boarded over underneath so that only the spine-beam is visible. There is a labelled cheese-room at first-floor level.

Coalbrookdale

Rose Cottage (SJ 669042)
Now one of the *in situ* exhibits of the Ironbridge Gorge Museum, this is reputedly the oldest surviving timber-framed dwelling in the Dale. The building began as a two-bayed house. There is a date of 1636 on the dormer window, probably indicating an insertion date. A large central

fireplace has a hood above which slopes on all four sides. It probably served a bloomery, but in 1636 the building was extended upwards, and further alterations took place in 1642. The initials of Lord Brook appear on the lintel of the fireplace. A stone-built extension was added to the front elevation but this appears to have been intended only for storage, there is no access from outside. An original unglazed window with an ovolo-moulded king mullion survives with a sliding shutter. Rose Cottage may have begun as a lodge between Wenlock Abbey and Madeley Court. Adaptation for industrial use followed and then it was further adapted for a dwelling. Following the decline of the iron industry it was converted into four cottages.[44]

Condover

Yew Tree Cottage (SJ 494060)
A T-shaped house consisting of a hall and service range with an added solar at the south end. The hall range is cruck-built and one truss has a rearing mark or 'scotch'—rare in cruck houses.[45] The hall has an inserted chequerboard ceiling.

Moat Farm, Stapleton (SJ 456036)
An old moated site, first recorded c.1350. The present house consists of two units at right angles to each other. Each is brick-cased, and, because of the rising ground, one is taller than the other. The taller unit stands on a stone plinth which probably relates to the early site. Each has a central stack, that of the lower range giving a lobby-entry. It probably dates from the early 17th century, but it contains moulded ceiling beams of mid-16th century date. The central boss is thought to be the work of 'carver' Hill in the 19th century. There is also an early Jacobean overmantel with inlay panels and classical motifs. A framed gatehouse was demolished in the 1930s.[46]

The Old School House (SJ 494060)
A cruck hall, truncated at the central truss, has a box-framed crosswing with cusped V-struts above the collar. It is reputedly the home of Richard Tarleton, court jester to Elizabeth I.[47]

Condover Court

Condover Court (SJ 494060)
Formerly called 'The Small House' to distinguish it from Condover Hall, this was probably the home farm. Although refurbished in 1878 (date on stack) it retains the complete lay-out of a medieval hall-house with a cruck-built range consisting of a two-bayed hall, two service bays and a box-framed crosswing. All the units are dendro-dated to 1445. The hall is notable for the quality of the central truss, but the decoration is reserved for the wind-braces which are cusped. There are two smoke-louvre positions, one in the hall and one in a service bay; there is no spere-truss. Entrance was directly into the lower bay of the hall.[48]

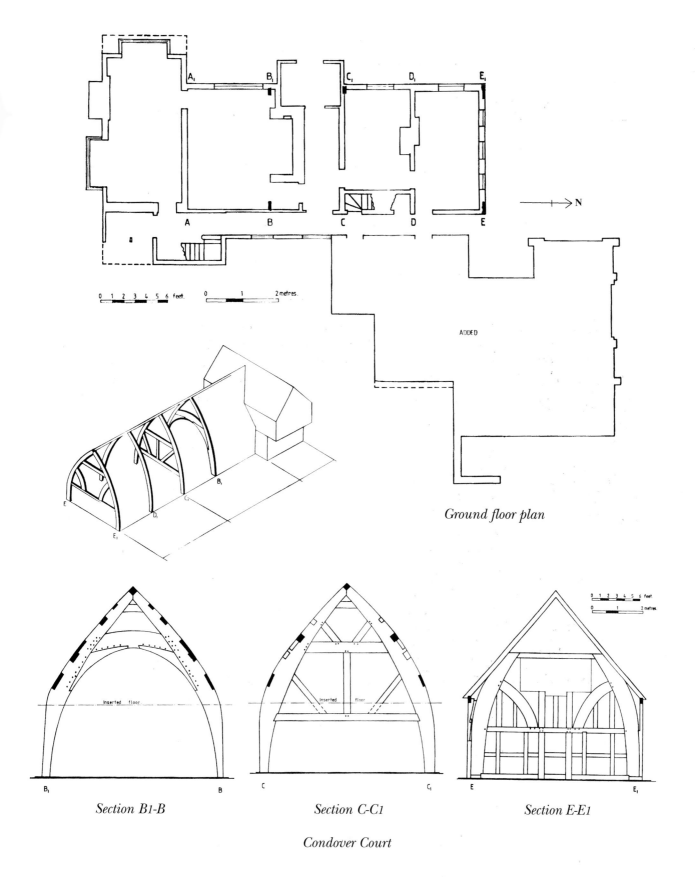

Ground floor plan

Section B1-B

Section C-C1

Section E-E1

Condover Court

421

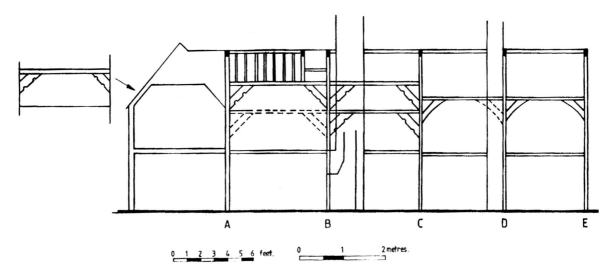

Section showing position of windbraces, Condover Court

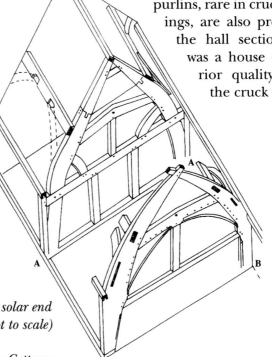

2 Ryton Grange Cottages (SJ 488035)
No.2 consists of the remains of a two-bay cruck hall and the fossilised remains of a solar bay to the west. The service end has been replaced by a separate cottage—No.1. The central truss in No.2 is notable for the inclusion of a low beam with a central strut, a crossed apex and no wall-posts. The windbraces vary in form, those in the solar are connected with notched-lap joints. Threaded purlins, rare in cruck buildings, are also present in the hall section. This was a house of superior quality within the cruck genre.[49]

Chamber over the hall at Condover Court showing the central truss, louvre position and cusped windbraces

Upper Bay of hall and solar end (part reconstruction, not to scale)

2 Ryton Grange Cottages

422

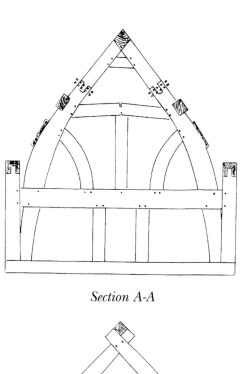

Section A-A

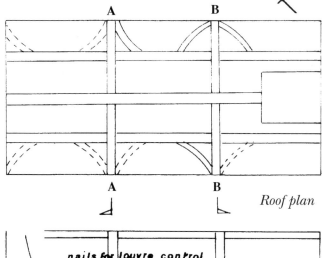

Roof plan

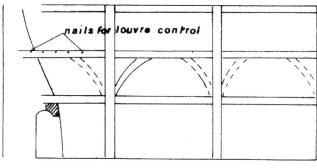

nails for louvre control

Long section looking south-east

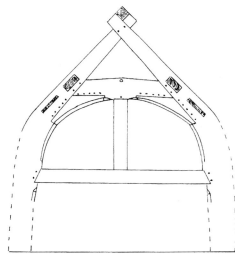

Section B-B

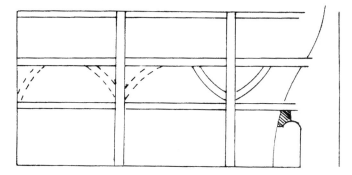

Long section looking north-west

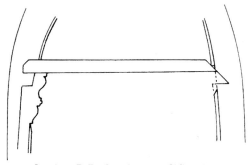

*Section B-B showing modifications
to low beam and cruck*

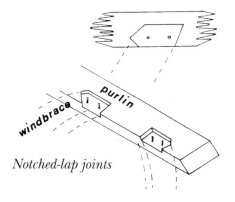

windbrace   purlin

Notched-lap joints

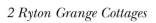

2 Ryton Grange Cottages

Wheathall (SJ 498038)

The three-bay symmetrical brick unit which faces the road and has a datestone WD 1721 (William Daker) replaced the service area of an earlier cruck-built hall of two bays and a box-framed crosswing. The central truss of the hall survives and is typical of the quality work noted in Condover parish. The upper and lower bays of the hall are differentiated on the central truss by having ovolo moulding on the 'high' side and a plain chamfer on the 'low' side. There is evidence for a canopy above the dais at the upper end of the hall. The two-bayed solar cross-wing remains reasonably intact. It is close-studded and has a tie-and-collar-beam roof with king-and-queen-strut uprights. A curious alcove in the outside wall has a pointed-arched stone lintel finished with quarter-round moulding.[50]

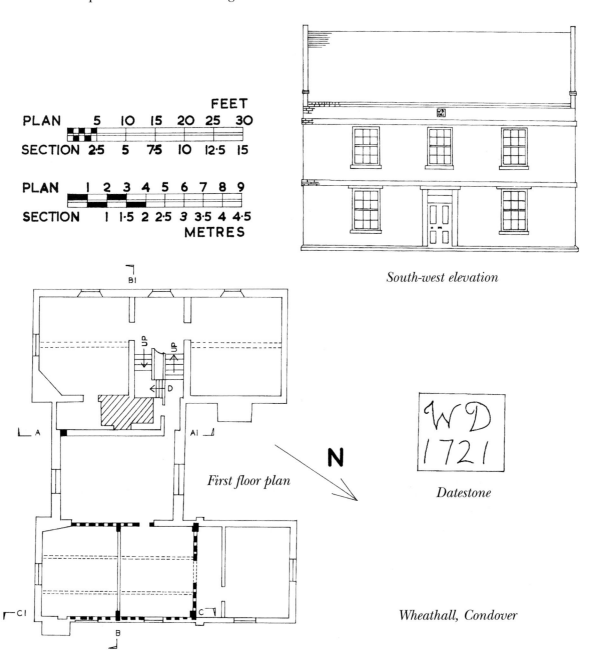

South-west elevation

First floor plan

N

Datestone

Wheathall, Condover

424

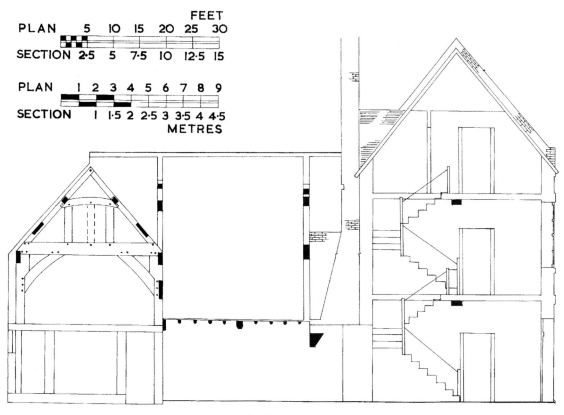

PLAN 5 10 15 20 25 30
SECTION 2·5 5 7·5 10 12·5 15

PLAN 1 2 3 4 5 6 7 8 9
SECTION 1 1·5 2 2·5 3 3·5 4 4·5
METRES

Section B-B1

CROSS SECTION
OF MOULDING ON
ARCHED BRACE.
ACTUAL SIZE.

1 INCH

BLOCKED
WINDOW

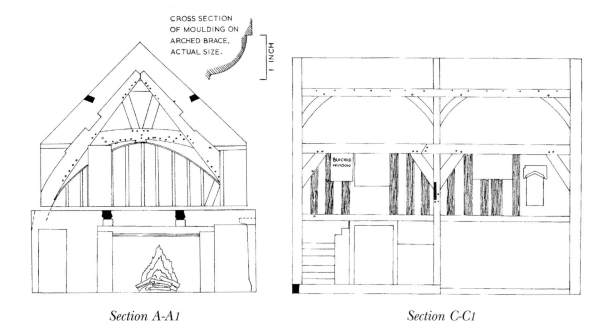

Section A-A1

Section C-C1

Wheathall, Condover

425

Cound

Blacksmith's Shop, Venus Bank (SJ 554059)
A box-framed two-up, two-down cottage which has evolved from a single-cell dwelling. Now in use as a pig-sty and situated behind the later smithy.[51]

Cruck Barn, Golding

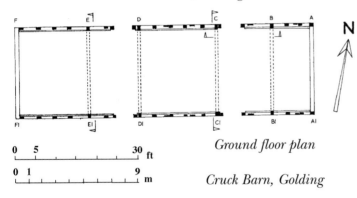

Ground floor plan

Cruck Barn, Golding

Upper Cound, Fulway Cottage (SJ 552036)
Originally, this was a small single-cell structure with very heavy close-studding all round. It gives the impression of being an important building of some kind—perhaps a chapel. Later it received an inserted floor and a stack and had a cottage attached to it, making two one-up, one-down dwellings. The older unit is dendro-dated to 1603 and the inserted ceiling to 1640. Both cottages were abandoned as dwellings and were used for implement storage.[52]

Golding, Cruck Barn (SJ 544034)
At the entrance to Golding Hall is a well-preserved cruck barn of five bays, originally three. The two inner trusses were open and the outer trusses had hipped ends. The closed trusses have no posts and therefore the cruck blades are not in alignment. It seems to have been a multi-purpose building, not a threshing barn.[53]

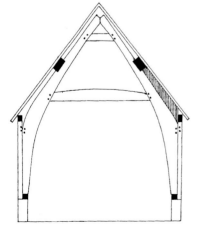

Section C-C1 (D-D1 similar)

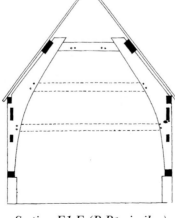

Section E1-E (B-B1 similar)

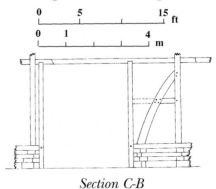

Section C-B

Golding Hall (SJ 544034)

A 'gentleman's residence', this H-shaped stylish brick house conceals close-studding on the east wing and hall area, dendro-dated to 1660. This phase includes a hewn jetty and a lobby-entry. Shortly afterwards, in 1668 (datestone), a prestigious parlour wing was completed in brick. Later the framing was brick-cased to make symmetrical façades to the front and back. The complex includes a fine cruck barn, granary, dovecote and a sunken garden.[54]

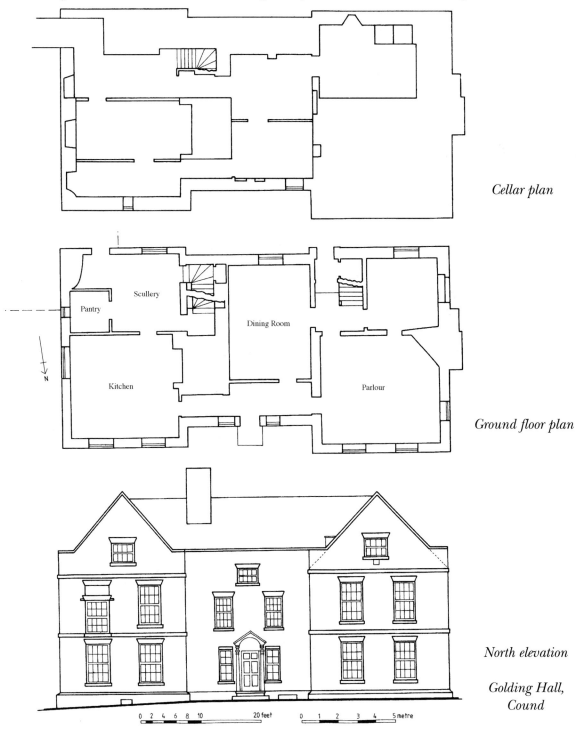

Cellar plan

Ground floor plan

North elevation

Golding Hall, Cound

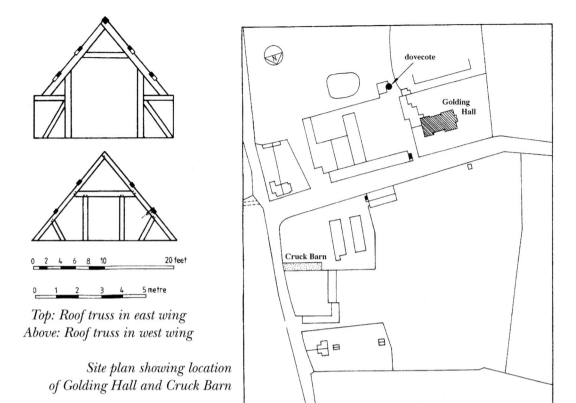

Top: Roof truss in east wing
Above: Roof truss in west wing

0 2 4 6 8 10   20 feet

0   1   2   3   4   5 metre

*Site plan showing location
of Golding Hall and Cruck Barn*

Golding Hall, Cound

0   50   100   200 feet   0 10 20 30 40 50 metres.

Culmington

2 Shaw bank, Craven Arms (SO 463834)
Basically a two-bay stone cottage with a rear out-shot for sleeping. The north bay is ceiled and has a cooking range with a bread-oven at the side. The south bay has an open roof and appears never to have had an upper floor. It may have housed livestock. There are no stairs—access to the room over the north bay was by ladder. This and many other cottages in Shaw Bank were built to house workers at the lime kilns at Knowle and belonged to the Stokesay estate.

Dawley

Hinkshay Row (SJ 697075)
Dawley was one of the east Shropshire coalfield settlements which was absorbed by the new town of Telford. Most of the rows of industrial cottages, some back-to-backs, were demolished. Hinkshay Row was such an example—375ft. long it contained 38 cottages each less than 10ft. wide.[55]

11, 15, 15a, Shop adjacent, Holly Road & Fairfield, Little Dawley (SJ 685060)
This group of buildings included many features of interest including crucks, wallpaintings, old shop fronts, an inn and two wattle-and-daub smoke-hoods ('fumbrells'). They gave a good indication of living patterns at the start of the Industrial Revolution. Part of the complex has been reconstructed at Blists Hill Museum.[56]

Ivy Farm, Little Dawley (SJ 682060)
One of the few remaining timber-framed buildings in the area. At first a 1¹/₂-storied hall with a projecting crosswing in square-framing and a large central stack, there have been several extensions.[57]

Diddlebury

Lydehole, Diddlebury

Lydehole (SO 521821)
A two-bayed, end-baffle-entry, 1¹/₂-storied, 17th-century, timber-framed cottage. One room was heated, the other end contained an unheated parlour and a dairy. There is an added bay in brick and a curious double-pile roofed porch.

Bouldon Farm (SO 546851)
An H-shaped farmhouse of stone and timber-frame, the west wing is added, but the hall and east wing are likely to be contemporary. The hall is single-bayed and smoke-blackened. Pegs on the purlins relate to the louvre control system.[58]

Bouldon Farm, Diddlebury, from the north-east

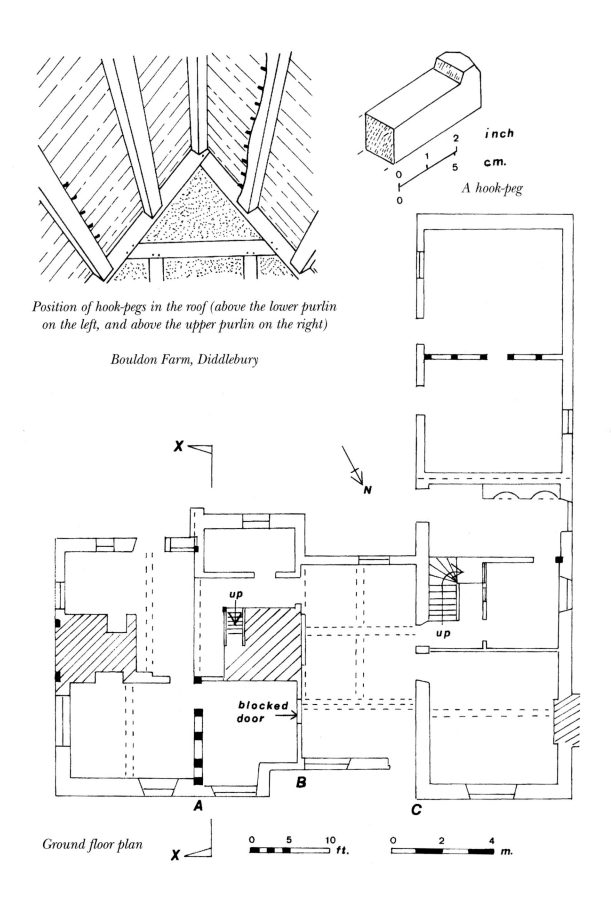

Position of hook-pegs in the roof (above the lower purlin on the left, and above the upper purlin on the right)

Bouldon Farm, Diddlebury

A hook-peg

inch

cm.

X

N

up

up

blocked
door

A

B

C

Ground floor plan

X

X

0   5   10   ft.

0   2   4   m.

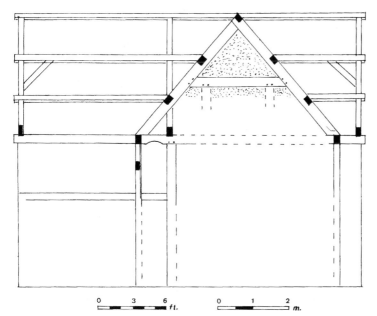

Bouldon Farm, Diddlebury, section X-X

Little Sutton Farm, Diddlebury

Glebe Farm (SO 506854)

An H-shaped farmhouse, originally all timber-framed, of late 17th-century date. Later stone casing was applied to the hall and service wing, but the parlour wing has exposed square-framing with inverted jowls to the corner posts. The plan is completely medieval, the only concessions to its time are the two-storied hall, the corner fireplace and the carved and moulded staircase.

Little Sutton Farm (SO 616831)

Now known as Sutton Court Farm, the house is a good example of the evolved H-plan and shows the hall losing its importance though retaining the cross passage element. The difference in the function of the two crosswings is expressed in the framing pattern: square-framing to the service wing and close-studding to the parlour wing. Wallpaintings occur in the latter.[59]

Sutton Court (SO 513824)

This is a large house, stone-built and basically U-shaped, but with many additions. There are several good fireplaces and over-mantels—the dining room was the courtroom and has a fireplace of c.1605 whilst the fireplace in the hall is dated 1473, but the date is unlikely to be authentic. The double linen-fold panelling in the passage is said to have come from Stirling Castle c.1900 and matches exactly the panelling in the hall. It is chiefly notable for its associations with the Powell family and their cultural trends. A fine Music Room was added in 1912 and distinguished visitors included Dame Nelly Melba, Sir F.P. Tosti etc. External features include impressive topiary and a perry press dated 1734 with the initials IPMP.[60]

Lawton Baskerville (SO 513839)

'Baskerville' relates to a family of that name who occupied the site between 1227 and 1400 and had a mill there in 1227.[61] Lawton is a D.M.V. site and a causeway connects it to Diddlebury. The house has much 19th-century work but the brickwork may replace earlier framing.

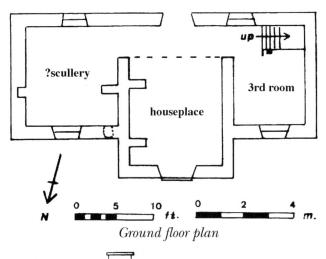

Ground floor plan

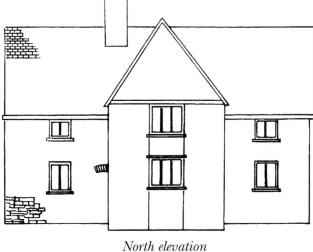

North elevation

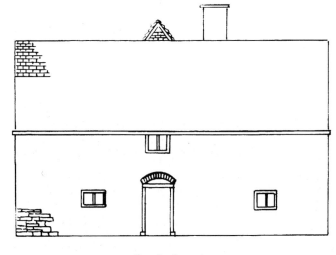

South elevation

Jack Clee's Cottage, Diddlebury

Jack Clee's Cottage (SO 528830)

An isolated, stone-built, three-bayed and two-storied house with a central stack providing back-to-back chimneys for the houseplace and the ?scullery. The latter contains a bread-oven. Third room was unheated. The house is backed by Suttonhill Coppice and has fine panoramic views from the front. The front of the house has architectural pretensions with a projecting central bay and symmetrical windows, but the back is 'cottage-like'. The floor joists and beams are of European larch, the floorboards of poplar and the roof timbers mostly of larch with some oak.

North Sutton House (SO 516833)

An H-shaped house, now mostly stone-clad. A stone building at the rear, probably the original detached kitchen, has been converted to become a separate cottage.

Ditton Priors

The Hyde (SO 625902)

Box-framed throughout and four-bayed; the stack bears a crest but no date. The room at the south end has a remarkable inserted ceiling, chequerboarded and moulded (cf. Wolverton). The stack occupied a whole bay and is said to have contained a dog-wheel.

Middleton Lodge, Middleton Priors (SO 623903)

A large three-storied house, basically stone-built and roughcast over when two distinct units were amalgamated. The Howard family owned the house and had their Catholic chapel in the part marked with a plaque dated 1845. The chapel was in use until 1974. An altar covering written by Clare Howard in 1890 reads 'The work was an antependium belonging to William Howard, Lord Stafford, executed on Tower Hill, 29th December 1680'.

North Farm, Middleton Priors (SO 625906)
A box-framed, 17th-century farmhouse, originally three-bayed with a central stack and 1½-storied. The houseplace has intersecting spine-beams with pyramid stops. On the side of the stack is a dog-wheel recess.

Derrington West (SO 606908)
A stone-built, two-storied farmhouse with two rear wings, one of which is a stair turret.

Donington

Humphreyston Hall (SJ 818051)
A complex house, basically of a continuous building programme begun in 1471 (dendro date).[62]

Lower Dairy House (SJ 806045)
Basically a box-framed, 17th-century farmhouse, now brick-clad. The two-bay hall has a central truss having a tie-beam now cut through and giving the impression of cruck spurs. There is no smoke-blackening.

Eardington

Moor Riddings Farm (SO 714909)
This house is probably the surviving cross-wing, of a larger complex. Close-studding to ground floor and square-framing above with long straight tension braces to each storey. Moor Riddings features in a 'Quit Rent' ceremony in the Royal Courts of Justice, London each year when the Corporation of London pays to the Crown the rent of a billhook and a hatchet.[63]

Easthope

Crowther's House (SO 567953) Hall and crosswing, each of cruck construction. The hall has been truncated at the central truss. A fireback is inscribed IWK 1701.

The Quit Rent ceremony for Moor Riddings Farm.
(Drawn by P. Gates, from Farmers Weekly *Nov. 1971)*

Moor Riddings Farm, Eardington

Crowther's House, Easthope

Crucks at right angles in Crowther's House, Easthope

Manor Farm (SO 566953)

Much of the timber-framed medieval manor house remains including the screens passage and spere-truss. The central truss of the hall has extended jowls to the posts, in effect making a form of jointed cruck. One plaster cast on the crosswing ceiling has the motto 'MAL MEV EST DEV DROIT' (Our lawful right is ill removed) but the cast has been applied upside down. Another, applied correctly, is purely decorative. There are cusped and nicked windbraces in the crosswing.

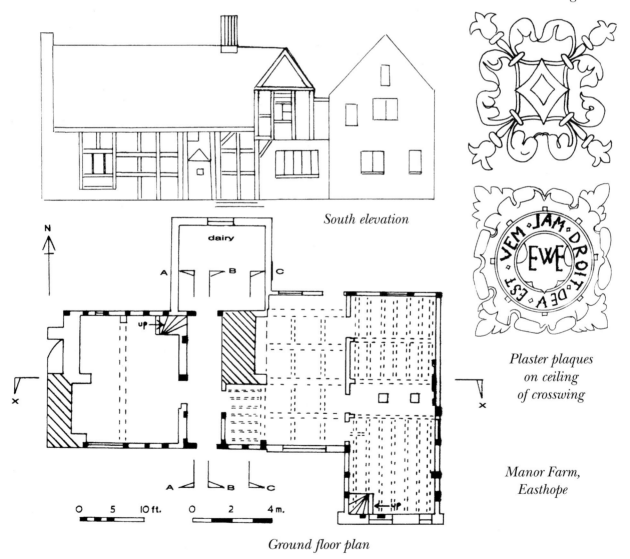

South elevation

Plaster plaques on ceiling of crosswing

Manor Farm, Easthope

Ground floor plan

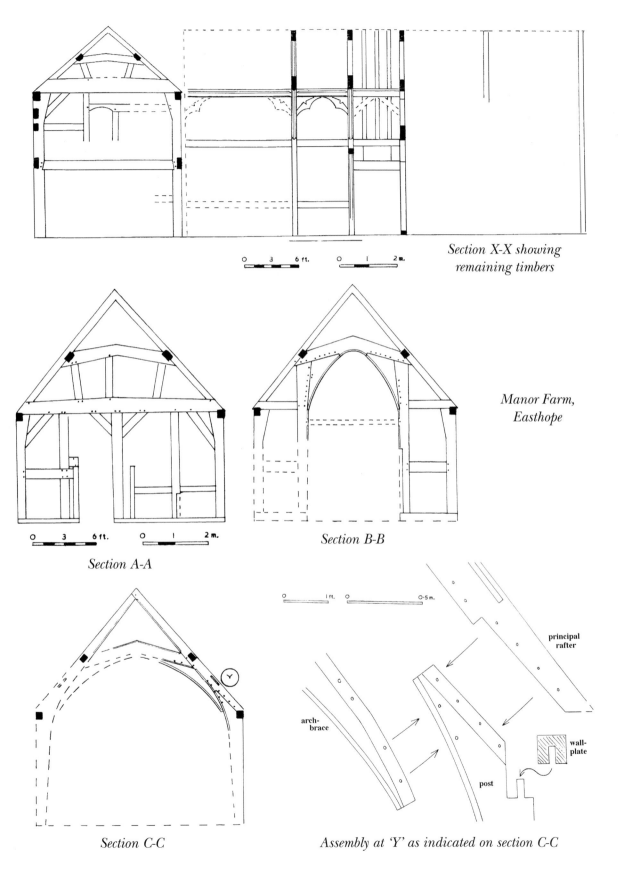

Section X-X showing
remaining timbers

0   3   6 ft.   0   1   2 m.

Manor Farm,
Easthope

Section A-A

0   3   6 ft.   0   1   2 m.

Section B-B

Section C-C

0   1 ft.   0   0·5 m.

principal
rafter

arch-
brace

wall-
plate

post

Assembly at 'Y' as indicated on section C-C

435

Cottage Farm (farm building) (SO 565953)

Two trusses of a medieval hall house remain, each is aisled and dendro-dated to 1431. One is a spere-truss which incorporates a low beam and the other is the hall end truss, which has a central vertical post between the sill-beam and the tie-beam. Unilateral bracing is present on the crown-posts. Also surviving is a brick-cased crosswing, dendro-dated to 1454. This has four half-bays with cusped windbraces. The crosswing appears to be a replacement for an earlier service end. It later became a maltings and a kiln was added.[64]

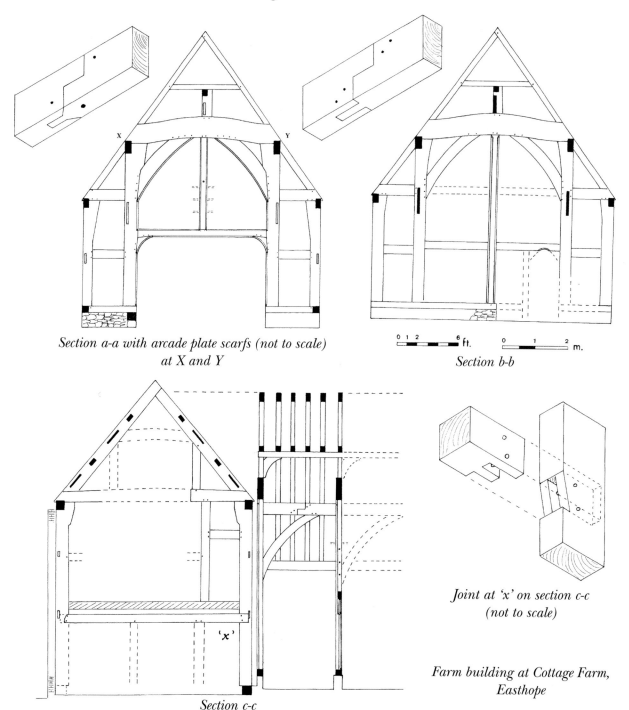

*Section a-a with arcade plate scarfs (not to scale)
at X and Y*

Section b-b

*Joint at 'x' on section c-c
(not to scale)*

Section c-c

*Farm building at Cottage Farm,
Easthope*

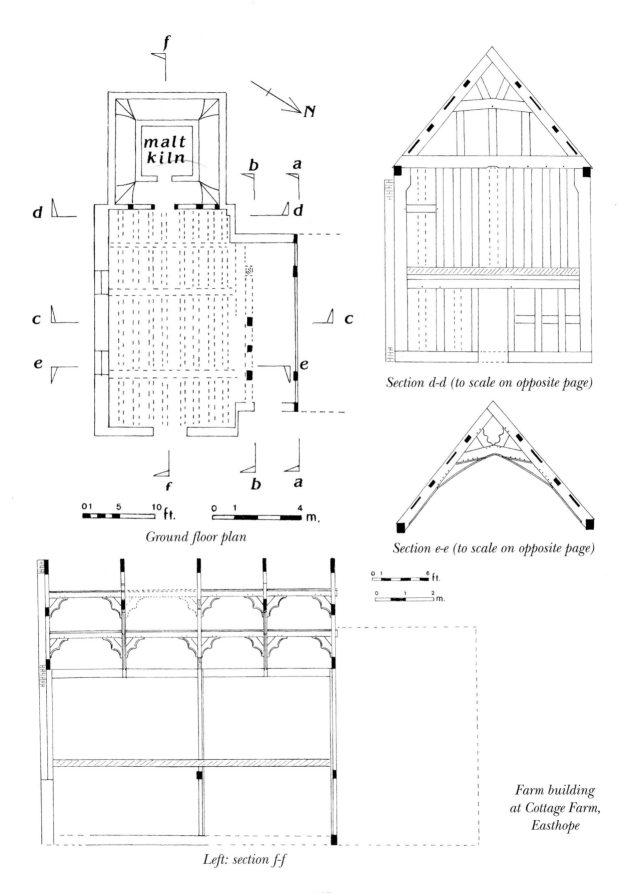

f

N

malt
kiln

b   *a*

d   *d*

c   *c*

e   *e*

f   *b*   *a*

0 1   5   10 ft.

0   1   4 m.

Ground floor plan

Section d-d (to scale on opposite page)

Section e-e (to scale on opposite page)

0 1   6 ft.

0   1   2 m.

*Farm building
at Cottage Farm,
Easthope*

Left: section f-f

437

Eaton Constantine

Baxter's House (SJ 598063)
Box-framed throughout, of hall and crosswing form, but the crosswing is probably a 17th-century replacement of the byre of a earlier longhouse. Ovolo moulding in the crosswing windows. This is the boyhood home of Richard Baxter, the Puritan cleric.

Plough Cottage (SJ 601064)
A box-framed 'yeoman'-type house of three bays and 1½ stories with added single-storey bays to the north and south. Originally built with a baffle-entry. This was once a public house, but had been converted into two cottages by 1870.

Baxter's House, Eaton Constantine

Eaton-under-Heywood

Wolverton (SO 471879)
The exterior is rendered over and whitewashed, but concealed within is a medieval hall house which has the standard three-part plan of hall-and-passage flanked by a lower service end and an upper solar crosswing. Outstanding features include the spere-truss which has lavish cusping, the central two-tier cruck central truss, the inserted ceiling in the hall which has the finest chequerboard design in Shropshire, the panelling in the solar, and the way in which the heating sequence can be traced from an open hearth, through to a smoke-hood and finally to a brick chimneystack. Home to the Jencks family for many years until the move to New Hall in the late 16th century. Dendro-dated to 1475 with the inserted ceiling *c.*1570.[65]

New Hall (SO 490892)
The ultimate H-plan house, still fully timber-framed with a mixture of close-studding and lozenge-work, though largely bricked over at present, and with a two-storied hall. All of one build, probably late 16th century, and notable for its wallpaintings, described in chapter 13.

Hatton Farm (SO 468903)
A possible longhouse. At the upper end is a crosswing with close-studding which has two bays divided by a passage, one wall of which is a post-and-pan screen. The two-bay cruck structure at the opposite end has a central truss with an arch-braced collar-beam and notched lap-joints. Smoke-blackened.

Middle Farm, Hatton (SO 468903)
This and Upper Farm are close together and share farm buildings. Middle Farm was newly built in the 17th century, of hall-and-crosswing form, timber-framed but now roughcast. The

parlour has a good chequerboard ceiling. The communal barn is 10-bayed and timber-framed with much reused timber.

Ticklerton Hall (SO 485908)

H-shaped and brick-walled, but of several different building phases. The earliest is *c.*1500 of which part of a close-studded screen survives. Much bolection moulding. The grounds contain the remains of a brick dovecote.

Harton Manor (SO 483886)

The early 17th-century part of the house has rectangular panelling and cusped lozenge work in the large dormer-gable. The date of 1615 appears on the brick star-shaped stack. Two internal fireplaces have dated slabs. That in the upper room reads IN ANNO DOMINI 1615 RWCAWTH (Richard Ward and his wife). In the lower room only the date and initials appear.

Dovecote at Ticklerton Hall

Each have stone moulded jambs with the moulding continuing across the wooden lintel. There is a Jacobean-style staircase with heavy twisted balusters. A large cross-wing was added in the 18th century which has Flemish bonding, two plat-bands, casement windows and internal decorative plasterwork.

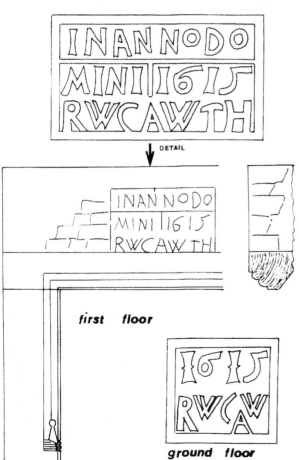

Harton Manor, Eaton-under-Heywood
Above: detail of gable panel (not to scale)
Left: details of fireplaces (not to scale)

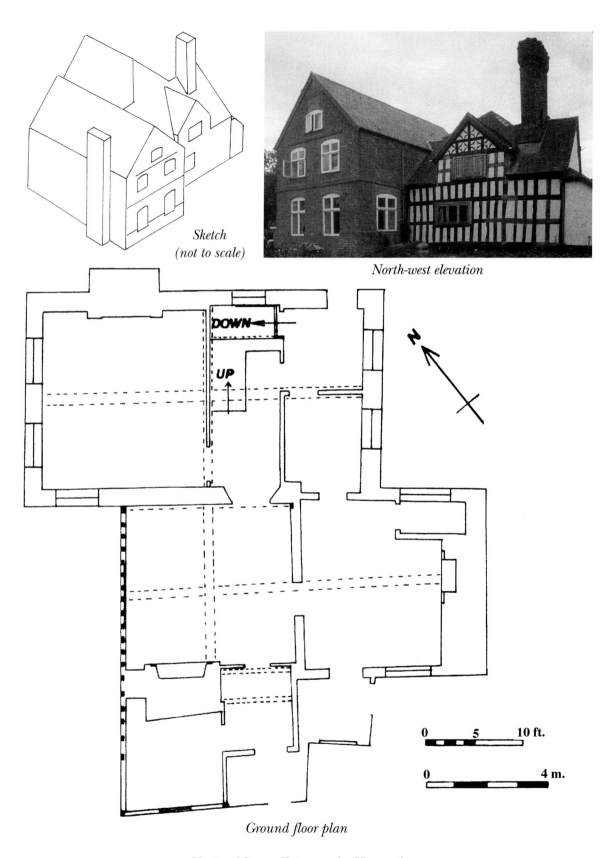

*Sketch
(not to scale)*

North-west elevation

DOWN

UP

0   5   10 ft.

0   4 m.

Ground floor plan

Harton Manor, Eaton-under-Heywood

Harton Farm (SO 482885)
A T-shaped house, box-framed with square-framing to the hall and rectangular panelling to the crosswing. The latter has a jetty, long straight tension braces, spiked and cusped lozenge-work and a pentice roof. The massive central stack in the hall range has star-shaped stacks. The hall roof has straddled purlins.

Provost's House, Edgmond

Edgmond

Provost's House (SJ 719063) The old Rectory is stone-built with some 14th-century masonry surviving, including three service doors with elaborate moulding in the screens passage. A problematic aperture at first-floor level, also moulded, may represent a large original window and there are the remains of another in a broom cupboard.

Caynton House (SJ 705219)
A stylish three-storied brick farmhouse with end chimneys, five bays wide with a recessed centre bay. The sash windows have thin glazing bars and the doorway has ionic pilasters and a segmental fanlight. There are two flanking two-storied wings. The building has continuous plat-band, cornice and parapet roof. *c.*1780-90.

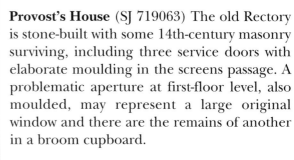

Service doorways in Provost's House, Edgmond

Ellesmere Rural

Old Marton Hall (SJ 347339)
A timber-framed house of *c.*1600, now brick-cased. In the gable the chimneystack, which does not project, is given emphasis with some elaborate brick arches forming an external feature. The staircase has shaped flat balusters and a string which is carved with a type of 'Greek key' pattern. The square newel post is also carved with a geometric pattern.

Staircase at Old Marton Hall, Ellesmere Rural

Old Groves, Eastwick (SJ 379375)

Now a two-bayed 1½-storied cottage, the central cruck-truss has a low beam which has decorative detail on one side suggestive of a coved dais truss, but there are many problems of interpretation.

Plas Warren, Dudleston (SJ 338389)

A brick-built H-shaped house of c.1730-40, but with earlier work inside including a gilded female figure holding a shield on the inner face of a bracket supporting a beam on the ground floor.

Sodylt Farm, Dudleston (SJ 345406)

U-shaped house, apparently box-framed, but the wings have been grafted onto a cruck-built house. Good cellar with ashlar stone.

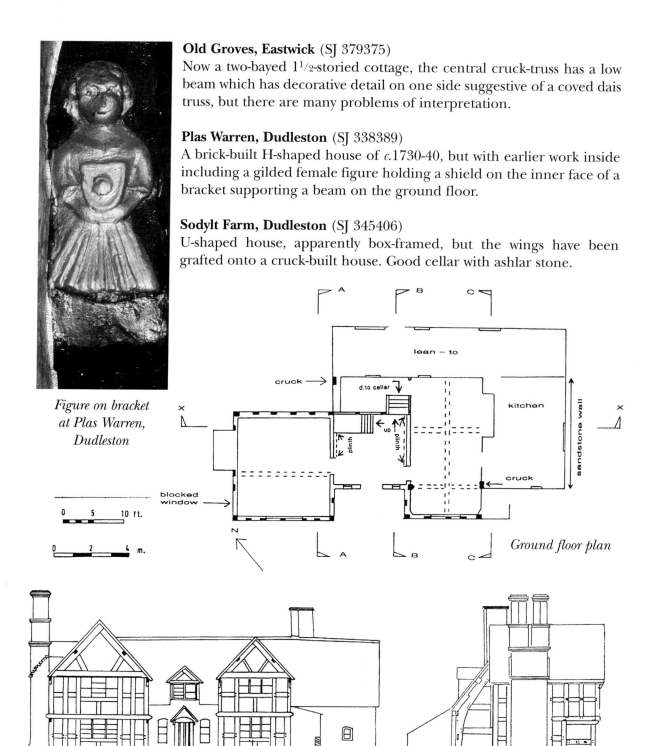

Figure on bracket at Plas Warren, Dudleston

Ground floor plan

South-west elevation

North-west elevation

Sodylt Farm, Dudleston, Ellesmere Rural

442

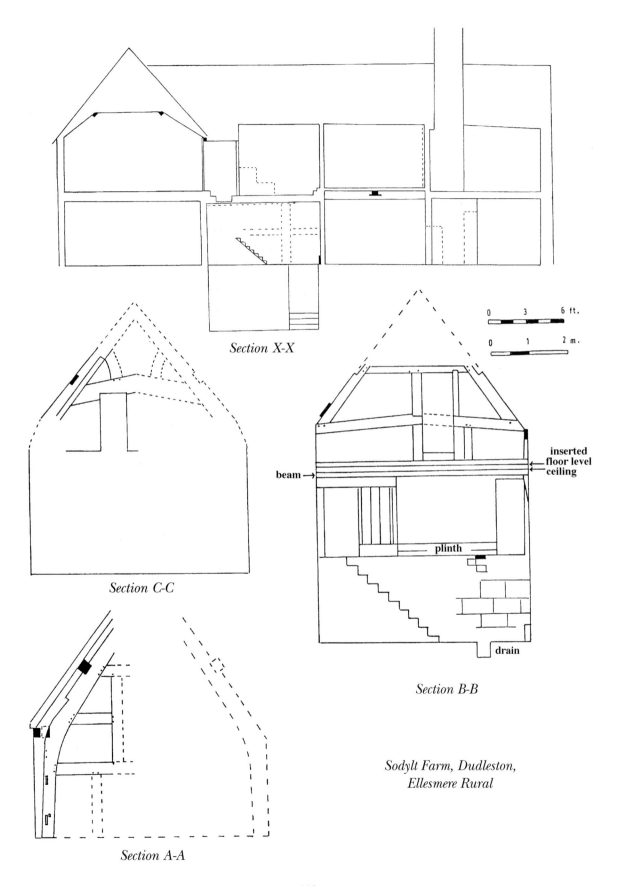

Section X-X

0 3 6 ft.

0 1 2 m.

Section C-C

inserted
floor level
ceiling

beam →

plinth

drain

Section B-B

Section A-A

Sodylt Farm, Dudleston,
Ellesmere Rural

443

Ercall Magna

Ercall Park (SJ 583175)
A gentleman's residence in a prime position which was originally plain-fronted but later altered on the ground floor to provide projecting bay windows and a pillared porch entry. It has a good 18th-century staircase with cast iron balusters. The dining room has a carved overmantel with two panels of inlay work and three carved human figures.

Poynton Manor (SJ 570178)
The house is timber-framed, of different dates, partly jettied but difficult to assess. The gable of one barn contains a three-light perpendicular window, probably surviving from a 15th-century chapel. Another has three cruck trusses, one of which has a bare-faced lap dovetail joint at the collar/blade junction. The collar extends to support the purlin. Thus the blades are held in a grip which tightens if there is torsion during rearing.

Farlow

The Lowe (SO 632805)
This is now an H-shaped stone farmhouse, but the large crosswing appears to have been a separate house. It has a through passage and suggestions of a dais end. There is a well preserved cider mill in the farm buildings.

Lower Ingardine (SO 629813)
Basically box-framed and jettied, this house assumed its present brick H-shape *c.*1800, but kept the original entrance position at the lower end of the hall. The original crosswing was jettied on three sides.

Ford

Oak Cottage (SJ 415138)
This building contains a two-bay open hall of cruck construction, the central truss of which is particularly fine with triple cusping above the collar.

Stockfield, Alberbury Road (SJ 391133)
The cottage perpetuates the name 'Stokes', a pre-conquest settlement, one of the medieval manors of Eyton (Eyton Stokes). This was originally a 17th-century, timber-framed, single-storied cottage with one room heated and the other not, but has been enlarged and given an end baffle-entry.

Great Ness

Alderton Hall (SJ 385174)
A two-storied projecting porch suggests that this house was once E-shaped. The date of 1591 on a carved overmantel in an upper room with the initials R.H. refers to Richard Heylin, a royalist who surrendered the house to the Roundheads. The carving has classical details.[66]

Top Farm, Kinton (SJ 369197)
This is a stone-built ginny-ring with an apsidal end and slate roof among the farm buildings.

Grinshill

Woodstile (SJ 539232)
The house is appropriately named, for it is brick-built but with painted on timbers. Even the end out-built stacks have had the treatment. An older unit at the rear has genuine framing.

Habberley

Habberley Hall (SJ 397035)
Originally a rectangular house, it was jettied on four sides with the central section open to accommodate a smoke-hood. It was later floored over and the fire removed to an out-built stack at the rear of the hall. Dendrodated 1555. Two timber-framed wings were added in 1593 by William Leighton; the inscription reads 'This House builded as you see A.D. 1593 by W.L.', but this

Ginny Ring at Top Farm, Kinton

Woodstile, Grinshill

may be a later version of the original. A bedhead inscribed GOD BLES USAL WL 1593 AL is recorded in a compilation of notes from various people with an interest in Habberley.[67]

The Old Mill (SJ 403036)
The mill was reconstructed in 1839, but on the north side is a single-cell cruck structure which could be the remains of the miller's house, here in 1370. Originally hipped at either end and with a central hearth, a row of pegs on the west purlin suggest the means of controlling the louvre.

Hadley

Apley Castle (SJ 654133)
Derelict, but under brick and plaster are the remains of the moated 14th-century Charlton house. It was stone-built with a ground-floor hall, screens passage and two service doors. There is a solar at the upper end and a chapel at first-floor level. This has a double-lancet window, an ogee-headed piscina, and painted walls including a female saint figure on one side of the altar.

Hanwood

The White House (SJ 445096)

This is the only house in the village to display timber-framing. Once a farm, it later housed a butcher's shop which had its own slaughterhouse and clemming house. The former is now a sitting room, a feature of which is a tree trunk whose roots disappear into the ground. The house is post-Civil War, T-shaped and originally with a lobby-entry. The stack may have housed a dog-wheel.

Harley

Harley Court (SJ 597018)

This was the miller's house and the detailing, including monk-bond brickwork, reflects his social standing. *c*.1780.

No.3 (SJ 597015)

Retaining its thatched roof, this cottage appears to be a straightforward example of 17th-century square-framing. But internally there are four bays, an ogee-headed doorway and an apparent gap which suggests that two buildings have been amalgamated. The panels are filled with split-laths instead of the usual wattle-work which suggests that at least the two bays nearest to the church were a barn.

No.6 (SJ 596016)

Basically a two-bayed 17th-century, yeoman-type farmhouse, timber-framed but always brick-nogged. It has a central stone stack and a lobby-entry. Thought to be the old Unicorn inn in 1615. A bay has been added to the south-east.

Rowley Cottages (SO 594998)

These are a pair of brick-built back-to-back farm labourers' cottages built between 1890 and 1910 for the Duke of Cleveland.[68] An identical pair are at the foot of Harley Bank. Each cottage has a porch, living room, kitchen and pantry downstairs and three bedrooms. There is lateral through ventilation, but no back door. The rear wall of each cottage is the dividing wall. Outside is a privy block with a pigsty and store and a large garden. Though now modernised, these were originally superior to the average industrial back-to-backs.

Rowley Farm Cottages, Harley

Hodnet

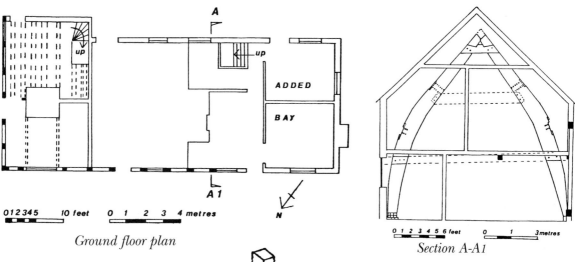

?Wine store at Hawkstone Farm, Hodnet

Hawkstone Abbey Farm (SJ 567303)
A farmhouse built in 1787 by the Hawkstone estate in gothic style; the kitchen has a cheese oven chute.

Hawkstone Farm, Marchamley (SJ 595295)
A T-shaped house with one cruck blade remaining. It includes a good range of 19th-century farm buildings with a structure built into the side of an old motte. It seems too large for an ice house although it could have supplied a large household. Could it have been connected with wine-making? There was a short-lived attempt by the estate at growing a vineyard.

Ground floor plan

Section A-A1

19-21 Drayton Road (SJ 614286)
The three cottages represent the subdivisions of a medieval cruck-built hall-house which has a contemporary box-framed solar wing and a later bay added to the hall. No.19 occupies the wing which is two-storied and two-bayed, demarcated by large curving arch-braces. The rear room still has large close-set joists, laid flat. The hall (no.21) was 20ft. (6.1m.) long, single-bayed and probably with a croglofft (sleeping platform) at the lower end. Here the cruck truss is relatively crude and adzed on both sides. The whole is dendro-dated to 1467.

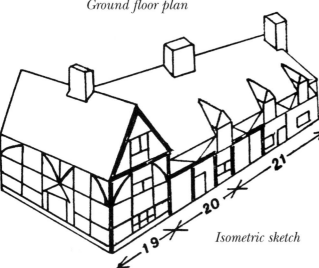

Isometric sketch

19-21 Drayton Road, Hodnet

Hopesay

Brook House (SO 394834)
Although basically a two-storied stone-built house, two mezzanine floors give four levels plus cellars. It was a mill, probably the work of John Griffiths (d.1756) for his own use. His tomb is in Hopesay churchyard. He was nicknamed 'Ingenious John' and also built The Fish (see below). The fireplace in the main room has a classical appearance and is likely to be his work. There is an interesting ha-ha wall. There was a cider mill, whilst some buildings, partially underground and with massive stone uprights, still survive.

The Fish (SO 396840)
This is one of a group of three houses, each with a 'Fish' element in its name. It was probably the work of John Griffiths (see above).

Low House, Broome (SO 401808)
Here the jetty is of similar construction to that at Clungunford Farm. The hall has a chequer-board ceiling. Two sickle-handles and a hammer were found embedded in a wattle-and-daub wall in a bedroom.

Hopton Cangeford

Castle Cottage (SO 548804)
This is a modern name for a single-bayed, stone houseplace of 1½ stories and a two-bay cross-wing in square-framing. Beyond the houseplace is a single-storied bay which housed cattle within the present owner's memory.

Little Wood (SO 557806)
A courtyard complex with the earliest part of the farmhouse, c.1650, occupying the south-west range and farm buildings completing the lay-out.

Lesser Poston (SO 538820)
A farmhouse which seems to have evolved from a medieval quality house with an open hall flanked by two crosswings. It was rebuilt in the 17th century and given a two-storied hall with remarkable carved ceiling beams. Later it was stone-walled and reduced in size and status.

Upper Wood (SO 553811)
A stone-built, T-shaped farmhouse. The crosswing is 2½-storied and the 'hall' is two-storied. The crosswing has a projecting porch with a side-entry and a studded door with a datestone of 1668 with the initials LIM (Littleton family) over the porch; the dressings are in brick. The spine-beams in the main room intersect and have cyma/pyramid stops. The kitchen stack contains numerous bake-ovens, hearths and boilers which all converge on one flue; there is also an underground kitchen.

Datestone at Upper Wood

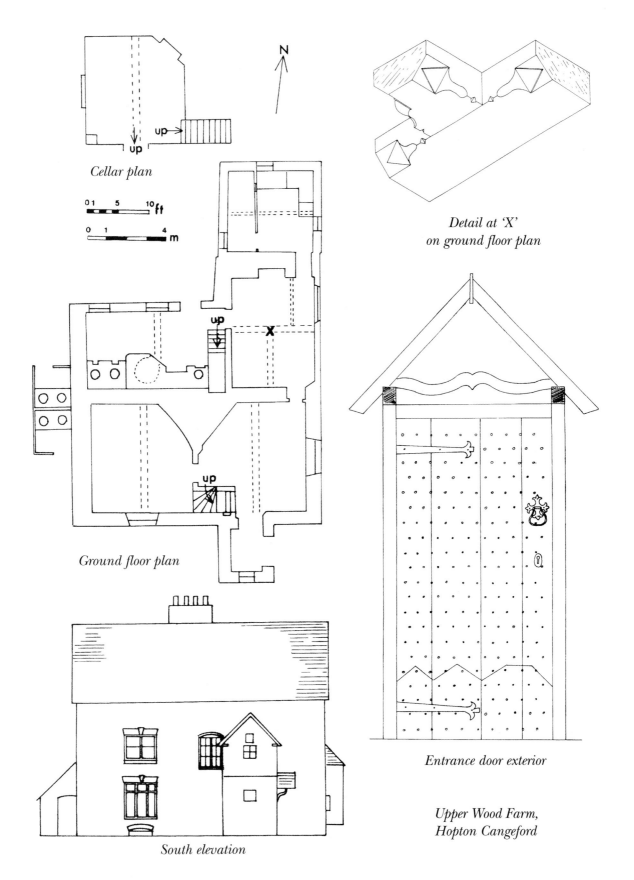

Cellar plan

0 1   5   10 ft

0   1   4 m

Detail at 'X'
on ground floor plan

up

up

X

up

up

Ground floor plan

Entrance door exterior

Upper Wood Farm,
Hopton Cangeford

South elevation

449

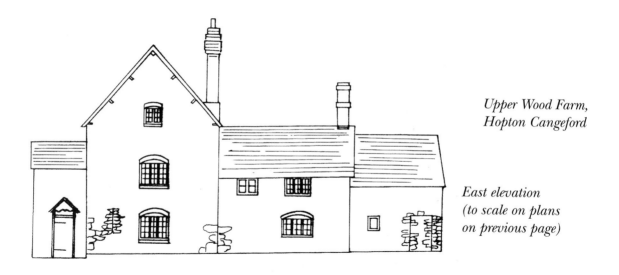

*Upper Wood Farm,
Hopton Cangeford*

*East elevation
(to scale on plans
on previous page)*

Hughley

Hollybank Villa (SO 562961)
A square-framed, two-bayed and 1½-storied cottage which may have begun as a single-celled squatter's cottage with a croglofft. It has an end baffle-entry at present, but the large stack may once have been out-built.

Ironbridge

The Swan Inn (SJ 668035)
Two parallel warehouse-type structures form a projecting wing to the inn. There are three upper crucks in the earlier wing and two in the other. The complex became a maltings and there is a large kiln at the north end, complete with malting floor. There are five different types of malting tiles, some are stamped 'Stanley Bros of Nuneaton'.[69]

Ightfield

Ightfield Hall Barn (SJ 601394)
This is basically box-framed but incorporating some reused crucks. Originally five-bayed with an added bay at the south end and an out-shot along the long rear wall. Dendro-dated 1567.[70]

Jackfield

The Tuckies (SJ 692024)
A large complex, mostly brick and stone, and much sub-divided. The house was leased by the Earl of Dundonald, of Tar Tunnel fame. The tunnel was intended to link the Severn in Madeley with mines in the Blists Hill area, but a spring of natural bitumen with medicinal properties was struck, and this was marketed instead. In 1800 it was the home of William Reynolds, the famous ironmaster. Some original features survive including the staircase with cone-shaped finials and newels. The balusters are not turned, but hand-carved. In the hall is a fixed handbasin backed with blue Delph tiles and fed from a hand-filled lead storage tank above.[71]

Kemberton

Kenyon-Slayney houses and cottages (SJ 73 04)
These are houses on the estate. Some are staff houses (11, 12, 13), built *c.*1670 and modernised. Others are farms (Hall Farm, The Cedars, 1722; and Kemberton House *c.*1713).

Kenley

Houses on Kenley Common
(SO 55 98)
Mostly squatters' cottages in origin, built of stone or timber-framed, mostly plastered over. Originally single-storied 1½-bays with out-built stack. Each squatter had a trade— wheelwright, weaver etc.—and each grew hemp. The weaver's cottage had a two-room plan and was built by an ancestor of the present owner. Hemp was taken to Mr. Carter's weaving sheds where it was made into the coarse linen known as 'hurden'. From there it went by pack-donkey to Hanwood for bleaching. The sheds have been demolished.[72]

Weaver's House, Kenley (squatter origin)

Kinlet

Earnwood Farm (SO 737805)
Identical in plan-form to Bush House, Chetton (see above).

Tippers (SO 735818)
This is a three-bay box-framed house which was cased with brick at different times. The out-built stack incorporates a so-called 'priest's hole' or probably a garderobe. There is a local style of brick bonding in part of the house. 'Tippers' or 'Tiphouse' comes from the name of a lawyer, a 'known speculator in concealed lands' from the time when catholics were barred from owning property. His reward was possession of the house.[73]

Kinnerley

The White House, Kynaston (SJ 353202)
A 17th-century 'husbandman-type' house of longhouse derivation. It has a houseplace and small parlour at the upper end whilst the lower bay is a byre. There is no direct access from house to byre, but a small window in the dividing stone wall gives visual access. It has an integral dairy out-shot at the rear.

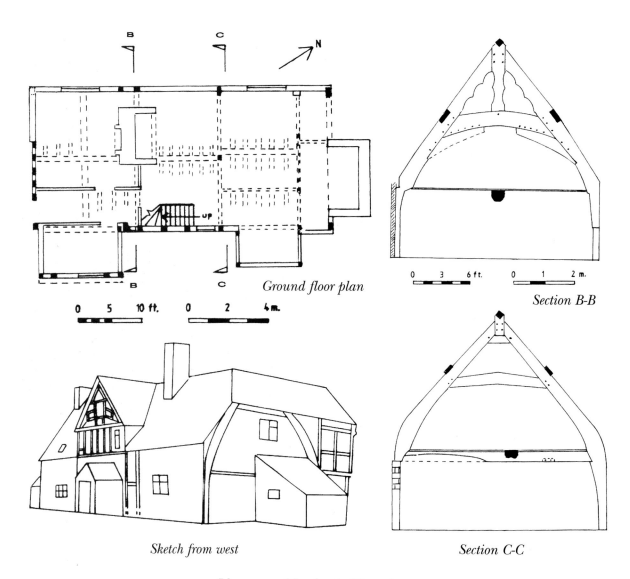

Ground floor plan

Section B-B

Sketch from west

Section C-C

Llwyn-y-go, Maesbrook, Kinnerley

Llwyn-y-go, Maesbrook (SJ 315212)
This is basically a three-part plan cruck-built house of which four cruck trusses survive and represent a two-bay open hall and storied end. The central open truss has an arch-braced cambered collar-beam with a cusped king-post above the collar. The tops of the crucks are also cusped. At the rear are two projecting 17th-century box-framed wings making a ¹/₂H-shaped plan. Many subsequent additions.[74]

Leebotwood

St. Mary's Church (SO 471986)
Although the policy of this book is to exclude churches, an exception is made in the case of the one remaining medieval truss in Leebotwood. Noteworthy are the carved *amphisbaenae* (mythical winged dragon with a head at each end) (see alongside) in the spandrels formed by

the collar and the arch-braces. They also occur at Llananno church in Radnorshire and in Much Wenlock Priory where they appear as foxes.

Penkridge Hall (SO 490976)
On the perimeter of the D.M.V. site of Lydley Hayes, this box-framed, two-storied house was built by Rowland Whitbrooke in 1590. Part of the stone basement is likely to have been a concealed chapel. The Whitbrookes were known catholics and a concealed stair connects the chapel with the fireplace above. The plan of the

Amphisbaenae *in Leebotwood church*

superstructure is simply two rooms on each floor, one small and one large. There are two garderobes, one of which is clearly exposed, fine panelling, fragments of wallpainting and a fireplace with double-ovolo-and-quirk moulding. The attic has 32 windbraces and a partitioned-off cubicle, the purpose of which is not known. Externally the framing displays a mixture of the 'Shrewsbury school' and the 'Ludlow school' with the 'Ludlow lazy jetty' a distinctive feature. Also surviving is the detached kitchen, now enlarged and converted to a cottage.

Leighton

Eye Farm (SJ 602052)
An isolated two-storied, box-framed, three-part plan-in-line house which seems to have been built with an open hall and screens passage, although this is debatable. A large chimneystack, built in two phases, blocks the passage and creates a lobby-entry. The small solar end was originally unheated, but a front chimney has been added. In the Raby Castle documents is a lease dated 1559, a condition of which specifies that a new house is 'to have a hall with a chamber over and a cross chamber at the end and a 3-tunnel

West elevation of Eye Farm, Leighton

chimney'. The house was to be built within 10 years. This only partly fits the present house, but there it may be that the specification was not carried out.

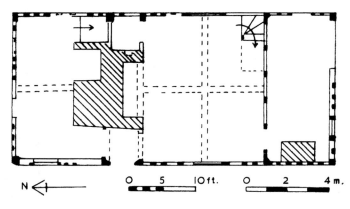
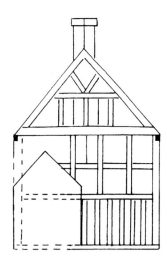

Eye Farm, Leighton
Left: ground floor plan; right: north elevation

Lilleshall

Barrack Houses (SJ 734165)
This row of 12 single-celled (originally *c*.20), brick-built industrial cottages was one of several in the area. They were built originally to house single men working in the limestone quarries, but later housed whole families. One row further to the east has been converted to attractive single-storey dwellings and there are other examples.[75]

Lilleshall Grange (SJ 730145)
A former granary, four-bayed and three-storied, stone-built and with a dated tablet, 1653. There is much reused stone and timber, presumably from the abbey.

9 Church Road (SJ 726152)
A 17th-century yeoman-type farmhouse, 1½-storied, three-bayed and square-framed, three panels high, with a lobby-entry. A text-book example of its kind.

Cruck truss in Lower House Farm, Little Ness

The Cottage (SJ 725149)
The little settlement at the south-west end of the village appears to have started as a squatters' site, and The Cottage is a typical example. Although much enlarged it began with a large stack and one room to the north-west.

Little Ness

Lower House Farm (SJ 407197)
Interlocked with a complicated set of later buildings are four bays of a cruck house in which a

two-bay open hall incorporating a low beam can be identified. The whole may have been a long-house. The central truss has crucks measuring 2ft. 6in. (0.76m.) at the elbow, but very plain.

Little Wenlock

Upper Huntington Farm (SJ 653081)
Externally the house presents a two-storied, three-bayed appearance; brick-built and with three dormer-gables, but internal details suggest that it was timber-framed and that the layout was that of a hunting lodge with a large hall and a small parlour at ground level. There are remarkably good moulded ceiling beams in the hall.

Llanfair Waterdine

Trebert (SO 256757)
Though ruinous, this seems to have been the manor house of a D.M.V. One truss is either a spere-truss or the central truss of the hall. It has much cusping and is smoke-blackened.

Llanyblodwell

Tanat House (SJ 240229)
A five-bayed, two-storied, double-pile house with a stone frontage of 1747 onto an earlier structure. The rear unit has three pairs of upper crucks in the roof. A main structural wall runs through the centre, dividing the front and rear units, and is broken by two chimneystacks and an octagon lantern.

Longnor

Moat House (SJ 494002)
Undoubtedly the finest box-framed house in the county. A detailed description is given in chapter 4.

Loppington

Blacksmith's Arms (SJ 470292)
An 'inn-and-blacksmith' complex at the entrance to the village.

Newholme (SJ 464286)
A stone-built, two-bay, two-storied cottage, now cement rendered. The cement is worked to resemble 'antique' timbers giving a square-framed effect and painted black and white, even the 'pegs' are imitated in cement. This process has been noted elsewhere in north Shropshire.[76]

Spenford House (SJ 472295)
This is either a T- or L-shaped house with a box-framed, two-bay, two-storied parlour unit at the front which is square-framed and four panels high. The gable has close-studding to the ground floor, square-framing to the upper storey and diagonal studding to the attic. It is notable for its hewn jetty.

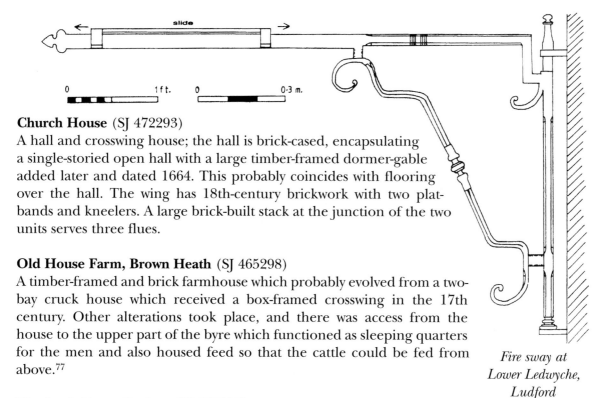

Church House (SJ 472293)

A hall and crosswing house; the hall is brick-cased, encapsulating a single-storied open hall with a large timber-framed dormer-gable added later and dated 1664. This probably coincides with flooring over the hall. The wing has 18th-century brickwork with two plat-bands and kneelers. A large brick-built stack at the junction of the two units serves three flues.

Old House Farm, Brown Heath (SJ 465298)

A timber-framed and brick farmhouse which probably evolved from a two-bay cruck house which received a box-framed crosswing in the 17th century. Other alterations took place, and there was access from the house to the upper part of the byre which functioned as sleeping quarters for the men and also housed feed so that the cattle could be fed from above.[77]

Fire sway at Lower Ledwyche, Ludford

Hatchett's Farm, Burlton (SJ 458261)

Now an L-shaped complex, it is an amalgamation of two box-framed houses, brick-cased and much altered. At the rear is a stair wing and a separate outside stair to the mens' room.

Ludford

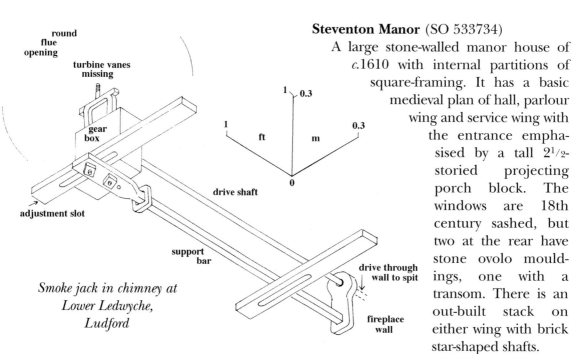

Smoke jack in chimney at Lower Ledwyche, Ludford

Steventon Manor (SO 533734)

A large stone-walled manor house of *c.*1610 with internal partitions of square-framing. It has a basic medieval plan of hall, parlour wing and service wing with the entrance empha-sised by a tall 2½-storied projecting porch block. The windows are 18th century sashed, but two at the rear have stone ovolo mould-ings, one with a transom. There is an out-built stack on either wing with brick star-shaped shafts.

Lower Ledwyche (SO 536746)
A three-storied farmhouse, brick-built throughout in English garden wall bond. The front unit is five-bayed but with an asymmetrical entrance. The sash windows are of about 1800. There are industrial king-post trusses in the roof. The fireplace in the main room has an iron 'sway' and a spit-rack, but in the chimney is an almost complete smoke-jack—only the rotor blades are missing. The house appears to be in an elevated position on an old moated site.

Lydbury North

The Red House (SO 365860)
Once a coaching inn on the old Craven Arms to Bishop's Castle road, the name reflects its unusual brick construction. It is symmetrically planned with two identical square rooms each with one smaller square room leading off on each level. Four-storied, with the recessed entrance at first-floor level reached by a flight of steps. The original kitchen occupied the whole of the south side of the lower

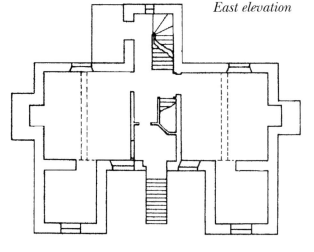

East elevation

0 1 2 3 4 5 10 feet.   0 1 2 3 4 metres.

Ground floor plan

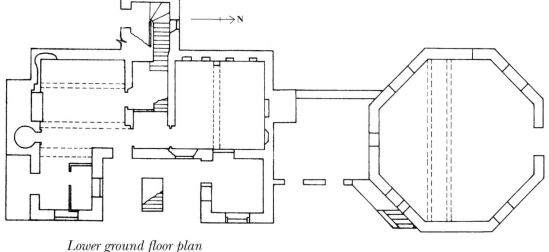

Lower ground floor plan

The Red House and cockpit, Lydbury North

ground floor, and the well, bake-oven, pump and cooking range survive. Close to the house is a stone octagonal cockpit with a wood-shingled roof. The house and the cockpit have associations with Clive of India who owned the mansion of Walcot nearby.[78]

Plowden Hall

Plowden Hall
(SO 7375866)
Home of the Plowden family since the time of the crusades this is a 'key' Shropshire building, displaying building phases of each century since the 14th. The earliest part, a base-cruck hall which has a crown-post roof of superior construction, is dendro-dated to 1302. A solar wing was added in 1454 and this has lavish cusping in its roof trusses. 'Lawyer Plowden's wing' was added in the late 16th century. His memorial is in Temple church in London. Never fully modernised, the house remains an unsurpassed example of English house evolution.[78]

Lea Castle Farm, Lydham
Top left: Woven oak panels in the barn; lower left: Goose-pens; right: Stairs to the mens' room

Walcot (SO 348850)

Within the grounds of the mansion is a stone 'beehive' dovecote with dormers and a central lantern. Also a very good range of farm buildings.

Lydham

Lea Castle Farm (SO 352893)

The house was modernised in the late 19th century and incorporates brickwork on the frontage, but there are older stone walls and fragments of timber-framing. A datestone of 1560 has been moved to the front. The present kitchen preserves a stair-ladder to the mens' room. The farm buildings include good barns, cowsheds and some goose-pens. The remains of the castle are joined onto the farmhouse at the rear, but they form a separate unit.

Madeley

King Charles' Barn, Church Street (SJ 695043)

Two ranges set at right angles, the so-called King's Barn flanking Church Street on the south side. This is box-framed, with five main bays plus two added at the west end. Originally it was single-storied, but has been excavated below floor level to full storey height and underpinned with cast iron pillars. The trusses are of different forms and incorporate some unusual carpenters' marks. The street frontage has inserted dormer windows with Y-type tracery and cast iron lattices. The other unit has a brick exterior of two dates. The better brickwork is dated 1765, suggesting that this was when a five-bay cruck barn was converted to a coachhouse. This unit is also excavated and underpinned.

Market Drayton

This town suffered from a major fire in 1651 and a group of timber-framed buildings appear to date from the rebuilding and to have survived subsequent fires and modernisation. They vary in size but in plan they are consistently of two bays with a central stack. Styling takes the form of close-studding with a mid-rail to the ground floor, herringbone-work above and, if a third storey is included, this has lozenge work. Within this group or closely related to it are the following seven examples:

Sandbrook Vaults, Shropshire St. (SJ 675342)

Dated HRE 1653, box-framed and jettied at two levels. The styling is as described above and the main bressumer is carved along its length with paired stylised dragons with protruding tongues, very similar to those on a plaque at Hazlewood Farm, Darliston, in Prees parish which is dated 1655, and to those on a frieze in the hall at Bitterley Court of a similar date.

*Bressumer with dragons
at Sandbrook Vaults, Market Drayton*

Tudor House, Cheshire St. (SJ 675342)
This also is dated 1653 and adjoins the above. The construction is similar but the decoration on the bressumer is simpler, consisting of a wave theme with leaves. Tudor House returns, forming the corner with Cheshire Street.

Cheshire Cheese Inn /Gingerbread Café (SJ 664333)
Situated on the corner of High Street and Cheshire Street this property, said

Sandbrook Vaults

to date from 1664, conforms to the design described above.

The Crown Inn (SJ 676344)
On the corner of Queen Street and Stafford Street, this also conforms to the design, the close-studding with mid-rail being displayed prominently along the Queen Street elevation.

9 Stafford Street (SJ 677344)
Although the timbering has largely gone this is a small version of the design set gable-end on to the street. Single-storied with use made of the roofspace.

27 Shropshire Street (SJ 675342)
Similar to the above, but retaining close-studding to the gable end and with square-framing at the sides.

The Star Hotel, Stafford Street (SJ 673346)
Dated 1669 but still fully timber-framed with diagonal strutting to the second storey and cusped and spiked lozenges to the twin gables. A projecting two-storied porch has a slightly different pattern above the window.

The Old House, Shropshire Street (SJ 675341)
A stylish house, probably built by the Corbet family soon after a fire in Shropshire Street in the 1670s. Many of the timbers are reused and show signs of charring. Of brick, the five-bay frontage has a projecting central bay which extends to accommodate a large semicircular pediment to the central dormer. The symmetrical façade does not relate to the internal plan which consists of two rooms on each floor, one large and one small. The original kitchen is in the cellar but a service extension was added at the rear and this contains a cream oven.

The Old House, Shropshire Street

Most of the windows have been renewed but the original ones which survive at the rear have ovolo-moulded sashes. The house has good panelling with bolection moulding in the parlour.

Plas Gwynne, Shropshire Street (SJ 674341)
Basically a box-framed townhouse of the 1660s, the house is now brick-cased and rendered, with timbers exposed only in the gable. The gap between the framing and the casing can be seen behind the window shutters. The cellars are excavated from the natural sandstone. A central stone stack serves two rooms on each floor and one fireplace in the attic which contains a concealed chamber—a priest's room? The ground-floor parlour fireplace has a stone over-mantel with acanthus leaf relief carving. Wallpaintings in an upper room are described in chapter 13. The house was built by Philip Cotton who was involved with the slave trade. A good inventory exists and names the rooms which still relate to the plan. It is possible that there are the remains of a dog-wheel in the kitchen. Five spits are listed.

Kilnbank Croft (SJ 674339)
Mostly 19th century of brick and stone, but interesting because it incorporates an old barn which was hewn from the natural rock that forms the walls on three sides. On one side the rock is to wall-plate level and on another to the windowsill.

34 Great Hales Street (SJ 680344)
A late medieval box-framed house well disguised with a Victorian brick 'skin' on the front and on the south side, but on the north side the jettied lateral wall has close-studding to both upper and lower stories and a brattished bressumer. The 'hall' section has quarter-round moulding on the wall-plate. The complex may have been U-shaped originally; the south wing is now a separate house. In no.34 the modern hall has a floor of decorative Maw's tiles.

Melverley

Foxglove Cottage (SJ 328185)
Once the village shop, this is basically a box-framed single cell cottage with an end chimney baffle-entry. Although much altered and extended, it preserves the remains of a wattle-and-daub smoke-hood or 'fumbrell'.

Ensdon House (SJ 415169)
A double-pile, brick-built, five-bay and $2^1/_2$-storied farmhouse of *c.*1770. The three central bays project and terminate with a lighted gable pediment. The windows have been altered, but two venetian windows at ground level in the side wall seem original. It was once a coaching inn on the A5 and the large stableblocks relate to this phase.

Monkhopton

Great Oxenbold (SO 594920)
Built as a 'retreat' for the prior of Wenlock in 1247 this farmhouse consists of two parts, his hall and chapel. A detailed account has been published.[80]

Montford

Grafton House (SJ 432190)

The older part of the house appears to be a surviving crosswing from an earlier complex. It is square-panelled, five panels high, and is a two-bay unit with a central stack, *c.*1620. The tie-beam is slightly jettied and has ovolo moulding with pyramid stops. Supporting ornamental brackets have a scroll pattern and entwined hearts. In the courtyard the cobbled surface has a motif dated S.E. 1754. This may date the 18th-century addition to the house.

More Farm, More

More

More Farm (SO 340922)

An L-shaped box-framed farmhouse of *c.*1600-20. The hall is comparatively small and is two-storied. The crosswing is the prestigious unit, and this has all rectangular framing with a jettied gable, moulded tie-beam and carved brackets. An added porch has the inscription 'Repaired MDCCCXLIX'. At the rear is a full-length stair turret with a central chute presumably for hoisting grain.

Church Farm (SO 344915)

Two timber-framed gables face the road, each with close-studding and a mid-rail, but they seem to be of different dates and one has a hewn jetty. There is no front door and the rear of the house is unlike the front. There is a lobby-entry and the girding-beam has brattished moulding. The southern unit is possibly the older and contains a chequerboard ceiling in the main room. The other unit has elaborately moulded beams which suggest a reuse. An extension at the rear of the northern unit has stencilled decoration on each wall that is described in chapter 13. The farm buildings are on a courtyard plan and include a granary with a dog kennel incorporated in the steps.

Moreton Say

Oldfields Farm (SJ 629364)

The remains of a base-cruck two-bay hall and its dais end remain in the complex. A detailed account has been published.[81]

Munslow

21 Hungerford (SO 539895)

Of nondescript appearance and much enlarged and altered from its original cruck-built form, the cottage is remarkable for having a square-framed truss with wattle-and-daub infill dividing

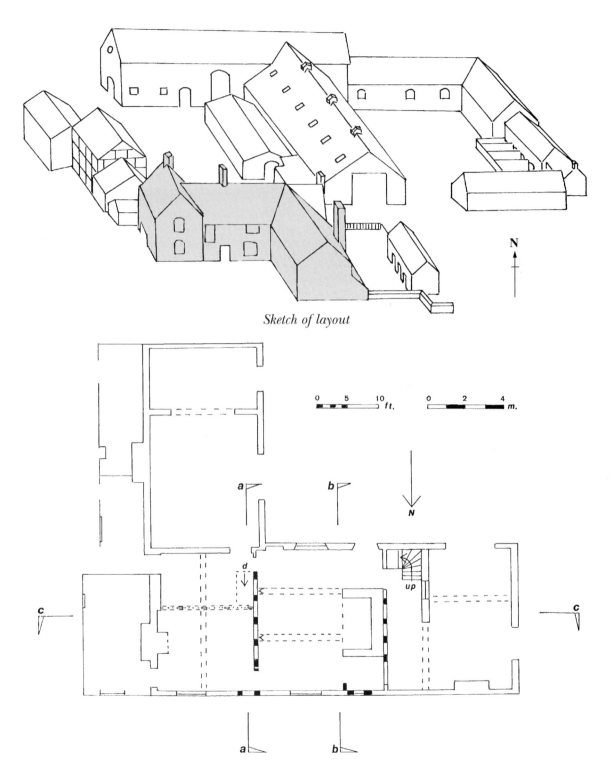

Sketch of layout

Ground floor plan of the house (shaded on the sketch plan above). The sketch plan was taken from an earlier aerial photo before some alterations were done to the house, so there are some differences

Oldfields Farm, Moreton Say

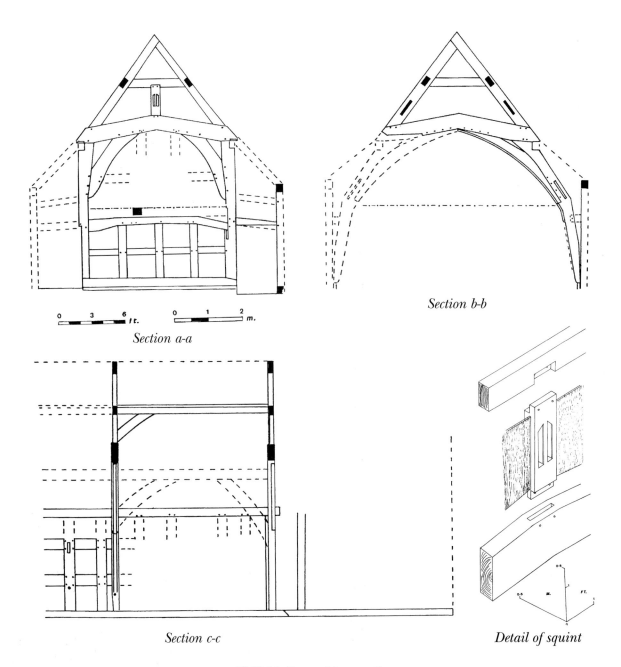

Section a-a

Section b-b

Section c-c

Detail of squint

Oldfields Farm, Moreton Say

the space longitudinally. This suggests either that it was designed as two back-to-back single-cell dwellings or became such later.

The Old School (SO 523875)

Stone-built and three-storied, this is basically a 17th-century 'hall-and-crosswing' house to which has been added a 19th-century school block in a matching style. The older range is dated BAI [John and Alice Baldwin] 1658 and has chamfered mullioned and transomed windows, a bolection-moulded fireplace and two ovolo-moulded spine beams in a ground-floor room.

Munslow Farm (SO 524974)

A farmhouse of two distinct parts. The northern unit is stone-built and two-storied with a hipped roof. This unit probably replaced an earlier house to which was added the brick southern unit which was a self-contained parlour wing, *c.*1660-70. The stone block contains a fireplace over which is a spit-rack and housing for a dog-wheel. The brick unit is built with a bond consisting mostly of two rows of stretchers and one row of headers and stretchers. The ground-floor window has sliding shutters and there is a 17th-century staircase with turned balusters and a string. The remarkable set of painted cloths is described in chapter 13.

The Forester's Lodge, Upper Millichope (SO 521894)

A stone-built, first-floor hall house of the late 13th century with walls 6ft. (1.83m.) thick. Traditionally the home of the head forester in a royal hunting preserve who was required to provide venison for the priory at Much Wenlock. Many features relate to comfort and to defence. Particularly significant are two windows in the hall which have fitted window seats, decorative moulding—and draw-bolts. Strangely the massive joists of both floors, wrought from whole or half trees very closely spaced, which were thought to be original features, yielded dendro dates of 1450 and 1633. Presumably the latter date was when refurbishment took place and the carpenters simply copied the form of the original.[82]

Myddle

Several houses in Myddle can be related to the transplanted houses mentioned in Richard Gough's *History of Myddle* written in 1701. They are the subject of a published article.[83] Others are mentioned in chapter 2 and a further selection includes:

Castle Farm (SJ 469236)

The present house is a modern replacement, but most of the farm buildings relate to the old house. They include a triple-bay stone cart-shed and a brick granary over another stone cart-shed. This has a dog kennel in the steps. Among others is a smaller brick building which has a swill-chute at ground level and steps to the upper floor. Its purpose is unclear. The remains of Myddle Castle are contained within the curtilage of the farm.

Newton Farm, Newton-on-the-Hill (SJ 485234)

This is Gough's old home, now much extended and roughcast, but basically a stone-built, two-storied and two-bayed farmhouse with a lobby-entry. It has what Gough would call an 'apart-ment' forming the first addition, perhaps accommodation for an elderly relative, and this contains a recognisable fumbrell (for illustrations see overleaf).

Houlston Manor (SJ 479248)

In Gough's time this was Broomhurst Farm, a brick-built, four-bayed and two-storied farmhouse of double-pile plan. The farm lands, like others in the area, are claimed from a drained mere. Cheese production was paramount. There are some dated bricks (1913) in the farm buildings.

2 Lower Road (SJ 481226)

Sandstone roadside cottage, now two-up, two-down but originally 1^1/$_2$-storied with a single ground-floor room and an end chimney. This is probably a survivor from Gough's time (see photo overleaf).

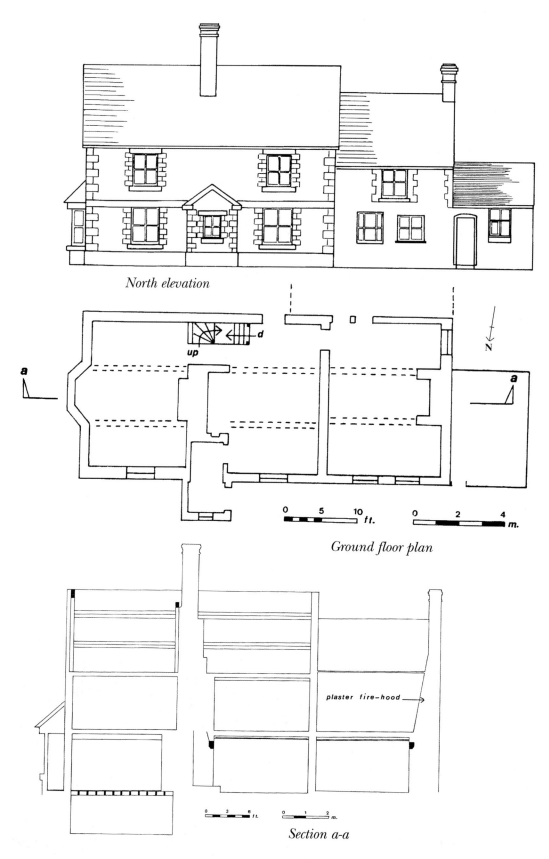

North elevation

Ground floor plan

up

d

N

a

a

0 5 10 ft.

0 2 4 m.

plaster fire-hood

0 3 6 ft.

0 1 2 m.

Section a-a

Newton Farm, Newton-on-the-Hill, Myddle

2 Lower Road, Myddle

Balderton Hall (SJ 482239)
A timber-framed, H-shaped farmhouse with additions. Gough said 'William Nicolas built most part of Balderton Hall - viz all except that crosse building called the kitchen end'. This would be *c.*1570-80 and the 'crosse end' is likely to be one of the rear wings. The hall ceiling has joists running front to back for about two-thirds of the area and side to side for the rest. There is no obvious reason for this. A large out-built stack on the west wing incorporates a fire window at both upper and lower levels.[84]

Alderton Farm (SJ 496241)
A three-bayed and two-storied farmhouse of double-pile plan with an M-shaped roof, each unit hipped at one end and gabled at the other. Flemish-bonded brickwork. The farm buildings include a ginny-ring.

The Warren (SJ 491222)
At one time the village shop and post office, this is basically a small sandstone cottage, 1½-storied and two-bayed with an attached byre and pigsties. In the late 1590s the Egertons, then lords of the manor, established a warren and appointed a warrener/labourer who also sold ale.[85]

Smithy Cottage (SJ 472238)
A three-bay, 1½-storied sandstone cottage with a brick-vaulted sandstone cellar. It is said that at one time this was an inn called the Three Crowns on account of the crown-shaped chimney pots, two of which remain in the garden. By 1851 it was The Blacksmith's Arms. Gough said that 'Zacharias [Wolph] was a blacksmith and built a Smyth's shop on the side of Myddle hill near the towne's end'. The smithy is opposite the house.[86]

The Toll House, Marton (SJ 445239)
The Marton Road was improved and turnpiked in 1829. This dates the toll-house which is of stone and with characteristic wide overhanging eaves. It has a five-sided frontage to the road, whilst the straight back gives the cottage a curious 'chopped off' appearance.

The Toll House, Marton

467

Marton Hall (SJ 443238)

A large E-shaped house in red sandstone, built in 1914 in Tudor style with mullioned and transomed windows for Colonel Gosling, but he was killed in the war. Over the front door is the family crest with the motto 'JE TIENS FERME' (I hold firm), and over the rear door is a plaque with three squirrels among branches, oak leaves and acorns. It is remarkable how the craftsman has worked the rough local sandstone to such fine detail.

The Tan House, Marton (SJ 440238)

Built by Thomas Atcherley, a tanner, of the old Marton Hall in the early 17th century, this is basically a single-storied, three-bayed, square-framed building which has had a large dormer inserted.[87]

Burlton Lane Farm (SJ 465249)

A good courtyard range of farm buildings, timber-framed, mostly with reused timbers, and always brick-nogged.

Neen Savage

Detton Hall (SO 666795)

A large farmhouse complex of piecemeal development, the earliest unit is a two-storied timber-framed wing on the west side. This has a pronounced three-sided jetty and is probably the parlour wing to a vanished hall. It is dendro-dated to 1575-6. A linking block contains a 17th-century open-well staircase in which are panels pierced with geometric shapes. Then comes a dendro-dated (1625-59) hall with chamber above which was extended shortly afterwards by a service wing which contains the mens' room. This has a separate compartment (possibly for a senior member) and a fireplace. The wing is served by a spiral oak staircase in its own turret. A feature of Detton Hall is its four chimneystacks, one of which has diaper brickwork.[88]

Detton Hall, Neen Savage, its staircase below

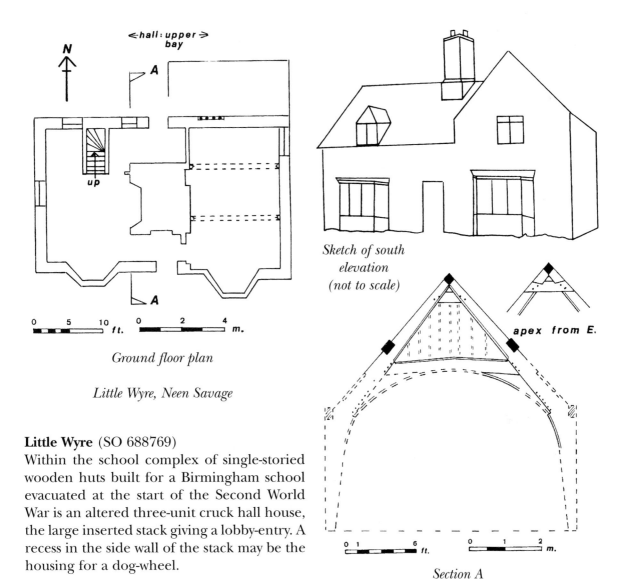

<hall : upper > bay

N

A

up

A

0 5 10 ft. 0 2 4 m.

Ground floor plan

Little Wyre, Neen Savage

Sketch of south elevation (not to scale)

apex from E.

0 1 6 ft. 0 1 2 m.

Section A

Little Wyre (SO 688769)
Within the school complex of single-storied wooden huts built for a Birmingham school evacuated at the start of the Second World War is an altered three-unit cruck hall house, the large inserted stack giving a lobby-entry. A recess in the side wall of the stack may be the housing for a dog-wheel.

Stone House Farm (SO 664772)
An H-shaped farmhouse dated 1639 and thought to be by Thomas Winn. Now it has a symmetrical appearance, but the windows are much altered and there is an arched stone doorway on the east wing with the inscription T T 0 A T and T T 0 E T.

Neenton

Churchyard Farm (SO 636876)
A box-framed house of *c*.1620 of the 'hall-and-crosswing' plan, but as the wing does not project there is a continuous bressumer serving a shallow jetty and this has double-ovolo-and-quirk moulding. The moulding is repeated on the principal rafter. The upper room in the wing has striking wallpaintings, for which see chapter 13.

Bank Farm (SO 641882)

A 17th-century, square-framed farmhouse of two-up, two-down design with a lobby-entry, but there is an added bay in brick which is partially underground and fitted out as a kitchen and dairy.

Hall Farm (SO 637879)

A stone-walled T-shaped farmhouse. Apart from the interest of the crucks in the cross piece of the T and also in the barn, the stem of the T contains the remains of an open hall and here it seems that the hall was heated by an open hearth against the central truss which had a smoke-hood to draw the smoke. Only one side is blackened.

Newport

The Guildhall, High Street (SJ 746189)

If Newport can be said to have a 'key' building it is surely the Guildhall. For many years sub-divided into three tenements it has recently been restored. The Guildhall itself is the south wing, set gable-end on, close-studded and containing four bays, the two central bays forming a fine open hall with mouldings and a highly decorative roof having cusped and pierced quatrefoil windbracing, an open entrance bay and a floored bay beyond the hall. This unit is dendro-dated to 1487. An extension was built at right-angles to it in 1546 and this had a lobby-entry. Both units contain wallpaintings (see chapter 13). In Victorian times a 'matching' wing in brick with applied timbers was added at the northern end and the whole was 'unified' to resemble a fully-developed medieval timber-framed house.[89]

East elevation of The Guildhall complex, Newport

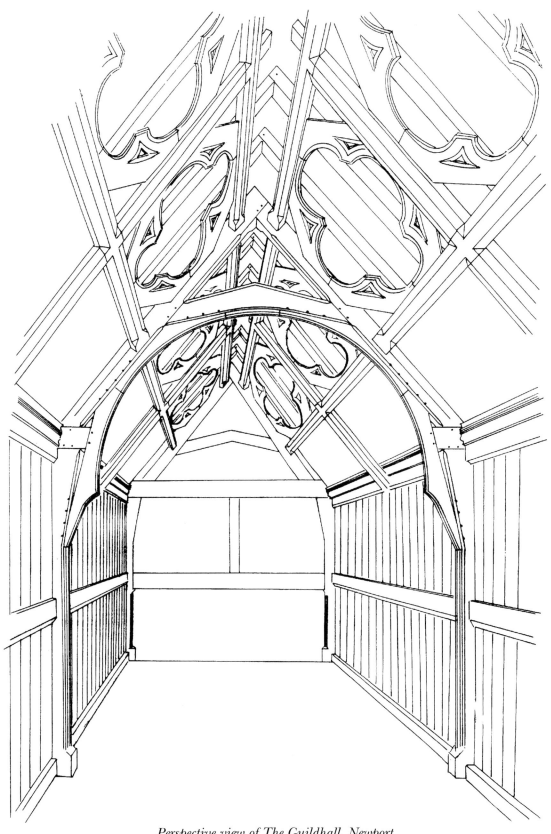

Perspective view of The Guildhall, Newport

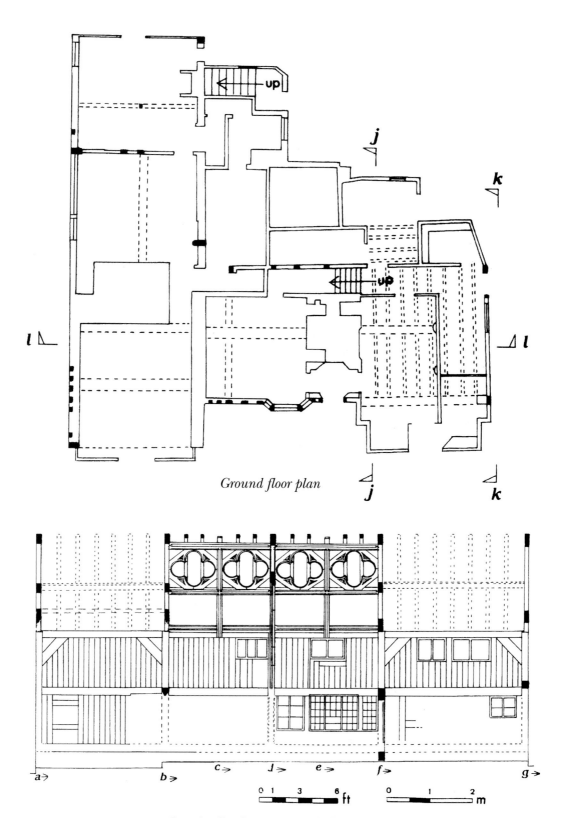

Ground floor plan

0 1 3 6 ft

0 1 2 m

Longitudinal section m-m looking south

The Guildhall complex, Newport

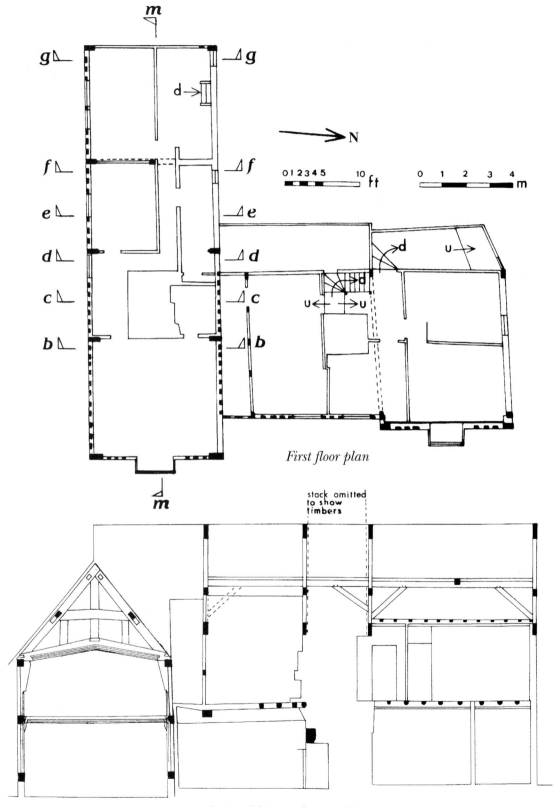

First floor plan

stack omitted
to show
timbers

Section l-l (to scale opposite)

The Guildhall complex, Newport

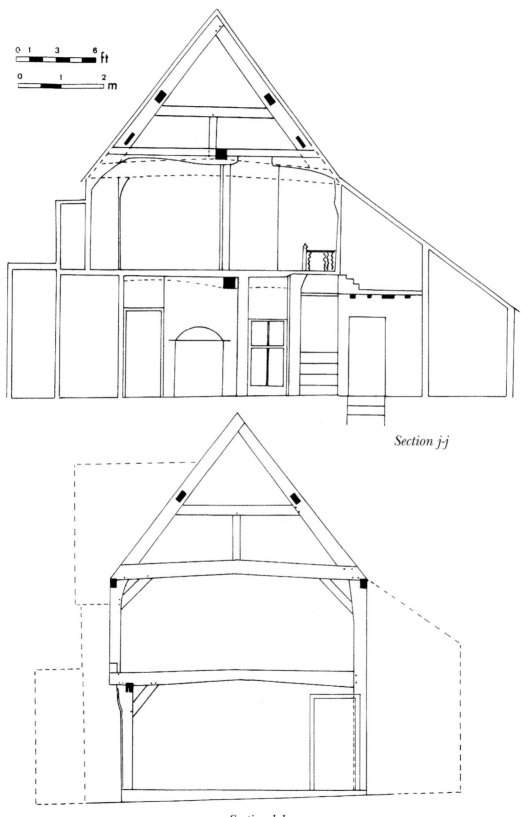

Section j-j

Section k-k
The Guildhall complex, Newport

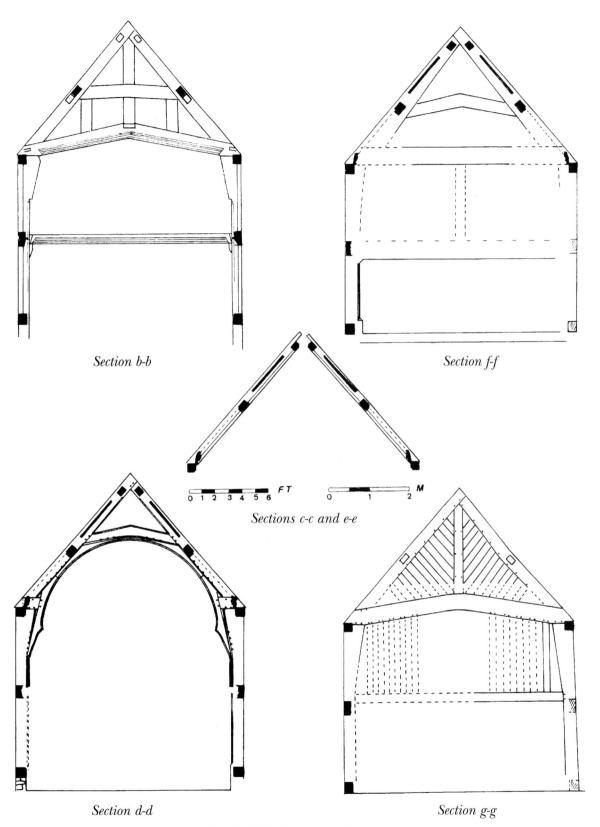

Section b-b

Section f-f

Sections c-c and e-e

FT
0 1 2 3 4 5 6

M
0 1 2

Section d-d

Section g-g

The Guildhall complex, Newport

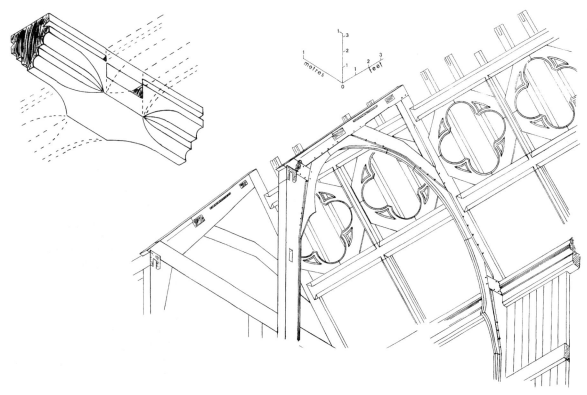

Reconstruction of central bays with inset of moulded joists reused as rafters in east bay

The Guildhall, Newport

Salter's Hall, Newport

Salter's Hall (SJ 742192)
Adjoining St. Peter and St. Paul's catholic church in Salter's Lane, this is the residence of the priest. In 1832 Joseph Potter and Son built the church and remodelled the Hall. Some 17th-century work remains inside and there is an echo of a still earlier screens passage. J. Salter was an eminent lawyer and a member of the Council in the Marches and it is no accident that St. Winefred has a window in the church—the Salters had salt-mining rights centred at Holywell in Flintshire. In 1521 he was Sheriff of Shropshire, but in 1579 the Council was ordered to investigate the well and to destroy it if its waters were not medicinal.[90]

11 Upper Bar (SJ 746186)

In its original form this was box-framed throughout and consisted of a three-bayed and two-storied hall range, jettied towards the street, with a single-bay parlour wing roofed at right angles but not projecting beyond the rectilinear hall. Though much disguised with roughcast and plaster, it represents an early example of suburban development in the town. Probably early 17th century.

20-24 St. Mary's Street (SJ 745192)

Though much altered and sub-divided the combined properties comprise six timber-framed bays of roughly the same size: 12ft. (3.7m.) square. Stylistically the framework suggests a date *c.*1560-80 and may represent post-Reformation building on the site of the medieval college of St. Mary, possibly taking the form of shops at ground level with jettied chambers above.

34 St. Mary's Street (SJ 745192)

This property is typical of the 'unit' house with a shop at the front and a parlour and kitchen behind. It has a narrow frontage, extends down the burgage plot and has a side-passage entry.[91] At the upper-floor level the shop extends across the passage. Little framework

Fish smoking house at 34 St. Mary's Street, Newport

is exposed. In the cellar there is a stretch of stone walling which does not relate to the present structure and could be the remnant of a medieval building, perhaps relating to the parish church. A tall, narrow brick building to the rear of the plot is a fish-smoking house. It is known that the property was once owned by a fishmonger.

Possible gallery at rear of 91 High Street, Newport

91 High Street (SJ 744193)

At the rear of the lateral wall there is a marked overhang supported by a carved bracket, suggestive of the remains of a spinning or knitting gallery of some kind. Its neighbour, no.93, is another side-passage house.

The old Star Inn, High Street (SJ 746190)

Contained in the building about 3ft. (0.9m.) from the present building line is a bressumer relating to an earlier framed house. It has ovolo moulding and is weathered.

The soffit has mortices indicating that the ground floor was close-studded. Its position suggests that the High Street was once even wider than it is at present.

Ivydene, Lower Bar (SJ 745193)

The early 18th-century frontage is clearly an attempt to emulate the larger building—Beaumaris House of 1720—which stood opposite. Encapsulated within Ivydene is a box-framed earlier house, the roof-line of which is exposed at attic level. Many building phases may be identified and a rear wing contains the entrance hall and staircase. The balusters are of cast-iron worked as decorative panels, and cast iron window frames are present in the east gable. At one time this wing was used as a school. A service block accommodates a trap-house, grooms' quarters and a bake-oven.

Norbury

Hardwick Hall (SO 369906)

A timber-framed house of three or four main phases, the earliest of which retains three cruck trusses. Two later units form a double-pile plan, but they are not contemporary. A large, elaborate, two-storied and jettied porch was added to the cruck range and this has concave lozenge work, diagonal strutting and rectangular panels. It was the home of the Ambler family from the 1580s to the 1900s.

Bellaport Old Hall in 1927

Norton-in-Hales

Bellaport Old Hall
(SJ 709405)

A Z-shaped isolated farmhouse, stuccoed. It was probably constructed from salvaged stone and brick from the old Bellaport which reputedly occupied the mound in the field in front of the house. The present house once had crow-stepped gables. Bellaport was the home of the Cotton family of Alkington Hall, Whitchurch. Sir Rowland Cotton and his wife, Lady Frances, have their tomb in Norton church.[92]

Bellaport Hall Farm (SJ 698407)

Reputedly the Home Farm to Bellaport, it is brick-built with two small projecting wings and a recessed front. There is an abundance of curvilinear gables, which also occur on the stable-block. They are reminiscent of the crow-stepped gable treatment at Bellaport Old Hall and at Alkington Hall—clearly a Cotton preference. Like the Old Hall, the Hall Farm has the site of another house in close proximity. In this case it was known as Bellaport Towers on account of the many turrets that it displayed.[93]

Ridgwardine Manor (SJ 680382)

A full recording of this house has been published.[94]

The Hayes, Oswestry
Left: front door of 1656; above: chimneys

Onibury

Padmore (SO 464794)
A medieval hall house with some unique features, it was destroyed in 1980. A detailed account has been published.[95]

Oswestry

The Hayes (SJ 282302)
Stone-built of Sweeney Mountain sandstone, this building is of unusual cruciform shape centred on a large 10-flue chimneystack with octagonal shafts. All the older windows are single mullion-and-transom with ovolo moulding. It has a good front door and moulded doorcase with a flattened four-centre arch. There are some good fireplaces, one is dated DRM 1656 (Ralph Davenport) and this could date the house. The fireplace at ground-floor level is earlier and has probably been imported—it has a carved overmantel with dolphins and carvings similar to those of the Ludlow school of carpentry. It also has a central carved rose.[96]

Oswestry Rural

Bryn-y-Pentre, Trefonen (SO 238260)
At the back of the present house is the earlier dwelling, a slightly superior cruck-trussed long-house, now used for storage. The central truss has a cambered collar-beam supporting a king-post which supports the ridge. There is no cusping, but the whole truss is chamfered. There is a large inserted stack, a croglofft, evidence of a cross passage and of access to the byre (illustrations overleaf).

479

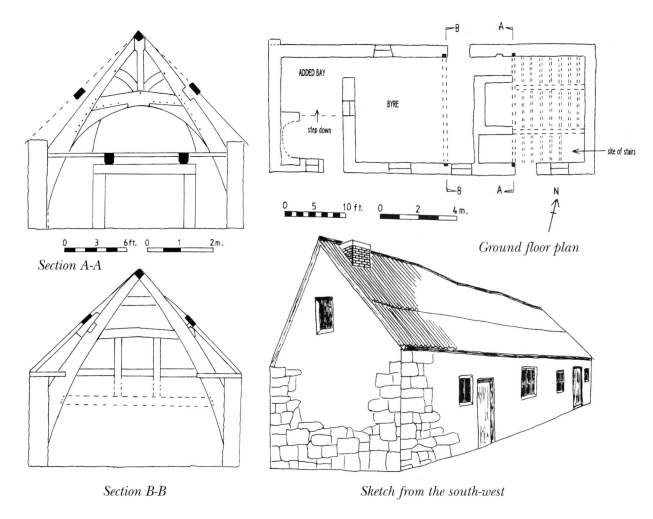

Section A-A

Ground floor plan

Section B-B

Sketch from the south-west

Bryn-y-Pentre, Oswestry Rural

Gibraltar Inn, Treflach Wood (SJ 261252)

Said to have been a farmhouse in 1605 this building became an inn in 1750, taking its name from a reward given to a serving officer at the second or third storming of Gibraltar. It has longhouse origins with a hayloft above the byre.[97]

Heated garden wall at Llanforda Hall

Llanforda Hall Gardens
(SJ 265290)

This is included because part of the walled garden which remains from the 1780 house retains its heating from a fireplace which circulated hot air through the cavity wall. The bricks are laid in a random bond with lime mortar. Coping stones top the walls. Edward Lhuyd, the botanist / scientist, lived at Llanforda Hall.[98]

Llwyn-y-Maen (SJ 272283)
This is included for the courtyard 'model farm' layout of the farm buildings by Sir Watkins Williams Wynne, a 'great improver', probably in 1844 (date on the pigsties). Built of local limestone the walls are insulated with chaff between the inner and outer skins. There is an underground waterwheel dated 1851 which was in use until the 1960s for powering a milking machine. There was probably an earlier wheel: Edward Lluyd's notes include a 'pump house'.

Farm buildings of 1844 at Llwyn-y-Maen

East Farm, Crickheath (SJ 293230)
A box-framed, T-shaped farmhouse with a mixture of close-studding and square-framing. The side-entry porch was added in 1677 and has the initials R L and decorative baluster work. The kitchen contains the remains of a smoke-hood (fumbrell) and has a bake-oven.

Crickheath Hall (SJ 290230)
A timber-framed, U-shaped house of *c.*1600, currently symmetrical. It has a remarkable carved bressumer which encompasses the three units (see chapter 4). Internal features include an ovolo-moulded window in the parlour wing and a four-centre stone fireplace with mouldings in an upper room. Both projecting wings are 2^{1}/$_{2}$-storied, giving extensive attic accommodation.

Pimhill

Albrighton Hall (SJ 495182)
Now a hotel, this building is entirely brick-built, two-storied with attics. The six-bayed frontage has a hipped roof and overhanging eaves. There is good diaper work on the (east) front and on the (south) garden front. There are many notable tall chimneystacks, some with eight shafts. Interior details include a staircase with turned balusters, carved woodwork, embroidered wall panels and heraldic carvings incorporating the Ireland crest. Thomas Ireland is thought to have built the house *c.*1630. He was sheriff of Shropshire and a descendant of Robert Ireland who built Ireland's Mansion in Shrewsbury.

Lea Hall (SJ 493211)
Mostly built in English bond with vitrified headers forming diaper work, this is a stylish U-shaped house of 1584 (dated overmantel). Some blocked stone mullion-and-transom windows remain and these have straight chamfers and 'slotted-in' mullions. There are three-shafted star-shaped out-built stacks to each crosswing. Internally the partition walls are timber-framed and small internal jetties supported by scroll brackets occur on either wing. The great parlour has a classical overmantel with the date and the initials LRE (Richard and Elenor Lea), and there is some good panelling. It is thought that the plan of the house may have been reversed.

A brick dovecote, apparently coeval with the house, octagonal in plan and fully operational with a potence and over 400 nesting boxes is a feature to the west of the house.

Pitchford

Pitchford Hall (SJ 547043)
The house is well-known and Pevsner gives a lengthy description of it, but a few historical notes may be of interest. It is probably on the site of a lost village called Little Eton. The church contains many 12th-century features and may be the original church. John Sandford began work on the present hall soon after 1549, but there is evidence in the west wing of an earlier, crown-post roof construction. Sandford was warden of the Carpenters' Guild in 1545 and a freeman of Shrewsbury. The Ottley family seem not to have been on the scene before the 16th century. Royalists in the Civil War, Sir Francis was knighted in 1642 and made governor of Shrewsbury Castle in 1643. The famous tree house in the grounds is first referenced in 1714, but the 'cult of melancholy' which inspired tree arbours is a late 16th-century phenomenon and they are not associated with the type of formal gardens which were being laid out at Pitchford in 1714. There were paintings in the tree house in the style of the Italian Renaissance, but delicate plasterwork in the style of Thomas Farnolls Pritchard currently dominates the interior.[99]

New Top Farm (SJ 531037)
A box-framed two-storied farmhouse of three bays, *c.*1620. Reputedly this was one of the houses moved from the grounds of Pitchford Hall.

Pontesbury

Brookgate Farm, Plealy in 1992 (after restoration)

Brookgate Farm, Plealy
(SJ 424068)
A house remarkable for the combination of a single-bayed cruck hall and a contemporary elaborate spere-truss which has cusping, jowelled posts and a central boss. It is dendro-dated to 1490. There is a close-studded dais screen. The function of the two ends has changed—the original solar end later became a kitchen and was extended to the rear 1533-81, and the service end was replaced with a square-framed parlour wing of 1612. The position of the original hearth is *c.*5ft. from the spere-truss. Some original roofing slabs were recovered. They are similar to 'Harnage' but probably came from the Long Mountain.[100]

Sibberscot Barn (SJ 427077)
The current manor house is a box-framed hall and crosswing house, originally jettied but later brick-cased and with a two-storied porch. Its predecessor was a three-bayed cruck structure,

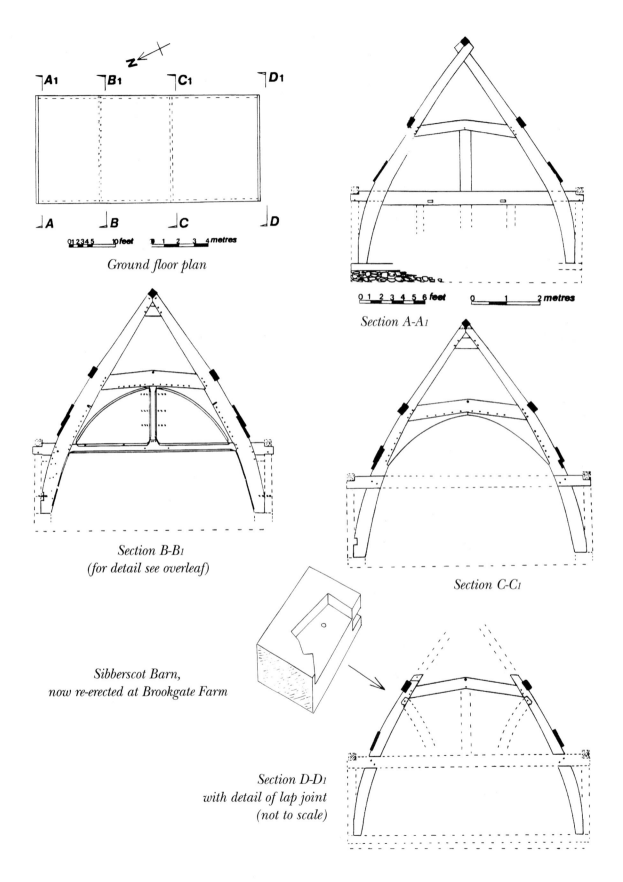

Ground floor plan

Section A-A1

Section B-B1
(for detail see overleaf)

Section C-C1

Sibberscot Barn,
now re-erected at Brookgate Farm

Section D-D1
with detail of lap joint
(not to scale)

483

Brookgate Farm, Plealy
Top: spere-truss; below: hall end truss

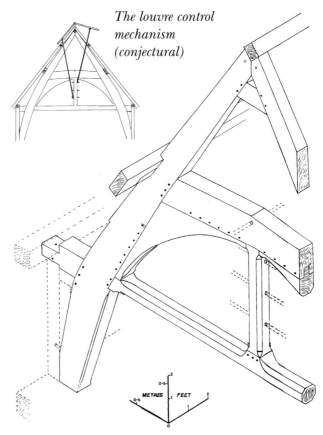

The louvre control mechanism (conjectural)

Detail of truss B-B₁

Sibberscot Barn

converted to a barn. This contained a truss with a low beam, chamfered on all four arrises and with an integral central upright pierced from side to side with three large dowel holes. The building collapsed in 1983 but has been reconstructed in the grounds of Brookgate Farm (above).[101]

Newnham Farm, Yockleton (SJ 411100)

A symmetrical three-storied farmhouse of five bays, end chimneys and an added porch with four Tuscan columns. There is also a three-storied rear block dated NIM 1723 (John Nicholls). Probably the whole L-shape was raised to three stories in the early 19th century. A stableblock is dated NRE 1780 and there is a tall brick rectangular dovecote. This has a pitched roof with coping stones and kneelers. Newnham is a township which has shrunk to this single farm since the 17th century.[102]

Upper Farm, Asterley (SJ 373069)

Now used as a barn, this is a five-bay cruck building, probably a longhouse originally. It has unusual cranked windbraces.[103]

Cruckmeole Old Hall (SJ 430095)

A complicated house of piecemeal development and once divided into four cottages. The east wing has square-framing, c.1625, with a two-storied and jettied porch. One unit has a lobby-entry with shaped doorheads to the rooms on either side. They are chamfered only on the entry side. A panelled room has a dated fireplace relating to the central stack. This has the initials W.P. ANO DOM 1588 (Phillips family). The jambs are of stone and the moulding is continued across the lintel in typical Shropshire fashion. Another fireplace has double-ogee-and-quirk moulding; again the moulding is continuous. Mural decorations are described in chapter 13.[104]

Lea House, Lea Cross SJ 416085)

Formerly known as 'Lea Farm', the house contains the remains of a medieval unit which had close-studding and a king-and-queen-post roof. Possibly it was a two-bay wing relating to an earlier hall, but the supposed cruck is a corner post which has a large jowelled head, 2ft. (0.61m.) across.[105] The fragmentary wall paintings are described in chapter 13.

The Poplars (SJ 401055)

A three-bayed and two-storied ex-farmhouse, built with Monk-bonded brickwork and flat-headed sash windows of 12 or 16 lights. The roof has coping stones and kneelers; there are rear chimneys. The house is probably of the late 18th/early 19th century and the range of farm buildings is contemporary and has the same bonding. They comprise mostly cow-houses, but an upper granary is included and this has two dog kennels in the steps.

Prees

Descriptions of many of the houses in Prees parish have been published.[106] Not included was:

Manor House (SJ 567350)

This is one of three houses in Prees which lay claim to the title. It is of brick, two-storied and of lobby-entry plan with a later kitchen wing built at the rear. From here a divided staircase serves the whole house. At one time the house functioned as the Poorhouse and it is thought that the staircase relates to the segregation of the sexes. In the main block one room is smaller and has a fireplace designed for cooking. At the upper level the remains of a timber-framed truss set in the opposite plane appear to be a relic from a former structure on the site.

Hazlewood Farm, Darliston (SJ 580335)

A drawing of the framework which was briefly exposed in 1987 is included in chapter 4. (cf. Sandbrook Vaults, Market Drayton.)

Preston-upon-the-Weald-Moors

Hoo Hall (SJ 685148)

An L-shaped farmhouse, mostly brick-cased, but framing remains on the crosswing frontage. Here there is a mixture of lozenge-work, close-studding and square panelling. The house is remarkable for the amount and quality of the internal plasterwork in the great chamber. This includes the Eyton family crest and a frieze with acorns, pomegranates, beasts and birds and a recurring human male figure with outstretched arms holding wavy staffs. The farm buildings include a ginny-ring.

Richard's Castle

Skirmisham House, Overton (SO 504720)

Once known as Scrummagem Cottage, the house has been modernised, but when occupied by Percy Robinson (d.1970) it was a two-up, two-down, with attics. He still used the detached kitchen, which included a stockroom and a dairy (since converted to a bungalow), and the outside privy.

Ruckley and Langley

Cottage (SO 531999)

Derelict in 1973, the cottage is of two distinct builds. The eastern bay is stone-built, 1½-storied with a dormer window. A large stone stack with a bake-oven was added at the rear. Some of the stones are dressed and may be of Roman origin. A two-bay timber-framed bay was added to the west side and this was later stone-cased. The framing has 17th-century carpenters' marks and there is an out-built brick stack on the gable. The windows and the door have brick arches.

Langley Hall, rear

Langley Hall (SJ 539002)

The present farmhouse is a replacement of the old Hall which was still standing in 1868.[107] Sited outside the Gatehouse, it is built of Hoar Edge Grit with red sandstone dressings. The front elevation is asymmetrical and has a porch with a mock Tudor, four-centre, arched doorway in the three-storied porch. The rear has three disparate wings including a complete two-storied kitchen block. The roofs have shaped polychrome tiles. A notable essay in Victorian architecture, truly eclectic.

Langley Gatehouse (SJ 539002)

The Gatehouse to the old Hall (above). A complex building, part stone, part timber-framed, but basically of two building phases. To the first belongs the stone archway and the masonry on either side of it. The archway gave access to the Hall and was clearly intended to impress. The rear presents a timber-framed façade, much of which is later. Opinions differ considerably regarding dating.[108]

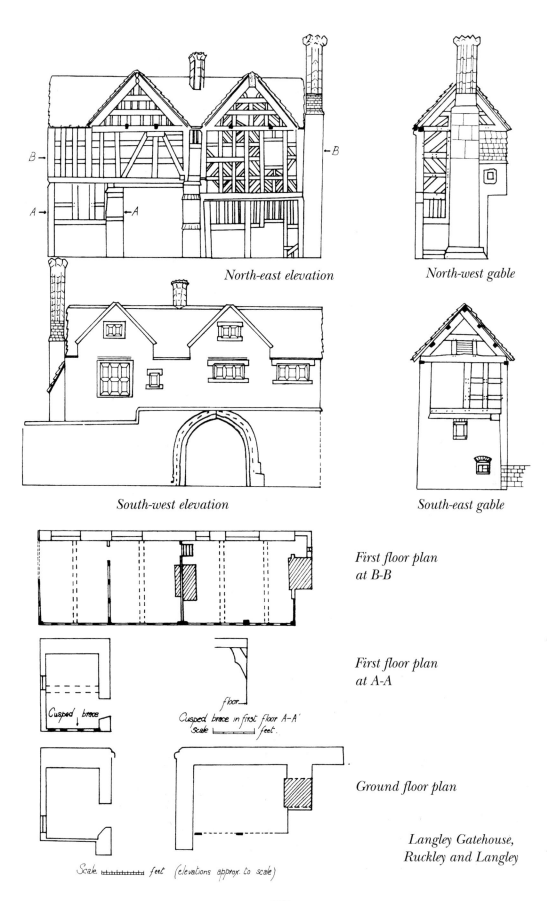

North-east elevation

North-west gable

South-west elevation

South-east gable

First floor plan
at B-B

First floor plan
at A-A

Cusped brace

floor

Cusped brace in first floor A-A'
scale ⊢————————⊣ feet.

Ground floor plan

Langley Gatehouse,
Ruckley and Langley

Scale ⊢┼┼┼┼┼┼┼┤ feet (elevations approx. to scale)

487

Rushbury

Stanway Manor Farm (SO 531915)
The house has been modernised and reduced in size. The farm buildings are laid out on a 19th-century model-farm plan and the dairy cattle units were served by a railway (cf. Honnington Grange, Lilleshall and Crow Leasowes, Bitterley). Some stretches of the rail network remain. There is good brickwork, the best of which is in English bond and so differs from the house. The floorboards above the granary are 2in. thick, grooved along the length and held together with metal tongues.

Stanway Manor (SO 527913)
A Victorian farmhouse dated 1868 with polychrome brickwork thought to be by James Brooks (1825-1901).

Rushbury Manor (SO 514319)
Not to be confused with Manor Farm, Rushbury Manor is neither a farm nor a manor house. It has overtones of a fashionable town house of the early-to-mid-17th century

Track of railway at Stanway Manor

with its triple-gabled frontage. Here the framing consists of fairly close studding divided by vertical rails. There is evidence that the stonework in the lower stages is a replacement for framing and that the doorway was centrally placed. At the rear the framing is simpler. Other features include some good panelling, a newel staircase, and fireplaces where the double-ovolo moulding on the stone jambs continues across the wooden lintel in typical Shropshire fashion. In the 19th century it was converted into three cottages, but it is now restored.[109]

Wilderhope Manor (SO 545928)
This is a National Trust property used as a Youth Hostel. What follows is additional to the description given by Pevsner. The walls are of Aymestrey and Wenlock limestone, but the quoins, mullions and drip-moulds are of Hoar Edge Grit. It has grouped chimneys, probably originally all with star-shaped shafts. Diaper brickwork on the plinth below the shaft, the bulk of the stacks are in stone. The roof slabs seem to be a mixture of Corvedale and Harnage. Over a ground-floor fireplace is what is said to be a bow-rack for holding 13 bows, but could easily be

a spit-rack. At the rear, in addition to the stair turret, there is a garderobe turret. The stableblock is said to be coeval with the house, *c.*1586, but is brick-built.

Coats Farm (SO 525925)
A large box-framed farmhouse, dendro-dated to 1486. Hall-and-crosswing plan, the crosswing being a later replacement for the service end of the hall. All units have close-studding including a former external kitchen,

Coats Farm

now integrated. There is an added porch. The screens passage is intact with doors at either end. The hall has a fine central truss with arch-braces reaching past the wall-plate. Most of the spere-truss is intact. The hall has an inserted chequerboard ceiling; the louvre position is apparent in the roof.[110]

Hall Farm, Wall-under-Heywood (SO 50992)
An H-plan house with a cruck-built hall and two box-framed crosswings. One wing has mural decorations which are described in chapter 13.

Shelvock farmyard

Ruyton-XI-Towns

Shelvock (SJ 372241)
Shelvock is one of the XI townships. The house appears to be coeval with the dated farm buildings which are planned around a large courtyard. A plaque on them reads T.B. and M.B.O. 1860. In the middle of the courtyard is a stone tower said to be a (gun) powder house, for at one time a range of the buildings served as a barrack block. All the units are stone-built.

Pinfold Cottage & Sycamore Cottage, Wykey (SJ 391250)
Originally a two-bay single-storied cottage, probably with an end baffle-entry. It is box-framed, of *c.*1640. Extended by one bay to the west to provide a smaller cottage and the roof raised by a half-storey to give a uniform 1¹/₂ stories to both cottages.

Eardiston House (SJ 371250)
The farm buildings are in a courtyard complex. Grinshill stone is used for the lower storey and square-framed above with brick infill. There is an ulenlok in gable end.

Smithy House

Smithy House (SJ 392223)
This was originally a three-bayed house with a lobby-entry; two-storied and square-framed. A double-storied porch has been added and the original door blocked up. The smithy at the southern end was later raised to two stories and incorporated into the house. A large timber-framed lean-to at the rear must have been added shortly afterwards. There is an 'Alliance' insurance plaque with the number 2129; the policy

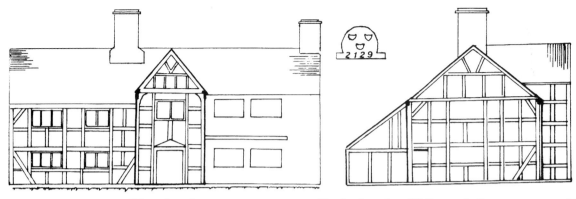

West elevation

North elevation & firemark (latter not to scale)

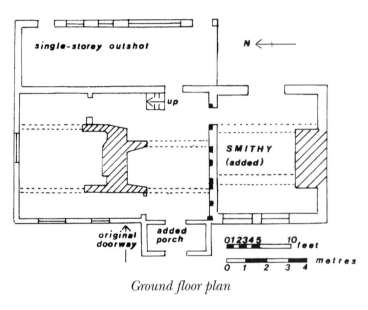

Ground floor plan

Smithy House

is dated 23 July 1800 under the name of William Birch who was then a farmer. A thatched roof is recorded then, and he insured the building for £600 at an annual premium of £1 3s. 3d.

Powis House (SJ 394222)
At one time a public house called The Powis Arms, it is now a brick-fronted, three-bayed, three-storied house but basically one of a row of 17th-century timber-framed cottages. Powis House has a lobby entry with the stairs behind the stack. In the late 18th century the cottages were raised to three stories and given brick frontages. The rear was also raised, but there the brickwork is laced with timbers. There is a rear brew-house with a room over.

Pradoe (SJ 359248)
This house was brick-built in Flemish bond in 1785, and is three-storied, five-bayed, double pile with a hipped roof. Later alterations were by Carline of Shrewsbury.[111] There are touches of T.F. Pritchard's style, but it is not known whether there is a family connection with the Rev. Pritchard for whom it was built. The farm buildings are grouped around a courtyard and include a granary, stables, cowsheds, a threshing barn with a slate floor, drift house, slaughter house, pigsties, dairy, brewery etc.; also a semi-basement bathroom with a slate bath and furnace. There is a remarkable set of wall tiles in the dairy, probably of late 18th century date. The chapel of ease built by Rhode Hawkins in 1860 was commissioned by Thomas Kenyon to save local people the long trek to the village church.[112] Its roof is described in chapter 5. 120m. east of Pradoe is an ice house, probably of the early 19th century—an earth mound covering a red-brick structure. Steps on the east side lead down to a segmental-headed tunnel.

Shawbury

Nos. 2-3, Muckleton (SJ 594213)
Now called Lane End Cottage, the block was, until recently, divided into two dwellings. Of two distinct parts, no.2 is a medieval crosswing to a hall which was replaced by no.3 in 1620 (date over door). The crosswing is box-framed and has a crown-post roof dendro-dated to 1371-2. The outer framing includes very large, curved angle-braces in either storey. No.3 is close-studded throughout and has a mid-rail in the upper storey. The gable has quatrefoil patterning and there is a hewn jetty on the three exposed sides. Internally the spine-beam carries a pyramid stop.[113]

Witheford Grange, Little Witheford (SJ 562193)
A three-bayed, box-framed, parlour wing added to an earlier range to produce a T-shaped plan with entry into a staircase lobby (cf. similar examples in chapter 12). At the rear of the house is a later extension in which the brickwork is treated to give the impression of more headers being used than is the case.

Sheriffhales

The Manor (SJ 756120)
Basically a box-framed, three-part plan house, but much altered after the Second World War and with pseudo-framing on the exterior. It has a 17th-century, two-storied porch with quatre-foil panels and flat balusters.

Six Corners (SJ 759121)
This and three similar houses in Church Road appear to be brick-cased, box-framed, three-part plan houses, each $1^1/_2$-storied.

Chadwell Grange (SJ 783143)
A three-bayed farmhouse, brick-built with end chimneys. $2^1/_2$-storied, but the roof may have been raised. It has two plat-bands, a sandstone plinth and is dated SM 1731.

Shifnal

Evelith Mill (SJ 743052)
The house is brick-cased enclosing an earlier timber-frame. The gap between the two is pronounced. Now a stylish front, three-bayed, two-storied and with shallow, hipped roof and a pillared porch. At the rear of the house is the mill, brick-built and three-storied. After the future Charles II's escape from Boscobel, he and Richard Penderel went in disguise to Evelith where they were challenged by the miller. They fled, but unknown to them, the miller was a Royalist and the mill was full of Royalist refugees from the battle of Worcester. Some of the caves nearby are brick-lined and were used as bake-ovens. Thus the process of wheat-to-flour-to-bread was continuous.

Hatton Grange (SJ 766045)

A description is given in Pevsner, to which can be added that the house was built after 1762 and the bay windows and the porch on the west front are additions. One fireplace is similar to that at 17 Green End, Whitchurch, which probably has Pritchard connections. Hatton Grange is the only extant country house firmly attributable to Pritchard.[114]

Shipton

Thatched Cottage (SO 563916)

Of cruck construction and with a thatched roof, this is basically a two-bay cottage with an end chimney and later additions. Two cruck trusses are present, that in the end gable terminating above collar-beam level which indicates that the hipped end is an original feature. The other truss is closed, suggesting that the plan simply consisted of a single-bayed hall, open to the roof, and a floored parlour or service end.

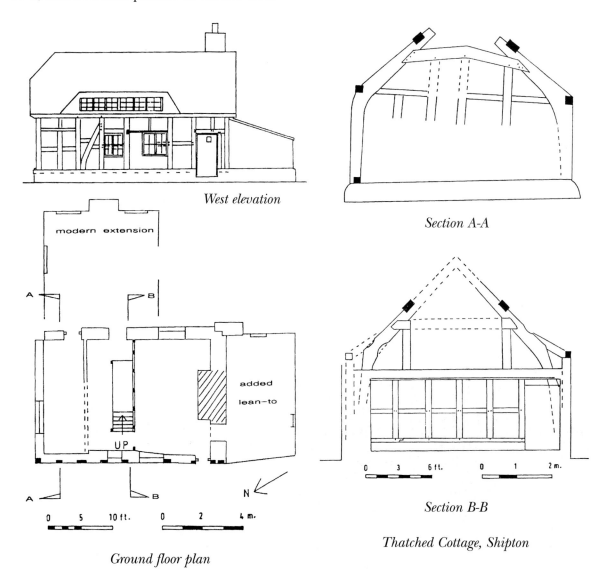

West elevation

Section A-A

Ground floor plan

Section B-B

Thatched Cottage, Shipton

492

Shrawardine

12, 13 & 14 The Critt (SJ 398152)
Though much altered, these cottages were once a medieval cruck-built hall house. No.14 has an added bay at the end, and its wallpaintings are described in chapter 13.

Silvington

Upper House Farm (SO 619797)
Two distinct ranges comprise the present farmhouse; the older is a three-bayed, square-framed range of medieval date which contains evidence for a smoke-louvre. Access to the upper rooms is from a flight of stone steps from the farmyard. The later 18th-century house is set at right angles to the older house and is taller. It is stone-built, two-storied, three-bayed and has gable-end chimneys, parapet gables and kneelers. It contains a dog-leg staircase with shaped, flat balusters.

Stanton Lacy

The Hope (SO 512784)
The Hope is a valley above Stanton Lacy, on the lower slopes of Brown Clee and the settlement here has squatter origins. The straker road from the open fields of Stanton Lacy climbs towards the common grazing grounds ('straker' is the name given to roads leading to such commons), and the ridge-and-furrow of the open fields can be seen from the settlement. Seven houses remain in The Hope, of which three are thatched including one in a ruinous state. No.10 is a longhouse, stone-walled but with framed partitions. It is clear that the out-built stack was built first. The original houseplace was one large room, 24ft. x 12ft. (7.3m. x 6.7m.), but this is now sub-divided. A wing has been added at the rear to provide a kitchen. There was no through passage; the cattle probably had a separate entrance. The eastern side of the byre later became a dairy. There was direct access from the northern end of the houseplace into the byre and from the byre into the hay store. 'Bowl-holes' or angled ventilation slits are present in the store which has an added calf-kit (calf-house) at the northern end.

Squatter's cottage, Lower Hayton

Lower Hayton Cottage (SO 511811)
A box-framed, single-bayed, 1½-storied cottage with an added bay in stone. Massive out-built stack. This is a typical squatter's cottage.

Lower Hayton Farm (SO 503808)
A two-storied, five-bayed farmhouse in which one end of the roof is hipped, the other gabled. Most of the framing is concealed either by roughcast, brickwork or stonework. There are two added wings at the rear. Externally the roof is in one plane, but structurally one end is roofed at right angles and the timbers are older and more

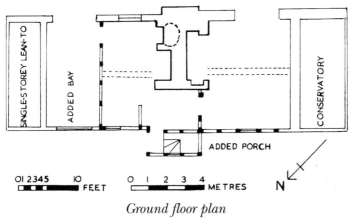

Ground floor plan

North-west elevation

Lower House Farm, Stanton Long

Middle Shadymoor Farm, Stapleton

substantial. A large extension was added in the 17th century and this still has a through passage and chimney-backing-on-the-entry plan. The remains of the older house then became the parlour end.

Stanton Long

Manor House (SO 572906)
A T-shaped farmhouse with walls of part brick and part stone. The brickwork in the front of the cross-wing is of an unclassified bond: three rows of stretchers and one row of two headers and a stretcher. There is a basement kitchen and dairy. The 'hall' range contains a chequerboard ceiling.

Lower House Farm (SO 575908)
Basically a two-bayed and $1\frac{1}{2}$-storied, square-framed house with a central stack and lobby-entry. It has been extended in more recent times but an early addition is the framed porch with side-entry.

Stapleton

Middle Shadymoor Farm
(SJ 459027)
A typical example of the type of newly-built, isolated, 17th-century farmhouse—box-framed, three panels high and with a thatched roof. Now of three bays, it was probably built as two-bayed with a lobby entrance.[115]

Netley Old Hall (SJ 465019)
Probably built by Thomas Phillips in 1619, the hall section of the house was reduced in size and the crosswing restored in 1965. The gable of the latter is a good example of the 'Shrewsbury school' of carpentry, with a jetty supported with carved brackets, S-braces and close-studding with a mid-rail. But there is little decorative work. The long side wall is brick-cased and forms the main entrance. A fine

494

Netley Old Hall, Stapleton

Overmantel at Netley Old Hall

Jacobean overmantel incorporates numerous human figures and is dated 1619.[116]

St. Martin's

Almshouses (SJ 326368)
A block of six single-storey dwellings built for '6 poor women' of brick with stone dressings. A central projection has a pediment and the date of 1810, but the charity was founded in 1698 by Sir John Trevor of Brynkinalt, Speaker of the House and Master of the Rolls in the time of William III and Queen Anne.

Pentre Morgan (SJ 340370)
A two-storied, brick-built, five-bayed, symmetrically-fronted farmhouse with two out-built gable stacks. These have recessed panels and the central bay of the house is also recessed. There is an elaborate newel post with the date 1668, which may indicate the date of a major rebuild. Most of the timbers inside appear to be reused including four pairs of crucks which were used as roof trusses.

Escob Farm (SJ 307362)
Esgob is the local name, the full name being Er'w'r Esgob. This is basically a cruck-built hall house of four bays with later additions and alterations. Probably of mid-15th-century date, it received an inserted stack in the 17th century, creating a lobby-entry. Noteworthy is the central truss of the hall which has an arch-braced collar-beam above which is lavish cusping forming a quatrefoil design flanked by two trefoils. The house is thought to have been the property of the bishops of St. Asaph.[117]

Stoke St. Milborough

Moor Farm (SO 565801)
A box-framed, H-plan house, probably of early 17th-century date. A two-storied hall, but the entrance is still at the lower end with a through passage. There is close-studding with a mid-rail on both upper and lower stories. There is a kitchen and dairy in the service wing, and great and small parlours in the upper wing. The hall has beams with ovolo moulding. The chim-

neystack of the hall/parlour has a renaissance-arch motif in the brickwork while the service wing stack is star-shaped. There is a cellar with a fireplace under the parlour. Owing to a road realignment the original front of the house is now at the rear.

Newton Farm (SO 589822)

This is basically a stone-built longhouse variant. There was a door from the upper-floor level of the house to the upper part of the byre (hay store) so that the cattle could be fed from above. The door and the hay-shutes are now blocked and a transverse feeding walk is used. The house is built on two different levels.

Newton Farm

Lower House Farm, Cleedownton (SO 582806)

Stone-built, three-storied plus attics, but only two bays wide, the farmhouse has end chimneys with out-built stacks and framed internal partitions. The walling stone is a mixture of local sandstone and a conglomerate known as cornstone. The windows, where original, are stone-framed, recessed, with two or three lights and stone straight-chamfered mullions. The plan consists of two large rooms at the front and two smaller behind and is consistent at each level, but the position of the staircase between the two smaller rooms provides access to all the rooms, obviating the need for intercommunicating doors—a significant advance in plan design. At the rear is a stone, two-storied building with a large fireplace which is now used as a farm building. This probably combined the original detached kitchen, mens' bothy and a byre.

East Farm, Cleedownton (SO 582808)

A cruciform-shaped house, two-storied, with a large chimneystack in the crossing. Mostly stone-walled, but the rear gable of the crosswing is stone to eaves level with early brickwork above. The return wall consists of brickwork typical of the 19th-century Rouse-Boughton estate, but embedded in this is the remains of a framed truss of a low single-storied building. The roof of the main range is two-bayed, but each bay is subdivided by two original half-intermediates which are not aligned on either side, but staggered. The hall has two spine-beams with stepped single-ovolo moulding and run-out stops.

The Leasowes (SO 598826)

An example of an isolated squatter's cottage on the boundary of the parishes of Stoke and Wheathill. Originally the cottage consisted of a room 12ft. 9in. x 11ft. 9in. (3.89m. x 3.58m.) which incorporated a large corner chimney, and which had a half-storey above. This was later extended and a byre attached, but there was no direct access from the house to the byre.

Stoke Court (SO 571820)

A stone-built, three-bayed, two-storied house with end chimneys. The front elevation has an applied brick skin, probably commissioned by Lord Lyttleton, Chancellor of England, *c.*1700 who then owned the house. Classic Grinshill stone arched porch and steps. The brick-arched cellars have cobble and stone-flagged floors. A fine Jacobean overmantel in a ground-floor room is said to have come from Ludlow Castle.[118] The **Malthouse**, which is attached to the west side of the house, is intact and has brick-vaulting, a furnace chamber and specially made brick joists laid across the vaulting to support the malting floor on which the final part of the processing was done. The joists measure 1ft. 10in. x 22in. x 5in. (0.56m. x 0.63m. x 0.13m.). The wetting-vat is on the ground floor and there is a first-stage malting floor for germination.

Above: Stoke Court
Below: the malt kiln floor at Stoke Court

Bockleton Court (SO 578833)

Though basically two-storied, this house has two front projecting gables of three full stories, clearly added to give the house status. The larger gable on the right accommodates a porch. A third gable does not project and has a window at the top. At the rear close-studding with two rails survives and inside are two dragon-beams indicating that the framed house was jettied on three sides. The fashionable stone front was added as part of a major refit in the 17th century. The doorframe of the porch has double-ovolo-and-quirk moulding and the door itself is heavily iron-studded with iron hinges and brackets.

The Lower Bush, Blackford Cottage (SO 587826)

Stone-built, 1½-storied, basically two-up, two-down, the cottage is built on sloping land so that the back is single-storied, and it probably began as a simple two-roomed dwelling. The kitchen has a large corner chimneystack; the parlour has a bed recess below the staircase.

The Lower Bush, Blackford Cottage

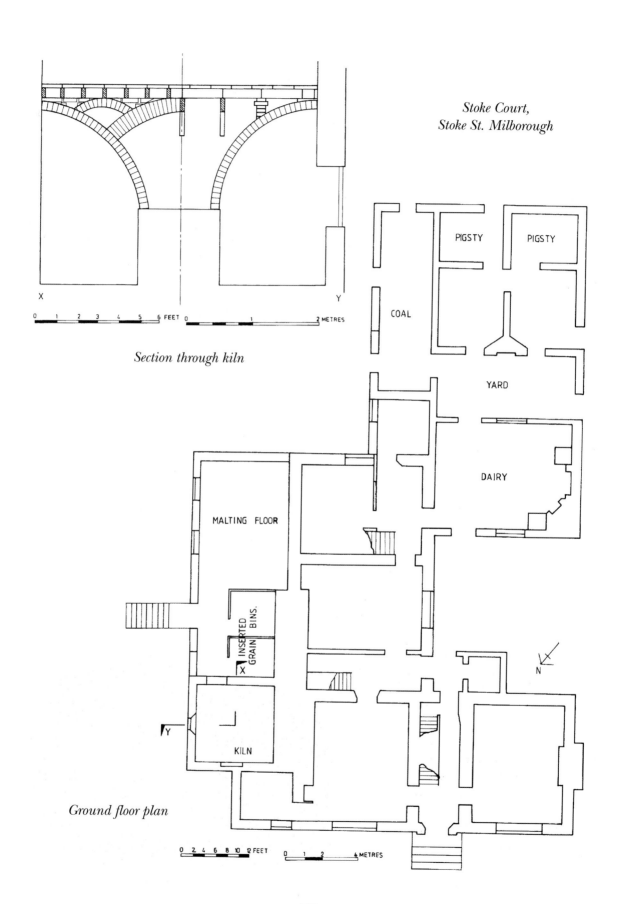

Stoke Court,
Stoke St. Milborough

PIGSTY PIGSTY

COAL

YARD

X   Y

DAIRY

0 1 2 3 4 5 6 FEET 0   1   2 METRES

Section through kiln

MALTING FLOOR

INSERTED GRAIN BINS.

X

N

Y

KILN

Ground floor plan

0 2 4 6 8 10 12 FEET 0 1 2   4 METRES

498

Although this room has a fireplace a stack was never provided. Smoke escaped via a shaped hole in the wall, but two wooden plugs show where some kind of smoke extractor was fitted.

Downton House Cottage, Cleedownton (SO 584805)
Inscribed and dated MRR 1822 this is a rare example of an early 19th-century farm-worker's cottage. Two-up, two-down and built of sandstone with some cornstone, one bedroom is a landing-type. The kitchen has an open grate, boiling copper, bread-oven and ash-pit. Additions include a single-storey range beyond the kitchen and a rear lean-to providing a bedroom and a pantry with a setlas.

Downton House Cottage, Cleedownton

Stoke-on-Tern

Petsey (SJ 636276;)
A box-framed farmhouse, dated 1634 on the two-storied porch. The two-storied hall range has an entry at the lower end, with a parlour crosswing. All these units are jettied and close-studded, and the upper stories have a mid-rail. A large service wing on the east is an addition and has its own entry. The porch had an oriel window, the supporting bracket with a carved human male head remains. The door is planked and studded and has strap hinges. Prominent at the rear are the staircase wing and a corner stack with brick lozenge work serves corner fire-places in the parlour wing. Internally the main spine beam and the intersecting beams are ovolo-moulded and the main beam has elaborate cyma-with-ovolo-and-bars stops. The wall-paintings are described in chapter 13.

Stottesdon

Wrickton Mill Cottage (SO 644856)
A cruck-built hall house, now stone-clad and 1½-storied. The large inserted stack created a lobby-entry (see drawings overleaf). One of the three cruck trusses is clearly the central truss of a two-bay hall, and there are pegs on the rafters for the control of the louvre. The chamfered beam of the inserted ceiling carries an elaborate stop.

Hall Farm (SO 627829)
Sited immediately to the west of the church, the house is basically a rectangular, stone-walled block, the walls in

Hall Farm, Stottesdon

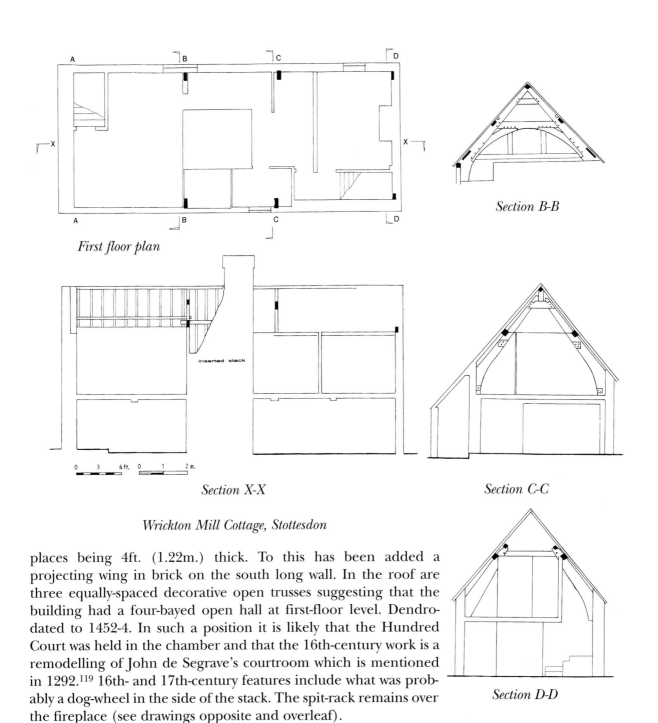

First floor plan

Section B-B

Section X-X

Section C-C

Wrickton Mill Cottage, Stottesdon

Section D-D

places being 4ft. (1.22m.) thick. To this has been added a projecting wing in brick on the south long wall. In the roof are three equally-spaced decorative open trusses suggesting that the building had a four-bayed open hall at first-floor level. Dendro-dated to 1452-4. In such a position it is likely that the Hundred Court was held in the chamber and that the 16th-century work is a remodelling of John de Segrave's courtroom which is mentioned in 1292.[119] 16th- and 17th-century features include what was prob-ably a dog-wheel in the side of the stack. The spit-rack remains over the fireplace (see drawings opposite and overleaf).

Sutton Maddock

Brockton Cottage (SJ 7200035)
A T-shaped house, basically timber-framed but much altered. The stem of the T has exposed framing with cut-back heads to the posts, and a massive out-built stack.

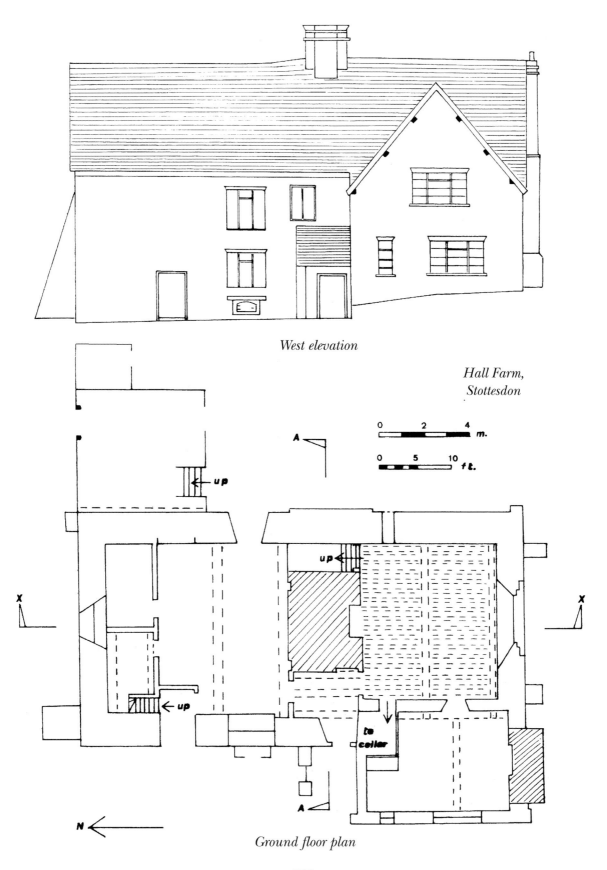

West elevation

Hall Farm,
Stottesdon

0   2   4   m.

0   5   10   ft.

up

up

up

to
cellar

A

A

X

X

N

Ground floor plan

501

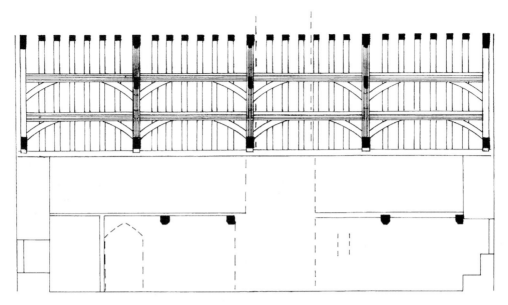

Section X-X

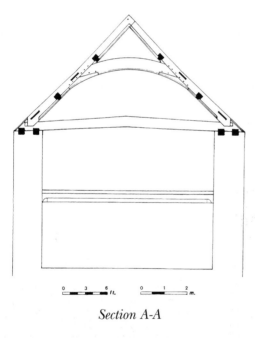

Section A-A

Hall Farm, Stottesdon

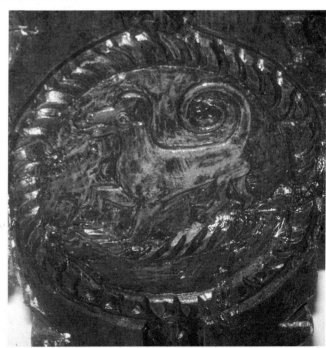

Talbot hound carving in Brockton Park

Brockton Court (SJ 722033)
A large house, brick-built with stone dressings and a hipped roof. A plaque on the side wall reads 'FWF 1678'.

Brockton Park (SJ 722036)
The modest three-bay brick exterior conceals a room which has decorative ceiling beams with carved medallions. One is a double-headed eagle with the initials R.F. and I.F. Another is a talbot hound and a third is the Prince of Wales' feathers. They probably relate to the Forester

family from nearby Willey, the beams perhaps belonging to an earlier house on the site. **The barn** was built *c.*1860 and is of good quality brick with industrial king-post trusses. It has been tastefully converted to a house.

Old Vicarage Cottage (SJ 723015)
A two-storied, three-bayed house with a brick exterior. It is L-shaped with two end chimneys. It was originally the vicarage. Some medieval framework remains internally. One truss was probably at the dais end of the hall and this has cusped and chamfered braces in the framing, whilst another seems to be the remains of a central truss of a two-bay solar crosswing. This may have had crown-post roof construction, but there is no evidence of the usual downbracing. There is no smoke-blackening. It is clear that the two units were built separately; the carpentry is similar, but there is a 6in. gap between them. The stack on the west side is stepped and includes some narrow hand-made bricks. That on the east side is smaller and later and contains one brick with a scratched date of 1877. This may indicate a date for the casing.

Old Vicarage Cottage and, below, its dais truss

Tibberton

Tibberton Grange (SJ 685190)
A number of large farmhouses in the area were built by the Marquess of Stafford, later to become the Duke of Sutherland, who had vast holdings in Shropshire. Tibberton

Tibberton Grange of 1810

Grange is dated 1810 and is, perhaps, the most stylish. Three-storied and brick-built with end chimneys, the building is three-bayed with a pillared porch and two single-storied wings. The fenestration remains intact, the ground-floor windows having semicircular arched heads.

Tibberton Manor (SJ 691198)

Another Marquess of Stafford house, brick-built, three-storied and three-bayed with end chimneys. Dated 1795 and with a pedimented porch entrance. The ground-floor windows have been replaced with Victorian bays.

Tugford

Baucott Manor (SO 540874)

Originally box-framed but later cased in stone and extended to form a T-shaped house. The extension is dated 1652 and has the initials S.I.E.R. The tie-beams probably relate to the earlier house.

Holdgate Castle Farm (Mrs. Stackhouse-Acton) now known as Hall Farm

Hall Farm, Holdgate (SO 563896)

The house is grafted onto the remaining round tower of Holdgate Castle and was probably built from salvaged stones in the 17th century, but there are timber-framed partitions inside suggestive of a screens-passage plan. The bay to the northeast is dated 1763 and appears to be an extension. The motte survives and has an 18th-century ice house built into its base which measures 10ft. x 5ft. (3.05m. x 1.52m.) and has an arched brick roof.

Uppington

Avenue Farm (SJ 600095)

The present farmhouse is 19th century and brick-built, but attached to it is a large brick-walled building which has an expansive roof-line and low walls. Within are the remains of a cruck-trussed building which may represent the earlier house or a large tithe barn. One truss carries a low beam and an arch-braced collar-beam.[120]

Upton Cressett

Upton Cressett Hall (SO 655942)

Upton Cressett is a classic example of an upland deserted medieval village with virtually only the Manor House and the church surviving. The site is moated. Basically the house is box-framed, though later encased in brickwork. Dendro-dated to 1431, the hall was originally open to the roof. It retains a remarkable aisled truss and is crown-post roofed. Another aisled truss is present, but the vital central truss is missing, raising the question of whether the whole unit was aisled or had a base-cruck in the middle. At right angles to the hall is the solar crosswing of similar date which has a roof of queen-posts and open arched-braced collar-beams. The crosswing was built first. Some of the brickwork, including two impressive chimneystacks, is dated 1580 and this could also date the brick gatehouse which contains interesting plaster-

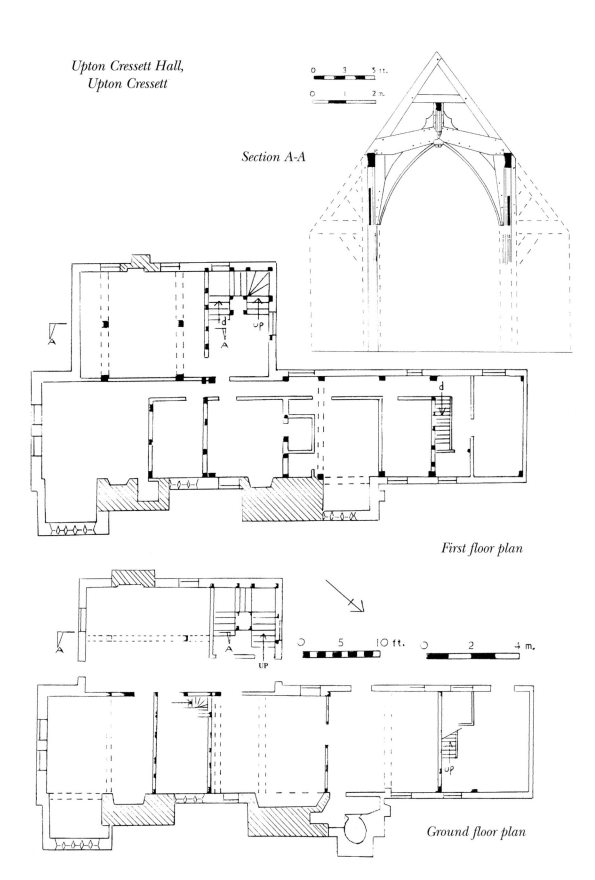

Upton Cressett Hall,
Upton Cressett

0   3   5 ft.

0   1   2 m.

Section A-A

First floor plan

5   10 ft.

2   4 m.

UP

Ground floor plan

505

work, mouldings and distaff holes. The church was built probably by the Upton family as a private chapel. Later it became a parish church. It contains Norman and 13th-century features and a Norman font.[121] (See also illustration on rear cover).

Upton Magna

Cruck Cottage (SJ 553125)
Dendro-dated to 1269, with a later remodelling in 1425, this is covered extensively elsewhere in this book.[122]

The Old Shop, Somerwood (SJ 553155)
Now restored and extended, in 1977 it was possible to trace the development from a single-celled, framed unit with an open hearth at one end and accommodation for a cow at the other, through the addition of a croglofft and a fumbrell to further improvements and enlargement. The fumbrell has been retained.[123]

Old Rectory (SJ 554124)
A 19th-century supra-vernacular rectory by G.E. Street, it has very fine brickwork which has never been repointed and looks new. Some hipped and some double-hipped roofs. There is cavetto moulding on the French windows.

Waters Upton

The Old Rectory (SJ 634195)
A brick-built double-pile house of 1765, dated by the deeds in an agreement between the Bishop of Lichfield and the rector. Parlour, hall and study are at the front, kitchen and brew-house are behind.

Wellington

The Falcon (SJ 640108)
This hostelry/former farm has had a chequered history, opening first as an inn, The Haygate, between 1625 and 1693,[124] to become a coaching inn on Telford's London-Holyhead road (now the A5). The house is brick-built, the front façade is three-storied and four-bayed but with a central doorway which has a pillared porch. There is a hipped roof. The ground-floor windows have been altered. The date JC 1767 (Cludde family) is on one chimney. One attic has a plaster floor.

Newdale (SJ 674096)
This area was cleared for opencast mining in the 1950s. It had been an industrial settlement established by the Darby family in 1759 and included rows of back-to-back houses, a Quaker meeting house, warehouses and a later school. Some survived into the 1970s.[125]

Wem

Many of the houses in Wem and Wem Rural are described in a recent publication and are therefore not included here.[126]

Westbury

Upper Lake, Asterley (SJ 371068)

Two bays of a cruck hall house survive, dendro-dated to 1545/6. Beyond these a moulded beam in a later unit has details suggesting that it once functioned as a dais beam, while an upper room at the southern end of the plan has a corner fireplace with carved jambs and a lintel incorporating classic blank arches and three human figures. There are many other interesting features.[127]

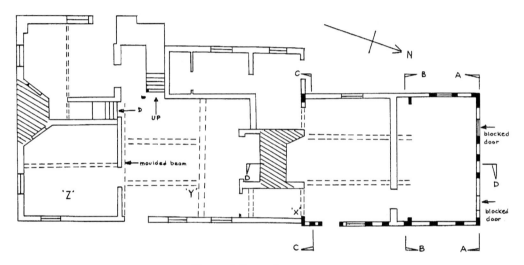

Ground floor plan

West elevation   *East elevation*   *North elevation*

Upper Lake, Westbury

507

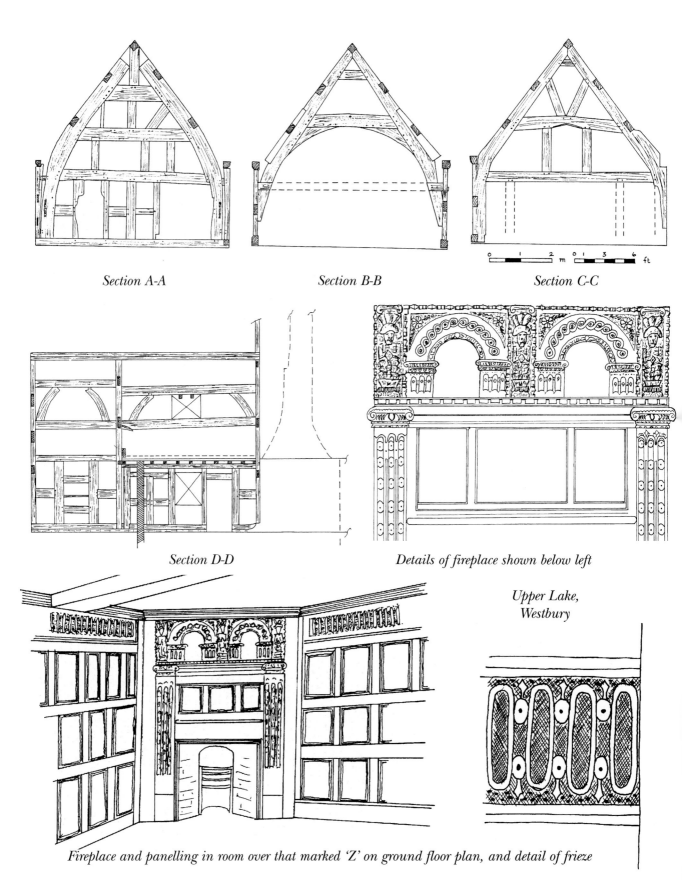

Section A-A

Section B-B

Section C-C

Section D-D

Details of fireplace shown below left

*Upper Lake,
Westbury*

Fireplace and panelling in room over that marked 'Z' on ground floor plan, and detail of frieze

Lower Farm, Hem Lane, Westley (SJ 363070)
A 17th-century, square-framed farmhouse, four panels high. The main bay is the kitchen which has a gable stack. The other bay is unheated and divided into a dairy and a store. There are two added bays to the rear. It was derelict in 1965, but has since been restored.[128]

Derelict Cottage by Yew Tree Farm, Stoney Stretton (SJ 377092)
Last occupied in 1838, this is a three-bayed, 1¹/₂-storied cottage, originally box-framed and thatched. The western bay is now open to the roof, but with evidence of a byre with a hay-loft above. The middle bay is divided into a dairy and a parlour, and the third bay is the houseplace. The fireplace had a hood and there is a bread-oven with what is possibly a smoking-chamber above. The standard of the carpentry is good and, surprisingly, there are stencilled wallpaintings which are described in chapter 13.

Stoney Stretton Manor (SJ 383095)
The plan is that of a cruck-built, two-bay, open hall, with a screens passage and service end and with a contemporary box-framed crosswing. It is now all brick-cased and there is an inserted stack in the lower bay of hall.

Interior of hall at Stoney Stretton Manor, Westbury

West Felton

Home Farm, Sandford (SJ 343235)
A U-shaped house, apparently of three different builds, but the symmetrical brick front is the result of 17th-century remodelling of an earlier cruck-built house. The brickwork has irregular bonding.

Tedsmore Hall (SJ 367254)
A large country house, built in 1768, possibly in brick, for Richard Bulkeley-Hatchett. It was remodelled in 1819 for Thomas Bulkeley-Owen and service wings were added in 1878. The early 19th-century remodelling is thought to include the stone cladding, finials, mullion-and-transomed windows which were removed later, gothic ceilings and doorframes. The billiard room/library is of 1854. There are some good internal features including fire-places by Carline of Shrewsbury.[129]

The Nursery (SJ 346258)
This was Dovaston House, the home of the famous naturalist, John Dovaston, who was a friend and biographer of Thomas Bewick (1753-1828). Many of

The Nursery, West Felton

The Cider House at The Nursery

Dovaston's pioneering botanical plants and trees survived until the 1980s when the house was demolished. A fine range of farm buildings included a cider house, still containing its wheel and press, a cattle byre with slate slabs for partitions, a stable and coachhouse dated 1877 with a Venetian window and a hoist above, etc.

Wheathill

Silvington, Manor (SO 621789)

Although it seems that a 17th-century stone house has been grafted onto the solar of a medieval hall house there are openings in the rear wall which suggest that fragments of the old hall remain. The stone is the same throughout. The solar is at first-floor level, reached by a flight of outside steps. The undercroft has large flat-laid joists. An inscription in the gable reads 'hvfrf*m*'. In the gable wall is a window with foiled tracery and there is a possible garderobe at the side of the fireplace.

Silvington Manor, Wheathill

Doctor's Cottages (SO 620818)

Two cottages, originally one three-bayed house, box-framed and stone-cased, but a cruck-truss was found embedded in the stone casing of a collapsed gable corner. A pentice roof protects the ground-floor windows, one of which has ovolo moulding.

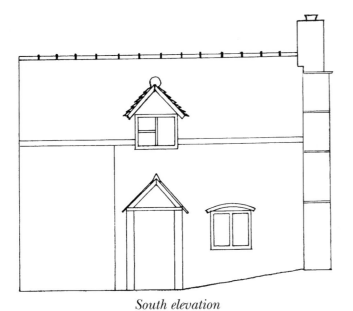

South elevation

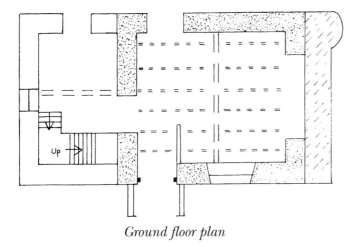

First floor plan

Ground floor plan

Yew Tree Cottage, Wheathill

Malthouse Farm (SO 613819)

A stone-built complex, mostly late 18th/early 19th century with an attached malthouse, until recently used as a Youth Hostel, which has a curious form of tie-beam. Instead of a continuous beam, there is a space in the middle and the two ends are turned upwards, resembling the bowl of a pipe. Another has an industrial king-post in which a long iron bolt goes through the tie-beam into the king-post where it is held by a captive nut housed in a slot which is cut back to reach the bolt hole. Similar forms have been noted in the surrounding area.

Yew Tree Cottage (SO 602823)

Built of Dhustone, originally a one-up, one-down squatter's cottage with a large out-built stack. Later extended to two-up, two-down, but still with only one room heated. A period-piece cast iron range by E. Bluck of Ludlow remains in use.

Whitchurch

Most of the houses in area of Whitchurch are described in a recent publication.[130] In addition:

Whitchurch Rural

Tilstock Hall Farmhouse (SJ 541376)

A house of three distinct phases. Initially a box-framed 17th-century range with square-framing and a large central stack with grouped star-shaped shafts and oversailing capping. A brick wing was then added which incorporates a porch with ovolo moulding. A datestone dated 1682 M.R.M. was removed from the front, but is preserved. Finally a large T-shaped brick extension added to the front in 1861. This has the initials G.S.C., probably Geoffrey Causer.

Wistanstow

Round House, Cwm Head (SO 420882)
A stone-built, two-storied round house with an octagonal roof and a central chimney. It has a heavy iron chain around it, but it is not known whether this is to stop it spreading or is symbolic.

Bressumer detail at Affcot Manor

Affcot Manor (SO 454864)
Basically this is a T-shaped house consisting of a two-bayed open hall of *c.*1500 with the addition of a late 16th-/early 17th-century parlour crosswing. The latter is jettied and has cusped and spiked lozenge work in the gable and stylish carving on the bressumer which includes a central Tudor rose. The wing is served by a tall 'Tudor'-style stack with star-shaped shafts. A brick service wing was added at the opposite end *c.*1800.

The purlins and rafters over the lower bay of the hall are smoke-blackened and there is a curious jointing of the purlin: the original purlin butts up to the end frame and a short length of timber is scarfed onto it to extend it into an added bay where it appears as a clasped protruding purlin. Two large 'keys' secure the joint. Some of the windbraces are inverted. The farm buildings include a stylish summer house with a pigeon loft above, a granary, stables and a range of timber-framed and brick-nogged cow-houses.

Palace Barn (SO 410853)
This large stone-built barn is in an extremely isolated position, three-bayed, but the third bay is probably an addition. The timber trusses inside appear to be 17th century, but the stone walls seem to be earlier. There are triangular ventilation holes. The barn is said to have been the property of the Bishop of Hereford, hence its name.

Castle Farm, Cheyney Longville (SO 417848)
The farmhouse is mostly of the 17th century, but it is part of a courtyard plan approached through a gatehouse across a moat. Within the courtyard at least two, possibly three, stone-built, first-floor halls have been identified. One has a large hall, approx. 33ft. x 15ft. (10m. x 4.6m.), approached by a flight of steps, and with a small inner solar, approx. 10ft. x 15ft. (3m.

x 4.6m.), the two connected by a 'Caernarvon'-arched doorway and lit only by slit windows; the other has a blocked pointed arched doorway at ground level and a traceried, two-light window which is square-headed, stone-mullioned and trefoiled. The two are linked by another stone block which has arched doorways at ground level. The whole complex is difficult to assess, but Sir Hugh Cheyney had licence to crenellate in 1395 and much of it could date from then. Other features include an ulenlok in the gable of the first hall and this building also has a plaster and wood hood which proved only to serve a later washing-copper at ground level. In the inner courtyard is a ginny-ring and the remains of a cider press. The ginny-ring was used for crushing oats as well as apples. The outer courtyard contains farm buildings among which is a long barn on graduated staddle-stones with a granary at one end.[131]

Withington

Church Farm (SJ 577129)

Though divided and largely disguised with brick cladding, this is basically a two-bayed open hall with a contemporary solar crosswing, probably of late 15th-century date. Later the hall was fitted with a smoke-bay against the central truss. The main posts in the hall all have jowelled heads and the central truss has arch-braces to a cambered tie-beam. The solar crosswing is two-bayed and two-storied with close-studding to face the church and the village. It contains wallpaintings, described in chapter 13. (Drawings of the farm are to be found on the following two pages.)

Wollaston

The Green Farm, Winnington (SJ 315119)

A three-bay, cruck-built house, which may have been truncated, with a modern brick wing. The inserted fireplace in the hall has a mantelbeam with symbolic carvings, depicting from left to right: a man on his side in 17th-century costume with a feather in his cap, a wyvern with scales in *amphisbaena* form (a mythical winged dragon with a head at either end), the legs of Man, another wyvern in the same form, a heart pierced from the left with an arrow and from the right with a spear, an upright sword, some interlacing, a couple with a loving cup, a hind, a lion with a human head and lastly what is thought to be old Welsh script. Presumably symbolic of Welsh culture, but not understood, other examples of similar but not identical mantel-beams are found at Llwynmelyn in Trewern (SJ 287111) and Gwernfyda in Llanllugan (SJ 045017), each in Montgomeryshire, and some of the carvings on the Communion rail at Llanvair Waterdine church in Shropshire are also comparable.[132]

Detail of carved mantel-beam at The Green Farm, Wollaston

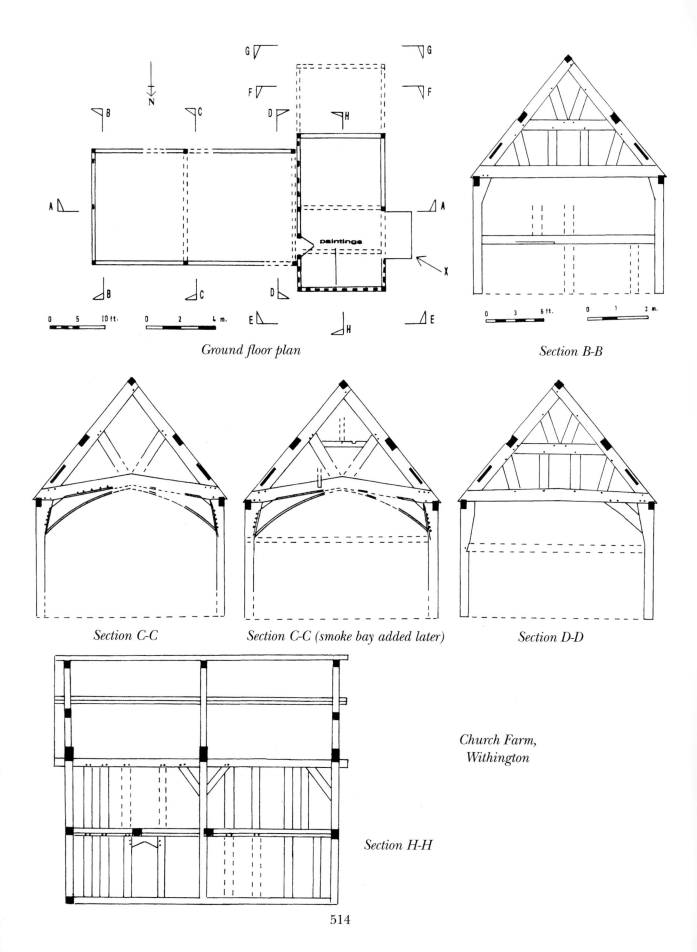

Ground floor plan

Section B-B

Section C-C

Section C-C (smoke bay added later)

Section D-D

Church Farm,
Withington

Section H-H

514

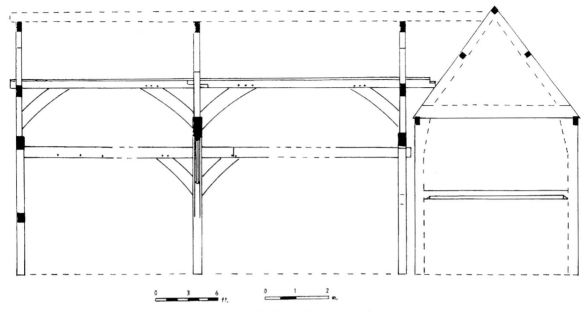

Section A-A (with own scale)

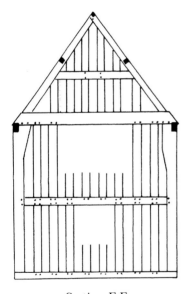

Section E-E

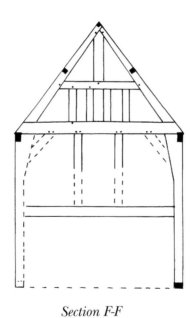

Section F-F

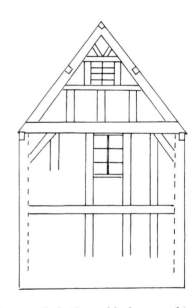

Section G-G (from old photograph)

Church Farm,
Withington

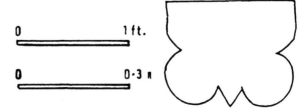

*Details of reused stone
in stack at X*

Woolstaston

Bowdler's House, 38 & 39 Woolstaston (SO 453984)

A three-part plan house consisting of a two-bay cruck hall and a contemporary box-framed crosswing with a crown-post roof, dendro-dated to 1398-1400, the crosswing being built first. The central truss of the hall has an integral low beam with a central upright, the whole truss ornamented with quarter-round moulding. The hall has an inserted ceiling, with multi-round moulding on the beams, thought to be recycled from elsewhere, and a large inserted stack which at one time served both the hall and a small smithy introduced into the end bay. There is a flattened ogee-arched doorway between the hall and the solar wing. A cruck barn is located within the curtilage alongside the road (see drawings opposite).[133]

Worfield

Bradney Farm (SO 769959)

At present a four-bay house with a crosswing and various extensions and with a lobby-entry at the lower end. Internally are the remains of a two-bay cruck hall, dendro-dated to 1487, in which the chamfering on the central truss is taken higher on the high side—a subtle distinction between the social orders. Also noteworthy is the louvre control—on the low side a cleat is supported by three pegs of the saddle, and an opening in the back allows a rope or chain to pass through. In the ridge is an iron hook to which one end of the rope was attached; with the other end a person could adjust the louvre (see drawings this page and overleaf).[134]

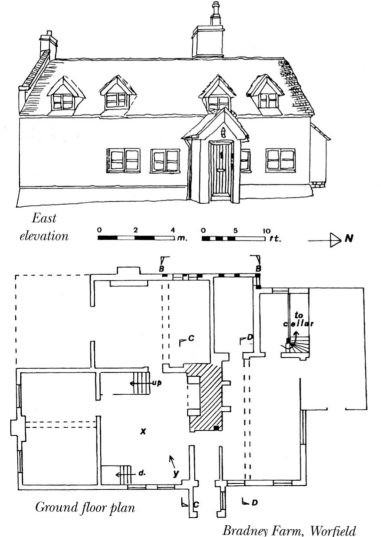

East elevation

Ground floor plan

View from north (not to scale)

Bradney Farm, Worfield

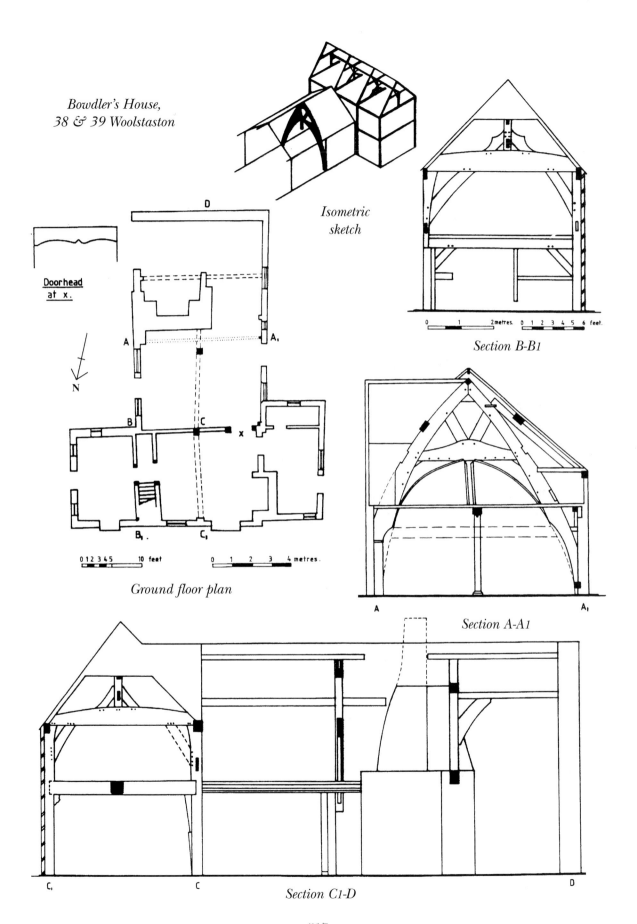

Bowdler's House,
38 & 39 Woolstaston

Isometric
sketch

Doorhead
at x.

N

D

A   A₁

B   C   x

B₁   C₁

0 1 2 3 4 5   10 feet

0   1   2   3   4 metres.

Ground floor plan

0   1   2metres.   0 1 2 3 4 5 6 feet.

Section B-B1

A   A₁

Section A-A1

C₁   C   D

Section C1-D

517

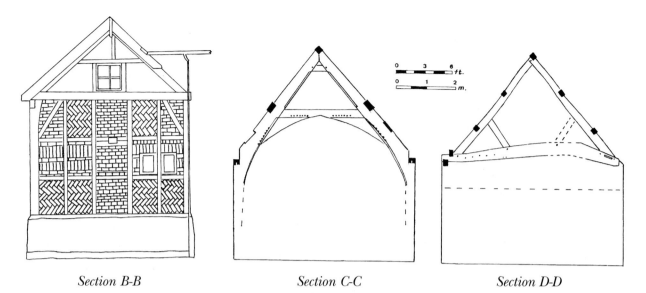

Section B-B   *Section C-C*   *Section D-D*

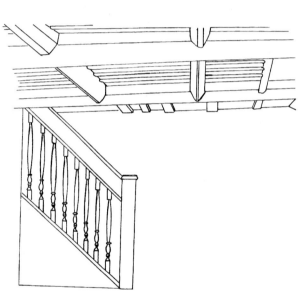

Ceiling plan at X on ground floor plan   *View from Y on ground floor plan*

Bradney Farm,
Worfield

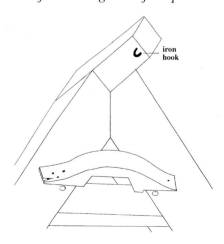

iron
hook

Detail of low side of C-C
(not to scale)

518

Lower Hall (SO 759957)

The house is now stripped of its stucco and the framing exposed. Mostly close-studded with mid-rails, it is of double-pile form and jettied all round.[135]

'Tailor's Platform' at Lower Hall, Worfield—reputedly where the itinerant tailor worked when he came to make clothes for the family

Stableford Farm, Ackleton
(SO 759985)
Within the farm buildings complex are two of special interest. One is a single-storied building at present used for stabling, the other is a large two-storied granary over a storage area with an elaborate cart-entry arrangement. Each employ a form of laminated cruck construction. The larger (five bays) use the 'upper-cruck' mode and the smaller use the 'full cruck'. There are seven laminates on each 'blade', those in the granary are slightly more elaborate, having rounded edges. In both cases the crucks cross at the top and are tied back in different ways. At ground level the granary has cast-iron pillars. The date must be *c*.1840-60, the period of 'high farming', a time of high grain prices when there was heavy investment and much innovation including, perhaps, steam threshing.

Worthen

Hogstow Farm (SJ 362007)
This complex is difficult to interpret. At one time it seems to have consisted of three dwellings. At the northern end is a square-framed unit, two panels high, in which the fireplace contains a bake-oven and a washing copper. This projects from the rest of the range which is part brick and part stone. A houseplace, parlour and dairy may be identified within the brick part, but a 5ft. (1.5m.) passageway accommodating the entrance and stairs poses problems. The stone part seems to have incorporated stabling.

Meadowtown Hall (SJ 312012)
A square-framed farmhouse, originally 1½-storied but now two-storied, four-bayed and with a lobby-entry, but the original entrance seems to have been next to the central truss of the hall. The latter has a chamfered transverse floor-beam supported by small curved angle-braces. It is undivided below. The plan includes an unheated parlour and a pantry to the north of the hall and a kitchen to the south of the chimneystack. The ground level drops sharply to the north.

Binweston Farm (SJ 301041)
Here the cow-house, clearly the earlier house, is on the opposite side of the road to the present house. It is of four-bayed cruck construction and the central truss of the hall is chamfered and

has arch-braces to the collar-beam. The house which superceded it seems to be *c.*1500, but has been enlarged several times. There is little relationship between the front and the back, the front having two jettied crosswings and a mixture of square-framing, close-studding, and lozenge work. The north wing seems to be a modification of a two-storied porch, jettied on three sides and with vine-leaf carving on the tie-beam. Most striking are the jettied end of the solar at the west end which because of an added bay now forms an internal feature, the inserted chequer-board ceiling in the hall which has double-tenon joints, and a number of shaped doorheads. Altogether an 'ambitious' house.

West Buxton Farm, Stiperstones (SJ 352001)
Basically a two-bayed, 1½-storied house with a central stack and lobby-entry. Built of random rubble limestone walls, it has an an attached byre in timber-framing, but it is not a longhouse. There is an added lean-to at the rear and an added crosswing at the southern end.

Gazebo at Orleton Hall

Wrockwardine

Orleton Hall (SJ 635114)
The ancillary buildings include the Gatehouse which was timber-framed and jettied on all sides. Now mostly brick, each chimney carries a plaque. One is dated 1766 and the other is said to be 1588, but is not obvious. The basic structure must pre-date 1588. In an upper room is a stencilled wallpainting which is described in chapter 13. The **dovecote** is of brick, octagonal and retains its potence, and the **gazebo** is elevated, in Chinese style, with 'keyhole' windows. There is also a stableblock dated 1735.[136]

Leaton Grange from the south-west

Leaton Grange (SJ 613114)
The oldest part of the complex is the crosswing at the west end. This is probably the solar wing to a medieval hall which has been replaced. It has crown-post roof construction, dendro-dated after 1313, and is unusual in having hipped ends. The central truss is intact at upper-floor level and has chamfered posts with jowelled heads, a

cranked, chamfered and rebated tie-beam and chamfered arch-braces. There are many additions to the house, from the 16th to the 19th centuries. From 1891 to 1905 the house was used as 'The Colonial Training Home for Girls' where destitute girls were trained for domestic service in the colonies.[137]

The Church Farm (SJ 624120)

This is a brick-built farmhouse of *c*.1800, two-storied, with a three-bay frontage and deep overhanging eaves. The front is symmetrical apart from the end chimneys; one is larger than the other. The brickwork is in Flemish bond and there are projecting, straight, rectangular corner pilasters. A distinctive feature is the fenestration. Five large windows with segmental heads are all of the 'Yorkshire' horizontally-sliding sash type. The roof over the main range has two trusses of the 'industrial king-post' type.

29 Charlton, Wrockwardine

The Summer House,
Eyton-on-Severn, Wroxeter

29 Charlton (SJ 600114)

A cottage which has every appearance of a squatter's dwelling: box-framed, single-storied with a large stone stepped out-built stack and a thatched roof. Very little altered except for the contrivance of a half-storey for a bedroom and a kitchen at the rear.

Wroxeter

The Summer House (SJ 573062)

This is all that remains of Sir Francis Newport's 1607 mansion. There were two summer/banqueting houses, one is incorporated into Eyton Farm, the other is freestanding, octagonal, open-arched below and floored above. Attached to it is a higher octagonal turret, three-storied and with an ogee cap. Towards the lane both units are in brickwork with white sandstone dressings. The brickwork incorporates some diaper patterning. The inner faces of both units show as red sandstone with the same white sandstone dressings. There is a flat roof with a stone balustrade on the lower unit which has mullioned and transomed windows. On the turret they are recessed two-light windows. In his later years the Shrewsbury architect, Thomas Farnolls Pritchard (1723-1777) occupied the building.[138]

Tithe Barn Cottage, Eyton-on-Severn, Wroxeter

Tithe Barn Cottage (SJ 575062)
This probably began as a barn belonging to Sir Francis Newport's 1607 mansion. There is a date of 1607 on the door lintel, but in modern numerals. Typical 17th-century with square-framing, five panels high and an added wing which has a stone lower storey and brick above. Added lean-to in brick at the rear. The whole is covered with 'Harnage' flags. There is a two-storied porch, also in square-framing. This seems to be a continuation of the framing on the long wall, but returns half-way along the gable. The whole is an essay in the use of Shropshire's three main building materials, timber, stone and brick—with indigenous roofing thrown in.

Appendix 1   Shropshire Buildings with Crucks

True Crucks

Grid Ref	State	Use	No.	Apex	Half-Hip	Blade Curve	Arch Brace	Source Publ.	Name	Parish, Name, Notes
SO 535956		E	2	B		C			SER	Acton Round, Church Porch
SJ 374115		D	5			E		VCH	MMO	Alberbury, Little Wollaston, Grange Farm
SJ 376140		A	2	E, F3		C		VCH	MMO	Alberbury, Lower Eyton Farm, was house
SO 526705		D	3	B		C			MMO	Ashford Carbonell, Nos. 8,9,10
SO 626828	R	A	2			C	*		MMO	Aston Botterell, Heywood Farm, Barn
SO 645949		D	3	L1, E		C			MMO	Aston Eyre, Ousley Barns (threaded purlins, no ridge)
SJ 423220		D	1			C			MMO	Baschurch, 7 Church Road
SJ 422212		D	4			E			MMO	Baschurch, Milford Cottages
SJ 426210	D								JTS	Baschurch, Prescott
SJ 422219		D	2	A		E			JTS	Baschurch, The Hollies
SO 367757		D	1	B		E	*	PEV	MMO	Bedstone, Manor (VEA, GAL, Dendro-dated 1448, no ridge purlin)
SJ 516079		D	1					VCH	MMO	Berrington, 118 Betton Abbots, (Spindle Cottage)
SO 323885		D	1	B		E		GAL	MMO	Bishop's Castle, Church St., Harp House
SO 323885	D	D	1	G					MMO	Bishop's Castle, 61 Church St.
SO 323883		A	1	L2		E			MMO	Bishop's Castle, The Bull Barn, now garage
SO 323887	D	D	2			C			JWT	Bishop's Castle, 4 Harley Jenkin St.
SO 319871		D	1	L2		E	*	GAL	MMO	Bishop's Castle, Colebatch, Swallow Beck Cottage (was Ivy Cottage)
SO 542776		D	3	A		C			MMO	Bitterley, Middleton, 2 & 3 Brookhouse Cottages
SO 543775		D	2	L2		C			MMO	Bitterley, Middleton, 1 Brookhouse Cottages
SO 539773		A	1	B		C			MMO	Bitterley, Middleton, Quarry Farm, barn, possibly was house
SJ 654207		D	1	A		C	*	VEA	MMO	Bolas Magna, Meeson Farm (has low-beam. Dendro-dated 1502)
SO 615699		D	2			C			MMO	Boraston, Homeside
SO 717930		C	4			C	*	VEA	MMO	Bridgnorth, Low Town, Brit. Legion, was warehouse. Dendro-dated 1392-1422
SO 492793	D	D						BRA	MMO	Bromfield, Prior's Halton Farm
SO 354738		D	3	B,D		C	*		MMO	Bucknell, The Post Office
SO 355742		D	1			C			MMO	Bucknell, Lower House Farm
SO 490964		D	3	L2		C	*	SHA	MMO	Cardington, Shootrough Farm. Dendro-dated 1422
SO 485965		D	3			E			MMO	Cardington, Comley, Comley Cottage
SO 514953		A	4			C			MMO	Cardington, Gretton, Court Farm, barn
SO 499946		A	1	D		E			MMO	Cardington, Willstone Farm, barn
SJ 664202		D	3	B		E			MMO	Cherrington, Cherrington Green, Long Acre
SJ 664202		D	3	A		E			MMO	Cherrington, 7 Cherrington Green
SJ 664202		D	3	L2		E	*	SHN	MMO	Cherrington, 8-9 Cherrington Green (No. 44, 1973)
SO 666202	D.R.	A	1			C		VEA	HHA	Cherrington, Cherrington Manor; Outbuilding, Dendro-dated 1537-57
SO 291974		D	4	G		C	*		MMO	Chirbury, Priest Weston, Old Smithy
SJ 425024		D	3					VCH	HMO	Church Pulverbatch, White Horse Inn (2 cruck ranges at right-angles)
SJ 425011		D,A	4	B		C	*	VCH	MMO	Church Pulverbatch, Shepton Fields (has low-beam)

True Crucks Grid Ref	State	Use	No.	Apex	Half-Hip	Blade Curve	Arch Brace	Source Publ.	Name	Parish, Name, Notes
SO 443918		D						VCH	MMO	Church Stretton, Little Stretton, Manor House
SO 444916		D	1			E			MMO	Church Stretton, Little Stretton, Bircher Cottage
SO 443919		D	1			E			MMO	Church Stretton, Little Stretton, Ragleth Inn
SO 431908		D	2	L2		C	*	PEV	MMO	Church Stretton, Minton, Longmynd House Farm, VCH
SO 456914		D	1			C		VCH	MMO	Church Stretton, Ragdon Farm
SO 563844		D	1	L2		C			MMO	Clee St. Margaret, Lower Brook House
SO 654784		D	2	L2			*	SHA	MMO	Cleobury Mortimer, Catherton Cottage (Vol.65, 1987. Dendro-dated 1485)
SO 304808		D	2			C		GAL	MMO	Clun, Clun Farm, (scarfed crucks. poss. 2 units at right-angles)
SO 303808		D	2	B				GAL	MMO	Clun, 17-19 High St. (has low beam)
SO 303811		D	1	B		C		GAL	MMO	Clun, Little Hospital, No. 2
SO 270824		D	1						MMO	Clun, Little Hall
SO 246820		D	5	B		C		GAL	JWT	Clun, Newcastle-on-Clun, Lower Spoad
SO 246820		A	4	E		C		GAL	JWT	Clun, Newcastle-on-Clun, Lower Spoad, barn
SO 247823		D	1			C		GAL	MMO	Clun, Newcastle-on-Clun, Old Plough
SO 326768		D	2	L2		C	*	VEA	HHA	Clun, Pentre Hodre (GAL, now Timber Croft, low beam. Dendro-dated 1465)
SO 303808		D	3			C		GAL	MMO	Clun, Sun Inn
SO 316758		D	4	L2		C		GAL	MMO	Clun, Chapel Lawn, Bryn Cambric
SO 360828		D	3	C		E		SMA	MMO	Clunbury, 25 Kempton (April 1957, 32. GAL, VEA, Dendro-dated 1474)
SJ 51 03	D	D						VCH	MMO	Condover, Cantlop, Lightgreen Coppice
SJ 494057		D	1	L2		C	*	VCH	MMO	Condover, Church House
SJ 495058		D	2	L2		C		VCH	MMO	Condover, 4-5 Church St (extended crucks)
SJ 495058		D	3	L2		C		VCH	MMO	Condover, 7 Church St.
SJ 495061		D	4	L2	*	C	*	VCH	MMO	Condover, Condover Court (VEA, dendro-dated 1445)
SJ 488035		D	2	L2, D			*	VCH	MMO	Condover, Gt. Ryton, 2 Grange Cottages
SJ 494060		D	1				*	VCH	MMO	Condover, Old School House
3J 498038		D	1	L2		C		VCH	MMO	Condover, Wheathall Farm
3J 495060		D	3	L2		C		VCH	MMO	Condover, Yew Tree Cottage
3J 544034		A	4	B		E		VCH	MMO	Cound, Golding, barn
SJ 558050	D	A	4					VCH	MMO	Cound, Rectory, tithe barn
SO 684059		D	2			C			MMO	Dawley, 15 & 15A Little Dawley
SO 498867		D	2	E		C			JWT	Diddlebury, Fernhall Mill
SO 607893		D	2			C	*		MMO	Ditton Priors, Botwood, (now workshop)
SJ 345406		D	2			C			MMO	Dudleston, Sodylt Farm
SJ 335384		D	2	G		C			MMO	Dudleston, Old Vron Farm
SO 567953		D	4	A	*	C	*	PEV	MMO	Easthope, Crowther's House (2 cruck ranges at right-angles)
SO 471879	R	D	2			C		SHA	MMO	Eaton-under-Heywood, Wolverton (in added crosswing)
SO 468903		D	1	L2		E	*		MMO	Eaton-under-Heywood, Marshbrook, Hatton Farm
SO 468903		D	1	E		E			MMO	Eaton-under-Heywood, Hatton, Upper Farm
SJ 722194		A	1	C					MMO	Edgmond, Stackyard Lane, Sunnyside, outbuilding
SJ 379375		D	2	E		C			MMO	Ellesmere Rural, Eastwick, Old Groves

Grid Ref	State	Use	No.	Apex	Half-Hip	Blade Curve	Arch Brace	Name	Source Publ.	Parish, Name, Notes
SJ 342343		D	2	G		C		CRY		Ellesmere Rural, Newnes, Dick Whittington's Cottage
SJ 570178		A	3	C		C		MMO		Ercall Magna, Poynton Manor, barn
SJ 631175		D	2	F1		C		CRY		Ercall Magna, 29 Crudgington
SJ 415138		D	3				*	JTS	VCH	Ford, Oak Cottages
SJ 373195		D	2	AA				MMO		Great Ness, Nesscliffe, Kinton, Kinton Cottage
SJ 522234		D	1	L2		C		ASN		Grinshill, Bromhaul
SO 571707		D	2			C		MMO		Greete, Lower Cottage
SJ 398036		D	3	A	**	C		EBE		Habberley, 1-2 Habberley (now Pear Tree Cottage)
SJ 403036		D	2			E		MMO		Habberley, The Old Mill
SJ 614286		D	1	L1		C		MMO	VEA	Hodnet, Drayton Road, No.20 (Dendro-dated 1467)
SJ 595295		D	1			C		MMO		Hodnet, Hawkstone Farm
SO 400809		D	3			E		MMO		Hopesay, Aston-on-Clun, 2 Broome
SJ 672034	R	D	1			C		MVO	SHN	Ironbridge, 23 High St. (No.38, 1970)
SJ 563008		D	1			E		MMO		Kenley, Old Post Office
SO 715775		D	3	L2	*	E	*	FCH	MCB	Kinlet, Silligrove
SJ 313212		D	4	G	*	E	*	MMO	EVH	Kinnerley, Maesbrook, Llwyn-y-Go
SJ 323228		D	3	B		E		MMO		Kinnerley, 1-2 Osbaston
SJ 324193	D	D	3	A		C	*	SRJ	SHA	Kinnerley, Tyr-y-Coed, (Vol.56, 1959)
SJ 545272		A	2			C		MMO		Lee Brockhurst, Manor Farm, barn
SO 475985		D	3	E		E	*	MMO	VCH	Leebotwood, Pound Inn
SO 475985		D	2			C		MMO		Leebotwood, 11 Leebotwood, Rose Cottage
SJ 604062		D	1			C		ASN		Leighton, Garmston, Pear Tree Cottage
SJ 407197		D	3	L2		C	*	MMO		Little Ness, Lower House Farm (has low-beam)
SJ 645068		D	2			C		MMO		Little Wenlock, Rose Cottage
SO 239799	R	A	1			C		MMO	VCH	Llanfair Waterdine, Llantroft, byre
SO 256757		D	3	B		C	*	MMO	GAL	Llanfair Waterdine, Trebert
SO 214786	R	A	2			C		MMO	GAL	Llanfair Waterdine, Coed-y-Hendre, barn
SO 268743	R	A	2					MMO	GAL	Llanfair Waterdine, Roadside barn, reused crucks for tie-beams
SJ 239229								PSM		Llanyblodwel. Erwbant
SJ 428058	R	D						MMO	VCH	Longden, Longden Hall Farm
SJ 424047		D	2			C		MMO	VCH	Longden, Oaks, Lower Farm
SJ 465298		D	2			C		MMO	SHA	Loppington, Brown Heath, Old House Farm (Vol.63, 1985)
SJ 469293		D	2	G				MMO	PEV	Loppington, Holly Cottage
SJ 463310	R	A	1			C		HHA		Loppington, Holywellmoor House, (from Pontesbury, tithe Barn 1)
SO 313848		A	1					HHA		Lydbury North, Acton, Acton House, barn
SO 328857		D	2	L2		C		MMO	GAL	Lydbury North, Brockton, No.28
SO 35 86	D	A	5		*			MMO		Lydbury North, Leas Meadow Farm, barn
SO 314905		A	1					HHA		Lydham, Lower Broughton, barn
SJ 696044		D	1	C		C		MMO		Madeley, 44 Church St.
SJ 695043		A	5	F2	**	E		MMO		Madeley, Church St, King Charles' Barn

True Crucks

Grid Ref	State	Use	No.	Apex	Half-Hip	Blade Curve	Arch Brace	Source Publ.	Name	Parish, Name, Notes
SO 291866		A	2	E		C		GAL	MMO	Mainstone, Cwm Colbatch, byre
SJ 593296		D	2			C			MMO	Marchamley, Old School House
SJ 676341	R	D	2						MMO	Market Drayton, Old School House
SJ 674343	R	A	1						MMO	Market Drayton, Frogmore Road, barn
SJ 375051		D	4						JWT	Minsterley, Crown & Sceptre
SJ 429162		D	1			E			MMO	Montford, 2 Forton
SO 333930		D	2			E			MMO	More, Lower Bent Farm
SO 622998		D	2			C			MMO	Much Wenlock, 18 High St.
SO 622998		D						HEF	MMO	Much Wenlock, 17 High St.
SJ 623000		D	3	G,H		S		HEF	MMO	Much Wenlock, St. Owen's Well House (VEA, Dendo-dated 1415)
SO 624999		D	6	L2,H	**	E	*	VEA	MMO	Much Wenlock, 25-28 Barrow St. (VEA, terrace, Dendro-dated 1435)
SO 623999		D	1			C			MMO	Much Wenlock, 24, Barrow St.
SJ 647022		D	1			E			MMO	Much Wenlock, Wyke Farm Cottage
SO 510867		D	2	B		C	*	SHA	JWT	Munslow, Aston Munslow, White House, (Vol.58, 1966)
SO 512867		D	1			C			MMO	Munslow, Aston Munslow, No.7
SO 522877		E	2	C		C			JWT	Munslow, Church Porch
SO 539895		D	1			C			MMO	Munslow, 21 Hungerford
SO 398912		2				C	*		MMO	Myndtown, Asterton, Home Farm
SO 688769		D	1	L1		C	*		MMO	Neen Savage, Little Wyre
SO 639882		A	5			C			MMO	Neenton, New House Farm, barn
SO 637879		D	2			C			MMO	Neenton, Hall Farm
SO 637879	R	A	1			C			MMO	Neenton, Hall Farm, barn
SJ 744195		D	1	L2,A		C			MMO	Newport, Chetwynd End, King's Head (1 blade, with low-beam)
SO 369906		D	3						MMO	Norbury, Hardwick Hall
SJ 288294	R	D	1			E			HHA	Oswestry, Welsh Walls, Holbache Museum
SJ 312250		A	2			C	*		MMO	Oswestry Rural, Maesbury, The Fields, barn, was house
SJ 312246		D	1			C			MMO	Oswestry Rural, Maesbury, Coed-y-Rae
SJ 299246		D	2	L2		C			ASN	Oswestry Rural, Morton, 2 Redwith Cottages
SJ 215239		A	3	L2,G		C	*		PSS	Oswestry Rural, Pen-y-Bont, Pentre Mawr, barn
SJ 238260		D				C			MMO	Oswestry Rural, Trefonen, Bryn Pentre
SJ 530043	D	D	1					VCH	MMO	Pitchford, Mill Cottages
SJ 375070	D	D	6	B	*	E		VCH	JWT	Pontesbury, Asterley, Upper House Farm, now barn
SJ 399059	D	D	2					EVH	MMO	Pontesbury, Birch Row
SJ 398060		A	2	B		E		VCH	JWT	Pontesbury, Challoner's Barn
SJ 401061	D,R	A	4					VCH	MMO	Pontesbury, Tithe Barn, 1 (reused as tie-beams)
SJ 400059		D	1					VCH	MMO	Pontesbury, Plough Inn and Garage
SJ 425068	D	D	3	L2	*			VCH	JWT	Pontesbury, Plealy, Brookgate Farm (VEA Dendro-dated 1490)
SJ 425067								VCH	MMO	Pontesbury, Plealy, Plealy Farm, (Old Farm) fragment
SJ 423069		A	3	B				VCH	JWT	Pontesbury, Plealy, Gallier's Farm, barn
SJ 426076	D	D	4	L2,D	*	C	*	VCH	MMO	Pontesbury, Sibberscot, barn, was house, (now at Brookgate Fm.)

True Crucks

Grid Ref	State	Use	No.	Apex	Half-Hip	Blade Curve	Arch Brace	Source Publ.	Name	Parish, Name, Notes
SJ 558333	D	D	3	B		C		SHN	JWT	Prees, Cross End (No.36, 1969)
SJ 557335		D	2	A,C		C	*	VEA	MMO	Prees, Manor Cott. (Dendro-dated 1551-2, pub. in *Vern. of Whitchurch*, 1999)
SJ 589155		D	1			C			MMO	Rodington, Rodenhurst Hall
SJ 589155		A	1	E		C			MMO	Rodington, Rodenhurst Hall, barn
SO 509925		D	3	H,E		C			JWT	Rushbury, Wall-under-Heywood, Hall Farm
SJ 39 22									JTS	Ruyton-XI-Towns
SJ 306362		D	5	B,E,G		C	*	NMR	MMO	St. Martin's, Escob Farm (cusped crucks)
SJ 306362		A	2	B		C		NMR	MMO	St. Martin's, Escob Farm, barn
SJ 327384		A	1	B		C			MMO	St. Martin's, Ifton Hall Farm, barn
SO 340370	R	D	4			E			MMO	St. Martin's, Pentre Morgan
SJ 321385	D	A	1	B		C			MMO	St. Martin's, Pen-y-Bryn, Upper House Farm, barn
SJ 565214		D	2	G					JWT	Shawbury, House
SO 563917		D	3	B	*	E			JWT	Shipton, cottage
SJ 398152		D	2	B		E			MMO	Shrawardine, The Critt, 13 & 14
SJ 498125		D	3			C		VEA	JWT	Shrewsbury, 18-19 Abbey Foregate (Dendro-dated 1408)
SJ 498125		D	3	F1		C		VEA	JWT	Shrewsbury, 20-21 Abbey Foregate (Dendro-dated 1430)
SJ 487129		D	2	B		E	*	PEV	MMO	Shrewsbury, 92 Frankwell
SO 435988		A	4	L1		C		VCH	JWF	Smethcott, Betchcott, Middle Farm (perhaps house, now barn)
SO 435988		A	3	B		C		VCH	JWT	Smethcott, Betchcott, Middle Farm, barn
SO 434995		D	4			C		VCH	JWT	Smethcott, Picklescott
SO 574909		D	3	A		E			SER	Stanton Long, The Malthouse
SO 567823		E	2	B		C			CRY	Stoke St. Milborough, Church Porch
SJ 640278		D	1			C			MMO	Stoke-upon-Tern, Stoke, Farmhouse
SO 436817		D	3	E		C	*	ABC	MMO	Stokesay, Stokesay Castle, hall, VEA (Dendro-dated 1284-5)
SO 698834	R	A	6	L1		E	*		MMO	Stottesdon, Chorley, Lower Farm, barn
SO 644856		D	3	A,G		C	*		MMO	Stottesdon, Wrickton Mill Cottage
SJ 600095		D	1	A		C			MMO	Uppington, Avenue Farm
SJ 553125		D	1	S					JTS	Upton Magna, No.3
SJ 553125		D	2		*	E		VEA	JTS	Upton Magna, No.12 (Now Cruck Cottage; Dendro-dated 1269)
SJ 554126	D	D							JTS	Upton Magna, third
SJ 529287		D	1	C		C	*		MMO	Wem, Aston Bridge Farm (pub. in *Vern. of Whitchurch*, 1999)
SJ 372068		D	2	C		E		VCH	MMO	Westbury, Westley, Upper Lake (Dendro-dated 1545-6)
SJ 383095		D	3			C		VCH	JWT	Westbury, Stoney Stretton Manor Farm
SJ 343235		D	1			C		GOR	MMO	West Felton, Sandford, Home Farm
SO 620818		D	1			E			MMO	Wheathill, Doctor's Cottages
SJ 543413		D	1	A		C			CRY	Whitchurch, 6, Dodington (pub. in *Vern. of Whitchurch*, 1999)
SJ 545411	D	D	3						MMO	Whitchurch, Porter's Yard
SJ 545410	R.D.		1						MMO	Whitchurch, rear of White Bear, stable/store "
SJ 544410	D	D	2						MMO	Whitchurch, cottage behind Whittinghams, "
SJ 544410	D	D	4						MMO	Whitchurch, rear of Swan Hotel, "

True Crucks

Grid Ref	State	Use	No.	Apex	Half-Hip	Blade Curve	Arch Brace	Source Publ.	Name	Parish, Name, Notes
SJ 543415	D							MMO	MMO	Whitchurch, rear of Bull Ring Vaults "
SJ 543415	D							MMO	MMO	Whitchurch, outbuilding to White Lion "
SJ 545415	D							MMO	MMO	Whitchurch, cottages behind Fountain House "
SJ 546415	D		1½					MMO	MMO	Whitchurch, cottage in Paradise Row "
SJ 534412	D		2					MMO	MMO	Whitchurch, cottage in Wrexham Rd. "
SJ 540416	D		6					MMO	MMO	Whitchurch, Newtown "
SJ 540416	D							MMO	MMO	Whitchurch, Newtown "
SJ 541417	D		4					MMO	MMO	Whitchurch, Yardington "
SJ 586405	D		1	G		C		MMO	MMO	Whitchurch, R. Ash, Ash Wood, (VEA Dendro-dated 1550) "
SJ 316119	D		2	E,H		C	*	VCH	JWT	Wollaston, Winnington, The Green Farm
SO 453984	D		2	H		C	*	VCH	JWT	Woolstaston, No.38, Has low-beam (VEA Dendro-dated 1399-1400)
SO 453984	A		4	H		C		VCH	JWT	Woolstaston, No.38, barn
SO 759985	A		4			C		VEA	MMO	Worfield, Ackleton, Stableford Farm (19c. laminated crucks)
SO 769959	D		1	L2	*	C		VEA	MMO	Worfield, Bradney Farm (Dendro-dated 1486)
SO 769959	R		1			C		VEA	MMO	Worfield, Bradney Farm
SJ 301042	D		5	L2		C	*		MMO	Worthen, Binweston Farm, now barn
SJ 301042	R		1	F3		C			MMO	Worthen, Binweston Farm, barn
SJ 563082	D		1	G		C			ASN	Wroxeter, 1-2 Glebe Cottages
SJ 398102	A		6	G		C		VCH	JWT	Yockleton, Bank Farm, barn

Possible Crucks

Grid Ref	State	Use	No.	Apex	Half-Hip	Blade Curve	Arch Brace	Source Publ.	Name	Parish, Name, Notes
SJ 42 21	D							VCH	JTS	Baschurch, Elsdon
SJ 52 05	D							VCH	MM	Berrington, Cantlop, Bendigo, (VCH, Vol. 8, 18)
SJ 494059	D							VCH	MMO	Condover, Condover Green, Arbour House
SJ 443062	D							VCH	MMO	Longden, Hall Farm, outbuilding
SJ 415085	D							VCH	MMO	Pontesbury, Lea, Lea Farm
SJ 398100	D							VCH	MMO	Yockleton, Upper House Farm (fragment, possible cruck)

Jointed Crucks

Grid Ref	State	Use	No.	Apex	Half-Hip	Blade Curve	Arch Brace	Source Publ.	Name	Parish, Name, Notes
SO 566953	D		1			C	*		HHA	Easthope. Manor Farm

Short Curved Feet

Grid Ref	State	Use	No.	Apex	Half-Hip	Blade Curve	Arch Brace	Source Publ.	Name	Parish, Name, Notes
SO 323889			1			E			MMO	Bishop's Castle, 2 The Square, rear

Upper Crucks

Grid Ref	State	Use	No.	Apex	Half-Hip	Blade Curve	Arch Brace	Source Publ.	Name	Parish, Name, Notes
SO 455896	A		4			C			HHA	Acton Scott, Hall Farm Museum, barn
SO 760845	D		1			C		VEA	MMO	Alveley, Bell Inn (V.A. 29;)
SO 760845	A		3			C		VEA	MMO	Alveley, Bell Inn, Granary, (V.A. 29, Dendro-dated c.1824)
SO 629854	A		2			E			MMO	Aston Botterell, Chatmore Farm, barn
SO 738931	D		3			E		VGR	MMO	Bridgnorth, 42 Riverside

Grid Ref	State	Use	No.	Apex	Half-Hip	Blade Curve	Arch Brace	Source Publ.	Name	Parish, Name, Notes
SO 717932		D	1			E		VGR	MMO	Bridgnorth, 59 High St.
SO 716932		D	2			E		VGR	MMO	Bridgnorth, 13a St. Mary's St.
SO 356740		D	1						MMO	Bucknell, Old Farm
SO 356740		A	1	D					MMO	Bucknell, Old Farm, barn
SJ 666202		A	1	C					MMO	Cherrington, Cherrington Manor, granary
SO 566844		C	1	D		C			MMO	Clee St. Margaret, The Steppes
SO 548835		A	4			S			MMO	Clee St. Margaret, Cold Weston Court, barn
SO 512825		A	2			C			MMO	Diddlebury, Little Sutton
SO 484909		A	2						HHA	Eaton-u-Heywood, Ticklerton, Upper Farm, granary, (stilted crucks)
SO 468903		A	3	E		E			MMO	Eaton-u-Heywood, Hatton, Upper & Middle Farms (shared building)
SJ 594174		D	3	E		E	*	HEF	ASN	High Ercall, High Ercall Hall (no ridge)
SO 394834		D	2						MMO	Hopesay, Brook House
SJ 668035		A	3			E		IAR	MMO	Ironbridge, Swan Inn, malthouse, 1 (west)
SJ 668035		A	2			E		IAR	MMO	Ironbridge, Swan Inn, malthouse, 2 (east)
SO 268743		A	2	E		E			MMO	Llanfair Waterdine, roadside barn, (also has reused crucks)
SJ 240299		D	3	D		C		VCH	MMO	Llanyblodwel, Tanat House
SJ 443062		D	1						MMO	Longden, Hall Farm
SO 512745		D	1			E		LRP	MMO	Ludlow, 5 Broad St, de Grey's Cafe
SO 513749		A	3			E			MMO	Ludlow, 139A Corve St
SO 513749		A	1						MMO	Ludlow, 137 Corve St
SO 615987		D	1			E		VCH	MMO	Much Wenlock, Bourton Road, No.5
SO 621997		A	1					VCH	MMO	Much Wenlock, Bourton Road, The Old Malthouse
SJ 399058		A	2	E		E			MMO	Pontesbury, Tithe Barn, 2
SJ 408080		D	1						MMO	Pontesbury, Hinton, Hinton Farm (Vol.8, 258)
SJ 493212		A	3			E			ASN	Preston Gubbals, Lea Hall, outbuilding
SJ 488125		D	1						ASN	Shrewsbury, Claremont Buildings, No.1
SJ 498128		A	2			E			MMO	Shrewsbury, Frankwell, Fellmongers
SJ 493123		D	2			E		VEA	MMO	Shrewsbury, 2 Milk St. (Dendro-dated 1655)
SJ 490125	D	D	1			E		JTS	MMO	Shrewsbury, 5 Hill's Lane
SJ 554127		D	1			E		EVH	MMO	Upton Magna, No.8
SJ 542417		D	2			C			MMO	Whitchurch, Church St., Horse & Jockey; (pub. in *Vern. of Whitchurch*, 1999)
SJ 542416		D	1						MMO	Whitchurch, 23, High St., (stilted crucks)
SJ 544413		A	1			E			MMO	Whitchurch, 25, Dodington (over Tack-room)
SO 759985		A	4			C			MMO	Worfield, Ackleton, Stableford Farm, (19c. laminated crucks)

Base Crucks

Grid Ref	State	Use	No.	Apex	Half-Hip	Blade Curve	Arch Brace	Source Publ.	Name	Parish, Name, Notes
SO 642848		D	1			C	*	VEA	MMO	Aston Botterell, The Bold (SHA, Dendro-dated 1320-54)
SO 771936		D	1			C	*	VEA	MMO	Claverley, High Grosvenor (SHA, Dendro-dated 1375-77)
SO 376866		D	1			C	*	VEA	MMO	Lydbury North, Plowden Hall (SHA, Dendro-dated 1302)
SJ 629364		D	1	E		C	*	VEA	MMO	Moreton Say, Oldfields Farm (pub in *Vern. of Whitchurch*, 1999) no ridge
SO 624999		D	1			C	*	VEA	MMO	Much Wenlock, 23, Barrow St (Dendro-dated 1327-30)

Base Crucks

Grid Ref	State	Use	No.	Apex	Half-Hip	Blade Curve	Arch Brace	Source Publ.	Name	Parish, Name, Notes
SO 623998	D		1			C	*	VEA	MMO	Much Wenlock, High St., Barclay's Bank (SHA, Dendro-dated 1408)
SJ 543414	D		1			C			MMO	Whitchurch, Watergate, The Old Eagles (pub. in *Vern. of Whitchurch*, 1999)

Base Cruck Variants

Grid Ref	State	Use	No.	Apex	Half-Hip	Blade Curve	Arch Brace	Source Publ.	Name	Parish, Name, Notes
SO 606795	D		1	F2		C	*	SHA	MMO	Bitterley, Cleeton Court
SO 471879	D		1	F2		C	*	VEA	MMO	Eaton-under-Heywood, Wolverton (SHA, Dendro-dated 1475)
SO 698834	D		1	L2		C			MMO	Stottesdon, Chorley, Lower Farm

Total (All kinds) @ September 2001- 273

Codes:

State
R Reused
D Demolished

Use
E Ecclesiatic
A Agricultural
D Domestic

Blade Curve
C Smooth curve
E Elbowed

Apex Joints
See Glossary

Abbreviations:

ABC R.A. Cordingley, Art Bulletin, 1963, (45)
ASN A. Snell
BRA British Architect, May 1881
CRY Miss C. Ryan
EBE Mrs E. Beaton
EVH Mercer, English Vernacular Houses, 1976
FCH F.W.B. Charles
GAL The Gale of Life, 2000
GOR L. Gore
HEF H.E. Forrest
HHA H. Hand
IAR Institute of Industrial Archaeology
JTS J.T. Smith
JWT J.W. Tonkin
LRP Ludlow Research Papers
MBC F.W.B. Charles, Medieval Cruck Building
MMO Mrs M. Moran
NMR National Monuments Record
PEV Pevsner, Buildings of England, Shropshire
PSS P. Smith, Supplements to Welsh Lists after HWC
SER S.E. Rigold
SHA Shropshire Archaeological Society, Transactions
SHN Shropshire Archaeological Society, Newsletter
SMA Shropshire Magazine
SRJ S.R. Jones
VCH Victoria County History
VEA Vernacular Architecture (Journal)
VGR Mrs V. Grose

Appendix 2   The Shropshire Dendrochronolgy Project

By Daniel Miles, Oxford Dendrochronology Laboratory

Introduction

After more than two decades spent working on the vernacular buildings of Shropshire, Madge Moran had become increasingly frustrated by the lack of firmly dated buildings in the county on which to develop a typological chronology. By 1990, only a few timber-framed buildings had been sampled, and only two yielded any useful data.

Encouraged by the successes enjoyed by Sarah Pearson with the Royal Commission project in Kent, and Nat Alcock with the Leverhulme Cruck Project, Madge felt it was time to try and redress the balance in Shropshire. Despite unsuccessful applications to both the Leverhulme Trust and the Society for Medieval Archaeology, she was able to engender support from a wide range of academic as well as private individuals. She was greatly aided in this initially by two people in particular—Eric Mercer, late of the Royal Commission of Historic Monuments, and George Baugh of the Shropshire Victoria County History. Together they wrote numerous grant applications, sent pleading letters, and generally badgered and bullied until grants were received or pledged from the following national bodies: the British Academy, the Society of Antiquaries of London, the Royal Archaeological Institute, and the Vernacular Architecture Group. On a local level, grants were received from Shropshire County Council and the Roy Fletcher Fund. Several other groups contributed towards specific buildings.

Once funds were in place to date some two dozen buildings, we were fortunate enough to be selected as the dendrochronologists in 1992 and enjoyed a good working relationship with the group during the following decade. Initially, D. Haddon-Reece provided assistance in the Laboratory, and from 1996 Michael Worthington began, helping both on site as well as in the lab. One other person must be mentioned, for the work would not have progressed as far if it were not for the indefatigable services of Henry Hand. Not only did he record and draw many of the houses sampled, but accompanied us to virtually every building assisting with reassuring the owners, moving furniture, loading and unloading equipment, crawling into the most cramped of roof-spaces to bring the one piece of missing equipment, and providing transport in the trusty veteran Range Rover. All of this he gave freely and without complaint, and we all owe him a huge debt of gratitude. It also needs to be said that Madge Moran provided the accommodation throughout the ten years of fieldwork, much of the transport, and all of the meals, every one worthy of three Michelin stars.

Preliminary tree-ring work to the Shropshire Dendrochronology Project 1972-91

Prior to 1992, Shropshire was a quiet backwater in the development of dendrochronology. But this was not as a result of a late start, for some of the earliest efforts at tree-ring dating in Britain were carried out in the county in 1972 by V. Siebenlist-Kerner from Munich. As part of a project to make a chronology for Wales and western England, two buildings were sampled in the county. These were the Bear Steps complex in Shrewsbury and the Church of St. Michael, Alberbury. At the Bear Steps, previous restoration works by F.W.B. Charles in the 1960s allowed the collection of a number of offcuts, one of which dated and produced a felling date of 1576.[1] Although the provenance of the samples taken during the repairs is not known, more recent work funded by English Heritage has found a purlin in the gallery with the same felling date.[2] Samples from

Alberbury Church included timber from the tower and the pews, but none was dated. Siebenlist-Kerner's original hand-written data sheets for both sites were recently discovered in the archive of Dr. John Fletcher at the Oxford Dendrochronology Laboratory, and the transcription and re-analysis of this material may enable further samples to be dated in the future. Dr. Fletcher was an early pioneer of the science of dendrochronology and had quickly appreciated its potential in studying the development of timber-framing, investigating the medieval buildings of the Oxford region between 1974 and 1986.

Back in Shropshire, a decade passed between the dating of the first and second buildings. In 1982 the Bucknell Barn at Craven Arms was moved to Burleydam (Cheshire) and four timbers were sampled by the Tree-ring Laboratory at Liverpool Polytechnic, to be combined to form a 182-year chronology ending in 1595.[3] However, none of the samples retained any evidence of sapwood, therefore a felling period could not have been any earlier than 1606.

Between 1985 and 1987, excavations in the former precincts at Shrewsbury Abbey revealed a number of oak and alder waterlogged samples. Only one of the oak samples dated, a pile with incomplete sapwood which had a heartwood/sapwood boundary date of 1256.[4] Taking into account surviving sapwood, and the lower sapwood estimate of 11-41 rings, this timber produced a felling date range of 1269-97. In 1990-91 St. Winifred's Well, Woolston was being repaired and the Landmark Trust commissioned some tree-ring dating which produced a much reduced date range of 1478-82.[5]

Shropshire Dendrochronology Project 1992-2002

By the time the first phase of fieldwork commenced, grants were received from the British Academy, the Society of Antiquaries, Shropshire County Council, the Royal Archaeological Institute, the Vernacular Architecture Group, and the Victoria County History (Shropshire). This first session commenced on 18 October 1992, and included Moat House, Longnor (1467), Great Oxenbold, Monkhopton (1247), Brookgate Farm, Plealy (1490), and Condover Court (1443). The results of the first 12 buildings were published in 1993.[6] The buildings also included the fattest cruck at 23 Barrow Street Much Wenlock (1327-30), the most awkward roof to access at the Guildhall, Ludlow (1411), and the dirtiest roof at the Guildhall, Newport (1487).

The second year's work during 1993 included 14 buildings.[7] Notable among these are the two most derelict buildings in the Shropshire survey at Fulway Cottage, Cound (1603), and Cottage Farm, Easthope (1430). At 55 Sheinton Street, Much Wenlock (1246-80), were found the oldest tree-rings in a Shropshire building reaching back to AD 881, showing that this building must have been built of trees in excess of 400 years old.

The third year of the project saw 15 buildings dated.[8] Star buildings included the most moulded cruck at Manor Farm, Bedstone (1448/9), and the earliest crucks to be found in the Shropshire, and the second oldest in the whole of Britain, at Upton Magna (1269).

Although the project was intended to conclude after three years of fieldwork, further funding from the Owen Family Trust allowed a fourth year of fieldwork to date another 13 buildings.[9] By 1995 some 54 buildings had been dated, and an interim regional chronology—SALOP95 —constructed. This comprised 71 individual sites mainly from Shropshire and surrounding counties, as well as the regional chronology by Giertz Siebenlist-Kerner. Ten of the components were by other laboratories. This chronology extended from AD 946 to 1745 and despite its rough and ready fabrication, was found to be extremely robust and invaluable in helping to date other buildings in the county.

Although the fourth year was projected to be the conclusion of the project, further contributions from private individuals as well as another grant from the Owen Family Trust, allowed a further 11 buildings to be dated during a fifth year of work.[10] This was greatly bolstered by support from English Heritage in commissioning major projects at the Bear Steps complex in Shrewsbury, Wistanstow Church and Stokesay Castle. At Wistanstow, the north transept roof produced a felling date range of 1200-1222, making it the earliest dated timber structure in Shropshire.[11] At Stokesay Castle, over ten phases of work were identified and dated, extending back as early as 1262.

During 1997, a sixth year of field work comprising six buildings was undertaken before funds ran out.[12] This was partially due to the contribution of Time Team in dating Hall Farm, Aston Eyre, and for the National Trust in commissioning the crown-post roof at Home Farm, Attingham (1385/6). A useful late contribution to the Shropshire building chronology was made by the malt-house or granary at the Bell Inn, Alveley (1753/4, extended 1824).

Although it looked as though 1997 was to be the final year of the project, further funding from English Heritage, groups in Bridgnorth, and in particular a phased grant from the Shrewsbury Civic Society allowed a further nine buildings to be dated.[13] Three more buildings were dated during an eighth year in1998, thanks also to a grant from the Marc Fitch Fund and North Shropshire District Council.[14] The Marc Fitch grant was specifically for completing the dating of Shropshire's crown-post roofs.

With the grant from the Marc Fitch Fund and Shrewsbury Civic Society, a ninth year of field-work during 2001 allowed a further nine buildings to be dated.[15] This total was greatly enhanced by work in Clungunford by English Heritage commissioning work on the nave roof of the church, and the local PCC commissioning complementary work on the chancel and north vestry aisle roofs. A further six buildings in the parish were dated through a Local Heritage Initiative grant administered by Alick and Fiona Barratt and a local individual.[16]

After ten years of fieldwork, some 105 individual buildings had been dated, encompassing 180 individual construction phases. Considering the original project was only intended to run for three years and date some 24 buildings, this is nothing short of an outstanding achievement for Madge Moran who organised the project, and to all those people and grant-giving bodies, from all walks of life, who have contributed financially as well as in kind. Here, one can truthfully say that the project not only snow-balled, but positively avalanched.

Work outside the Shropshire Dendrochronology Project 1992-2002
The dendrochronological record of Shropshire would not be complete without mentioning the independent work of other labs and researchers which during the last decade, dating six other buildings. Sheffield Dendrochronology Laboratory have dated Langley Gatehouse to 1606/7,[17] Ightfield Hall Farm Barn, Ightfield to 1567,[18] a sill beam from Newton Mill, Craven Arms to after 1596,[19] and the nave roof of St. Swithin's Church, Clunbury to 1494/5.[20] Nigel Nayling whilst at Sheffield dated various phases ranging from the fourteenth to the seventeenth century in the tower of Shrewsbury Abbey,[21] and from Lampeter Dendrochronology Laboratory dated the nave roof at St Marys Church, Bromfield, to after 1559 and supporting the inscribed building date of 1577, and identifying a number of later repairs in the following century.[22]

The sampling strategy
Given the wide-ranging scope of the project, a sampling strategy was chosen that focused more on dating as many buildings as possible rather than on chronology building. Generally, one would

look to taking between 8 and 10 samples per building phase. However, this would have resulted in perhaps half as many building phases being dated. Instead, it was decided to spread the sampling further by averaging between 4 and 6 samples per phase, with some of the subsidiary phases being represented sometimes by as little as a one or two samples. Of course, sampling was often reduced to this level by the lack of suitable ring sequences within the timbers available. Obviously, the primary strategy in selecting samples within a structure was to choose those with ring sequences that were likely to date. When these were of marginal quality, more than the average number would be taken, if they were available, to increase the likelihood of the site dating. Another factor determining sample depth is the presence of sapwood. To better understand the probable construction date of any phase of building, as many samples as possible with complete sapwood need to be taken. However, in any typical timber-framed building only one or two, and rarely more than five or six, samples with complete sapwood would survive the initial conversion of the timbers and subsequent degradation and attrition over the ensuing centuries. Therefore, a priority in sampling was always to try to obtain as many samples as possible with bark edge and high ring counts.

Normally, a series of buildings would be given preliminary assessments of their dendrochronological potential. It is often the case that the most important building from a building historian's point of view offers the dendrochronologists the least dating potential. However, from the outset, the buildings were chosen for sampling beforehand and were assessed and either sampled or rejected on the same day. Remarkably, it was not until half-way through the project that a building was rejected on the grounds of having insufficient potential. Throughout the course of the project, only a few buildings were rejected at assessment stage. These included Brook House Farm and 12 High Street, both in Much Wenlock. Three other building phases failed to date: The crown-post hall roof at Bear Steps, Shrewsbury, the Bell Inn at Alveley, and the base cruck at Oldfields Farm, Moreton Say. Other buildings failed to have primary timbers date, such as at 15 Bridge Street, Bridgnorth, or only had timbers without any sapwood date, such as at Leaton Grange, Wrockwardine. Only two householders refused entry—one in Ludlow was particularly worried that it might result in her receiving a blue plaque!

This high success rate is due primarily to the quality of the timber in Shropshire. Early on, it was discovered that the buildings in the south of the county were far more dateable than those to the north-east. This is primarily due to geographical reasons, in that the south-west is very hilly with slow-grown timber, whereas the north-east tends to be flat, resulting in fast-grown complacent trees. Given this distribution, resources tended to be concentrated on the southern half of the county where the success rate was better (see distribution map opposite).

Dendrochronology has, through multiple felling dates within individual sites, shown that trees used in any one building were rarely felled all at one time. Indeed, evidence suggests that the trees required were often felled over a period of two or three years. Of course there are some examples, albeit with only two or three felling dates each, which were found to have been felled in the same year and season, such as 12 and 13 Upton Magna, where both crucks were felled in the summer of 1269, and at the Forester's Lodge, Upper Millichope, where two later phases of replacement joists had two felled in the winter of 1450/51, and three from the summer of 1633.[23] At Meeson Farm, Bolas Magna, a cruck, purlin, and collar were all found to have been felled in the winter of 1502/3.[24] These were probably all felled at one time from a single woodland source. Often, there will be a variation within a single year, for instance at the Porch House, Bishop's Castle, four timbers were found to have been felled between winter 1564/5 and spring 1565.[25] What is far more common is to find variations over a year or two.

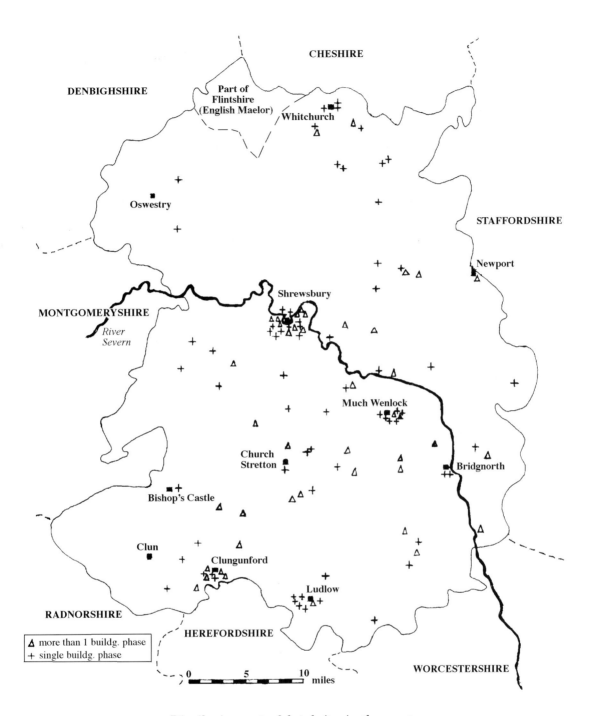

Distribution map of dated sites in the county

However, more extreme examples were often found, as at Stokesay Castle, where the main range of buildings were found to have 11 felling dates ranging from spring 1285 to spring 1290.[26] However, even smaller buildings were found to have a wide variation in felling dates, as at Abcott Manor, Clungunford, where one rafter was found to be felled in the spring of 1543, and another in the summer of 1546, as was a ridge piece, and at Lane End Cottage, Muckleton, where a crown-post dated to the winter of 1367/8, and a principal post to the winter of 1371/2.[27] Probably the most diverse example is at Brookgate Farm, Plealy, where a single phase produced no less than seven different felling dates for as many timbers, ranging from spring 1487 to summer 1490.[28]

Whilst the example from Stokesay Castle is most likely due to stockpiling during large, extended building campaigns, the other examples are all rural in nature, and from not necessarily exceptionally large houses. In other counties where extensive fieldwork has been carried out, such as Hampshire, the rural houses tended to have more consistent felling dates, whereas larger or urban projects tended to have wider date ranges.[29] In Shropshire, however, variation in felling dates were found to be equally common in the country as in the town. This illustrates the need to obtain as many samples with complete sapwood as possible to avoid the very real risk of sampling the one timber which had been stockpiled a few years earlier, thereby allowing an earlier construction date to be inferred. Ideally, had unlimited funding been available, or more timbers retaining sound sapwood, it would have been preferable to take more samples where available. But as this was not the case, a lack of refinement in the interpretation of felling dates in some circumstances has been considered acceptable when viewed in the overall scope of the project.

Another inherent danger in any dendrochronological study is the presence of re-used timbers. Generally, careful study of the timberwork prior to sampling will identify second-hand timbers, but occasionally even appearances can be deceiving. For example, Old Hall Farm, All Stretton, consists of a cross-wing of 1565, and a lobby-entry range of 1630. However, one of the principal rafters with no obvious signs of reuse dated to 1533.[30] This clearly illustrates why single samples from buildings are not ideal, especially if one accidentally happens on a rogue timber from an earlier structure. Repairs can be equally confusing, but are generally more easily identifiable, unless the building had undergone more extensive dismantling and reconstruction using second-hand timbers from elsewhere.

Unquestionably, the project has been a great success, and, as chapter 14 shows, has enabled an evaluation based on scientific fact, rather than guesswork, to be made of Shropshire's vernacular buildings. Enthusiasm shows no sign of abating, and we look forward to continuing this very valuable exercise in Shropshire.

The Shropshire Dendrochronology Project was funded by the following:

Grant-giving bodies
British Academy (three grants)
Fletcher Fund
Ludlow Civic Society
Ludlow Research Group
Marc Fitch Fund
North Shropshire District Council (two grants)
Owen Family Trust (three grants)
Royal Archaeological Institute
Shrewsbury Civic Society
Shropshire Archaeological and Historical Society
Shropshire County Council (two grants)
Shropshire Victoria County History
Society of Antiquaries
Vernacular Architecture Group

The following have wholly commissioned the dating of their buildings:

Mr. & Mrs. M. Barker	Bradney Farm, Worfield
Alick and Fiona Barratt	Abcott Manor, Clungunford
	Bird in the Rock Tea Rooms
	Church Farm, Clungunford
	Clungunford Farm
	Rowton Grange, Clungunford
Bridgnorth Civic Society	All Forces Club, Bridgnorth
Bridgnorth Historical Research Group	15 Bridge Street, Bridgnorth
Clungunford PCC	Clungunford Church (chancel and north vestry)
Mrs. S. Crow	Cherrington Manor
	Meeson Farm, Bolas Magna
English Heritage	2 Milk Street, Shrewsbury
	Abbot's Lodgings, Buildwas Abbey
	Stokesay Castle
	The Old Mansion, Shrewsbury
	Timber Croft, Pentre Hodre, Clun
	Upper Lake, Westbury
	Wistanstow Church
	Clungunford Church (nave)
Mr. R. Hartley	Golding Hall
Mrs. M. Harvey	Bodenham's, Ludlow
Mr. A. Jones	Meeson Hall, Bolas Magna
The Landmark Trust	St. Winifred's Well
The Millichope Trust	Upper Millichope
The National Trust	Home Farm, Attingham
Newport Town Council	Newport Guildhall

North Shropshire District Council   28 Watergate, Whitchurch
Lt. Cdr. J. Oldham-Malcolm   Leaton Grange, Wrockwardine
Mr. E. Ratcliff   Detton Hall, Neen Savage
Mr. Bill Sheridan   The Bell Inn, Alveley
Mr. Brian Taylor   Sycamore Farm, Clungunford
Time-Team C4   St. Owens Well House, Much Wenlock

                                       55 and 56 Sheinton Street, Much Wenlock
                                       Hall Farm, Aston Eyre
                                       High Ercall Hall, High Ercall

The following have made contributions to the dating of individual buildings:
Michael and Jacqui Bond   Shootrough, Cardington
Mr. Louis DeWet   Prior's Hall, Wenlock Abbey, Much Wenlock
Mr. J.W. Fearnall   Alkington Hall, Whitchurch
Mr. T. Holmes   Bowdlers House (38/39) Woolstaston
Mr. & Mrs. A. Ketchen   14 Callaughton, Much Wenlock
Peter & Margaret Richards   Moat House, Longnor
Sir Hugh Ripley   Bedstone Manor
Shropshire VCH   25-28 Barrow Street, Much Wenlock
Time-Team C4   Prior's Hall, Wenlock Abbey, Much Wenlock

                                       25-28 Barrow Street, Much Wenlock

Mr. E.A. Windsor   Park Farm, Alkington

Glossary

Aedicule:	An opening framed by two columns supporting an entablature and a pediment
Arcade-plate:	Longitudinal timber set along the tops of arcade posts in an aisled building
Arris:	The line along which two timber surfaces meet
Ashlar:	Stone worked to a fine finish. Also applied to fine jointing
Baffle-entry:	Similar to a lobby-entry. Progress is inhibited by the side of the chimneystack and rooms are accessed to the right and left. Strictly, in the 'baffle' entry there are no doors to the rooms
Bay:	The area between two main frames of a building, used as a unit of measurement, *e.g.* 'two-bay hall'
Blazon:	In heraldry the science or rules of coats-of-arms
Bolection moulding:	A moulding which projects beyond the surface of the panel, frame or feature
Box-frame:	Timber-framing in which posts and beams form a 'box' which supports the roof directly and in which the walls are integral. *cf.* 'Cruck'
Brace:	In timber-framing a strengthening timber set diagonally
Arch-	Curved and usually used in pairs; in roof construction, between wall or post and tie or collar above; in wall-framing between post and rail or wallplate above
Passing-	A lengthy timber, passing other truss components
Scissor-	Two timbers crossing diagonally, usually applicable to roof construction
Tension-	In wall-framing between post and rail or sill below
Wind-	In roofs usually set in pairs between principals and side purlins to resist wind pressure and to stiffen the construction. Can be straight, curved or cranked. Often decorative and sometimes tiered
Byng:	In Shropshire a feeding walk in a shippon (cow-house)
Cadency mark:	In heraldry the emblem or symbol of younger sons
Cavetto Moulding:	A hollow moulding
Chamfer:	The surface formed by cutting off a square edge, usually at 45°
Cheese Oven Shute:	In small-scale cheese-making the cheeses were kept in a cupboard by the side of the fireplace (the oven). They were then hauled by means of a rope up the chute into the cheese storage room
Clemming house:	Where beasts are 'clemmed' (starved) prior to slaughter
Closed Truss:	A cross-frame in which the spaces between the timbers are filled, usually with wattle-and-daub. Openings may be left for doors and windows
Collar-beam:	A transverse timber connecting rafters or cruck blades at a point below the apex and above the tie-beam
Collar-purlin:	The longitudinal timber supported by the crown-post. Often the only lengthwise stiffening in crown-post roof construction. Sometimes called the 'collar-plate'
Cornice:	The uppermost member of the entablature, projecting above the frieze. The moulding running round a room at the junction of the walls and ceiling
Console:	A form of bracket with a uniform front width and S-shaped profile, the lower curve smaller than the upper
Copyhold:	In law, a right to hold land the title of which is taken from a copy of the manorial court roll. Virtually freehold
Croggloft:	A built-in sleeping shelf in an otherwise open unit. A Welsh term
Cross Passage:	Entry and exit through opposed doorways and with a wall or partition on the hall side. Sometimes 'Through Passage'
Crown-post:	The upright central timber standing on a tie-beam and supporting a crown-plate or collar-purlin. It does not rise to the apex and is usually braced four ways. Usually not associated with side purlins

Crow-stepped gable: Where the stone or brick slopes of the gable are arranged in steps

Cruck: A pair of inclined timbers, usually wrought from a single tree, forming an arch. The roof is supported on the back of the cruck 'blades' and the walls are independent. There are many variants. See chapter on 'Cruck Construction'. *cf.* 'box-frame'

Apex Joints:

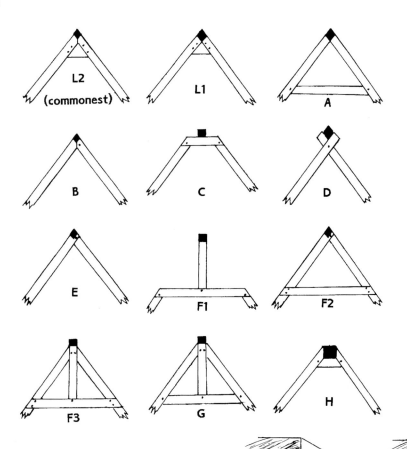

Cyma Recta moulding: An S-shaped moulding with the concave part uppermost (see near right)

Cyma Reversa moulding: As above, but with the convex part uppermost (see far right)

Dendrochronology: The science of sampling and analysing timbers to determine the tree-ring growth pattern and thus arrive at the felling date which is virtually the building date

Dentil eaves moulding: Projecting bricks or stones at eaves level resembling teeth

Diaper work: In brickwork where vitrified headers are used to create a lozenge or diamond-shaped patterning

Double-pile form: Two parallel blocks with a common dividing wall. Can be roofed in various ways, but usually separately

Dragon-beam: Beam running diagonally across the ceiling to support jetties on two adjacent sides of an upper floor

Drift-house: The open area (roofed) between two ranges of farm buildings where laden carts could stay overnight. Often forms the entrance to the farm buildings

Eared surround:	The surround of a door or window where extensions at the head resemble squared ears. Sometimes 'lugged'. Popular in 18th- century work
End baffle-entry:	Where the entry faces the side of the internal end chimneystack
Entablature:	In classical architecture the superstructure of an Order, consisting of architrave, frieze and cornice
Face-peg:	When the joint is secured by driving in the peg(s) from the fair surface
Fan-light:	The semi-circular window over a door. The glazing-bars are arranged in the shape of a fan. Popular in 18th-century work
Fire-window:	A window giving visual access to an inglenook
Finial:	Upright ornament at the apex of roofs, pediments, gables, etc.
Frieze:	Any band of ornament or walling immediately below a cornice
Ginny-ring:	Horse-engine house or wheelhouse; a round, square or polygonal building connected to a threshing barn, where power to drive the machinery was provided by horse(s) or oxen in circulatory movement
Girding beam:	The horizontal beam in a framed wall, at the level of an upper floor
Guilloche:	A classical ornamental form consisting of two or more intertwining bands of circles
Hood mould:	A projecting moulding over the heads of arches. Sometimes used for dripstones over windows to deflect rainwater
Houseplace:	The term used for the main (floored) living room in 17th-century documents (replacing 'hall'). Sometimes shortened to 'house'
Jetty:	The projection of an upper storey beyond the lower storey. See chapter 4
Jowelled feet:	Where the feet of posts (as opposed to the heads) are thickened
King Post:	An upright timber standing in the centre of a tie-beam and rising to the apex of the roof
King-strut:	As above, but not rising to the apex
Kneeler:	A short coping stone set horizontally at the foot of the gable slope to stop the coping stones on the slope from slipping down. Sometimes decorative
Knopped Colonettes:	Small columns or pilasters with capitals resembling bunches of leaves or flowers
Lamb's Tongue Stops:	The stops worked on the end of chamfered beams, resembling a lamb's tongue. Also called cyma, ogee or scroll
Mason's Mitre:	In stonework where the horizontal member overlies the vertical, the mouldings meeting at the intersection. Different from a 'carpenter's mitre' where the joint is at an angle to both members
Metope:	Part of a classical frieze; the spaces between the triglyphs
Modillion:	Projecting rectangular brackets in the cornices of classical styles
Monk-bond:	Two stretchers and one header in each course of bricks
Mouchettes:	Curved dagger-like motifs often found in conjunction with quatrefoil tracery
Mullions:	The vertical members between the lights of a window. They may be moulded or of square section set diagonally
Notched-lap joint:	A joint fashioned to resist withdrawal by having a notch cut in one side. They take various forms
Outshut:	A subsidiary unit attached to a house, usually under a lean-to roof. Sometimes called 'outshot'
Ovolo moulding:	Moulding which has a egg-shaped profile, usually combined with a fillet when used in window mullions. The late 16th-/17th- century successor to the medieval quarter-round
Ovolo and Quirk moulding:	As above, the fillet is sometimes called the quirk
Pentice roof:	The lean-to roof over an adjoining subsidiary building
Pilaster:	A shallow pier-like rectangular column which is attached to a wall. Usually made of stone but Ruabon Pilasters are made from the bright red bricks produced at Ruabon in Denbighshire

Plank-and-Muntin:	A solid wood wall or partition made from upright timbers (muntins) into whose grooved sides planks of thinner scantling are slotted
Plat-band:	A band of projecting brick or stonework usually on the front of a building. Its function is two-fold: to hide the joist-ends and/or to give relief to an otherwise plain frontage
Post-and-pan:	As Plank-and-Muntin above
Potence:	The revolving ladder in a dovecote to enable the keeper to access the nesting-boxes
Purlin:	A lateral roof timber supporting the rafters. There are many types
Queen-posts:	Paired posts set on a tie-beam and supporting the purlins. May be straight or raking
Queen-struts:	As above, but supporting the collar-beam
Quoins:	Raised dressed stones or bricks at the corners of buildings. Used for effect
Rat-trap brickwork:	Where the bricks are laid on edge, saving on bricks, mortar and time. So called because the cavities so formed between the leaves resembled traps
Sallied abutment-joints:	Joints which incorporate obtuse angular projections where the two timbers of the scarf meet
Scantling:	The measured size or dimensions of a timber
Scarf-joint:	The joining together of two short timbers to make a longer one. The technique varies greatly
Stop-splayed:	A slant or bevel finished with a decorative stop
Setlas:	A raised platform, usually arched below, on which dairy vessels were kept
Shippon:	In Shropshire, a cow-house
Spere-Truss:	The fixed decorative truss at the low end of a hall, usually of aisled form. Access to the hall was through the 'nave' section. 'Spere' is old English for 'Screen'. It seems to have been a status symbol
Spur:	A short timber connecting a cruck blade to the wallpost or wallplate. Not common in Shropshire. Can also be used for the short timber tenoned into the post and supporting a jettied structure
Squinted butts:	Oblique (not right-angled) joints where the two timbers of the scarf meet
Staddle-stones:	Mushroom-shaped stones used to raise granaries above ground level to deter vermin
Tie-beam:	The main transverse beam connecting opposite walls at wallplate level. Applies to box-frames and crucks
Transom:	A horizontal member dividing an opening, usually a window
Ulenlok:	The 'owl-door' (Germ. 'eule' (owl) and 'loker' (locker)) to enable the domestic owl to access the roof space to deal with vermin
Vitrified header:	A 'header' is a brick laid end-on as opposed to 'stretcher'. A vitrified header is a brick which has been subjected to excess heat during firing, thus changing its colour and texture. Glass-like
Voussoir:	A wedge-shaped stone or brick forming part of an arch
Wallplate:	The horizontal timber at the wallhead to which the roof trusses and rafters are fixed
Wealdon House:	Where the open hall and the two storied end bays are roofed in one plane. The hall is usually recessed, the ends jettied and the eaves continuous. Designs and sizes can vary
Witness mark:	Any residual mark giving evidence of a former feature

References

Abbreviations used

Antiq. J.	*The Antiquaries Journal*
Archaeol. J.	*Archaeological Journal*
Bod. Lib.	Bodleian Library (Oxford)
B.U.F.A.U.	Birmingham University Field Archaeology Unit
Cal. Pat. Rolls	Calendars of Patent Rolls
C.B.A.	Council for British Archaeology
C.R.O.	Cheshire Record Office
C.S.V.F.C.	Caradoc and Severn Valley Field Club
D.O.E.	Department of the Environment
E.H.	English Heritage
E.P.N.S.	English Place-name Society
H.M.S.O.	Her Majesty's Stationery Office
I.G.M.A.U.	Ironbridge Gorge Museum Archaeology Unit
L.R.P.	*Ludlow Research Papers*
L.H.R.G.	Ludlow Historical Research Group
L.S.L.	Local Studies Library, Shrewsbury (Now part of the Shropshire Records and Research Centre)
N.M.R.	National Monuments Record
O.S.	Ordnance Survey
O.U.P.	Oxford University Press
pers. comm.	personal communication
P.C.C.	Prerogative Court of Canterbury
P.R.O.	Public Records Office
R.C.A.H.M.W.	Royal Commission on Ancient and Historical Monuments in Wales
R.C.H.M.	Royal Commission on Historical Monuments (of England)
Shrews. Chron.	*Shrewsbury Chronicle*
S.N.L.	*Shropshire Newsletter*
S.R.O.	Salop (Shropshire) Record Office (Now the Shropshire Records and Research Centre)
S.A.S.	Shropshire Archaeological Society (now Shropshire Archaeological and Historical Society)
S.R.R.C.	Shropshire Records and Research Centre
Soc. Arch. Hist.	The Society of Architecural Historians
Soc. Med. Archae.	The Society for Medieval Archaeology
T.A.M.S.	*Transactions of the Ancient Monument Society*
T.S.A.(H.)S.	*Transactions of the Shropshire Archaeological (and Historical) Society*
V.A.	*Vernacular Architecture* (Journal of the Vernacular Architecture Group)
V.A.G.	Vernacular Architecture Group
V.C.H.	*The Victoria History of the County of Shropshire / Staffordshire*
W.A.A.G.	Whitchurch Area Archaeological Group (Now Whitchurch History and Archaeology Group)

Chapter 1 Defensive Houses

1. B. Trinder, *A History of Shropshire*, Phillimore (1983), 19
2. M.D. Watson, Gazetteer of Moated Sites in Shropshire, *T.S.A.S.* Vol. LXV (1987) 1-11
3. *V.C.H. Shropshire*, Vol.8 (1968), 141, 246
4. M.D. Watson, Medieval Moated Sites in Shropshire, *West Midlands Archaeology*, C.B.A. Group 8, no.24 (1981), 42
5. M. Salter, *The Castles and Moated Mansions of Shropshire*, Folly Publications (1988)
6. *V.C.H. op. cit.*, 188, 9
7. R. Radford, Acton Burnell Castle, S*tudies in Building History*, ed. E.M. Jope, Odhams (1961), 94-103; Rev. J.D. La Touche, Stokesay Castle, *T.S.A.S.* Vol.1, (1878), 311-332; *V.A.* Vol 28 (1997), 160, 161, 163
8. S.R.R.C. D 71.4, J.T. Smith, *Shrewsbury Topography*

& *Architecture*, B'ham Uni. Thesis, (1953), Vol 1, 160-166

9. *ibid.*, 166-173
10. *ibid.*, 148-160
11. *ibid.*, 173-175
12. C.A. Ralegh Radford, *Studies in Building History*, ed. E.M. Jope, Odhams (1961), 94-103
13. M. Moran, Great Oxenbold, *T.S.A.H.S.*, Vol 72 (1997), 9-25; *V.A.* Vol 24 (1993), 57, 59; W.F. Mumford, *Wenlock in the Middle Ages* (1977), *passim*; H.E. Forrest, *Old Houses of Much Wenlock*, (1915), 70 (Unreliable, but subsequent accounts eg. N. Pevsner & M. Wood are based on it)
14. M. Moran & D. James, *The Forester's Lodge*, guide book (1986); *V.A.*, Vol 26 (1995), 70, 72
15. H.E. Forrest, Some Old Shropshire Houses, *T.S.A.S.* Vol 46, (1931-32), 80-84
16. *V.A.* Vol 28 (1993), 56, 8; (see also chapter 6)
17. F. Stackhouse-Acton, *The Garrisons of Shropshire*, (1867), 39,
18. *ibid.*
19. Anon, *T.S.A.S.*, Vol I (1878), 119-123
20. *ibid.*
21. M.O.H. Carver (ed), Two Town Houses in Medieval Shrewsbury, *T.S.A.S.* Vol 61 (1983), 46-68
22. *V.A.* Vol 25 (1994), 32, 34; D.H.S. Cranage, *Archaeologia* Vol 72 (1922), 105-132, *et al.*
23. *V.A.* Vol 28 (1997), 168,9
24. *V.A.* Vol 27 (1996), 104,5
25. W.F. Mumford, *op.cit.*, 53
26. H.E. Forrest, *op.cit.*
27. M.E.C. Walcott, Cheyney Longville, *T.S.A.S.*, Vol I (1878), 119-128
28. F. Stackhouse-Acton, *op.cit.*
29. Similar ceilings, overmantels and/or inscriptions have been noted at Wilderhope Manor, Easthope Manor, Belswardyne, Plaish Hall, Upton Cressett Gatehouse and Old Hall, Hughley. At Buildwas and Easthope the lettering is anti-clockwise, indicating that when the mould was carved allowance for reversal was not made. Probably a travelling craftsman, using wooden moulds, was working on the more important houses in the area in the late 16th century
30. N. Pevsner, *Shropshire*, Penguin (1958), 210; C. Hussey, Wenlock Abbey, *Country Life*, April 20th 1907, 558-564, Dec. 1st, 8th & 15th 1960; P.A. Faulkner, Domestic Planning from the Twelfth to the Fourteenth Centuries, *Archaeol.J.*, Vol CXV (1958), 167, 169; W.F. Mumford, *op. cit.*, *passim*; M.Wood, *The English Mediaeval House*, Phoenix (1965), *passim*, H.E. Forrest, *Old Houses of Wenlock* (1915), 32, 33
31. W.F. Mumford, *op.cit.*, 33,40

32. P.A. Faulkner, *op.cit.*, 169,170
33. J.T. Smith, Stokesay Castle, *Archaeol.J.*, Vol CXIII, (1957), 211, 214; F.W.B. Charles, *Medieval Cruck Building and its Derivatives*, Soc. Med. Archaeol, Monograpgh 2 (1967), 24; R.A. Cordingley, *Stokesay Castle: The Chronology of its Buildings*, The Art Bulletin, Vol XLV, 2, (June 1963), 100
34. P.A. Faulkner, *op.cit.*
35. F. Stackhouse-Acton, *The Castles and Old Mansions of Shropshire*, (1868), 31
36. E. Mercer, Domus Longa and Long House, *V.A.*, Vol 3, (1972), 9,10
37. H.W.R.O. *Glebe Terriers*, 11/31 (Westbury); 10/13 (Cold Weston); 13/3 (Aston Botterell); 9/25 (Clun); 14/17 (Church Stretton); *V.C.H.* (*Shropshire*) Vol X (1998), 113. I am grateful to George Baugh for the Church Stretton ref. I have used modern spelling in the text
38. I. Peate, The Welsh House, *Y Cymmrodor*, Vol XLVII (1940)
39. M. Moran, Padmore, Onibury, Shropshire, *Archaeol.J.*, Vol 142, (1985), 340-60
40. *V.C.H. op.cit.*, 133, pl. facing p.54. The child, 2nd. left, is now Mrs. Lewis who owns the photograph and remembers the longhouse in use
41. *ibid.*
42. M. Moran, Padmore, *op.cit.*
43. *V.C.H. op.cit.*, 33; V.A.G. Conference booklet (1982), 3
44. N.W. Alcock & M. Moran, Low Open-Truss Beams (MantelBeams): Problems of Function & Distribution, *V.A.*, Vol 15, (1984) 47-55; *V.C.H. op.cit.*, 256
45. *V.A.* Vol. 31 (2000), 106
46. M. Moran, Two Early Timber-Framed Houses in Shropshire, *T.S.A.H.S.* Vol 68 (1993), 79-92; *V.A.* Vol 24 (1993), 56,58
47. M. Moran, Catherton Cottage, Hopton Wafers, *T.S.A.S.*, Vol 65 (1987), 45-9; V.A. Vol 27 (1996), 103, 105
48. N.M.R. Report and Plans
49. V.A.G. Conference booklet (1982), 25
50. D. Bilbey, *Church Stretton*, Phillimore (1985), fig. 154
51. Photograph *c.*1896, *penes* Mr. Tom Wilding of All Stretton, shows the house before the addition of the upper storey
52. M. Moran, *Vernacular Buildings of Whitchurch & Area*, Logaston Press (1999), 171-8
53. *ibid.*, 247
54. *ibid.*, 89-94
55. M. Moran, The Old Shop, Somerwood, *T.S.A.S.* Vol 64 (1985), 69-75
56. C. Ryan & M. Moran, Old House Farm, Loppington, *T.S.A.S.* Vol 63 (1985), 11-16

Chapter 2   Stone Houses

1. P. Toghill and K. Chell, Shropshire Geolog-Stratigraphic and Techtonic History, *Field Studies* 6, (1984), 59; M.A. Scard, *The Building Stones of Shropshire*, Swan Hill Press (1990), *passim*
2. J. Plymley, *A General View of Agriculture in Shropshire*, (1803)
3. R. Gough, *The History of Myddle*, ed. D. Hey, Penguin edn. (1981), 107; M. Moran, Re-erecting Houses in Shropshire in the Late Seventeenth Century, *Archaeol. J.*, Vol 146, (1989), 543, 4
4. R. Gough, *op.cit.*, 185; M. Moran, *op.cit.*, 550
5. I am grateful to Mr. Cyril Taylor of Bridgnorth, the last occupant, for information. The Apley estate converted the caves into a cottage for his great-grandfather who acted as custodian for the adjoining chapel cave. I also wish to thank Frank Foxall for help with the Hermitage complex and for access to a rare interior photograph of Mr. Taylor's former home
6. H. Smith, Bridgnorth Hermitage, *T.S.A.S.* Vol 1, (1878), 159-72
7. The painting was in the possession of the late Mr. Morley-Tonkin, but its present whereabouts are unknown
8. anon, quoted in Thomas Cox, *Magna Brittanica*, Shropshire, (1727), 670
9. R. Gough, *op.cit.*, *passim*
10. *ibid.*, 32. I wish to thank Peter Icke for his help with the Myddle houses, and all the householders who kindly allowed me to examine their homes
11. D.M. Bills and E. & W.R. Griffiths, *Kinver Rock Houses*, ed. H. Parsons, Elda Publications, 26, High St., Kinver, n.d.
12. K. Downes, *Grinshill Stone Quarries*, dissertation for B.A. (Hons) degree, Univ. of Durham (1980), 16; D.B Thompson. *A Guide to the History & Geology of Quarrying at Localities along the Natural History Trail in Corbet Wood, Grinshill, N. Shropshire*, Clive & Grinshill Conservation Committee (1995), *passim*
13. Info. from the late C.A. Harley
14. J.B. Oldham, *A History of Shrewsbury School 1552-1952*, Blackwell, (1952), *passim*
15. M. Moran, Langley Gatehouse, *S.N.L.*, 38, (June 1970)
16. I.D. Mercer, The Geography of the Alberbury Breccia, *Field Studies*, Vol 1, no.1, (1959)
17. I wish to thank Sir Michael Leighton of Loton Park for permission to examine Keeper's Cottage. The park is not open to the public
18. Permission to visit the quarry must be obtained from Mr. C.C. Edwards of Freehold Farm, Norbury
19. I am grateful to Andrew Jenkinson for geological data on 'Harnage Slate'
20. J.B. Lawson, Harnage Slates and other roofing materials in Shrewsbury and neighbourhood in the late medieval and early modern period, *T.S.A.S.*, Vol LXIV, (1985), 116-18
21. Paperback ed., Faber, (1972)
22. J.B. Lawson, *op.cit.*
23. M.O.H. Carver (ed.), Two Town Houses in Medieval Shrewsbury, *T.S.A.S.*, Vol 61 (1983), 32, 33
24. *ibid.*, 60. 68 (fn.9)
25. *V.C.H. Shropshire* Vol 8 (1968), 86
26. R.A. Meeson, *Madeley Court*: Interim Report, (1978-9)
27. M. Moran, Great Oxenbold, Monkhopton, Shropshire, *T.S.A.H.S.*, Vol 72 (1997), 9
28. T.C. Cantrill, Geological report on Uriconium, *Archaeologia Cambrensis*, Vol 86, (1931) 87-98
29. I am grateful to Dr. Peter Toghill for information on this point
30. The area of the hall was excavated in 1986 by R. Meeson, N. Baker and C. Moffett
31. I. Peate, *The Welsh House*, Y Cmmrodor, Vol XLVII (1940), 151; D.B. Hague & C. Warhurst, Excavations at Sycharth Castle, Denbighshire, 1962-3, *Archaeologia Cambrensis* (1966), 108-127

Chapter 3   Cruck Construction in Shropshire

1. E. Mercer, *English Vernacular Houses*, H.M.S.O. (1975), 97
2. C. Hart & C. Raymond, *British Trees in Colour*, Michael Joseph (1973), 28, 29. For a comprehensive study see M.G. Morris & F.H. Perring (eds.), *The British Oak*, Classey, (1974)
3. Sir Cyril Fox, *The Personality of Britain*, Nat. Lib. of Wales, (1947)
4. Sir Cyril Fox & Lord Raglan, *Monmouthshire Houses*, Part I, Nat. Mus. of Wales (1951), 38
5. *V.A.*, Vol 28 (1997), 160, 163; *ibid.*, Vol 26 (1995), 70, 72
6. I am grateful to Richard Harris for elucidation on this point
7. N.W. Alcock, *Cruck Construction, An Intro. & Catalogue*, C.B.A. Research Report, No. 42 (1981)
8. V.C.H. (*Shropshire*), Vol 8, O.U.P. (1968), *passim*
9. N.W. Alcock, *op.cit.*, 7,96
10. F.W.B. Charles, *Medieval Cruck Building & its Derivitives*, Soc. for Med. Archaeol., Monograph Series, 2 (1967), 18, Fig. 3C
11. M. Moran, *Vernacular Buildings of Whitchurch & Area*, Logaston Press (1999), 59-62, 151-162, 171-178
12. E. Mercer, *English Vernacular Houses*, HMSO (1975), pl 64; M. Moran, Catherton Cottage, Hopton Wafers, *T.S.A.H.S.*, Vol 65, (1987), 45-9;

RCHM Historic Buildings Report, 1995

13. J.T. Smith, Cruck Distributions: An Interpretation of some Recent Maps, *V.A.*, Vol 6 (1975), 3-18; N.W. Alcock, *op.cit.*,

14. V.C.H. *supra*, 69, entry in the Close Roll, 1242-47, 97

15. E.A. Gee, The Chronology of Crucks, *T.A.M.S.*, New Series, Vol 22, (1997), 9-26

16. B.L., Egerton Ms. 3712 f54v n.d., 'pro opera unius domus de viginte pedibus et meremium inter furcas quatuordecim pedis' (Wombridge Cartulary). I am grateful to Dr. David Cox of the V.C.H. for this ref.

17. S.R.R.C. 356/MT 551. I am grateful to Michael Faraday for this ref. and translation. Though no regnal year is given on the lease the evidence of the names of the witnesses shows beyond reasonable doubt that this can be dated 25 Ed. I, ie. 1296-7 (Faraday)

18. P.R.O. Just. 1/737 (1272). I am grateful to Michael Faraday for this ref. and translation

19. Hereford Cathedral Library 4836, Dean & Chapter endowments; S.R.R.C. 6001/4411, E.H. Martin, Ms. *History of the Parish of Diddlebury*; I am grateful to Dr. Martin Speight for this ref. See M. Speight, *Some Diddlebury Houses and their History*, (2000), 9

20. S.R.R.C. Deeds, 2796, Manor of Armegrove

21. S.R.R.C. 1037/25/10, Jasper More Papers. I am grateful to Dr. Martin Speight for this ref.

22. S.R.R.C. Deeds, 9136, m (42), Condover Court Roll, 3rd May Henry VI 'ac posuit fimem ad pedem cuiusdam furce per quam furca predicta corrumpitur ad dampnum suum de xxs'

23. *idem.*, See also G. Baugh, A Forged Manor Court Roll, S.A.S. News Bulletin, 16 (Autumn 1982), 11

24. T.S.A.S. 3rd Series, Vol 10 (1910), 69-70, Worfield Churchwardens' Accounts 1581-2. I am grateful to Robert Taylor for this ref.

25. *V.C.H. supra*, 18

26. E. Mercer, *op.cit.*, 97

27. J.T. Smith, Medieval Roofs: A Classification, *Archaeol. J.*, CXV (1958), 111-49; N.W. Alcock & M.W. Barley, Medieval Roofs with Base-crucks and Short Principals, *Antiq. J.*, 52 (1972) 132-68; J.W. Tonkin, Social Standing & Base-Crucks in Herefordshire, *V.A.*, Vol 1 (1970), 7-11, *et al.*

28. N.W. Alcock, *op.cit.* (fn 7.), 4, 7

29. *ibid.*, 4

30. R.W. Brunskill, *Timber Building in Britain*, Gollancz, (1985), 65

31. E. Mercer, *op.cit.*, 96, 97

32. E.D.H. Williams, Jointed Crucks, *V.A.*, Vol 8 (1977), 826-9

33. P. Smith, *Houses of the Welsh Countryside*, H.M.S.O. (1975), 515-6, map 44

34. *ibid.*, 403, map 14; E.D.H. Williams, *op.cit*, 827

35. M. Moran, *op.cit.* (fn 11), 71-4

36. *ibid.*, 187-94

37. M. Moran, The Medieval Parts of Plowden Hall, *T.S.A.S.*, Vol 59, (1973/4), 263-71

38. M. Moran, Two Early Timber-Framed Hall Houses in Shropshire, *T.S.A.H.S.*, Vol 68 (1993), 72-8

39. M. Moran, High Grosvenor, Claverley, *T.S.A.H.S.*, Vol 70, (1995), 202-8

40. W.F. Mumford, *Wenlock in the Middle Ages*, Mumford, 1977

41. S.R. Jones, Tir-y-Coed, *T.S.A.S.*, Vol 56 (1957-60), 149-57

42. M. Moran, *op.cit.*, (fn 36), 79-92

43. M. Moran, Cleeton Court, Cleeton St. Mary, *T.S.A.S.*, Vol 65, (1987), 41-4

44. SRRC D.O.E. Relisting (1980)

45. N.W. Alcock, *op.cit.*, (fn 7), 61

46. I. Homes, The Agricultural Use of the Herefordshire House and its Outbuildings, *V.A.*, Vol 9, (1978), 12-16

47. M. Trueman & A. Jones, Malting and the Swan Inn, Archaeology in Ironbridge, *I.G.M.A.U.*, (1985-6), 28-33

48. R.A. Cordingley, Stokesay Castle, *Art Bulletin*, Vol. XLV, 2, (June 1963), 99; E. Mercer, *op.cit.*, 97

49. M. Moran, Padmore, Onibury, Shropshire, *Archaeol. J.*, Vol 142, (1985), 349-53

50. J.W. Tonkin, The White House, Aston Munslow, *T.S.A.S.*, Vol 58, part 2, (1966), 147

51. J.T. Smith, Stokesay Castle, *Archaeol. J.*, Vol 113, (1957), fig 9

52. E.D.H. Williams, *op.cit.*, 828-9

53. M. Moran, *op.cit.*, (fn 11), 11-14

Chapter 4   Box-framed and Jettied Houses

1. *V.A.* Vol 26 (1995), 69, 70-71

2. *V.A.* Vol 26 (1995), 69, 71-72; *V.A.* Vol 32 (forthcoming)

3. *V.A.* Vol 32 (forthcoming)

4. *V.A.* Vol 25 (1994), 31, 33

5. *V.A.* Vol 25 (1994), 32, 34; Owen & Blakeway, *History of Shrewsbury* Vol 2 (1825), pl opp 267

6. A pen-and-ink drawing by Joseph Humphreys, 1846, after Varley. The original is held at Shrewsbury Schools. I am grateful to James Lawson for this example

7. *V.A.* Vol 26 (1995), 69, 71; M. Moran, *Vernacular Buildings of Whitchurch & Area*, Logaston Press (1999), 171-8

8. *V.A.* Vol 26 (1995), 69, 72

9. *V.A.* Vol 31 (2000), 105

10. M. Moran, *op.cit.*, 55, 61

11. *V.A.* Vol 24 (1993), 57, 58; *V.C.H. Shropshire*, Vol 8 (1968), 108, 109

12. F.W.B. Charles, *The Conservation of Timber Buildings*, Hutchinson (1984), 84

13. L.F. Salzman, *Buildings in England down to 1540*, Oxford (1952), 205
14. *ibid.*
15. M. Moran, *op.cit.*, 179-186
16. *V.A.* Vol 26 (1995), 69, 72
17. M. Moran, *op. cit.*, 219-224
18. pers. comm. D. Miles
19. as fn 5
20. *V.A.* Vol 26 (1995), 69, 71; D.J. Lloyd & M. Moran, *The Corner Shop, L.R.P.* 2 (1978)
21. *V.A.* Vol 26 (1995), 69, 71
22. E. Mercer & P. Stamper, Beslow Hall: The Demolition of a Rival to Pitchford, *T.S.A.H.S.*, Vol 65 (1987), 56-63
23. *R.C.H.M.*, Report, (June 1998). Dendro dating was commissioned by R.C.H.M.
24. M. Moran, *op.cit.* (1999), 195-212; *V.A.* Vol 27 (1996), 104, 106
25. Much has been written on Wealden Houses. The late R.T. Mason coined the term in *Framed Buildings of the Weald* (1964)
26. R. Harris, Jetties, *V.A.* Vol 21 (1990), 33-36; For most of what follows here I am indebted to Henry Hand
27. E.L.N. Viollet-le-Duc, *Dictionnaire raisonné de l'architecture francais, XI au XV siècle* (1867-70)
28. *V.A.* Vol 28 (1997), 160, 163
29. *V.A.* Vol 24 (1993), 57, 59; H. Hand, The Axial Jowled Post in Shropshire, *V.A.* Vol 20 (1989), 38; *V.A.* Vol 24 (1993), 56, 58
30. *V.A.* Vol 28 (1997), 160, 162
31. *V.A.* Vol 26 (1995), 69, 71-72
32. *V.A.* Vol 26 (1995), 69, 72
33. M. Speight, The Great House, *L.R.P.*, 4 (1980)
34. R. Harris, *op.cit.*, 34
35. *V.A.* Vol 27 (1996), 27, 105
36. *V.A.* Vol 27 (1996), 102, 104
37. *V.A.* Vol 32 (forthcoming)
38. *V.A.* Vol 25 (1994), 32, 34
39. *V.A.* Vol 29 (1998), 121
40. *V.A.* Vol 28 (1997), 160, 162-163

Chapter 5 Roof Construction

1. P. Smith, *Houses of the Welsh Countryside*, H.M.S.O., (1975), 80
2. C. Fox, *The Personality of Britain*, Nat. Lib. of Wales, (1947), map B
3. R.A. Cordingley, British Historical Roof-types and their Members: A Classification, *Trans. Ancient Mon. Soc.*, Vol 9 (1961), 73-130
4. *ibid.*, 75
5. *V.A.* Vol 28 (1997), 161, 163, 105-6
6. *V.A.* Vol 24 (1993), 56, 58
7. *V.A.* Vol 28 (1997), 161, 163
8. F.W.B. Charles, Medieval Cruck Building and its Derivitives, *Soc. Med. Archae.*, Monograph 2, (1967), 4
9. *ibid.*
10. J.W. Tonkin, The White House, Aston Munslow, *T.S.A.S.* Vol 58, part 2 (1966), 148
11. R.A. Cordingley, Stokesay Castle, *The Art Bulletin*, Vol XLV, no.2, (June 1963), 91-107; *V.A.* Vol 28 (1997) 160, 161, 163
12. N.W. Alcock, *Cruck Construction*, C.B.A. Research Report, 42, (1981), 96
13. For The Bold see M. Moran, Two Early Timber-Framed Hall Houses in Shropshire, *T.S.A.H.S.* Vol 68 (1993), 72-8; *V.A.* Vol 26 (1995), 68, 70. For 3-4 Broad St. Ludlow see R. Shoesmith & R. Morris, *3-4 Broad Street, Ludlow*, City of Hereford Archaeology Unit, (Sept. 1998); *V.A.* Vol 26 (1995), 69, 71. For Plowden Hall see M. Moran, The Medieval Parts of Plowden Hall, *T.S.A.S.* Vol 59, part 3 (1973-4), 263-71; *V.A.* Vol 24 (1993), 57, 59. For The Nag's Head see *V.A.* Vol 26 (1995), 69, 72
14. M.O.H. Carver, ed. Two Town Houses in Medieval Shrewsbury, *T.S.A.S.* Vol. 61, (1983) 51, 52
15. R.C.H.M., *City of York*, Vol 5, Central Area, H.M.S.O. (1981) lxx
16. M. Moran, High Grosvenor, Claverley, Shropshire, *T.S.A.H.S.*, Vol 70 (1995), 202-8
17. D.J. Lloyd and M. Moran, The Corner Shop, *L.R.P.* 2, (1978)
18. P. Smith, *op.cit.*, 81
19. *V.A.* Vol 26 (1995), 70, 72
20. J.T. Smith, Medieval Roofs: A Classification, *Archae.J.*, Vol CXV, (1958), 111-149; J.M. Fletcher & P.S. Spokes, The Origin and Development of Crown-Post Roofs, *Med. Archae.*, Vol 8 (1964), 152-183; G. Bailey and B. Hutton, Crown-Post Roofs in Hertfordshire, *Herts. Local Hist. Council*, (1966); J.T. Smith, The Reliability of Typological Dating of Medieval English Roofs, in R. Berger, ed., *Scientific Methods in Medieval Archaeology*, (California, 1970), 25859; J. Munby, M. Sparks & T. Tatton-Brown, Crown-Post and King-Strut Roofs in South-East England, *Med. Archae.*, Vol XXVII (1983), 123-135
21. E. Mercer, *English Vernacular Houses*, R.C.H.M. (1975) 7995
22. D.H.S. Cranage, *An Architectural Account of the Churches of Shropshire*, (1900), 1053
23. J.T. Smith, *op.cit.*, (1958), 123,4
24. *ibid.*, 143
25. F. Stackhouse-Acton, *Castles and Mansions of Shropshire*, (1868), 30
26. J.T. Smith, *op.cit.*, (1958), 130
27. M.O.H. Carver, ed., *op.cit.*, (1983), 51, 52
28. M. Moran, Padmore, Onibury, Shropshire, *Archaeol. J.*, Vol 142 (1985), 340-60

29. S.R. Jones, Sheffield Lodge Farm, Staffs. An Altered Hall-House of Medieval Date, *Trans. S. Staffs Archae. & Hist. Soc.*, Vol X (1968), 69
30. *V.A.* Vol. 31 (2000), 107
31. M. Moran & H. Hand, Great Binnal, Astley Abbotts 1460, *V.A.* Vol 27 (1996), 62, 63, 102
32. *V.A.* Vol 27 (1996), 102, 104
33. *V.C.H. Shropshire*, Vol 8, (1968) pl facing 111
34. *V.A.* Vol 25 (1994), 31, 33-4
35. *V.A.* Vol 24 (1993), 57, 58; *V.C.H., op.cit.*, 1089, pl facing 111; *V.A.G. Conf. Booklet* (1982), 18
36. D. Lloyd, Broad Street, Ludlow, *L.R.P.* 3, (1979), *passim*
37. *ibid.*
38. *V.A.* Vol 28 (1997), 168, 169
39. *V.A.* Vol 24 (1993), 57, 58
40. *ibid.*, 57, 59, fn 13
41. *ibid.*, 57, 59
42. M. Moran, Padmore, Onibury, Shropshire, *Archaeol. J.,* 142, (1985), 340-60
43. *V.A.* Vol 27 (1996), 104, 105; *V.A.G. Conf. Booklet,* (1982), 21
44. M.O.H. Carver, *op.cit.*
45. *V.A.* Vol 28 (1997), 168, 170; H.E. Forrest, *The Old Houses of Shrewsbury, Wilding,* (rep. (1972) of 1935), 27, 28
46. *V.A.* Vol 27 (1996), 104, 105-6
47. *V.A.* Vol 25 (1994), 33, 35
48. *V.A.* Vol 23 (1992), 49, 50
49. M. Moran, *The Vernacualar Buildings of Whitchurch & Area*, Logaston Press (1999), 117-22
50. *ibid.*, 95-100
51. B. Coulton, pers. comm.; see also J. Lindsay, *A History of the North Wales Slate Industry*, David & Charles, (1974), 118; E. Wilson, *The Ellesmere and Llangollen Canal*, Phillimore, (1975), 84-6
52. S.R.R.C., 3365/2537, Shrewsbury Borough Records
53. *V.C.H. op.cit.* 104, 279, *passim*
54. *V.C.H. Shropshire*, Vol X (1998), 132
55. *ibid.*, 271
56. *V.C.H. Shropshire*, Vol XI (1985), 231, 260
57. B. Trinder, *The Industrial Revolution in Shropshire*, Phillimore, (1973), 99
58. B. Trinder & J. Cox, *Yeomen & Colliers in Telford*, Phillimore, (1980), 287, 438
59. M. Moran & J. Barton, *Overton Hall; A Handsome House*, Logaston Press, (2000), 22

Chapter 6 Ludlow Houses: The Medieval Period

1. D.J. Lloyd and P. Klein, *Ludlow, A Historic Town in Words and Pictures*, Phillimore (1984), 12
2. T. Wright, *History of Ludlow*, (1852), 34
3. C. Platt, *The English Medieval Town*, Secker and Warburg, (1976), 33-36
4. M.E. Speight and D.J. Lloyd, Ludlow House and Their Residents, *L.R.P.* 1, (1978), 2
5. Lloyd and Klein, *op.cit.* (1984), 13
6. D.J. Lloyd, *The Parish Church of St. Laurence*, Ludlow P.C.C. (1980), 3
7. P. Klein and A. Roe, The Carmelite Friary, *L.R.P.* 6, (1988), 4, 5
8. Lloyd and Klein, *op.cit.* (1984), 96
9. D.J. Lloyd, *Historic Ludlow*, Studio Press, n.d., 4
10. *ibid.*, 3; E.W. Ganderton and J. Laford, *Ludlow Stained and Painted Glass*, (1961), 46-53
11. *V.C.H. Shropshire*, Vol.2 (1973), 134-140
12. D.J. Lloyd, Broad Street, *L.R.P.* 3, (1979), 10, 43
13. *ibid.*, 11, 12, 13
14. Cal. Pat. Rolls, 1234-47; 35; C.J. Train, *The Walls and Gates of Ludlow*, L.H.R.G., (1999), 4-12
15. R. Morriss, *Barnaby House, Ludlow*, Heref. Archaeol. Series, 98 (1991); *V.A.* Vol 28 (1997), 168, 169; *V.C.H. op.cit.*, 150; Lloyd and Klein, *op.cit.*, (1984), 64; V.A.G. Conference booklet (*Ludlow*), (1982), 5
16. *V.A.* Vol 24 (1993), 56, 58
17. R. Shoesmith & R. Morriss, *3/4 Broad St, Ludlow*, City of Heref. Archaeol. Unit, (Sept. 1988); *V.A.* Vol 26 (1995), 69, 71
18. *V.C.H., op. cit.*, 134-40; *V.A.* Vol 24 (1993), 57, 58
19. M. Moran, Padmore, Onibury, Shropshire, *Archaeol. J.,* Vol 142, (1985), 340-60
20. D.J. Lloyd & M. Moran, The Corner Shop, *L.R.P.* 2, (1978); *V.A.* Vol 26 (1995), 69, 71
21. *V.A.* Vol 24 (1993), 57, 58; D.J. Lloyd, *The Concise History of Ludlow*, Merlin Unwin (1999), 53; Lloyd & Klein, *op.cit.*, 122, C. Liddy, The Palmers' Guild Window, *T.S.A.H.S*, Vol 72 (1997), 26-37; *et. al.*
22. D.J. Lloyd, *op.cit.*, (1999), 90; *V.A.*, Vol 28, 168, 169
23. D.J. Lloyd, *ibid.*, 60
24. *V.C.H., op.cit.*, 147-50; D.J. Lloyd, *Country Grammar School*, private publication, (1977); D.J. Lloyd, *op.cit.*, (1999), 57, 58 et. al.
25. D.J. Lloyd, *op.cit.* (1999), *passim*; Lloyd & Klein, *op.cit.*, 108
26. D.J. Lloyd *op.cit.* (1979), 43,45,49
27. *ibid.*, 31,32,40
28. V.A.G. Conf. booklet (*Ludlow*) (1982), 8, 9
29. D.J. Lloyd, *op.cit.*(1979), 19, 43, 46, 67
30. V.A.G. Conf. booklet (*Ludlow*) (1982), 16, 17
31. D.J. Lloyd, *The Concise History of Ludlow*, Unwin, (1999), 60,61
32. D.J. Lloyd, *op.cit.* (1979), 43, 45, 65
33. Lloyd and Klein, *op.cit.*, (1984), 124
34. M. Speight, The Great House, *L.R.P* 4 (1980)
35. ex.info. from D.J. Lloyd
36. *ibid.*
37. *ibid.*
38. *V.C.H., op.cit.*, 108-9; 111-14

Chapter 7   Ludlow Houses: The Post-Medieval Period

1. Statute, Henrici Octavi, 1535, 'An Act for reparing and amending of the townes of Glocester, Nothyngham, Northampton, and other Capit.'
2. P. Williams, *The Council in the Marches of Wales under Elizabeth I*, Uni. of Wales Press, (1958)
3. M.D.G. Wanklyn, *Landed Society and Allegiance in Cheshire and Shropshire in the First Civil War*, Manchester Ph.D., (1967), 42
4. D.J. Lloyd, P. Howell, and M.Richards, The Feathers, *L.R.P.* 5, (1986), 6, 7, 48
5. V.A.G. Conference booklet Ludlow, (1982), 19
6. T. Wright, *History of Ludlow*, (1852), 415
7. D.J. Lloyd and P. Klein, *Ludlow, A Historic Town in Words and Pictures*, Phillimore, (1984), 70
8. T. Wright, *op.cit.*, 415-17
9. Lloyd and Klein, *op.cit.*, 41; D.J. Lloyd, *The Concise History of Ludlow*, Unwin, (1999), 60, 61
10. *ibid.*, 42, 43; C.A.J. Skeel, *The Council in the Marches of Wales*, London (1903), 188
11. H.T. Weyman, Some Account of the Early History of the Foxe Family, *T.S.A.S.*, 2nd Series Vol 12, (1900) 113-90
12. P. Williams, *op.cit.*, 159
13. Lloyd and Klein, *op.cit.*, 43; *Welsh Folk Museum Handbook* (1974), 8, 9
14. D.J. Lloyd, Broad Street, *L.R.P.* 3, (1979), 48, 60
15. *V.C.H. Shropshire*, Vol.2 (1973), 95
16. D.J. Lloyd, (1979) 45
17. Lloyd and Klein, *op.cit.*, 87
18. V.A.G. (1982), 17
19. Lloyd and Klein, *op.cit.*, 104
20. D.J. Lloyd, *Historic Ludlow*, Studio Press, n.d., 9
21. Lloyd and Klein, *op.cit.*, 50
22. M. Speight, *Ludlow in Old Picture Postcards*, European Library, (1983), 50
23. ex info. D.J. Lloyd
24. C.A.J. Skeel, *op.cit.*, 129-79
25. D.J. Lloyd, (1979), 48, 55
26. *ibid.*, 37,46
27. Lloyd and Klein, *op.cit.*, 43
28. D.J. Lloyd, (1979), 19, 48; V.A.G. (1982) 12
29. Basil Stallybrass, a reputable architect/ craftsman was employed by Henry Mahler in 1909 to refurbish The Old Bell House, to landscape the gardens and to create a shell grotto. The plasterwork done at this time is of excellent quality, as is the fireplace in the great chamber. Stallybrass worked with Detmar Blow, a leading exponent of the 'Arts and Crafts Movement' on Little Ridge in Wiltshire and on other country houses. He was an exponent of the best S.P.A.B. principles and his restoration of Quennel House, Plaistow, Sussex is testimony to this
30. V.A.G. (1982), 18, 19
31. D.J. Lloyd, (1979), 29, 38
32. Parkinson and Ould, *Old Cottages, Farmhouses and other Half-timbered buildings in Shropshire, Herefordshire and Cheshire*, Batsford, (1904), plates XXI, XXII; M. Speight, *op.cit.*, 61; Owen and Blakeway, *History of Shrewsbury*, (1825), Vol 1, pl opp 356; D.J. Lloyd, P. Howell and M. Richards, *op.cit.*, 7, 13, 52
33. D.J. Lloyd, P. Howell and M. Richards, *op.cit.*,
34. Lloyd and Klein, *op.cit.*, 48
35. D.J. Lloyd, (1979), 14, 15
36. The painting is in Ludlow Museum
37. D.J. Lloyd, (1979), 31
38. *ibid.*, 33
39. H. Weyman, *Ludlow in Bye-Gone Days*, (1913), 70-1
40. V.A.G. (1982), 22, 23
41. D.J. Lloyd, P. Howell and M. Richards, *op.cit.*, 43f; (SRRC 356/30, 170)
42. V.A.G. (1982), 24
43. M.E. Speight and D.J. Lloyd, Ludlow Houses and their Residents, *L.R.P.* l, (1978), 13
44. D.J. Lloyd, (1979), 54
45. Speight and Lloyd, *op.cit.*, 12
46. Lloyd and Klein, *op.cit.*, 98
47. D.J. Lloyd, (1979), 38, 50
48. D.J. Lloyd, *Historic Ludlow*, Studio Press, n.d.
49. W. Watkins-Pitchford, *The Shropshire Hearth Tax Roll, 1672*, Shrop. Archaeol. & Parish. Reg. Soc., (1949), 167

Chapter 8   Stokesay Castle Gatehouse & Ludford House

1. *V.A.*, Vol 28 (1997), 161, 162
2. D.L. Gregory, *John Abel of Sarnesfield*, C.S.V.F.C., (1980), 14
3. Local Govt. Extension order no. P1708
4. A. Oswald, Ludford House, Shropshire, *Country Life*, (2-9-49), 682-6; J. Ionides, *Thomas Farnolls Pritchard of Shrewsbury*, Dog Rose Press, (1999), 183-6 & *passim*
5. *V.C.H. Shropshire*, Vol II, (1973) 101
6. D.J. Lloyd, Broad Street, *L.R.P.* 3, (1979), 20
7. M. Carver (ed.) Two Town Houses in Medieval Shrewsbury, *T.S.A.S.* Vol 61, fig 37
8. eg. A. Kendall, *Elizabeth I*, Wayland, (1973), 40
9. H.T. Weyman, *Ludlow in Bye-Gone Days*, Onny Press reprint 1972, 56
10. D.J. LLoyd, *op.cit.*, 48; J. Ionides, *op.cit.*, 166-9, & *passim*
11. *V.C.H.*, *op.cit.*; H.T. Weyman, Ludford, *T.S.A.S.* Vol. 49 (1937-8) 217-39

Chapter 9 Shrewsbury Houses: The Medieval Period

1. W.G. Hoskins, *Local History in England*, Longmans, (1984) 227-280
2. J. Morris (gen.ed.) *Domesday Book (Shropshire)*, Phillimore, (1986), 252 a, c
3. Owen and Blakeway, *History of Shrewsbury*, Vol 1 (1825) 128; *ibid.*, Vol 2, 132

4. K.M. Kenyon, *Wroxeter Roman City*, H.M.S.0., (1949), 1

5. P. Toghill, *Geology in Shropshire*, Swan Hill Press, (1990), 131

6. Owen and Blakeway, *op.cit.*, 36-39

7. U. Rees, *The Cartulary of Haughmond Abbey*, S.A.S. and Uni. of Wales Press, (1985), 198-9, deeds 1050, 1052; B. Champion, pers. comm.

8. M. Wood, *The English Mediaeval House*, Phoenix, (1965), 262, pl. VII D

9. Shrewsbury Heritage Project, 2nd Interim Report, B.U.F.A.U., (n.d.-1986?) SRRC, D61 vf

10. SRRC, C73vf M/F 69a, J. Buckler's drawings, *passim*; Owen's Shrewsbury, MS 200, *passim*

11. Owen, *Some Account of Shrewsbury*, (1808), rep. Morten (1972), 484-90

12. Cal. Pat. Rolls 1324-27, 178, 1325; J. Buckler's drawings, *op.cit.*, 146, 147; *Old Prints of Shrewsbury*, SRRC, D66/5328, 76

13. Owen and Blakeway, *op.cit.*, Vol 2, 318

14. *Old Prints of Shrewsbury*, *op.cit.*, 77

15. *The Changing Face of Shrewsbury*, Shrops. County Lib., (1977), 14

16. H. Owen, *op.cit.*, 525

17. *Paintings and Drawings of Shrewsbury*, SRRC, MS 5326

18. H. Owen, *op.cit.*, 465, 6; J. Buckler, *op.cit.*, 178

19. L.S.L., Mallinson neg. 638

20. B. Champion, pers. comm; N. Baker, S.A.H.S. Newsletter, Spring 1995

21. N. Baker, *The Archaeology of the Charles Darwin Centre*, B.A.F.A.U., (1988), SRRC, D61, vf

22. J.B. Blakeway, The Topographical Hist. of Shrewsbury, *T.S.A.S.*, 3rd series, Vol 7 (1905), 315

23. H. Owen, *op.cit.*, 464, 474

24. M. Carver, (ed.) Two Town Houses in Medieval Shrewsbury, *T.S.A.S.*, Vol LXI, 1983

25. Gawsworth Hall, Macclesfield, *TA.M.S.*, Vol 11, (1963), 90

26. Bod. Lib., MS Gough, Shropshire 12, fo 98. I am grateful to B. Champion for this ref; *V.A.* Vol 31 (2000), forthcoming

27. M. Carver, *op.cit.*

28. F.A. Girling, *English Merchants' Marks*, O.U.P., (1964); B. Champion, *Everyday Life in Tudor Shrewsbury*, Shrewsbury Books (1994), 73

29. J.H. Parker, *Some Acc. of Dom. Archit.in England from Ed. I to Rich. II*, Vol 2, (Oxford), (1855), 306

30. J.A. Morris, An Early Medieval Building behind the Barge Inn, *T.S.A.S.*, 4th series, Vol XII (1929-30), Misc. XIX

31. U. Rees, *op.cit.*, deeds 966-1094

32. J.B. Blakeway, *op.cit.*, Vols 5, 6, 7

33. D. Cromarty, The Shrewsbury Lay Subsidies 1297-1332, *West Midland Studies*, Vol 18, (W'ton Poly.), 1985

34. M. Moran, *Bear Steps*, (1982), Shrewsbury Civic Society; *V.A.* Vol 28 (1997), 160, 162-3

35. Ancient Mon. Lab. Report 24/96 R.C.H.M; R. Morriss, The Old Mansion, Shrewsbury - An Outline Analysis, *Mercian Heritage*, Ser. 7 (1995); *V.A.* Vol 27 (1996), 93, 94

36. Owen & Blakeway, *op.cit.*, Vol 1, 420

37. H. Owen, *op.cit.*, 526

38. *V.A.* Vol 26 (1995), 69, 71-2

39. D. Park, Courtauld Inst. of Art, in a report to Alan Snell of Arrol & Snell, Shrewsbury, the architects who were responsible for the discovery. The painting has been conserved by a team from the School of Hist. and Archaeol., Uni. of Wales, Cardiff. I am grateful to Arrol & Snell for access to these and other reports.

40. J.L. Hobbs, *Shrewsbury Street Names* (1954), 46

41. SRRC, MS 5326, *supra*, 50

42. *V.A.* Vol 26 (1995), 69, 72

43. *ibid.*; Tenurial details, W.A. Champion, John Ashby and the History and Environs of the Lion Inn, Shrewsbury, *T.S.A.H.S*, Vol 75 (2000), 59-63

44. T.C. Mendenhall, *The Shrewsbury Drapers and the Welsh Wool Trade in the XVI & XVII centuries*, O.U.P., (1953), 82; Owen, *op.cit.*, 325-8; SRRC, D97/5317, 212

45. M.C. Hill, *The History of Shropshire's Many Shirehalls*, Salop C.C. (1963), 1-2

46. *ibid.*, opp 2; D.J. Lloyd and M. Moran, The Corner Shop, *L.R.P.* 2, (1987), 23; *Shrews. Chron.* 20 May 1898, 46; B. Champion, *op.cit.*, 16

47. *V.A.* Vol 25 (1994), 32, 34

48. Owen & Blakeway, *op.cit.*, Vol 2, 266

49. SRRC, 3365/387 m 1d. I am grateful to B. Champion who first discovered and translated the document, and to G. Baugh for discussing the interpretation with me.

50. Ancient Mon. Lab. Report 25/96 R.C.H.M.; H. Owen, *op.cit.* 536; *V.A.* Vol 27 (1996), 93, 94, 95

51. SRRC, deed 6000/9391; Owen & Blakeway, *op.cit.*, Vol 1, 272-3; *V.A.* Vol 28 (1997), 168, 170

52. *V.A.* Vol 31 (2000), 107

53. *V.A.* Vol 23 (1992), 10-14

54. SRRC, Box (Bridge St.); Lloyd Neg. 228

55. L.C. Lloyd, *The Inns of Shrewsbury*, Shrop. County Lib., Reprint, 1976, cover illustration

56. H. Hand, The Axial Jowled Post in Shropshire, *V.A.* Vol 20 (1989), 38

57. SRRC, Box 8 (Castle St.), print 4131; N.B.R. AA 62/3836; See also the chapter on Roof Construction in this work

58. J.T. Smith, *Shrewsbury: Topography and Domestic Architecture to the middle of the 17th Century*, B'ham Uni. M.A. thesis, 2 Vols., (1953). Copy in SRRC, D71.4. The present work owes much to Smith's researches

59. H.E. Forrest, *Old Houses of Shrewsbury*, Wilding, (1935); J.B. Blakeway, *op.cit.*

60. J.B. Blakeway, *ibid.*, Vol 3, 315

61. E.L. Cutts, *Scenes and Characters of the Middle Ages*, London, (1926), 535

Chapter 10   Shrewsbury Houses 16th- and 17th-Century Houses

1. Statute, Henrici Octavi 1535: 'An Act for Repairing and amending the townes of Glocester, Nothyngham, Northampton, and other Capit'

2. W.A. Champion, The Shrewsbury Lay Subsidy of 1525, *T.S.A.S.*, Vol. LXIV (1985), 45

3. SRRC, D64. Acc. 5319, *Early Chronicles of Shrewsbury*, 1372-1603, part transcription of Dr. Taylor's MS by Rev. W.A. Leighton, 24, 25, 26, 31, 44; *Municipal J.*, 2 Dec. 1955, 3269-3270; For a recent acc. see R. Cromarty, The Water Supply in Shrewsbury 1550-1835, *T.S.A.H.S.*, Vol 75 (2000) 15-48. Mr. Cromarty cites the earliest date as 1555

4. J.B. Lawson, John Sandford of Shrewsbury and Pitchford, Carpenter; *T.S.A.S.*, Vol. LXIV (1985), 119-20

5. W.A. Champion, John Ashby & the History & Environs of the Lion Inn, Shrewsbury, *T.S.A.H.S.*, Vol 75 (2000), 59; the model was made by N. Sanders

6. SRRC, C73 of M/F 69a, (J. Buckler's drawings), 146

7. *ibid.*, 172

8. Owen, *Some Account of Shrewsbury* (1808), rep. Morten, 1972, 536. Owen calls the building the Old Post Office inn, but this stands in a court-yard to the rear and is probably adapted from an ancillary building; Owen and Blakeway, *The History of Shrewsbury*, (1825) Vol. I, 532; *V.A.* Vol 27 (1996), 93, 94, 95

9. H.E. Forrest, *Old Houses of Shrewsbury*, Wilding, (1911), rep. 1972, 48; see also *Shrews. Chron.* 4 April 1913 for Forrest's sketch of the date-bearing tie-beam

10. A.T. Gaydon, The Old Co-Op, (formerly the String of Horses), Frankwell, Shrewsbury, *S.N.L.* 37, Dec. 1969, 2630

11. Pers. comm. Mr. J. Lawson

12. SRRC, J. Buckler, *op.cit.*, 164

13. Owen, *op.cit.*, 533-5

14. Owen and Blakeway, *op.cit.*, Vol I, facing 405; H.E. Forrest, *op.cit.*, 85

15. Owen, *op.cit.*, 535-6

16. L.C. Lloyd, *The Inns of Shrewsbury*, Shrops. County Lib., rep. (1976), 18

17. R. Gradidge, Stylish in its Return, *Country Life*, 10 Oct. 1991, 100

18. SRRC, MSS 2737

19. *T.S.A.S.* Vol. LXI, (1983) 53-4

20. H.E. Forrest, *Shrewsbury Burgess Roll*, (1924), 258

21. H.E. Forrest, *Old Houses of Shrewsbury*, *supra*, 65

22. SRRC, D 64.5, *supra*, 43

23. J.A. Morris, Demolition in Hill's Lane, *T.S.A.S.* Vol XII (1929/30), xviii (Misc.); SRRC, Mallinson neg. 771

24. H.E. Forrest, *Shrewsbury Burgess Roll*, *supra*, 263; Pers. comm. Mr. J. Lawson

25. Owen, *op.cit.*, 436-41

26. SRRC, C04 3410, *Shropshire Notes and Queries*, Vol 4 (1895), 109-10

27. J.B. Oldham, *A History of Shrewsbury School 1552-1952*, Oxford, (1952), 31-4

28. Owen & Blakeway, *op.cit.*, Vol I, 562; Owen, *op.cit.*, 518-22; J.B. Lawson, Harnage slates and other roofing materials in Shrewsbury and neighbourhood in the late medieval and early modern period, *T.S.A.S.*, Vol LXIV (1985), 116

29. Owen, *op.cit.*, 524

30. Owen & Blakeway, *op.cit.*, Vol I, opp 298 (an engraving by E.P. Owen); J. Buckler, *op.cit.*, 144; Watercolour by T. Shotter Boys in Rowley's House museum

31. *V.A.* Vol 32 (2001), forthcoming

32. *V.A.* Vol 31 (2000), 107

33. SRRC, Frankwell Box 2/2, prints 217, 1859; N.B.R. photo *c.*1943

34. H.E. Forrest, Thornes Hall, *T.S.A.S.* 4th series, Vol VIII (1920) 260-6

35. Owen & Blakeway, *op.cit.*, Vol I, opp. p.356; D. Lloyd, P. Howell & M. Richards, The Feathers, *L.R.P.* 5, (1986), 52; Parkinson & Ould, *Old cottages, farmhouses and other half-timbered buildings in Shropshire, Herefordshire & Cheshire*, Batsford (1904), pls XXI, XXII

36. V.A.G. Conference booklet (1982), 13

37. SRRC, D66/5328

38. Owen & Blakeway, *op.cit.*, Vol I, 420; H.E. Forrest, *Old Houses of Shrewsbury*, *supra*, 16, 70-2

39. SRRC, J. Buckler, *op.cit.*, 155

40. Many artists depicted these buildings. T. Shotter Boys' work is held by the Shrewsbury museum service.

41. L.C. Lloyd, *op.cit.*, 12

42. E.N.V. Lloyd, The history of Millington's Hospital, C.S.V.F.C., (1982)

43. SRRC, J, Buckler, *op.cit.*, 1

44. SRRC, D 71.4, J.T. Smith, *Shrewsbury: Topography & Domestic Architecture*, (M.A. Thesis, 1953), Vol 2, 365

45. R. Leighton, Extracts from a MS book at Sweeny Hall, *T.S.A.S.*, Vol 7, (1918-19), 125

Chapter 11   Much Wenlock

1. *V.C.H. Shropshire*, Vol 10 (1998), 399

2. *ibid.*, 405; *V.C.H. Shropshire*, Vol 3 (1979), 354

3. *V.C.H. Shropshire*, Vol 2 (1973), 39
4. *V.C.H. Shropshire*, Vol 10 (1998), 436; W.F. Mumford, *Wenlock in the Middle Ages* (1977), 112
5. *V.C.H. Shropshire*, Vol 10 (1998), 406
6. *V.A.* Vol 25 (1994), 32, 34
7. *ibid.*
8. H.E. Forrest, *Old Houses of Wenlock* (1915), 37
9. *V.A.* Vol 24 (1993), 57, 59
10. H. Hand, The Axial Jowled Post in Shropshire, *V.A.* Vol 20, (1989), 38
11. C.A. Hewett, *The Development of Carpentry 1200-1700*, David & Charles, (1969), 174
12. *V.A.* Vol 24 (1993), 57, 59; S.R. Jones, Tir-y-Coed, *T.S.A.S.*, Vol 56 (1957-60), 149-57
13. R.C.H.M. Report, (June 1988), dendro-dating was commissioned by the R.C.H.M.
14. *V.A.* Vol 25 (1994) 32, 34; M. Moran, A Terrace of Crucks at Much Wenlock, *V.A.* Vol 23, (1992), 13; *T.S.A.S.* 1st ser. vi, 105; H.E. Forrest, *op cit.*, 36
15. N.W. Alcock & M. Moran, Low Open-Truss Beams (Mantel-Beams): Problems of Function and Distribution, *V.A.* Vol 15 (1994), 47-55
16. W.F. Mumford, *op.cit.*, 28-30; *V.A.* Vol 25 (1994), 32, 34; *V.C.H. Shropshire*, Vol 10 (1998), 410; M. Wood, *The English Mediaeval House*, Phoenix (1965), pl 16; J.H. Parker, *Some Account of Domestic Architecture in England from Edward I to Richard II* (1853), opp 340
17. M. Moran, Great Oxenbold, Monkhopton, *T.S.A.H.S.* Vol 72, (1977) 9-25
18. *V.A.* Vol 25 (1994), 32, 34; M. Moran, A Terrace of Crucks at Much Wenlock, *op.cit.*, 10-14
19. F.W.B. Charles, Scotches, Lever Sockets and Rafter Holes, *V.A.* Vol 5 (1974), 21-24
20. *V.C.H. Shropshire*, Vol 10, (1998), 402, 416, 417, 446; *ibid.*, Vol 2 (1993), 192
21. *ibid.*, Vol 10, 413
22. *ibid.*, 405; F.W.B. Charles, *The Conservation of Timber Buildings*, Hutchinson (1884, rep. 1986), 172-92; W.F. Mumford, *op.cit.*, 124; H.E. Forrest, *op.cit.*, 31, 32; I am grateful to Glyn McDonald for helpful discussion on the Guildhall
23. *V.A.* Vol 28 (1997), 168, 169; W.F. Mumford, *op.cit.*, *passim*

Chapter 12   The Transitional House in Shropshire

1. *V.A.* Vol 24 (1993), 57, 59; *Regional Variations in Timber-Framed Buildings*, Essex C.C. (1998), 109
2. E. Mercer & P. Stamper, Plaish Hall & Early Brickwork in Shropshire, *T.S.A.H.S.* Vol 66 (1989), 90-96
3. M. Moran, *Vernacular Buildings of Whitchurch & Area*, Logaston Press (1999), 151-62, 171-78; *V.A.* Vol 25 (1994), 31, 33; *V.A.* Vol 26 (1995), 69, 71
4. *V.A.* Vol 26 (1995), 69, 71
5. M. Moran, Two Early Timber-Framed Hall Houses in Shropshire, *T.S.A.H.S.* Vol 68 (1993), 79-92; *V.A.* Vol 24 (1993), 56, 58
6. M. Moran & A. Snell, The Old Shop, Somerwood, *T.S.A.S.* Vol 64 (1985), 69-75
7. S.R.R.C. D 71.4, J.T. Smith, *Shrewsbury Topography and Architecture*, B'ham Uni. Thesis (1953), Vol 1, 148-60
8. C.A. Ralegh Radford, Acton Burnell Castle, *Studies in Building History*, (ed. E.M. Jope), Odhams, (1961), 97
9. E. Mercer & P. Stamper, *op.cit.*
10. as fn 5
11. *V.A.* Vol 26 (1995), 69, 70-1; *V.A.* Vol 25 (1994), 31, 33 & M. Moran, High Grosvenor, Claverley, *T.S.A.H.S.* Vol 70 (1995), 202-8; *V.A.* Vol 28 (1997), 168-9
12. M. Moran, *Vernacular Buildings of Whitchurch & Area*, Logaston Press (1999), 219-24
13. D. Lloyd, P. Howell, M. Richards, The Feathers, *L.R.P.* 5, (1986)
14. M. Moran, *supra*, 41-6, 63-70
15. E. Mercer, *Conf. Booklet for Soc. of Archit. Historians* (1988), 56, 57

Chapter 13   Painted Decorations in Shropshire Houses

1. D. Park, *The King's Head Wall-Painting*, report to Arrol & Snell from the Courtauld Institute of Art (1987); D. Watkinson, *Conservation of Wall-Paintings in the King's Head Public House*, Shrewsbury, report from the conservation team, Univ. of Wales, Cardiff (1989); J. Davies, *The Wall-Painting at the King's Head*, report, (1988)
2. *V.A.* Vol 26 (1995), 69, 71, 72
3. *V.A.* Vol 29 (1998), 121
4. H.E. Forrest, *Old Houses of Shrewsbury*, (1911), 76
5. *Shrewsbury Chronicle*, 7 Sept. 1956, 6
6. F.R. Reader, Tudor Domestic Wall-Paintings, part II, *Archaeol. J.*, 93 (1936), 232-3, pl vii
7. Cf. painting at Althrey Hall, Flints., see P. Smith, *Houses of the Welsh Countryside*, 2nd ed., H.M.S.O., (1988), pl VII
8. *V.A.* Vol 31 (2000), 105
9. M. Faraday, Ludlow 1085-1660; *A Social, Economic & Political History*, Phillimore, (1991), 114, 116
10. M. Moran, *Vernacular Buildings of Whitchurch & Area*, Logaston Press (1999), 75-88
11. T. Beck, *The Embroiderers' Flowers*, David & Charles (1992) 34, 39, 149. Henry Lytes makes this clear in his 'A Nievve Herbal' (1578). He calls it 'the clove gillofer'.
12. C. Hassall, Report no. W175c, Dec. 2000 (Paint Analysis at 28, Watergate, Whitchurch). I am grateful to Mrs. K. Baird for her help and co-operation with this example; *V.A.* Vol 32 (2001), forthcoming

13. M. Moran, High Grosvenor, Claverley, Shropshire, *T.S.A.H.S.* Vol. 70 (1995), 202-8

14. M. Moran, Shootrough Farm, Cardington, Shropshire, *T.S.A.H.S.*, Vol 74 (1999), 43-50; *V.A.* Vol 27 (1996), 103, 105

15. *V.C.H. Shropshire*, Vol. XI, (1985), 218

16. *V.A.* Vol 25 (1994), 31, 33-34

17. D. Lloyd, Broad Street, *L.R.P.* 3, (1979), 19

18. *V.A.* Vol 24 (1993), 57, 59

19. M.E. McClintock & R.C. Watson, Domestic Wall-Painting in the North-West, *V.A.* Vol 14, (1983), 55-8

20. Mrs. Stackhouse-Acton, *Castles & Old Mansions of Shropshire*, (1868), 14-16; *V.A.* Vol 31 (2000), 105

21. D. Lloyd & P. Klein, *Ludlow: A Historic Town in Words & Pictures*, Phillimore, (1984), 65, 80, *passim*

22. G.E. & K.R. Fussell, *The English Countryman*, Melrose (1955), pls. 62 - 65

23. *V.C.H. Shropshire*, Vol XI, (1985), 312; N. Pevsner, *The Buildings of England (Shropshire)*, Penguin, (1958), 222. The present owner cannot recall having seen the datestone

24. N. Joyce, Sophisticated Stencils, *Old House J.*, (Feb. 1992), 58-62; M. Moran, *op.cit.*, 111-16

25. E. Mercer & P. Stamper, Plaish Hall & Early Brickwork in Shropshire, *T.S.A.H.S.* LXVI, (1989), 90-96

26. B.M. Added Ms., 36378, f.214; SRRC., C73 vf M/F 69a, 214

27. R. Gough, *Sepulchral Monuments in Great Britain*, part 1, (1786), cxxvi, fn 1

28. B.L. cell mark 7815, d12, E.L. Blackburne, *Sketches, Graphic, Descriptive Etc for a history of the decorative painting applied to English Architecture during the Middle Ages*, (1847), 25. I am grateful to A.C. James for this ref.

29. T. Watts, *Cheap Print and Popular Piety*, Cambridge, (1991), 188, 191. I am grateful to J. Lawson for this ref.

30. A. Rodger, Roger Ward's Shrewsbury Stock: An Inventory of 1585, *The Library*, 5th series, 13 (1958), 252. (Copy held in SRRC., D 86 vf)

31. F.E. Matley-Moore, Painted Cloths, *Trans. Worc. Arch. Soc.*, 3rd Series, Vol 8, (1982), 73-9. This was a pioneering study; several writers have since expanded the theme. For details of the technique and the differences between stained and painted cloths see see O. Baker, *In Shakespeare's Warwickshire*, (1937), 121-153

32. F.E. Matley-Moore, *ibid.*, 73

33. S.R.R.C., qH 55.5, S. Watts, Whitchurch Probate Inventories 1535-1650, in 2 Vols, n.d; M. Moran, *op.cit.*, 17-24

34. B. Trinder & J. Cox, *Yeomen & Colliers in Telford*, Phillimore, (1980), 99

35. S.R.R.C., 1831 (uncat.). I am grateful to J. Lawson for this ref. We are unable to explain 'wier trees'. 'Syle' has several different meanings; here it probably means 'seal'

36. M. Peele, Shrewsbury Drapers' Inventories, *T.S.A.S.* Vol LII, (1947/8) 237

37. T. Midgley, (1949). The note is contained in the 'Midgcley Papers', a collection *penes* D.J. Lloyd

38. G. Jackson, *Shropshire Word Book* (1879, rep. 1982), 204, 205, 218

39. F.E. Matley Moore, *op.cit.*, 75, 76, 77

40. Pers. Comm. R. de Peyer & S. Price. See also Birmingham Museum and Art Gallery Information Sheet on Blakesley Hall, n.d.

41. A dissertation for a Ph D. on the subject is being prepared by Kathryn Baird. In it she researches aspects such as pigments, pattern books, personalities, costs, distribution etc. I am grateful to her for sharing so many of her findings with me

Chapter 14   Dendrochronology in Shropshire

1. Acknowledgements are made on pp.*ix-x*

2. M. Moran, *Bear Steps*. A guide published by Shrewsbury Civic Society (1982)

3. Vols 24 (1993) onwards

4. Baillie, M.G.L. and Pilcher, J.R., 'A simple cross dating program for recording research', *Tree Ring Bulletin*, 33, 1973, 7-14

5. A version of this and other programmes were written in BASIC by D. Haddon-Reece, and latterly rewritten in Microsoft Visual Basic by M.R. Allwright and P.A. Parker.

6. Miles, D.H., and Haddon-Reece, D., 'List 54 - Tree-ring dates', *V.A*, 24, 1993, 54-60

7. Hillam, J., Morgan, R.A., and Tyers, I., 'Sapwood estimates and the dating of short ring sequences', in *Applications of tree-ring studies: current research in dendrochronology and related areas* (ed. R.G.W. Ward), BAR Int Ser, 333, Oxford, 1987, 165-85

8. Miles, D.H., 'The interpretation, presentation, and use of tree-ring dates', *V.A.*, 28, 1997, 40-56. This estimate has continued to be used, although the issue of sapwood estimates in general has now become the subject of a doctoral thesis at Oxford, with the hope that estimates may be revised even further. Nevertheless, the 1997 estimate has allowed some reduction in the sapwood ranges produced prior to this date, and these have been updated on the Laboratory's web-site www.dendrochronology.com where all buildings published in *Vernacular Architecture* have been reproduced on line. Any further developments and refinements in dates already published will be presented here.

9. K. Sandall, Aisled Halls in England and Wales, *V.A.* Vol 6, (1975), 20; see also fig 1

10. N. Hill and D. Miles, The Royal George, Cottingham, Northamptonshire: An early Cruck Building, *V.A.* 32, (2001), 62-7, 77

11. M. Moran, Great Oxenbold, Monkhopton, Shropshire, *T.S.A.H.S.* Vol 72 (1997), 9-25

12. M. Moran, Two Early Timber-Framed Hall Houses in Shropshire, *T.S.A.H.S.* Vol 68 (1993), 72-92

13. D.J. Lloyd and M. Moran, The Corner Shop, *L.R.P.* 2, (1978)

14. R. Morriss & P. Napier, The Abbot's House, Butcher Row, Shrewsbury, *Hereford Archeol. Series*, 200 (1994)

15. M. Moran, The Medieval Parts of Plowden Hall, *T.S.A.S.* Vol 59, part 3, 264-271

16. N.W. Alcock, *Cruck Construction: An Introduction and Catalogue*, CBA Research Report, Vol 42 (1981), 96, fig.2

17. R.A. Cordingley, Stokesay Castle, Shropshire: The Chronology of its Buildings, *The Arts Bulletin*, Vol 45 (1963), 2

18. M. Moran, *Vernacular Buildings of Whitchurch & Area*, Logaston Press, (1999), 61-62, 154, 155, 157, 173

19. M. Moran, *op.cit.*, (1993)

20. M. Moran, A Terrace of Crucks at Much Wenlock, *V.A.* Vol 23 (1992), 10-14

21. M. Moran, Catherton Cottage, Hopton Wafers, *T.S.A.H.S.* Vol 65 (1987), 45-49

22. S.O. Addy, *The Evolution of the English House*, (1898), 75

23. E. Mercer, *English Vernacular Architecture*, H.M.S.O., (1975), 92

24. S.R. Jones, Tir-y-Coed: A Fifteenth Century Farmhouse in the Parish of Melverley, Salop, *T.S.A.S.* Vol 56, (195760), 154

25. *V.C.H. Shropshire*, Vol X (1998), 92

26. M. Speight & D.J. Lloyd, Ludlow Houses and their Residents, *L.R.P.* 1, (n.d. - *c*.1977), fig 1

27. N.W. Alcock & M. Moran, Low Open-Truss Beams (Mantel-Beams): Problems of Function and Distribution, *V.A.* Vol 15 (1984), 47-55

28. J.T. Smith, Stokesay Castle, *Archaeol. J.* Vol 63 (1957), 211-14

29. C.R.J. Currie, Archaic Roofs in Hereford and Worcester, *V.A.* Vol 21 (1990), 18-32

30. E.H.D. Williams, Church Houses in Somerset, *V.A.* Vol 23 (1992), 15-23

31. M. Moran & D. James, *The Foresters' Lodge, Upper Millichope*, (private pub., n.d. (*c*.1985))

32. E. Mercer, Soc. of Architectural Historians of Gt. Britain, Conf. Booklet, (1988), 27-8

33. SRRC, 3365/387 m, l, d

34. SRRC, 6000/9391

Chapter 15   Gazetteer

1. H.E. Forrest, *Old Houses of Wenlock* (1915), 54

2. *ibid.*, 53,54; F. Stackhouse-Acton, *Castles and Old Mansions of Shropshire* (1868), 40; *V.A.* Vol 29 (1998), 121

3. *V.C.H. Shropshire*, Vol 8 (1968), 197, 198; E. Blore, Wattlesborough Tower, *Archaeol. J.* XXV, (1868), 98

4. J. Hunt & M. Stokes, Sculpture and Patronage in a Shropshire Manor: A Group of XII-century Sculptures from Alveley, *Jn. of Brit. Archaeol. Ass.* Vol CL (1997), 27 47; M. Moran, The Bell Inn, Alveley, *V.A.* Vol 29 (1998), 85-87, 121

5. M. Moran & H. Hand, Great Binnal, Astley Abbotts, *V.A.* Vol 27 (1996), 62, 63, 102

6. J.W. Tonkin, The White House, Aston Munslow, *T.S.A.S.* Vol 58 part 2 (1966), 140-152

7. A. Gomme, Stanwardine Hall, *Soc. of Archit. Hist*, Conference booklet (1988), 23, 25

8. M. Moran, Re-erecting Houses in Shropshire in the late Seventeenth century, *Archaeol. J.* Vol 146, (1989), 538-553

9. Census return (1841) Condover N., Bayston Hill, District 16, 1-4

10. N. Pevsner, *Shropshire* (1958), 133

11. *The Gale of Life*, Logaston Press (2000), 144

12. *ibid.*, 133-4; *V.A.* Vol 31 (2000), 105

13. *ibid.*, 144

14. *ibid.*, 143

15. *ibid.*, 143

16. *ibid.*, 144

17. F. Stackhouse-Acton, *op.cit.*, 63; N. Pevsner, *op.cit.*, 116-117; M. Moran & I. West, *V.A.G.* Conference booklet (1982), 27

18. *V.A.* Vol 27 (1996), 102, 104

19. J. Ionides, *Thomas Farnolls Pritchard of Shrewsbury*, Dog Rose Press (1999), 124-127, *passim*

20. M. Moran, Cleeton Court, Cleeton St. Mary, *T.S.A.S.* Vol 65 (1987), 41-44;

21. *V.A.* Vol 27 (1996), 103, 104-105

22. *V.A.* Vol 31 (2000), 106

23. P. Smith, *Houses of the Welsh Countryside*, H.M.S.O. (1975), 457

24. J. McCann, Enquiry into the Design and Use of Dovecotes, *Trans. Anc. Mon. Soc.* Vol 35 (1991), 136

25. *V.A.* Vol 27 (1996), 103, 105

26. as fn 8, 551-3

27. D.H. Robinson, *The Sleepy Meese*, Waine (1988), 94, 95; *V.A.* Vol 31 (2000), 106

28. *V.C.H. Shropshire*, Vol 8 (1968), 132, 135, pl. opp. 111

29. *ibid.*, 131

30. *ibid.*, 133, 134, pl. opp. 54; N.W. Alcock & M. Moran, Low Open Truss Beams (Mantel Beams): Problems of Function & Distribution, *V.A.* Vol 15 (1984), 54

31. *V.A.* Vol 26 (1995), 69, 71
32. *V.A.* Vol 25 (1994), 32, 33; M. Moran, High Grosvenor, Claverley, *T.S.A.H.S.* Vol 70 (1995), 202-208
33. *V.A.* Vol 27 (1996), 103, 105; N.W. Alcock & M. Moran, *op.cit.*, 47-55; M. Moran, Catherton Cottage, Hopton Wafers, *T.S.A.S.* Vol 65 (1987), 45-49
34. *The Gale of Life*, Logaston Press (2000), 149
35. N.W. Alcock & M. Moran, *op.cit.*, 47-55; *The Gale of Life*, *op.cit.*, 148
36. *ibid.*, 149; *V.A.* Vol 31 (2000), 106
37. *ibid.*, 149
38. *ibid.*, 148
39. *ibid.*, 152
40. *ibid.*, 151; M. Moran & I. West, *op.cit.*, 24
41. M. Moran & I. West, *op.cit.*, 23
42. *The Gale of Life*, *op.cit.*, 144-5; M. Moran & I. West, *op.cit.*, 42
43. *ibid.*, 146; *ibid.*, 29; A. & F. Barratt, Clungunford, *950 Years of a Rural Community*, Alfi (2000), 121-5; ; H.E. Forrest, *Some Old Shropshire Houses and their Owners* (1924), 106-110; Owen & Blakeway, *History of Shrewsbury*, (1825), 140; *V.A.*, Vol 33 92002), 95-6
44. W.G. Muter, *The Buildings of an Industrial Community*, Phillimore (1979), 25, p1 36
45. F.W.B. Charles, Scotches, Lever Sockets & Rafter Holes, *V.A.* Vol 5 (1974) 21-24
46. *V.C.H. Shropshire*, Vol 8 (1968), 163
47. *ibid.*, 33; M. Moran & I. West, *op.cit.*, 2
48. *idem.*; *ibid.*, 3; *V.A.* Vol 24 (1993), 56, 58
49. *V.C.H. Shropshire*, Vol 8 (1968), 35
50. *ibid.*, 36
51. *ibid.*, 61; M. Moran & I. West, *op.cit.*, 6
52. *V.A.* Vol 25 (1994), 31, 33; M. Moran & I. West, *op.cit.*, 11
53. M. Moran & I. West, *op.cit.*, 6
54. *V.C.H. Shropshire*, Vol 8 (1968), 64; *V.A.* Vol 25, (1994), 31, 33; M. Moran & I. West, *op.cit.*, 7
55. B. Trinder, *The Industrial Revolution in Shropshire*, Phillimore (1973), 324; *V.C.H. Shropshire*, Vol 11 (1985), 109, pl 42
56. *Ironbridge Archaeological Series*, 20 (1998), *passim*
57. *ibid.*, 5, (1987), *passim*
58. H. Hand, Purlin Hook-Pegs in the Open Hall House, *V.A.* Vol 19 (1998), 43
59. See chapter 13
60. Pers. comm. Mrs. Harvey
61. Pers. comm. Paul & Brian Beck
62. *V.A.* Vol 27 (1996), 103, 105
63. S. Smith, Keeping tally with a blunt billhook, *Farmers Weekly*, 5 Nov. 1971, 85
64. *V.A.* Vol 25 (1994), 31, 33-34
65. M. Moran, Two Early Timber-Framed Hall Houses in Shropshire, *T.S.A.H.S.*, Vol 68 (1993), 79, 92; *V.A.* Vol 24 (1993), 56, 58

66. Pers. comm. Mrs. Richie
67. *V.A.* Vol 26 (1995), 69, 71; *V.C.H. Shropshire*, Vol 8 (1968), 240; *T.S.A.S.*, 1st Series, viii (1885), 196-7
68. Pers. comm. Mr. C.A. Eade, Agent for Lord Barnard
69. *Archaeology in Ironbridge 1985-6*, I.G.M.A.U. (1986), 28-33
70. *V.A.* Vol 30 (1999), 124
71. *Archaeology in Ironbridge 1985-6*, I.G.M.A.U. (1986), 35
72. *V.C.H. Shropshire*, Vol 8 (1968), 94; Pers. comm. Miss Carter whose ancestor built Weaver's Cottage
73. Kinlet Newsletter 1967
74. E. Mercer, *English Vernacular Houses*, H.M.S.O. (1975), 1969 pl 64
75. D.R. Adams & J. Hazeley, Survey of the Church Aston - Lilleshall Mining Area, *Shropshire Mining Club*, Report 7 (1970), 38
76. M. Moran, *Vernacular Buildings of Whitchurch & Area*, Logaston Press (1999), xviii
77. C. Ryan & M. Moran, The Old House Farm, Loppington, *T.S.A.S.*, Vol LXIII, (1985). 11-16
78. M. Moran & I. West, *op.cit.*, 26
79. M. Moran, The Medieval Parts of Plowden Hall, *T.S.A.S.*, Vol LIX, part 3 (1973/4), 264-271; *V.A.* Vol 24 (1993), 57-9
80. M. Moran, Great Oxenbold, Monkhopton, Shropshire, *T.S.A.H.S.*, Vol LXXII (1997); *V.A.*, Vol 24 (1993), 57, 59
81. M. Moran, *Vernacular Buildings of Whitchurch & Area*, Logaston Press (1999), 187-194
82. M. Moran & D. James, *The Forester's Lodge, Upper Millichope, Shropshire*, priv. pub., n.d.
83. M. Moran, Re-erecting Houses in Shropshire in the Late Seventeenth Century, *Archaeol. J.*, Vol 146 (1989), 538-553
84. R. Gough, *The History of Myddle*, ed. D. Hey, Penguin repr. (1981), 216-218
85. *ibid.*, 60-61
86. *ibid.*, 170
87. *ibid.*, 89
88. *V.A.* Vol 28 (1997), 168, 169-170
89. *V.A.* Vol 24 (1993), 57, 59
90. Owen & Blakeway, *op.cit.*, Vol 1, 292; P. Williams, *The Council in the Marches of Wales under Elizabeth I*, Uni. of Wales Press (1958), 93
91. J. Summerson, *Architecture in Britain 1530-1830*, Penguin (1953), 56
92. M. Moran, *Vernacular Buildings of Whitchurch & Area*, Logaston Press (1999), 209
93. painting, *penes* Mrs. Smith
94. M. Moran, *Vernacular Buildings of Whitchurch & Area*, Logaston Press (1999), 225-238
95. M. Moran, Padmore, Onibury, *Archaeol. J.* Vol 142 (1985), 340-360

96. L.C. Lloyd, The Hayes, Oswestry, *T.S.A.S.*, Vol 56, part 3 (1960), 295-307
97. Pers. comm. Mr. P. Hagan
98. B.F. Roberts, *Edward Lhuyd, The Making of a Scientist*, Uni. of Wales Press (1980); S. Leighton, *Shropshire Houses Past and Present* (1901), 23
99. *V.C.H. Shropshire*, Vol 8 (1968), 118, 119, 120; P. Stamper, *Historic Parks and Gardens of Shropshire*, Shropshire Books (1996), *passim*; J.B. Lawson, John Sandford of Shrewsbury and Pitchford, *T.S.A.S.* Vol 64 (1985), 119, 120; J. Ionides, *op.cit.*, 51, 52; J. Morris, *Domesday Book (Shropshire)*, Phillimore (1986), 3f
100. *V.A.* Vol 24 (1993) 58, 59; *V.C.H. Shropshire*, Vol 8 (1968), 255
101. N. Alcock & M. Moran, *op.cit.*, 47-55
102. *V.C.H. Shropshire*, Vol 8 (1968), 260
103. *ibid.*, 257; M. Moran & I. West, *op.cit.*, 25
104. *ibid.*, 259
105. *ibid.*, 258, 259
106. M. Moran, *Vernacular Buildings of Whitchurch & Area*, Logaston Press (1999), 171-186, 242-246
107. F. Stackhouse-Acton, *Castles and Old Mansions of Shropshire* (1868), 29-31
108. *ibid.*; *Langley Gatehouse*, Hereford Archaeol. Series. 143 (1992); M. Moran, Langley Gatehouse, *S.N.L.*, 38 (June 1970); *V.A.* Vol 24 (1993), 47, 48
109. M. Moran & I. West, *op.cit.*, 22
110. *ibid.*, 21; *V.A.* Vol 27 (1996) 104, 105
111. H. Colvin, *A Biographical Dictionary of British Architects 1660-1840*, Murray (1978), 187
112. *Ibid.*, 187, 408
113. *V.A.*, Vol 33 (2002), 98, 99
114. J. Ionides, *op.cit.*, *passim*
115. *V.C.H. Shropshire*, Vol 8 (1968), 164
116. *ibid.*, 163
117. R.C.H.M. Historic Building Report (Oct. 1995), NBR no. 94166
118. Pers. comm. Mrs. Whiteman
119. *V.A.* Vol 27 (1996), 104, 105-6; R.W. Eyton, *The Antiquities of Shropshire* (1856), Vol 4, 152
120. N.W. Alcock & M. Moran, *op.cit.*, 54
121. V. Bellamy, Upton Cressett Hall, *Country Life* (April 11 2002), 108-113
122. *V.A.* Vol 26 (1995), 70, 72
123. M. Moran, The Old Shop, Somerwood, *T.S.A.S.* Vol 64 (1985), 69-75
124. *V.C.H. Shropshire*, Vol 11 (1985), 309
125. B. Trinder, *op.cit.*, 319; *Newdale, Shropshire*, Ironbridge Archaeol. Series, 12 (1987)
126. M. Moran, *Vernacular Buildings of Whitchurch & Area*, Logaston Press, (1999) 247-250
127. *V.C.H. Shropshire*, Vol 8 (1968), 306; *V.A.* Vol 31 (2000), 107
128. *idem.*

129. H.E. Forrest in *Shropshire*, Mate (1906), 144
130. M. Moran, *Vernacular Buildings of Whitchurch & Area*, Logaston Press (1999)
131. 'F.S.A.', Cheyney Longville, *T.S.A.S.* Vol 1 (1878), 119-123
132. P. Smith, *op.cit.*, 2nd ed. (1988), figs 158 a, b
133. *V.A.* Vol 26 (1995), 70,72; *V.C.H. Shropshire*, Vol 8 (1968), 171; N.W. Alcock & M. Moran, *op.cit.*, 54
134. *V.A.* Vol 28 (1997), 107, 169, 171
135. *Country Life*, 13 June 1952, 1816-1819; *ibid.*, 3 March 1977, 492-494
136. *V.C.H. Shropshire*, Vol 11 (1985), 312, pl.5; P. Stamper, *op.cit.*, 51, fig. 35
137. *ibid.*, 308, 322; *V.A.* Vol 21a (1998), 88, 89, 122-123
138. F. Stackhouse-Acton, *op.cit.*, 44-45; P. Stamper, *op.cit.*, 9-10; H. Colvin, *op.cit*, 662, 663

Appendix 2
The Shropshire Dendrochronolgy Project

1. Siebenlist-Kerner, V., 'The Chronology, 1341-1636, for certain hillside oaks from Western England and Wales', in *Dendrochronology in Europe* (ed. J.M. Fletcher), BAR, 51, 1978, 157-61
2. Miles, D.H., and Worthington, M.J., 'Lists 81 and 83 - Tree-ring dates', *V.A.*, 28, 1997, 159-81
3. Leggett, P.A., Hibbert, F.A., Hughes, M.K., Fletcher, J.M., and Morgan, R., 'Tree-ring dates for buildings with oak timber', *V.A.*, 13, 1982, 48
4. Groves, C., *Tree-ring analysis of timbers from Shrewsbury Abbey, Shropshire, 1985-1987*, Anc. Mon. Lab. Rep., 194/88
5. Haddon-Reece, D., and Miles, D.H., 'List 43 - Tree-ring dates', *V.A.*, 23, 1992, 48-51
6. Miles, D.H., and Haddon-Reece, D., 'List 54 - Tree-ring dates', *V.A*, 24, 1993, 54-60
7. Miles, D.H., and Haddon-Reece, D., 'List 56 - Tree-ring dates', *V.A.*, 25, 1994, 28-36
8. Miles, D.H., and Haddon-Reece, D., 'List 64 - Tree-ring dates', *V.A.*, 26, 1995, 60-74
9. Miles, D.H., and Haddon-Reece, D., 'List 72 - Tree-ring dates', *V.A.*, 27, 1996, 97-102
10. Miles, D.H., and Worthington, M.J., 'Lists 81 and 83 - Tree-ring dates', *V.A.*, 28, 1997, 159-81
11. Miles, D.H., *The tree-ring dating the north transept, Holy Trinity Church, Wistanstow, Shropshire*, Anc. Mon. Lab. Rep., 1998, 60/98
12. Miles, D.H., and Worthington, M.J., 'List 92 - Tree-ring dates', *V.A.*, 29, 1998, 121-23
13. Miles, D.H., and Worthington, M.J., 'List 109 - Tree-ring dates', V.A., 31, 2000, 105-17
14. Miles, D.H., and Worthington, M.J., 'List 118 - Tree-ring dates', *V.A.*, 32, 2001, 81-2
15. Miles, D.H., and Worthington, M.J., 'List 128 - Tree-ring dates', V.A., 33, 2002, 94-9

16. Barratt, A. and Barratt, F., *Clungunford - 950 years of a Rural Community*, Alfi Productions, London, 2002

17. Hillam, J., and Groves, C., *Tree-ring dating of oak timbers from Langley Gatehouse, Shropshire*, Anc. Mon. Lab. Rep., 1993, 23/93

18. Groves, C., *Dendrochronological analysis of Ightfield Hall Farm Barn, Ightfield, Whitchurch, Shropshire*, Anc. Mon. Lab. Rep., 1997, 91/97

19. Hillam, J., *Tree-ring analysis of timbers from Newton Mill and Newington Bridge, Craven Arms, Shropshire*, An. Mon. Lab. Rep., 1997, 6/98

20. Tyers, I., *Tree-ring analysis of oak timbers from The Church of St. Swithin, Clunbury, Shropshire*, Anc. Mon. Lab. Rep., 2000, 8/2000

21. Nayling, N., *Tree-ring analysis of oak timbers from Shrewsbury Abbey Church*, Anc, Mon, Lab, Rep,, 1999, 39/99

22. Nayling, N., *Tree-ring analysis of timbers from the nave roof of the Church of St. Mary the Virgin, Bromfield, Shropshire*, Anc. Mon. Lab. Rep., 2000, 69/2000

23. Miles, D.H., and Haddon-Reece, D., 'List 64 - Tree-ring dates', *V.A.*, 26, 1995, 60-74

24. Miles, D.H., and Worthington, M.J., 'List 109 - Tree-ring dates', *V.A.*, 31, 2000, 105-17

25. Worthington, M.J., and Miles, D.H., *The tree-ring dating of The Porch House, 33-5 High Street, Bishop's Castle, Shropshire* Anc. Mon. Lab. Rep., 2000, 72/2000

26. Miles, D.H., and Worthington, M.J., 'Lists 81 and 83 - Tree-ring dates', *V.A.*, 28, 1997,159-81

27. Miles, D.H., and Worthington, M.J., 'List 128 - Tree-ring dates', *V.A.*, 33, 2002, 94-9

28. Miles, D.H., and Haddon-Reece, D., 'List 54 - Tree-ring dates', *V.A.*, 24, 1993, 54-60

29. Roberts, E., *Hampshire Houses 1250-1700: Their Dating and Development*, Hampshire County Council, 2003

30. Miles, D.H., and Haddon-Reece, D., 'List 72 - Tree-ring dates', *V.A.*, 27, 1996, 97-102

Index

For ease of finding individual properties, these are both listed alphabetically by individual name and by parish where the major properties that feature in the book are also separately identified. Where properties generally have a number rather than name, they are listed under the relevant town or village, the list then including all the properties mentioned in the settlement. This applies for Bishop's Castle, Bridgnorth, Church Stretton, Hodnet, Ludlow, Market Drayton, Much Wenlock, Newport, Shifnal and Shrewsbury. Cruck construction, Jetty, Stone for building, Roofs, and the Transitional House are listed with various sub-entries. Painting and carving is listed under Decoration. Numbers in italics relate to pages carrying illustrations.

Mercia: The Anglo-Saxon Kingdom of Central England
by Sarah Zaluckyj

Of the three great Anglo-Saxon kingdoms in Britain before the advent of 'England'—Northumbria, Mercia and Wessex—Mercia has long deserved its own history. Northumbria had Bede, Wessex had the *Anglo-Saxon Chronicle*, but Mercia has largely to be explored through the eyes of others.

This book attempts to redress this gap. Using the fragmentary chronicles that refer to the kingdom, inferring from lost sources utilized by later medieval chroniclers, extracting information from the charters, letters and other documents of the period that have survived and incorporating the growing amount of information gained from archaeological excavations carried out over many years across the breadth of Mercia, this book provides a study of how the kingdom emerged from the Dark Ages in the late 6th and early 7th centuries and grew into a power to be reckoned with by the popes in Rome and the Carolingian empire from the late 8th century, a position of strength from which it subsequently declined.

At its greatest Mercia stretched from the Humber in the north to south of the Thames, controlling parts of Wiltshire, Hampshire, Surrey and Berkshire, along with Kent and Essex. Its remit ran from the Welsh Borders to East Anglia. London was its main port, Tamworth its 'capital', and many of the towns that subsequently became county towns were developed. Mercia became recognized for its learning and for its industry, arguably the most important commodity of which was salt. It gained much of its central revenue from trade through the port of London and the extensive saltworks at Droitwich. Councils and synods were held at venues throughout the kingdom, often in large timber halls. Monasteries were founded with great enthusiasm, royal saints and their cults blossomed, trade and coinage developed in periods of stability.

Yet warfare never seems to have been far away. Initially this served to carve out the core of Mercia (primarily Staffordshire) under its earliest kings, the most notable of whom was Cearl, then to extend the territory south-westwards into Worcestershire and Herefordshire under Penda, and east-wards into the east midlands as far as Cambridgeshire. Alliances were made in the 7th century with the Britons of Wales to counteract the power of Northumbria with whom warfare was waged over many years. East Anglia, the territory from which the original Mercians may have come or, at least, through which they passed, was at different times its ally, its enemy or a client province. Mercia was often in conflict with Wessex throughout its history and in later years with Kent. Friendship with the Welsh deteriorated into warfare on that frontier and led to the building of the famous Offa's Dyke.

A period of stability and exercise of diplomacy under Offa and Coenred, for example, saw Mercia playing a role on the Continental stage, before a royal family, seemingly weakened by purges carried out by Offa, started to lose control of the south-eastern part of the kingdom. Yet, for many years Mercia remained a cohesive entity, until the advent of Scandinavian incursions caused the kingdom to buckle and, with the fall of Burgred, be split into the Danelaw and English Mercia, with client kings in the latter. Gradually Mercia came to recognize that its interests lay in working with Wessex and so emerged the idea of an 'English' kingdom, and the demise of that of Mercia.

320 pages, paperback with over 180 photographs and plans
Price £14.95
ISBN 1 873827 62 8

The Mortimers, Lords of the March
by Charles Hopkinson & Martin Speight

Occupying a central position on the English-Welsh border and in the Welsh March, or *marchia Wallie*—the parts of Wales under Anglo-Norman control, an area with its own Custom and Law, the Mortimers have long deserved their own history. Too often they crop up as an adjunct to the histories of English kings (and in one case, Empress) or of relations with Wales. There is the notable exception of Edward IV, but he carried the Mortimer name by choice, his grandmother being Anne Mortimer, the sister of the last male heir of the line.

The early history of the family is difficult to untangle due to a shortage of reliable sources, yet this book manages to set the period out in some detail. Once the Mortimers gained a foothold in the March, and particularly after the loss of Normandy to France, they readily switched their attentions to acquiring a Celtic empire, building up huge territorial acquisitions not just in Wales but also in Ireland in addition to their English estates. Most members of the family sought to increase their power base and standing, none more so than Roger (IV) who was instrumental in the deposition of Edward II, lived with Edward's queen and created himself earl of March. But he was not alone. Indeed, one great advantage of this book is that it shows how over time the family managed its relationship with the king, worked their estates, and dealt with the continual problem of young heirs and their wardship, so as to increase and augment their position.

This book details the lives of all the Mortimer heirs, along with other members of the family, and of branches of the family at Richard's Castle, Chelmarsh and Chirk. But it is more than just a chronicle of the family's history. Chapters also deal with the family's relations with the Welsh, which were not simply one of warfare and acquisition, but also of inter-marriage and of seeming interest in the Celtic world; with the spread and organization of their estates; with their activity in castle-building and borough creation.

Charles Hopkinson is a farmer living in Herefordshire who writes and lectures on various aspects of history. It was almost 40 years ago that his interest in the Mortimer family was roused during a visit to Wigmore Castle and subsequent years of research have led to his contribution to this book.

Martin Speight read History at University College London, where he gained his Ph.D. in 1969. He taught at Ludlow Grammar School and its successor, Ludlow College, from which he retired as Head of History in 1997. A founder of the Ludlow Historical Research Group and a former Mayor of Ludlow, he has published a number of short books and articles on the history of the area.

Hardback £19.95   288 pages   Paperback £12.95
ISBN 1 873827 78 4   over 100 illustrations   ISBN 1 873827 53 9

Also from Logaston Press

The Pubs of Ludlow & neighbouring villages
by Tony Hobbs

'Whenn they hadde drokyn i-nowe of wyne that was in tavernys and in othyr placys they ulle ungoodely smote owte the heddys of the pypys and hoggys hedys of wyne, that men wente wete-schede in wyne, and thenn they robbyd the towne, and bare a-waye beddynge and clothe and othyr stuffe and defoulyd many wymmen.'

This is one of the first records of the effect of too much drinking in Ludlow, albeit after the collapse of the Yorkist forces at Ludford Bridge in 1459, when Royalist troops used the opportunity to celebrate a bloodless victory. Fortunately, much subsequent drinking in the pubs, inns and taverns of the town and its neighbourhood has had more socially acceptable consequences. But even the supposedly good and great could not always resist going too far—writing about the town in the early 17th century, when the Council in the Marches was based in the castle and town, Richard Baxter noted that 'the town was full of temptations, through the multitude of persons (councillors, attorneys, officers and clerks) and much given to tippling and excess'.

This book details the history surrounding the many drinking houses that have existed in Ludlow over the years, not just those that remain in existence today. It is full of stories of buildings, landlords, customers, beers, ghosts, a beer-drinking Jackdaw that gurgled back his ale, brewing, mulling, and activities arranged by inns—or the Licensed Victuallers of Ludlow themselves, such as a 'Miraculous Menagerie with flying rabbits and guinea pigs; transformation of vegetables into lozenges; and enchanted fruit'.

The first two chapters set the scene, detailing changes in licensing hours and laws over the centuries, the history of local breweries and attitudes to drink. The town is then split up into sections and the book adopts the form of a walking tour discussing the pubs that have existed on the selected route. The final two chapters describe hostelries in the surrounding villages.

Tony Hobbs was born in a pub in London and subsequently ran a hostelry in Hythe, Kent. His interest in beer and inns developed further when walking from Land's End to John O'Groats in 1997 (a journey about which he wrote in his book, *One Pair of Boots*) after which he moved to north Herefordshire where he still lives.

224 pages, paperback, with over 150 illustrations
Price: £9.95
ISBN 1 873827 83 0

Also from Logaston Press

Sir Samuel Meyrick & Goodrich Court
by Rosalind Lowe

Sir Samuel Rush Meyrick was the founding father of the systematic study of arms and armour. Although he died more than 150 years ago, his name is still revered by enthusiasts all over the world. His last days were spent in Herefordshire, where his magnificent collection of arms, armour and antiquities could be visited in his mock Gothic castle called Goodrich Court. The collection is now largely dispersed, but the British public can still see some of the choicest pieces at the Wallace Collection and at the British Museum.

Goodrich Court was not to the taste of William Wordsworth and other admirers of the Picturesque, particularly as it overpowered the ivy-clad towers of Goodrich Castle nearby. Those who made the tour of the building described in this book were rather more impressed. When the Meyrick family moved on, the Court enjoyed seventy years as a grand house until its idyll was brought to an end by the Second World War. After sheltering Felsted School during the war, it remained empty and forlorn until demolished in 1950. Its exotic gatehouse still remains alongside the A40 trunk road between Ross and Monmouth to intrigue the modern traveller.

Sir Samuel and the Meyrick collection played an important role in the early 19th century movement towards historical accuracy in the portrayal of correct costume in works of art and the theatre. Artists such as Bonington, Cooper, Corbould, Cottingham and Haydon sketched the armour: the architect William Burges bought items from the collection and was surely influenced by Sir Samuel's views on medieval decoration. Meyrick's lavishly illustrated works were an unparalleled source for later writers, and he published many historical articles. He is better known in Wales as the editor of the genealogical collections of the 16th century herald Lewys Dwnn.

Sir Samuel's story, and that of Goodrich Court and its treasures is no dry antiquarian tale, but full-blooded and sometimes humorous. His life was a roller-coaster of public acclaim and private tragedy, played out against the military and political movements of the pre-Victorian age. Although respected for his scholarship by the royal family and the public at large, he was no stranger to scandal and controversy. At the moment of his greatest triumph he sowed the seeds of his own painful death.

Rosalind Lowe has lived in Goodrich for nine years, in a house once owned by Sir Samuel Meyrick. Her childhood was spent in the old county of Breconshire in Wales, before a professional life spent in the computer and oil industries. She now writes on the archaeology and history of Herefordshire.

320 pages, paperback, with over 100 black and white and 30 colour illustrations
Price: £17.50
ISBN: 1 873827 88 1

Forthcoming titles from Logaston Press

Tewkesbury Abbey: History, Art & Architecture
edited by Richard K. Morris & Ron Shoesmith

This is the first major book to appear on Tewkesbury Abbey for over a century and the most wide-ranging ever to be written on the subject. The book is designed to be attractive to the general readership; it is written in an accessible style and is well illustrated. It also presents new research in sufficient depth to be of interest to specialists in church architecture and archaeology. The project was initiated by the Revd. Michael Tavinor to celebrate the 900th centenary of the arrival of Benedictine monks at the abbey (1102-2002), and it brings together 18 authors, all of them acknowledged experts in their respective fields and in their acquaintance with the abbey. They shed new light on many aspects of the abbey's history, life and art—the Clarence bones, the Founders' Book, the archaeological excavations in Abbey Meadow, the incumbencies of 20th-century vicars, to name just a few examples. The book's style follows that of: *A Definitive History of Dore Abbey*, and *Ludlow Castle: its History and Buildings*, two earlier Logaston Press titles (both still in print in 2003, paperback editions only, at £14.95 each).

Over 150 black and white and 30 colour illustrations
Due to be published November 2003

English Vernacular Architecture: The Shropshire Experience
by Eric Mercer

This book is the work that Eric Mercer had all but completed when he died. In 23 chapters it will detail Shropshire's vernacular architecture, following themes of ecclesiastical and secular architecture.

Due to be published November 2003

The Folklore of Shropshire
by Roy Palmer

Roy Palmer presents the folklore of the county as a series of themes that embrace landscape, buildings, beliefs, work, seasons and people. Each chapter can stand alone or the book can be read as a whole.

Due to be published in 2004